MEDIA

AN INTRODUCTORY ANALYSIS OF AMERICAN MASS COMMUNICATIONS

The Second Edition

Peter M. Sandman
The University of Michigan

David M. Rubin
New York University
at Washington Square

David B. Sachsman
Livingston College
Rutgers—The State University
of New Jersey

PRENTICE-HALL, INC., ENGLEWOOD CLIFFS, NEW JERSEY

Library of Congress Cataloging in Publication Data

SANDMAN, PETER M
  Media: an introductory analysis of American mass
communications.

  Includes bibliographies and index.
  1. Mass media—United States.   I. Rubin, David M.,
joint author.   II. Sachsman, David B., joint author.
III. Title.
P92.U5S24   1976   301.16'1'0973   75-31602
ISBN 0-13-572586-0
ISBN 0-13-572578-X (pbk.)

*To Suzy, Tina, and Judy, our wives
And to William L. Rivers, our teacher*

10 9 8 7 6 5 4 3 2

PRENTICE-HALL, INTERNATIONAL, INC., London
PRENTICE-HALL OF AUSTRALIA, PTY. LTD., Sydney
PRENTICE-HALL OF CANADA, LTD., Toronto
PRENTICE-HALL OF INDIA PRIVATE LIMITED, New Delhi
PRENTICE-HALL OF JAPAN, INC., Tokyo
PRENTICE-HALL OF SOUTHEAST ASIA PTE. LTD., Singapore

Contents

iii

PART II   RESPONSIBILITY   *75*

Foreword

Trying to avoid the products of the mass media is like trying to avoid daylight: You can do it, but only with an effort so demanding that it reaches the point of absurdity. Except for those who plan to enter monasteries, all college students will be immersed in the media for the rest of their lives. It follows that all—not just those who will become newspaper reporters, television producers, and filmmakers, but also those who will be lawyers and stockbrokers and morticians—should learn about the strengths and the flaws of mass communication, what it can do for them, and what it can do *to* them.

Not so long ago schools and departments of journalism and communication were content to deal only with prospective reporters, advertising salesmen, filmmakers, and others who were trying to learn to work in the media. The skills and techniques courses that make up the bulk of the curricula of that time were designed to *train* rather than to educate. There was precious little in those journalism programs that appealed to students who wanted a career outside the mass media. Now, however, programs almost everywhere offer at least a few courses—some offer a great many—that teach all comers *about* the world of mass communication. The result is surely better-informed practitioners and more knowledgeable laymen.

This book is completely in tune with the trend to broad-gauge journalism education. The authors are not at all concerned here with teaching how news stories, magazine articles, and television documentaries are written and edited. They *are* concerned with how the structures of these forms—and the structures of the industries that produce them—create a world of shadows and reality. This is the keynote throughout: What are the effects of the forms, practices, habits, and biases of the media today?

How can a teacher express public pride in the work of his students without seeming immodest? From 1967 to 1971, the authors of this book were my students in a Ph.D. program called Public Affairs Communication. I worked closely with them (and played poker with them) all those years. Paying tribute to their book may thus be unseemly —a bit self-appreciative. But I do consider this a fine book, and I believe that I can escape any suspicion of self-appreciation by recording that Peter Sandman, David Rubin, and David Sachsman were excellent writers and thinkers before they became my students. I have been paying tribute to their work from the beginning. And I thank them. For a teacher, happiness is a bright student.

WILLIAM L. RIVERS
Stanford, California

Preface

We began writing the first edition of this book in 1969 because we saw two crucial gaps that needed to be filled.

First, we wanted to produce a text that did not assume its readers were planning a career in journalism. Though we saw the serious need for better-informed journalists, we believed that the need for better-informed readers and viewers was at least as critical. Consumers of mass communication, we felt, need to know what it is doing for them, what it is doing to them, and what they can do about it.

Second, we wanted to produce a text that would itself embody the characteristics of the best of modern journalism—solid evidence, written in a light style, structured by forthright interpretation. Even an introductory book, we insisted, should be thoroughly documented, thoroughly readable, and thoroughly interpretive.

Many things have happened to the media since the first edition was published in 1972. Perhaps the most important change is a phenomenal growth in consumer interest in the process and effects of mass communication. This interest has been fanned by the media's successes and by their failures—by Watergate exposés and by media inattention to minorities and women, by "Sesame Street" and by television violence. Today, more people than ever before are aware of the media as a social and political institution that affects their lives. More people than ever before are trying to affect the content of the media. And more people than ever before are considering communications careers.

The goal of this second edition is identical with the goal of the first—to help media consumers and future media professionals understand the media, so that the former can consume more cautiously, so that the latter can perform more effectively, and so that both can join in the struggle to improve the content of the mass media.

PETER M. SANDMAN
DAVID M. RUBIN
DAVID B. SACHSMAN

Introduction

Communication involves the sharing of information, attitudes, and experiences. While interpersonal communication is a delicate process controlled jointly by the source and the receiver, mass communication is much more brutal and one-sided. The mass communication audience—you—has little control over content; sources and the media themselves make most of the content decisions. In the United States, those decisions are determined mainly by the profit motive, leavened with some concern for social responsibility.

COMMUNICATION

Communication is the process of transmitting a message from a source to an audience via a channel. Consider, for example, a conversation, the most common kind of communication. The person who speaks is the source. The person who listens is the audience. What is transmitted is the message. And the spoken voice carried through the air is the channel.

Now consider a more complicated example, an article in a newspaper. The message is everything the article says, everything it implies, and everything a reader might infer from it. The audience is everybody who reads the article or even glances at it. The source is everybody who contributes in one way or another to the article; this includes the newsmakers who are quoted, the reporter, the editor, and even the proofreaders and printers. The channel is, of course, the printed word, the newspaper itself.

What is a communication *medium?* Strictly speaking, a medium is a channel—the spoken word, the printed word, or whatever. But the term is often used to mean both the channel and the source, and sometimes even the message. It includes everything that reaches the audience. When we speak of the "mass media," for example, we usually mean not only the channels of mass communication but also the content of those channels and the behavior of the people who work for them.

Wilbur Schramm thinks of communication as a sharing process. He puts it this way:

Communication comes from the Latin *communis,* common. When we communicate we are trying to establish a "commonness" with someone. That is, we are trying to share information, an idea, or an attitude. At this moment I am trying to communicate to you the idea that the essence of communication is getting the receiver and the sender "tuned" together for a particular message.[1]

Effective communication, then, is communication that succeeds in establishing Schramm's "commonness" between the source and the audience. Communication is perfectly effective when the audience receives precisely what the source intended it to receive.

Anything that interferes with effective communication can be called "noise." This bit of jargon is borrowed from electrical engineering, where "noise" refers literally to the static in an electrical system that lessens the precision of the transmission. A misspelled word, a fuzzy TV picture, and an ink splotch are all examples of noise in a communications channel. Similarly, a speaker who uses words the audience doesn't know is an example of "source noise."

Most of the noise in a communication system is contributed by neither the source nor the channel, but rather by the audience. People are enormously proficient at ignoring, misinterpreting, and misremembering communications that for one reason or another don't appeal to them. At least three psychological strategies are relevant here:

- *Selective attention.* People expose themselves primarily to communications they like. If you are not interested in buying a car, you will read very few automobile advertisements. If you are interested, you'll probably read all the ads you can. But once you settle on a Plymouth, you are likely to read only the Plymouth ads.
- *Selective perception.* Once exposed to a communication, people tend to interpret it so as to coincide with their own preconceptions. If you show a middle-class audience a drawing of a white man brandishing a razor in the face of a black, many will "see" the razor in the hand of the black instead.
- *Selective retention.* Even if they understand a communication, people tend to remember only what they want to remember. After reading a balanced discussion of Soviet Communism,

anti-Communist students recall mostly the drawbacks of the system, while pro-Communist students tend to remember mostly its advantages.

Most communications are controlled by the source. When a teacher lectures to a class, it is the teacher, not the class, who decides what will be said. Selective attention, selective perception, and selective retention are the principal methods open to the audience for controlling the message. If a student is bored or offended by what the teacher is saying, he or she may tune the teacher out and think about something else. Or the student may unconsciously misinterpret the lecture, perhaps "hearing" that there will be one term paper when the teacher has said there will be two. Or the student may simply forget those parts of the message that are least appealing, such as the reading assignment. The teacher is likely to take a dim view of these lapses, but he or she is just as guilty as the students. In grading papers, for example, teachers tend to "see" the right answers in the papers of students whose work they admire.

Selective attention, selective perception, and selective retention are universal. They add a tremendous amount of noise to nearly every communication. The source can easily control what is said, but the source cannot control what the audience hears, or thinks it hears.

Audience noise is most potent when the message is controversial; simple and unthreatening messages, on the other hand, tend to be received relatively "clear." As a result, it is next to impossible for any communication to convert an audience from one viewpoint to another. It is much easier to create a new viewpoint where none existed before. And it is easier still to communicate information that tends to support the established viewpoint of the audience. All communicators—advertisers, politicians, reporters, even teachers—must work within these constraints.

So far we have talked about communication as if it were a one-way street; the message moves in a straight line from the source to the channel to the audience. In reality, every good communication system must work both ways. The mechanisms for transmitting messages backward from audience to channel, from audience to source, or from channel to source are known as "feedback loops." When a television actor checks the monitor to see how he looks on the screen, he is getting feedback from the channel. When an actress reads her fan mail, she is getting feedback from the audience. And when the network management looks over the show's ratings, it too is getting feedback from the audience.

The technical vocabulary of communication will be used sparingly in this book. Of course we'll be talking a lot about sources and audiences, but very little about channels, and even less about "noise," "selective attention," "feedback loops," and the like. Nevertheless, these are vitally important concepts to bear in mind. When we speak later about the influence of news bias, we will be describing a kind of noise. When we discuss the ineffectiveness of editorials, we will be referring to a special case of selective attention. And when we complain about the problem of public control of the media, we will be noting the absence of sufficient provision for feedback.

MASS COMMUNICATION

Interpersonal communication is the process of transmitting information, ideas, and attitudes from one person to another. Mass communication is the process of transmitting information, ideas, and attitudes to many people, usually through a machine. There are several important differences between the two.

First, the sources of a mass communication have great difficulty gearing their message to their audience. They may know the demographic statistics of the audience—its average age, its average socioeconomic status, etc.—but they cannot know the individual quirks of each individual reader, listener, and viewer.

Second, mass-communication systems typically include much weaker feedback loops than interpersonal communication systems. When you talk to friends, you can usually tell whether they are listening, whether they understand, whether they agree or disagree, and so forth. All this is impossible in mass communication.

Third, the audience of a mass communication is much more likely than the audience of an interpersonal communication to twist the message through selective attention, perception, and retention. People turn off the TV (literally or figuratively) if they don't like what it's saying. It's a lot harder—though still possible—to turn off someone talking to you.

Fourth, and perhaps most important, mass-communication systems are a lot more complicated than interpersonal communication systems. Each message (an article in a newspaper, for example) may have as many as a dozen sources, with different points of view and different goals for the communication. The channel, too, is typically a complex organization (such as a newspaper), composed of many individuals, whose viewpoints and goals may vary widely. Every mass communication is in a sense a committee product.

All four of these factors tend to lessen the effect of a mass communication on its audience. The power of the mass media is based on the size of their audience, on their ability to reach millions of people in one shot. But in dealing with any individual member of that audience, you'd be a lot more effective if you sat down together for a chat.

When people sit down for a chat, however, the things they talk about and the attitudes they express are often derived from the mass media. In 1940, Paul Lazarsfeld and his colleagues studied the voting behavior of a group of citizens in Erie County, Ohio. They discovered, to their surprise, that very few people decided how to vote on the basis of information learned directly from the mass media. Most voters made up their minds as a result of interpersonal communications—conversations with a friend, a neighbor, a union leader, a spouse.

Only a minority of Erie County's citizens made significant use of the media for voting information. Members of this minority then sat down with their friends and neighbors and transmitted the message of the media through interpersonal communication. Lazarsfeld called these minority members "opinion leaders." He concluded that "ideas often flow from radio and print to opinion leaders and from these to the less active sections of the population." [2] This is known as the "two-step flow" theory of mass-media influence.

More recent research has shown that even the two-step flow theory is oversimplified. A more accurate term might be "multi-step flow." For every field of interest (politics, fashion, economics, moviegoing, etc.) there are apparently certain people who make great use of the media for information and guidance. These opinion leaders then communicate with each other, crystalizing their views into a consistent stance. Later they transmit this attitude to lesser opinion leaders, who also make use of the mass media but not so much. The recipients compare what they get from the media with what they get from their opinion leaders, then pass the combination on down the line. Eventually the message reaches that large segment of the population that makes little or no direct use of the media.

Opinion leadership, by the way, is not usually a general trait. Each of us is an opinion leader for some groups of people and some topics, and a follower for many other groups and topics. The two main characteristics of opinion leaders are that they pay greater than average attention to the mass media, and that they are respected by their followers. Like any other kind of leader, an opinion leader must not get too far ahead of the group. If an opinion leader's distillation

of media content conflicts too strongly with the group's customs and norms, the group is very likely to find itself another leader.

In the field of labor relations, the multi-step flow might run something like this: A group of union leaders, all inveterate newspaper readers, agree that they are opposed to the president's plan for wage and price controls. They pass this information on to the shop stewards, who have followed the issue casually on television. The shop stewards pass it on to the rank and file, who have a hazy understanding of the problem. And the rank and file pass it on to their friends and family.

The information chain for, say, birth-control methods would be quite different. A male union leader is unlikely to read about the medical hazards of the pill and then pass the information along to his shop stewards. He is far more likely to hear about it from his wife, who heard about it from a woman friend or co-worker, who read about it in the paper. The principle, however, is the same. The direct effect of the mass media on labor relations and contraception is comparatively minor. But the indirect impact is huge.

AMERICAN MASS COMMUNICATION

The American system of mass communication has at least three characteristics that distinguish it from systems in other countries.

1. Pervasive influence.
2. Freedom of the press.
3. Big-business media.

None of these characteristics is unique. There are other countries with powerful media, other countries with free media, other countries with profit-oriented media. But the United States embodies all three traits to an extent unmatched in the rest of the world.

1. Pervasive Influence. A fish could no

more tell you what it is like to live out of water than an American could tell you what it is like to live without mass communication. As soon as American children are old enough to distinguish between two different makes of midget racing cars or fruit-flavored brands of toothpaste, they are bathed in a constant stream of messages from radio and television. They approach the daily newspaper through the comics or sports section; these lead them to comic books and sporting magazines, and then perhaps to more serious books and magazines.

By the time they enter kindergarten, most American children have already been exposed to hundreds, perhaps thousands of hours of radio and television. They have attended dozens of movies and browsed through scores of children's books. They have cut pictures out of magazines and scowled at the newspaper in unconscious imitation of their parents. All these experiences have taught them something—something about literacy, perhaps, something about violence, something about America. They are in a real sense children of the mass media.

For most adults, meanwhile, the mass media constitute the only advanced education they receive after high school or college. It is obvious that the media offer every American a continuous course in modern world history. But it is not so obvious, perhaps, that the very basics of community living come to us through the media: births, weddings, deaths, weather reports, traffic accidents, crimes, sales, elections.

It is hard to imagine an efficient system of democratic government without an equally efficient system of mass communication. Citizens would learn of new legislation only after it passed, and then only if they visited their representative in Washington. Incumbents would probably serve for life, because

---

REALITY AND PSEUDO-REALITY

In 1922, the distinguished political columnist Walter Lippmann wrote a book on *Public Opinion*. He began the book this way:

> There is an island in the ocean where in 1914 a few Englishmen, Frenchmen, and Germans lived. No cable reaches that island, and the British mail steamer comes but once in sixty days. In September it had not yet come, and the islanders were still talking about the latest newspaper which told about the approaching trial of Madame Caillaux for the shooting of Gaston Calmette. It was, therefore, with more than usual eagerness that the whole colony assembled at the quay on a day in mid-September to hear from the captain what the verdict had been. They learned that for over six weeks now those of them who were English and those of them who were French had been fighting in behalf of the sanctity of treaties against those of them who were Germans. For six strange weeks they had acted as if they were friends, when in fact they were enemies.

Lippmann's point is that much of what we know about our world and our relationship to it reaches us indirectly, through media rather than personal experience. This indirect information may come quickly or slowly; it may be true or false; we may interpret it accurately or inaccurately. But "whatever we believe to be a true picture, we treat as if it were the environment itself." Thus Lippmann begins his analysis of public opinion with this axiom: "We shall assume that what each man does is based not on direct and certain knowledge, but on pictures made by himself or given to him."

Lippmann called his first chapter "The World Outside and the Pictures in Our Heads." Decades before television, he insisted that society is molded by the interaction between media content and the media audience.[3]

no challengers could make themselves known to the electorate. Corruption would go largely unchecked. News of foreign affairs would remain the monopoly of the president and the State Department. And on the local level, mayors would be free to run their cities as personal fiefdoms. Political information is political power. Without the mass media to transmit such information, the American people would be powerless.

Dwarfing even the educational and political roles of the American media is their entertainment function. Television offers a seemingly unending stream of westerns, thrillers, comedies, and star-studded specials. Radio spins records and conversation. Newspapers lighten the weight of the news with puzzles, advice to the lovelorn, comics, sports, and back-fence gossip. Books, magazines, and films supply entertainment packages for more specialized audiences. The Number One source of recreational activity of almost every American is the mass media.

Of course the media are pervasive in other countries as well. Transistor radios are always among the first manufactured products to be imported into any unindustrialized area of the world. Newspapers and government-sponsored radio and TV stations follow soon afterward. Nevertheless, few observers would dispute that Americans are more a product of their media than any other people in the world.

2. *Freedom of the Press.* The American government was founded on a radical political theory: representative democracy. According to this strange notion, the people of a nation should control the government by electing officials to carry out their will. The mass media necessarily play a central role in representative democracy. It is through the media, presumably, that the people get the information they need to decide what they want their officials to do. And it is through the media, presumably, that the people find out if their officials are doing it.

For this reason the First Amendment to the U.S. Constitution forbids the government to make any laws "abridging the freedom of the press." When it was first written, this provision was unprecedented. Other governments had assumed the right of the king to put a stop to any publication he deemed damaging to the nation. The American Constitution denied Congress and the president this fundamental right. The real threat to a democracy, so the argument went, is a mass-media system in chains. As long as every publisher (though not necessarily every reporter) is free to print whatever he or she wants to print, the truth will make itself clear, the people will be informed, and the democracy will flourish.

Today, many foreign governments have copied our First Amendment into their constitutions, and some even practice the freedom they preach. The American government, meanwhile, restrains its media with the laws of libel, obscenity, and privacy, the licensing of broadcast stations, the postal regulations, and so forth.

Despite these limitations, there is no mass-media system in the world today that is more free from government interference than the American system. In recent years, a number of very high officials have attacked the media for "irresponsible" opposition to government policy. Some have interpreted these attacks as attempts to control the press, and so they may be. But it is a testimonial to the almost incredible freedom of the American media that the attacks are limited mostly to speeches, denunciations, and largely futile attempts at intimidation. The government can *do* relatively little. You need only consult the latest news of national politics for fresh evidence of America's freedom of the press.

The purpose of a free press, you will remember, is to insure that the people will be well-informed. Well, we have a free press. Do we have an informed population? Pollster George Gallup often quotes a survey of college graduates which found that only four in ten could name the two senators from their own state; only half could cite a single difference between capitalism and socialism; only half had an accurate idea of the population of the United States; and only one in three could list five of the Soviet Union's satellite countries in Eastern Europe.[4]

The notion that freedom of the press is the basic requirement for an informed population is known as the "libertarian theory." The authors of the First Amendment firmly believed that if every newspaper were free to print precisely what it wanted to print, somehow truth would emerge victorious from its open confrontation with falsehood. The only responsibility of the media was to tell it the way they saw it. The only responsibility of the government was to leave the media alone.

In recent years, many observers have begun to question the libertarian theory. In its place they have proposed a social responsibility theory of the press. That is, they argue that the American mass media must recognize their obligation to serve the public—to be truthful, accurate, and complete; to act as a forum for conflicting viewpoints; to provide meaningful background to the daily news; etc. Social responsibility theorists claim that if the media do not voluntarily live up to their obligations, then they must be forced to do so by the government.

Though the social responsibility theory is gaining in popularity and influence, it is not yet established. The American mass media today are free—free to serve the public or not as they choose.

3. Big-Business Media. Perhaps the strongest weapon in the arsenal of the social responsibility theorists is the Big Business emphasis in the modern American media. The United States is one of the few countries in the world whose major media are all privately owned. Like General Motors and U.S. Steel, American newspapers, magazines, and broadcast stations spend much of their time worrying about stockholders, dividends, and profits. They may have too little time left for worrying about service to the public.

Like every business, the mass media have a product to sell. In the case of the book and film industries, the product is the medium itself; part of the price of a book or movie ticket is the manufacturer's profit. For the rest of the mass media, the product is you. Newspapers, magazines, and broadcast stations earn their considerable profits by selling your presence and your attention to advertisers. Articles and programs are just a device to keep you corralled, a come-on for the all-important ads.

The inexorable trend in American business is toward monopoly—toward bigness and fewness. The mass media are no exception. Chains dominate the newspaper and magazine industries. The three networks have an iron grip on television programming. The book business is dominated by a few giant companies on the East Coast, the movie business by a few giant companies on the West Coast. Competing with the biggies in any of these fields is incredibly costly and hazardous.

Several conclusions follow from these facts. First, since the American media are businesses first and foremost, they are likely to choose profit over public service when the two come into conflict. Second, since the media are owned by business-oriented people, they are likely to reflect a business-oriented notion of what's good for the public—which may not be everybody's notion. Third, since the media are close to monopolies, they are likely to offer the audience only a single viewpoint on public affairs, instead of the rich conflict of viewpoints envisioned by the Founding Fathers. And fourth, since the media make competition extremely difficult, they are likely to "black out" positions and groups of which they disapprove.

Pervasive influence, freedom of the press, and the profit motive—this is the combination that makes the American mass media unique. Nowhere else is such a powerful social force so little controlled by government, so much controlled by self-interest.

THE FOUR FUNCTIONS

The mass media in general, and the American mass media in particular, have at least four basic functions to perform. They are:

1. To serve the economic system.
2. To entertain.
3. To inform.
4. To influence.

We will consider each in turn.

1. To Serve the Economic System. The fundamental economic purpose of the mass media in the United States is to sell people to advertisers. The articles in your newspaper and the programs on your radio and TV sets are merely "come-ons" to catch and hold your attention. Advertisers buy that attention from the media, and use it to sell you their products and services. In the process, both the media and the advertisers earn substantial profits.

It is possible to conceive of a mass-media system not dedicated to profit through advertising. Such systems exist, in fact, in many countries. The British Broadcasting Corporation (BBC), to give but one example, is financed in part by a special tax on radio and TV sets. It accepts no ads and earns no profits. Even in this country there are non-profit broadcast stations and publications—not many, but a few. And of course some of the profit-making media, such as books and movies, earn their money directly from the audience. But the most influential media in the United States are fueled by advertising.

This dependence on advertising has many important implications for media content, which is inevitably designed to attract the sort of audience advertisers need in the sort of mood advertisers want. But advertising is also important for its own sake. Through advertising, the mass media bring buyer and seller together. Advertising creates the demand for new goods and increases the demand for old ones. It thus helps keep the engine of industry running. No one knows exactly how much of the U.S. gross national product is the result of advertising in the mass media, but most economists agree that advertising's contribution to the GNP is substantial. Regardless of whether we approve or disapprove of advertising, this service to the economic system is certainly a central function of the American mass media.

2. To Entertain. Entertainment is by far the biggest service of the American mass media. This is especially true from the viewpoint of the audience. Political scientists may evaluate a television program in terms of how much information it imparts. Advertisers may ask what kind of climate for persuasion it offers. Station owners may wonder how much profit it brings in. But with rare exceptions, viewers want to know only how entertaining it is.

Television is undoubtedly the nation's Number One entertainment medium, but film and radio are not far behind. When the movie *Love Story* opened in December of 1970, it broke the house record in 159 of the 165 theaters in which it was shown. The film grossed over $2,400,000 in its first three days. As for radio, the average American family owns at least two receivers in the home and a third in the car. Why do people go to movies and switch on the radio? To be entertained.

Even the print media succeed or fail largely in terms of their entertainment value. The best-seller lists for hardback and paperback books usually include a few works of significance and value. But the bulk of every list is always pure entertainment, and even the "important" books must be entertaining to succeed. Magazines, too, must season their informational content with a heavy dose of fun and games. The least entertaining of the mass media is undoubtedly the newspaper. Yet even that offers the reader dozens of comics, humor and gossip columns, and human-interest features in every issue.

Because the public demands entertainment from its media, the media owner who wants to succeed has no choice but to try to be entertaining. Many critics have deplored this fact, complaining that mere entertainment was a waste and a degradation of media potential. Such an attitude ignores the important social role played by entertainment— the transmission of culture, the enlargement of perspectives, the encouragement of imagination, etc. And even the most virulent opponents of media entertainment must admit that the opportunity to relax and unwind is vital. Entertainment is not merely an economic necessity for media owners; it is an integral, essential function of the media.

But that is far from the whole story. The media have other functions besides entertainment. Moreover, the media *choose* the kinds of entertainment they wish to use. They are subject to criticism for their choices.

It is extremely difficult to come up with a clear-cut standard for distinguishing between "good" entertainment and "bad" entertainment. Nonetheless, most observers will agree that in some sense *Harper's* is better than *True Romances,* "Sesame Street" is better than "Bugs Bunny," and Hemingway is better than Erle Stanley Gardner. The media must cater to public tastes, but they also help to mold public tastes. If the media choose violence, or pornography, or the lowest of lowbrow culture, then they must take responsibility for the choice.

3. To Inform. Entertainment may be what the public wants from its mass media, but information is probably their most important function. No doubt many people read *Time* and *Newsweek,* say, because they find them entertaining; and certainly the newsmagazines try to entertain their readers. But the best newsmagazine is not necessarily the most entertaining one. It is the one that successfully conveys the most information.

The power of the mass media to inform is almost incredible. On November 22, 1963, at 12:30 in the afternoon, President John F. Kennedy was assassinated. Within half an hour, two-thirds of all Americans knew of the event. Ninety percent knew within an

---

WHAT WE WATCH

Judged by the ratings, the following were the most popular TV shows in early January, 1974:

1. "All In The Family" (CBS)
2. "Sanford & Son" (NBC)
3. "The Waltons" (CBS)
4. "M*A*S*H" (CBS)
5. "Maude" (CBS)
6. "Hawaii Five-O" (CBS)
7. "World of Disney" (NBC)
8. "CBS Friday Movie" (CBS)
9. "Mary Tyler Moore" (CBS)
10. "NBC Sunday Mystery Movie" (NBC) [5]

Every show on the list is entertainment. We learn from these shows, of course—everything from wartime medical techniques to the lifestyle of lower-middle-class New Yorkers. And we pick up attitudes from them too—toward doctors and detectives, criminals and cowboys, hippies and housewives. What we learn may be true or false; the attitudes we absorb may be humane or oppressive. But none of that is what the shows are "about." They are entertainment.

---

hour, and 99.8 percent had heard the story by early evening.[6] Some got the news directly from the mass media; others were told by family, friends, or strangers on the street, who had themselves heard it on the media.

There was an immediate rush to radio and television for more detail. During the days that followed, 166 million Americans tuned in to the assassination story on television. The average TV set was on for roughly eight hours a day.[7]

Most of the news supplied by the mass media is more routine than a presidential assassination. Weather reports, stock listings, and movie timetables are among the best-read features in your daily newspaper—and among the most informative. We tend to dismiss these services not because they are unimportant, but because they are easy to prepare. Similarly, news reports of natural disasters, crimes, accidents, and the like are genuinely useful. Since they are standard fare for the media and difficult to handle poorly, scholars pay them very little attention—perhaps less attention than they deserve.

The more difficult a story is to cover, the less likely the media are to cover it well. The informational problems of the media are many and varied. Is a story so complicated that no reporter can understand it, much less repeat it? Is it so technical that few readers are likely to enjoy it or finish it? Does it require days of hard-nosed investigative digging among sources who would much rather keep their mouths shut? Might it insult or embarrass an advertiser, an important newsmaker, a friend of the publisher, or even a reader? Such stories may or may not be more important than the easier ones. But because they are difficult to cover, the way they are handled is a good measure of the media's responsibility to their informing function.

Perhaps the most important information of all is information about the government. The purpose of the First Amendment, after all, is to insure that the media will be free to report and criticize the actions of government officials, free to inform the public

about public affairs. When a television station carries live the speech of a president, it is performing a valuable public service. When it offers intelligent commentary on the content and meaning of that speech, it is performing a much *more* valuable public service.

It is worth mentioning that everything in the mass media is in some sense informative, whether or not it is intended that way. Even a soap opera tells us something (true or false) about how people live, how they dress and talk and solve problems.

For centuries, Italy was a country with two different populations: the wealthy, cosmopolitan North and the poor, rural South. The two were so different they even spoke different dialects, and were almost completely unable to understand one another. Then, in 1954, nationwide Italian television was introduced. In just a few years, television began to unify the country.

A university professor comments: "Some intellectuals call television the 'opium of the people.' That may be so in a city like Milan or Turin. But can you imagine a modern bathroom appearing on TV screens from Naples southward?" And a historian adds: "There's been more change in Italy's linguistic situation in the past fifteen years than in the century since Rome became the capital." [8]

The bulk of this book is devoted to an assessment and explanation of the informational performance of the American mass media. This is not because media owners, or advertisers, or audiences consider information the most important role of the media. Many don't. We do.

4. To Influence. The power of the mass media to change people's minds directly is very limited. People don't like to have their minds changed, and so they ignore or misinterpret attempts to do so—usually successfully. If influence were limited to changing people's minds directly, the media would not be particularly influential.

But influence is more subtle than that. When William Randolph Hearst's *New York Journal* championed the war against Spain in 1898, he didn't achieve very many conversions. But through slanted news coverage and sensational writing, the *Journal* did manage to help create a climate of war fever. No doubt most readers viewed Hearst's style of journalism as entertainment and information, not influence. Yet he helped make them go to war.

More than a century before Hearst, Thomas Paine wrote a political pamphlet called *Common Sense,* urging an American Revolution. And about 75 years after Hearst, in 1968, Richard Nixon engineered a series of television advertisements, urging his election as president. Paine didn't convert many Tories, and Nixon didn't win over many Democrats. But Paine did succeed in crystalizing the incoherent resentments of many colonists into a consistent revolutionary ideology. And Nixon succeeded in crystalizing the incoherent frustrations of many Americans into a Republican vote. So Paine got his revolution, and Nixon got the White House. The mass media played a vital role in the success of both men.

The most obvious and prevalent example of mass media influence is advertising. Media ad campaigns have a lot going for them. Through careful intermixture with entertainment and informational content, they gain a captive audience. Through bold colors and imaginative graphics, they make you pay attention. Through catchy slogans and constant repetition, they make you remember. Through irrelevant appeals to sex, snobbism, and the good life, they make you buy.

The very existence of newspapers, magazines, radio, and television testifies to the persuasive power of advertising. For if the ads were unsuccessful, there would be no ads. And if there were no ads, there would be no newspapers, magazines, radio, and television in the form we know them.

Not every media attempt to influence the public is successful, of course. Politicians and manufacturers may spend millions on the media and still lose out to the competition. Editorialists and polemicists may devote page after page to an urgent plea for action, and get no action. Not every revolutionary book foments a revolution; not every TV appeal to voters captures the White House. But it is nearly impossible to foment a revolution without a book, to win the White House without a TV appeal. The persuasive power of the mass media, though limited, is undeniable.

The remainder of this chapter is devoted to exploring the impact of mass media on society, especially the impact of American mass media on American society. This is an enormously complex and confusing topic.

Before we begin, consider the following facts that have already been mentioned:

1. Mass media pervade the lives of all Americans, adults as well as children; we are all in some sense products of our media.

     but

2. The media audience can easily avoid conversion to new attitudes (and even exposure to unpleasant truths) by ignoring, misunderstanding, or forgetting what it doesn't want to know.

     but

3. We learn from entertainment too, and are influenced by fiction and "straight" news as well as by intentional persuasion.

     but

4. Sources of mass-media content cannot gear their messages to individuals in the audience, and cannot easily judge how the audience is responding in time to change the message accordingly.

     but

5. Interpersonal communication is often based on information and attitudes that opinion leaders have absorbed from the mass media.

     but

6. The mass media are so complex, and so diverse in their sources and channels, that no single viewpoint is likely to dominate the media for long.

but

7. Even though advertising and propaganda are not always successful, they achieve enough that few manufacturers or ideologues would try to do without them.

An adequate picture of the impact of American media on American society must make sense of all these conflicting facts.

———————

The persuasive power of the mass media is neither as great as the alarmists warn us nor as little as the optimists assure us. The media are rarely able to convert their audience to an opposing viewpoint overnight, but they can reinforce old attitudes, create brand new ones, and in time even achieve some change. Readers and viewers are active participants in this process, using the media for their own purposes and needs. This may protect us from specific influence attempts, but it does not keep the media from creating the reality in which we live and to which we respond. The media "environment" plays as big a role in the lives of many Americans as the first-hand environment of their own experience.

PERSUASION AND PROPAGANDA

People have thought about the effects of communication on attitudes and behavior at least since the time of Aristotle. And the special power of mass communication to change the way we think, feel, and behave has been a source of concern (especially to governments) since the invention of the printing press. But the modern science of communication research was born out of psychology, sociology, and political science only in the 1930s. There were two immediate reasons for its quick development at that point in history. First, advertisers wanted to know how to spend their money more effectively. And second, American intellectuals were worried about the propaganda efforts of Nazi Germany.

The research tradition that developed over the next thirty years was devoted to answering one basic question: What factors determine how much impact a particular piece of communication will have on the attitudes of its audience? Hundreds of books and thousands of journal articles were written about various aspects of this question.

By way of example, here is a more or less random list of six findings from this type of research:

1. It is usually better to state your conclusions explicitly than to let your audience draw its own conclusions.[9]

2. Arguments presented at the beginning or end of a communication are remembered better than arguments presented in the middle.[10]

3. Emotional appeals are often more effective than strictly rational ones.[11]

4. When dealing with an audience that disagrees with your position, it helps to acknowledge some validity to the opposing view.[12]

5. Attitude change may be greater some time after a communication than right after it.[13]

6. High-credibility sources (such as doctors) provoke more attitude change than low-credibility sources (such as patients), even if the reason for the credibility has nothing to do with the topic of the communication.[14]

These findings—and hundreds more like them—were very helpful to advertisers, who used them to design more effective ads. They were very helpful to the war effort, which used them to counter Nazi propaganda and later to produce Allied propaganda. And they are still very helpful to marketing experts, political candidates, and anyone else interested in using communication to change people's attitudes.

But as the studies accumulated, attitude change turned out to be a more complicated phenomenon than the early findings had seemed to imply. Later research had to specify the conditions under which the various "principles" of attitude change did or did not hold true. As time went on, and more and more conflicting findings turned up, it became harder and harder to specify which principles were valid under which conditions.

Researchers began to suspect that there was something fundamentally wrong with the way they were studying the effects of communications. In fact, there were at least four things wrong with it.

First, the majority of the early studies were conducted in the laboratories of academic social scientists, using students as subjects. Whole theories of communication emerged from the unpaid efforts of undergraduates in introductory psychology courses. This was convenient for the researchers and made for neat, methodologically controlled studies—but it was unreal. The occasional pieces of real-world research almost invariably found much less attitude change than the lab studies had led everyone to expect. The complexities and counter-pressures of reality just couldn't be duplicated in controlled laboratory experiments.

Second, most of the studies dealt with topics of some intellectual importance but practically no audience involvement—such as dental hygiene, currency devaluation, or the future of movie theaters. The way attitudes are changed around these sorts of topics turned out to be almost irrelevant. Most propagandists were interested in more gut-grabbing topics, such as race prejudice, "welfare statism," or the upcoming presidential election. Audiences already had strong emotional commitments on those issues, and a speech on race relations yielded a lot less attitude change than one on the future of movie theaters. Advertisers, meanwhile, were interested in topics of zero intellectual interest to the audience, like the choice of a breakfast cereal. By 1965, Herbert E. Krugman was arguing that people are influenced by advertising without paying attention, and without changing their attitudes at all.[15]

Third, most attitude-change research was based on an oversimplified model of how attitudes are related to information and behavior. Many studies assumed that if the audience learned the message, its attitudes would therefore be changed. Even more studies assumed that if attitudes (as expressed on a questionnaire) were changed, behavior would inevitably change too. By the 1960s these assumptions were falling apart. In 1964, Jack B. Haskins surveyed twenty-eight different studies of information, attitudes, and behavior, and concluded that there was "no relationship between what a person learned, knew, or recalled on the one hand, and what he did or how he felt on the other." [16] In the same year, Leon Festinger reviewed the meager research literature on how attitudes affect behavior, and found no evidence of a consistent relationship there either.[17]

Fourth, the early research on attitude change virtually ignored the audience. All the care and creativity went into figuring out the different effects of different kinds of sources, channels, styles of presentation, etc. The audience was viewed as just being there, passive, receiving the message and then changing or not changing depending on the source's skill and know-how. But in fact, people are not just sponges who soak up media content. We *use* the media for our own purposes, and we are therefore active participants in the communication process. How the media affect us depends very largely on who we are and how we are using the media.

In a sense, everything that was wrong with traditional communication research resulted from underestimating the audience. You know that you respond differently to an experiment in a psych class than to an editorial on television. You know that your views on currency devaluation are more thoughtful than your views on breakfast cereals, and less emotional than your views on race prejudice. You know that you can learn things without believing them, believe things without doing them, and do things without learning or believing them. It took communication researchers thirty years to acknowledge these truths fully, because for thirty years they concentrated on the source and the message and almost ignored the audience.

THE MEDIA AUDIENCE

Most Americans, it must be said, are happy with their mass media. They have complaints, of course—too much depressing news, too many commercials, and so forth. But on the whole they are quite satisfied. When survey researchers go into the field and ask people what they would like from the media that they are not already getting, almost invariably the response is "Nothing." It is possible, of course—perhaps even likely—that there are public needs which are not adequately served by the mass media. But if so, the public is largely unaware of them.

What, then, are the public needs that are served by the media? In other words, what do we use our media for, what functions do they fulfill in our lives?

Play is obviously one of the most important ways we use the media. From the very first time your parents read you a story, you have been taught that media use is fun. And for most of us it *is* fun. Not just explicit entertainment, either—many people watch commercials and read newspapers for pleasure, and certainly advertisers and reporters work hard to make their writing pleasurable. At least one scholar, William Stephenson, argues that fun is both the greatest impact and the greatest public service of the media; his book is called *The Play Theory of Mass Communication*.[18] Other observers complain that media "escapism" distracts people from more active sorts of entertainment and from the serious problems of the day. But no one denies that we use our media for play.

Time-filling is related to play, but a lot more passive. When New York's newspapers went on strike in 1945, Bernard Berelson asked people what they missed. Most readers talked about the importance of newspapers as part of the routine at certain points in their daily schedule—over the breakfast table, for example, or while commuting to and from work. They resented the disruption in their lives caused by the strike, and many resorted to scanning cereal boxes or subway ads just to have something to read.[19] Similarly, we listen to the radio while driving and the TV while doing chores mainly to fill up the time.

Media use also serves a number of social needs for the audience. Conversation requires a steady supply of topics to keep it going, and the media are a reliable source; you can always talk about this morning's news or last night's TV. Many magazines are purchased for the social status they confer when mentioned in passing or spread out on the coffee table. Television gives families a chance to spend time together peacefully. People go to movies to get away from their kids, or to get away from their parents, or to get close to someone else.

Innumerable psychological needs are met

THE AUDIENCE IS PEOPLE

Not only do people use the media for different purposes at different times. They also have different personalities—and our personalities greatly affect how we respond to a persuasive argument. Authoritarian people are more easily persuaded than independent thinkers, especially by a high-status source. People with high IQs are more influenced by logical arguments than people with low IQs, but they are less influenced by emotional ones. Some psychologists have even suggested that persuasibility is itself a personality trait.

Age, sex, income, social class, occupation, and other demographic variables also influence our response to persuasion. So do the groups we belong to or want to belong to. The mass-media audience is made up of real people who lead real lives, not robots who do whatever the media tell them.

---

by the media as well. Studies have shown, for example, that when family fights break out, children turn to television for solace; when their egos are bruised by failure, they read more "Superman"-type comic books. Similarly, many women use serials for vicarious enjoyment of open emotion, while many men use racy magazines for vicarious enjoyment of open sex. The catharsis of a Shakespeare tragedy, the violence of a shoot-'em-up western, and the self-confidence of a news commentator all meet important psychological needs in the audience.

Information-seeking is another reason why people turn to the media. Not just news, but also quiz programs and advertisements capture our attention in part because they offer us information. And one early study found that people went to movies partly in order to learn how higher-status Americans dress, behave, and make love.[20] Sometimes the information is sought for its own sake; our society considers it a civic virtue to be well-informed whether you take action or not. Sometimes the information is sought for reassurance—people who just bought a Ford, for instance, read Ford ads to collect information showing they made a wise choice. Sometimes the information satisfies a psychological need, or confers social status. And sometimes it's just useful: Why, after all, do you read the weather forecast?

Finally, people use the media for guidance in problem-solving. When a decision needs to be made, we seek out not only relevant information but also relevant influence. We look for someone to tell us what to decide. Self-help books, editorials, advice columns, "how-to" articles, and the like obviously meet this need for help. Other sorts of media content meet it less obviously. A classic study of radio soap operas, for example, found that many listeners used the shows for guidance in their everyday activities. One faithful follower commented: "If you listen to these programs and something turns up in your own life, you would know what to do about it." [21]

We have listed several reasons why audiences use the mass media: play, time-filling, social needs, psychological needs, information-seeking, and guidance. What happens to your attitudes in response to an attempt at persuasion will depend largely on whether you are paying attention for fun or for status, for information or for reassurance, for guidance or just to kill time.

The media entertain us when we want to play. They pass the time for us when we are bored. They help us relate to each other or avoid each other. They make us feel better about ourselves. They provide us with information when we are looking for it. They tell us what to do when we need guidance. There's nothing covert or manipulative about any of this. It's what we want from our media, and it's what our media do for us. Persuasion is a sideline.

PERSUADING THE AUDIENCE

What, finally, can we say about the impact of the mass media on our attitudes and behavior? Can we do any better than Bernard Berelson's truism: "Some kinds of *communication* on some kinds of *issues,* brought to the attention of some kinds of *people* under some kinds of *conditions,* have some kinds of *effects.*"? [22] Yes.

First of all, conversion through the mass media is extremely rare. Hundreds of social philosophers have worried about it, hundreds of researchers have looked for it, but it just doesn't happen very often. In fact, the opposite is far more likely. Regardless of the issue, the mass media usually reinforce the existing attitudes and lifestyles of their audience. They are far more often a force for stability than a force for change.

The active participation of the audience insures that this will be true. People very seldom want to be changed; we usually want to be reassured that what we believe and do is what we should believe and do. Conversion is not one of the ways we use the fact, it is inconsistent with several of them—it isn't fun, it doesn't pass the time innocuously, and it creates psychological and social conflicts instead of resolving them. Selective attention enables us to avoid communications that might threaten our personal status quo. Selective perception helps us misinterpret those we can't avoid, and selective retention helps us forget those we can't misinterpret. Our group memberships and allegiances keep us from straying too far from the group's norms. We talk mostly to people who agree with us, and we use mostly the same media they use. The diversity of the media assures that a threatening communication will soon be supplanted by a supportive one. And the media's profit motive guarantees that most communications will pander to our prejudices, not challenge them. In the face of all this, conversion is highly unlikely.

The fact that the media tend to reinforce our attitudes is itself an important effect. Our views are strengthened by ammunition from the media. They give us new facts to cite, new sources to quote, and above all a sense that we are right and others agree with us. Imagine a hot local debate over a school bond issue, where the bulk of the news happens to favor the supporters. Most opponents probably won't be converted—but that isn't really necessary. If the supporters are getting lots of reinforcement from the media, they'll be much more likely to speak up in conversations with their friends, and to vote on election day. Lacking this reinforcement, opponents of the bond issue are more likely to keep quiet and forget to vote. A crucial piece of every persuasion strategy is to increase the fervor of your allies and dampen the enthusiasm of your enemies. This the media do very, very well.

And what about issues with a lot less audience involvement than voting, such as the choice of a breakfast cereal? Here the audience has no strong attitude, perhaps no attitude at all. We rarely seek out information or guidance on breakfast cereals, but we

don't resist it either—we barely pay attention to it when it comes our way. Through repetition alone, an advertiser can thus build in our minds a sense of the product's appropriateness. And so when we go to buy a cereal, or a detergent, or anything else we don't much care about, we usually buy an advertised brand—not because we believe it's better (we don't believe anything about it, really), but just because we've heard of it and it somehow "seems like a good one." An established attitude, a habit, a group norm, a recommendation from a friend, a bad experience with the product, or just about any other influence can overcome this "learning without involvement." But if nothing else is happening and we don't bother to think about it, mere repetition in the media is enough to determine what we buy.

Advertisers don't have to rely only on low-involvement repetition for their impact. They know that we use the media to satisfy our needs, and they know that the media are good at reinforcing our values. Nothing is easier than tying a product to those needs and values. And so we get the toothpaste ad that promises social and sexual success in return for our purchase. Of course the needs triggered and reinforced by the ad—sex, status, and the like—are not really satisfied by switching toothpastes. We know the connection posited by the ad is irrational; we don't really believe that Ultra Brite gives us sex appeal. But unless there's an opposing influence somewhere in our social environment, the reinforcement of our sexual needs and values is often enough to make us switch to Ultra Brite.

Once we make the switch, we may begin to feel a bit silly. People like to have reasons for what they do, even if what they do isn't reasonable. So we start looking for information that will make sense of our new behavior [23]—and suddenly we're reading Ultra Brite ads with unusual interest. In the case of Ultra Brite, it probably won't work. We can't find any information that one toothpaste is better than another (maybe because

WHAT DO YOU KNOW ABOUT WOLVES?

The power of the media to change us through mere repetition is not limited to advertising. There are thousands of noncommercial topics about which we could care less, about which we know almost nothing, and about which everything we know comes from the media. If what the media tell us on these topics is always the same, and if nothing in our non-media environment says anything different, we will predictably wind up believing what we're told. It may or may not be true.

For example, what do you know about wolves? Apart from zoos, most Americans today have absolutely no personal experience with wolves, nor are they something we talk a lot about with our friends and neighbors. Nearly everything we know and think about wolves comes to us from the media. It starts with "Little Red Riding Hood" and "The Three Little Pigs." It continues with the Wolfman and his imitators, and with references to the "wolfish leers" of oversexed men and the slyly disguised threat of a "wolf in sheep's clothing." It ends with our constant battle to "keep the wolf from the door." These and similar metaphors are constantly repeated in the media, from which we pick them up for conversational use. Little wonder, then, that most Americans consider wolves to be vicious, destructive, cunning, dishonest animals. Ecologists know that this image is untrue (wolves hunt only for food, and seldom attack people or pigs), and that it leads to some very unwise extermination programs. But ecologists don't often write for the media.

We are not very committed to our image of wolves, so it is easy to overcome. A 1969 NBC documentary called "The Wolf Men" was seen by more than 24 million people, and resulted in 16,000 letters urging natural resources agencies to protect the wolf.[24] But without such an opposing influence, even a casual, low-involvement image can significantly affect our attitudes and behavior.

---

it isn't), and so the only thing that keeps us using Ultra Brite is habit and the constant repetition of those sexy ads.

But suppose the new behavior is something a little more defensible, like recycling used newspapers, cans, and bottles. Many people start recycling for the same sorts of irrational reasons that determine their choice of a toothpaste—peer pressure, pressure from their children, etc. But once they start, they begin looking for information to make sense of what they're doing. And they find it in the media. News about the value of recycling probably doesn't do much to get people started; for that you need the sort of manipulative persuasion found in toothpaste ads. But news is absolutely essential to help us make sense of what we are already doing, and thus to keep us doing it.

Information in the media also helps us apply our existing attitudes to new circumstances. News of the Watergate scandals, for example, didn't make people any more opposed to political corruption than they already were, but it did focus that opposition on the behavior of Richard Nixon. Similarly, the information that a product contributes to pollution can't create an attitude against pollution—but if you're already worried about pollution, that information can turn you against the product. As early as 1948, Paul F. Lazarsfeld and Robert K. Merton acknowledged this role of the media; they called it canalization.[25]

We have listed five ways that media content can affect our attitudes and behavior:

1. The media can provide ammunition to sup-

port our attitudes, thus increasing our commitment.

2. On low-involvement issues where there are no competing influences, mere repetition in the media can change our behavior directly.

3. By catering to our existing needs and values and linking them to a new behavior, the media can get us to act without changing our attitudes.

4. Information in the media can be used to justify or rationalize behavior initially based on needs, building attitudes to support that behavior.

5. The media can relate an existing attitude to a new object by providing information that ties the two together.

None of these five effects is inconsistent with the general principle that the media are more a force for stability than a force for change. All five involve reinforcement, not conversion. Yet they do change what we believe and what we do.

There is a sixth effect of the media which is not based on the reinforcement notion. It is true that when a communication conflicts with our current attitudes, we tend to ignore or reject it. But psychologists have found that every attitude has a so-called "latitude of acceptance" around it. A communication that falls within our latitude of acceptance is *not* ignored or rejected. In fact, people see such a communication as closer to their own views than it really is, and as a result their own views move in the direction of the communication.[26] A piece of information that is just barely consistent with our original attitude will thus shift the attitude slightly—and a more extreme piece of information now becomes acceptable. With careful planning and a thorough knowledge of the audience, it is thus possible to guide people slowly toward a whole new value system.

To do this intentionally would be a serious violation of journalistic norms. But the media sometimes stumble into it—and we gradually adjust to the notion that homo-

sexuals are unfairly persecuted, or that environmental pollution endangers humanity. But the process doesn't usually work. It requires a near-monopoly on media content, with nobody trying to push attitudes in the opposite direction. It requires the support (or at least the non-opposition) of interpersonal communication and group norms. And even then, people whose initial attitudes are not in tune with these views won't integrate the relevant information; their attitudes will move in just the opposite direction, or not at all.

THE IMPACT OF MEDIA

So far we have talked about the impact of the mass media only in terms of persuasion. We have seen that the alarmists are wrong in attributing to the media the power to convert us from our most deeply held beliefs in a few carefully manipulated minutes. But we have also seen that the media can reinforce our attitudes and values, build new ones on issues we don't care much about, and even change us some over the long haul.

As you might have guessed, persuasion is by no means the only impact of the media on our society. It's the one that gets most of the research, but there are others. We will talk about four of them:

1. Agenda-setting.
2. Norms and culture.
3. Modeling.
4. Apathy.

Our discussion will be short, not because these topics are any less important than persuasion, but because a lot less is known about them.

1. Agenda-Setting. On any given day, the typical metropolitan newspaper or broadcast station has available more than ten times as much ready-to-go content as it has space or time to use. The media are therefore obliged to play the role of gatekeepers, deciding what information to transmit and how much emphasis to give it. The editorial decision that a particular event is not news is a self-fulfilling judgment; if the news media ignore it, then it cannot be news. Conversely, any event given major play in the mass media becomes by definition a major event. There is plentiful evidence that the media audience absorbs the "agenda" of the newspaper front page and the TV news show far more completely than it absorbs their content. In this sense, even when the mass media do not tell us what to think, they tell us what to think about.

Any group that has ever tried unsuccessfully to get news of its activities into the media can testify to the importance of agenda-setting. As Lazarsfeld and Merton put it in 1948, "the mass media confer status on public issues, persons, organizations, and social movements" merely by reporting them.[27] In the 1960s, the media may or may not have changed the racial attitudes of white Americans (the evidence is mixed)— but for sure the media convinced us all that racial discrimination is something important to think about. What will be important to think about in the late 1970s? Most people will be watching the media to find out.

The agenda-setting function is not confined to news. In 1972, television and movie entertainment quietly began dealing with themes such as women's liberation, abortion, and homosexuality. Most of these shows probably didn't change many people's attitudes, but their cumulative impact over several years made an important contribution to getting us thinking about those issues.

Of course the media don't usually do their agenda-setting on purpose. In fact, the media get *their* agendas mostly from the public; reporters tell us about what they think we're interested in, not what they think we should be interested in. Still, the media are often ahead of the audience in their interests, and they help bring the audience along.

2. Norms and Culture. The media tell us what our norms are. American society is made up of many subcultures, divided by age, income, religion, geography, etc. Most of our personal contacts are with people who share our subculture, but through the media we interact with those from other cultures as well. How argumentative, how flirtatious, and how drunk can you be at a party and still stay within the bounds of good taste? Which grievances justify a fist fight, and which should be settled less violently? When is an adolescent old enough to stay out all night? What is the proper attitude for a "right-thinking" American to hold toward Communist China, extramarital sex, and cheating on one's income tax? How often should you wax your car? The media suggest answers to these questions, which may or may not be the same answers our friends and neighbors propose.

The result is a tendency toward the homogenization of culture. The media expand our horizons by telling us what other people do, and in the process they make us more like those other people. In a variety of ways— in language, in dress, in child-rearing practices, in ethical standards—Americans become more and more alike every year, largely because of the influence of the media. Some subcultures, of course, are strong enough to withstand the homogenizing assault of the mainstream American media. But in the battle between cultural diversity and the melting pot, the media are securely on the side of the pot.

3. Modeling. The media not only tell us what other people are doing; they also tell us how we can do it too. Long before most children are ready to go to kindergarten, they have already picked up many behavior patterns their parents never taught them—from television. Kids frequently imitate the posture and vocabulary of their favorite TV hero. More important, they pick up the hero's style of dealing with people and situations as well. And how many adults, for that matter, have modeled pieces of their own behavior in precise imitation of Humphrey Bogart or Raquel Welch, Walter Cronkite or Mary Tyler Moore?

Most of the research on modeling has centered on the effects of media violence, a key issue to many critics of the media. In one typical series of experiments, children watched films of an adult model aggressively kicking or punching a pop-up "bo-bo doll." When the children were later intentionally frustrated (by having their toys taken away) and then put in a room with a bo-bo doll, sure enough they kicked it and punched it more than kids who had seen a different film.[28] They had learned from the model how to abuse the doll. In much the same way, scores of airplane hijackers learned from the media how to vent their feelings most effectively.

The evidence is not conclusive that violence in the media makes us *feel* more violent. But media violence does set a very tolerant norm for us, telling us that physical aggression is All-American. And through modeling, media violence teaches us new and satisfying ways to be violent ourselves. That's enough.

4. Apathy. We have talked a lot about the things the media make us do. What about the things the media keep us from doing?

At the most obvious level, most of us spend more than four hours a day passively watching television, reading newspapers or magazines, or listening to the radio. One of the most common criticisms of the mass media is that they replace genuine participation with a kind of vicarious, passive pseudo-experience. The result, it is charged, is an apathetic and uninvolved public.

This argument is usually made about media entertainment, especially television, but it may apply to news as well. News in the media is mostly raw, uninterpreted information. In their effort to be objective, reporters seldom tell us what we should do with the information, or even what we could do with it. The speed of modern mass communication and the complexity of the world's problems encourage us to conclude that informed action is impossible, and perhaps even inappropriate. Let the government handle it.

The very format of media news presentations is aimed at rewarding the reader, listener, or viewer for the mere act of reading, listening, or viewing. Reporters are taught to "round out" their stories, to work at creating the impression that all relevant questions have been asked and answered, that the job (reporter's and audience's) is done. The result may be a redefinition of the obligations of a citizen. Instead of feeling obliged to do something about the world's problems, we may come to feel that it's enough just to know what the problems are. G. D. Wiebe calls this the syndrome of "well-informed futility." [29] Most of us call it apathy.

Lazarsfeld and Merton described this vitally important impact of the media back in 1948:

> Exposure to [a] flood of information may serve to narcotize rather than to energize the average reader or listener. . . . The individual reads accounts of issues and problems and may even discuss alternative lines of action. But this rather intellectualized, rather remote connection with organized social action is not activated. The interested and informed citizen can congratulate himself on his lofty state of interest and information and neglect to see that he has abstained from decision and action. . . . He comes to mistake *knowing* about the problems of the day for *doing* something about them. His social conscience remains spotlessly clean. He *is* concerned. He *is* informed. And he has all sorts of ideas as to what should be done. But after he has gotten through his dinner and after he has listened to his favored radio programs and after he has read his second newspaper of the day, it is really time for bed.[30]

Agenda-setting, norms and culture, modeling, and apathy have little to do with persuasion. But they have a lot to do with our lives, and with the media's impact on our lives.

Quite apart from their content, the very existence of the mass media affects our lives. Such effects are difficult or impossible to document, but anyone who has lived through the introduction of radio in a primitive village or the introduction of television in an American small town knows that they are real. More than anyone else, Marshall McLuhan has directed our attention to the impact of media as social phenomena regardless of their content.

MEDIA AS ENVIRONMENT

Every moment of our waking lives, we learn from our environment. Some of this learning is through our rational faculties. Some of it is through our senses, our intuition, and our feelings. We learn from the smell of the air in a meadow or on a city street. We learn from the conversations, glances, and half-glances of the people we meet. We learn from the feeling in our muscles after a hard workout. All of these are educational materials, inputs to the human biocomputer.

Before the invention of the printing press, people spent nearly all of their time experiencing life in these ways. Before the invention of television, most of us spent a good deal of our time doing so. Even today, very few people live their lives entirely in the mass media. But more and more of our time, especially our leisure time, is devoted to the pseudo-reality of the media instead of the genuine reality around us.

This *must* make a difference. Think about watching television for four hours a night—just sitting there, eyes wide, body still, room dark, other people reduced to vague shadows, images pouring into your brain. Regardless of what's *on* the tube, all those hours in front of it must have some kind of impact.

Communication researchers have seldom studied these sorts of questions, because there was (and is) no methodology to study them rigorously. Until the 1960s, what little we knew about the effects of media irrespective of content came to us from anthropologists, who recorded the reactions of primitive cultures to new communication technologies.

Consider this excerpt from a book by Edmund Carpenter, describing his experiences in the village of Sio, in New Guinea:

> We gave each person a Polaroid shot of himself. At first there was no understanding. The photographs were black & white, flat, static, odorless—far removed from any reality they knew. They had to be taught to "read" them. I pointed to a nose in a picture, then touched the real nose, etc. . . .

Recognition gradually came into the subject's face. And fear. Suddenly he covered his mouth, ducked his head & turned his body away. After this first startled response, often repeated several times, he either stood transfixed, staring at his image, only his stomach muscles betraying tension, or he retreated from the group, pressing his photograph against his chest, showing it to no one, slipping away to study it in solitude. . . .

When we projected movies . . . there was absolute silence as they watched themselves, a silence broken only by whispered identification of faces on the screen. . . .

When we returned to Sio, months later, I thought at first we had made a wrong turn in the river network. I didn't recognize the place. Several houses had been rebuilt in a new style. Men wore European clothing. They carried themselves differently. They acted differently. . . . In one brutal movement they had been torn out of a tribal existence & transformed into detached individuals, lonely, frustrated, no longer at home—anywhere.[31]

Except for anthropologists, no one wrote very much about the impact on culture of the very existence of mass media. Then, in 1964, a Canadian scholar named Marshall McLuhan published his book, *Understanding Media*. McLuhan's thinking relies heavily on the ideas of another Canadian scholar, Harold Innis—but it was McLuhan who first popularized those ideas.

Trained in engineering and English literature, McLuhan was (and is) an intellectual eclectic. He ignores the findings of social science even when they support his ideas. He does not bother to prove his statements with evidence, but rather illustrates them with examples—drawn from such varied sources as James Joyce and professional football. The reaction of traditional scholars to these tactics is summed up by critic Dwight Macdonald:

One defect of *Understanding Media* is that the parts are greater than the whole. A single page is impressive, two are "stimulating," five

raise serious doubts, ten confirm them, and long before the hardy reader has staggered to page 359 the accumulation of contradictions, nonsequiturs, facts that are distorted and facts that are not facts, exaggerations, and chronic rhetorical vagueness has numbed him to the insights. . . .[32]

These accusations do not seem to bother McLuhan, who claims that his unrigorous style is ideally suited to the world of television. Nor do they bother his disciples, who number in the thousands.

THE MEDIUM IS THE MESSAGE

McLuhan's central assertion is that "the medium is the message." The customary distinction between the two, he argues, is mythical. What a medium communicates, quite apart from its content, is the nature of the medium itself. "Our conventional response to all media, namely that it is how they are used that counts, is the numb stance of the technological idiot. For the 'content' of a medium is like the juicy piece of meat carried by the burglar to distract the watchdog of the mind."[33] McLuhan entitled one of his later books *The Medium Is The Massage,* purposely turning the title into a pun in order to emphasize that the real "message" of a medium is the way it pokes, jabs, and kneads its audience—not what it says.[34]

Media for McLuhan are extensions of one or more of the five senses. Face-to-face speech (the oldest of the media) extends all five senses. Print extends only the eye, radio the ear. Television is an extension of both the eye and the ear. (Elsewhere, McLuhan insists that TV is primarily a tactile medium, but he never makes clear the meaning or significance of the remark.) The impact of a medium is determined by which senses it extends and the way it extends them.

Media, says McLuhan, are either "hot" or "cool." This is a crucial distinction for McLuhan, and he describes it lucidly:

There is a basic principle that distinguishes

a hot medium like radio from a cool one like the telephone, or a hot medium like the movie from a cool one like TV. A hot medium is one that extends one single sense in "high definition." High definition is the state of being well filled with data. A photograph is, visually, "high definition." A cartoon is "low definition," simply because very little visual information is provided. Telephone is a cool medium, or one of low definition, because the ear is given a meager amount of information. And speech is a cool medium of low definition, because so little is given and so much has to be filled in by the listener. On the other hand, hot media do not leave so much to be filled in or completed by the audience. Hot media are, therefore, low in participation, and cool media are high in participation or completion by the audience. Naturally, therefore, a hot medium like radio has very different effects on the user from a cool medium like the telephone.[35]

A hot medium is hot, in other words, because it provides a lot of information and requires little audience participation. A cool medium is cool because it provides little information and requires a lot of audience participation. Print, film, radio, and nylon stockings are hot. Telephone, modern art, and open-mesh stockings are cool. Television is cool, too—a fuzzy collection of tiny dots that the viewer must connect and fill in.

McLuhan wants to know only two things about any medium: which senses it extends, and whether it does so in high definition (hot) or low definition (cool).

RETRIBALIZATION

History for McLuhan is divided into three stages. The first may be called the "tribal" stage. It is characterized by local, oral communication within each tribe or community. Person-to-person speech is, in McLuhan's view, a cool medium, involving all five senses. It thus requires the maximum amount of participation.

The second stage begins with the invention of the printing press. Print, of course, is the hottest of McLuhan's media, and extends only one sense: the eye. Instead of participation and involvement, it requires dispassionate attention to the words on the page. James W. Carey notes that "the desire to break things down into elementary units . . . the tendency to see reality in discrete units, to find causal relations and linear serial order . . . to find orderly structure in nature" can be traced to the influence of print.

Carey goes even further: "To live in an oral culture, one acquires knowledge only in contact with other people, in terms of communal activities. Printing, however, allows individuals to withdraw, to contemplate and meditate outside of communal activities. Print thus encourages privatization, the lonely scholar, and the development of private, individual points of view." [36]

In addition, McLuhan says, print created the price system—"for until commodities are uniform and repeatable the price of an article is subject to haggle and adjustment." [37] Print is also responsible for the growth of nationalism, because it permitted "visual apprehension of the mother tongue and, through maps, visual apprehension of the nation." [38] All these effects, taken together, McLuhan calls detribalization.

McLuhan's third stage begins with the invention of television. TV, he tells us, is a cool medium; it requires its audience to participate. TV is also an extension of at least three senses—the visual, the aural, and the tactile. Through television, involvement has once again become a fundamental part of the communication process. Instead of the "tribal village" of the first stage, we are faced now with a "global village," mediated by television. We are in the process of being "retribalized" by television.

Most adults can't take it. "We are no more prepared to encounter radio and TV in our literate milieu than the native of Ghana is able to cope with the literacy that takes him out of his collective tribal world and beaches him in individual isolation. We are as numb in our new electric world as the native involved in our literate and mechanical culture." [39]

But in McLuhan's view, anyone born after 1950 doesn't need retribalizing. He or she grew up with television, and hence has always been a member of the tribe. "Print man," writes Tom Wolfe, "always has the feeling that no matter what anybody says, he can go check it out. . . . He can *look* it up. . . . The aural man is not so much of an individualist; he is more a part of the collective consciousness; he *believes*." [40] James Carey summarizes McLuhan's views this way:

> The generational gap we now observe by contrasting the withdrawn, private, specializing student of the fifties with the active, involved, generalist student of the sixties McLuhan rests at the door of television. . . . The desire of students for involvement and participation, for talking rather than reading, for seminars rather than lectures, for action rather than reflection, in short for participation and involvement rather than withdrawal and observation he ascribes to the reorchestration of the senses provoked by television. [41]

The impact of television is so enormous that McLuhan does not hesitate to assert that it "has begun to dissolve the fabric of Amercian life." He has recommended, apparently quite seriously, that TV be banned in the United States before it destroys the country by driving us "inward in depth into a totally nonvisual universe of involvement." [42]

TRUTH AND FANTASY

Is McLuhan right? Certainly he is right about some things. The mass media do have far-reaching effects on society, effects too broad to be measured in the experiments of social scientists. And at least some of those effects, it seems, stem from the nature of the

media themselves, irrespective of content. McLuhan has looked at the history of civilization from a new perspective. Much of what he sees no one else has seen.

Much of what he sees probably isn't there. Listen to critic Tom Nairn: "Take the example of the so-called 'global village.' To anyone who can extricate himself from the McLuhanite trance for a few seconds, it is reasonably clear that the existing global village was created by European imperialism, not by television; that it is not a 'village,' but a cruel class society tearing humanity in two; that the techniques which made it, and sustain it, are overwhelmingly pre-electronic— private property and the gun; and that the *actual* use made of media like television in our society, far from pushing us toward a healing of the gap, reinforces our acceptance of it. . . ." [43]

Or listen to critic Richard Kostelanetz, talking about the notion that the medium is the message: "The fifth rerun of *I Love Lucy* is a considerably different TV experience from a presentation of George F. Kennan addressing the Committee on Foreign Relations on the War in Vietnam; and I doubt if many people watching Kennan stayed with that channel when Lucy appeared in his stead. Even on the medium which has perhaps the narrowest range of quality, content does count." [44]

McLuhan and his disciples share a complete disdain for evidence. One of the distinctions between print and broadcasting, according to McLuhan, is that print follows a linear one-thing-at-a-time sort of logic, while broadcasting is global, everything-at-once. As a result, McLuhanites claim, Western Civilization is now undergoing a change from a linear lifestyle to a global one. This is, in the language of social science, a testable hypothesis. But McLuhan and his followers do not bother to test it, or even to find out whether it has already been tested. Instead, they simply point out that baseball, a linear game, is now less popular than football, a global game. Q.E.D. If you want more proof than that, you are obviously a linear personality, unfit for the television age.

Evidence for McLuhan's propositions turns up in unexpected places. Professor John Wilson of the African Institute of London University, for example, tried to use a movie to teach African villagers how to read. He found, to his surprise, that these people did not "see" the film the same way he did. In each scene of the movie, they picked out a familiar object like a chicken and fastened on that, switching to a different object only when the scene switched. They made no effort to connect the scenes or follow the story line.[45] Several studies of children watching television have produced intriguingly similar results. The children did not focus on the whole screen as their parents did; instead, they scanned the screen for details to fasten on.[46] Perhaps television is retribalizing us after all.

To summarize Marshall McLuhan in a single paragraph (and only a linear mind would try): He is impossible to understand, difficult to accept, and dangerous to ignore. He is one part nonsense, one part insight, and several parts unproved supposition. All the social science Ph.D's in the country could spend their lifetimes testing McLuhan's guesses—and maybe they should.

Notes

1 Wilbur Schramm, "How Communication Works," in *The Process and Effects of Mass Communication,* ed. Wilbur Schramm (Urbana, Ill.: University of Illinois Press, 1954), p. 3.

2 Paul F. Lazarsfeld, Bernard Berelson, and Hazel Gaudet, *The People's Choice,* 2nd ed. (New York: Columbia University Press, 1948), p. 151.

3 Walter Lippmann, "The World Outside and the Pictures in Our Heads," *Public Opinion* (New York: Macmillan, 1922), ch. 1.

4 George Gallup, "The Importance of Opinion News," *Journalism Educator,* Fall, 1966, p. 113.

5 *Variety,* January 23, 1974, p. 31.

6 Wilbur Schramm, "Communication in Crisis," in *The Kennedy Assassination and the American Public: Social Communication in Crisis,* ed. Brad-

ley S. Greenberg and Edwin B. Parker (Stanford, Calif.: Stanford University Press, 1965), pp. 14–15.

7 A. C. Nielsen Co., "TV Responses to the Death of the President," pamphlet, New York, 1963.

8 "Talking Like a Native," *Newsweek,* March 9, 1970, p. 57.

9 C. Hovland and W. Mandell, "An Experimental Comparison of Conclusion Drawing by the Communicator and by the Audience," *Journal of Abnormal and Social Psychology,* 47, 1952, 581–88.

10 P. Tannenbaum, "Effect of Serial Position on Recall of Radio News Stories," *Journalism Quarterly,* 31, 1954, 319–23.

11 G. Hartmann, "A Field Experiment on the Comparative Effectiveness of 'Emotional' and 'Rational' Political Leaflets in Determining Election Results," *Journal of Abnormal and Social Psychology,* 31, 1936, 94–114.

12 C. Hovland, A. Lumsdaine, and F. Sheffield, *Experiments on Mass Communication* (Princeton: Princeton University Press, 1949).

13 *Ibid.*

14 C. Hovland and W. Weiss, "The Influence of Source Credibility on Communication Effectiveness," *Public Opinion Quarterly,* 15, 1951, pp. 635–50.

15 Herbert E. Krugman, "The Impact of Television Advertising: Learning Without Involvement," *Public Opinion Quarterly,* 29, 1965, 349–56.

16 Jack B. Haskins, "Factual Recall as a Measure of Advertising Effectiveness," *Journal of Advertising Research,* 4, 1964, 2–8.

17 Leon Festinger, "Behavioral Support for Opinion Change," *Public Opinion Quarterly,* 28, 1964, 404–17.

18 William Stephenson, *The Play Theory of Mass Communication* (Chicago: University of Chicago Press, 1967).

19 Bernard Berelson, "What 'Missing the Newspaper' Means," in *Communication Research 1948–1949,* ed. P. F. Lazarsfeld and F. N. Stanton (New York: Harper, 1949), pp. 111–29.

20 H. Blumer, *Movies and Conduct* (New York: Macmillan, 1933).

21 Herta Herzog, "Motivations and Gratifications of Daily Serial Listeners," in *Process and Effects of Mass Communication,* ed. Wilbur Schramm, pp. 50–55.

22 Bernard Berelson, "Communications and Public Opinion," in *Mass Communications,* ed. Wilbur Schramm (Urbana, Ill.: University of Illinois Press, 1960), pp. 527–43.

23 Leon Festinger, *A Theory of Cognitive Dissonance* (New York: Harper and Row, 1957).

24 David L. Erickson and G. Norman Van Tubergen, "The Wolf Men," *Journal of Environmental Education,* Fall, 1972, pp. 26–30.

25 Paul F. Lazarsfeld and Robert K. Merton, "Mass Communication, Popular Taste and Organized Social Action," in *Mass Communications,* ed. Wilbur Schramm, pp. 492–512.

26 Muzafer Sherif and Carl I. Hovland, *Social Judgment* (New Haven: Yale University Press, 1961).

27 Lazarsfeld and Merton, "Mass Communication," pp. 492–512.

28 A. Bandura and R. H. Walters, *Social Learning and Personality Development* (New York: Holt, Rinehart and Winston, 1963).

29 G. D. Wiebe, "Mass Media and Man's Relationship to His Environment," *Journalism Quarterly,* Autumn, 1973, pp. 426–32, 446.

30 Lazarsfeld and Merton, "Mass Communication," pp. 492–512.

31 Edmund Carpenter, *Oh, What a Blow That Phantom Gave Me* (New York: Holt, Rinehart and Winston, 1973), pp. 132–33.

32 Gerald Emanuel Stearn, ed., *McLuhan: Hot and Cool* (New York: Signet Paperback, 1967), p. 205.

33 Marshall McLuhan, *Understanding Media* (New York: Signet Paperback, 1964), p. 32.

34 Marshall McLuhan, *The Medium Is the Massage* (New York: Bantam Books, 1967).

35 McLuhan, *Understanding Media,* p. 36.

36 Raymond Rosenthal, ed., *McLuhan Pro and Con* (Baltimore: Penguin Books, 1968), pp. 285–86.

37 Marshall McLuhan, *The Gutenberg Galaxy* (Toronto: University of Toronto Press, 1962), p. 164.

38 Rosenthal, *McLuhan Pro and Con,* p. 286.

39 McLuhan, *Understanding Media,* p. 31.

40 Stearn, *McLuhan: Hot and Cool,* p. 37.

41 Rosenthal, *McLuhan Pro and Con,* p. 288.

42 Stearn, *McLuhan: Hot and Cool,* pp. 270–71, 291.

43 Rosenthal, *McLuhan Pro and Con,* p. 150.

44 *Ibid.,* p. 220.

45 McLuhan, *The Gutenberg Galaxy,* pp. 36–37.

46 Stearn, *McLuhan: Hot and Cool,* p. 37.

Suggested Readings

KARLINS, MARVIN and HERBERT I. ABELSON, *Persuasion.* New York: Springer Publishing Co., 1970.

KLAPPER, JOSEPH, *The Effects of Mass Communication.* New York: The Free Press, 1960.

LIEBERT, ROBERT M. *et al., The Early Window: Effects of Television on Children and Youth.* New York: Pergamon Press, 1973.

McLUHAN, MARSHALL, *The Gutenberg Galaxy.* Toronto: University of Toronto Press, 1962.

———, *Understanding Media.* New York: Signet Paperback, 1964.

ROSENTHAL, RAYMOND, ed., *McLuhan: Pro and Con.* Baltimore: Penguin Books, 1968.

SCHRAMM, WILBUR, ed., *Mass Communications,* 2nd ed. Urbana, Ill.: University of Illinois Press, 1960.

———, *Men, Messages, and Media: A Look at Human Communication.* New York: Harper & Row, 1973.

———, and DONALD F. ROBERTS, eds., *The Process and Effects of Mass Communication,* 2nd ed. Urbana, Ill.: University of Illinois Press, 1971.

STEARN, GERALD EMANUEL, ed., *McLuhan: Hot and Cool.* New York: Signet Paperback, 1967.

PART I
DEVELOPMENT

The trouble with history is that you have to know a lot about the present before the past seems useful or relevant. And yet you can't really understand the way things are until after you have discovered how they got that way. Ideally, then, everyone would read this chapter twice—once now, to get a feel for the development of the media; and again after finishing the rest of the book, to get the background of the problems that will be discussed later.

If you haven't read the rest of the book yet, the best you can do is to try to keep your own catalogue of important issues and how they grew. There are dozens of them, all discussed some place later on, but let us suggest a few of the most crucial ones here:

1. *Trends in government control.* For many centuries, all governments maintained strict control over the media. Then they began to loosen the reins, allowing greater and greater measures of freedom of the press. How and why did this happen? Was it entirely a good thing? How has it affected the nature of the media today?

2. *Trends in individuality.* Throughout most of their history, the media have been very much the tools of individual writers and editors, who disagreed violently with each other and competed viciously for the allegiance of the public. This is much less true today. What caused the change? How has it affected the tone and function of the media? What can be done about it?

3. *Trends in the audience.* The mass-media audience in the seventeenth century was limited to the literate upper class. Slowly it expanded to include merchants, factory workers, immigrants, farmers. How have the media adapted to these new audiences? Which ones have tried to reach all the public, and which have specialized in certain classes or groups? What implications does this have for democratic processes?

4. *Trends in technology.* Books were the first mass medium, followed by newspapers, then magazines, then film and radio, and finally television. Along the way came such revolutionary technological advances as the high-speed press and the telegraph. How has each new medium affected the older ones? Have the media made use of technology, or merely succumbed to it? How can they be expected to respond to future developments?

5. *Trends in influence.* At various points in history, the mass media have influenced the course of social change in many different ways—and have, in turn, been influenced by

social change. What determines the power and influence of the media? Are they aware of their power? Do they use it wisely?

6. *Trends in news definition.* How the media define the word "news" determines the topics they cover and the way they cover them. How has this definition changed over time? What caused the changes? Which is the "right" definition?

7. *Trends in partisanship.* The principal goal of the mass media has varied greatly throughout their history. Sometimes it has been to inform, sometimes to entertain, sometimes to persuade, and sometimes merely to make money. And quite often media owners and media consumers have disagreed about the role of the media. How did these variations come about? What effects did they have on the content of the media? What should be the main function of the media?

8. *Trends in professionalism.* Media owners once viewed themselves as professional advocates; today they are more profit-oriented. Reporters and editors, on the other hand, were once mere employees; today they see themselves as professionals. Why did this turnabout take place? In what ways has it affected the structure and content of the media? How, if at all, is the conflict resolved?

This is only a partial list. Make your own as you go along. Above all, bear in mind the three basic questions of any historical survey: How did things get to where they are? How else might they have turned out? And where are they likely to go in the future?

Chapter 1
Development

Today's mass media, like all complex social institutions, have developed over a period of centuries. The events of each century had a lasting effect on the structure and performance of the media. To understand the modern media in the United States, then, it is necessary to examine their roots in medieval Europe, Elizabethan England, and colonial America.

Medieval Europe was a land-based society. The fundamental economic and social unit was not the city or the country, but the self-sufficient feudal manor. Travel from one manor to another was extremely difficult. Except for churchmen, soldiers, and cutthroats, it was also pretty pointless. Literacy was equally irrelevant. The local serf tilled his land. The local lord managed his serfs. The local priest memorized and recited his prayers. Neither serf nor lord nor priest had any reason to be interested in events beyond the horizon.

Throughout the Middle Ages, the monasteries had a virtual monopoly on literacy. Dutifully the monks hand-copied and hand-illustrated their meager supply of books. Some of the most beautiful were sold to the secular elite, who used them as decorations and status symbols. But it was an unusual nobleman who could do more than admire the colorful designs of his Bible.

Feudal society began to crack in the thirteenth century. Towns and then cities grew up midway between the great manors. They were inhabited by a new middle class —independent merchants and artisans. The nobles soon learned the advantages of trade. Messengers traveled from the manors to the cities with money and surplus crops; they returned with cattle, weapons, woodwork, cloth, and luxuries of all sorts. They returned also with news: news of war, news of taxes ordered by a faraway king, news of a special bargain in satin or spices.

Oral messages were painfully inaccurate. Written ones were better. So monks were assigned or persuaded to teach the sons of feudal landowners to read. In time the family Bible became no longer merely a piece of decoration; it was a book.

Learning was suddenly a valuable commodity. Dozens of universities were founded throughout Europe, to teach the sons of the nobility their Latin. The artisans and traders in the cities, meanwhile, taught themselves to read the vernacular—German,

20,000 B.C.	Cave painting, the earliest form of written communication, reflects prehistoric people's conception of their surroundings.
3500 B.C.	The Sumerians of Mesopotamia develop cuneiform, the first known pictographic writing.
3100 B.C.	The Egyptians develop hieroglyphics.
2500 B.C.	Papyrus, a paperlike substance made from reeds, is invented in Egypt. It quickly replaces clay as the main writing material.
1800–1600 B.C.	The first real alphabet is developed in the Mideast. It will eventually be carried by the Phoenicians to Greece.
1580–1350 B.C.	The first book, *The Book of the Dead,* is written in Egypt.
540 B.C.	The first public library is founded in Athens.
200–150 B.C.	The Greeks perfect parchment, a new writing material made from animal skins.
100 B.C.	A full-fledged publishing system develops in Rome. Parchment scrolls are copied and sold. Public libraries, copyright laws, and some government censorship already exist.
48 A.D.	Roman soldiers invade Alexandria and sack its library, destroying over 500,000 scrolls.
105	An inexpensive method for making paper is perfected in China.
150	For the first time, parchment is folded into pages to make books instead of scrolls.
400	After the fall of Rome, Catholic monasteries become the sole centers of learning in Europe. They will retain their monopoly for 800 years.
676	The Chinese art of papermaking has spread through Persia to the Arabs. Not until the thirteenth century will it be introduced into Europe.
1221	The Chinese develop movable type made of wood.
1200–1400	The Renaissance of learning in Europe. Fifty great European universities are founded during this period.
1445	The Chinese construct copper movable type.
1450	Johann Gutenberg of Mainz, Germany, introduces metal movable type to Europe. Six years later he will print the famous Gutenberg Bible, ushering in the European age of printing.

French, Spanish, or English. Both groups, the upper class and the middle class, demanded more and cheaper books.

Whenever a new need develops in society, an industry is likely to emerge to meet that need, for a profit. Just as television today "gives the public what it wants," so did printing in the fifteenth century. The illuminated manuscripts of the monasteries were incredibly beautiful, but they were also incredibly expensive. What the fifteenth-century reader wanted was lots and lots of books—cheap, portable, and permanent. There was a healthy market for books. The printing industry developed to exploit that market.

The first printing presses were modeled

after wine presses. Words and illustrations were carved into large wooden blocks. The blocks were inked, then covered with a sheet of paper. Pressure was applied (by a screw-and-lever arrangement) until the paper picked up an inked version of the carving. The result was, literally, a block print.

This method was infinitely faster and cheaper than the hand-illumination of the monks, but it was still pretty inefficient. After a few hundred impressions the letters began to crack and a new block had to be carved. In the 1440s, Johann Gutenberg found a better way: movable metal type. Gutenberg manufactured individual pieces of metal type for each letter of the alphabet. Hundreds of such pieces were wedged together into a wooden form to make up a single page. After the first page was printed, the type was reorganized into the words of the second page. No new "carving" was required.

By 1500, more than 15 million copies of 35,000 different titles were in circulation throughout Europe. Nearly all of them were printed by Gutenberg's method with movable metal type.

But the greatest literary need of the commercial classes was not for books, but for news. By the middle of the sixteenth century, many large companies found it useful to circulate handwritten newsletters among their employees and favored customers. These newsletters naturally stressed shipping and financial transactions, but they also included news of political events that might affect the business community.

The first printed news reports were "newsbooks," like the 1513 English pamphlet that recounted "the trewe encountre of the battle of Flodden Field." Most were printed by the government. In the 1560s, for example, the government of Venice produced a series of reports on the war in Dalmatia. Sold for one gazetta (a small coin), these publications came to be known as "gazettes."

By the early 1600s, German, Dutch, and Belgian printers began publishing their own regular newspapers, aimed at the commercial audience in various European cities. Most were one-page weeklies, concentrating almost entirely on financial news. The outbreak of the Thirty Years War in 1618 greatly increased the demand for political news as well. Printers cheerfully went along with the trend, and newspapers started looking a little like newspapers.

AUTHORITARIAN ENGLAND

William Caxton, an English merchant, was also a curious man. He traveled to the European continent to study the new craft of printing. In 1476 he returned to England with a printing press.

For nearly fifty years, Caxton and his successors printed whatever they liked without government interference—books, newsletters, even political satires and street ballads. Then, in 1529, King Henry VIII decided to take control of the printing industry. Every printer, he decreed, must have a royal patent (a license) to set up shop. Licensed printers held their patents only so long as what they printed continued to please the king. Certain books were absolutely forbidden; many others were known to be "questionable." In return, English printers were granted local monopolies, while on the national level imported publications were outlawed.

To all intents and purposes, Henry "nationalized" the English printing industry. His reasons seem more religious than political from today's perspective, but at the time there was little reason to distinguish between the two. In 1529, Henry was a devout Catholic, a king by "divine right." He controlled the press mainly in order to halt the distribution of heretical Protestant tracts. Four years later, Henry broke with the Vatican and founded the Church of England. He now controlled the press in hopes of banning Catholic writings. When Queen Mary came to the throne in 1553, Catholicism again became the state religion in England, and Protestant writings were again forbidden. Five years later Queen Elizabeth re-established the Church of England, and outlawed the publications of both Catholics and Puritans. Religion was *the* political issue of sixteenth-century England. It was an issue that made books dangerous and government control inevitable.

Despite the penalties, unauthorized "broadsheets" describing particular political events were openly hawked on the streets of London. So were ideological "newsbooks," pamphlets, and the like. As the literary blackmarket grew, government reaction intensified. In 1584 William Carter was hanged for printing a pro-Catholic pamphlet—perhaps the first English martyr to freedom of the press.

By 1610, regularly appearing newspapers were common on the European continent, but in England they were unknown. The English broadsheets came out irregularly and reported only a single event. This lack wasn't remedied until 1620, when Nathaniel Butter began importing Dutch newspapers (printed in English). A year later, Butter teamed up with printer Thomas Archer to pirate the news from the Dutch papers. These earliest newspapers contained only foreign news, concentrating on the Thirty Years War. They were immensely successful.

Unfortunately, King James I felt that the Thirty Years War was an affair of state, not

CHRONOLOGY

1476	William Caxton establishes the first printing press in England.
1529–1530	Henry VIII forbids the publication of certain books, and requires all English printers to obtain royal licenses, the start of authoritarian control over the press.
1550	The major trading companies of Europe circulate handwritten commercial newsletters among their employees and customers.
1609	The first primitive weekly newspaper appears in Germany, followed soon by weeklies in Holland and Belgium.
1620	Nathaniel Butter imports Dutch newspapers and distributes them in England. Called "corantos," the papers specialize in foreign news.
1621	Butter and Thomas Archer print the first English coranto, which soon meets with government repression. Nicholas Bourne joins the team, and government permission is obtained for *The Continuation of Our Weekly Newes,* the first regular newspaper in England.
1644	English poet John Milton publishes *Areopagitica,* advocating a free marketplace of ideas and urging an end to press licensing.
1694	England abandons licensing of the press.
1702	The first English language daily newspaper, the *Daily Courant,* appears in London.
1709	The first modern copyright law is enacted in England.
1712	England adopts the Stamp Tax, a heavy tax on newspapers and other publications.
1709–1720	Richard Steele, Joseph Addison, and Daniel DeFoe produce the *Tatler,* the *Spectator,* and *Mist's Journal,* collections of magazine-type essays in newspaper format.

to be discussed or debated by mere citizens. In 1621 he ordered Butter and Archer to stop carrying news of the war. The order was ignored, and Archer was imprisoned. Butter then joined up with Nicholas Bourne, and petitioned the king for permission to print a weekly newspaper. They agreed to submit the text of their paper to the government for advance approval. Such precensorship was to become a hallmark of authoritarian control over the press.

Butter and Bourne published their first issue in September of 1621. Entitled *The Continuation of Our Weekly Newes,* the paper carried the legend: "Published With Authority." It ran only one page, on a sheet a little smaller than a piece of typewriter paper. As soon as he was released from jail, Archer joined the team. From 1621 to 1632, *Our Weekly Newes* was the only official weekly newspaper in England.

The decade of the 1630s was marked by intense conflict between King Charles I and the English Parliament. By 1640 Parliament was clearly the winner. It celebrated and consolidated its power by granting increased civil and religious liberties to the nation, including a relaxation of press censorship. Poet John Milton was among those whose voices were raised in favor of freedom of the press. In his monumental *Areopagitica,* Milton argued:

> Truth and understanding are not such wares as to be monopolized and traded in by tickets and statutes and standards. We must not think to make a staple commodity of all knowledge in the land, to mark and license it like our broadcloth. . . . Give me the liberty to know, to utter, and to argue freely according to conscience, above all liberties. . . And though all the winds of doctrine were let loose to play upon the earth, so Truth be in the field, we do injuriously, by licensing and prohibiting, to misdoubt her strength. Let her and Falsehood grapple; who ever knew Truth put to the worse, in a free and open encounter.[1]

Spurred on by the new permissiveness, a series of daily reports called "diurnals" developed throughout England. They chronicled the tail end of the conflict between Parliament and Crown. That conflict ended in the mid-1640s with the Puritan Revolution. A victory for Parliament, the revolution soon proved a defeat for freedom of the press. Its leader, Oliver Cromwell, quickly established himself as a virtual dictator of England. Unlicensed printers were harshly dealt with, while licensed printers were subjected to incessant censorship. Ironically enough, it was John Milton himself who became the nation's chief censor under the Puritan regime.

The restoration of the monarchy under Charles II brought no immediate improvement for the press. But the power of the king was on the wane, and libertarianism was in the air. Instances of censorship were rare throughout the 1670s and the 1680s, and in 1694 licensing of the press was abandoned completely. By the time the *Daily Courant,* England's first daily newspaper, was founded in 1702, the English press was more or less free to write what it pleased, so long as it avoided criticizing the government. The journalism of England in the early eighteenth century was to serve as a model for the young printers who introduced newspapers to the American colonies.

COLONIAL AMERICA

Two of the Pilgrims who landed in Plymouth in 1620 were skilled printers. They had published illegal Protestant tracts in England, and watched the production of primitive newspapers in Holland. But they brought no press with them to the New World. They realized that their tiny outpost in the wilderness would have neither the time nor the need for newspapers.

The Massachusetts Bay Colony, which settled Boston in 1630, was larger, wealthier, and better educated than Plymouth. All Puritan children were taught to read, and the brightest boys were sent to Harvard College to prepare for the ministry. In 1638 the first printing press in the New World was established at Harvard to produce religious texts.

In England the Puritans had been revolutionaries; in Massachusetts Bay they were the Establishment. Like other Establishments of the time, they feared that a free press might threaten the government and promote religious heresies. Printing was therefore strictly controlled. By the mid-1600s, various presses in Massachusetts had published lawbooks, volumes of sermons, poetry, and a history of the colony. But it was not until the last decade of the century that a printer dared to produce anything resembling a newspaper.

Benjamin Harris had come to Boston in 1686, after publishing a number of seditious pamphlets in England. In 1690 he printed the first issue of *Publick Occurrences,* a three-page newspaper roughly 6 × 9 inches in size. Featurey by today's standards, the paper included the following item of special interest:

> The Christianized *Indians* in some parts of *Plimouth* have newly appointed a day of Thanksgiving to God for his Mercy in supplying their extream and pinching Necessities under their late want of Corn, & for His giving them now a prospect of a very *Comfortable Harvest.* Their Example may be worth Mentioning.[2]

The paper also gossiped about the presumed immorality of the king of France, and complained that the Indian allies of the British had mistreated French prisoners. These were bold topics—perhaps too bold. The colonial governor and the Puritan elders immediately ordered the paper suppressed. *Publick Occurrences,* America's first newspaper, died after one issue.

By 1700, the thriving commercial city of Boston was ripe for a second try. John Campbell, the local postmaster, met the need for news with a handwritten newsletter, which he distributed to shippers, farmers, mer-

chants, and government officials throughout the colonies. Campbell was in an ideal position to run a newspaper. As postmaster, he was the first one to get a look at the English and European papers. Moreover, his postage-free "franking privilege" enabled him to send his newsletters through the mail without charge. Throughout the colonial period, the job of postmaster was closely linked to that of publisher.

In 1704 Campbell began printing his newsletter. Aptly called the *Boston News-Letter,* it was precensored by the governor and "Published by Authority." The single-page paper, printed on both sides, was sold by subscription only. By 1715 Campbell had perhaps 300 regular readers.

The *Boston News-Letter* was strictly a commercial newspaper. It emphasized local financial news and foreign political developments, the latter pirated directly from English papers. A smattering of births, deaths, and social events made Campbell's paper even more appealing to the economic elite of the colonies—but it was not a publication for the average citizen or the intellectual. As a commercial paper, the News-Letter was an obvious candidate for advertising. The very first issue carried this notice:

> This News-Letter is to be continued Weekly, and all Persons who have Houses, Lands, Tenements, Farms, Ships, Vessels, Goods, Wares or Merchandise, &c to be Sold or Let; or Servants Run-away, or Goods Stole or Lost; may have the same inserted at a Reasonable Rate, from *Twelve Pence* to *Five Shilling*s. . . .[3]

Before long, Campbell was earning a considerable profit from ads.

After losing the postmaster job in 1719, Campbell decided to continue printing his newspaper without the franking privilege. The new postmaster, William Brooker, hired printer James Franklin to publish his own paper, the *Boston Gazette.* Competition had come to the colonies, and both papers were livelier as a result.

Two years later Franklin left the *Gazette*

and established a third newspaper, the *New England Courant.* Franklin was an intellectual of sorts. His interests were secular and political, not religious or commercial. The articles and essays in the *Courant,* often written under pseudonyms, viciously attacked the Puritan clergy and its control over the Boston government. The third regular newspaper in Massachusetts was anti-Establishment.

Among the staff of the *Courant* was Franklin's younger brother Benjamin, an apprentice printer. Apparently without his brother's knowledge, Ben Franklin was also the author of several satirical essays in the paper, run under the byline "Silence Dogood." In 1722 James Franklin was jailed for three weeks for his attacks on the government, and "Silence Dogood" came out with an eloquent plea for freedom of the press. James soon got out of jail, discovered the identity of "Dogood," and jealously ordered his teenage brother to stick to the printing end of the business.

The *Courant* kept up its attacks on church and state, and in 1723 Franklin was ordered to submit his paper for precensorship. He got around the command by making Ben titular publisher, a tactic that enraged the religious leadership of the colony but amused its citizens. Franklin was arrested for contempt of the censorship order, but he was so popular that the government (headed by Increase Mather and his son Cotton) didn't dare to try him. He was soon released and resumed control of the newspaper. Precensorship had failed in Massachusetts; it would never again succeed.

The American colonists were, by and large, an independent lot. Schooled in religious dissent, they took naturally to political dissent as well. At the end of the first quarter of the eighteenth century, most colonial governments still had licensing and precensorship laws on the books. But they were seldom invoked, and almost never invoked with success. The *New England Courant* was the first outspoken anti-Establishment newspaper in America—but it was by no means the last.

The first American printing press outside Massachusetts was brought to Philadelphia by William Bradford in 1685. A book publisher, Bradford found the censorship laws in that Quaker city too stiff for comfort. So in 1693 he moved his press to New York. Bradford's son Andrew soon returned to Philadelphia, and in 1719 he established the *American Weekly Mercury.* The *Mercury* was the first American newspaper outside Boston, and the third regularly published paper in the colonies.

Never as outspoken as Franklin's *Courant,* the *Mercury* was nevertheless in constant trouble with the government of Philadelphia. Bradford was ordered "not to publish anything relating to or concerning the affairs of this Government, or the Government of any other of His Majesty's Colonies, without the permission of the Governor or Secretary of this Province."[4] Bradford often disobeyed the order. Once, after an especially damning satire, he was arrested. But by this time the spirit of liberty was strong even in Quaker Philadelphia, and Bradford was never prosecuted.

Young Ben Franklin, meanwhile, was bored with working for his brother in Boston. In 1723, shortly after James Franklin was released from prison, Ben ran away to Philadelphia. Six years later he founded the weekly *Pennsylvania Gazette.* A shrewd politician, Franklin managed to publish the brightest and wittiest paper in the colonies without government interference.

In 1741, Franklin inaugurated his *General Magazine;* not to be outdone, Andrew Bradford began the *American Magazine* in the same year. Neither was successful. The American public was not yet ready for such heavy doses of philosophical and literary commentary.

When Andrew Bradford left New York for Philadelphia, William Bradford stayed behind. In 1725 he followed his son's example and founded New York's first newspaper, the *New York Gazette.* The poorly printed two-page paper carefully avoided antagonizing government officials. But stronger papers soon developed in New York: the *Weekly Post Boy,* the *Evening-Post*—and the historic *New York Weekly Journal.*

By the end of the 1720s, a political power struggle was underway in New York, between the rising middle class and the Tory Establishment, headed by Governor William Cosby. In 1733 the leaders of the anti-administration group decided that they needed a newspaper to champion their cause. They founded the *New York Weekly Journal,* and asked printer John Peter Zenger to be its editor.

Zenger immediately set about attacking Cosby and the aristocracy, urging a more representative government for New York. Twice Cosby asked the grand jury to indict Zenger for seditious libel (criticizing the government), and twice the grand jury refused. Finally, Cosby's council issued its own warrant for Zenger's arrest, and in November of 1734 the crusading editor was sent to jail.

His *Journal* missed only one issue. Later editions were dictated to his wife through a "Hole of the Door of the Prison." [5]

The Zenger case came to trial in August, 1735. Andrew Hamilton, a famous lawyer nearly eighty years old, was brought in from Philadelphia to handle the defense.

Hamilton began by admitting that Zenger had, in fact, published the articles in question. Under existing law, that should have been the end of the case; criticism of the government, whether true or false, was illegal. As the prosecuting attorney explained: "I think the jury must find a verdict for the King; for supposing they [the libels] were true, the law says that they are not the less libelous for that; nay, indeed, the law says their being true is an aggravation of the crime."

It was precisely this point that Hamilton disputed. He argued what was then a novel legal contention: "The words themselves must be libelous, that is, *false, scandalous, and seditious* or else we are not guilty."

CHRONOLOGY

1638   The Puritans establish the first printing press in America at Harvard College.

1685   William Bradford brings to Philadelphia, and later to New York, the first printing press in America outside Massachusetts.

1690   Benjamin Harris publishes the first American newspaper, *Publick Occurrences.* It is suppressed by Boston authorities after one issue.

1704   John Campbell's *Boston News-Letter* becomes the first regularly published newspaper in America.

1719   William Brooker and James Franklin found the *Boston Gazette;* Andrew Bradford establishes the *American Weekly Mercury* in Philadelphia.

1721   James Franklin emphasizes political and social criticism in his *New England Courant.*

1725   William Bradford founds the *New York Gazette,* the first newspaper in New York.

1729   Benjamin Franklin begins publishing the *Pennsylvania Gazette* in Philadelphia.

1735   John Peter Zenger, publisher of the *New York Weekly Journal,* is acquitted on charges of seditious libel. After Zenger, colonial juries will refuse to convict journalists for printing the truth, however injurious to the government.

1741   The *General Magazine* and *American Magazine* are founded in Philadelphia. Both are unsuccessful.

The judge sided with precedent and the prosecutor, ruling that truth was irrelevant. He refused even to let Hamilton try to prove Zenger's anti-government accusations. Hamilton then appealed directly to the jury:

> The question before the court and you, gentlemen of the jury, is not of small nor private concern, it is not the cause of a poor printer, nor of New York alone. . . . It is the cause of liberty . . . the liberty both of exposing and opposing arbitrary power (in these parts of the world, at least) by speaking and writing truth.[6]

The jury returned a verdict of not guilty, and Zenger was released.

The importance of the Zenger trial is not that it established a new legal principle. In fact, truth was not officially accepted as a defense in seditious libel cases until the Sedition Act of 1798. What the Zenger trial proved is that the average American colonist —in this case the jury—was unalterably opposed to authoritarian government. The trial recognized and solidified the role of the colonial press as critic of government and defender of liberty. It thus paved the way for the important part the press was to play in bringing about the American Revolution.

The American press in the last half of the eighteenth century was less interested in news than in comment—philosophical, social, literary, and political. Most colonial newspapers were quickly radicalized by the hated Stamp Act, and thereafter they led the cry for Independence. After the Revolution, the papers split into two camps: the elite Federalists and the populist Republicans. Each newspaper was written for readers who agreed with it; no newspaper tried to be objective in the modern sense. Political partisanship was to characterize the American press until well into the nineteenth century.

THE REVOLUTIONARY PERIOD

There were twelve newspapers in the American colonies in 1750, serving a population of just over one million. By 1775, the population would rise to 2.5 million, while the number of newspapers would jump to 48. Five successful magazines would be established during this period, and innumerable book publishers. The American mass media were thriving.

The typical newspaper of the times was a four-page weekly, 10×15 inches in size. The paper was rough foolscap imported from England; it was mottled and ugly, but surprisingly durable. Headlines were rare, and illustrations rarer still. A hand press was used to produce perhaps 400 copies of each issue.

The content of such a newspaper was mostly philosophical-political essays. Even reports on specific local events were generally written in essay form—but most "articles" were not tied to an event at all. Libertarianism was the philosophy of the day. Every colonial newspaper devoted considerable space to reprints of English and French libertarian tracts, not to mention the wisdom of home-grown philosophers.

The English Stamp Act of 1765 provided a new focus for these libertarian essays: the evil of King George. The Stamp Act imposed a heavy tax on paper; it thus hit newspaper publishers harder than anyone else. Not that the tax itself was anything new. It was first levied against *English* newspapers in 1712. Still, never before had the English government imposed such a tax on American newspapers, and the colonial press was unanimous in its opposition to this "taxation without representation." Several papers announced that they were suspending publication in protest. They later reappeared without nameplates, claiming that they were broadsides or handbills and thus exempt from the tax. Before long they resumed their original titles, but no colonial newspaper ever carried the required stamp or paid the required tax.

The Stamp Act was repealed in 1766—but it was too late. The experience of uniting in opposition to the established government is a heady one. From that experience the colonial press never recovered. After 1765, most

American publishers were committed to Revolution in one form or another. Their newspapers were devoted to that cause.

The *Boston Gazette,* often edited by Samuel Adams, was typical of the militant papers of the day. With each new imposition of British rule, Adams and other radical writers throughout the colonies strove to stir up resistance. The following is the "lead" of the *Gazette*'s story on the "Boston Massacre" of 1770. It is thoughtful and contemplative, but hardly unbiased:

> The Town of Boston affords a recent and melancholy Demonstration of the destructive Consequences of quartering Troops among Citizens in a Time of Peace, under a Pretence of supporting the Laws and aiding Civil Authority; every considerate and unprejudic'd Person among us was deeply imprest with the Apprehension of these Consequences when it was known that a Number of Regiments were ordered to this Town under such a Pretext, but in Reality to inforce oppressive Measures; to awe and controul the legislative as well as executive Power of the Province, and to quell a Spirit of Liberty, which however it may have been basely oppos'd and even ridicul'd by some, would do Honor to any Age or Country.[7]

To be sure, there were some moderates and even Royalists among American publishers. John Dickinson, for example, published his influential "Letters from a Farmer in Pennsylvania" in the *Pennsylvania Chronicle* of 1767–1768. A businessman, Dickinson resented English control over American foreign trade. But he was unalterably opposed to revolution.

Yet men like Dickinson could do little to halt the effect of revolutionaries like Sam Adams—or Tom Paine, editor of the *Pennsylvania Magazine,* whose pamphlet "Common Sense" sold 120,000 copies in the spring of 1776.

By 1775, war had become inevitable. Publishers were forced to choose sides, becoming either radical Patriots or steadfast Loyalists; there was no middle ground left. Isaiah Thomas, editor of the *Massachusetts Spy,* headlined his article on the Battle of Lexington: "The shot heard round the world." His lead paragraph left no doubt where he stood:

> Americans! forever bear in mind the BATTLE OF LEXINGTON!—where British troops, unmolested and unprovoked, wantonly and in a most inhuman manner, fired upon and killed

---

CHRONOLOGY

1765 Colonial newspapers refuse to pay the tax imposed by the English Stamp Act—thus taking a giant step toward radicalization.

1767 John Dickinson publishes the first of his moderate "Letters from a Farmer in Pennsylvania" in the *Pennsylvania Chronicle.*

1770 Boston publisher John Mein is attacked by Patriot leaders and forced to fold his Tory *Boston Chronicle*—a sign of growing polarization.

1772 Sam Adams, a regular contributor to the radical *Boston Gazette,* organizes the Committees of Correspondence, a network of agents "covering" events throughout the colonies on behalf of the Patriot press.

1773 James Rivington founds *Rivington's New York Gazetteer,* the most powerful Tory newspaper of the Revolution.

1776 Tom Paine's pamphlet, "Common Sense," is widely circulated throughout the colonies; the Declaration of Independence is carried on the front page of most colonial newspapers; the Revolution begins in earnest.

a number of our countrymen, then robbed, ransacked, and burnt their houses! nor could the tears of defenseless women, some of whom were in the pains of childbirth, the cries of helpless babes, nor the prayers of old age, confined to beds of sickness, appease their thirst for blood!—or divert them from their DESIGN of MURDER and ROBBERY! [8]

At first, the war was hard on both Patriot and Tory newspapers. Neither were allowed to publish or circulate in territory controlled by the enemy. But as the Thirteen United States of America won victory after victory, the Loyalist press quickly disappeared. Wartime commerce, meanwhile, brought heavy loads of lucrative advertising to the pages of revolutionary newspapers. And public interest in the war itself gave some Patriot papers as many as 8,000 readers. The end of the Revolution left the American mass media—books, magazines, and newspapers—stronger than ever before. They had waged a battle, and they had won.

THE PARTISAN PRESS

The Revolutionary War had united rich and poor in the common cause of independence. But as soon as the war ended, this unity ended as well. Merchants, bankers, manufacturers, and large property owners—the "aristocracy" of America—urged the establishment of a strong central government. Small farmers and wage earners, on the other hand, feared the power of the monied interests; they supported a loose confederacy of local governments.

The agrarian-labor types were in control at the close of the war. The Articles of Confederation they passed in 1781 gave nearly all the power to the states. Without even the right of taxation, the new national government was too weak to cope with the postwar economic depression. Moreover, the propertied classes soon gained control of the various state legislatures. In 1787 they convened the Philadelphia Constitutional Convention to rewrite the Articles of Confederation and

strengthen the federal government. The delegates to that Convention were nearly all propertied men, advocates of strong national government. The new Constitution reflected their aims and interests.

Once the Constitution was written, it was sent to the states for ratification. The battle was joined. The conservative, monied group now called itself the Federalists; the agrarian-labor bloc was known as the Anti-Federalists or Republicans. Again, newspapers throughout the thirteen colonies (now the thirteen states) were forced to choose sides. One was either a Federalist or a Republican; once more, there was no middle ground.

Alexander Hamilton, James Madison, and John Jay wrote a total of 85 essays urging ratification of the Constitution. Collectively called *The Federalist,* these essays first appeared in the *New York Independent Journal.* They were carried by Federalist newspapers throughout the nation, and were circulated in pamphlet and book form as well. Anti-Federalist papers responded by publishing Richard Henry Lee's *Letters from the Federal Farmer,* which opposed the Constitution as a document of the propertied classes.

One bone of contention was the conspicuous absence in the new Constitution of specific guarantees of individual rights, including the right of freedom of the press. Nine of the thirteen states already provided for such freedom in their state constitutions, and the Federalists presumably felt that that was enough. The Federalists were not by nature sympathetic to press freedom; the Constitution itself was debated in strict secrecy. As Alexander Hamilton wrote:

What is Liberty of the Press? Who can give it any definition which does not leave the utmost latitude for evasion? I hold it to be impracticable; and from this I infer, that its security, whatever fine declarations may be inserted in any Constitution respecting it, must altogether depend on public opinion, and on the general spirit of the people and of the Government.[9]

The Republicans, by contrast, believed freedom of the press to be crucial to the survival of American democracy. Thomas Jefferson, by birth an aristocrat but by choice a "friend of the common man," was the acknowledged leader of the Republicans. In a letter to a friend, Jefferson wrote:

> The basis of our government being the opinion of the people, the very first object should be to keep that right; and if it were left to me to decide whether we should have a government without newspapers, or newspapers without a government, I should not hesitate a moment to prefer the latter.[10]

In 1788, after a year of bitter strife, the Constitution was finally ratified. The Federalists easily dominated the first Congress of the new nation. In an effort to reunify the country, they proposed a Bill of Rights. It included what is now the First Amendment: "Congress shall make no law . . . abridging the freedom of speech or of the press." In 1791 the Bill of Rights was ratified by the states and became law.

The Bill of Rights did little to bridge the gap between the two factions. General George Washington was the unanimous choice for President. His Vice President was John Adams, a Federalist. His Secretary of the Treasury was Alexander Hamilton, also a Federalist. His Secretary of State was Thomas Jefferson, leader of the Republicans. Throughout the Washington administration, Federalists and Republicans were at each other's throats.

Not content with the support of independent publishers, both parties established "house organs" to serve as direct pipelines between political leaders and their followers. Federalist funds were responsible for John Fenno's *Gazette of the United States* and Noah Webster's *American Minerva,* both in New York. Hamilton personally set editorial policy for both papers. Not to be outdone, Jefferson appointed Philip Freneau official translator for the State Department, in return for Freneau's agreement to publish a

Republican party organ in Philadelphia. Policy for Freneau's *National Gazette* was personally set by Jefferson. Other publishers throughout the country looked to one or another of these newspapers for guidance on how to handle the news.

In 1796, Federalist John Adams was elected President; Jefferson, the loser, became Vice President. The most divisive issue of the moment was the war in Europe between France and England. The Republicans, who had applauded the populist French Revolution several years earlier, supported France. The Federalists, with control of both the presidency and Congress, supported England. The United States prepared to go to war against France.

With war fever at its highest, and rival journalists brawling in the streets, the Federalists made their move to squelch the opposition. In 1798, Congress passed the Sedition Act. Under the Act, it became a federal crime to publish any false criticism of government officials.

The Sedition Act is remembered for two conflicting reasons. On the one hand, it established the "Zenger principle" by explicitly accepting truth as a defense; only *false* criticisms of the government were illegal. On the other hand, it was also the most outstanding piece of repressive legislation in the early history of the United States.

The Federalists used the Sedition Act to purge the nation of anti-Federalist thought. Federalist editors were allowed to continue their defamatory attacks on Jefferson and his supporters—but seven leading Republican editors were prosecuted and convicted for similar invective against the Federalist leadership. The plan backfired. In 1800, public resentment of the Sedition Act helped sweep Jefferson into the presidency. War preparations were immediately halted, and in 1801 the Sedition Act was allowed to lapse.

The last quarter of the eighteenth century was the heyday of the Partisan Press. There were no words so insulting that Federalist and Republican editors were unwilling to use them to describe their enemies. Benjamin Franklin Bache (grandson of Ben Franklin) was publisher of the strictly Republican *Philadelphia Aurora*. In 1797, he celebrated the retirement of George Washington in the following terms:

> The man who is the source of all the misfortunes of our country is this day reduced to a level with his fellow-citizens, and is no longer possessed of power to multiply evils upon the United States. . . . Every heart in unison with the freedom and happiness of the people, ought to beat high with exultation that the name of Washington from this day ceased to give a currency to political iniquity and to legalized corruption.[11]

This was too much for William Cobbett, the Federalist editor of *Porcupine's Gazette*, also in Philadelphia. Putting aside politicians for the moment, Cobbett attacked Bache directly:

> He spent several years in hunting offices under the Federal Government, and being constantly rejected, he at last became its most bitter foe. Hence his abuse of general Washington, whom, at the time he was soliciting a place, he panegerized up to the third heaven. He was born for a hireling, and therefore when he found he could not obtain employ in one quarter, he sought it in another. . . . He is an ill-looking devil. His eyes never get above your knees.[12]

Neither of these quotations, by the way, comes from an "editorial." Throughout the eighteenth century and well into the nineteenth, it was customary for newspapers to intersperse news and opinion, often within the same article. By 1800, a few papers, including the *Aurora,* had set aside page two as an editorial page of sorts—complete with the editorial "We." But opinions were found on the other pages as well. Objectivity in the modern sense simply wasn't a characteristic of the Partisan Press.

Almost without exception, the dedicated Federalist and Republican newspapers were weeklies. There was no need to hurry a vituperative essay into print; next week would do as well as tomorrow. Urban merchants, on the other hand, were desperate for daily reports on ship arrivals and other commercial news.

The first American daily newspaper was the *Pennsylvania Evening Post and Daily Advertiser,* founded in 1783. A year later the *Pennsylvania Packet and Daily Advertiser* appeared. It was a better newspaper than the *Post,* and despite its expensive price (fourpence), it soon forced the competition to fold. In 1785, two more dailies appeared —the *New York Morning Post and Daily Advertiser,* and the *New York Daily Advertiser.* By 1800, there were twenty daily newspapers in the United States.

As their names imply, the new daily papers depended heavily on advertising. Many were able to fill sixteen out of twenty columns with ads, leaving only four for news. This was all right with their readers, who often found the advertisements as useful as the editorial copy. They cheerfully paid as much as eight dollars a year (roughly the cost of a barrel of flour) for subscriptions. The *New York Daily Advertiser* pioneered the use of half-inch-high headlines in its ads; large type would soon be used for news headlines as well.

The partisan weeklies flourished right along with the commercial dailies. By 1800, there were roughly 200 weeklies in operation, all but a few dozen of them founded after the Revolution. Subscriptions averaged $2.50 a year; the number of subscribers averaged 600 to 700. As much as half the space in a successful weekly might be advertising.

Most of these weeklies served small cities and towns, pirating their news from the larger metropolitan papers. They were able to survive largely because of the Post Office Act of 1792, which set a low one-cent rate for the mailing of newspapers. The Act also provided that publishers could exchange their papers by mail without charge, enabling frontier papers to get all their news free.

The government supported the newspaper industry in other ways as well. Perhaps the most important subsidy was the legal printing contract. Key newspapers in each state and territory were paid to reprint the texts of various laws. This plum was handed out strictly along party lines, as a form of political patronage. Scores of influential frontier papers could never have started without their government printing contracts.

Between 1800 and 1830, the American media prospered, but they changed very little in character. Some of the commercial dailies turned partisan, while some of the partisan weeklies went daily—and dozens of new weeklies were founded every year. By 1830, then, there were three kinds of newspapers in America: (1) A handful of strictly commercial dailies; (2) Roughly sixty partisan metropolitan dailies; and (3) Well over a thousand small-town and frontier weeklies, most of them partisan.

Improvements in printing enabled publishers to produce as many as 1,100 impressions an hour. The extra capacity was seldom needed—the average daily still circulated only a thousand copies, and weekly circulation was lower still. The cost of the average newspaper rose to six cents an issue, the same as a pint of whiskey. Headlines improved the appearance of the typical paper, while the use of part-time "correspondents" in Washington and elsewhere improved its quality. But the overall look of the page was still very gray, and most of the content was still essays and commentary.

The magazine and book industries also thrived. Most of the hundred-odd magazines in business in 1830 neglected politics and concentrated on literary and social comment. Typical were the *Port Folio* (founded in 1801), the *North American Review* (1815), and the *Saturday Evening Post* (1821). The *Post,* an immediate success, was made up of

CHRONOLOGY

1783   The first American daily newspaper, the *Pennsylvania Evening Post and Daily Advertiser,* is published in Philadelphia.

1787   Federalist newspapers print *The Federalist,* a series of essays by Alexander Hamilton and others urging ratification of the Constitution. Republican papers respond with Richard Henry Lee's *Letters from a Federal Farmer.*

1789   *The Triumph of Nature,* the first native American novel, is published.

1791   The First Amendment to the Constitution is ratified, guaranteeing freedom of the press from congressional censorship.

1792   The Post Office Act grants newspapers special low mailing rates.

1798   The Federalist Congress enacts the Sedition Act in an effort to restrain Republican newspapers. The invention of the iron press permits printers to make as many as 250 impressions per hour.

1801   The Jefferson administration allows the Sedition Act to lapse.

1811   Fredrich Koenig of Germany invents a steam-driven cylinder press, capable of producing 1100 impressions per hour.

1821   The *Saturday Evening Post* is founded, the first successful magazine to appeal to women as well as men.

1822   A crude but permanent photograph is produced in France. By 1839 the process will be practical.

1827   The Washington Hand Press is invented; it will cross the continent and give the frontier nearly all its newspapers.

fiction and poems, essays, and regular columns on morals and religion. Although most books sold in the United States were still printed in England, by 1820 more than 40,000 titles written and published by Americans had appeared. Among the best-sellers were histories (John Marshall's *Life of Washington*), political commentaries (*The Federalist*), and novels (James Fenimore Cooper's *The Spy*).

The American mass media in 1830 were healthy and flourishing, but they were nevertheless the property of the privileged classes. Books, magazines, and newspapers were not designed to appeal to the working class. They were too expensive, for one thing. For another, they were too literate. What did a dock worker in New York care about the price of wheat on the Philadelphia commodity market or the latest antics of a famous novelist? The population of the United States in 1830 was twelve million. The total circulation of all the newspapers in the country was well under two million.

The times were ripe for a newspaper for the masses.

───────────────

By 1830 the urban working class was the largest potential newspaper audience in America. The papers that emerged to meet the needs of that audience were cheap and readable, stressing human-interest features and objective news over political partisanship. These were the first genuinely mass media in the country, and they quickly became the most influential. Other kinds of newspapers survived (the partisan press, the frontier press, the elite press), but they were clearly secondary in importance.

THE PENNY PRESS

The Industrial Revolution began in America early in the nineteenth century. Thousands of farm children and recent immigrants flooded the cities of the eastern seaboard in search of factory work. This new urban working class soon demanded—and received—the right to vote. The workers used their suffrage

to institute tax-supported public schools, and by 1830 most of them knew how to read. But they couldn't afford the newspapers of the period, nor were they interested in shipping and commercial news.

On September 3, 1833, Benjamin Day published the first issue of the *New York Sun*. He greeted his audience with these words:

> The object of this paper is to lay before the public, at a price within the means of every one, ALL THE NEWS OF THE DAY, and at the same time afford an advantageous medium for advertising. . . .[13]

Day's definition of news was much broader than that of the commercial and political newspapers of his time. It included whatever might entertain the masses—especially human-interest features. The first issue of the *Sun* carried this story on page one:

> *A Whistler.*—A boy in Vermont, accustomed to working alone, was so prone to whistling, that, as soon as he was by himself, he unconsciously commenced. When asleep, the muscles of his mouth, chest, and lungs were so completely concatenated in the association, he whistled with astonishing shrillness. A pale countenance, loss of appetite, and almost total prostration of strength, convinced his mother it would end in death, if not speedily overcome, which was accomplished by placing him in the society of another boy, who had orders to give him a blow as soon as he began to whistle.[14]

Everything in the *Sun* was designed with the urban masses in mind. Day chose a type face nearly twice as large as the opposition's. He cut the paper down to three columns per page, a far more readable format than the customary jumble of five or six columns. More important, Day filled the *Sun* with entertaining features. Perhaps the most entertaining was George Wisner's "Police Office," a daily round-up of local crime news. Wisner was the first police reporter in American journalism. He was one of the first reporters of any kind.

The key to the *Sun*'s financial success was marketing. Recognizing that the urban masses could not afford six cents for a newspaper (nor an annual subscription at almost any price), Day sold the *Sun* on the street for a penny a copy. Newsboys bought the paper for 67 cents a hundred, then filled the downtown area with cries of crime and violence—on sale for only a penny. By 1836 the *Sun* had a daily circulation of more than 30,000.

The success of the *Sun* spawned dozens of imitators throughout the East. But the three most important ones were right in New York: the *New York Herald,* the *New York Tribune,* and the *New York Times.*

James Gordon Bennett founded the *Herald* in 1835. He matched the *Sun* crime for crime and sensation for sensation, and then some; in 1836 the *Herald* turned the murder of a local prostitute into a national issue. But Bennett was not content with just the working-class audience. He challenged the middle-class press as well, with up-to-the-minute coverage of commercial, political, and foreign news. Bennett's private pony express carried first-hand reports from Washington, and European news intercepted in Newfoundland. When Samuel Morse's telegraph was perfected in 1844, the *Herald* became one of its biggest customers.

Such newsgathering techniques were costly, and Bennett was forced to charge two cents for his paper. The public was apparently willing to pay the price. The *Herald*'s extensive (and expensive) coverage of the Mexican War gave a giant boost to both circulation and advertising. By 1860 the *Herald* was the richest newspaper in America, selling 60,000 copies a day.

Horace Greeley's *New York Tribune,* founded in 1841, proved that a penny newspaper could succeed without sensationalism. Greeley's large editorial staff included correspondents in six American cities, plus Europe, Canada, Mexico, Central America, and Cuba. In place of scandal, the *Tribune* offered solid news coverage and a zesty editorial page. Greeley campaigned against slavery, whiskey, tobacco, debt, and numerous other evils both personal and political. A special weekly edition of the *Tribune* circulated nationwide—200,000 copies a week by 1860.

The *New York Times* was a latecomer to the Penny Press, founded by Henry J. Raymond in 1851. Almost from the first, the *Times* was the most "elite" of the mass-market newspapers. Its news was well-balanced and well-edited, and there was plenty of it—with special attention to foreign affairs. The *Times* was not yet the "paper of record" for the United States, but it was on its way.

The Penny Press began with sensationalism and human interest. By mid-century it was the "two-penny" press. The human interest continued unabated, but the sensationalism began to disappear; it was replaced with hard national and international news.

In 1848 six New York newspapers banded together to share the cost of telegraphing national news from Washington and European news from Boston. The organization they formed, the Associated Press of New York, soon became a wire service for the entire nation. Newspapers throughout the country purchased the news reports that AP prepared in Washington and Boston. Since the member papers represented a variety of editorial viewpoints, AP could satisfy them all only by having no viewpoint of its own. Objectivity had come to American journalism.

Now it was left to each newspaper to add its own interpretation or bias to the AP story. Many did just that—but many more didn't bother. Before long, newspapers in Atlanta, Chicago, and New York were carrying identical, unbiased reports. The change was startling. The following wire article on the Supreme Court's Dred Scott decision was carried by the *New York Times* in 1857. It is impossible to tell from the article where the *Times* stood on slavery:

The opinion of the Supreme Court in the DRED SCOTT case was delivered by Chief

1830	*Godey's Lady's Book* is founded, a monthly magazine especially for women.
1830–1833	Englishman David Napier perfects the Koenig steam press, producing thousands of impressions per hour.
1833	Benjamin Day publishes the *New York Sun*, the first of the penny newspapers, designed for the working class.
1835	James Gordon Bennett starts the *New York Herald* with $500. The two-cent paper will appeal to both the workers and the middle class.
1840	A German process for making paper from wood pulp permits truly mass-market publishing.
1841	Horace Greeley's *New York Tribune* stresses hard news and editorials instead of sensationalism.
1844	Samuel F. B. Morse perfects the telegraph.
1846	The rotary or "lighting" press is invented; it costs $25,000—but can produce 20,000 impressions an hour.
1848	Six New York newspapers form the Associated Press of New York to pool telegraph costs. Other papers with varying political views will soon tie onto the AP, forcing it to report the news objectively.
1850	*Harper's Monthly* is founded, with an emphasis on science and travel.
1851	Henry J. Raymond publishes the *New York Times,* with an initial investment of $100,000. Paul Julius Reuter establishes the first commercial wire service in Europe.
1857	*Harper's Weekly* is founded, using dramatic engravings to report national news.
1860	The Government Printing Office is established; partisan newspapers lose the patronage of federal—but not local—governmental printing.

Justice TANEY. It was a full and elaborate statement of the views of the Court. They have decided the following important points:

First—Negroes, whether slaves or free, that is, men of the African race, are not citizens of the United States by the Constitution. . . .[15]

The magazine and book industries, meanwhile, followed the same trends as newspapers—appealing to the mass market first through sensationalism and human interest, and later through solid news coverage. *Godey's Lady's Book* (founded in 1830) was one of the first of a host of monthlies for women. *Graham's* (1840) stressed the special interests of men. *Harper's New Monthly Magazine* (1850) concentrated on science, travel, and current events, while the *Atlantic Monthly* (1857) had a more literary flavor. Weekly periodicals like *Gleason's Pictorial* (1851) and *Leslie's Illustrated Newspaper* (1855) attracted readers with woodblock illustrations of fires, railroad accidents, and the like. *Harper's Weekly* (1857) added dramatic engravings of more important national events.

The fortunes of book publishing rose with the appearance of great American authors. Emerson, Thoreau, Poe, Cooper, and Whitman were read by "everyone." So were scores of sentimental novels—and Harriet Beecher Stowe's blockbuster, *Uncle Tom's Cabin.*

The second third of the nineteenth century witnessed the development of several crucial journalistic trends—mass-circulation newspapers and magazines, human-interest stories, and objectivity. But the Partisan Press was by no means dead during this period. It was kept alive first by the issue of Jacksonian Democracy, and later by the even more divisive issue of slavery.

As early as 1837, an abolitionist editor died for his views. He was Elijah Lovejoy, editor of the *St. Louis Observer,* a strident anti-slavery weekly. Lovejoy was forced by public pressure to move his presses across the river to Alton, Illinois. Three times his office was ransacked—but still he refused to moderate his words. Finally, the editor was murdered by an angry mob. The *Liberator,* a Boston abolitionist paper edited by William Lloyd Garrison, headlined the story:

Horrid Tragedy!
BLOOD CRIETH!
Riot and Murder at Alton.

By the outbreak of hostilities in 1861, the American mass media were once more divided. Almost without exception the Southern newspapers supported slavery and secession, while most Northern papers were firmly opposed to both. Once again, there was no middle ground.

The Civil War was covered as no American war had ever been covered before. More than 150 newspaper and magazine reporters scoured the Northern front for news, while the well-organized Press Association of the Confederate States of America served Southern newspapers from the other side of the line.

Freedom of the press is not designed for a nation at war with itself. Civil War censorship was strict. In 1861, Union officials discovered that Confederate spies were masquerading as Northern reporters, sending back military secrets in the form of "news" telegrams. The Union army quickly issued an order forbidding telegraph companies from sending reports on military activity without prior government approval. The rule was almost certainly unconstitutional, but this was wartime, and the Supreme Court declined to rule on the matter.

Military officials used their censorship powers not only to protect military secrets but also to preserve their own reputations. The war between the generals and the reporters was nearly as violent as the war between the North and the South. In 1863, correspondent Thomas W. Knox described the Northern defeat at Vicksburg for the *New York Herald:*

> Throughout the battle the conduct of the general officers was excellent, with a few exceptions. General Sherman was so exceedingly erratic that the discussion of a twelvemonth ago with respect to his sanity was revived with much earnestness. . . . With another brain than that of General Sherman's, we will drop the disappointment at our reverse, and feel certain of victory in the future.[16]

Sherman immediately had Knox court-martialed as a spy. The reporter was found guilty only of ignoring the censorship regulations, and was handed a light sentence. But Sherman succeeded in having him banished from the front lines for the remainder of the conflict.

In 1864, the *New York World* and the *Journal of Commerce* mistakenly published a forged presidential proclamation, ordering the draft of 400,000 men. The government retaliated by closing down both papers for a two-day period. Consistently "Copperhead" (pro-Southern) newspapers, meanwhile, were stormed by mobs and forced to quit publishing. It was the same in the South. The *North Carolina Standard* argued that the war benefited only the wealthy; its office was destroyed by a Georgia regiment. Freedom of the press, it seems, was a concept for peacetime only.

The Civil War was the first American war to be covered by photographers. Photography had already become a practical process by 1839, as a result of the experiments of Frenchmen Joseph Niepce and Louis Daguerre. But subjects had to remain motionless for more than a minute, which effectively limited photography to portrait work and landscapes. In 1855, New York portrait photographer Mathew Brady experimented successfully with the quicker wet-plate photographic process invented by Frederick Scott Archer. On the eve of the Civil War, Brady put his flourishing business aside and asked President Lincoln's permission to produce a photographic history of the conflict.

Brady and his associates turned wagons into darkrooms and set out to cover the war. In some 3,500 photographs—of generals, common soldiers, and the horrors of battle—they put the Civil War in focus. Though Brady was the nation's first great news photographer, the media of his day were not able to reproduce his photos. Until photoengraving was invented in 1878, newspapers and magazines had to rely on artists' drawings and woodcuts instead. As a result, many newspaper illustrations during the Civil War carried the credit line, "From a photograph by Brady."

The Civil War brought about several major changes in American journalism. For one thing, Washington D.C. became the most important news center in the country—a role it still plays. Reporters had been covering the Capitol since 1822, and the *New York Herald* had established the first Washington bureau in 1841. But when war came the number of reporters in Washington more than doubled, and for the first time a journalist was assigned to cover the White House. From the Civil War on, more news came out of Washington than any other American city.

Reporters at the battlefronts, meanwhile, were suspicious of the new telegraph machine. Fearful that their entire dispatch might not get through, they made sure to put the most important information first, leaving details and "color" for later. The rambling, roughly chronological news style of the early 1800s gave way to this tighter structure, which we now call the "inverted pyramid" style.

Telegraph reports from the front were often transmitted in spurts. Instead of waiting for the rest of the story, editors began setting these "bulletins" in headline type while the details were still being written. Such many-decked headlines became characteristic of the mid-nineteenth-century press.

A final result of the war was the development of the feature syndicate. Ansell Kellogg, publisher of a weekly in Baraboo, Wis-

CHRONOLOGY

1831 William Lloyd Garrison founds the *Liberator* in Boston, the most influential of the abolitionist newspapers.

1837 Abolitionist editor Elijah Lovejoy is killed by a pro-slavery mob in Alton, Illinois.

1850 Horace Greeley's *New York Tribune* adopts the cause of abolition, the first major daily to do so.

1851 Robert Barnwell Rhett, editor of the *Charleston Mercury,* is elected to the Senate. Rhett will lead the Southern fight for secession.

1852 Harriet Beecher Stowe's *Uncle Tom's Cabin,* formerly serialized in newspapers, becomes a best-selling book, arguing forcefully against slavery.

1861 The Civil War begins. Both sides immediately institute strict military censorship of war correspondents.

1862 The Press Association of the Confederate States of America is founded.

consin, was short of printing help in his backshop. So he arranged for the *Wisconsin State Journal* in Madison to send him sheets of war news, ready to fold into his own paper. One side was left blank so that Kellogg could add local copy or advertisements. Seeing a good thing, Kellogg later moved to Chicago and started his own syndicate service. By 1865 he had 53 clients.

Some of these trends can be seen in the following article from the *New York Times* of April 15, 1865, reported by Associated Press correspondent Lawrence A. Gobright:

AWFUL EVENT

President Lincoln Shot by an Assassin

The Deed Done at Ford's Theatre Last Night

THE ACT OF A DESPERATE REBEL

The President Still Alive at Last Accounts

No Hope Entertained of His Recovery

Attempted Assassination of Secretary Seward

DETAILS OF THE DREADFUL TRAGEDY

WASHINGTON, Friday, April 14—12:30 A.M. The President was shot in a theatre tonight and is, perhaps, mortally wounded. . . .[17]

TRANSITION

In a sense, the history of the United States starts over again at the end of the Civil War. The last third of the nineteenth century was characterized by three vitally important trends: industrialization, immigration, and urbanization.

Between 1865 and 1900, the national wealth of the country quadrupled, while manufacturing production increased sevenfold. This was the age of steel, oil, railroads, and electricity; the age of expanding factories and a growing labor movement. Meanwhile, the population more than doubled, from 35 million in 1865 to 76 million in 1900. Much of the growth was due to immigration, averaging as many as half a million new residents a year. Most of the immigrants, naturally, remained in the large cities on the East Coast, where jobs were plentiful for the unskilled. In the generation from 1860 to 1900, the population of New York City alone grew from slightly over a million to 3.4 million.

Inevitably, the American mass media changed with these conditions. By 1900, there were 2,326 daily newspapers in the country, roughly six times the number in 1865. More important, newspapers geared themselves more and more for the blue-collar reader, especially the urban immigrant. They were cheap and easy to read, filled with bold headlines, exciting artwork, human-interest stories, and editorials that championed the rights of the working classes. These developments were to culminate in the turn-of-the-century "New Journalism" of Joseph Pulitzer, William Randolph Hearst, and E. W. Scripps.

Of course not all American publishers were busy cultivating the urban mass market. The frontier press, for example, had no mass market to cultivate. Many Western weeklies survived on circulations of only a few hundred. A few such papers were lucky enough to attract superlative journalists. Mark Twain, for instance, worked for several years as a reporter for the *Territorial Enterprise* of Virginia City, Nevada. But most frontier newspapers made do with more ordinary talent. Their pages were dominated by government proclamations (paid legal advertising) and reports on the activities of local civic groups.

The elite press, meanwhile, pursued the specialized interests of its readers with little regard for national trends. Every large city supported at least one newspaper devoted to commercial and financial news, plus a second paper that stressed the conservative, business-oriented attitude toward the events of the day. Intellectuals could subscribe to any of hundreds of literary magazines. For political and social commentary they might read *The Nation,* a weekly magazine founded by E. L. Godkin in 1865. *The Nation* consistently lost money (in more than a hundred years of continuous publication, it has never once earned a profit), but it was (and is) a highly influential vehicle for liberal political philosophy.

The elite press and the frontier press were important, but it was the mass-circulation newspaper that was to change the course of American journalism. Industrialization, immigration, and urbanization created the mass market. Publishers did their best to capture it.

They could never have succeeded without the help of dozens of inventors and engineers. The following technological developments all took place between 1860 and 1900, making possible a truly mass-circulation newspaper:

1. The first transatlantic cable is completed, permitting up-to-the-minute news reports from overseas.

2. The telephone is invented, speeding the flow of information from news source to newsroom.

3. The web perfecting press is developed, capable of simultaneously printing both sides of a continuous roll of paper.

4. The electric press and the color press are introduced, increasing production speed to 48,000 12-page papers per hour.

5. Improved paper-making techniques reduce the price of newsprint from $246 a ton in 1870 to $42 a ton in 1900.

6. The development of the electric light bulb makes after-dinner reading possible, stimulating an upsurge in evening newspapers.

7. The typewriter is invented and adopted by the Associated Press and many large newspapers.

8. The linotype machine is patented, immediately tripling the speed of typesetting.

9. Halftone photoengraving is perfected, enabling newspapers and magazines to print photographs in addition to drawings and woodcuts.

All this newfangled equipment cost money —a lot of money. A single high-speed press might cost as much as $80,000; linotype machines, photoengravers, and even typewriters added to the bill. In 1835, James Gordon Bennett had started the *New York Herald* with a capital investment of $500. In 1895, William Randolph Hearst paid $180,000 for the printing plant of the *New York Journal.* And in 1901, *Editor & Publisher* magazine estimated that it would take at least a million dollars to launch a daily newspaper in New York. In order to run a "modern" newspaper, then, the turn-of-the-century publisher *had* to attract a mass audience. A high-speed press is simply too expensive to stand idle; it must be used to capacity, or it loses money.

Metropolitan newspapers need a mass audience to survive, but they seldom earn their profits directly from that audience. The profits come from advertising. It is doubtful that mass-circulation newspapers would have been possible without the invention of the department store.

Until the 1860s, newspaper advertising was mostly of the "classified" variety—brief, solid-type notices of products for sale. Then department stores began to replace neighborhood merchants as the chief source of goods. Besides the convenience of buying everything in one place, they offered fixed prices, credit, and free delivery. They also offered the first standardized, uniform-quality merchandise—the same hat or tin of flour in Boston as in Chicago. Suddenly newspapers were inundated with two new kinds of advertising: ads from the department stores (special on soap flakes at John Wanamaker's), and ads from the manufacturers whose brand names the stores carried (our chewing tobacco is better than their chewing tobacco). By 1880, advertising accounted for nearly half of newspaper gross revenue. By 1910, the figure would be two-thirds.

Most of this advertising was aimed at women—then as now the main customers for consumer goods. This was a boon for the women's magazines of the period (*Ladies' Home Journal, Woman's Home Companion, McCall's*). It also forced the daily newspapers to supply more material of presumed interest to women: fashion, cooking, society, etc. This was not the last time that the American mass media would tailor their content to the needs of advertisers.

A publisher who has sunk a few hundred thousand dollars into a printing plant wants to get as much use out of it as possible. Morning newspapers thus began printing afternoon editions as well. With improvements in home lighting in the 1870s, these became evening editions. By 1890, evening newspapers outnumbered morning ones two to one.

The same logic led to the development of the Sunday edition. Publishers were happy to have another use for their presses, while retailers were eager to reach the reader on a no-work day. Since there was little real news over the weekend, the Sunday papers were filled with features, short fiction, comics, and the like. They soon outstripped their parent dailies in size, circulation—and profit.

By the mid-1880s, industrialization, immigration, and urbanization had progressed to the point where, for the first time, a truly mass market existed for newspapers. By the mid-1880s, also, technological improvements and retail display advertising had developed sufficiently to permit publishers to exploit that market. It was the era of Big Business

in American history. And the mass media were about to become a big business themselves.

The period from 1880 to 1910 produced a revolution in American journalism. Joseph Pulitzer and William Randolph Hearst created the nation's first truly mass-circulation newspapers, reaching heights of sensationalism never matched before or since. E. W. Scripps founded the first of the great newspaper chains, helping to transform journalism into a Big Business. Powerful wire services introduced standardization in newspaper content, while magazines like McClure's offered readers their first and finest taste of persistent full-length muckraking.

JOSEPH PULITZER

Joseph Pulitzer came to America from Hungary to fight in the Union army. Instead, he wound up as a newspaper reporter in St. Louis. In 1878, he founded the *St. Louis Post-Dispatch*. The paper was an immediate success, and by 1883 Pulitzer had saved enough money to try the "big time." He moved to New York and bought the *World*—a sober, commercial paper with a circulation of 20,000.

In his very first issue, Pulitzer announced that the *World* would be sober no longer:

> There is room in this great and growing city for a journal that is not only cheap but bright, not only bright but large, not only large but truly democratic—dedicated to the cause of the people rather than to that of the purse potentates—devoted more to the news of the New than the Old World—that will expose all fraud and sham, fight all public evils and abuses—that will battle for the people with earnest sincerity.[18]

Two weeks later Pulitzer began to fulfill his promise. The Brooklyn Bridge was dedicated, and the *World* launched its first crusade: no tolls. In the months that followed, the paper exposed and denounced the New

1863   William Bullock introduces the web perfecting press, which prints both sides of a continuous roll of paper.

1865   E. L. Godkin founds *The Nation,* an elite weekly opinion magazine.

1866   The first successful transatlantic cable is completed.

1868   Charles A. Dana buys the *New York Sun,* and turns it into a lively combination of political activism and feature writing.

1869   The N. W. Ayer & Son advertising agency is founded to help advertisers buy newspaper space.

1871   The *New York Times* and *Harper's Weekly* (through cartoonist Thomas Nast) break the story of Tammany Hall corruption in New York government—an early example of muckraking journalism.

1876   Alexander Graham Bell invents the telephone.

1878   Thomas A. Edison develops the first phonograph. Frederick E. Ives introduces a practical method for halftone photoengraving; the technique will not be widely used for newspaper photography for another twenty years.

1879   Edison invents the incandescent bulb (electric light). John Wanamaker of Philadelphia buys the first full-page newspaper advertisement for his department store.

1885   Ottmar Mergenthaler files a patent for the first linotype machine.

York Central Railroad, the Standard Oil and Bell Telephone monopolies, political bribery, tenement housing conditions, inheritance tax loopholes, vote-buying, and civil service corruption—all on the front page.

Pulitzer's *World* also offered solid news coverage—but so did many other newspapers. What was special about the *World* was its exposés, its human-interest stories, and its stunts.

Averaging sixteen pages an issue, the paper was filled with gossip, scandal, and sensational tidbits of all sorts. Headlines were lively, and illustrations were plentiful: crime scenes (X marked the spot), disaster drawings, political cartoons, etc. The *World* promoted itself in every issue, using coupons, contests, and assorted other gimmicks. Pulitzer led the drive to build a pedestal for the Statue of Liberty, and sent an expedition to rescue a pioneer woman from Indian captors. He designed and executed some of the first public opinion polls. He invented the man-in-the-street interview. He sent columnist "Nellie Bly" (Elizabeth Cochran) to improve on Jules Verne by circling the globe in only seventy-two days. All to build circulation.

In 1884, one year after Pulitzer took over, the *World*'s circulation hit 100,000. Ten years later the figure, including both morning and evening editions, topped 400,000. Pulitzer's formula (news + human interest + stunts + editorial crusades) was a resounding success. It would be widely imitated.

WILLIAM RANDOLPH HEARST

While a student at Harvard, William Randolph Hearst was fascinated by the sensationalism of Pulitzer's *World.* He begged his father, owner of the *San Francisco Examiner,* to let him try the same trick. Daddy went along, and the *Examiner* had a new, 24-year-old publisher.

"Wasteful Willie" spent a small fortune transforming the paper into an exciting medium for the masses. He used special trains to get his reporters to the scene first, and hired the finest and most sensational writers he could find, whatever the cost. News for Hearst was defined as anything that made the reader say "Gee whiz"—and the columns of satirist Ambrose Bierce and sob-sister "Annie Laurie" (Winifred Black Bonfils) more than filled the bill. Within a year the *Examiner* had doubled its circulation. In 1893 it overtook the staid *San Francisco Chronicle* to become the most successful newspaper in the West.

Young Hearst was eager to battle Pulitzer on the *World*'s home turf. Financed by the family fortune (earned through precious metals, not newspapers), he purchased the *New York Morning Journal* in 1895. Scandal, gossip, sex, and pseudo-science immediately began to fill the pages of the *Journal*. Hearst spent wildly to acquire an all-star line-up, hiring, among others, most of the staff of the *World*'s Sunday edition. The *Journal*'s circulation rose to 150,000, and several advertisers dropped Pulitzer to take advantage of Hearst's cheaper ad rates.

A few years before, Pulitzer had hired R. F. Outcault to draw the first cartoon comic, "The Yellow Kid of Hogan's Alley," for his Sunday edition. Printed in color, the strip was very successful. When Hearst stole Outcault from the *World,* Pulitzer hired himself another artist. Both newspapers now carried "The Yellow Kid." The competition between the two comics came to symbolize the entire Hearst-Pulitzer circulation war, and gave that war a name: yellow journalism.

By 1897, both the *World* and the *Journal* were publishing morning, evening, and Sunday editions. Hearst's daily circulation matched Pulitzer's at 700,000; his Sunday circulation of 600,000 was coming close. In the struggle for readers, no feature was too silly to run. A typical article from the Sunday *World* was headlined "Does Tight Lacing Develop Cruelty?" The story began:

The wearing of tight corsets will lower the moral character of the most refined woman. It will make her cruel. It will lead to morbid impulses—perhaps to crime. It will wholly destroy in her the naturally gentle and humane impulses of the feminine character.

Tight lacing, we are told, compresses the solar plexus. . . . By reflex action the compression of the corset disturbs the entire nervous system—and the victim proceeds to descend from her lofty mental heights and to grovel in the depths of nervous depression.[19]

Yellow journalism reached its high point as the *World* and the *Journal* (and dozens of imitators across the country) covered the Cuban struggle against Spanish colonial rule. Hearst, in particular, intentionally built up war fever in order to build up circulation—and his competitors played the same game. It is probably unfair to claim that the *Journal* single-handedly started the Spanish-American War, but certainly Hearst did his share.

In 1897, Hearst sent writer Richard Harding Davis and artist Frederic Remington (both nationally famous) to cover the Cuban story first-hand. Nothing much was happening, and Remington cabled Hearst for permission to come home. The publisher is supposed to have replied: "Please remain. You furnish the pictures and I'll furnish the war." And so he did. One issue of the *Journal* carried a Remington sketch of a naked Cuban woman surrounded by leering Spanish officers, supposedly searching her clothes while on board an American ship. The banner headline read: "Does Our Flag Protect Women?" The *World* piously revealed that no such incident had ever happened—and then went out in search of its own atrocity stories.

When the battleship Maine exploded mysteriously in Havana harbor, both papers pulled out all the stops. The *Journal* devoted its whole front page to the story. "Destruction of the war ship Maine was the work of an enemy," it announced—and then went on to offer a $50,000 reward for proof of the claim. The *World* discovered "evidence" that a Spanish mine was responsible. Both news-papers passed the one-million circulation mark. Weeks later the war began.

NEWSPAPER CHAINS

In 1873, James E. and George H. Scripps founded the *Detroit News*. In 1878 Edward Wyllis Scripps started the *Cleveland Press.* During the next twelve years the three brothers added the *Buffalo Evening Tele-graph,* the *St. Louis Chronicle,* the *Cincinnati Post,* and the *Kentucky Post.* The first mod-ern newspaper chain was born.

E. W. Scripps quickly proved the most talented of the three brothers. His formula was simple. Find a city with weak news-papers and an editor with strong ideas. Start a new paper from scratch, emphasizing human-interest stories and an occasional cru-sade, always on behalf of the working class. Pay your top editor $25 a week until the paper shows a profit, then give the editor a huge block of stock. And sit back and wait.

Not every Scripps paper succeeded, but the successes far outweighed the losers. By 1914, the Scripps-McRae League was publisher of 23 newspapers across the country. Scripps himself wrote the editorials for all his papers. The chain was further unified by the United Press Association (a wire service), plus a fea-ture syndicate and a science service. Readers of Scripps papers from coast to coast were offered identical national news and editorials.

E. W. Scripps was not primarily a business-man. He was sincerely dedicated to his cru-sades for the common people, and so hated pressure from advertisers that he twice ex-perimented with adless papers. Nevertheless, Scripps proved that a large chain of news-papers, run from afar, could earn immense profits for its owner. Later chain publishers were often more interested in the profits than in news and editorial influence.

Until 1900, William Randolph Hearst owned only two newspapers, the *San Fran-cisco Examiner* and the *New York Journal.* Then, obviously impressed by Scripps' suc-cess, he began to make up for lost time. First came papers in Chicago, Boston, and Atlanta, then two new ones in San Francisco—all be-fore 1917. Between 1917 and 1921, the Hearst chain acquired six properties. Seven more were added in 1922, and sixteen more by 1934.

Even more than Scripps, Hearst preferred power to profit. He built his chain partly to further his political ambitions in the Demo-cratic Party. And he ran his papers with an iron hand. They were as fanatically anti-war and anti-Ally in 1916 as they had been pro-war and pro-Cuban in 1897. Hearst person-ally directed local crusades for his member papers, and led them on the first great "red hunt" after the Russian Revolution. The chain was united by two wire services—Inter-national News Service and Universal Service. Other Hearst subsidiaries included King Features (now the largest feature syndicate in America) and *American Weekly,* a Sunday supplement that was stuffed into every Hearst paper.

Hearst rule was healthy for some news-papers, deadly for others. In search of top-flight staffs and no competition, Hearst often bought out and merged or folded the op-position papers. In Chicago, the *Herald* and *Examiner* became the *Herald-Examiner;* in Boston, the *Daily Advertiser* was merged into Hearst's *Record.* Came the Depression of the 1930s, the Hearst chain found that it had overextended its financial reach, and began killing its own papers in a frantic economy drive. At one time or another, Hearst owned forty-two newspapers. By the time he went into semi-retirement in 1940, the chain was down to seventeen. Seven of the others had been sold. The remaining eighteen were dead.

WIRE SERVICES

The development of mass-circulation daily newspapers greatly increased the importance of the wire service—how else could a paper get the news of the world quickly and cheaply? For thirty-four years after its founding in 1848, the Associated Press was the only wire service in America (aside from the short-lived Confederate group during the Civil War). A loose cooperative of regional services (New England AP, Western AP, etc.), the Associated Press was actually run by the New York AP. It used its power to set rates and news policies that favored the needs of New York newspapers. It also enforced a rule whereby any member newspaper could blackball a competitor from AP membership.

By 1882 the need for a second wire service was obvious. A new group, calling itself the United Press, was organized to meet that need. Soon it had enrolled non-AP papers in nearly every major city. But this was the age of monopoly. Instead of competing with the new service, the Associated Press decided to make a deal. A secret agreement was negotiated; UP promised not to encourage any new papers in AP cities, and both services agreed to share their news reports.

Word of the agreement eventually leaked out to the Western AP members (already unhappy with New York's management), and in 1890 a government investigation was launched. Embarrassed, the New York group bolted to the United Press, leaving the Westerners in charge of the AP. They quickly incorporated as the Associated Press of Illinois.

Melville E. Stone was drafted as general manager of the newly organized AP. Stone managed to work out exclusive news-exchange contracts with the European press services, severely hampering the UP operation. In 1897 the United Press was forced into bankruptcy. Again the country was left with only one national wire service.

In 1900 the Illinois Supreme Court ruled that the AP was not entitled to blackball would-be members. In response, the company left Illinois and incorporated in New York. The membership protest right (blackball) survived until 1945, when the U.S. Supreme Court finally outlawed it.

In the meantime, a newspaper without an AP membership had only two alternatives. It could buy out a member paper, or it could start its own wire service. In 1907, E. W. Scripps founded the United Press Association, and Hearst followed in 1909 with the International News Service. Instead of issuing memberships, these services sold their reports to subscribers. In 1958 they merged. The resulting United Press International had little trouble competing successfully with the Associated Press.

THE MUCKRAKERS

In October of 1902, *McClure's* magazine printed the first of a nineteen-part series on "The Rise of the Standard Oil Company." Written by Ida Tarbell, the series revealed a number of secret agreements—kickbacks, rebates, and the like—between Standard Oil and the railroads. The public was inflamed, and the government brought suit against the oil company under the Sherman Anti-Trust Act. As a result of the first great magazine crusade, Standard Oil was fined $29 million.

That same issue of *McClure's* also carried an article by Lincoln Steffens on "Tweed Days in St. Louis." It was a part of Steffens' "Shame of the Cities" series, which exposed political corruption in Minneapolis, Pittsburgh, Chicago, Philadelphia, and New York, as well as St. Louis.

McClure's was by no means the only crusading magazine of the period. Others included *Cosmopolitan, Everybody's, Pearson's, Hampton's, La Follete's Weekly,* and the *American Magazine. Collier's* magazine was also partial to exposés. In 1911 it began a fifteen-part series by Will Irwin on "The American Newspaper." Highly critical of weak-kneed publishers and strong-armed advertisers, the series is among the earliest and finest examples of journalism exposing journalism.

Theodore Roosevelt, who had complimented the early magazine exposés, later turned against them. He called their writers "muckrakers," claiming that like the Man with the Muckrake in Bunyan's *Pilgrim's Progress,* they ploughed through the filth without ever seeing the positive side of life. In time, the reading public came to agree, and the crusading magazines began losing circulation. By World War I, Americans were more interested in the features and light fiction to be found in publications like *Munsey's* and the *Saturday Evening Post*. The opinion magazines had had their day. Never again would they be so popular or so influential.

Muckraking is a cyclical phenomenon, and it did not disappear for good when World War I began. Some sixty years later, the social disquiet and political scandal of the 1970s would give rise to a similar spurt of investigative journalism, led this time by a few newspapers and newsmagazines. With Watergate as its centerpiece, muckraking in the 1970s would once again stress the themes of industrial greed and government corruption.

What happened to American journalism between 1880 and 1910 may well be the heaviest irony in media history. For the first time, a truly mass-circulation newspaper industry was able to develop—made possible by urbanization, immigration, industrialization, technological improvements, and retail display advertising. And such an industry did develop. Media barons like Hearst and Pulitzer combined the human-interest emphasis of the Penny Press with the crusading zeal of the Partisan Press, and came up with a wholly new kind of journalism: the Yellow Press. What they produced was uniquely suited to the needs and wants of their mass audience.

But yellow journalism was also big-time journalism. By 1897, Pulitzer's *World* had a circulation of more than 700,000 copies a day. The paper was valued at $10 million, employed a staff of 1300, and earned an annual profit of nearly a million dollars. Hearst's *Journal* was just as big. And dozens of smaller newspapers, with circulations hovering around the 100,000 mark, were quite big enough to consider themselves full-fledged businesses.

When a newspaper becomes a business, its owners begin to think like business executives. The bigger the paper gets, the more money it makes, the more it struggles to get still bigger and make still more money.

The heyday of yellow journalism was the late 1890s. By the turn of the century, newspapers were already becoming perceptibly less sensational. They still ran light human-interest stories, but they no longer bally-hooed them with giant headlines. They still planned and led crusades, but they no longer dared to raise new and controversial issues. The change was due partly to public resentment of Hearst, whose passionate invective was accused of inciting the assassination of President McKinley in 1901. But it was far more the result of a growing business orientation on the part of American publishers. The "people's newspapers" were turning middle-class.

Magazines like *McClure's* picked up the cudgels for a while, but soon reverted to features and fiction. The most pressing social issues of the day were already being handled through legislation, and the public's appetite for muckraking was waning.

By 1915, the most typical newspaper article was not a feature or an exposé, but a concise, objective news report supplied by the Associated Press. The most typical newspaper was not the *World* or the *Journal*, but one of the small-city afternoon dailies owned by Scripps —readable, responsible, and immensely profitable. The most prestigious newspaper in the country was, again, not the *World* or the *Journal*, but Adolph S. Ochs' *New York Times*—accurate, voluminous, and dull.

Historians Harry J. Carman and Harold C. Syrett summarize the period this way:

> As the circulation of the large urban dailies reached unprecedented figures, many of them became huge enterprises that in all essential features were similar to the large corporations of industry and transportation. . . . Despite important exceptions, the increasing financial success of the larger papers often resulted in a corresponding growth of a conservative outlook in their editorial columns. This view was succinctly expressed by Arthur Brisbane, a

1873   The Scripps family founds the *Detroit News,* the first newspaper in the first great newspaper chain.

1878   Joseph Pulitzer establishes the *St. Louis Post-Dispatch;* a series of popular crusades soon makes it the most popular evening paper in that city. E. W. Scripps starts the *Cleveland Press.*

1882   The United Press is organized to compete with the Associated Press.

1883   Pulitzer buys the *New York World,* adds human interest, gossip, and crusades, and within a year is selling 100,000 copies a day. Cyrus H. K. Curtis begins publishing the *Ladies' Home Journal;* by 1903 its circulation will top the one-million mark.

1887   William Randolph Hearst takes over the *San Francisco Examiner* and begins to transform it into a mass-market newspaper.

1889   The *World* publishes the first regular newspaper comics section.

1890   Western publishers take over the Associated Press; the New York AP joins the United Press.

1895   Hearst buys the *New York Journal* to compete directly with Pulitzer.

1896   Adolph S. Ochs takes over the undistinguished *New York Times;* he will buck the trend by stressing accuracy, objectivity, and depth.

1897   The United Press goes into bankruptcy.

1897–1898   Competition between Pulitzer and Hearst leads to sensational "yellow journalism," culminating in coverage of the Cuban insurrection and the Spanish-American War.

1902   *McClure's* magazine presents the first great magazine exposé, a 19-month attack on Standard Oil. E. W. Scripps founds the first national feature syndicate, the Newspaper Enterprise Association.

1904   Ivy Lee founds the first modern public-relations firm in New York.

1907   Scripps organizes the United Press Association to compete with the Associated Press; two years later Hearst will add a third wire service, the International News Service.

1911   Will Irwin begins a 15-part muckraking series in *Collier's* on "The American Newspaper."

1914   Hearst forms the King Features Syndicate.

Hearst employee: "Journalistic success brings money. The editor has become a money man. 'Where your treasure is, there your heart will be also.'" As journalism became more and more a big business, there was also a noticeable development toward standardization. The press services supplied the same news to all their customers, and syndicates furnished many papers with the same cartoons, comic strips, photographs, and feature stories. Equally striking evidence of the trend toward standardization was the formation of several newspaper chains that had papers in several cities under a single management. . . .[20]

The era of yellow journalism left a legacy of many characteristics still to be found in today's newspapers: large headlines and pictures, Sunday comics, human-interest features, public-service crusades. It also left a tradition of stunts and sensationalism that still influences many editors. But the greatest effect of the yellow journalists was paradoxical: They produced the first Big Newspapers, and thus inevitably turned newspapering into a Big Business. Pulitzer, Hearst, and Scripps might best be described as "crusading press barons." Today we have press barons galore, but few crusaders.

The history of the mass media before the twentieth century is the history of printing—newspapers, magazines, and books. Then came the new media: first film, next radio, and finally television. These upstarts quickly began to compete with the established media, forcing them to change their character in order to retain their influence. Television in particular had—and continues to have—a tremendous effect on all the other media.

NEW MEDIA

The existence of the motion picture rests on the 1824 discovery that the human eye retains an image for a fraction of a second longer than the picture actually appears. If a slightly different picture is substituted during this brief interval, the illusion of motion results.

In 1903, almost eighty years later, Edwin S. Porter produced the first American commercial film with a plot. *The Great Train Robbery* was eight thrilling minutes of stunt-riding and gunfighting. Suddenly film was a realistic medium, a worthy competitor of the legitimate theater.

Until 1912, no American film ran longer than fifteen minutes. This was the decision of the Motion Picture Patents Company, an industry association that apparently felt there was no market for films of more than one reel. The Patents Company also ruled that film actors should not be identified—since a

well-known performer might demand higher wages. And it established the National Board of Censorship to insure that member producers did nothing to offend the moviegoer.

Then, in 1912, Adolf Zukor purchased the American rights to a four-reel production of *Queen Elizabeth,* starring Sarah Bernhardt. The Patents Company refused to distribute the film through normal channels (nickelodeons and store shows), so Zukor persuaded the Lyceum Theatre in New York to run it. The movie later toured the country, and Zukor founded Paramount Pictures with the profits.

Three years later, D. W. Griffith produced *The Birth of a Nation,* incorporating a sympathetic approach to the Ku Klux Klan. It ran twelve reels (nearly three hours), and had a special score performed by a symphony orchestra. Griffith's film gripped its audience as no movie had before, and as few have since. Race riots followed its presentation in several cities; Woodrow Wilson called it "like writing history in lightning." [21] Film was now a force to be reckoned with.

During the next decade, the movie industry moved west to Hollywood, where it found lower taxes and better shooting weather. The Patents Company weakened and dissolved. The feature film replaced the one-reeler, and the "first run" movie theater replaced the nickelodeon. Moviegoers came to idolize certain performers—Mary Pickford, Lillian and Dorothy Gish, Lionel Barrymore, William S. Hart, Fatty Arbuckle, Douglas Fairbanks, Charlie Chaplin. The appearance of any of these stars guaranteed a box-office hit.

By the mid-1920's, movies were Big Business—slick, commercial, and very profitable. But a new competitor was already on the scene: radio.

Radio owes its existence to the "wireless telegraph," invented by Gugliemo Marconi in 1895. The wireless was fine for dots and dashes, but voice transmission was impossible until 1906, when Lee De Forest perfected the vacuum tube. Four years later, De Forest dramatically broadcast the voice of Enrico

Caruso from the stage of New York's Metropolitan Opera House.

Experimentation continued during World War I, and in 1919 Westinghouse engineer Frank Conrad began broadcasting music throughout the Pittsburgh area. Listener response was enthusiastic; Westinghouse immediately started advertising its crystal sets "to hear Dr. Conrad's popular broadcasts." In 1920, the station was christened KDKA.

The *Detroit News,* meanwhile, was running what was to become radio station WWJ in order to gain goodwill and help sell newspapers. Publishers in Kansas City, Milwaukee, Chicago, Los Angeles, Louisville, Atlanta, Des Moines, and Dallas soon followed suit. Department stores ran radio stations to promote their goods. So did manufacturers like AT&T, General Electric, and of course Westinghouse.

From the very beginning, news was an important part of broadcasting. KDKA's first transmission was the 1920 election returns. In 1922, the Associated Press decided that radio might soon constitute a major threat to the newspaper business, so it ruled that AP reports could not be carried on radio. Station-owning publishers rebelled against the rule, complaining that their competitors would use the UP or INS reports anyhow. Although AP tried to reserve its 1924 election returns for the print media only, some three million families learned of the victory of Calvin Coolidge via radio. AP soon joined the other wire services in supplying news to broadcast stations.

Meanwhile, New York station WEAF was discovering, rather to its surprise, that radio could earn money. In 1922 the station's owner, AT&T, began selling time to advertisers. Word spread quickly, and the race for broadcast licenses was on. Plans to develop radio as a nonprofit public-service institution were abandoned. In 1921 there had been only 30 commercial radio stations; by 1923 there were more than 500.

Radio networks developed to meet the needs of national advertisers. By 1925, AT&T already operated a chain of 26 stations, stretching from New York to Kansas City. RCA, Westinghouse, and General Electric (all radio manufacturers) were working together to organize a competing network. In 1926, AT&T agreed to sell out to its rivals in return for a monopoly over all network relays, the lines that connect member stations. The National Broadcasting Company was founded as an RCA subsidiary to run the new operation. The old AT&T network became the NBC "red network," while the original Westinghouse-RCA-GE network was called the "blue network." Coast-to-coast programming began in 1927, under the leadership of NBC head David Sarnoff. Three years later, Westinghouse and GE were forced out of network operation by an antitrust suit, and Sarnoff took over control of RCA.

The competing Columbia Broadcasting System was founded in 1927 by the Columbia phonograph record company. William S. Paley soon became its president, and by 1929 CBS was making money.

In 1927 there were 733 stations in the nation. Many of them found it necessary to skip around from frequency to frequency, searching for a clear one where they could broadcast without interference. Inevitably, the more powerful stations were smothering their weaker rivals. The radio industry and the listening public asked the federal government to clear up the interference problem by assigning each station its own frequency. Congress accepted the responsibility. The Radio Act of 1927 gave a five-person Federal Radio Commission the power to regulate all broadcast transmissions.

The job of the FRC was to grant licenses for the use of specific frequencies renewable every three years. Licensees were expected to act in the "public interest, convenience, or necessity." [22] The implicit power of censorship through license renewal expressed in these standards has been used only rarely (and very hesitantly) by the Commission.

In order to put a stop to signal interference, the FRC eliminated more than a hun-

1824 Peter Mark Roget discovers the principle of motion pictures—that the human eye retains an image briefly after the picture is gone.

1839 Louis Daguerre and Joseph Niepce develop a practical photographic process.

1877 Eadweard Muybridge and John D. Issacs use 24 cameras in sequence to photograph a race horse in action.

1884 George Eastman introduces roll film, leading in 1888 to the easy-to-operate Kodak camera.

1889 Edison and William K. L. Dickson develop a sprocket system for motion pictures.

1895 Systems for projecting motion pictures on a screen are developed simultaneously in several countries. Gugliemo Marconi transmits wireless telegraph signals for one mile.

1901 Marconi sends wireless signals across the Atlantic.

1903 *The Great Train Robbery* becomes the first American movie with a plot.

1906 Lee De Forest perfects the vacuum tube, making possible radio voice transmissions.

1912 Adolf Zukor presents the four-reel movie *Queen Elizabeth,* starring Sarah Bernhardt. Congress passes the Radio Act of 1912 to prevent individual ham operators from interfering with government transmissions.

1915 D. W. Griffith produces *The Birth of a Nation,* the longest and most powerful film to date.

1919 Westinghouse engineer Frank Conrad begins broadcasting music throughout the Pittsburgh area.

1920 Westinghouse obtains a license for station KDKA in Pittsburgh.

1922 New York station WEAF begins selling airtime to advertisers. The Associated Press refuses to allow the broadcasting of AP reports. In an effort to avoid government censorship, the movie industry establishes a production code and self-censorship procedures.

1923 The Eveready Battery Company prepares and sponsors its own hour-long show on WEAF; a year later it will produce the show on a national network.

1926 AT&T turns its radio network over to a joint RCA-Westinghouse-GE consortium, leading to the development of the RCA-controlled National Broadcasting Company.

1927 The Columbia Broadcasting System is organized to compete with the NBC network. The Radio Act of 1927 establishes a five-person Federal Radio Commission to license broadcasters and prevent signal interference.

---

dred stations, leaving the total number at roughly 600. "Clear channels" were established to allow selected urban stations to reach distant rural areas with no stations of their own. Most of these highly lucrative channels soon fell into network hands.

The film and radio industries both experienced a surge of tremendous growth in the 1920s. What were the print media doing during that decade?

America may have entered World War I reluctantly, but American newspapers entered with enthusiasm. Even the isolationist Hearst chain abandoned its campaign for neutrality after the 1917 declaration of war. Throughout the nineteen months of fighting, anti-German propaganda dominated the press.

The government did what it could to insure that dominance. President Wilson appointed former newsman George Creel to head the Committee on Public Information. The C.P.I. issued over 6,000 patriotic press releases during the course of the war, most of which were faithfully carried by the nation's press. The Creel Committee also established "guidelines for voluntary censorship" on touchy subjects such as troop movements.

In addition, Congress passed a series of laws aimed at putting a stop to "treasonous" publications. These laws culminated in the Espionage Act of 1917 and the Sedition Act of 1918. The latter outlawed, among other things, "any disloyal, profane, scurrilous, or abusive language about the form of government of the United States, or the Constitution, military or naval forces, flag, or the uniform of the army or navy of the United States." [23] No attempt was made to invoke the Sedition Act against mainstream publishers; it was used instead to stifle the socialist and German-language press. Mainstream publishers, after all, minded their manners. When the war was over, *The Nation* magazine was moved to comment:

> During the past two years, we have seen what is practically an official control of the press, not merely by Messrs. Burleson and Gregory [heads of the Post Office and Justice Department] but by the logic of events and the patriotic desire of the press to support the government.[24]

The end of World War I was the start of the Roaring Twenties. It was a sensational decade—jazz and flappers; Prohibition, speakeasies, and gangsters; Mary Pickford and Douglas Fairbanks; Charles Lindbergh and the Prince of Wales; Jack Dempsey, Red Grange, and Babe Ruth; Leopold and Loeb; Sacco and Vanzetti. The Roaring Twenties virtually cried out for a renaissance in yellow journalism.

The cry was answered with a new kind of newspaper: the tabloid. Tabloids may be recognized by their small size (easy to carry on the subway), their small number of columns (seldom more than five), and their extensive use of photography (often the whole front page). The first modern American tabloid was the *New York Daily News,* founded by Joseph M. Patterson in 1919. The *News* offered its readers a steady diet of sex and crime, luridly illustrated and simply written. By 1924 it had the largest daily circulation of any newspaper in America.

Typical of the *News* approach to news was the paper's 1928 front-page photo of the execution of convicted murderer Ruth Snyder. The heavily retouched picture filled the entire page, with the following caption:

> WHEN RUTH PAID HER DEBT TO THE STATE!—The only unofficial photo ever taken within the death chamber, this most remarkable, exclusive picture shows closeup of Ruth Snyder in death chair at Sing Sing as lethal current surged through her body at 11:06 Thursday night. . . . *Story and another electrocution picture on page 3.*[25]

Dozens of tabloids appeared in major cities throughout the country in the 1920s, modeled on the *News* formula of sex and violence. Some died off, but many survive to this day, often with very healthy circulation figures. Though tabloids obviously exert great influence on their readers, they are viewed by journalists and students of journalism almost as a quirk, quite separate from the mainstream of American publishing. The *New York Daily News* still has the highest newspaper readership in the United States, and as a *news*paper it has greatly improved since the 1920s—but not one university in a hundred receives and microfilms the paper.

Like the Penny Press and the Yellow Press, the Tabloid Press built its circulation on people who had not regularly read a daily newspaper—immigrants and blue-collar workers. Mainstream newspapers ignored the tabloids, sticking firmly to the standards of accuracy, objectivity, and responsibility established before the war. The finest example of this tradition was the *New York Times,* published by Adolph S. Ochs and edited by Carr V. Van Anda.

The *Times* strove in every issue to be a "newspaper of record," correct, careful, and complete. Its motto was "All the News That's Fit to Print." An unwritten corrolary was "and not a *word* of interpretation." According to the *Times* ethic, interpretation was like bias, unworthy of a newspaper that prided itself on straight reporting.

Not every newspaper in the 1920s was a miniature *New York Times,* but except for the tabloids nearly every newspaper secretly wished it was. The wire services helped to point the way. In an effort to please publishers with all sorts of viewpoints, AP, UP, and INS tried to write without any viewpoint. The wire story—an assortment of accurate but uninterpreted facts—became the epitome of good newspaper journalism. Occasionally every paper would lapse into sensationalism or bias or interpretation, and some papers lapsed more than others. But every paper (tabloids aside) tried to lapse as little as possible, to stick as best it could to the straight and narrow path of objectivity.

American journalists now considered themselves members of a full-fledged profession. In 1922, the editors of the major daily newspapers organized the American Society of Newspaper Editors. The group had its first annual meeting in 1923, and immediately adopted a seven-point code of ethics, known as the "Canons of Journalism." The Canons stressed sincerity, truthfulness, accuracy, impartiality, fair play, decency, independence, and fidelity to the public interest. They were extremely general and strictly voluntary. The Canons were an expression, not of what newspapers were, but rather of what newspapers thought they ought to be. They were thus indicative of a major transition in American journalism, from the free-wheeling libertarian theory of the nineteenth century to the more sober "social responsibility" theory of the twentieth.

But the social responsibility of the press, according to the Canons of Journalism, was limited to telling the truth about the news. Nothing was said about interpreting the news, giving it meaning, or making sense of

---

CHRONOLOGY

1917 World War I begins, and American newspapers willingly accept "voluntary" censorship at the hands of the Creel Committee.

1918 Congress passes the Sedition Act and other laws which were used to stifle the socialist and German-language press.

1919 The war ends, and Joseph M. Patterson founds the *New York Daily News,* the first of the sex-and-violence tabloids.

1922 DeWitt Wallace begins publishing *The Reader's Digest,* destined to become the largest general-interest magazine in the world.

1923 The American Society of Newspaper Editors adopts the Canons of Journalism, an expression of the "social responsibility" of the press. Henry R. Luce and Briton Hadden found *Time* magazine, the first of the modern weekly newsmagazines.

1924 H. L. Mencken establishes the *American Mercury,* an outspoken and frequently obstreperous magazine of opinion.

it for the reader. Editors and publishers would soon discover that this limited notion of responsibility was not enough.

As newspapers grew more "responsible," they also diminished in number. Competition and economic pressures caused the death of many papers. Intentional consolidation at the hands of media barons killed others. Still others died simply because there was no longer any need for them; as newspaper content became more and more standardized, readers cared less and less which paper they read. In 1910, there were 2,200 English-language dailies in the United States, serving 1,207 cities. By 1930 there were only 1,942 dailies serving 1,002 cities. During the same period, the number of American cities with competing daily newspapers plummeted from 689 to 288. These trends would continue in the decades ahead. By 1960, the number of daily newspapers would be stabilized at 1,763; the number of cities with competing dailies would be down to a mere 61 and still decreasing.

The magazine industry, meanwhile, grew less and less concerned with news and public affairs. The muckraking magazines of the turn of the century either folded or reverted to features and fiction. So did most of the serious magazines of opinion that had flourished before the war. They were replaced for a while by H. L. Mencken's *American Mercury*. Founded in 1924, the *Mercury* was outspoken and sensational, the magazine equivalent of a tabloid. Other new entries of the 1920s included the *Reader's Digest* (1922), the *Saturday Review of Literature* (1924), and the *New Yorker* (1925).

The major exception to the retreat of magazines from the real world was *Time*, founded by Henry R. Luce and Briton Hadden in 1923. Both were young men in their twenties; both wanted to publish a weekly magazine that would make sense of the news. "People are uninformed," they argued, "because no publication has adapted itself to the time which busy men are able to spend on simply keeping informed." [26] *Time*'s interpretations of the news were slick, facile, and often misleading—but it *did* interpret the news. It thus satisfied a need that would become increasingly acute in the years ahead.

DEPRESSION AND AFTER

On October 29, 1929, the New York stock market crashed—heralding the Great Depression, the New Deal, and a revolution in American life. Every institution was significantly changed by the events of the 1930s, and the mass media were no exception.

The Depression cut heavily into newspaper revenue, but radio continued to grow and prosper. In 1932, the American Newspaper Publishers Association voted to combat the electronic competition by cutting off its supply of news. ANPA asked the wire services to stop selling news to radio stations, except for brief announcements that would stimulate the sale of newspapers. It also recommended that member papers start treating their radio logs as advertising. The wire services and most major newspapers supported the boycott, and radio was on its own.

CBS immediately set up news bureaus in New York, Washington, Chicago, Los Angeles, and London. Within a few months, daily newscasts by H. V. Kaltenborn and Boake Carter were supplying CBS affiliates with an adequate replacement for the wires. The NBC news service wasn't nearly as good, but many local stations didn't really care—they simply stole their news reports out of the early editions of local newspapers. Several lawsuits by the Associated Press clearly established the illegality of this practice. But AP couldn't afford to sue half the radio stations in the country.

The boycott was a failure. A compromise Press-Radio Plan was worked out in 1934, granting stations the right to ten minutes of wire news a day. It wasn't enough. Radio wanted more, and was willing to pay for it. In 1935, UP and INS agreed to sell complete news reports to stations. AP soon followed suit. Today, both major services have special radio wires. AP services 3,400 U.S. broadcast clients (and only 1,750 publications), while the UPI wire goes to 2,300 stations (and only 1,600 publications).

Radio soon became *the* mass medium for spot news. The vacuum tube has a tremendous advantage over the printing press: speed. It warms up faster; it requires no typesetters and no delivery trucks. Radio can have a story on the air minutes after the event; newspapers take hours. By the end of the 1930s, it was obvious to editors that the "scoop" and the "extra" were obsolete. Newspapers could still serve the public by supplying the details of the news, or the significance of the news—but radio was bound to get there first with the news itself.

Thus interpretive journalism was born. It was pioneered in the 1910s and 1920s by columnists like David Lawrence (*New York Evening Post*), Mark Sullivan (*New York Herald Tribune*), and Frank R. Kent (*Baltimore Sun*). It was picked up by the feature syndicates in the early 1930s, making national figures of such pundits as Walter Lippmann, Heywood Broun, and Drew Pearson. All these people did their best to tell newspaper readers "the news behind the news."

Interpretive journalism made it to the front page in 1933, when the United States went off the gold standard. This was far too complex a subject to report "straight." President Roosevelt sent a group of White House economic advisers over to the press room to help reporters understand the meaning of the move. The reporters were grateful, and interpretive news articles (with or without the help of presidential advisers) soon became commonplace.

Consider, for example, this "news lead" from a 1935 issue of the *Buffalo* (N.Y.) *Evening News:*

WASHINGTON, Aug. 15.—A scratch of a pen by the Chief Executive Wednesday extended to approximately a fourth of America's population some measure of federal protection from the vicissitudes of life.

It was the signing by President Roosevelt of the nation's first social security legislation, re-garded by the President more than any other action taken during his administration as the heart of the New Deal.[27]

A sidebar to the story began: "Here are some examples of how the new social security program will operate. . . ." This was the kind of reporting that radio couldn't do.

What radio *could* do was offer the country a varied diet of news and entertainment. Performers like Amos 'n' Andy, Jack Benny, Rudy Vallee, and Kate Smith entertained millions of Americans throughout the Depression. Kaltenborn's news broadcasts and President Roosevelt's "fireside chats" proved the medium's potential for more than pap. So did live coverage of the Spanish Civil War, and of innumerable sporting events. By the end of the decade, William L. Shirer in London and Edward R. Murrow in Vienna (later in London as well) were reporting the rise of Nazism *as it happened,* to a public that had learned to expect its news instantly.

As radio thrived and newspapers turned more interpretive, the film industry discovered sound. The first full-length talking picture, *The Jazz Singer* starring Al Jolson, was produced by Warner Brothers in 1927. It was an instant success. Sound movies single-handedly rescued the film industry from the doldrums caused by radio competition. By 1929, nearly half of the nation's 20,000 movie theaters were equipped to handle sound. Paid admissions rose from 60 million a week in 1927 to 110 million a week in 1929. By the early 1930s, the silent film was dead.

Movie magnates had other problems to worry about. Censorship was by far the biggest. The public outcry against "dirty movies" was fed as much by stories of corruption and immorality in Hollywood as it was by the films themselves. In 1922 the major studios had founded the Motion Picture Producers and Distributors of America, headed by Will H. Hays. The "Hays Office" did its best to forestall government censorship by instituting self-censorship instead. The tactic was only partially successful. It stopped the government (by and large), but it didn't stop the Legion of Decency, established by a group of Catholic laypeople in 1934. It wasn't until the late 1950s that movie producers discovered that the public would support a good film (and sometimes a bad film) even if it lacked the Legion's seal of approval.

Newsreels were standard movie theater fare throughout the 1920s and 1930s. Though newsreel news was often two or three weeks old, it had the tremendous advantage of including both pictures and sound. Newsreels remained popular until the advent of television.

The motion picture industry of the 1930s produced movies in waves—musicals, then prison pictures, then screwball comedies, then biographies, etc. As World War II drew near, Hollywood went to war. From the beginning, the Nazis were the villains. When the United States entered the conflict in 1942, war movies were turned into frank propaganda for the Allies.

The biggest development in the magazine world, meanwhile, was the success of *Life* magazine, first published by Henry R. Luce in 1936. Capitalizing on the public taste for big photographs nurtured by the tabloid papers in the 1920s, *Life* was an immediate circulation and advertising success. Alfred Eisenstaedt, Thomas McEvoy, Peter Stackpole, and others filled the pages of the new magazine with a visual record of American lifestyles.

Margaret Bourke-White was probably the greatest photographer on *Life*'s team. A veteran of industrial photography and Luce's business magazine *Fortune,* she produced a nine-page photo essay for the first issue of *Life,* recording the lives of workers who were building the Fort Peck Dam in Montana. In succeeding years she was to travel a million miles for *Life* and *Fortune.* She photographed the Nazi bombing of Moscow, was the first woman photographer accredited by the U.S. armed forces in World War II, and shocked the world with her photographs of Nazi concentration camps. Margaret Bourke-

White captured a whole generation of history in her lens.

World War II was radio's "finest hour." Kaltenborn left CBS to head the NBC news team in Europe, but no one at NBC could match the impact of Edward R. Murrow, broadcasting from London for CBS. "Neutral" Americans listened in awe as Murrow narrated, blow by blow, the Battle of Britain. For newspapers, meanwhile, the war was a repeat of World War I: massive reporting of battles, scant reporting of issues, and voluntary self-censorship of military details.

This, then, is how the American mass media stood at the end of World War II. Radio was fat and sassy, with both the number of stations and the amount of advertising expanding rapidly. It offered listeners a potpourri of news, culture, sports, and lowbrow entertainment. Newspapers were also doing well, the beneficiaries of consolidation, monopoly ownership, and the postwar boom. Most combined their straight news with interpretive stories, features, backgrounders, syndicated columns, and editorials. Magazines were slick and profitable, geared to entertaining the mass market and little more. So were movies. And even the book industry was earning money, especially with its paperback and textbook lines.

Then came television.

Television had its start in the 1920s, but it didn't begin to develop seriously until after the war. Then, in just a few years, it transformed itself from an experiment into a way of life. In revenue, in circulation, and in the devotion of its audience, television quickly became the mass medium of the mid-twentieth century. All other media have been forced into subordinate roles.

TV DEVELOPS

In 1923, Vladimir Zworykin invented the iconoscope and the kinescope, the basis for

1922   The Motion Picture Producers and Distributors of America is founded.

1927   Warner Brothers produces the first sound movie, *The Jazz Singer,* starring Al Jolson.

1929   The stock market crashes and the Depression begins.

1931   Political columnist Walter Lippmann begins publishing in the *New York Herald Tribune;* his column is soon syndicated throughout the country.

1932   The American Newspaper Publishers Association and the wire services refuse to sell news to radio. Drew Pearson and Robert S. Allen begin their free-wheeling syndicated political column, "Washington Merry-Go-Round."

1933   The U.S. goes off the gold standard, and reporters turn to interpretive journalism in order to make sense of the event. The American Newspaper Guild, the first union for journalists, is founded in Cleveland.

1934   Congress passes the Communications Act, establishing a seven-person Federal Communications Commission to oversee the electronic media. The Legion of Decency is organized to fight "dirty" movies.

1935   UP and INS agree to sell news to radio stations. Time, Inc. introduces *The March of Time,* a superior newsreel series that includes analysis and interpretation.

1936   *Life* magazine is founded and is instantly successful.

1940   The Associated Press establishes a special radio wire. Edward R. Murrow describes the Nazi blitz of London on CBS radio.

1942   The United States enters the war, and issues a voluntary but detailed Code of Wartime Practices for the American Press.

1943   Under pressure from the FCC, NBC sells its "blue chain" to Lifesaver king Edward J. Noble; it is renamed the American Broadcasting Company and becomes the nation's third network.

---

television transmission and reception respectively. Philo Farnsworth added the electronic camera, and Allen B. Dumont contributed the receiving tube. General Electric put them all together, and in 1928 founded the first regular television station, WGY, in Schenectady, New York. By 1937, there were seventeen such experimental stations on the air.

The development of the coaxial cable in 1935 enabled these early TV stations to hook up into a primitive "network" in order to broadcast special events. They did so for the opening of the New York World's Fair, for the 1940 nominating conventions, for several football and baseball games, and for at least one speech by President Roosevelt.

In 1939 the *Milwaukee Journal* applied for a commercial TV license. The Federal Communications Commission pondered the notion of commercial television for a few years, finally approving the license in 1941. Ten commercial stations, including the *Journal*'s, appeared within a year, and immediately began soliciting ads. When war broke out in 1942, the FCC put a "freeze" on TV development: no new licenses, no new receivers to be manufactured, and a limited schedule for stations already on the air. Only six of the ten 1941 pioneers lasted through the war.

The influence of government over broadcasting was becoming increasingly important. In 1934 Congress had replaced the five-person Federal Radio Commission with a seven-person Federal Communications Commission, responsible for television, telephone, and telegraph as well as radio. Like the FRC before it, the FCC viewed its job as a maintenance function: dividing up the spectrum and preventing interference. But there were more applicants for radio licenses than there was space on the radio band. The Commission was forced to choose between applicants, to decide which would best serve "the public interest, convenience, and necessity."

It simply wasn't possible for the FCC to confine its duties to technical matters. In 1939, for example, the Mayflower Broadcasting Corporation applied for the license of radio station WAAB, arguing that the frequent editorials of the current WAAB licensee were not in the public interest. After much thought, the Commission agreed. Mayflower was denied the license on other grounds, but WAAB was ordered to stop editorializing. This 1941 "Mayflower decision" outlawing broadcast editorials stood until 1949, when the Commission changed its mind and reversed the ruling. The so-called "fairness doctrine," requiring broadcasters to give fair treatment to all sides in a controversy, developed out of the Mayflower confusion.

Even when it confined itself to technology, the FCC had a vast impact on the future of broadcasting. The Commission spent the war trying to decide what to do about two new media—television and frequency modulation (FM) radio. FM had been invented by Edwin H. Armstrong in 1933; Armstrong's experimental station was on the air in Alpine, N.J., by 1939. Like television, FM boomed in the early 1940s. Like television, it was "frozen" by the FCC during the war.

In 1945 the Commission made its crucial decision. It moved FM "upstairs" to another part of the spectrum (making all existing FM receivers obsolete), and opened up more space for thirteen commercial television channels instead. The move set FM back nearly twenty years. NBC, which had encouraged its affiliates to apply for TV licenses, was elated. CBS was badly hurt; it had put its money on FM instead.

Once a favorable decision had been made, television growth was fast and furious. In 1948 the FCC reassigned Channel 1 for nonbroadcast services, and again ordered a freeze on channel allocations, this time to study the interference problem and the possibility of color television. The Korean War prolonged the freeze until 1952. Nevertheless, some 15 million families purchased TV sets during the freeze in order to watch the 108 stations then on the air. They saw Milton Berle's debut in 1948 on a 13-station NBC network. They saw Ed Sullivan on CBS for the first time that same year. They saw baseball's World Series as it happened. They saw news and public affairs broadcasting, too, notably the Kefauver Committee investigation into organized crime. And they saw some fine theater—"Philco Playhouse," "Goodyear Playhouse," Gian-Carlo Minotti's opera *Amahl and the Night Visitors*. But mostly they saw "I Love Lucy" and "Your Show of Shows"; "Arthur Godfrey's Talent Scouts" and "Kukla, Fran, and Ollie"; "The Web," "The Front Page," "The Big Story," and "The Cisco Kid."

And they saw ads—hour after hour of ads —for cars and appliances, for cigarettes and detergents, for banks and insurance companies, for presidential aspirants Eisenhower and Stevenson.

When the freeze was lifted in 1952, television grew quickly. The development of microwave relays made coast-to-coast hookups practical for the first time, and the networks were quick to employ them. By 1961 there were 548 television stations in the country, broadcasting to 60 million receiving sets (in 89 percent of all American homes). Of these stations, 205 were affiliated with CBS, 187 with NBC, and 127 with

ABC; only 29 stations had no connections with any network. The average TV station in 1961 earned a profit of 15 percent. The average TV set was left running for at least five hours a day, 365 days a year.

Television changed little in the 1960s and early 1970s. It grew, of course. By 1975, more than 66 million homes (97 percent) had at least one TV set. And the 1959 quiz show scandals forced the three networks to produce most of their own programs, instead of letting the advertisers do it for them. But aside from that, TV content in 1975 was much the same as TV content in 1965 and 1955: one-tenth news and public affairs, one-tenth drama and culture, and four-fifths ads and light entertainment.

To the extent that TV changed at all in the 1960s and early 1970s, it changed at the hands of the Federal Communications Commission. In the early 1970s, for example, the FCC adopted a series of rules requiring local stations to carry something other than network programming in prime time. The Commission also proposed or enacted several restrictions on radio-TV and print-broadcasting combinations in a single market. These steps were designed to alleviate the two biggest problems of American television today: the bland homogeneity of entertainment programming, and the economic and political danger of monopoly.

Meanwhile, the FCC continued to arbitrate the demands of technological innovations that could (at least potentially) revolutionize the broadcast industry. The RCA system for color television got the final go-ahead in 1953; by 1970, 40 percent of all American homes had a color TV set, and by 1973 fully 60 percent had color TV. A huge slice of the spectrum was set aside in 1952 for ultrahigh frequency (UHF) television. UHF developed slowly until 1962, when the FCC asked Congress to require all new TV sets to include UHF receivers. Then it grew quickly; by 1973, 324 out of a total of 927 television stations were UHF. Educational television was also given a boost by the Commission, which

set aside special channels for noncommercial use. There were 230 such stations in operation by 1973.

Color, UHF, and educational TV are practical and important developments, but the greatest potential for change is in cable and satellite television. Either one could revolutionize broadcasting—cable by permitting the growth of thousands of additional local channels, satellites by permitting the growth of dozens of national and international networks. But revolutionary potential doesn't always lead to revolutionary change. Cable and satellites are not new inventions, after all. The first substantial cable TV system was set up in 1950, bringing television to Lansford, Pa. Satellite transmission began twelve years later, with the launching of Telstar in 1962. Today, cable is still used mostly to improve TV reception in mountainous rural regions and skyscraper cities. Satellites are used for international viewing of funerals, world conferences, inaugurations, Olympic Games, and the like.

Why haven't cable and satellites had the revolutionary impact that was predicted for them? Much of the responsibility belongs to the FCC. Throughout the 1960s, the Commission intentionally slowed the development of both innovations. Instead of cable and satellites, it put its chips on the maintenance of network-dominated broadcasting and on the slow but steady growth of UHF.

In the early 1970s, however, the FCC decided to give cable and satellites a better break. In 1972, it adopted new rules to encourage cable while still protecting the economic security of over-the-air broadcasters. In the same year, it broke the monopoly over domestic communications satellites held by Comsat (a semi-public corporation dominated by AT&T), and announced that other companies were free to orbit their own systems.

Still the revolution did not occur. Many independent cable TV companies ran into serious financial problems; the cost of wiring a city for cable proved higher than expected,

1923   Vladimir Zworykin invents the iconoscope and the kinescope, the basis for television.

1928   The first experimental TV station, WGY, begins operation in Schenectady, New York.

1933   Edwin H. Armstrong invents FM radio.

1934   Congress passes the Communications Act, establishing a Federal Communications Commission with authority over television as well as radio.

1935   The first coaxial cable is built between New York and Philadelphia, making TV hook-ups possible.

1939   Armstrong begins operating his experimental FM radio station in Alpine, N.J.

1941   The FCC issues the first ten commercial TV licenses. The Mayflower decision outlaws broadcast editorials.

1942   The FCC puts a wartime freeze on TV and FM development.

1945   The freeze ends; the FCC decides to encourage television and downgrade FM radio.

1946   The FCC "Blue Book" obligates broadcasters to include some public affairs programming.

1948   Once again the FCC freezes TV development; this time the delay will last until 1952.

1949   The FCC reverses the Mayflower decision; broadcasters may "editorialize with fairness."

1950   The first commercial cable TV system begins serving the mountainous community of Lansford, Pa. The FCC authorizes experimental "pay TV" and approves the CBS system for color television.

1951   The first transcontinental microwave relay connects TV stations in New York and San Francisco.

1952   The FCC provides for the future development of 70 ultrahigh frequency (UHF) television channels, reserving many of them for nonprofit and educational use.

1953   Reversing its earlier decision, the FCC approves the RCA (NBC) color TV system, because it permits noncolor sets to receive color programming in black and white.

1959   The quiz show scandals force the networks to forbid advertisers to produce their own shows.

1962   The Telstar satellite makes live international broadcasting possible. A prolonged and inconclusive experiment with pay TV is begun in Hartford, Conn. At the FCC's request, Congress requires UHF receivers on all new televsion sets, starting in 1964.

1966   The FCC asserts control over cable television and passes restrictive regulations designed to encourage UHF at the expense of cable.

1968   The FCC authorizes commercial pay TV.

1970   The FCC adopts rules to encourage local prime-time programming; these will prove largely unsuccessful.

1972   The FCC adopts new rules governing cable TV, which are designed to encourage cable growth while still protecting over-the-air broadcasters. But financial problems and consumer disinterest slow (in some cases halt) the growth of cable.

1974   The Justice Department urges the FCC to consider not renewing licenses of selected stations owned by newspapers in the same community.

1975   The FCC rules that new newspaper-broadcast combinations in the same market will no longer be approved.

---

and urban viewers were less than enthusiastic about the extra channels and clearer reception offered (for a price) by cable. Over-the-air broadcasters continued lobbying to protect their interests at the expense of cable. And the networks, the phone company, and Western Union moved very cautiously into satellites, making sure to protect the current domination of the three networks and the current profitability of the land lines that serve them.

As of 1975, cable and satellites were growing—slower than expected and later than expected, but they were growing. Will they continue to grow, and in what directions? The future of television in the 1980s will depend largely on what the FCC and the companies involved do about cable TV and satellite TV in the next few years.

THE OLD MEDIA RESPOND

Television revolutionized American life. Naturally, it revolutionized the other mass media as well.

Part of the revolution was economic. In 1950, the infant TV industry received only 3 percent of all money spent on advertising. Newspapers got 36 percent; magazines, 9 percent; and radio, 11 percent (the other 41 percent went to billboards, direct mailings, and the like). In 1968, by contrast, TV received 18 percent of the advertising dollar. Newspapers were down to 29 percent, magazines to 7 percent; radio to 6 percent. If you eliminate local ads and billboards and the like, the figures are even more impressive. In 1939, national media advertising was almost evenly divided: 38 percent for newspapers, 35 percent for magazines, and 27 percent for radio. In 1968, this was the division: television, 49 percent; magazines, 25 percent; newspapers, 19 percent; radio, 8 percent. Television was rich. Everyone else, at least comparatively, was fading.

But economics are only half the story. Television did (and does) a superlative job of satisfying the public's appetite for spot news and light entertainment. No other medium could possibly compete with TV in those areas. The older communications industries were forced to rebuild their formats along new lines.

Radio was the hardest hit. Audio news programming could not help but suffer as the networks became more and more TV-oriented. Edward R. Murrow's "Hear It Now" turned into "See It Now," and radio documentaries disappeared almost completely. The networks continued to supply stations with hourly spot news reports, but the rest of the news operation was geared for TV and TV alone. Moreover, the melodramas, soap operas, comedy shows, and variety programs that had comprised the bulk of radio time soon became standard fare on television instead. The local station was left with hour after hour to fill on its own—on a dwindling budget and limited advertiser support.

For a while it seemed to some that commercial radio might die. Instead, radio became the "low-key" medium of the 1960s and 1970s, unspectacular but steady. News, sports, and music were the winning combination for thousands of stations. Others chose to specialize: all-rock, all-classical, all-news, or all-talk. Still more specialized stations aimed their shows at one or another minority group—blacks or chicanos, teens or commuters. Whatever the format, it was always low-budget. An engineer, two or three disc jockeys, and someone to sell ads were all the average station needed.

Radio never regained the "importance" it had had before television, but it did manage to retain its popularity. Between 1950 and 1973, the number of AM radio stations in the country rose from 2,086 to 4,395. The number of radio sets reached an incredible 354 million—more than a radio and a half for every man, woman, and child. No home, car, or beach blanket was without one.

Because it was less profitable to begin with, FM radio recognized the threat of television a little sooner than AM. By 1950 it was already gearing itself for specialized audiences, offering high-quality reception and highbrow music. During the 1960s the FCC did its best to promote the development of FM. It authorized stations to broadcast in multiplex stereo, and required them to originate some of their own programming. Aided by these policies, the number of FM stations grew from 753 in 1960 to 2,936 in 1973.

The movie industry had enough problems even before television. A 1949 Supreme Court decision forced film producers to sell off their chains of movie theaters. This solved the antitrust problem of combined production and distribution, but it also cut deeply into Hollywood revenues. The political purges and anti-Communist witch-hunts of the early 1950s added to Hollywood's headaches.

When television came along, the movie companies declared a fight to the finish. Film stars were not allowed to appear on TV, and the studios refused to sell their old films to the rival medium. But it was soon obvious that the public would no longer pay to see Grade B movies when equivalent fare was available on television. One by one, the great studios reversed their positions. They sought windfall profits by selling their old movies to be shown on the tube, and urged their stars to trade TV appearances for plugs. Finally, the large companies agreed to produce programs specifically for the television screen. The major studios were now part of the electronic medium.

Because routine movies wouldn't sell any more, the film industry turned in desperation to giant wide screens, stereophonic sound, and multimillion-dollar epics. To save money, these pictures were often produced abroad. And still they lost money. In 1950, there were 474 actors, 147 writers, and 99 directors under contract to the major studios. By 1960 the figures were down to 139 actors, 48 writers, and 24 directors. Three studios (RKO, Republic, and Monogram) stopped production entirely, and some 6,000 movie theaters shut down. Traditional Hollywood sank into what can only be described as a slow death. The back lots of many once-prosperous studios are now apartment complexes.

Into the struggling movie market came the independent producers, Europeans as well as Americans. Their topical, low-budget films struck a responsive chord in the increasingly youthful theater-going public. They intentionally violated the industry's code of self-censorship, fighting (and winning) their case in court. Taboos about drugs, sex, violence, and language disappeared. While the large studios lost vast sums on spectaculars like *Cleopatra,* independent producers filled movies houses with low-budget films like *Easy Rider.*

But then the trend reversed again. *Airport* and *Patton* were box-office successes despite their big budgets and general-interest approaches. By 1974, the movie industry was as diverse as it had ever been, with low-budget topical films and big-budget general films competing successfully with each other for the moviegoing audience. But thanks to television, the moviegoing audience was smaller than ever before. It was a rare Hollywood studio that could stay afloat without selling old movies to TV and making new movies especially for TV. Feature films had become almost a sideline of the film industry.

Television hit the magazine business almost as hard as it hit radio and film. Magazines, after all, are largely dependent on national advertising, also the main support for network TV. Moreover, television tended to satisfy the public demand for light entertainment and illustrated news—the two main staples of magazine content.

The result: General-interest magazines began losing money. Soaring production costs and postal rates added to their difficulties, until one by one they folded—*Collier's, Coronet, American, Look,* the *Saturday Evening Post,* and finally *Life.* By 1975 only the *Reader's Digest* was left. For the moment at least, the mass-circulation general-interest magazine was dead.

Other kinds of magazines did better. Newsmagazines like *Time* and *Newsweek* offered background and interpretation as well as straight news, and thus survived the rise of television. The "quality" magazines (*National Geographic, New Yorker,* and the like) were little damaged by TV, and the same was true of the women's magazines (*Ladies' Home Journal, McCalls, Good Housekeeping*). All these publications seemed to prosper throughout the 1960s and early 1970s.

By and large, the most successful magazines were the most specialized; television was unable to steal either their audience or their advertisers. Leaders in the specialty fields range from *Playboy* to *Scientific American,* from *Business Week* to *Better Homes and Gardens,* from *Women's Wear Daily* to *Sports Illustrated,* from *Successful Farming* to *Rolling Stone.* Ironically, the most successful of all the specialized magazines was *TV Guide.*

Television's effect on the book industry was indirect, but powerful. As soon as the first TV station was erected in a city, public library use and bookstore sales began to decline. People simply weren't using as much leisure time for reading; they spent more time with the tube instead.

Broadly speaking, there are three kinds of books. Textbooks are sold directly to primary and secondary schools, or through college bookstores to students. Mass-market paperbacks are sold by the millions through drugstores, supermarkets, and the like. Trade books are sold through ordinary bookstores; they include the majority of the 40,000 new books published evey year, both paperbacks and hardcovers, fiction and nonfiction.

Textbooks and mass-market paperbacks are immensely profitable. Trade books earn much less. Most Americans today read only two kinds of books: what they have to read in school, and the lightest of light fiction and equally light nonfiction.

Surprisingly enough, the mass medium least affected by the rise of television was the newspaper. TV did cause a precipitous drop in the newspaper's share of national advertising, but this was more than balanced by an increase in local ad linage. The growth of "cold type" offset printing helped many smaller papers cut costs, while the larger ones (to the extent permitted by the labor unions) turned to computerized typesetting and other labor-saving devices.

The 1950s and 1960s witnessed a tremendous explosion in suburban living, opening up new markets for new publishers. Suburban newspapers like *Newsday* (on Long Island) built huge circulations in just a few years. Such papers were often among the most profitable in the country. Residents depended on them for neighborhood news (which television couldn't provide), and every new shopping center meant thousands of dollars more in advertising.

The development of regional printing facilities, meanwhile, led to the growth of the country's first truly national newspapers: the *Wall Street Journal* and the *Christian Science Monitor.* The *New York Times* con-

1940 *Newsday* is founded in suburban Long Island; twenty years later it will soar to leadership in both circulation and advertising revenue.

1945 Bernard Kilgore takes over the *Wall Street Journal*; by 1965, under his guidance, the newspaper will have a national circulation of 800,000.

1948 Radio ad revenue reaches its peak and begins to decline.

1949 The Supreme Court forces movie companies to sell off their theater holdings. The film audience reaches a peak of 90 million tickets a week; by 1968 it will be down to 21 million a week.

1950 The Intertype Corporation comes out with its "fotosetter," making offset newspapers feasible.

1951 Edward R. Murrow's documentary "Hear It Now" leaves radio for television, becoming "See It Now."

1953 Twentieth Century Fox produces "The Robe," the first of the wide-screen Cinemascope spectaculars.

1955 The major film studios begin selling old movies to television; they will sell nearly 9,000 of them by 1958.

1956 *Collier's* becomes the first of the big mass-circulation, general-interest magazines to fold.

1958 United Press and International News Service merge to form United Press International; both UPI and AP begin moving interpretive articles.

1960 Editor John Denson of the *New York Herald Tribune* leads the trend toward magazine-style layout.

1961 The FCC approves multiplex stereo for FM radio.

1963 Several metropolitan daily newspapers begin setting type by computer.

1964 The FCC rules that AM-FM radio combinations must run different programs on the two stations at least half the time.

1966 The *New York Herald Tribune, World-Telegram & Sun,* and *Journal-American* merge to form a single afternoon paper. The result of the merger, the *World Journal Tribune,* will die in 1967.

1969 *Easy Rider,* a low-budget topical film, is a smash at the box office. In 1970, *Airport* and *Patton,* big-budget general-interest films, will be even more successful, but production for television will earn Hollywood its only steady and secure income.

1971 The Supreme Court permits the *New York Times* and other papers to print the Pentagon Papers.

1972 *Life* magazine dies, while specialized magazines thrive. *Penthouse* successfully seeks some of the *Playboy* market.

1973 The *Washington Post* sticks with the Watergate story and wins a Pulitzer Prize for its efforts. The Supreme Court rules that states may set obscenity standards.

tinued as a national paper of sorts. It was the nation's "newspaper of record"—and no legislator, public library, or university could do without it.

In the face of these trends, the metropolitan daily suffered but survived. There were still enough readers and advertisers in the inner city to support at least one morning and one evening paper—and by the mid-1960s very few cities had more than that number.

The existence of television news forced some changes in newspaper content, but they were little more than the continuation of changes already begun in the face of radio news. Now it was television as well as radio that could reach the public with a bulletin before any newspaper had a chance. All the more reason for newspapers to go the way they were already going—interpretive and featurey, the details of the news and the news behind the news. The trend simply intensified. In keeping with their content, many papers followed the lead of the *New York Herald Tribune* and moved to a simplified, uncluttered, magazine-style layout. And even the wire services backed off the who/what/where/when concept of journalism and began moving some interpretive stories. The typical American newspaper is still far from a daily edition of *Time,* but it appears to be moving in that direction.

Though the content of newspapers changed little because of television, their impact may have changed greatly. Researchers have found that many of the most widely read items in today's newspapers have nothing to do with "news." They are the weather report, the advice column, the movie listings, the TV log, the sports results, and the ads. Most of the hard news available to Americans every day is published in newspapers, not broadcast on TV. But the average American seldom reads it. Most of us get most of our news from television.

Something else happened in the early 1970s that cannot be traced to the influence of television. The media and the government fought an all-out battle, and the media won. The battle had its beginnings in the events of the late 1960s—especially the war in Vietnam and the antiwar movement at home. Covering the issue of war was a consciousness-raising experience for the media, forcing them to deal seriously with concepts like imperialism, repression, and government credibility. When the scandals of the Nixon administration began to emerge, the media were prepared to cover them aggressively. The president was prepared to fight just as aggressively against that sort of coverage, and so the battle was joined.

The period from the discovery of the Watergate break-in in 1972 to the resignation of President Nixon in 1974 was fraught with dangers—the danger that the government would succeed in its efforts to intimidate the media, the danger that the media would become permanent and reckless enemies of the government, the danger that the public would lose all its faith in either or both. By 1975 the crisis seemed to be over. But as the rediscovered tradition of muckraking continued into the Ford administration, the dangers remained.

This, then, is how the American mass media stand as of 1976. Newspapers are profitable little monopolies, moving toward interpretive news but read mostly for their ads and service items. Books have failed to attract a mass audience, except for light paperbacks and required school texts. Magazines are becoming more and more specialized, while those that can't make the switch have died. Movies are torn between spectacular blockbuster gambles and safer, low-budget topical productions; many are planned with TV in mind. Radio has settled on a low-key, background approach that earns steady if unimpressive profits. And television—television is for viewers a way of life, and for owners a license to print money.

Notes

[1] John Milton, *Paradise Lost and Selected Poetry and Prose,* ed. Northrop Frye (New York: Rinehart & Co., 1951), pp. 486–500.

[2] Edwin Emery, ed., *The Story of America* (New York: Simon and Schuster, Inc., 1965), p. 3.

[3] James Playsted Wood, *The Story of Advertising* (New York: The Ronald Press Co., 1958), p. 45.

[4] Frank Luther Mott, *American Journalism,* 3rd ed. (New York: The Macmillan Co., 1962), p. 25.

[5] Emery, *Story of America,* p. 5.

[6] Louis L. Snyder, and Robert B. Morris, *A Treasury of Great Reporting* (New York: Simon and Schuster, Inc., 1949), pp. 21–24.

[7] Emery, *Story of America,* p. 10.

[8] Snyder and Morris, *Treasury of Great Reporting,* pp. 29–30.

[9] *The Federalist,* LXXXIV, in Mott, *American Journalism,* p. 145.

[10] Paul L. Ford, ed., *The Writings of Thomas Jefferson* (New York: G. P. Putnam's Sons, 1892–99), II, p. 69.

[11] *Aurora,* March 6, 1797, in Frederick Hudson, *Journalism in the United States* (New York: Harper & Brothers, 1873), pp. 210–11.

[12] Emery, *Story of America,* p. 27.

[13] *Ibid.,* p. 44.

[14] *Ibid.,* p. 44.

[15] *Ibid.,* p. 61.

[16] Thomas H. Guback, "General Sherman's War on the Press," *Journalism Quarterly,* Spring, 1959, pp. 172–73.

[17] Emery, *Story of America,* p. 80.

[18] *The World,* May 11, 1883, in Mott, *American Journalism,* p. 434.

[19] Emery, *Story of America,* p. 107.

[20] Harry J. Carman and Harold C. Syrett, *A History of the American People* (New York: Alfred A. Knopf, Inc., 1958), II, p. 228.

[21] Arthur Knight, *The Liveliest Art* (New York: Mentor Books, 1957), p. 35.

[22] Radio Act of 1927.

[23] Mott, *American Journalism,* pp. 623–24.

[24] *Ibid.,* p. 625.

[25] Emery, *Story of America,* p. 184.

[26] Edwin Emery, *The Press in America,* 2nd ed. (Englewood Cliffs, N.J.: Prentice-Hall, Inc., 1962), p. 645.

[27] Emery, *Story of America,* p. 203.

Suggested Readings

BARNOUW, ERIK, *A Tower in Babel* (Vol. I—to 1933). New York: Oxford University Press, Inc., 1966.

———. *The Golden Web* (Vol. II—1933–1953). New York: Oxford University Press, Inc., 1968.

———, *The Image Empire* (Vol. III—from 1953). New York: Oxford University Press, Inc., 1970.

EMERY, EDWIN, *The Press in America* (3rd ed.). Englewood Cliffs, N.J.: Prentice-Hall, Inc., 1972.

———, ed., *The Story of America.* New York: Simon and Schuster, Inc., 1965.

KENDRICK, ALEXANDER, *Prime Time: The Life of Edward R. Murrow.* Boston: Little, Brown and Co., 1969.

KNIGHT, ARTHUR, *The Liveliest Art.* New York: Mentor Books, 1957.

MOTT, FRANK LUTHER, *American Journalism* (3rd ed.). New York: The Macmillan Co., 1962.

POLLACK, PETER, *The Picture History of Photography.* New York: Harry N. Abrams, Inc., 1969.

SIEBERT, FRED S., THEODORE PETERSON, and WILBUR SCHRAMM, *Four Theories of the Press.* Urbana, Ill.: University of Illinois Press, 1956.

SNYDER, LOUIS L., and RICHARD B. MORRIS, eds., *A Treasury of Great Reporting.* New York: Simon and Schuster, Inc., 1949.

———, *Luce and His Empire.* New York: Dell Publishing Co., 1972.

SWANBERG, W. A., *Citizen Hearst.* New York: Bantam Books, Inc., 1961.

TALESE, GAY, *The Kingdom and the Power.* New York: World Publishing Co., 1969.

PART II
RESPONSIBILITY

The Introduction and first section of this book dealt with the impact and history of the mass media. By this point it should be clear that, if nothing else, the media are important.

We turn now to the question of responsibility. Which individuals, groups, and institutions in this country determine the course of the mass media? Which ones wield its enormous power? Which will decide its future history? If the media themselves are important, then these questions are also important.

In the next seven chapters we will examine the following sorts of control over the media:

1. *Self-control* through professional codes and ethical standards.
2. *Internal control* at various points in the media bureaucracies, from publisher and station manager down to reporter and assignment editor.
3. *Monopoly control* through chains, conglomerates, networks, and other forms of media monopoly.
4. *Advertiser control,* whether directly through pressure from individual advertisers or indirectly through media recognition of broad business needs.

5. *Source control* through secrecy, news management, and other techniques for the manipulation of media content before it reaches the media.
6. *Government control,* including the massive influence of law and the even more massive influence of the federal regulatory agencies.
7. *Public control* through letters to the editor, ratings, and many less passive techniques.

It is the firm opinion of the authors that the first and the last items on this list—self-control and public control—are far too weak. The remaining five are too strong, or misapplied, or both. If we were forced to rank the seven forms of control from the most dangerous down to the least, we would tend toward the following order:

1. Too much monopoly control.
2. Too little public control.
3. Too much source control.
4. Misapplied government control.
5. Too little self-control.
6. Too much and misapplied internal control.
7. Too much advertiser control.

Others might propose a different order, but few would object to the general picture of media control outlined here. The American mass media today are run largely by giant monopolies, which impose homogeneity and greatly reduce the diversity of media content. Major sources of information, both private and governmental, possess tremendous power to control the news they make. Through courts, regulatory agencies, and informal policies, the federal government exercises considerable influence on the present conduct of the media, and almost total control over their future course. Well-placed employees within the media are in a position to make their weight felt in surprising ways. Advertisers are permitted to demand special favors as well as overall formats suitable to their needs. Ethical standards, meanwhile, exert little influence, and public opinion is almost totally powerless to affect the media.

Two vital points must be made with respect to the interplay of these seven factors. They are emphasized here because they will be largely ignored in the following chapters, as the forms of media control are treated one at a time.

1. *The dynamics of media control are an ongoing process, and may change dramatically from decade to decade.* In the 1950s, for example, monopolies were a far less serious problem than they are today. Media tended to be somewhat less responsive to the public—and they were much more responsive to the demands of advertisers. The implications of government control over broadcasting were just beginning to be recognized —and so was the importance of professional and ethical standards. It is difficult to guess what the patterns of media control will be like in the 1980s and 1990s, but it is unlikely that they will resemble too closely today's patterns.

2. *The various forms of media control are in conflict, not balance, and often help keep each other in check.* Consider, for example, the interplay of government and monopoly control. A television network is a dangerous monopoly, an incredible concentration of power in the hands of a few people. Yet only the networks are strong enough to defy the government when it demands—even more dangerously—that newscasters be kinder in their commentary on the misuse of government authority. The power of the federal regulatory agencies, conversely, is frightening when applied to something so delicate as the First Amendment. Yet only the government has the necessary strength to forbid newspapers to own broadcast stations in the same city—perhaps an even more frightening First Amendment infraction.

Pluralism is central to a democracy. The goal of a social critic or policy-maker should always be to equalize power, to play off one influence against another in the hope that freedom will be the winner. If all seven forms of media control on our list were equally powerful, there would be no danger. It is only when one or two of the seven usurp the power of the others and upset the dynamic tension that we need to worry.

Chapter 2
Self-Control

Like other professions, journalism is greatly influenced by ethical standards. Unlike other professions, however, journalism has avoided codifying its ethics into clear and usable rules. The various professional codes of the mass media tend to concentrate on truisms and trivia, ignoring the real ethical problems faced by working journalists. Procedures for making individual journalists accountable to the public or the profession—not only to their boss—are just now beginning to be established.

Gabe Pressman, a television newsman for WNEW in New York, has said that: "As a group, reporters have really never formalized their ethics. Yet I think that the best of them have always followed the strictest code of ethics, a code that would compare with what the medical and legal professions have established. It's a dedication to uncovering the truth, to communicating the information to people . . . to reporting the news without prejudice." [1]

Pressman is right, of course, and yet he ignores the vital difference between journalism and other professions like medicine and law. Because they have formalized their ethics into codes, doctors and lawyers are able to enforce them; if necessary they can expel from their ranks an unethical member. An unethical journalist, on the other hand, can be fired only by the boss, not by other journalists. Sociologists claim that two of the defining characteristics of a profession are a code of ethics and rules of enforcement. Journalism has neither.

MEDIA CODES

Every mass-media group has its code of ethics, including even the Comics Magazine Association of America. Almost without exception the codes are mere collections of platitudes.

The oldest, shortest, and broadest of the codes is the Canons of Journalism, adopted by the American Society of Newspaper Editors in 1923. The seven "canons" are entitled Responsibility; Freedom of the Press; Independence; Sincerity, Truthfulness, Accuracy; Impartiality; Fair Play; and Decency. The canons themselves are no more specific than their titles. "Responsibility," for example, reads as follows:

> The right of a newspaper to attract and hold readers is restricted by nothing but considerations of public welfare. The use a newspaper

makes of the share of public attention it gains serves to determine its sense of responsibility, which it shares with every member of its staff. A journalist who uses his power for any selfish or otherwise unworthy purpose is faithless to a high trust.[2]

There is nothing in the Canons of Journalism (or in the 1975 revised version) that a publisher or editor need fear—but just to be on the safe side journalists are not required to subscribe. And should a newspaper or a reporter "violate" a provision—whatever that might mean—there is no punishment or means of enforcement.

The other four major media codes (for movies, radio, television, and comic books) were all developed in the face of public pressure and criticism. They were designed to forestall government regulation by substituting self-regulation instead. As a result, they are negative rather than positive, and more specific than the Canons of Journalism —but only a little.

Consider the Television Code, adopted by the National Association of Broadcasters in 1952. It starts with sections on "Advancement of Education and Culture," "Responsibility Toward Children," and "Community Responsibility"—all very broad and very trite. Then comes the meat of the code, a list of "general program standards." These are almost exclusively concerned with guaranteeing that nobody is ever offended by anything on television. They include such items as:

6. Respect is maintained for the sanctity of marriage and the value of the home. Divorce is not treated casually as a solution for marital problems. . . .

9. Law enforcement shall be upheld and, except where essential to the program plot, officers of the law portrayed with respect and dignity. . . .

11. The use of animals both in the production of television programs and as a part of television program content, shall at all times, be in conformity with accepted standards of humane treatment. . . .

18. Narcotic addiction shall not be presented except as a vicious habit. The administration of illegal drugs will not be displayed.[3]

After the general program standards comes another collection of platitudes, this time on the desirability of good news and religious programming. The final section is devoted to advertising standards. It contains the most specific and potentially the most valuable provisions of the code—items like: "Commercial material, including total station break time, in prime time shall not exceed 17.2% (10 minutes and 20 seconds) in any 60-minute period." [4]

Enforcement of the Television Code is almost nonexistent. The NAB has a Code Review Board which awards a seal of approval to any station that subscribes to the code and obeys it. The seal is customarily flashed, with a brief explanation, at sign-on and sign-off; farmers and insomniacs are thus able to get a quick look at it. The only penalty for a station that does not subscribe to the code or does not follow it is denial of permission to exhibit the seal.

Here's how it works. In 1957 the Code Review Board outlawed TV ads for hemorrhoid remedies. When "enforcement" of the ban began in mid-1959, 148 stations were advertising Preparation H, a hemorrhoid remedy; 84 of them were code subscribers. After two weeks 17 stations resigned from the code rather than drop the ads, and 21 more continued the ads and lost the seal. Only 46 out of 148 stations agreed to conform to the code.[5] Eventually the code itself was liberalized to permit the ads.

TV broadcasters like their code the way it is—toothless. In the late 1950s, the FCC toyed with the idea of regulating the amount of time stations could devote to commercials. It proposed a rule that precisely duplicated the Television Code's own standards. The TV industry vehemently objected, and the Commission backed down. So the standards are still voluntary.

The radio, motion picture, and comic book codes are just as unenforced and unenforceable as the Television Code. They are, in fact, remarkably similar. All are designed to avoid offending the public, and thereby to avoid the threat of government regulation. None of them offers much help to the media owner or journalist with a real ethical problem to deal with.

A number of publishers and broadcasters have tried to fill the gap with their own in-house codes. Useful though these may be, they are not an adequate substitute for professional standards. In-house codes come in the form of instructions from the boss, not standards from the profession. Having your employer tell you what to do is not at all the same thing as having your peers tell you what ought to be done.

ACCOUNTABILITY

The issue is essentially one of accountability. Journalists as a group have a strong sense of responsibility to the public, a deep conviction that what they do has significant impact on society and should therefore be done responsibly. When two reporters get together for lunch, their conversation is surprisingly likely to center on ways to make news coverage more accurate, complete, and ethical. No other occupation devotes as much time and energy to criticizing its own work.

Many journalists, in other words, *feel* responsible to the public. But they are *not* responsible to the public. Their readers and viewers do not elect them and cannot fire them. The government does not license them or set standards for their behavior. Nor are individual reporters systematically responsible to the journalism profession. You cannot become a lawyer unless the Bar Association accepts you; you cannot remain a lawyer unless the Bar Association continues to accept you. At least in theory, the Bar Association exercises its power on behalf of the public. Unqualified lawyers are turned away; unscrupulous lawyers are thrown out. Journalism has no such mechanisms. You

become a journalist when you declare that you are one, and you remain a journalist as long as you keep declaring that you are one. It is hard to think of another occupation of comparable importance to society that exercises so little formal control over itself.

But the individual journalist does not stand alone in solitary splendor either. A reporter is not accountable to the public, the government, or the journalism profession, but the reporter is directly accountable to the boss—the publisher or broadcast station owner. The ethics of American journalism, then, are ultimately in the hands of the people who own our media.

There are two important implications of all this. First, journalism has absolutely no way to get rid of an irresponsible practitioner. No matter how unethical a reporter may be, he or she may continue on the job until fired by the boss. The second implication is more subtle, but no less important: Responsible journalists have no professional codes to insulate them from the occasionally irresponsible demands of their employers. If a hospital director asks a doctor to do something unethical, the doctor can cite chapter and verse of medical ethics as justification for refusing. A journalist in the same position has no comparable support system for opposing the employer's demands.

Of course professional standards often insulate a practitioner from clients as well as from employers. The standards of the American Medical Association and the Bar Association do not always seem to have the public interest at heart. But as long as reporters are not directly accountable to their readers and viewers, accountability to their colleagues seems a vast improvement over total subservience to the boss.

How, then, can journalism be professionalized? Four current trends—all still in their infancy—seem to be moving in the right direction. These are (1) the reporter power movement; (2) unions; (3) the growing use of media ombudspersons; and (4) press councils. We will consider each in turn.

THE JOURNALISM REVIEWS

The growing professional feeling of journalists is best expressed by the spectacular rise of journalism reviews since the 1960s. These monthly or bi-monthly critiques of national and local media performance are written and edited—and read—by reporters in their off-duty hours.

The granddaddy of them all is the *Columbia Journalism Review,* begun in 1961. Its goals, as stated in the first issue and quoted in each issue thereafter, are "to assess the performance of journalism in all its forms, to call attention to its shortcomings and strengths, and to help define—or redefine—standards of honest, responsible service. . . . [Also] to help stimulate continuing improvement in the profession and to speak out for what is right, fair, and decent." CJR is now published every two months, and has collected some of its best pieces in a book entitled *Our Troubled Press.*

The battles between police and reporters at the 1968 Democratic Convention in Chicago led to the founding of the *Chicago Journalism Review,* the first of many local reviews. Others were started in Philadelphia, St. Louis, Houston, Southern California, Honolulu, and even Alaska.[6] Among the most ambitious of the reviews is *[MORE],* a New York City monthly edited by former *Newsweek* staffer Richard Pollak. Despite a circulation of 20,000, *[MORE]* is in financial trouble; like nearly all the journalism reviews, it is in constant danger of folding.

The existence of journalism reviews demonstrates the strong urge of journalists to be professionals. But the fact that the reviews are mostly shoestring operations demonstrates that journalists are not yet professionals. Even at their best, journalism reviews cannot force the media to improve; they can only criticize and suggest. And their circulation, remember, is confined mostly to journalists themselves. Public criticism of the media—and the accountability that such criticism might engender—is somewhat rarer.

Public media criticism has a distinguished history in the United States. In 1911, for example, Will Irwin wrote a long series of perceptive articles about the press for *Collier's* magazine. Many of Irwin's charges are still valid today, and the old articles have been collected by Clifford F. Weigle and David G. Clark for The Iowa State University Press under the title *The American Newspaper.* Irwin's spiritual successor was the late A. J. Liebling, who wrote a regular *New Yorker* column called "The Wayward Press" from 1944 to 1963. Liebling's best columns are available in *The Press,* published by Ballantine. By contrast, most of the best media criticism written today appears in journalism reviews, not in mass magazines (and certainly not in newspapers or on TV). In an effort to professionalize, reporters are exposing their dirty linen to each other, but not usually to the American people.

---

1. Reporter Power. The reporter power movement had its birth in Europe, and even today is much stronger there than in this country. At *Le Monde,* a highly respected French newspaper, 40 percent of the capital is held by a "corporation of journalists" working at the paper. The majority of the company is controlled by editorial personnel, who use their power to discourage purchase of the rest by those who would use the paper for monetary gain alone. In addition, *Le Monde* has established a supervisory council and an editorial staff committee to represent the viewpoints of journalists on financial and policy issues.[7] Other European publications, such as *Le Figaro* in France and *Stern* in Germany, have similar arrangements.

In the United States, only a handful of

newspapers (and no major broadcast stations) share their stock with editorial employees in large enough amounts to affect decision-making. But by the early 1970s, American journalists had begun to organize for at least an advisory role. In 1972, for example, the *Minneapolis Star* and *Tribune* agreed to meet monthly with committees of reporters to discuss "matters affecting relations between employees and the employer," including issues of professional responsibility, ethics, and news judgment.[8] Similar channels have been established (or are being agitated for) at a dozen other newspapers, as well as the networks, wire services, and newsmagazines.

2. Unions. For the reporter power movement to grow in the United States, media owners will have to relinquish voluntarily some of the control that traditionally accompanies ownership of a business. Probably the most likely vehicle through which this can occur is the collective bargaining process. There are three unions to which journalists now belong in substantial numbers—the American Newspaper Guild (newspaper writers), the Writers Guild of America (broadcast writers), and the American Federation of Television and Radio Artists (broadcast on-the-air talent).

Historically, all three have been "bread-and-butter" unions, confining their efforts to the pursuit of higher wages, better fringe benefits, more job security, and the like. This just may be changing. Charles Perlik, national head of the Newspaper Guild, told a 1973 journalism convention in Washington that his union was beginning to include in its contract proposals a clause forbidding management to change a reporter's story without the reporter's permission, unless it also removed the byline. Of course journalists at many newspapers and broadcast stations, particularly the smaller ones, are not unionized at all. Still, union interest in professional ethics is an encouraging sign.

But there are important differences between unionization and professionalization. For years, the International Typographical Union and other unions of backshop personnel have battled against the introduction of computer typesetting and automation of all sorts in the newspaper industry. In so doing, these unions have been quite properly protecting the jobs of their members. But as a by-product, they have also slowed the technological progress of newspapers, and have cost the papers money that might otherwise be spent on improved news coverage. The Newspaper Guild has been generally neutral in the automation war, but many Guild reporters would feel duty-bound to honor an ITU picket line. Worker solidarity would take precedence over the professional obligation to inform the public.

Meanwhile, media unions have many unintended effects on news coverage. Consider these three examples from broadcasting:

1. Contracts between the TV networks and AFTRA provide for an additional fee each time a reporter appears on camera. That seems fair enough. But it gives reporters an incentive to work themselves into the story, and to cover as many different stories in a day as they can. And it gives management an incentive to keep reporters off camera whenever possible. Both tendencies may hurt the quality of coverage.

2. In 1971, conservative columnist William F. Buckley, Jr. objected to a closed-shop agreement between AFTRA and RKO General, which used to produce Buckley's program, "Firing Line." According to the agreement, Buckley would have to join the union if he wanted to keep appearing on TV. Buckley refused, arguing that it was unconstitutional to require someone to belong to any organization as a condition for the exercise of free speech. The appeals court disagreed.[9]

3. In San Francisco and several other big cities, the contracts between local radio stations and technical unions provide that a station may not broadcast an ongoing event unless an audio engineer is present to record

it. This means the station cannot simply send out a reporter with a tape recorder. As a result, budget-conscious stations often send the engineer alone, leaving the reporter free to cover something else.

In many European countries, unions of journalists are working to resolve these conflicts between bread-and-butter issues and professional ones. American media unions, newly interested in professionalism, have just begun to see the conflicts, not yet to resolve them.

3. Ombudspersons. A media ombudsperson reviews the performance of the medium, handles complaints from readers or viewers, explains newsgathering procedures, and mediates controversies that arise between the reporting staff and management. The concept originated in Europe; in this country the *Washington Post* and the *Louisville Courier-Journal* are among the pioneering papers. A study conducted by Keith Sanders of the University of Missouri School of Journalism found that, as of 1973, only 9 percent of the daily newspapers in the U.S. employed an ombudsperson. Most of these were the larger papers of 100,000 circulation or more.[10]

The value of an ombudsperson is that he or she is paid to think, full-time, about questions of quality and ethics. Is the medium doing its job? Has it been accurate? Has it been fair to its source and audience? Have reporters been forced to distort their stories to serve the interests of management? The ombudsperson thus represents another step toward establishing and enforcing a stronger code of performance for journalism.

4. Press Councils. Sweden established its national press council in 1916. Made up of both laypeople and journalists, the press council undertook to monitor the performance of the news media, investigate complaints brought by the public or by government officials, and publicize the results. Britain's national press council, established in 1952, was organized along the same lines.

In the late 1960s the U.S. moved timidly to catch up. The first U.S. press councils were purely local affairs, in small cities such as Cairo, Illinois, and Redwood City, California. Minnesota was the first state to establish a statewide press council. And in 1973, with the help of the Twentieth Century Fund, a National News Council was founded with headquarters in New York.

At its head is William B. Arthur, a former editor of *Look* magazine. Among the fifteen members are a former U.S. Senator, a Louisiana attorney, a Memphis clergyman, and people from various branches of the media. Like most of the local press councils, the National News Council has no power to fine a medium or fire a reporter. It has only the power of persuasion and publicity—and it must rely on the news media themselves for the latter.

Despite its weakness, the Council has faced considerable hostility from the nation's publishers and broadcasters. Some, like Arthur Ochs Sulzberger of the *New York Times,* view the Council as simply "regulation in another form," and oppose it as a potential threat to freedom of the press.[11]

So far the council in Minnesota and the National News Council have had little impact. The latter offered to investigate charges by the Nixon administration that the TV networks were guilty of biased reporting on the Watergate scandals, but the White House declined to cooperate by listing precisely which items it felt were biased. Still, the very existence of press councils in the United States indicates a growing concern over journalistic ethics, standards, and accountability.

THE DILEMMA OF OBJECTIVITY

The most serious ethical problem confronting reporters and editors is also the most common. It is expressed in questions like these: How do I approach the story? Whom do I interview? What do I ask? What do I lead with in my first paragraph? What do I

In response to increasing government regulation, the advertising industry followed the traditional pattern of other mass media by setting up, in 1971, the National Advertising Review Board to police the industry from the inside. The Board is composed of thirty representatives from companies that advertise in the media, ten from ad agencies, and ten more from the public. Its investigative arm is the National Advertising Division of the Council of Better Business Bureaus.

The NARB works like a press council, studying complaints from the public and from companies with competitive products. In its first two and a half years of operation, it processed only 600 complaints. By contrast, Canada's advertising board dealt with over a thousand complaints in the first four months of 1973 alone.[12]

Besides the small number of complaints handled, the NARB has been criticized for taking too long to reach a decision (an average of ten months), and for not adequately publicizing its existence or its findings. A 1974 study by the Missouri Public Interest Research Group concluded that the Board had not had a significant impact on fraudulence in advertising.[13]

Nonetheless, the Board does occasionally rule against an advertiser. In 1973, for example, it criticized a Schick Flexamatic campaign because the ads didn't say which competitors were tested against the Schick, and because they falsely implied that the Schick would give a close shave to all men at all times. Schick said it would abide by the panel's recommendations "in the interest of industry self-regulation and continued cooperation with the NARB."[14]

---

leave out? What headline do I write? How long do I let the story run? Which stories do I put on the front page? The conventional answer to all these questions is "Be objective"—which is about as useful as telling a batter to hit a home run, please.

Most journalists today aim at objectivity—and often fail. When the home team wins 6–4, it has "thumped" the opposition. When the home team loses 6–4, it has been "edged." That crowd of demonstrators marching on City Hall is "unruly, vicious, and dangerous." The same crowd celebrating a World Series victory is "jubilant, ecstatic, and playful." Words have connotations as well as denotations; they imply more than they mean. And reporters have values and attitudes as well as eyes and ears; they must interpret what they see and hear. As long as journalism is produced by people and expressed in words, complete objectivity is impossible.

The former editor of the *New York Times*

Sunday magazine, Lester Markel, argues the same point:

> The reporter, the most objective reporter, collects fifty facts. Out of the fifty he selects twelve to include in his story (there is such a thing as space limitation). Thus he discards thirty-eight. This is Judgment Number One.
>
> Then the reporter or editor decides which of the facts shall be the first paragraph of the story, thus emphasizing one fact above the other eleven. This is Judgment Number Two.
>
> Then the editor decides whether the story shall be placed on Page One or Page Twelve; on Page One it will command many times the attention it would on Page Twelve. This is Judgment Number Three.
>
> This so-called factual presentation is thus subjected to three judgments, all of them most humanly and most ungodly made.[15]

Everything Markel says is true. Yet it is still possible for a reporter and an editor to at least try to put aside their prejudices and strive for fair and balanced news. Kenneth Stewart, a longtime journalist and journalism educator, writes: "If you mean by objectivity the absence of convictions, willingness to let nature take its course, uncritical acceptance of things as they are (what Robert Frost calls the 'isness of is'), the hell with it. If you mean by objectivity a healthy respect for the ascertainable truth, a readiness to modify conclusions when new evidence comes in, a refusal to distort deliberately and for ulterior or concealed motives . . . all well and good." [16]

INTERVIEW ETIQUETTE

The following is taken from a radio interview with Senator Strom Thurmond, conducted in 1964 by newsman Robert Fargo. The Senator had just stated that there were communists teaching in the nation's public schools.

FARGO: Will you name one? Will you name one? Will you name one teacher without your congressional immunity. . . .

THURMOND: No, I'm not. . . .

FARGO: Name one teacher. . . . Name one school in the United States of America that has ever been indicted and convicted in a Federal grand jury of subversion, sedition, or anything else. Name one right here. I ask you, right now.

THURMOND: I. . . .

FARGO: That's my final question.

THURMOND: I could name . . . I could name . . . I could name. . . .

FARGO: Name one. . . . Name one right here.

THURMOND: Many of. . . .

FARGO: Name one, right here.

THURMOND: I am not indulging. . . .

FARGO: Name one.

THURMOND: You have asked your question. I'm now answering it if you'll. . . .

FARGO: Name one. Name one. I'm asking you to name. . . .

THURMOND: Keep quiet.

FARGO: I'm asking you to name one, right here and now, without congressional immunity.

THURMOND: Are you now through asking your question? I'll attempt to answer it. My answer is that I am not indulging in personalities. . . .

FARGO: All right, I'll take your refusal right here.

THURMOND: I have not indulged. . . .

FARGO: What you have pointed out is very, very important.

THURMOND: If you'll wait until I get through. . . .

FARGO: A smear is very important. Name one.

THURMOND: Who do you represent? Who do you represent?

FARGO: Name one.

After the exchange, Senator Thurmond demanded, and received, an apology from the station's general manager. Most of the journalists present agreed that Fargo had acted unethically and inexcusably, trying to "get" the Senator rather than get the news. Said one: "This one shallow-minded tirade could undo months of dedicated work by the majority." [17]

Even in these terms, it can be argued that objectivity is a false god. All too often, objectivity means writing in such a way that the reader or viewer cannot tell where the reporter's sympathies lie. If the reporter does in fact have sympathies and those sympathies are in fact influencing the story, this simply makes the prejudice less obvious. Sociologist Gaye Tuchman argues that journalistic objectivity is essentially a "strategic ritual," designed not to keep the story from being biased but rather to keep the story from seeming biased. Reporters who talk to representatives of both sides in a controversy, who quote and attribute every judgment they use, who start the story with who/what/where/when and only then go to why, Tuchman argues, are thereby protecting themselves from criticism.[18] The story may be no less misleading for all its objectivity, but it is safer.

And suppose a reporter is somehow successful in keeping his or her values from influencing the story. Is this necessarily good? What is the value of having humane and concerned journalists if they hide their humanity and concern when they set out to cover the news? Was objectivity a good thing in the 1950s, when it forced the media to be "fair" to the incredibly unfair allegations of Senator Joseph McCarthy? Ultimately, why should a conservative reporter be "fair" to the scourge of Communism? Why should a radical reporter be "fair" to the capitalist Establishment?

On the other hand, the notion of objectivity does impose a useful discipline on journalists. Even if it is unattainable and sometimes a bit hypocritical, objectivity as a goal reminds reporters that they are paid to tell us about events, not about their own feelings; that they are obliged to talk to all sides in a dispute before writing their story; that they should resort to volatile language sparingly and only where it is justified. Objectivity is journalism's cautious response to its own power. In limiting the reporter's freedom to guide the audience, objectivity also limits the reporter's freedom to misguide the audience.

Whether or not it is a false god, objectivity is certainly a fairly new one. In the late eighteenth century and well into the nineteenth, most newspapers were openly partisan in their news judgments. It wasn't until the first wire service was born in the 1840s that objectivity became a part of American journalism. And even then it was assumed that a subscribing newspaper would add its own unique bias to the wire reports if it had the time. Often newspapers didn't have the time. Local reporters copied the neutrality of the wires, and objectivity eventually became the defining characteristic of responsible journalism.

Wire-style objectivity dominated the media for decades. But by the 1930s, the world had become too complicated a place for journalists to report it solely in police-blotter facts. In 1933 the United States went off the gold standard, and a confused group of Washington reporters faced the task of telling the nation about it. President Roosevelt sent over some of his economic advisers to help the reporters understand the move, and together they tried to explain it to the country. Some journalism historians point to that day as the birth of interpretive reporting in the U.S.[19]

Interpretive journalism reports not only the facts but also explanation and analysis of the facts. Can objectivity stretch this far? In the 1930s, most editors said no. As late as the mid-1960s, the wire services were still resisting the trend toward interpretive reporting. But journalism professor (and former newspaper editor) Carl E. Lindstrom expresses the more common view today. Lindstrom sees interpretive reporting as simply the addition of new kinds of facts —"historical, circumstantial, biographical, statistical, reflective"[20]—that can throw added light on the events of the day. Though objectivity is often considered more difficult to achieve in interpretive articles than in "straight" writing, interpretation and objectivity are no longer viewed as inconsistent with one another.

While the battle over interpretive reporting was still raging, a new threat to objectivity emerged on the scene. In the late 1950s and early 1960s, a group of journalists, most of them working in New York, began experimenting with fiction techniques in their writing. Trying to report a different sort of "truth" to their readers, these men and women used a number of unconventional devices: narrative, unstructured styles; extensive dialogue; detailed scene-building; strongly evocative adjectives and verbs (including some they made up); playful punctuation; etc. Tom Wolfe has become a principal advocate of this approach, which is most often called the "New Journalism."

Wolfe points to a story about heavyweight boxer Joe Louis, which appeared in *Esquire* in 1962, as a trend-setter for the New Journalism. The author was Gay Talese, who later profiled the *New York Times* in *The Kingdom and the Power*. The beginning of the article sets it apart immediately from much of what was (and still is) typical of American journalism:

"Hi, sweetheart!" Joe Louis called to his wife, spotting her waiting for him at the Los Angeles airport.

She smiled, walked toward him, and was about to stretch up on her toes and kiss him—but suddenly stopped.

"Joe," she said, "where's your tie?"

"Aw, sweetie," he said, shrugging, "I stayed out all night in New York and didn't have time—"

"All *night!*" she cut in. "When you're out here all you do is sleep, sleep, sleep."

"Sweetie," Joe Louis said, with a tired grin, "I'm an ole man."

"Yes," she agreed, "but when you go to New York you try to be young again." [21]

Instead of merely describing the former champ, Talese took his readers behind the scenes, revealing conversations and thoughts, painting pictures, setting scenes. These became the trademarks of the New Journalists, as they tried to penetrate reality by breaking the bonds of objective journalism. Norman Mailer, Murray Kempton, Jack Newfield, Truman Capote, Gail Sheehy, Wolfe, Talese, and many others adopted this approach in their writing. So

---

REDPANTS AND SUGARMAN

As a narrative vehicle to tell the true story of prostitution and pimping in New York City, journalist Gail Sheehy created two composite characters—Redpants and Sugarman—based on her lengthy interviewing of street people. This is an old and honorable technique, permissible so long as the composites are realistic, quotations are not fabricated, and the reader is told that there is no Redpants or Sugarman.

The article appeared in 1971 in *New York* magazine, home-base of the New Journalism. Sheehy had written a paragraph early in the piece explaining the composite characterization, but her editor, Clay Felker, took it out because he felt it slowed up the narration. Said Felker (later): "I thought it was perfectly apparent one person couldn't do all that. . . . I made a major mistake." [22]

The *Wall Street Journal* brought the oversight to the attention of the public, much to the embarrassment of Sheehy and *New York*. The example has been used to damn all of the New Journalism, which is not really fair. But it does point up the absolute necessity of being honest with the reading or viewing public: Your audience must be told what is fact and what is fiction, what is truth and what is satire, what is exposé and what is fantasy.

did Daniel DeFoe several centuries ago, in his *Journal of the Plague Year*. The New Journalism is not entirely new. What *is* new is the large number of once-conventional reporters who now try to use some of these novelistic techniques in their daily writing.

Already the New Journalism is pretty much accepted in magazine writing (though many of the more traditional magazines won't touch it). But it is a raging battle in newspaper and broadcast reporting—and so far, at least, the New Journalists are losing.

Is the New Journalism anti-objective, unethical, and irresponsible? It depends on whom you ask. Some of the more fanatic New Journalists claim that both conventional novels and conventional reporting are now obsolete, to be replaced by the hybrid they have created. Critic Michael J. Arlen, on the other hand, faults the New Journalism for its "determination and insistence that we shall see life largely on [the New Journalist's] terms." [23] Arlen prefers to make his own judgments, based on the more dispassionate information provided by objective reporters. Jack Newfield, meanwhile, believes that separating journalism into these two camps is a pointless and destructive exercise. "There is only good writing and bad writing," says Newfield, "smart ideas and dumb ideas, hard work and laziness." [24]

However you feel about objectivity and the New Journalism, one thing is sure: The choice is up to you and your employer. The public and the journalism profession will have little or no influence on your decision.

In the absence of any meaningful sort of accountability to the public or the profession, journalists must resolve their ethical problems on their own —aided only by their employers. Among the hundreds of ethical dilemmas confronting the reporter, six seem especially important: (1) The right to privacy; (2) Confidentiality of sources; (3) The reporter as part of the story; (4) Conflict of interest; (5) The junket; and (6) Paying for the news. None of them is easily solved.

THE RIGHT TO PRIVACY

One of the most common ethical problems facing every reporter is the likelihood that your story may in some way injure the people you write about or those you get your information from. In 1965, for example, a *New York Times* reporter discovered that a prominent member of the American Nazi Party was of Jewish ancestry. The Nazi made it clear to the reporter that his "career" would be finished if this fact were revealed to the public. The *Times* ran the story anyhow, and the Jewish Nazi committed suicide. Was this a valid intrusion on his private life, or was it unethical?

During a mid-1950s murder trial, a reporter discovered that one of the jurors had been convicted on a misdemeanor homosexuality charge eleven years before. The press rehashed the old story, and even went so far as to interview the juror's wife. He soon asked to be excused from the jury. "I feel," he said, "I would be a subheadline as long as this trial goes on." Similarly, the year-old case of an army general court-martialled for accidentally revealing military secrets made headlines all over again when the general's son, a West Point cadet, died in a fire while on leave.[25] Are these two incidents less ethical than the Nazi example? If so, why?

In many European countries it is illegal even to mention the criminal record of a person who has been released and not been in trouble again. But in the United States this sort of rehash of old crimes is not only legal—it is extremely common.

Former criminals are not the only ones whose privacy is often invaded by the mass media. Broadcaster Robert Schulman recalls his cub reporter days, when he was often sent to the home of a recent widow to pick up a photo of her deceased husband. Once Schulman was the first to arrive, and had to tell the woman her husband was dead before asking for the picture.[26] TV reporter Gabe Pressman was in a New York airport when news arrived of a transoceanic plane crash. Pressman recalls how uncomfortable *he* was watching another TV reporter interview the shocked relatives—capitalizing on their sorrow for the sake of a "news" story.[27]

Does a person as famous as Jacqueline Kennedy Onassis have a right to privacy that can protect her (and her children) from the prying eye of the camera when she is in a public place? Photographer Ronald Galella made a career of photographing Onassis and her children. In 1972, wearied by Galella's attention, she took the case to court. Galella was ordered to stay at least 150 feet from Onassis and 225 feet from the children. The court later modified the decision to 25 and 30 feet—but agreed that even Jacqueline Kennedy Onassis had a right to some privacy.[28]

Privacy versus the public's right to know: That is the problem. Should photographers have chased down a grand jury witness in a gambling probe when the witness was avoiding publicity for fear of mob reprisals? Should reporters have printed the names of police doctors accused of brutality by a woman student arrested at a peace march? Should TV stations have run the film of two airplane crash victims, still strapped in their seats and still recognizable, floating in the water?

On the other hand, should the world's foreign correspondents have agreed in 1963 to keep the secret that Pope John XXIII was dying of cancer? The Vatican reporters protected the Pontiff from a five-month orgy of premature mourning—but they also hid from their readers and viewers a news event of worldwide importance.

In 1954 the mass media of San Francisco blacked out a local kidnapping story for sixty-one hours, at the request of the police and the victim's parents. Only after the kidnappers were caught did they report the story. Commenting on the silence, the chief of police stated that "The press deserves a large share of credit for solving this crime." The *San Francisco Chronicle* was reluctant to accept the praise. "Suppression of information," it editorialized, "is certainly not our business; it is the opposite of the proper function of a free press." [29] Had the victim been killed or the kidnappers escaped, the media might well have been criticized for their failure to inform the public. And if the kidnappers had added a second victim during the blackout, the criticism of the media would have been overwhelming. Was this an occasion when the media should have protected the privacy of their sources, or should they have warned the public of a kidnapper on the loose?

CONFIDENTIALITY OF SOURCES

On December 14, 1971, Henry A. Kissinger (then an assistant to President Nixon for national security affairs) was flying home from the Azores, accompanied by a large group of reporters. Much on his mind, and on the reporters' minds as well, was the ongoing war between India and Pakistan over the emerging nation of Bangladesh, which found the U.S. lining up with China, against Russia, in support of Pakistan. An impromptu briefing was arranged, on the understanding that reporters could use what they learned, but could not attribute it to Kissinger.

Under these terms, Kissinger was asked if the Soviet Union's support of India might endanger a planned Nixon trip to Moscow or otherwise strain U.S.-Soviet relations. He answered that if Soviet encouragement of Indian military action continued, "the entire U.S.-Soviet relationship might well be reexamined." Kissinger was using the media, as diplomats often do, to convey a position to another country without resorting to formal messages or policy statements. Because he was speaking anonymously, his negotiating freedom would not be curtailed—

yet Russia was sure to get the message. Reporters respected his wishes because they knew that without the promise of anonymity they would not have received even this background information.

But one newspaper, the *Washington Post,* decided that such a sensational threat should not be made anonymously. Despite Kissinger's request for confidentiality, the *Post* story the next morning quoted Kissinger by name. Later, the White House Correspondents Association rebuked the *Post,* and the paper privately apologized.[30]

These events highlight three points about the media's use of anonymous sources. First, it is so common a practice that formal rules have grown up to govern it. Second, breaking a source's confidence is something reporters never do lightly. And third, sometimes they feel they must.

Any journalist who engages in investigative reporting, political reporting, or police reporting (or covers anything more controversial than a Rotary Club picnic) is often asked by a news source not to reveal his or her name. Few reporters will refuse such a request. If they do, they run the risk of not getting the information at all. Carl Bernstein and Bob Woodward of the *Washington Post* could not possibly have learned as much as they did about the Watergate break-in and cover-up without promising anonymity to their sources. If the two reporters had revealed who was talking to them, the sources would have lost their jobs, or worse. Certainly other sources would have been much less likely to come forward.

Having promised to shield a source, a reporter is properly very, very reluctant to break the promise. Two years after the Watergate break-in, Woodward and Bernstein were still keeping quiet about the names of their sources, especially the talkative insider they nicknamed "Deep Throat." Even when they felt a source had lied to them (in which case a reporter's only way to get even is to divulge the name), they agonized over whether or not to break their

word.[31] Once a reporter gets a reputation as someone who won't keep a confidence, that reporter is finished as an investigator—and the public is the loser.

Many reporters have gone to jail rather than reveal a source. A famous example involved the TV columnist for the now-defunct *New York Herald Tribune,* Marie Torre. In 1959, Torre learned from a source at CBS that actress Judy Garland was refusing to appear in all of the many TV specials offered her by the network, because she was overweight. CBS, the source said, was planning to dump her as a result. Torre used the item in her column, but, as she had promised, did not name her source. Garland claimed it was all a lie, and brought a libel suit against CBS for damaging her reputation. The court ordered Torre to name her source at CBS. She refused, and was sent to jail for ten days.[32]

In the early 1970s, dozens of reporters across the country were suddenly faced with subpoenas demanding that they reveal the names of their confidential sources—on stories ranging from a serious investigation of the Black Panthers to a feature on drug abuse to a sensational piece on the celebrated Charles Manson murders. Many journalists felt this was intentional harassment of the press; others saw it as an effort by law enforcement officials to get the media to do their job for them. The result, in any case, was a great deal of legal and legislative jockeying around a reporter's right to protect confidential sources from government inquiry. We will discuss this issue in Chapter 7.

The issue here is not the right to protect your sources, but rather the ethics of protecting them. Faced with Marie Torre's dilemma, some reporters might well have concluded that providing the needed evidence was more important than shielding an executive gossip at CBS. And the *Washington Post* in the Kissinger case apparently felt that the public (and the Soviet Union?) had a right to know who was threatening a break with Russia. But the same newspaper absolutely refused to name its anonymous sources of Watergate information, a decision that most journalists would certainly endorse.

Of course, most reporters try not to promise anonymity if they suspect the source is abusing the privilege, or if they sense there may be a good reason later to reveal the name to the public or the courts. This is a good trick in itself, requiring something close to omniscience. And what do you do when you have promised anonymity, and now you feel the public interest would be better served by revealing the name? Most reporters keep their promise (and thus keep their reputation)—but not many do it happily.

THE REPORTER AS PART OF THE STORY

One day in 1957, a Pittsburgh reporter heard over the radio that the police were engaged in a shootout with a suspect trapped inside a house. The reporter telephoned the gunman, and after three calls convinced him to give himself up.[33] Question: Was this reporter acting as a journalist, or as a kind of assistant policeman?

The ethical problem of a reporter who gets involved in his or her own story is often a serious one. In the late 1960s Sanford Watzman was Washington correspondent for the *Cleveland Plain Dealer*. Watz-

man wrote a ten-part series for his paper on overcharging in defense contracts. Except for the Cleveland area, the series was ignored, so Watzman asked Ohio Senator Stephen Young to insert it into the Congressional Record. He also drafted a speech on the subject for Young, and sent a copy of the series to each member of Ohio's twenty-six-member congressional delegation. Finally, Watzman proposed corrective legislation to Wisconsin Senator William Proxmire and Ohio Representative William Minshall. Several months later "Watzman's bill" became a law.

Watzman apparently saw no conflict in the fact that he was a participant in the events he covered. "The test in my mind," he said, "is whether you do this on behalf of a special interest group or on behalf of the public." But Edward Barrett, former dean of the Columbia School of Journalism, is not so sanguine. He finds the reporter's dual role "very disturbing," though he "wouldn't put down a blanket prohibition against it." Barrett believes a reporter may be less objective under such circumstances, and therefore "has an obligation to disclose his involvement to his editors and probably to his readers."[34] As we shall see in Chapter 15, it is by no means unusual for a Washington correspondent to become a newsmaker as well as a news reporter. Very few of them ever mention it in their stories.

Reporters sometimes affect the news without intending to. After the assassination of

REPORTER TURNS STATESMAN

In October, 1962, ABC diplomatic correspondent John Scali received a telephone call from the Russian embassy in Washington. The caller asked Scali to relay to the State Department a new proposal for defusing the Cuban missile crisis, which was threatening to blow up into a third world war. For the next three days Scali was the major U.S. spokesman to the Soviet Union. It was he who met Russian official Alexander Fromin in a deserted hotel ballroom and called the new proposal "a dirty, rotten, lousy, stinking double cross." When the crisis was over, President Kennedy asked Scali to keep his own role a secret, which he did until Kennedy was assassinated the following year.[35]

President John F. Kennedy, hordes of reporters descended on the city of Dallas. Among other things, they demanded that suspect Lee Harvey Oswald be transferred from one jail to another in public, not in secret. The resulting confusion, many have charged, permitted Jack Ruby to slip by police and murder Oswald. This is a rare case. Much more common is the effect of reporters and television cameras on riots, demonstrations, and similar events. We will return to this problem when we discuss coverage of violence and crime in Chapter 16.

CONFLICT OF INTEREST

Conflict of interest results from the fact that a reporter is also a private individual. Consider, for example, the financial staff of a daily newspaper. They hear business news in advance of the general public, and are thus in a good position to make timely investments. They may also slant their coverage in order to benefit those investments, and may even be offered free stock in return for favorable news treatment. In 1963 the Securities and Exchange Commission found evidence that all three unethical measures were being practiced.

In order to curb such profiteering, the *Louisville Courier-Journal,* for example, instructs employees that they "must never use their position to obtain an advantage over the general public should a situation arise in connection with stock transactions." The *New Orleans Times-Picayune* goes even further, requiring that "no member of the financial news staff own any interest in any stocks or bonds which are listed in our tables or otherwise figure in financial page coverage." But many newspapers have no such policy, letting each reporter police his or her own investment practices. Explained John J. Cleary of the *Cleveland Plain Dealer:* "We feel that formalized rules

would not thwart an individual bent on shady practice."[36]

Not all conflict of interest cases are so obviously unethical. In 1968, network newsman Chet Huntley twice editorialized on radio against the Federal Wholesome Meat Act of 1967, which set standards of cleanliness for meat-packing plants. At the time, Huntley had a financial stake in Edmund Mayer, Inc., a New York City packing plant. The new law would have cost Mayer (and therefore Huntley) considerable sums of money. Should Huntley have revealed his financial holdings? Should he have been allowed to editorialize at all?

In 1973, syndicated film critic Rex Reed agreed to appear in an ad for the movie *Billy Jack,* which he had already reviewed favorably in his column. Reed did the ad not for money but because he was enormously enthusiastic about the movie. Yet the action raises, or could raise, suspicion in the public mind about Reed's objectivity and critical distance. Other film reviewers in New York, including Judith Crist, have been offered similar deals, but turned them down.[37]

The three television networks and all the stations they own and operate (as well as many newspapers) have a standing rule that prohibits reporters from publicly taking sides on behalf of any political candidate or party. Geraldo Rivera, a reporter for WABC in New York, was giving speeches on behalf of candidate George McGovern in 1972, and was ordered to stop. William Sheehan, director of TV news for the network, said Rivera's speech-making was "contrary to all our policies governing behavior of news personnel. There are no gray areas in such cases; they're all black and white."[38] The policy is nonpartisan. In 1970, Washington educational TV station WETA dismissed newsman William Woestendiek for potential conflict of interest after his wife was hired as press secretary for Martha Mitchell, wife of the then-Attorney General.

Must reporters take no part in political and civic activities during their off hours? And if they do take part, how can they preserve their objectivity and avoid conflicts of interest?

Because of low wages, newspaper reporters are often forced to "moonlight," taking a second job to help make ends meet. Since their major talent is writing, many reporters are hired as part-time publicity agents for local companies. Others wind up working for charities, political groups, and the like. Some even run for public office. Many metropolitan newspapers forbid all kinds of moonlighting except magazine free-lance writing. Most smaller papers have no policy at all.

The potential for conflict of interest in all these situations is obvious. But the alternative seems to be requiring that off-duty journalists do no writing.

THE JUNKET

In the space of one year, Aileen Ryan of the *Milwaukee Journal* was offered free trips to Spain (to look at olive groves), to Switzerland (a soup company plant), to Colorado (sheep ranches), and to Idaho (potato farms). She refused them all—which is the only unusual thing about her story.

A junket is a free trip arranged by a publicity agent for a reporter in the hope of reaping a complimentary article. Travel and business reporters get the most junket offers, but most journalists receive at least a couple in the average year. As PR man

---

SPORTS FREEBIES

In the course of a 1973 investigation into ticket scalping (the illegal sale of tickets above their printed price), the New York State Attorney General's office uncovered a Madison Square Garden "master freebie press list," outlining who was to get how many free tickets to Knicks (basketball) and Rangers (hockey) games. Sports editors of the three New York daily newspapers were receiving from six to a dozen free seats for every home game, with smaller numbers going to the wire services, many broadcast stations, and such super-commentators as Howard Cosell, Dick Schaap, and Bill Mazur. The three papers alone were getting nearly $65,000 a year in free tickets—not counting the gifts that might be sent to the homes of reporters at Christmastime.

While no one suggests that free tickets are enough to make very many writers slant their stories, the practice does provide access for the Garden's PR people when they are trying to drum up publicity for something less popular than a Knicks or Rangers game.

In the words of one Garden PR man, here's how it works: "I once had this bomb [unpopular] event I was pushing, and since I had been giving seats to one of the sports editors of an unnamed local paper for years, I was able to walk into his office and lay my cards on the table. I told him I really needed a favor. He had to bail me out. . . . He sat there and made me justify his putting it in the paper. But that was okay. That was my job. Once we agreed on an appropriate advance I wrote it and the paper printed it under the editor's byline. It stayed in the paper through all editions, as well. That's why make-up editors and composing room bosses have been on the freebie lists too." Presumably the story sold a few extra seats for the Garden's "bomb."

When informed of the freebies, *New York Times* Managing Editor A. M. Rosenthal ended the practice immediately. His counterpart at the *Daily News*, Mike O'Neill, said he would take it up with the paper's ethics committee.[39]

J. E. Schoonover puts it, the story that results from a junket "carries a stamp of objectivity and credibility no paid advertisement can match." [40]

Reporters deal with junkets in a number of ways. Some, like Aileen Ryan, never accept any at all. Many accept them only if the story is worth covering and cannot be covered in any other way; they try to put the generosity of the source out of their minds while writing the article. But some reporters accept just about every junket that comes their way, and as a matter of course repay their hosts by writing a favorable story.

Junketing has many close cousins—Christmas gifts, free movie tickets, dinners on the house, and so forth. A few of the better newspapers forbid employees to accept any favors of any sort from anybody. Some have open season on gifts and junkets, while most compromise somewhere in the middle.

The ethics of junketing are not as clear as most people imagine. The travel editor of a newspaper, for example, has far too low a budget to cover much of anything without some financial help from the travel industry. Very few papers can afford to send their reporters to away games unless the reporters can travel with the team at team expense. And only a purist would object to a war correspondent who hitches a ride with the army, or a film reviewer who declines to pay for movie tickets. Yet even these relatively benign sorts of favors undoubtedly raise ethical problems for reporters.

PAYING FOR THE NEWS

The media have been paying for news stories ever since the first circulation wars of the 1800s. In 1908, for example, explorers Robert E. Peary and Frederick A. Cook set out to reach the North Pole. The *New York Times* had its money on Peary; it had arranged for exclusive rights to his story. The rival *New York Herald* was backing Cook.

When both explorers claimed to have discovered the North Pole, a lively battle erupted in the New York press, each paper supporting its own man. Peary turned out to be right—but it was not that victory that made the *New York Times* the fine newspaper it is today.

It is well known in the mass media that certain types of public figures give "better answers" in interviews if there's some money in it for them. Professional athletes are often paid for broadcast interviews, and as a matter of course most guests on pregame and postgame shows receive cash or gifts. Elvis Presley among show business personalities, and Madame Nhu among jet-set politicians, have also demanded money for interviews. NBC paid $4,000 to interview former Nazi Baldur Von Schirach when he was released from Spandau Prison. And escaped Chinese violinist Ma Szu-tsung told *Life* magazine all about his experiences in Communist China—for a price.

In 1967, *Life* set a disturbing precedent by offering every U.S. astronaut $6,200 a year for the "personal" story of his involvement in the manned space program. Since the astronauts receive all their training and experience at the taxpayer's expense, there is reason to question the ethics of their selling exclusive rights to their story—and reason also to question the ethics of *Life* in making the offer. CBS made a similar offer to H. R. Haldeman in 1975, paying the convicted Watergate felon $25,000 (some say much more) for an exclusive interview.

There are at least three dangers in paying for the news. First, the less wealthy media may not be able to compete. Second, the cost will inevitably be passed on to the consumer. Third and most important, news sources may be tempted to sensationalize their stories—perhaps even invent them—in order to earn a higher price. In the late 1960s, a group of self-proclaimed revolutionaries asked CBS for $30,000 for the rights to film their invasion of Haiti. It soon became clear to the network that the

$30,000 would finance the invasion, or at least a landing on a strip of unpatrolled beach. No money, no invasion. CBS promptly backed out of the deal.[41] A congressional committee later investigated the incident. Its conclusions were highly critical of CBS, but it did not recommend any official action.

We have discussed just six ethical problems of the mass media, seven when you count the broader issue of objectivity. If space permitted, we could easily discuss dozens more. Perhaps it is an indication of the power of journalism that so many journalistic decisions and practices seem to raise ethical dilemmas.

Three points are worth emphasizing. First, none of these ethical problems is obvious or easy to solve. Second, most journalists do their best to solve them, to be as ethical as they know how. Third and most important, working journalists still receive very little help from their peers in deciding and enforcing ethical standards. If journalism is a profession, it is the only profession without a meaningful code of ethics.

Notes

[1] Gabe Pressman, Robert Lewis Shayon, and Robert Schulman, "The Responsible Reporter," *Television Quarterly*, Spring, 1964, p. 8.

[2] Canons of Journalism, in William L. Rivers and Wilbur Schramm, *Responsibility in Mass Communication*, 2nd ed. (New York: Harper and Row, 1969), p. 253.

[3] Television Code, in Rivers and Schramm, *Responsibility*, pp. 259–60.

[4] *Ibid.*, p. 268.

[5] Meyer Weinberg, *TV in America* (New York: Ballantine Books, 1962), p. 93.

[6] "The New Press Critics," *Columbia Journalism Review*, September/October, 1973, pp. 29–40.

[7] Shelley M. Fisher, "La Participation," [*MORE*], October, 1972, pp. 8–11.

[8] Richard Pollack, "The *Liebling Ledger* Comes Off the Press," [*MORE*], November, 1973, p. 4.

[9] "A Summary of Supreme Court Decisions," *New York Times*, December 24, 1974, p. 4.

[10] *Editor & Publisher*, December 1, 1973, p. 7.

[11] *New York Times*, December 1, 1972, p. 53.

[12] "Advertising: Regulation Efforts," *New York Times*, November 26, 1973, p. 51.

[13] "Advertising: N.A.R.B. Is Scored," *New York Times*, February 11, 1974, p. 57.

[14] "Advertising: Panel Hits Schick," *New York Times*, December 31, 1973, p. 29.

[15] William L. Rivers, Theodore Peterson, and Jay W. Jensen, *The Mass Media and Modern Society*, 2nd ed. (San Francisco: Rinehart Press, 1971), p. 188.

[16] Ken Macrorie, "Objectivity: Dead or Alive?" *Journalism Quarterly*, Spring, 1959, pp. 148–49.

[17] "Etiquette for Interviewers," *Columbia Journalism Review*, Winter, 1964, pp. 43–44.

[18] Gaye Tuchman, "Objectivity as Strategic Ritual: An Examination of Newsmen's Notions of Objectivity," *American Journal of Sociology*, January, 1972, pp. 660–79.

[19] William L. Rivers, "The New Confusion," *Progressive*, December, 1971, p. 26.

[20] Carl E. Lindstrom, *The Fading American Newspaper* (Gloucester, Mass.: Peter Smith, 1964), p. 63.

[21] Tom Wolfe, "The Birth of 'The New Journalism'; Eyewitness Report by Tom Wolfe," *New York*, February 14, 1972, p. 34.

[22] A. Kent MacDougall, "Clay Felker's *New York*," *Columbia Journalism Review*, March/April, 1974, pp. 36–47.

[23] Michael J. Arlen, "Notes on the New Journalism," *Atlantic Monthly*, May, 1972, p. 47.

[24] Jack Newfield, "Of Honest Men and Good Writers," *Village Voice*, May 18, 1972, p. 7.

[25] Gay Talese, *The Kingdom and the Power* (New York: Bantam Books, 1970), pp. 431–48. Ignaz Rothenberg, "Newspaper Sins Against Privacy," *Nieman Reports*, January, 1957, pp. 41–42.

[26] Pressman, Shayon, and Schulman, "The Responsible Reporter," p. 22.

[27] *Ibid.*, p. 10.

[28] *New York Times*, March 3, 1972, p. 33. *New York Times*, November 14, 1973, p. 35.

[29] Kenneth E. Wilson, "The Great Secrecy Case," *Nieman Reports*, April, 1954, pp. 3–6.

[30] John Osborne, "The Nixon Watch—Toilet Training," *New Republic*, January 1 and 8, 1972, pp. 16–17.

[31] Carl Bernstein and Bob Woodward, *All The President's Men* (New York: Simon & Schuster, 1974), pp. 189–90.

[32] Marie Torre, "Perspective on a Crisis," *AFTRA*, Spring, 1973, pp. 14–16.

[33] Curtis D. MacDougall, *Reporters Report Reporters*

(Ames, Iowa: Iowa State University Press, 1968), pp. 101–102.

34 Noel Epstein, "Capital Newsmen Often Play a Role in Creating the Events They Cover," *Wall Street Journal*, September 11, 1968, pp. 1, 23.

35 William L. Rivers, *The Opinionmakers* (Boston: Beacon Press, 1965), pp. 160–61.

36 Blaine K. McKee, "Reporters as Insiders: Financial News and Stock Buying," *Columbia Journalism Review*, Spring, 1968, p. 41.

37 *Variety*, November 21, 1973, p. 3.

38 *New York Times*, October 16, 1972, p. 75.

39 Nicholas Pileggi, "Freebies—Fringe Benefits of the Sporting Life," *New York*, June 18, 1973, pp. 53–56.

40 Frederick C. Klein, "Junket Journalism," *Wall Street Journal*, February 14, 1966, pp. 1, 12.

41 Bill Surface, "Should Reporters Buy News?" *Saturday Review*, May 13, 1967, p. 86.

Suggested Readings

ARONSON, JAMES, "On Assignment with WFBI," [*MORE*], February, 1972.

BARNETT, WILLIAM L., "Survey Shows Few Papers Are Using Ombudsmen," *Journalism Quarterly*, Spring, 1973.

DENNIS, EVERETT E. and WILLIAM L. RIVERS, *Other Voices*. San Francisco: Canfield Press, 1974.

"How Newspapers Hold Themselves Accountable," *Editor & Publisher*, December 1, 1973.

KLEIN, FREDERICK C., "Junket Journalism," *Wall Street Journal*, February 14, 1966.

MACRORIE, KEN, "Objectivity: Dead or Alive?" *Journalism Quarterly*, Spring, 1959.

MCKEE, BLAINE K., "Reporters as Insiders: Financial News and Stock Buying," *Columbia Journalism Review*, Spring, 1968.

"The New Press Critics," *Columbia Journalism Review*, September/October, 1973.

OFFER, DAVE, "The Guild Enters the Ethics Fray," *Quill*, October, 1974.

PILEGGI, NICHOLAS, "Freebies—Fringe Benefits of the Sporting Life," *New York*, June 18, 1973.

PRESSMAN, GABE, ROBERT LEWIS SHAYON, and ROBERT SCHULMAN, "The Responsible Reporter," *Television Quarterly*, Spring, 1964.

REISIG, ROBIN, "The Biggest Freeloaders Around," [*MORE*], May, 1972.

SURFACE, BILL, "Should Reporters Buy News?" *Saturday Review*, May 13, 1967.

TUCHMAN, GAYE, "Objectivity as Strategic Ritual: An Examination of Newsmen's Notions of Objectivity," *American Journal of Sociology*, January, 1972.

WILCOX, WALTER, "The Staged News Photograph and Professional Ethics," *Journalism Quarterly*, Autumn, 1961.

WOLFE, TOM, "The Birth of 'The New Journalism'; Eyewitness Report by Tom Wolfe," *New York*, February 14, 1972.

Chapter 3
Internal Control

The main qualification for owning a newspaper, magazine, or broadcast station in this country is enough money to buy it. Besides cash, mass-media owners have one other thing in common: power. By hiring and firing, rewarding and punishing, commanding and forbidding, an owner can control news content as much as he or she wishes. Most media owners use this power sparingly. A few resort to it freely; they view the media as convenient outlets for their own economic aims, personal whims, and ideological convictions.

Horace Greeley launched the *New York Tribune* in 1841. Greeley was greatly taken with the philosophy of French socialist Charles Fourier. For five years he preached Fourierism wherever he went—and so did the *Tribune*. Then he lost interest in the movement, and his paper never mentioned it again. Greeley was a teetotaler; the *Tribune* fought for prohibition. Greeley was opposed to capital punishment; the *Tribune* campaigned for its abolition. Greeley was a bitter enemy of slavery; so was the *Tribune*.

Joseph Medill bought into the *Chicago Tribune* in 1855, and by 1874 owned the majority of its stock. Medill was a firm be-

liever in simplified spelling, so for years the *Tribune* used words like "infinit," "favorit," and "telegrafed." Medill also attributed all natural phenomena to sunspots—until one day he read of the existence of microbes, which he immediately adopted as his new explanation. Soon after, a *Tribune* editor wrote that a plague in Egypt had been caused by sunspots. Medill went through the copy and crossed out each reference to sunspots, substituting "microbes" instead.

Greeley and Medill are typical of nineteenth-century publishers. They viewed their newspapers as extensions of themselves. Greeley knew that most New Yorkers are fond of alcohol—but he wasn't, so his paper wasn't either. Medill knew that most Chicagoans spell words the way the dictionary does—but he didn't, so his paper didn't either. Both men spent a great deal of time in their respective newsrooms, making sure that reporters and editors covered the news *their* way.

Today's metropolitan publishers belong to a different breed. Whether they own one newspaper or a chain of twenty, they are far more likely to be found in the "front office" than in the newsroom. They look after the financial health of the company, and let their professional employees look after the news.

Yet even today the mass-media owner retains almost absolute power to control news coverage—and sometimes that power is used.

POLICY

In 1967 David Bowers surveyed hundreds of newspaper managing editors throughout the country, asking them to assess the influence of their publishers. Bowers found that the larger the paper, the smaller the role of the publisher in day-to-day news coverage. This is presumably because metropolitan publishers are too busy with corporate affairs to waste much time looking over a reporter's shoulder. Nearly a quarter of the editors told Bowers that their publishers never entered the newsroom.[1]

Still, that leaves three-quarters of the publishers who did find their way into the newsroom from time to time. And there are plenty of ways for a publisher to influence news coverage without ever leaving the front office. Rodney Stark suggests some typical techniques. The publisher can: (1) Hire compliant reporters to start with; (2) Fire any reporter who produces articles the publisher doesn't like; (3) Demand that editors and reporters check with the front office on potentially controversial stories; (4) Personally write, edit, or rewrite copy from the newsroom; (5) Issue standing orders to downplay certain topics or people and emphasize others; and (6) Reward reporters who go along with all this by tolerating their absenteeism or alcoholism, by assigning them to "choice" stories, or by sending them on junkets.[2]

Publishers use these tactics to enforce "policy"—their notion of what the newspaper should and should not say. Though the evidence is mixed, most of the mass media appear to have some kind of owner-enforced policy. Charles Swanson, for example, asked reporters whether they agreed with the statement: "I am not aware of any definite fixed news and editorial policies of this newspaper." Only 24 percent agreed; the rest thought that such policies did in fact exist. Furthermore, 32 percent of the reporters told Swanson that they had had stories "played down or killed for 'policy' reasons," and another 16 percent were unsure.[3]

There are three reasons why a mass-media owner may wish to control news coverage, and each reason dictates its own sort of policy. Thus:

1. The economic interests of the company dictate a "business policy."

2. The individual likes and dislikes of the owner dictate a "personal policy."

3. The ideological convictions of the owner dictate a "political policy."

We will discuss each in turn.

1. Business Policy. Since modern media owners are most concerned with the financial health of their companies, it is scarcely surprising that more news is altered because of business policy than for any other reason. Even the most *laissez faire* publisher, Bowers found, is very interested in any article that might directly or indirectly affect newspaper revenue. Most such articles have to do with advertisers or potential advertisers. The daughter of a department store owner is charged with drunk driving—should the newspaper report it? A new shopping center would like its grand opening covered on television in exchange for a healthy spot advertising contract—should the station accept? A national magazine is asked to print a twelve-page "news" supplement written by a corporation PR department—is it worth the money? Such decisions are made every day, and usually by the owner or publisher.

Business policy is not a recent invention. In 1911 *Collier's* magazine ran an anonymous article, "The Confessions of a Managing Editor," in which the author unburdened his conscience by revealing the tight policy control of his boss. He told how caustic movie reviews were abandoned because they displeased a theater owner who advertised regularly; a harmless department store fire was reported so as to imply that the stock had been damaged, permitting the store to announce a "fire sale" in the next day's paper; a story on a local electric power monopoly was killed because the chairman of the power company was a major advertiser.[4] If this 1911 article were reprinted in 1976, few informed readers would sense any incongruity—the same abuses are still taking place.

When business policy doesn't concern advertisers, it usually involves investors. In the 1964 presidential campaign, for example, the fiercely pro-Goldwater *Manchester* (N.H.) *Union-Leader* editorially rebuked its own candidate for criticizing Teamster boss James Hoffa, who was subsequently jailed for jury tampering. The Teamsters, it seems, had a $2,000,000 investment in the paper, and Hoffa was to be treated nicely. Similarly, when Joseph Kennedy put $500,000 into the financially ailing *Boston Post,* the paper prudently switched its editorial endorsement to his son John.[5]

2. Personal Policy. Like everyone else, mass-media owners have friends, and like everyone else they do what they can to help their friends. In the case of the media, this means playing up stories that the friends are proud of (like a society wedding), and playing down or killing stories that the friends find embarrassing (like a divorce or an arrest). The friends of mass-media owners, by the way, tend to be leaders of the local business community. They are often in the news, so the owners have plenty of chances to do them favors.

Media owners are also subject to their own personal whims—and the privilege of indulging them. Walter Annenberg is a good example. Annenberg is owner of Triangle Publications, which publishes *TV Guide;* until 1970 he also owned the *Philadelphia Inquirer* and *News.* In addition, Annenberg is a man with strong likes and dislikes.

Veterans of the *Inquirer* newsroom recall Annenberg's "shit list," a collection of names never to be printed in the paper. Columnist Rose DeWolf once did an article on the Philadelphia-Baltimore Stock Exchange, quoting its president, Elkins Wetherkill, at length. Told that Wetherkill was on the list, she had to call him back and ask that all his quotes be attributed to an Exchange vice president. The president of the University of Pennsylvania, Gaylord P. Harnwell, was also on Annenberg's list. Each year Harnwell awarded the prestigious Wharton School gold medal to a distinguished alumnus; each year the *Inquirer* ascribed the presentation to an unnamed "university official." Other names banned from all Annenberg publications included Imogene Coca, Zsa Zsa Gabor, and Dinah Shore—a constant challenge for the staff of *TV Guide.* Even the Philadelphia 76ers basketball team was in Annenberg's bad graces. He limited the team to two paragraphs after each win, one paragraph after each loss.[6]

The personal predilections of a publisher usually do the reader more harm than good, but sometimes the tables are turned. The late William F. Knowland, former publisher of the *Oakland* (Calif.) *Tribune,* was a strong conservationist. As a result, the *Tribune*—in many ways a mediocre newspaper—was well ahead of other California papers in its coverage of environmental issues. Neighboring publishers were reluctant to mention corporate polluters by name; the *Tribune* seldom hesitated.

3. Political Policy. Many nineteenth-century publishers were ideologues; they purchased newspapers largely in order to advance a particular political or social philosophy. Most modern publishers, by contrast, are strictly business-oriented; they purchase newspapers in order to make money, and they seldom mount the soapbox.

A media owner who tries to change a reporter's copy too often is likely to face a newsroom revolution. There is a safer way to exercise policy influence—by leaving out a customary syndicated feature when it conflicts with the owner's ideological biases. This is probably the most common instance of political policy at work.

In 1974, for example, editor Charles Betts of the *Hartford Times* decided not to carry a particular "Doonesbury" cartoon strip because he felt it was an attempt to make fun of an embattled President Nixon and "considered it in extremely bad taste." [7]

Because of its political content, "Doonesbury" is often skipped for a day or two by publishers who disagree. So are many syndicated political columnists, from satirist Art Buchwald to muckraker Jack Anderson. On television, such censorship is even more common. For years, many Southern broadcasters refused to carry network documentaries on the civil rights movement. And in 1973 an episode of "Maude" in which abortion was sympathetically treated was passed over by dozens of disapproving station owners throughout the country.

There are exceptions, of course. During the 1968 Democratic presidential primary in Indiana, publisher Eugene Pulliam of the *Indianapolis Star* and *News* was often seen in the newsroom. The primary was a three-way race between Governor Roger D. Branigin (standing in for Lyndon Johnson), Robert Kennedy, and Eugene McCarthy. Pulliam supported Branigin.

From March 28 to May 7, 1968, Branigin received 1,048 column inches in the *Star* and *News*. Kennedy got 712 inches, and McCarthy 584 inches. Kennedy, the favorite, was on the front page of the two papers 17 times; Branigin was front-paged a total of 31 times. Shortly before the primary, syndicated columnist Joseph Kraft wrote a piece praising Kennedy. The *Star* ran it with the following editor's note: "This article by Joseph Kraft, long-time columnist friend of the Kennedy family, ridiculing Indiana, is typical of the propaganda being turned out by pro-Kennedy writers to push the candidacy of Senator Robert F. Kennedy." [8]

Political policy is not restricted to Democrats, or to newspapers. In 1968 Harold F. Gross, owner of WJIM-TV in Lansing, Michigan, ordered a total blackout on Democratic congressional candidate James A. Harrison. A reporter for the station told Harrison that he had been instructed, "I don't want to see that son-of-a-bitch Harrison on again for the rest of the campaign." The *Detroit Free Press* unearthed a number of similar abuses by Gross, and outraged Lansing citizens put pressure on the FCC to investigate the case. Gross's license renewal was held up pending the investigation. [9]

The publisher of the *Greensburg* (Pa.) *Tribune-Review* is Richard Mellon Scaife, a strong anti-communist. Shortly after the 1973 coup against Marxist President Salvadore Allende of Chile, the wire services moved a story quoting two evacuated U.S. tourists describing the execution of hundreds of Allende supporters. Managing editor Tom Aikens put the story on the front page of the *Tribune-Review*, but Scaife ordered it killed for the final edition. Why? He didn't like Allende's politics, and didn't want to damage the reputation of Allende's successors in the minds of Greensburg readers. [10]

But this sort of overt political bias is rare today, especially on major national and international issues. In the 1972 election, more than 70 percent of U.S. daily newspapers endorsed Nixon on their editorial page; 5

Newsmagazines are renowned for committee editing and the mammoth influence of policy on content. Much of this reputation stems from the record of *Time* magazine under the ownership of Henry R. Luce. In *Luce, His Time, Life, and Fortune,* author John Kobler paints the following picture of *Time's* coverage of Vietnam in the early 1960s:

> Operating in the area of national and foreign affairs like a state within a state, *Time* was seldom content to print news as its correspondents filed it from the scene. Such stories had to be pondered at New York headquarters in the light of Lucean policy decisions. There would be weighty conferences and staff luncheons resembling a convocation of the National Security Council by the President of the United States. Frequently, editors and executives would take quick fact-finding trips like Congressmen. . . . During a visit home in 1963 *Time's* Hong Kong correspondent, Stanley Karnow, was repeatedly asked by the big brass, "What's the alternative to Diem?" They seemed to feel that they ought not to criticize the beleaguered ruler unless they could propose a successor. *Time* should confine itself to reporting the war, said Karnow, instead of trying to make policy. He cut no ice.[11]

Luce was an ardent opponent of Red China. In an article on the Chinese economy, Karnow wrote that its failures resulted from "successive years of mismanagement, confusion, natural calamities and population pressures—and perhaps the sheer unwieldiness of China itself." Luce noted in the margin of the manuscript: "Too many explanations. The simple answer is Communism." Where Karnow commented that China had "exaggerated" its claims to economic progress, Luce changed the word to "lied." For "official statements," Luce substituted "official lies."

The Luce bias affected the reporting of domestic affairs as well. The week before Roosevelt's easy second win in 1936, an editor asked Luce why *Time* didn't tell its readers that Roosevelt was winning. Luce answered: "Because it might help him win." [12]

---

percent supported McGovern; and the rest made no endorsement. Yet news coverage of the campaign was hardly pro-Nixon—at least not in the amount of coverage given to each candidate. In fact, McGovern got slightly more newspaper space and broadcast time than the total allotted to Nixon himself plus the subordinates who did much of his campaigning for him.[13] On the other hand, the media almost ignored Watergate before the election (except for the *Washington Post* and CBS).[14] Was this an instance of political policy at work, or was it simply an inability to believe that the White House corruption was real? Probably the latter.

We have detailed three ways that mass-media owners control the news—business policy, personal policy, and political policy. The first is by far the most common. The third is probably the most dangerous. All three are important forms of media control.

SOCIAL CONTROL

In 1967, Lewis Donohew studied coverage of the Medicare issue in seventeen Kentucky daily newspapers. He related coverage to three factors: community need for Medicare, community attitudes toward Medicare, and publisher attitudes toward Medicare. His findings were surprising. The correlation between the attitude of the publisher and the kind of coverage was very high (.73), while the other two factors did not correlate significantly with coverage. In other words, newspapers whose publishers favored Medicare gave the issue favorable treatment and plenty of it—regardless of community attitudes or community needs. Papers with publishers opposed to Medicare, on the other hand, accorded it much less space and handled it much more critically.[15]

The important point here is that Donohew found almost no evidence of overt publisher influence on Medicare coverage. Apparently the Kentucky reporters and editors knew without being told what sort of news play would be most pleasing to their boss. And, without any direct orders, they provided it.

In a landmark essay on "Social Control in the Newsroom," written in 1955, sociologist Warren Breed reached essentially the same conclusion. Newspaper reporters, Breed argued, learn "by osmosis" which stories involve policy and how they should be handled. It is seldom necessary—and considered rather gauche—for an owner to issue an explicit policy manifesto.[16]

This view is supported by a disturbing experiment conducted on journalism students in 1964. The students were instructed to write news articles (based on fact sheets) for imaginary newspapers. They were told in advance what the editorial policy of "their paper" was toward that particular issue. In the overwhelming majority of cases, the students voluntarily biased their article in the direction of the paper's policy. Students whose own beliefs were farthest from policy made the greatest effort to go along. Those who agreed with the newspaper policy were actually more likely to be fair to the anti-policy view than those who were themselves anti-policy. On the other hand, business students with no training in journalism tended to be much less influenced by the policies of their imaginary publishers.[17]

The more you think about this study the more frightening it is. These were journalism students; today many of them are probably working journalists. Without the slightest hesitation, and largely without noticing what they were doing, they slanted the news the way they thought their employer wanted it slanted. If most reporters are like the subjects in this experiment, then there is really no need for owners to be crass about policy. All they have to do is let it be known how they like their news—and that's how they'll get it.

UNANIMITY

Suppose there are two independent newspapers in a city, and both publishers have a lot to say about how the news is covered. This is a bad enough situation even if the publishers are enemies. But suppose they're friends, suppose they play tennis together every weekend at the club, suppose they agree on almost every issue. Then the situation becomes much more dangerous.

It is a fact of life that mass-media owners are businessmen. Most of the important ones are, by definition, big businessmen. They are overwhelmingly white, upper-middle-class, urban males. Whether high-level corporate executives or self-made entrepreneurs, they inevitably share many of the same attitudes and opinions. To the extent that they influence news coverage, they are likely to influence it in the same direction.

The influence of policy, in other words, may be a consistent bias in the media—not just in one newspaper here and another TV station there, but in nearly every newspaper and nearly every TV station everywhere. This phenomenon has sometimes been called "country club journalism."

The arena in which this battle is customarily fought is politics. Many observers have charged that, while the country itself contains more Democrats than Republicans, the mass media are overwhelmingly Republican. In the 1952 presidential campaign, for example, 67 percent of the nation's newspapers (with 80 percent of the circulation) supported Eisenhower. Only 15 percent of the papers (with 11 percent of the circulation) endorsed Stevenson.[18] The split in the popular vote, of course, was much closer.

The newspapers showed their bias in four ways, aside from the endorsements:

1. They gave larger headlines to the favored candidate.

2. They ran more lead stories on the favored candidate.

3. They gave more prominent position to articles on the favored candidate.

4. They printed more quotations from the favored candidate, and more remarks praising him.

Though the Democratic newspapers were just as biased in 1952 as the Republican ones, most of the papers were Republican.

Political reporting has improved since 1952. A study of fifteen leading newspapers in 1960 and 1964, for example, revealed that the papers gave almost equal space to the Democratic and Republican presidential candidates. The Democrats got slightly more column inches, while the Republicans received slightly better placement.[19] The furor that followed the 1968 Indianapolis incident (see Page 99) indicates how unacceptable slanted political coverage is to today's journalists—at least during hot national campaigns.

Nevertheless, the similarity of most mass-media owners is cause for worry. Though coverage of national politics has improved, most media owners are still conservatives—and their conservatism is inevitably reflected in the media they own. Media owners are remarkably alike in viewpoint. When they influence news coverage through policy—whether business, personal, or political—that influence is likely to be close to unanimous.

It is hard to find two mass-media owners today as different from each other as, say, Horace Greeley and Joseph Medill. It is just as hard to find two owners as intimately involved in the day-to-day production of news. Modern publishers and broadcasters intervene only occasionally—but when they

do, their policy is predictably and conventionally that of Big Business.

Owners are potentially the most powerful individuals in the mass media, but most use their power sparingly. The vast majority of the important day-to-day news decisions are made by the staff—by reporters and editors. Certain positions within media bureaucracies inevitably involve tremendous influence over news content. Many of these are relatively low-level positions, in terms of status and salary. Their occupants are often unaware of their own power.

GATEKEEPERS

Every piece of news passes through many hands between the original source and the final consumer. A corporation, say, mails a press release to a local newspaper. A *mail clerk* opens the envelope, reads the release, and decides that it should go to the financial department. An *assistant financial editor* reads it and judges that it is worth the attention of the *financial editor*. The financial editor assigns the piece to a *reporter,* who goes out in search of more information. The reporter writes the story and submits it to an *assistant city editor,* who decides that it needs more flair, and therefore turns it over to a *rewrite specialist.* The revised article is checked over by the *night editor.* He or she makes a few changes, then gives the article to a *copy editor,* who corrects the grammar, writes a headline, and sends the manuscript to the *typesetter.* A *photographer,* meanwhile, is out taking a picture to accompany the article, and the *layout editor* is busy dummying it into the newspaper. Eventually the story is okayed by the *city editor* and the *managing editor.* Then it is printed.

In this simplified example, thirteen people got a crack at a single corporate release. Most of them had a chance to change the content of the article in significant ways; at least six of them could have ruled it out of the paper entirely.

Communications researchers refer to these thirteen individuals as "gatekeepers." A gatekeeper is any person in the newsgathering process with authority to make decisions affecting the flow of information to the public. The image is precisely that of a turnstile gatekeeper at a sporting event, who examines the qualifications of the people in line, and decides whether or not to let them in. The difference is that what gets let in or left out is not a person, but a piece of news.

Turnstile gatekeepers have very little room for flexibility. They are under orders to let in anyone with a ticket, and no one without a ticket. Occasionally mass-media gatekeepers are in the same position—the owner decides how a story is to be handled and an editor mechanically does the job. Most of the time, however, the owner remains neutral, so the editorial gatekeepers are left to make the decision. San Francisco journalist Lynn Ludlow puts it this way:

> On the surface the newspaper is organized along strict lines of authority and responsibility. The reporter is responsible to the city editor, who works under the policies of the managing editor, editor and publisher, etc. The insider knows, however, that . . . the man who actually does the work is actually setting his own strategy, tactics and policy a good deal of the time.[20]

We turn now to a few specific examples of mass-media gatekeepers.

THE TELEGRAPH EDITOR

Just about all state, national, and international news reaches the mass media via teletype, sent out by the Associated Press, United Press International, and other wire services. The job of the telegraph editor is to sort through this news and decide what to use.

It's an incredible job. A large metropolitan newspaper may subscribe to as many as 25 wires (including specialized ones like business news and weather). Out of maybe 2,500 separate news items a day, the metro telegraph editor must pick out 200 or so for use in the paper. Working pretty much alone, the telegraph editor must consider questions like: Did we have something about this in the paper yesterday? Is our competition using anything on it? Are we likely to get a better story later in the day, in time for our deadline? Is the story too narrow or technical to interest our readers? Does it need checking for a local angle? Are more important stories likely to come in later? Even if the story is good, do I have room for it?

On the basis of the answers to these questions, the telegraph editor either edits the wire copy for publication or tosses it into a giant wastebasket that waits beside his or her desk. Throughout the day, this editor is busy comparing, figuring, squeezing, and discarding—in short, gatekeeping.

In 1949 researcher David Manning White spent a week with the telegraph editor of a small Midwestern daily newspaper. The editor received a total of 11,910 column inches of copy from three wire services. He was able to use only 1,297 column inches, less than 11 percent. Exactly 1,333 stories were not used. Just under half of them, White reported, were discarded solely because of lack of space. Many of the rest were eliminated because the editor chose to print the same item from another wire service.[21]

Seventeen years later, in 1966, Paul Snider duplicated the White study, using the same telegraph editor. In the intervening time the paper had merged with its opposition and cut down to one wire service. (This is unusual; most newspapers get more wire copy than ever before.) As a result, the editor had only 1,971 column inches available during a five-day period. That was more than enough —he used only 631 inches, less than a third of the total.[22]

Telegraph editors have no universal standards or criteria to apply in deciding which wire stories to use. They invent their own—and each editor makes a different choice. Consider a 1959 study of wire copy in six small Michigan newspapers.[23] During a typical week, 764 wire stories appeared in at least one of the six papers. Only eight stories appeared in all six, and only four were on the front pages of all six. The total number of wire articles used ranged from 122 to 385; the number on the front page ranged from 45 to 105. One newspaper printed almost no international stories; another ran nearly as many foreign datelines as domestic ones. Every newspaper included at least a few articles that none of the other five bothered with.

Clearly, then, the telegraph editor is a gatekeeper of tremendous importance. Working under deadline pressure with little time for careful thought, each telegraph editor determines almost entirely what that paper will publish about the world beyond its own city limits.

OTHER MEDIA GATEKEEPERS

The telegraph editor is only one of dozens of mass-media gatekeepers. An entire book could be filled with gatekeeper studies of the various media. In the pages that follow we will discuss only a few of the more important or less obvious examples.

1. The Wire-Service Editor. Telegraph editors have plenty of news to choose from—but there is lots more they never see. Only a fraction of the stories prepared by AP and UPI reporters are put on the national wire each day. Every article must pass through a succession of local and regional wire-service editors, who decide whether it is important enough to teletype. Any one of these editors can kill the story.

In 1948 the Mississippi state legislature approved the creation of the Mississippi Bureau of Investigation, a special police force with wide discretionary powers. The AP and UPI Southern regional editors decided it was a minor story, so they kept it off the national wires. Press critic A. J. Liebling read about it in a New Orleans newspaper, and disagreed. Liebling's *New Yorker* articles on the M.B.I. started a national controversy. Only then did the wire services carry the story outside the South.[24]

2. The Reporter. No matter how many gatekeepers get their hands on a news item before it reaches the public, the one who influences that item most is the reporter. The reporter decides whom to interview and what questions to ask, where and how to cover an event, which facts to include and which to leave out. Editors can kill the story or cut it to ribbons, but only occasionally do they know enough to add or correct anything. The way a reporter sees an event is almost certain to be the way that event is described by his or her newspaper, magazine, or broadcast station.

But no two reporters see the same event in the same way. Most journalists try hard for objectivity, but they know before they start that they are doomed to failure. It is a fundamental law of psychology that people perceive the same stimulus in different ways, depending on their own attitudes, interests, and biases. If you support a political candidate, your estimate of the crowd at the rally will be larger than the estimates of opponents. If you disapprove of a war, you will see war crimes in actions that less critical observers view as unfortunate accidents. If you distrust college students, you will miss the evidence of legitimate grievances behind campus rebellions. Conscientious reporters do what they can to control these influences—but inevitably their opinions and feelings affect what they write.

3. The Headline Writer. The people who write headlines for newspaper articles tend to be hurried, harried, and often careless. Yet many readers never get further than the headline.

Even those readers who plow through an

entire article are greatly influenced by its headline. In 1953, Percy Tannenbaum planted a story about an imaginary murder trial in the *Daily Iowan,* a student newspaper. Tannenbaum used three different headlines. "Admits Ownership of Frat Murder Weapon" was intended to imply that the defendant was guilty. "Many Had Access to Frat Murder Weapon" seemed to imply innocence. And "Approach Final Stage in Frat Murder Trial" was neutral. Each reader saw only one headline, followed by the identical article in every case.

Tannenbaum then asked a sample of students whether they thought the defendant was guilty or innocent. This was their response:

	Guilty	Inno-cent	No Opinion	Total
Guilty headline	44	20	65	129
Innocent headline	29	38	65	132
Neutral headline	35	25	77	137

In all three groups, more people chose the "no opinion" answer than either of the other two. However, among the three groups, the "innocent headline" group was most inclined to feel that the defendant was innocent. And the "guilty headline" group was most inclined to feel he was guilty. Tannenbaum concluded that the headline "has a most definite effect on the interpretation of a story." He added: "The headline writer who recognizes the potentialities of the headline, and who is aware of the reading habits of the public, is certainly in a position to exert a significant influence upon the opinions of his audience." [25]

4. The Assignment Editor. Every mass medium has someone whose job it is to tell the reporters what stories to cover. Whatever the title, the person who makes the assignments is an important gatekeeper. Nothing gets covered unless the assignment editor asks someone to cover it.

William Whitworth offers this description of assignment editor Robert Northshield's role in preparing for the evening NBC network newscast:

> Assignments have been made the day before, by Northshield or by the show's producer, Lester Crystal. Correspondents are at work in other cities and other countries, and are in touch with Northshield and Crystal off and on all day. . . .
>
> By noon, Northshield has seen some film, discussed story ideas with his producer and with the Washington staff, spoken to a correspondent or two, and read as much wire copy as possible. These chores will occupy him throughout the day. . . . Northshield will begin trying to make a rundown—a list of the stories that will be used on the program, with an estimate of the time to be allotted to each—between three-thirty and four. Perhaps six or eight of these stories will be filmed or taped reports. . . . The twenty or so other stories will be briefer. . . . Shortly before five, Crystal holds a story conference with the writers and gives them their assignments. Each man's is likely to be brief—anywhere from thirty seconds to three minutes of copy. [26]

Assignment editors in network television are seasoned professionals. In radio and local TV, however, they are likely to be comparative newcomers. They receive much lower pay than on-the-air reporters, yet they—not the reporters—determine which stories are to be covered.

5. The Film Editor. The television film editor (or the radio tape editor) takes twenty minutes of an interview or press conference and cuts it down to a minute or less. The film editor's job is to pick the most important, pithy, memorable, and interesting statements of the news source—without distorting the meaning. This is an extremely difficult and vital task. Often it is performed by a trainee fresh out of college.

6. Other Media. When the editors of a small newspaper are unsure how to report a national story, they may well check to see what the big city papers did with it. When

Next to the headline, the lead of a news story—the first paragraph or two—is by far the most important part. Few readers get any further. The following excerpts all refer to the march on the Pentagon in October, 1967. Regardless of the articles that followed, these passages would create very different impressions of that event.

1. *Chicago Tribune,* October 22, 1967, page 1:

HURL BACK PENTAGON MOB

An estimated 4,000 to 5,000 anti-war demonstrators settled down in front of the Pentagon this evening, apparently planning to spend the night.

They were all that were left of an estimated 30,000 to 35,000 protestors who earlier in the day stormed the Pentagon and were hurled back by armed soldiers and club swinging United States marshals. They came close to breaking the doors they considered a symbol of militarism.

2. *Washington Post,* October 22, 1967, page 1:

55,000 RALLY AGAINST WAR;
GIs REPEL PENTAGON CHARGE

More than 55,000 persons demonstrated here against the war in Vietnam yesterday in what started out as a peaceful, youthful rally but erupted into violence at the Pentagon late in the day.

At one point, a surging band of about 20 demonstrators rushed into the Pentagon, only to be thrown out by armed troops.

Dozens of youthful demonstrators were arrested during two brief but angry melees at the Pentagon's Mall Entrance. Several thousand demonstrators surged across boundaries that the Government had prescribed.

3. *Time* magazine, October 27, 1967, page 23:

THE BANNERS OF DISSENT

[Starts with a physical and historical sketch of the Pentagon.] Against that physically and functionally immovable object last week surged a self-proclaimed irresistible force of 35,000 ranting, chanting protestors who are immutably opposed to the U.S. commitment in Vietnam. By the time the demonstration had ended, more than 425 irresistibles had been arrested, 13 more had been injured, and the Pentagon had remained immobile. Within the tide of dissenters swarmed all the elements of American dissent in 1967: hard-eyed revolutionaries and skylarking hippies; ersatz motorcycle gangs and all-too-real college professors; housewives, ministers, and authors; Black Nationalists in African garb—but no real African nationalists; nonviolent pacifists and nonpacific advocates of violence—some of them anti-anti-warriors and American Nazis spoiling for a fight.

4. *London Times,* October 23, 1967, p. 4.

BESIEGE THE PENTAGON

The anti-war demonstration continued outside the Pentagon and elsewhere today after a night of disorder and some violence. About 200 demonstrators marched on the White House this morning, but a strong police guard kept them at a distance.

The vast Defense Department building, which stands on 583 acres of lawn and car parks, was penetrated briefly yesterday by a few dozen youngsters. United States marshals, with clubs swinging, quickly turned their attack into a retreat.

a telegraph editor is swamped with copy, he or she looks to see what's on the wire-service list of the day's most important stories. When a radio disc jockey sits down to prepare the station's hourly five-minute news report, local stories are quietly borrowed from the front page of the nearest newspaper. In these and other ways, the larger and more established news media serve as gatekeepers of a sort for the smaller and less established ones.

There are many other gatekeepers in the mass media—from the writer who handles photo captions to the TV camera operator who decides where to point the lens, from the librarian who supplies background for stories to the rewrite specialist who adds sparkle to dreary copy. All of them have two things in common. First, they exercise a tremendous influence over the flow of news to the public. And second, they are largely unaware of their power. From time to time a publisher consciously sets policy. Working journalists unconsciously set policy minute by minute.

UNANIMITY AGAIN

The dangerous thing about mass-media owners is that they are all so much alike. Can the same charge be leveled against media gatekeepers? At least one observer, former Vice President Spiro Agnew, thinks it can:

> A small group of men, numbering perhaps no more than a dozen "anchormen," commentators and executive producers, settle upon the 20 minutes or so of film and commentary that is to reach the public. . . .
>
> We do know that, to a man, these commentators and producers live and work in the geographical and intellectual confines of Washington, D.C., or New York City—the latter of which James Reston terms the "most unrepresentative community in the entire United States." . . . We can deduce that these men thus read the same newspapers, and draw their

political and social views from the same sources. . . .

> The upshot of all this controversy is that a narrow and distorted picture of America often emerges from the televised news. . . .[27]

Though Agnew's comments here concentrated on television, he made it clear elsewhere that he feels the same way about most newspaper reporters. Media owners, we have charged, tend to be conservatives. Working journalists, Agnew replies, tend to be liberals. Both statements are overgeneralizations, but both are more true than false.

In July, 1972, the executive board of the American Newspaper Guild endorsed George McGovern for President, the first time the union leadership had ever endorsed a political candidate. Many politicians (and journalists) were furious about the endorsement, saying it compromised the integrity and credibility of reporters. Senator Barry Goldwater convincingly identified the move as evidence of "a built-in bias" in the media "in favor of radical Democrats."[28]

Agnew and Goldwater were not alone in their views. When George Romney was running for the Republican presidential nomination in 1968, many of the country's most influential political reporters refused to take his candidacy seriously. David S. Broder comments: "I often thought . . . as I saw Romney during his Presidential campaign, surrounded by our circle—men a generation younger than he, many of us with cigarettes in our mouths, drinks in our hands, and cynicism in our hearts—that he must have felt as helpless with us as I would feel if my fate or future as a journalist were being decided by a committee of Romney's colleagues among the elders of the Mormon Church."[29] Broder offers this description of the leading political reporters in Washington:

> Not only is the group small, but its characteristics make it a highly atypical group of Americans. Its members are all Easterners, by residence if not by birth. They are all college

graduates. They all enjoy, despite the low-paying reputation of newspapers, incomes well over the national median. Not one of them is a Negro. Only two are women. More of them vote Democratic and fewer of them regularly attend church, I would guess, than in a random sample of the population. None is under 30 and few, except for the columnists, are over 45. . . . I think I have said enough to indicate that they—or we, I should say—represent a narrow and rather peculiar slice of this society.[30]

In his book *The Boys on the Bus,* author Timothy Crouse offers numerous examples of the press corps' fundamental dislike for Nixon and identification with McGovern during the 1972 campaign.[31] Yet when McGovern's running-mate, Thomas Eagleton, was found to have a history of mental disorder, reporters were able to sweep aside their emotional and ideological ties. They wrote the story with enough accuracy and enthusiasm that it may well have played a role in Nixon's large victory.

That is the crucial difference between the bias of reporters and the bias of media owners. Working journalists are presumably trained to overcome their biases and present as balanced and objective a picture of the news as possible. And working journalists are indiscriminately enthusiastic about a big story, no matter whom it helps or hurts. Most mass-media owners have no such training, and no such enthusiasm. When publishers walk into their newsrooms, they generally do so for the express purpose of coloring the news to suit their taste. The gatekeepers who belong in that newsroom, on the other hand, are striving—with some success—not to color the news at all.

Fifty years ago political scientist Curtice N. Hitchcock wrote a review of Upton Sinclair's newspaper critique, *The Brass Check.* In his review, Hitchcock made the following statement:

Granted an adequate standard of professional journalism—a body of highly trained men com-petent to weigh news in terms of social significance and to present it adequately—the problem of control becomes one of turning the control over to them.[32]

The journalism profession has a long way to go yet before it satisfies Hitchcock's premise. But at least it is moving in that direction.

In the final analysis, the difference between owners and gatekeepers is this: Owners set policy (occasionally) in order to achieve their own business, personal, and political goals. Gatekeepers influence the news (constantly) despite their honest efforts to remain objective.

Notes

[1] David R. Bowers, "A Report on Activity by Publishers in Directing Newsroom Decisions," *Journalism Quarterly,* Spring, 1967, pp. 44–49.

[2] Rodney W. Stark, "Policy and the Pros: An Organizational Analysis of a Metropolitan Newspaper," *Berkeley Journal of Sociology,* Spring, 1962, pp. 14–15, 26.

[3] Charles E. Swanson, "Midcity Daily: News Staff and Control," *Journalism Quarterly,* March, 1949, p. 25.

[4] "Confessions of a Managing Editor," *Collier's,* October 28, 1911, p. 19.

[5] Ben H. Bagdikian, "News as a Byproduct," *Columbia Journalism Review,* Spring, 1967, p. 9.

[6] Edward W. Barrett, "Books" (Review of *Annenberg,* Gaeton Fonzi), *Columbia Journalism Review,* Spring, 1970, p. 56.

[7] United Press International (file #276A), Hartford, Conn., March 2, 1974.

[8] Jules Witcover, "The Indiana Primary and the Indianapolis Newspapers—A Report in Detail," *Columbia Journalism Review,* Summer, 1968, pp. 12–16.

[9] David Anderson, "Blackout in Lansing," *Columbia Journalism Review,* March/April, 1974, pp. 27–28.

[10] Patrick Carroll, "Mutiny in Greensburg," *Columbia Journalism Review,* January/February, 1974, pp. 41–42.

[11] John Kobler, *Luce, His Time, Life, and Fortune* (Garden City, N.Y.: Doubleday & Co., 1968), pp. 6–7.

[12] *Ibid.,* pp. 151, 177.

13 Robert G. Meadow, "Cross-Media Comparison of Coverage of the 1972 Presidential Campaign," *Journalism Quarterly,* Autumn, 1973, pp. 482–88.

14 James McCartney, "The Washington 'Post' and Watergate: How Two Davids Slew Goliath," *Columbia Journalism Review,* July/August, 1973, p. 22.

15 Lewis Donohew, "Newspaper Gatekeepers and Forces in the News Channel," *Public Opinion Quarterly,* Spring, 1967, pp. 62–66.

16 Warren Breed, "Social Control in the News Room," in *Mass Communications,* ed. Wilbur Schramm (Urbana, Ill.: University of Illinois Press, 1960), p. 182.

17 Jean S. Kerrick, "Balance and the Writer's Attitude in News Stories and Editorials," *Journalism Quarterly,* Spring, 1964, pp. 207–15.

18 Malcolm W. Klein and Nathan Maccoby, "Newspaper Objectivity in the 1952 Campaign," *Journalism Quarterly,* Summer, 1954, p. 285.

19 Guido H. Stempel, III, "The Prestige Press in Two Presidential Elections," *Journalism Quarterly,* Winter, 1965, p. 21.

20 Personal communication from Lynn Ludlow of the *San Francisco Examiner* to David M. Rubin, August, 1969.

21 David Manning White, "The 'Gate Keeper': A Case Study in the Selection of News," *Journalism Quarterly,* Autumn, 1950, p. 387.

22 Paul B. Snider, " 'Mr. Gates' Revisited: A 1966 Version of the 1949 Case Study," *Journalism Quarterly,* Autumn, 1967, p. 423.

23 Guido H. Stempel, III, "Uniformity of Wire Content of Six Michigan Dailies," *Journalism Quarterly,* Winter, 1959, p. 48.

24 A. J. Liebling, *The Press* (New York: Ballantine Books, 1961), pp. 126–43.

25 Percy H. Tannenbaum, "The Effect of Headlines on the Interpretation of News Stories," *Journalism Quarterly,* Spring, 1953, pp. 189–97.

26 William Whitworth, "An Accident of Casting," *New Yorker,* August 3, 1968, pp. 48–50.

27 Address of Vice President Spiro T. Agnew before the Midwest Regional Republican Committee, Des Moines, Iowa, November 13, 1969.

28 "Goldwater Scores Media on Guild's Endorsement," *New York Times,* July 20, 1972, p. 16.

29 David S. Broder, "Views of the Press: Political Reporters in Presidential Politics," *Washington Monthly,* February, 1969, p. 28.

30 *Ibid.,* p. 28.

31 Timothy Crouse, *The Boys on the Bus* (New York: Random House, 1972).

32 Curtice N. Hitchcock, "The Brass Check: A Study of American Journalism: By Upton Sinclair," *Journal of Political Economy,* April, 1921, pp. 343–44.

Suggested Readings

ANDERSON, DAVID, "Blackout in Lansing," *Columbia Journalism Review,* March/April, 1974.

BOWERS, DAVID R., "A Report on Activity by Publishers in Directing Newsroom Decisions," *Journalism Quarterly,* Spring, 1967.

BREED, WARREN, "Social Control in the News Room," reprinted in Wilbur Schramm, ed., *Mass Communications.* Urbana, Ill.: University of Illinois Press, 1960.

CARROLL, PATRICK, "Mutiny in Greensburg," *Columbia Journalism Review,* January/February, 1974.

FLEGEL, RUTH, and STEVE CHAFFEE, "Influences of Editors, Readers, and Personal Opinions on Reporters," *Journalism Quarterly,* Winter, 1971.

FONZI, GAETON, *Annenberg.* New York: Weybright and Talley, Inc., 1970.

KOBLER, JOHN, *Luce, His Time, Life and Fortune.* New York: Doubleday & Co., Inc., 1968.

STARK, RODNEY W., "Policy and the Pros: An Organizational Analysis of a Metropolitan Newspaper," *Berkeley Journal of Sociology,* Spring, 1962.

WHITE, DAVID MANNING, "The 'Gate Keeper': A Case Study in the Selection of News," *Journalism Quarterly,* Fall, 1950.

WITCOVER, JULES, "The Indiana Primary and the Indianapolis Newspapers—A Report in Detail," *Columbia Journalism Review,* Summer, 1968.

Chapter 4
Monopoly Control

The concept of freedom of the press is based on the conviction that truth somehow emerges from the conflict of many voices. But freedom can become a dangerous luxury when the number of voices falls to just two or three. The growth of giant media monopolies—networks, chains, conglomerates, and the like—has drastically reduced the diversity of media voices. This concentration of power in the hands of a few media "barons" represents a major threat to our First Amendment freedoms.

For six years WAVA was the only all-news radio station in the Washington D.C. area. Then, in 1968, WTOP switched to the same format. WAVA immediately complained to the Federal Trade Commission, charging that a dangerous media monopoly was in the making. WTOP, it pointed out, is owned by the *Washington Post,* the largest newspaper in the Capital and one of the most distinguished in the nation. Other *Post* properties include one of Washington's three network television stations, one of its largest FM radio stations, and *Newsweek,* an influential national newsmagazine. Working together, WAVA's management argued, the various *Post* outlets could establish a near-monopoly over the flow of news in the Washington area.

The *Post* responded that WTOP and other *Post*-owned media were free to cover the news as they wished, without corporate control. The FTC found this a persuasive answer. It dismissed the complaint, noting that its investigation "failed to produce any evidence of misuse of alleged monopolistic power possessed by the Washington Post Company." [1]

The FTC decision made sense. The *Post* really did allow its subsidiaries great editorial freedom. And with forty-four broadcast stations and three daily newspapers (since reduced to two), Washington offered much more media diversity than the average American city.

Nevertheless, there is an inherent danger to democracy any time a single owner controls more than one mass-media outlet. Freedom of the press is predicated on the belief that if people have access to a wide range of opinions and information, they will make intelligent decisions. Supreme Court Justice Oliver Wendell Holmes put it this way: "The best test of truth is the power of the thought to get itself accepted in the competition of the market." [2] It follows that the government should not be permitted to regulate the media. Let each paper and station cover the news however it likes, the theory goes, and the people will be able to figure out who's right and who's wrong.

The theory works only so long as Holmes' "market" remains competitive. The fewer the number of independent media outlets in a given location, the weaker the case for freedom becomes. Consider an extreme example. If there were only one newspaper publisher in the entire United States, it would obviously be very dangerous to leave that publisher free to decide how to cover the news. How could the people choose right from wrong if they had only one source of information? Every media combination brings us that much closer to this "one source" situation.

Some media owners may allow their outlets to disagree with each other for a while, but later they may change their minds—or sell their holdings to a new owner with stronger convictions. Competing media may supply the necessary diversity at first, but they too may eventually be purchased by a monopolist—or be forced to fold in the face of concentrated economic pressure. To be sure, some media combinations are more dangerous than others, and the *Washington Post* combine must be counted among the safest. Yet it is not entirely safe. No media combination is entirely safe.

Media combinations come in many forms, but there are four major varieties:

1. *Chains and networks*—two or more outlets in the same medium (television, newspapers, or whatever) but usually in different cities are owned or controlled by the same person or group.

2. *Cross-media ownership*—two or more outlets in the same city but in different media are owned by the same person or group.

3. *Joint operating agreements*—two separately owned newspapers in the same city arrange to combine certain operations, such as printing and advertising, and to split the profits.

4. *Conglomerates*—companies that are not primarily in the communications business own or are owned by mass-media outlets.

We will discuss each briefly in turn.

CHAINS AND NETWORKS

At the start of 1974, there were 1,780 daily newspapers in the United States. Of these, 977 were owned by chains. That comes out to 54.9 percent of all the daily papers in the country owned by people or companies that also own other newspapers.[3]

These were all-time high figures, but they are probably even higher today. In 1973 alone, fifty-two U.S. daily newspapers changed hands; forty-nine of these papers were purchased by newspaper chains.[4] In some states, more than 80 percent of the papers are now chain-owned. And the list of chain newspapers includes many of the nation's largest—the *New York Daily News,* the *Cleveland Plain Dealer,* the *Atlanta Constitution,* the *Detroit Free Press,* the *Philadelphia Inquirer,* etc. Bryce Rucker estimates that if current trends continue, chains will own virtually all the dailies in the country by 1990.[5]

Most newspaper chains consist of only two or three papers—but some are massive. The Thomson chain owns fifty-three American papers; Gannett has fifty-two; Newhouse, Knight, Copley, Scripps-Howard, Ridder, and Cowles all have well over ten apiece.[6] In July of 1974, Knight Newspapers, Inc. and Ridder Publications, Inc. announced an agreement in principle to merge. If the merger is eventually approved, it will unite sixteen Knight papers in seven states and eighteen Ridder papers in ten states, plus the Ridder-owned *New York Journal of Commerce.* The new chain will have a circulation of over 3.5 million on weekdays and more than 3.8 million on Sundays.[7] Worse still, it could pave the way for a British-style ownership pattern, with three or four monster chains owning most of the daily newspapers in the country.

Magazine chains are frequently tied to newspapers. The Hearst organization, for example, owns twelve papers, plus *Good Housekeeping, Cosmopolitan, Harper's Bazaar, Popular Mechanics,* and sixteen other magazines. Additional magazine chains in-

111

clude Time-Life, Cowles, and Fairchild; each owns several magazines at least, and some own newspaper or broadcasting interests.

Broadcasting chains are almost as old as broadcasting. But they are limited in size by the Federal Communications Commission, which sets a maximum for each owner of seven television stations (of which only five can be VHF), seven AM radio stations, and seven FM radio stations. In January, 1973, there were 286 chain owners of radio and TV stations in the country. Several were close to the FCC's twenty-one-station limit, including Metromedia, Westinghouse, RKO General, Storer, CBS, NBC, and ABC.[8] By 1970, in fact, these seven companies already owned a total of 125 broadcast outlets, nearly all of them in the nation's largest cities. Five of the six commercial VHF television stations in New York City, for example, are owned by one or another of these seven companies.

Cable television is also susceptible to chain ownership. The giants to watch as cable grows are TelePrompTer, Warner Communications, and the American Television and Communications Corporation.

Many people think of broadcast networks as a kind of chain, but there is an important difference. The links in a broadcast chain are all owned by the same person or company, while the links in a network may be separately owned. Nonetheless, networking can reduce the diversity of the media every bit as much as chains. If a network-affiliated station invariably takes most of its programming from the network, the fact that it isn't owned by the network makes very little difference to its audience.

Radio networks are not a major problem. More than two-thirds of the radio stations in the U.S.—including many powerful and profitable ones—have no network affiliation at all. And even the network affiliates do most of their own programming, relying on the nets principally for national news.

Television networks are another story. The three TV networks provide their affiliates throughout the country with nearly the whole day's programming. And most TV stations are network affiliates. This is especially true of commercial VHF television stations in the major markets—the most profitable and influential stations of all. At the start of 1973, NBC had 219 TV affiliates, CBS had 192, and ABC had 168. That's a total of 579 network-affiliated stations. In 1973, there were only 510 commercial VHF stations and 187 commercial UHF stations on the air in the U.S., a total of 697 commercial stations. A little arithmetic reveals that 83 percent of all commercial television was network-affiliated. Although the FCC allows the three networks to own only seven TV stations apiece, they nonetheless control the nation's television through their affiliates.

CROSS-MEDIA OWNERSHIP

At the close of the 1960s, a single owner controlled at least one television station and one newspaper in thirty-four of the fifty largest cities in the U.S. Overall, ninety-four television stations were owned by newspapers in the same city.[9] The situation quickly went from bad to worse. As of November, 1971, the U.S. had 231 newspaper-television or newspaper-radio combinations in the same city.[10] Today there are even more.

Of course there are also newspaper-broadcasting combinations in different cities, and even in different states. In January of 1973, newspaper or magazine publishers owned a total of 178 TV stations, 325 AM radio stations, and 171 FM radio stations.[11] Some authorities use the term "cross-media ownership" to describe all print-broadcasting combinations, even if the newspaper is thousands of miles from the station. But the greatest threat to media diversity occurs when one owner controls a newspaper and a station (or a radio and a TV station) in the same community, and many experts confine the term "cross-media ownership" to this especially dangerous situation.

And if you believe in media diversity, cross-media ownership *is* dangerous. Fifty-three communities are now served by only one commercial radio station and one daily newspaper, both owned by the same company. On the list are Santa Cruz, Calif.; Coeur D'Alene, Ida.; Alliance, Ohio; Gettysburg, Pa.; Stamford, Conn.; and Bethlehem, Pa. Ten cities have just one commercial TV station and one newspaper, both owned by the same company. These include Fort Smith, Ark.; Albany, Ga.; Akron, Ohio; Bluefield, W. Va.; and Cheyenne, Wyo.[12]

In the larger cities, cross-media ownership is often combined with chains and networks to produce nearly total control over local broadcasting. In Detroit, for example, one TV station is owned by ABC, one by the *Detroit News,* and one by Storer Stations, a chain. The top three stations in St. Louis are owned by CBS, the *St. Louis Post-Dispatch,* and the *St. Louis Globe-Democrat.* In Chicago, the three largest TV stations are owned by the networks; number four is the property of the *Chicago Tribune.* The Cox chain owns the *Atlanta Journal* and the *Atlanta Constitution,* plus one of the city's TV stations; the Storer chain owns another Atlanta TV station, and Pacific and Southern Stations, another chain, also owns one.

Until the FCC took the license for WHDH-TV in Boston from the now-defunct *Herald Traveler,* you had to go down to the eighteenth-largest broadcast market (Miami) before finding a single network-affiliated TV station that was not owned by some newspaper, chain, or network.[13] In all, more than 80 percent of the commercial VHF television stations in the country are owned by chains, newspapers, or networks. In eleven states every commercial VHF station is so owned.[14]

Concentration is strongest in the nation's small towns. In 1967, 83 percent of all communities with a population of more than 200,000 had at least one newspaper and one broadcast station that were not owned by the same company. This was true of only 71 percent of the communities of 10,000 to 200,000—and of only 25 percent of the communities with fewer than 10,000 residents.[15]

Cross-media ownership is not limited to the newspaper-broadcast combination. Within broadcasting, the majority of FM radio stations are owned by AM stations. Many of the larger AM stations, in turn, are owned by TV stations. Broadcasters own more than a third of the nation's cable TV systems; newspapers and movie theaters bring the total up to half.[16] Many newspapers own their own feature syndicates; a number of them publish local or national magazines as well. Several magazine companies, meanwhile, own broadcast chains, or newspapers, or both. Nearly half of the major book publishing houses either own or are owned by broadcasting, newspaper, or magazine interests. It is hard to imagine any field with more interconnections than the communications industry.

JOINT OPERATING AGREEMENTS

Albuquerque, New Mexico, has only two newspapers, the morning *Journal* and the afternoon *Tribune.* In 1933 the two papers negotiated, in secret, the first newspaper joint operating agreement. They arranged to do all their printing in one plant, and to employ a single business office, circulation department, and advertising department. Commercial expenses were split down the middle. At the end of each year the profits were to be divided according to a set ratio, regardless of either paper's circulation or advertising revenue.

By 1975, newspapers in twenty-three cities had established joint operating agreements. In the following list, the combinations that involve chain-owned newspapers as well are marked with a bullet:

- *Albuquerque Journal* and *Tribune*
  Anchorage Daily Times and *Daily News*
- *Birmingham Post-Herald* and *News*

Newspaper, magazine, and book publishers, accustomed to worrying about how to increase circulation, faced a new and frightening problem in late 1973: a shortage of paper. A survey by the Associated Press Managing Editors found that 63 percent of the nearly 500 newspapers polled dropped some news articles to save paper; 9 percent dropped advertising; and a handful cut back on circulation. The *Minneapolis Tribune* went so far as to cut out its crossword puzzle.[17] The publisher Knopf could not print enough copies of *Alistair Cooke's America* to fill orders.[18] The magazine *Saturday Review/World* had to go to press on two different stocks of paper. And a new magazine called *Rallying Point,* which had planned a first issue of 200,000 copies, could find only enough paper for 5,000.[19]

The shortages, which are likely to be around for some time, focused attention on the paper manufacturing industry and the giant companies that dominate it—International Paper, Westavco, Weyerhauser, Kimberly Clark, Crown Zellerbach, and St. Regis. In the early 1970s these companies were unwilling to invest in new plants because, they claimed, government price controls didn't permit a large enough return on their investment.[20] The high cost of constructing new mills, the increased international demand for paper, and the need to control air and water pollution at paper mills are additional reasons for the shortage.

But the most serious problem is the lack of competition. Some paper consumers accused the industry of hoarding paper until the end of the price freeze.[21] Others complain that the companies are making only the more expensive, higher-quality stocks.[22] Some have proposed government rationing of newsprint and other kinds of paper used by the media. Newsprint is rationed in several countries today—and newspapers friendly to those in power get more than their share, while some opponents of the government have had to fold for lack of paper. It's not an appealing solution.

Timber growers and paper mills seem a long way from the metropolitan newsroom. But corporate decisions in the paper industry may now have as much impact on media content as the decisions of reporters, editors, and publishers.

- *Bristol Herald-Courier* and *Virginia-Tennessean*
  Charleston Gazette and *Daily Mail*
- *Columbus Citizen-Journal* and *Dispatch*
- *El Paso Times* and *Herald-Post*
- *Evansville Courier* and *Press*
- *Fort Wayne Journal-Gazette* and *News-Sentinel*
- *Honolulu Advertiser* and *Star-Bulletin*
- *Knoxville Journal* and *News-Sentinel*
- *Lincoln Star* and *Journal*
- *Madison State Journal* and *Capital Times*
- *Miami Herald* and *News*
- *Nashville Tennessean* and *Banner*
  Oil City-Franklin Derrick and *News-Herald*
- *Pittsburgh Post-Gazette* and *Press*
- *St. Louis Globe-Democrat* and *Post-Dispatch*
- *Salt Lake City Tribune* and *Deseret-News*
- *San Francisco Chronicle* and *Examiner*
- *Shreveport Times* and *Journal*
- *Tucson Arizona Star* and *Citizen*
  Tulsa World and *Tribune.*[23]

Some of the advantages of the joint operating agreement are obvious: It reduces the cost of advertising sales, printing, and distribution. As long as the agreement is confined to these points it is harmless, even helpful. But many newspapers have used joint operating agreements as an excuse for manipulating advertising rates in such a way that no third newspaper can possibly develop. And a few papers have extended their cooperation to include news and editorials as well as advertising and circulation, posing a clear threat to media diversity.

CONGLOMERATES

A conglomerate is a company that operates in a number of different and unrelated markets. RCA owns the NBC television network; more than a dozen individual radio and TV stations; RCA records; and RCA television sets, phonographs, and tape recorders. That makes it a media monster of tremendous size, but not a conglomerate—all these holdings are in the communications industry. What makes RCA a conglomerate is its ownership of Hertz cars, Banquet frozen foods, Coronet carpets, and Cushman & Wakefield real estate as well. Similarly, CBS not only owns a network, a bunch of radio and TV stations, a record company, a publishing house, and the like; it also has a toy manufacturing firm (Creative Playthings) and a piano company (Steinway). It therefore qualifies as a conglomerate.

Most media conglomerates work in the other direction—they start out manufacturing something, then work their way into the media. There are many examples.

- Westinghouse manufactures nuclear reactor components, refrigerators, electric ranges, and high-pressure sodium lamps—and owns a chain of radio and TV stations.

- Norton Simon, Inc. owns Max Factor cosmetics, Wesson Oil, Canada Dry beverages, United Can Company—and *Redbook* magazine, and Talent Associates, a producer of prime-time television series.

- Litton Industries owns Monroe calculators, Ingalls Shipbuilding, Royal Medallion typewriters, oven and machine tool companies—and the Van Nostrand Reinhold book publishing firm, and twenty magazines.

- Gulf and Western owns machine tool companies, cigar manufacturers, zinc plants—and Paramount Pictures.

- Kinney National Service owns parking lots, funeral chapels—and comic books.

- Kaiser Industries owns gravel, aluminum, cement, and steel manufacturers, an aerospace research firm, a jeep company—and a group of UHF television stations.

The chief danger of media conglomerates is that they may use their communication outlets to advance the interests of their other operations. This is by no means a merely theoretical danger. Among the conglomerates that have worked to increase their media holdings in recent years are two that have often been the subject of unfavorable news coverage—the International Telephone and Telegraph Company (ITT), and the interlocking companies controlled by multimillionaire Howard Hughes. Both ITT and Hughes would gain immeasurably if they could control what the public knows and thinks about their operations. Ownership of the media is one obvious way to accomplish this goal.

AN OVERVIEW

The trend toward media combination might not be so serious if there were an ever-increasing number of media outlets. Unfortunately, this is not the case.

In 1790 there were only eight daily newspapers in the entire United States. By 1850 the number of papers had risen to 387. By 1900 it was up to 2,190, and in 1910 it hit a high of 2,433. Then the figure began to slip—to 2,042 in 1920, to 1,878 in 1940. Throughout the 1960s and early 1970s the figure was stable at 1,750 to 1,780 daily newspapers in the country—considerably fewer than in the 1890s.

There are many reasons why the number of newspapers declined in the first half of the twentieth century—increased operating costs, recurrent labor problems, competition from broadcasting, etc. But the most important reason was simply that newspapering became a business. When a publisher decides that earning money is more important than advocating a viewpoint, he or she naturally eliminates most of the ideological advocacy from the paper, and cares very little about the advocacy that is left. There is then no reason not to merge with another paper. One publisher is bought out and retires with a tidy profit; the other publisher gains a monopoly and thus increases the paper's profit.

The broadcast media, meanwhile, are limited in number by the technology of broadcasting. The spectrum has room for only so many stations. There are still more than 1,000 unclaimed TV frequencies available, but few are likely to prove profitable—so there are no takers.

So far we haven't said anything at all about the abuse of media monopolies. The very existence of these monopolies—of chains and networks, cross-media ownership, joint operating agreements, and conglomerates—represents a serious threat to the democratic process, even without abuses.

Every media monopoly possesses the dangerous power to advance its own interests at the expense of others—including the public. Many monopolists have used this power; others may do so in the future. It is not practical, however, to outlaw all forms of media combination. One must choose among evils, and for this purpose pro-monopoly arguments are instructive. So far, the federal government has taken some action against all the forms of media monopoly, but decisive action against none of them. Apparently it has not decided yet which forms are the most dangerous.

ABUSES OF CONCENTRATION

Any form of media combination reduces, at least in theory, the total number of independent voices that can be heard. It therefore runs contrary to the fundamental premise of the First Amendment, that if the people hear all sides they can make the right decision. As the Federal Communications

Commission phrased it: "Centralization of control over the media of mass communications is, like monopolization of economic power, *per se* undesirable." [24]

But the dangers of media monopoly are far more than just theory. Two specific abuses have frequently been documented: news management and unfair economic competition. We will offer a few examples of each.

1. News Management. Between 1926 and 1937, conservative George Richards acquired an impressive chain of AM radio stations, including major outlets in Detroit, Cleveland, and Hollywood. He left standing orders for all his news staffs to give no favorable coverage to President Roosevelt, but rather to depict the president as a lover of "the Jews and Communists." When Mrs. Roosevelt was in an auto accident in 1946, Richards ordered his stations to make it seem that she had been drinking. Local editors who refused to follow the Richards line were fired. [25]

A less ideological example of news management came to light in 1969, when the FCC began its investigation of KRON-TV, a local station owned and operated by the *San Francisco Chronicle*. Station employees testified that when the *Chronicle* and the afternoon *Examiner* formed a joint operating agreement in 1965, KRON failed to report the story. Returning the favor, the *Chronicle* grossly underplayed the events leading to the FCC hearings on KRON.

And *Chronicle* columnist Charles McCabe testified that a piece he had written deploring violence on television was "killed" by higher-ups at the paper. [26]

Karl Nestvold has studied the relationships between 128 newspapers and the radio stations they owned. He found that 25 of the stations were located right within the newspaper building. Over 40 of them used newspaper personnel on the air. And roughly half the stations had access to prepublication carbons of newspaper articles. [27] Regular readers of the newspapers in Nestvold's

During the 1972 presidential campaign, James M. Cox, Jr. directed his chain of eight newspapers to endorse Richard Nixon. This was one of the few times Cox had interfered with the editorial policy of his papers. Greg Favre, editor of the *West Palm Beach Post-Times*, resigned shortly after the editorial was run. Sylvan Meyer, editor of the *Miami News*, said that "as a newsman, I could not vote for Mr. Nixon," and also resigned some months later. And for the *Atlanta Constitution*, Cox's order marked the first time in the paper's history that it backed a Republican for president.[28]

study had little to gain from listening to the radio stations those newspapers owned.

In 1967 the International Telephone and Telegraph Company attempted to purchase the ABC network. Despite the fact that ITT was already a giant international conglomerate, the FCC approved the sale. Three commissioners dissented. "We simply cannot find," they wrote, "that the public interest of the American citizenry is served by turning over a major network to an international enterprise whose fortunes are tied to its political relations with the foreign officials whose actions it will be called upon to interpret to the world."

Their fears were borne out by ITT's conduct while the sale was under scrutiny by the FCC and the Justice Department. ITT officials phoned AP and UPI reporters and asked them to make their stories more sympathetic to the company position. A *New York Times* correspondent who had criticized the merger received a call from an ITT senior vice president. The man asked if she was following the price of ABC and ITT stock, and didn't she feel "a responsibility to the shareholders who might lose money as a result" of what she wrote.[29] If ITT was pressuring reporters now, one might ask, what would it do after it owned its own reporters to pressure? Fortunately, the Justice Department balked at the merger, and ITT eventually withdrew the offer.

2. *Unfair Economic Competition*. The *Examiner-Chronicle*-KRON combination can

be used to illustrate unfair competition as well as news management. Before 1965 the two newspapers were involved in a bitter circulation war for the morning San Francisco market. *Chronicle* owners used the profits from KRON to win the battle, forcing the *Examiner* to move to the afternoon and sign a joint operating agreement.

Once the agreement was reached, the *Chronicle* doubled its advertising rate, while the weaker *Examiner* raised its rate by about 50 percent. The joint rate for placing the same ad in both papers was set only slightly higher than the *Chronicle*'s rate alone. The *Chronicle* had a monopoly, so advertisers were forced to pay its doubled rate. It then made sense for them to pay just a little more and get into the *Examiner* as well. The result: Suburban afternoon papers that were hoping to compete with the *Examiner* suffered a loss in advertising linage. And, more important, metropolitan competition was rendered impossible.

Not every media combination has made use of its power to slant the news. Not every media combination has taken advantage of its economic muscle to squelch the opposition. But every media combination is capable of these things—and some have done them.

COMPETITION

The most common criticism of media combinations is that they reduce competition. This raises a vital question: Does media competition really produce better media?

The assumption of the critics is that competitive media tend to produce more aggressive journalists than noncompetitive ones. To test this hypothesis, Gerard Borstel examined news and editorials in four kinds of newspapers—independent papers with local competition, chain papers with local competition, independent papers without competition, and chain papers without competition. He found absolutely no differences of any sort. The chain and monopoly papers were every bit as good as the independent and competitive ones.[30] It can be argued, then, that competitive papers are simply "rivals in conformity," offering the public no real diversity of viewpoint.

There may even be some advantages to a monopoly. Paul Block Jr., publisher of both the *Toledo Blade* and the *Toledo Times,* states his case persuasively:

> For one thing, a newspaper which isn't competing against a rival can present news in better balance. There is no need to sensationalize. . . .
>
> Competing newspapers live in fear of each other. They may be stampeded into excesses by their fear of losing circulation to a competitor less burdened with conscience. . . .
>
> The unopposed newspaper can give its reader . . . relief from the pressures of time. Deadlines no longer loom like avenging angels just this side of the next edition. . . . There is more freedom from financial pressure on the business side. A single ownership newspaper can better afford to take an unpopular stand. It can better absorb the loss of money in support of a principle. . . .[31]

In a similar vein, the National Association of Broadcasters sponsored a study which tried to prove that cross-media ownership produces better, not worse, media. Author George Litwin interviewed owners, journalists, and citizens in six cities, three with strong cross-media ownership and three with independent media. He concluded that owners of two or more media are more likely than independent owners to adopt a hands-off policy, leaving the management of the station and the newspaper to professional journalists. In addition, Litwin said, giant media barons can afford a larger staff and more facilities, resulting in better news coverage.[32]

The advantages of newspaper chains have also been developed at some length. Here are eight of them. (1) Newsprint, ink, and other supplies can be purchased more cheaply in bulk. (2) One representative can sell national ads for the entire chain. (3) Standardized accounting methods turn up errors in individual papers that can be quickly corrected. (4) Editors and reporters can exchange ideas and criticize one another. (5) Valuable feature material can be obtained for the chain more easily and cheaply. (6) High salaries and employee stock benefits can be maintained more easily, even in hard times. (7) Costs can be cut by centralizing some business functions. (8) Staff members from different papers can be used to work on an important story for the entire chain. Many of the eight factors apply also to cross-media ownerships, joint operating agreements, and conglomerates.

There are rebuttals to all these arguments. Researcher Bryant Kearl, for example, has shown that monopoly media do not in fact use their added economic resources to improve performance. Specifically, he found that monopoly newspapers purchase no more wire services than competitive ones [33]— though wires are among the cheapest and easiest ways to improve a paper. Economics Professor Harvey Levin surveyed sixty joint newspaper-broadcast operations in 1954, and concluded that "no significant management economies seem to result from affiliation because the jobs of directing newspapers and radio or TV stations are markedly different." The main benefit of cross-media ownership, Levin found, is not increased profits, but rather increased economic security through diversification.[34]

Defenders of media monopoly always seem

to miss the central point. Obviously media combinations offer some advantages; otherwise there wouldn't be so many of them. No doubt a conscientious media baron can turn these advantages to the benefit of the public. No doubt some media barons have done so. The fact remains: Every case of media combination is one less independent voice in the community. If our independent media are not making sufficient use of their freedom, that is a serious problem, worthy of serious attention. But at least they *are* independent; when they do raise their voices, they don't all say the same thing. Diversity is the strength of democracy. And no media monopoly can supply diversity.

GOVERNMENT REGULATION

From what has been said about the dangers of media monopolies, it should come as no surprise that the federal government has made efforts to contain and restrict them. What is surprising is the weakness of those efforts, at least until the end of the 1960s. Let us examine the extent of government restraint on each of the four forms of media combination.

1. Chains and Networks. Commercial radio was barely out of its infancy when the Federal Communications Commission began to worry about broadcast networks. The big problem was NBC, which owned two of the three existing networks, serving a majority of the strong metropolitan stations. In 1941 the FCC finally acted, ordering that "no license shall be issued to a standard broadcast station affiliated with a network organization which maintains more than one network." [35] This forced NBC to get rid of its so-called Blue Network. Lifesaver king Edward J. Noble bought the holdings; they became the nucleus of what is now ABC.

The FCC took two other actions in the early 1940s, known jointly as the Duopoly Rule. First, it ordered that no licensee could operate two stations of the same kind (AM, FM, or TV) in the same community. Second, it put a limit on the number of stations throughout the country that one licensee could own. Today that limit stands at seven AM, seven FM, and seven TV (of which no more than five may be VHF). In the thirty-odd years since the Duopoly Rule, the FCC has done little to slow the growth of broadcast chains.

It didn't pay much attention to the networks, either, until the late 1960s. Since then, the Commission has tried to weaken the almost total control of the networks over the

---

ONE-CITY CHAINS

The Justice Department doesn't worry much about broad-based newspaper chains, but when the chains are local Justice begins to get interested. In 1968, for example, the department forced the *Los Angeles Times* to sell the *San Bernardino Sun and Telegram.* The two cities are only twenty-odd miles apart, and getting closer every year. Apparently Justice didn't want the *Times* to wind up owning both papers in the Southern California megalopolis.

Later that year, the department required the afternoon *Cincinnati Post & Times-Star* (a Scripps chain paper) to divest itself of the morning *Cincinnati Enquirer,* in order to "restore competition between downtown papers." [36] And in early 1970 it forced the *Chattanooga Times* to close its sister paper, the *Evening Post,* because the latter was started with the sole intention of driving the competing *News-Free Press* out of business. The *Evening Post* was deliberately published at a loss, Justice claimed, just to make it impossible for the *News-Free Press* to compete.[37]

nation's television diet. One result of this effort was a rule requiring local TV stations to carry at least half an hour of non-network content during prime time. But three networks still decide what most Americans watch on television most of the time. For the foreseeable future, the FCC is not likely to alter this basic fact of media monopoly.

The FCC, of course, can regulate only broadcasting; the government agency that watches over print monopolies is the Department of Justice, with the help of the Federal Trade Commission. From time to time Justice has opposed a particular newspaper sale or merger, but on the whole it doesn't object to newspaper combinations unless they are within a single city. In 1970, for example, the Justice Department approved the sale of *Newsday*, a large Long Island tabloid, to the Times Mirror Company of Los Angeles. That company already owned the *Los Angeles Times*, the *Dallas Times-Herald*, and assorted other publishing and broadcast properties—but the Justice Department didn't seem to mind. Mused one *Newsday* editor: "The *Times* has the best national reporting in the country for my money. But it's a long way from Long Island." [38]

2. Cross-Media Ownership. For many years, the FCC had no policy concerning the extent to which newspaper publishers should be permitted to operate broadcast stations. Instead, it decided cross-media applications on a case-by-case basis.

In 1938, for the first time, the Commission denied a newspaper applicant its license, awarding it to an independent instead. The Supreme Court intervened, holding that newspaper ownership was insufficient grounds for denying a license application or renewal. Eighteen years passed, and then in 1956 the FCC tried again. It picked an untried applicant with no media holdings over one with an extensive newspaper and broadcast chain. This time the courts upheld the Commission, ruling that diversity may be one factor—though not the sole factor—in deciding who gets a license. [39] But the Com-

mission seldom took advantage of its newly won power, and newspaper-broadcast combinations continued to flourish.

Then, in 1968, the Department of Justice entered the scene. It filed with the FCC a formal objection to the purchase of station KFDM-TV in Beaumont, Texas, by the owner of the only two Beaumont newspapers. Justice argued that the merger would substantially lessen the competition for advertising. Before the FCC could make up its mind, the application for transfer of the license was withdrawn.

Justice next presented to the FCC a legal rationale for moving against cross-media combinations on antitrust grounds. Combined ownerships, it submitted, "may facilitate undesirable competitive practices by which the 'combined' owner seeks to exploit his advantages over the single station owner." [40] Justice urged the FCC to take action against cross-media combinations.

To the shock of many broadcasters, the Commission agreed. In 1969 it refused to renew the license of Boston station WHDH-TV, owned by the *Boston Herald Traveler*. On several grounds, including media diversity, it awarded the license to a committee of local educators and business executives.

That was only the beginning. In 1970, the FCC adopted a rule it had proposed in 1968, providing that henceforth no licensee of a VHF television station could also own an AM or FM radio station in the same market. AM-FM and UHF-radio combinations would be considered on a case-by-case basis. This might have revolutionized broadcast ownership, but a grandfather clause provided that combinations already in existence could remain intact. The ruling thus produced practically no change at all in the major markets.

Also in 1970, the Commission announced a "declaration of proposed rulemaking"—a statement of what it hoped to do in the near future. The terms were severe: (1) Within five years all newspaper owners would be required to get rid of all their broadcast holdings in the same city; (2) After five years no owner of a television station would be permitted to operate a radio station in the same city; and (3) Any broadcaster who purchased a newspaper in the same city would be required to give up the broadcast license. Industry response to the bombshell was immediate. NBC, for example, announced that the FCC "is seeking a rule requiring divestiture (if not forfeiture) in the absence of any showing either of monopoly power or of any restraint of trade." [41]

But three years passed and the FCC took no further action on its proposed rule. By the end of 1973, it looked like the WHDH decision would stand in lonely isolation forever. Under the leadership of President Nixon and Chairman Dean Burch, the FCC no longer seemed enthusiastic about snatching away licenses from powerful broadcast potentates who happened to own newspapers. Then, in early 1974, the Justice Department again stepped in. It formally petitioned the FCC not to renew the licenses of stations whose ownership of other media allowed them to control more than 70 percent of local advertising revenue in a single market.

The cities immediately affected were St. Louis, Des Moines, and Minneapolis–St. Paul. In Minneapolis, for example, WCCO-AM-FM-TV is owned by Midwest Radio-Television, Inc.; ownership of Midwest is shared by the Minneapolis Star and Tribune Company, which publishes the two Minneapolis dailies, and Northwest Publications, Inc., which owns St. Paul's two daily papers.

The reasoning of the Justice Department was clear in the WCCO petition. "The ownership structure of Midwest collects together the two Minneapolis newspapers, the two St. Paul newspapers, the leading television station, the locally dominant radio station, and an FM station." WCCO-AM had nearly 50 percent of total local AM advertising revenue in 1972; WCCO-TV's share of total TV ad revenue was 35 percent. Combining newspaper and broadcast revenue for the St. Paul market, Midwest took in a whopping 84 percent. Said Justice: "We believe that the level of local media concentration is so

high that . . . the Commission should find that renewing the licenses challenged here would not be in the public interest." [42]

In early 1975, the FCC adopted a less extreme approach to cross-media ownership. Henceforth, it said, no new broadcast-newspaper combinations in the same community would be permitted. But existing ones could continue as long as there were competing stations serving the same audience. The Commission found only sixteen combinations around the country that failed to satisfy this criterion, and ordered them to get rid of either the paper or the station by 1980. No big-city combinations were listed.[43]

The Justice Department approach to cross-media ownership stresses dominance over advertising and other potential business abuses. It therefore threatens powerful combinations in major metropolitan areas. The FCC approach, on the other hand, concentrates on diversity of viewpoint and programming service, and therefore affects mostly small-city monopolies where there are no other stations at all. Broadcasters are understandably unhappy about both approaches, and are lobbying hard for protection. In 1974, the House (but not the Senate) passed a bill that would ban the FCC from selectively denying license renewal to newspaper owners of broadcast stations. The vote was 379–14. Similar legislation will undoubtedly be considered—and possibly be passed—in the years ahead.

Meanwhile, the FCC has been fairly vigilant about breaking up cross-media ownerships involving cable TV before they get established. The Commission has ordered the networks to get out of the cable business entirely, and television stations may not own cable systems in the same city. Divestiture was to be completed by August 10, 1975, and the FCC was pretty stingy about waiving the rules for specific licensees.[44]

3. Joint Operating Agreements. In 1965 the Justice Department filed suit against the *Tucson Arizona Star* and *Citizen,* charging that the two newspapers had entered into a joint operating agreement that violated antitrust laws. The papers were accused of price-fixing, profit-pooling, and creating a total monopoly over the daily newspaper business in Tucson. The U.S. District Court in Arizona agreed, and declared the agreement unlawful. The U.S. Supreme Court upheld the decision. The newspaper joint operating agreement (except for limited arrangements involving papers in genuine danger of folding) was dead.

It was born again in 1967, when Arizona Senator Carl Hayden introduced the Failing Newspaper Act, which explicitly legalized agreements like Tucson's. The act died in committee, but was reintroduced as the Newspaper Preservation Act. In 1970 it passed both houses of Congress and was signed into law.

The act was vigorously lobbied through Congress by the powerful newspaper industry. Proponents argued that only the joint operating agreement could keep weak metropolitan papers from folding, leaving their cities with just a single newspaper. The act, they said, was therefore an attempt to preserve competition and forestall monopoly.

Opponents saw it differently. They pointed out that in most American cities it is the *third* newspaper, not the *second,* that is in imminent danger of folding. They marshalled statistics to establish that any city with more than 200,000 population can support two independent newspapers. They concluded, as John J. Flynn put it:

> It is dangerous to think the bill is designed to preserve the struggling and crusading editor of yesteryear whose only devotion is to the noncommercial aspects of journalism. It is ridiculous to think that the bill is anything other than an open invitation to further concentrate an already overconcentrated industry, thereby destroying the few remaining independent editorial voices.[45]

Even if a newspaper is in danger of folding, many argued, the goals of democracy are better served by letting it fold than by propping it up with a joint operating agreement. A newspaper that cannot survive as one of two in a big city must be doing something wrong. Perhaps if it were allowed to fold another paper might take its place—and do a better job. At a minimum, weekly and suburban papers in the area would benefit from the increased availability of advertising.

Nevertheless, the Newspaper Preservation Act is now law, and joint operating agreements are legal once again.

Interestingly enough, there has not been any rush to form new joint operating agreements in the wake of their legalization. The number of such agreements remained constant from 1970 to 1974. Chains and cross-media ownerships are apparently more attractive to the average publisher than joint operating agreements.

4. Conglomerates. Neither the FCC nor the Justice Department nor any other government agency has a policy restricting the right of conglomerates to get into the media business. As the Justice Department's refusal to approve the proposed ITT-ABC merger demonstrates, the government is likely to balk when a giant conglomerate wants to take over a major media system. But conglomerates buy individual stations, newspapers, and magazines all the time, without any serious objections from the government. As long as a conglomerate builds its media holdings slowly, and doesn't violate the rules governing broadcast chains and cross-media ownership, it is reasonably safe.

CHOOSING AMONG EVILS

We have discussed four forms of media combination—chains and networks, cross-media ownership, joint operating agreements, and conglomerates. It is probably not feasible to outlaw them all. This is the age of Big Business, in communications as in all other industries. Critics of media monopoly must therefore decide which forms to fight, and which to leave alone as the lesser among evils.

The government, too, must make this decision. So far none of the four forms has been outlawed. Still, it is possible to examine the actions of the FCC, the Justice Department, and Congress, and to deduce from them how the government views the problem. The "official government ranking," from most dangerous to least dangerous, would probably look like this:

1. Cross-media ownership.
2. Chains and networks (mostly networks).
3. Conglomerates.
4. Joint operating agreements.

As of mid-1975, in short, the government is virtually at war against cross-media ownership within a single community. And it is actively chipping away at the power of the networks. By contrast, chains are nearly unregulated as long as they stay geographically spread out, and conglomerates are safe as long as they don't try to gobble up too big a piece of the media pie in one bite. Joint operating agreements, of course, are protected by law.

All this could change overnight. Congress could pass a law protecting cross-media ownerships; the Justice Department could start fighting chains more vigorously; the FCC could refuse to let conglomerates buy television stations.

Which form of media monopoly is really the most dangerous? The answer depends on what sort of danger worries you the most. In terms of local diversity, cross-media ownership is the most serious problem, because it limits the number of independent voices within a community, and thus directly threatens the free marketplace of ideas. In terms of national power, chains and networks are the most serious; they enable a single executive to decide what tens of millions of readers and viewers will be told. And in terms of the likelihood of intentional news bias, conglomerates are the most serious; a conglomerate with media holdings has the rare privilege of reporting about itself. Even joint operating agreements may be viewed

by some as the most serious problem, because of their ability to keep sick newspapers alive and prevent the growth of healthy, new ones.

Whatever priority you choose, one conclusion is clear: Diversity of viewpoint is vital to freedom of the press. And media monopoly—*every* form of media monopoly—is antithetical to diversity.

But there is yet another side to the issue. In periods of government misbehavior, the media often play a vital role by exposing evil in high places. The "Watergate Era" of 1972–1974 was such a period. It is at least arguable that the media need all the power that monopoly gives them in order to play this role in the face of government's inevitable efforts to muzzle the muckrakers. If it were not for networks, chains, and the like, the argument goes, the Nixon administration would have found it much easier to intimidate the media into silence.

Consider a typical example of government efforts to control media monopoly. In 1972, the Justice Department filed an antitrust suit against the three television networks, claiming that they exercised too much control over TV production. By using its own facilities to produce its own programs, the suit charged, a network can effectively control the price and supply of programs made by independent producers for sale to the networks.

It is clear that a limit on network production would increase the competitive power of the Hollywood studios and independent TV producers, and thus add to the potential diversity of television programming. It is also clear that such a move could significantly decrease network profits. The cost-cutting that would result, the networks claimed, would seriously weaken their news operations.[46]

In their 1973 response to the Justice Department suit, the networks went even further, invoking the First Amendment in defense of their production facilities. CBS, for example, claimed that the suit was an effort by the government to "restrain, intimidate and inhibit criticism of the President of the United States and his appointees," with no other goal than "harassing" the network.[47]

Will CBS tone down its criticism of the government in order to keep its production studios? And if it should lose its studios, would a that-much-weaker CBS be strong and wealthy and courageous enough to criticize the government quite so forcefully the next time? These are important questions to ask before urging more vigorous government regulation of media monopolies.

Yet the strength of America's media has traditionally been their diversity. A powerful government may successfully intimidate one or two or even a thousand papers and stations, but it cannot intimidate them all. And once the truth is out, shame and public pressure (and the competitive pressures of journalism) will force even the most timid media to carry it. The choice is between two kinds of strength: the strength of media monopolies so powerful that they can defy the government and single-handedly control the flow of ideas and information, or the strength of media variety so diverse that there is always at least one publisher or broadcaster who is willing to take the chance. The ideal future for the American media is probably somewhere in the middle.

Notes

[1] Richard L. Worsnop, "Competing Media," *Editorial Research Reports,* July 18, 1969, pp. 538–39.

[2] *Abrams v. United States,* 250 U.S. 616, 630 (1919).

[3] *Editor & Publisher,* February 23, 1974, p. 9.

[4] *Editor & Publisher,* December 29, 1973, pp. 24–32.

[5] Bryce Rucker, *The First Freedom* (Carbondale, Ill.: Southern Illinois University Press, 1968), pp. 21–23.

[6] *Editor & Publisher International Yearbook,* 1973, pp. 348–52.

[7] "Knight and Ridder Papers Plan Merger," *New York Times,* July 11, 1974, p. 37.

[8] *Editor & Publisher International Yearbook,* 1973, pp. A91–A98.

[9] Federal Communications Commission, "Further Notice of Proposed Rulemaking," 70–311 46096, March 25, 1970, para. 30–31.

[10] *Federal Communications Commission Annual Report,* Fiscal 1972, pp. 224–27.

[11] *1973 Broadcasting Yearbook,* p. 12.

[12] *Federal Communications Commission Annual Report,* Fiscal 1972, pp. 243–44.

[13] *1973 Broadcasting Yearbook.*

[14] Rucker, *The First Freedom,* p. 196.

[15] Guido H. Stempel III, "A New Analysis of Monopoly and Competition," *Columbia Journalism Review,* Spring, 1967, pp. 11–12.

[16] *Television Factbook* (Services Volume), 1973–1974, p. 84A.

[17] *New York Times,* October 9, 1973, p. 29.

[18] *New York Times,* Sunday Business Section, January 27, 1974, p. 11.

[19] *New York Times,* November 28, 1973, p. 73.

[20] *New York Times,* January 6, 1974, p. F71.

[21] *New York Times,* Sunday Business Section, January 27, 1974, p. 11.

[22] *New York Times,* November 28, 1973, p. 73.

[23] David M. Rubin, "Nothing Succeeds Like Failure," [*MORE*], June, 1975, pp. 18–20, 27.

[24] Federal Communications Commission, "First Report and Order," 70–310 46095, para. 17.

[25] Erik Barnouw, *The Golden Web* (New York: Oxford University Press, 1968), pp. 221–24.

[26] "McCabe Testifies at TV Hearings," *San Francisco Chronicle,* April 15, 1970, p. 6.

[27] Karl J. Nestvold, "Local News Cooperation Between Co-Owned Newspapers and Radio Stations," *Journal of Broadcasting,* Spring, 1965, pp. 145–52.

[28] "An 'Agonizing' Decision," [*MORE*], December, 1972, pp. 17–18.

[29] Nicholas Johnson, "The Media Barons and the Public Interest," *Atlantic,* June, 1968, pp. 44–46.

[30] Gerard H. Borstel, "Ownership, Competition and Comment in 20 Small Dailies," *Journalism Quarterly,* Spring, 1956, pp. 220–21.

[31] Paul Block Jr., "Facing Up to the 'Monopoly' Charge," *Nieman Reports,* July, 1955, p. 4.

[32] George H. Litwin and William H. Wroth, *The Effects of Common Ownership on Media Content and Influence,* National Association of Broadcasters, July, 1969, pp. 5–13.

[33] Bryant Kearl, "Effects of Newspaper Competition on Press Service Resources," *Journalism Quarterly,* Winter, 1958, p. 64.

[34] Harvey J. Levin, "Economics in Cross Channel Affiliation of Media," *Journalism Quarterly,* Spring, 1954, pp. 167–74.

[35] Barnouw, *The Golden Web,* pp. 170–71.

[36] Walter B. Kerr, "The Problem of Combinations," *Saturday Review,* October 12, 1968, p. 82.

37 "Antitrust Consent Decree Closes Chattanooga Post," *Editor & Publisher,* February 28, 1970, p. 9.

38 "Thank You, Mr. Smith," *Newsweek,* April 27, 1970, p. 94.

39 Christopher Sterling, "Newspaper Ownership of Broadcast Stations, 1920–1968," *Journalism Quarterly,* Summer, 1969, pp. 231–33.

40 Department of Justice Memorandum, August 1, 1968, p. 6.

41 Federal Communications Commission, "Further Notice of Proposed Rulemaking," 70–311 49069, March 25, 1970, para. 19.

42 *Variety,* March 6, 1974, p. 31.

43 I. William Hill, "FCC Bars Cross-Ownership, Breaks Up Media in 16 Cities," *Editor & Publisher,* February 1, 1975, p. 9.

44 *Variety,* January 24, 1973, p. 29. *Broadcasting,* September 10, 1973, pp. 44–45.

45 John J. Flynn, "Antitrust and the Newspapers, A Comment on S.1312," *Vanderbilt Law Review,* 1968–1969, p. 114.

46 *Wall Street Journal,* December 3, 1973, p. 2.

47 *New York Times,* December 22, 1973, p. 49.

Suggested Readings

BARNETT, STEPHEN R., "Merger, Monopoly and a Free Press," *Nation,* January 15, 1973.

BARNOUW, ERIK, *The Golden Web.* New York: Oxford University Press, Inc., 1968.

JOHNSON, NICHOLAS, "The Media Barons and the Public Interest," *The Atlantic,* June, 1968.

McCOMBS, MAXWELL E., "Mass Media in the Marketplace," *Journalism Monographs,* August, 1972.

MINTZ, MORTON, and JERRY S. COHEN, *America, Inc.* New York: The Dial Press, 1971.

RUBIN, DAVID M., "Nothing Succeeds Like Failure," [*More*], June, 1975.

RUCKER, BRYCE, *The First Freedom.* Carbondale, Ill.: Southern Illinois University Press, 1968.

STEMPEL, GUIDO H., III, "Effects on Performance of a Cross-Media Monopoly," *Journalism Monographs,* June, 1973.

Chapter 5
Advertiser Control

Most of the money in the mass media comes from advertising. If money means power, then advertisers must have enormous power to control the media. And they do. Surprisingly, they exercise that power only on occasion, and usually for business rather than political reasons. Advertiser control does have an effect on overall media performance, especially in broadcasting, but the effect is usually more subtle than most critics imagine.

Newspaper people are not easy to embarrass, but this time the *Denver Post* offices were filled with red faces. Someone had spirited an interoffice memorandum from the newspaper's files and published it. Addressed to the managing editor, the memo read as follows:

Regarding "editorial" commitment on advertising schedules for Villa Italia Shopping Center. . . .

I'm open to review on figures, based on Hatcher's [retail advertising manager] stated commitment of 25 per cent free space ratio to advertising, but believe this is reasonably accurate. . . .

We have since Feb. 2 . . . published in various sections of the *Post* 826 column inches of copy and pictures directly related to Villa Italia, through March 7.

Coverage beyond Monday (three days of grand openings . . . which we can't ignore and must cover with pix and stories) won't come close to the total commitment, but probably would put it over the half-way mark. If we did a picture page each day of the opening . . . we would be providing another 546 column inches and thus be beginning to get close to the commitment figure. . . .[1]

Why is this memo so damning? All it reveals, after all, is that the *Post* had promised the shopping center one inch of free "news stories" for every four inches of paid advertising—and that the paper was having trouble finding the necessary news angles. Such a commercial arrangement is straightforward, legal, and very common. It is also typical of the way advertisers influence the content of the mass media. The Villa Italia Shopping Center did not bribe the *Post* to support a particular political candidate, or even to fight for a zoning change it might have wanted. It simply purchased a little free space along with its ads. That seems harmless enough.

Nonetheless, the loss to *Denver Post* readers is clear. For one thing, they were falsely led to believe that the newspaper's editors considered Villa Italia an important news story. Moreover, in just over a month 826 column inches of genuinely important stories (roughly 30,000 words, the equivalent of a short novel) were eased out of the paper to make room for this disguised advertising.

WHO PAYS THE PIPER

Almost all American mass media are commercial. Some, like the book and motion picture industries, earn their revenue directly from the consumer. Most earn it—or at least the bulk of it—from advertising.

Newspapers: Sixty percent of the space in the average newspaper is devoted to ads, which account for three-quarters of the paper's income.

Magazines: A little over half of all magazine income is derived from ads, which fill just about half the available space.

Broadcasting: One-quarter of the nation's air time is reserved for commercial messages, which pay the entire cost of the other three quarters.

In 1972 advertisers spent $6.9 billion on newspapers; $4.1 billion on television; $1.5 billion on radio; and $1.4 billion on magazines. Each year the figures are larger. It is obvious that none of these media could exist in the form we know them without advertising.

Imagine that you are the Vice President for Advertising of Procter & Gamble, which in 1972 spent roughly $220 million on television advertising alone, much of it for daytime serials. Imagine also that the script for one of your serials calls for an episode in which the heroine goes swimming in detergent-polluted water and suffers a psychotic breakdown because of the slime. You would almost certainly feel tempted to ask the producer to skip that part, and you might well feel cheated if he or she refused. As far as we know P&G does not monitor TV shows before broadcast. But then, as far as we know no soap opera has ever featured the dangers of detergent pollution. With $220 million of Procter & Gamble's money at stake, no soap opera is likely to do so.

Advertisers pay the piper. If they want to, they can more or less call the tune.

IDEOLOGY VERSUS BUSINESS

In the late 1950s, General Motors signed with CBS to sponsor a series of television documentaries. When it was learned that the first program would be entitled "The Vice Presidency: Great American Lottery," the company guessed that the show might attack V.P. Richard Nixon. Nixon was a great favorite of many GM executives, so GM withdrew from the entire series.[2]

This anecdote has been told and retold many times over, and for good reason: It is rare. Advertisers almost never exercise their power, as GM apparently did, purely for ideological reasons. Their goal, after all, is to sell a product, and they pick their outlets on commercial grounds, not political ones. No matter how conservative a company may be, if it wants to sell to young people it will be pleased to have an ad in the middle of "Sanford & Son." Wherever the market is, that is where the advertiser hopes to be. In a 1962 speech, conservative business editor Donald I. Rogers described (and criticized) this devotion to circulation:

When businessmen place their advertising in Washington, where do they place it?

They place 600,000 more lines per month with the liberal, welfare-state loving *Post* than in the *Star,* and the poor old conservative *News* runs a poor—a very poor—third. . . .

The picture is no different here in New York. We find that the greatest amount of advertising placed by businessmen goes into the liberal *Times.* . . .

The influential conservative New York papers, the *Herald Tribune* and the *World Tele-*

gram & Sun, get very sparse pickings indeed from the American business community which they support so effectively in their editorial policies.[3]

Rogers urged the business establishment to support the papers that support business. He was ignored. As a result, the *Herald Tribune* and the *World Telegram & Sun* are now dead, victims of scanty advertising. The *Washington News* has been forced to merge with the *Star,* and the resulting *Star-News* still runs a distant second to the liberal *Post* in advertising linage. American advertisers simply will not pay to keep an ideo-

logical supporter in business. They pay to reach an audience, period.

Rogers considered the ideological neutrality of advertisers short-sighted. Perhaps it is, but it is also very fortunate for the independence of the media. Because of this neutrality, a newspaper, magazine, or broadcast station that attacks the business establishment will be kept in business *by* the business establishment, as long as it can attract an adequate audience. In the 1950s, for example, the *Milwaukee Journal* led the nation in advertising linage, despite its opposition to Red-baiting Joseph McCarthy and its support for Democrat Adlai Stevenson. Adver-

---

ADVERTISER BOYCOTT

William F. Schanen, Jr. was publisher of three weekly newspapers in suburban Ozaukee County, Wisconsin. For extra cash, he also did joblot printing for several smaller publications. These included conservative political, religious, and business newsletters—and *Kaleidoscope,* an underground newspaper serving Milwaukee's "hippie" community. *Kaleidoscope* wasn't very popular in Ozaukee County. Even Schanen often found it offensive, but he believed that "no printer should deny his facility to any . . . legal use."

Benjamin Grob, a local machine-tool manufacturer, disagreed. In 1969, Grob sent a letter to 500 influential Ozaukee advertisers, charging that Schanen "prints obscene literature for profit." Grob continued: "I will not buy space in his newspapers, and I will not buy from anyone who advertises in his newspapers. Ladies and gentlemen, I am looking for company."

Almost immediately, Schanen's gross advertising revenue plummeted from $4,000 a week to $700—a loss of $165,000 a year. At the start of the boycott, Schanen got moral and financial support from the National Newspaper Association, the American Civil Liberties Union, and other sympathizers.[4] But the help soon petered out, and Schanen was forced to sell off two of his three papers.

Schanen died in February, 1971, and his son, William F. Schanen III, took over the surviving *Ozaukee Press* and the fight. A few months later, *Kaleidoscope* folded. But the boycott continued until 1973, and the *Press* today is still a lot weaker than it once was. The younger Schanen continues to print underground papers in his backshop. He says "the Midwest has caught up with the rest of the country," and there is no talk of a second boycott.[5]

Boycotts are the most potent form of advertiser control—as well as the rarest. Ozaukee advertisers had no complaints about the selling power of Schanen's three newspapers. They didn't even object to the content of the papers. But they shared an ideological disapproval of a fourth paper, *Kaleidoscope,* which Schanen printed to earn some extra money on the side. Because of this disapproval, they nearly forced an "establishment" publisher to fold.

---

tisers agreed that the *Journal* was "anti-business," but Hearst's conservative *Milwaukee Sentinel* was a loser in the circulation race —and so the ads stayed with the *Journal.*[6]

Every underground newspaper today, from the *Berkeley Barb* to the *Great Speckled Bird* in Atlanta, depends for its survival on advertisements from the business establishment, especially record and film companies. The ideological tension between the underground paper and the large corporation is obvious. But that tension doesn't prevent businesses from putting their ads where they will help sales the most.

PATTERNS OF ADVERTISER CONTROL

The fact that most advertisers are ideologically neutral does not mean that they ignore the content of the programs they sponsor or the publications they appear in. Some companies, of course, are satisfied to pay for their ads and let it go at that. But many like to have at least a little say over what comes before and after.

There are at least four types of advertiser control over mass-media content:

1. The ads themselves.
2. Connecting the product to nonadvertising content.
3. Making the company and product look good, never bad.
4. Avoiding controversy at all costs.

We will discuss each of these in turn.

1. The Ads Themselves. It may be obvious, but it is worth emphasizing that nearly half the content of the mass media is written directly by advertisers—the ads. The average American adult is exposed to several hundred separate advertising messages each day. Many find their way into the language as symbols of our culture—"The Pepsi Generation," "The Dodge Rebellion," "Progress Is Our Most Important Product." Besides selling goods, these ads undoubtedly have a cumulative effect on American society. Philosopher Erich Fromm has defined Western Man as *Homo consumens*—Man the Consumer. If the description fits, the institution to blame is advertising.

Legally, a publication or station is free to reject most kinds of ads if it wishes, but as a practical matter only the most egregiously dishonest or offensive specimens are ever turned away. It is a strange paradox that advertisers have more power over the content of the media than the media have over the ads.

2. Connecting the Product to Nonadvertising Content. The clearest example of the blurred line between advertising and nonadvertising is the common newspaper custom of trading free "news stories" for paid ads, as in the *Denver Post* case already discussed. A parallel practice in the magazine world is the disguising of advertisements as editorial copy. The November, 1967, issue of the *Reader's Digest,* for instance, contained a special section advocating the use of brand-name drugs instead of the cheaper generic versions. The whole section was laid out to look like standard *Digest* fare. Only a small box at the end informed readers that it was paid for by the Pharmaceutical Manufacturers Association. Are readers confused by such ads? Evidently advertisers think so, for they pay dearly for the privilege of running them.

Nearly every newspaper has a department or two whose main purpose is to keep advertisers happy by giving them something "appropriate" to appear next to. Frequent offenders include the real estate section, entertainment page, church page, and travel and dining pages. There is nothing evil about a newspaper deciding to run, say, a weekly ski page. But if the only function of the page is to give skiing advertisers a place to locate— and if the page disappears when the ads fall off—then the editor's news judgment has been replaced by the business manager's. In his book *The Fading American Newspaper,* Carl Lindstrom calls these sorts of articles "revenue-related reading matter." [7] Many newspaper executives use another term: BOMs, or Business Office Musts. The reader, of course, pays the price—a steady diet of pap and puffery.

In broadcasting, the best way to connect paid and unpaid content is to hire the performer to do his or her own ads. It was Dinah Shore herself who sang, at the end of every show, "See the U.S.A. in your Chevrolet." Between monologues and interviews, Johnny Carson tells millions of viewers what to buy.

Almost from the beginning, network television newscasters refused to do commercials, believing that it was unfair and misleading to slide from a review of the day's action on Capitol Hill to a review of the reasons for taking Excedrin. Many local TV reporters are not so conscientious, however, and nearly all radio announcers are willing to alternate between news and commercials. Even on network TV news, some intermingling is permitted. NBC's coverage of the 1964 political conventions, for example, was sponsored by Gulf Oil. At the company's request, the luminous orange Gulf disc was installed behind every commentator's desk.

On this subject, the networks are a good deal less scrupulous in the morning than in the evening. The hosts on NBC's "Today" show, including superstar Barbara Walters, regularly do their own commercials. In 1974, NBC had trouble finding a replacement for Frank McGee on the show, because several top prospects refused to do the ads. Among those who said no were Tom Brokaw, NBC's White House correspondent, and Bill Moyers, former editor of *Newsday* and once Lyndon Johnson's press secretary. Jim Hartz, a reporter for WNBC in New York, finally accepted the job; he does the commercials. [8]

Blurring the line between news and advertising is intended to strengthen the credibility of the ads. It may also lessen the credibility of the news.

3. Making the Company and Product Look Good, Never Bad. Advertisers go to a great deal of trouble to look good in their ads; wherever possible, they would like to look good between the ads as well. It is sometimes possible. CBS reporter Alexander Kendrick recalls the case of a cigarette sponsor that "dictated that on none of its entertainment programs, whether drama or studio panel game, could any actor or other participant smoke a pipe or cigar, or chew tobacco, or even chew gum that might be mis-

---

CHET HUNTLEY AND AMERICAN AIRLINES

A recent, much-debated case of an advertiser trading on the credibility of a journalist involved former NBC anchorman Chet Huntley. In 1972, American Airlines offered Huntley roughly $300,000 a year to appear in ten commercials and narrate a series of American-sponsored TV specials on the U.S. Bicentennial.

Huntley had retired from NBC nearly two years before he signed the agreement with American. But a public-opinion study by the Doyle Dane Bernbach ad agency found that Huntley was still number two in response to the question: "Which newscaster do you believe the most?" (Walter Cronkite was number one.) It isn't hard to see why American wanted him as a pitchman. Said American Vice President Tom Ross: "It is important that this business become more believable. Chet Huntley is believable." NBC's John Hart, on the other hand, objected that trading on Huntley's image as a reporter "blurs the line of detachment that journalists have been trying to establish for years." [9]

Huntley died in the spring of 1974, and American Airlines had to find a different sales strategy. What will the bidding be like when Walter Cronkite retires from CBS?

---

taken for tobacco. Only cigarettes could be smoked, and only king-sized, but no program could show untidy ashtrays, filled with cigarette butts. . . ." [10]

Such policies are less common today, because for the most part advertisers no longer sponsor whole programs. Instead, they buy a minute here and a minute there (see p. 135), which makes it hard for them to exercise the careful control over program content they used to take for granted. But when an advertiser does decide to underwrite an entire show, this kind of control is often part of the package. If Bufferin sponsors a special television drama, the star is unlikely to take plain aspirin for her headache.

In addition, TV producers regularly accept products and services from various companies in exchange for a plug on the show. Chevrolet, for example, provides six free cars for use on "Mannix." The deal stipulates that only sympathetic characters are to drive the Chevys, and that they can't be used in collision scenes. Similarly, "Hawaii Five-0" often needs film of an airplane landing on the island. United Airlines pays the producers a substantial fee, estimated by one CBS source at $25,000 a year, to guarantee that all such shots will feature a United plane, thus plugging the airline's service to Hawaii.[11] Of course if the plot called for an airplane crash, a United plane would not be used.

When an airplane does crash, newspapers and news broadcasts must report it, and they even mention the name of the airline (though there was a time when they didn't). But if an airline ad is scheduled next to the news show, it is moved to another spot.

The subservience of news to advertising is reflected mostly in small favors. When someone commits suicide in a downtown hotel, many newspapers don't name the hotel. When a bigshot with a big ad account gets married, the story receives big play on the society page; when the bigshot gets divorced the story is often ignored. The names of shoplifters and embezzlers are printed, but whenever possible the names of the stores and businesses they stole from are not. But no advertiser today is powerful enough to make a major news organization kill an important story, just because the story reflects badly on the advertiser.

Advertisers keep trying, of course. In early 1972, the Bumble Bee Tuna people objected to CBS coverage of a congressional investigation of the fishing industry. The company felt that correspondent Daniel Schorr had paid too little attention to industry rebuttals on water pollution, chemical additives, monopoly, etc. So it instructed its ad agency not to buy any Bumble Bee spots on CBS stations in February and March. Richard Salant, head of CBS News, commented that "I do not recall ever having been faced before with so blunt an attempt by advertisers to influence news handling and to punish a news organization." [12] It didn't do any good. Coverage remained the same, and Bumble Bee returned to CBS in April.

But when the story is less important, or the news organization less major, the advertiser stands a better chance of winning. Soon after Chevron gasoline started advertising its "anti-pollution" F-310 additive in 1970, a *San Jose* (California) *Mercury* reporter attended a respiratory disease convention in San Francisco. Several of the expert participants were highly critical of the additive and advertising claims for its environmental benefits. The reporter wrote the story as a sidebar (a related feature running next to a piece of hard news) to the convention article. What followed, he says, was not typical of the *Mercury:*

The city editor at the time held the story for several days. I questioned him about [it] and he finally redlined [banned] it with the astounding comment: "Oh, hell. This isn't all that pertinent, and the firm has a big advertising campaign with us now. Maybe later." I have done some intensive research on my own on that score and have determined that it was his own second-guessing of management's desires rather than any kind of order from above that prompted his decision.[13]

When the FTC later charged that the F-310 ads were fraudulent, it became a major story, and the *Mercury* covered it well. (The charge was eventually dropped.)

In 1972, radio reporter Jim Lange decided to do some investigative journalism for WQWK-FM in State College, Pa. A tour of local stores revealed that many merchants were not posting base price lists as required by the Federal Price Commission. Lange reported this fact on the air. Enraged store-owners complained to the station's president, who then fired Lange for violating station policy by not checking a controversial newscast with management beforehand. Only after Lange filed a complaint with the FCC did the station modify its position and re-hire him.[14]

The requirement that reporters check out sensitive stories in advance, by the way, is typical of most newspapers and broadcast stations. Many such stories—and nearly all the really important ones—are printed or broadcast in the end. But their publication is often preceded by intensive and extensive debate with editors and executives. Reporters may not fear the outcome of that debate so much as they simply want to avoid the debate itself. Ignoring advertiser-related news

items is a lot easier than pushing them up through the hierarchy. The result, of course, is the same as if advertisers actually had a veto power.

4. Avoiding Controversy at All Costs. A major advertiser of breakfast foods once sent the following memo to the scriptwriters of the television series it sponsored:

> In general, the moral code of the characters in our dramas will be more or less synonymous with the moral code of the bulk of the American middle class, as it is commonly understood. There will be no material that will give offense, either directly or by inference, to any organized minority group, lodge or other organizations, institutions, residents of any state or section of the country, or a commercial organization of any sort. . . . We will treat mention of the Civil War carefully, mindful of the sensitiveness of the South on this subject. . . . There will be no material for or against sharply drawn national or regional controversial issues. . . . There will be no material on any of our programs which could in any way further the concept of business as cold, ruthless and lacking in all sentiment or spiritual motivation.[15]

The goal of this broad coat of whitewash is to give advertisers an antiseptic environment in which to sell their goods—an environment that nobody could possibly find

---

BITING THE HAND THAT FEEDS

The media today are a lot less subservient to advertisers than they were fifty or even ten years ago. A good example of this new-found independence was an April, 1973, CBS documentary entitled "You and the Commercial." Narrator Charles Kuralt took the viewer behind the scenes of television advertising. He showed market research efforts to make commercials more persuasive, and interviewed philosopher Erich Fromm on the suggestive power and social impact of advertising. He delved into the emotional topic of children's advertising, and noted that the average child sees 25,000 commercials a year and spends more time in front of a TV set than in school. He covered the laxness of government regulation, the luxuriousness of production budgets, and nearly every other aspect of the world of the TV commercial.[16]

Advertisers were unhappy about "You and the Commercial," as CBS knew they would be. It produced the show anyhow.

offensive. This is desirable for two reasons. First, advertisers are afraid that offended readers and viewers might project the controversy onto the ads too, and angrily buy their widgets from someone else. Second, advertisers believe that a sales pitch is most likely to be successful if the audience isn't thinking. Anything that wakes you up and makes you think—even if it doesn't offend you—may lessen the impact of the ads.

All this is especially important on television, which caters to a mass audience of millions that tends to view programs and commercials as all part of the same steady stream of stuff. In a celebrated incident in 1969, CBS was quick to edit out of the Merv Griffin talk show an appeal by actress Elke Sommer for postcards and letters to be sent to Mrs. Martin Luther King, calling for world peace. Comedian Carol Burnett made a similar appeal on the Christmas Day show and it, too, was censored. Peace, apparently, is a controversial issue. It threatens the narcotic sameness of television that helps us believe the commercials.

In 1972, David W. Rintels, a television writer and chairman of the Committee on Censorship of the Writers Guild of America, testified before the Senate Subcommittee on Constitutional Rights. He complained that writers of TV dramas were not allowed to touch certain topics. On medical shows, for example, the taboos included: the political lobbying of the American Medical Association; the quality and cost of hospital care, especially for the poor; medical education and the supply of doctors; and the need for national health insurance. Rintels read into the record a 1959 memo from the head of an ad agency to a CBS executive:

> We know that your series is striving mightily to do things that are different and outstanding so as a series it will rise above the general level of TV drama. This is fine, but since the series is a vehicle for commercial advertisers, it must also be extremely sensitive to utilizing anything, however dramatic, however different, however well done, if this will offend viewers.

> You know that we can never lose sight of the fact that the sole purpose for which an advertiser spends money is to win friends and influence people. . . . Narrow, prejudiced, ignorant, or what you will, though any part of the population may be, as a commercial vehicle the series must be ever alert not to alienate its viewers.[17]

Rintels summarized his point with a quotation from another writer, William Brown Newman (author of the original "Gunsmoke" script): "In television the writer's job is to write about nothing." [18]

The aversion of advertisers to controversy is largely responsible for the homogenized, sleepy quality of most television entertainment. The only opposing factor is the existence of a small audience that likes thoughtful drama. As we shall soon see, the television and advertising industries are reluctant to meet the needs of this audience very often.

Even more important than the homogenization of television entertainment, the effort to avoid controversy deters the news media from covering many problems of national significance. Once again, television is the biggest offender. Of course a major breaking story merits TV time no matter how controversial it is, but controversial documentaries and features are anathema to most advertisers. In his book *Television and The News*, critic Harry Skornia of the University of Illinois, Chicago Circle, lists these noteworthy subjects which he believes the broadcast media have ignored over the years in deference to advertisers: poverty in America; public utilities bilking the public; the harmful effects of liquor, tobacco, and coffee; air and water pollution; and the problems of labor in labor-management disputes.[19]

THREATS, BRIBES, AND UNDERSTANDINGS

When the average citizen thinks of advertiser influence, two images are likely to come to mind: the sumptuous party at which journalists are wined and dined into the "right" attitude, and the irate merchant who storms into an editor's office and threatens to withdraw all advertising unless. . . . Both images —the bribe and the threat—have some truth to them. There isn't an editor, reporter, or broadcaster of experience who hasn't experienced both at one time or another. But such tactics are too gauche, and so they tend to fail as often as not. In the mid-1950s, the *Wall Street Journal* managed to get the details on the new General Motors cars before the information was officially released. GM quickly cancelled $11,000 worth of advertising in retribution. The *Journal* was not intimidated, and published the story anyhow.[20]

More recently, St. Louis Cardinal owner Gussie Busch fired his radio commentator Harry Caray. The word went out that any station that hired Caray would not only get no ads from Busch's Budweiser beer, but also no business from the two largest advertising agencies in town. Months later Caray was back on the air in St. Louis—sponsored by Schlitz. The experiences of Bumble Bee Tuna and Jim Lange are further examples of intimidation that failed.

More subtle techniques are more effective, and always have been. During the oil pipeline wars of the 1890s, the Ohio press was highly critical of John D. Rockefeller's Standard Oil Company. The boss assigned his trusted "fixer," Dan O'Day, to sweeten the sour press. O'Day did not threaten anybody, nor did he offer any outright bribes. Instead, he planned a heavy advertising campaign for Mica Axle Grease, a very minor Standard product. Huge ads were purchased on a regular basis in every Ohio newspaper. Editors got the point: Don't bite the hand that feeds. After a year of receiving monthly checks from the axle grease subsidiary, most had quit knocking John D. and the parent corporation. Mica, by the way, became a top seller.[21]

Even this indirect sort of bribe is not often necessary. Over the years, editors have come to know what advertisers expect, and at least on minor stories they supply it without questioning. Nobody has to tell the copy editor of a newspaper to cut the brand name of the car out of that traffic accident article. Editors understand without being told that including the name might embarrass the manufacturer. They understand that embarrassing the manufacturer would be in "bad taste" for the newspaper. They understand that that just isn't the sort of thing one business (publishing) does to another business (automotive). Copy editors don't have to be threatened or bribed; such tactics would only offend and bewilder them.

Can you call this advertiser control? Only in the sense that in the back of every editor's mind is the need to keep advertisers happy. The local auto dealer, after all, doesn't even know that the newspaper copy editor is "censoring" the name of the car. Should the name slip in, the dealer would probably take no action at all. At worst, the topic might come up casually when dealer and managing editor met at the country club or the next Chamber of Commerce meeting. Certainly most auto dealers would not threaten to withdraw their ads over such a minor offense; they need the newspaper at least as much as the newspaper needs them. The important point is that this conflict of wills seldom takes place. Copy editors know their job, and so the brand of the car rarely gets into the traffic accident report.

BROADCASTING: A SPECIAL CASE

When radio was invented at the turn of the century, few thought it would ever be a profit-making medium, and fewer still expected it to earn its profit from advertising. Events reversed expectations:

1919: Dr. Frank Conrad begins the first regular entertainment broadcast, offering Pittsburgh crystal set owners a few hours of music each week.

1920: Westinghouse obtains the first commercial radio license, KDKA, also in Pittsburgh.

1921: Thirty commercial stations are in operation throughout the country.

1922: WEAF in New York sells the first radio advertisement.

1923: The Eveready Battery Company produces its own radio program, "The Eveready Hour," on WEAF.

1924: A "network" hook-up is arranged to broadcast "The Eveready Hour" on several stations at the same time.

By 1927, only eight years after the Conrad broadcast, "The Eveready Hour" was a part of a nationwide NBC radio network. It offered a varied diet of concert music, dance music, and drama. Programs were prepared jointly by the station, the company, and its advertising agency. They were submitted to the sponsor three weeks before air time, and if declared unsatisfactory they were revised or abandoned.

There were objections voiced to the delivery of the radio medium into the hands of the advertisers—but they were quickly outshouted by soaring profit curves. Throughout the 1930s and 1940s, advertisers and their agencies closely controlled the content of the programs they sponsored, and sponsored programs made up the bulk of network radio schedules. The job of the station was merely to sell the time and run the transmitter; the sponsor and its ad agency handled everything else. When commercial television was introduced in the late forties, this pattern of advertiser control and advertiser production was accepted from the very start.

By the late 1950s, the cost of even a single prime-time network television show had grown too big for all but the largest advertisers to afford. When the "quiz show scandals" at the end of the decade brought public pressure on the networks to accept responsibility for programming, broadcasters were only too happy to comply. It was good business as well as good politics. ABC set the trend by encouraging sponsors to scatter their ads among several different programs; NBC and CBS soon followed suit. By 1962 it was rare for a sponsor to produce its own show. Some continued to sponsor particular network-produced programs, while most settled for the ABC "scatter plan" system. This is still the pattern in broadcasting today.

Though the networks took over programming control from advertisers in the early sixties, they did nothing to alter the fundamental nature of the programs. Advertisers no longer write their own shows, but they still decide where to put their ads. A show without advertiser appeal is unlikely to be produced, unlikelier to be broadcast, and unlikeliest to be renewed for a second season.

To most Americans this sounds like a truism, an inevitable result of the free-market system. It isn't. Even within the context of commercial broadcasting, advertisers need not be all-powerful. In England, for example, sponsors are not permitted to choose where in the day's program schedule their advertising spots will be placed. They simply purchase so many minutes of television time, and the station decides which minutes to put where. British advertisers are free to utilize television or not as they like. But they can-

HOW MUCH FOR A MINUTE?

Advertisers pay the networks an incredible sum for the privilege of reaching you in your living room. In the 1973 season, the cost of one minute on "All In The Family" was $120,000. "M*A*S*H" was getting nearly $100,000 a minute, while advertisers paid a mere $80,000 for a minute on the Monday night football game. The Super Bowl went for an astounding $200,000 a minute. All these figures come out to about half a cent per viewer.

THE QUIZ SHOW SCANDALS

On June 7, 1955, emcee Hal March posed before the world's first "isolation booth" and announced to a massive CBS network audience: "This is The $64,000 Question." The era of big-money TV quizzes had begun. NBC countered with "Twenty-One," and within a year six similar programs were on the air.

"The $64,000 Question" was the invention of Revlon, Inc., a cosmetics firm, with some assistance from Revlon's ad agency, a few independent producers, and CBS. It was a package product: Revlon and its agency supervised the content of the show as well as the commercials, and paid CBS $80,000 for each half hour of network time. CBS had some say in how the show was run, but not much. The other quiz programs were similarly organized.

Syndicated columnist Steve Scheuer was the first to suggest that the shows were frauds, fixed to allow certain participants to win. Soon a former contestant on NBC's "Twenty-One" told a congressional subcommittee that he had been forced to lose to Charles Van Doren.

As a result, 1959 was a year of television soul-searching. Van Doren admitted that he had been fed the questions and answers for his $129,000 streak on "Twenty-One." The packagers of "The $64,000 Challenge," meanwhile, revealed that Revlon executives had personally decided which contestants to bump and which to keep. Both networks claimed to know nothing, fixing the blame on the sponsors, ad agencies, and producers. In November, 1959, CBS President Frank Stanton told a House subcommittee:

> I want to say here and now that I was completely unaware . . . of any irregularity in the quiz shows on our network. When gossip about quiz shows in general came to my attention, I was assured by our television network people that these shows were completely above criticism of this kind. . . . This has been a bitter pill for us to swallow. . . . We propose to be more certain . . . that it is we and we alone who decide not only what is to appear on the CBS Television Network but how it is to appear.[22]

Stanton kept his promise, as did the other two networks. Broadcasters resumed control of programming content, and the scandals since have been few and far between.

---

not pick their program, and therefore cannot influence programming to any great extent.

American television is designed to attract advertising, and advertising is designed to influence the largest possible audience. It follows that the great majority of TV programming must be aimed at the "mass market," at the lowest common denominator of public viewing tastes. The potential audience for a classical opera may be, say, one million viewers. The potential audience for a soap opera in the same time slot may be ten million. Naturally television will choose the soap opera, not the classical opera, to broadcast. The classical opera will not even be allotted one-tenth as much broadcast time as the soap opera (though it has one-tenth the potential audience)—for what advertiser would be willing to sponsor such a minority-interest program?

Even when advertisers can be found for small-audience shows, television stations are reluctant to broadcast them. A single "highbrow" program can force millions of viewers to switch to another channel; once switched, they may stay there for hours or even days. The ratings on adjacent shows are therefore lowered. Other advertisers begin to complain, and station profits begin to drop.

Exactly this happened to the Firestone Hour in the early 1960s. Sponsored by the Firestone Tire & Rubber Company, the classical music program had a consistently low rating. Firestone did not mind; it wanted an "elite" audience for its ads. But adjacent mass-market programs were suffering. After moving the show around a few times in an effort to reduce the adjacency problem, the network finally gave up and refused to continue the show. Companies like Bell Telephone and Xerox, which like to sponsor documentaries and cultural programs, have had similar difficulties finding a time slot.

In 1970, United Press International moved the following news item: "Armstrong Cork Co., whose Circle Theater was one of television's best known dramatic shows, said . . . it has dropped video advertising because the networks offer only childish programming." [23] Apparently Armstrong was unable to find a network willing to produce another Circle Theater.

Advertising revenue is at the heart of the debate over the quality of television programming. In the 1959–60 season NBC and CBS tried an experiment, offering several "high-quality" music and drama shows. ABC, financially weakest of the three networks, refused to go along. Instead, it chose that season to introduce its gory detective series "The Untouchables," plus ten westerns a week. Ratings were excellent and ABC closed the gap on its older rivals. The next season, NBC and CBS followed the ABC lead, with detective and western series galore. The experiment was over.

Comments critic Robert Eck: "In the audience delivery business, you do not have the luxury of setting either your standards or those of your audience. Instead, they are set for you by the relative success of your competitors." [24] This is another way of saying what NBC President Robert Kintner answered in response to the question "Who is responsible for what appears on network cameras?": "The ultimate responsibility is ours," Kintner replied, "but the ultimate power has to be the sponsor's, because without him you couldn't afford to run a network." [25]

Notes

1 "News for Advertisers: A Denver Case," *Columbia Journalism Review,* Summer, 1966, p. 10.

2 William L. Rivers and Wilbur Schramm, *Responsibility in Mass Communication,* 2nd ed. (New York: Harper and Row, 1969), p. 107.

3 Donald I. Rogers, "Businessmen: Don't Subsidize Your Enemies," *Human Events,* August 11, 1962, pp. 599–600.

4 Bernice Buresh, "Boycott Turns on Wisconsin Publisher," *Chicago Journalism Review,* September, 1969, pp. 7–11.

5 Telephone conversation between William F. Schanen, III and David M. Rubin, July 9, 1974.

6 Vern E. Edwards, Jr., *Journalism in a Free Society* (Dubuque, Iowa: William C. Brown, 1970), p. 176.

7 Carl E. Lindstrom, *The Fading American Newspaper* (Gloucester, Mass.: Peter Smith, 1964).

8 "NBC Will Replace McGee by July 31," *New York Times,* July 19, 1974, p. 70.

9 "Good Buy, Chet," *Newsweek,* April 10, 1972, p. 57.

10 Alexander Kendrick, *Prime Time* (Boston: Little, Brown & Co., 1969), p. 449.

11 Peter Funt, "How TV Producers Sneak in a Few Extra Commercials," *New York Times,* August 11, 1974, section 2, pp. 1, 15.

12 "Why You Won't See Bumble Bee Ads on C.B.S.-TV," *New York Times,* March 7, 1972, p. 79.

13 David M. Rubin and David P. Sachs, *Mass Media and the Environment* (New York: Praeger, 1973), p. 46.

14 "FM Newsman Irks Local Stores, Gets Fired; Beefs to FCC, Gets His Job Back," *Variety,* April 12, 1972, p. 2.

15 Dallas Smyth, "Five Myths of Consumership," *Nation,* January 20, 1969, p. 83.

16 "TV: Those Commercials," *New York Times,* April 26, 1973, p. 87.

17 David W. Rintels, "Will Marcus Welby Always Make You Well?" *New York Times,* Sunday edition, March 12, 1972, pp. D1, D17.

18 *Ibid.,* p. D17.

19 Harry Skornia, *Television and The News* (Palo Alto, Calif.: Pacific Books, 1968), pp. 87–90.

[20] Rivers and Schramm, *Responsibility,* pp. 108–109.

[21] Will Irwin, "Our Kind of People," *Collier's,* June 17, 1911, pp. 17–18.

[22] Fred W. Friendly, *Due to Circumstances Beyond Our Control* (New York: Random House, 1967), pp. 101–102.

[23] United Press International, April 8, 1970.

[24] Robert Eck, "The Real Masters of Television," *Harper's,* March, 1967, p. 49.

[25] "The Tarnished Image," *Time,* November 16, 1959, pp. 72–80.

Suggested Readings

CUNNINGHAM, ANN MARIE, "Sour Grapes," [*MORE*], November, 1974.

ECK, ROBERT, "The Real Masters of Television," *Harper's,* March, 1967.

MARTIN, TERRENCE L., "Wilting in the Heat," *Columbia Journalism Review,* May/June, 1974.

SKORNIA, HARRY, *Television and the News.* Palo Alto, Calif.: Pacific Books, 1968.

Chapter 6
Source Control

Only a small percentage of the news covered by the mass media comes from on-the-scene reporting. The vast majority must be obtained from news sources—often through interviews, even more often through mimeographed press releases and the like. Sources are seldom unbiased. In one way or another they usually try to control the form and content of the news they offer. Such news management on the part of both governmental and private sources has a tremendous effect on the nature of the news reaching the public.

Throughout his eight years in the White House, President Dwight Eisenhower depended heavily on his press secretary, James Hagerty. One of Hagerty's main jobs was covering up for his boss's longish vacations. *Time* magazine described the process:

> Hagerty struggled valiantly and, to a point, successfully in stressing work over play. . . . He took with him on trips briefcases full of executive orders, appointments, etc., and parceled them out daily to make news under the Augusta or Gettysburg dateline. He encouraged feature stories on the Army Signal Corps' elaborate setup to keep Ike in close touch with Washington. . . . He did anything and everything, in short, to keep the subjects of golf

and fishing far down in the daily stories about the President.[1]

If Hagerty had been working for General Motors, say, instead of Eisenhower, his job would presumably have been a little different. In place of diligence, he would have stressed the economic health of the company and the beauty of its new models. In place of vacations, he would have obscured price hikes and auto safety complaints.

But wherever they work, the purpose and technique of press secretaries and public-relations people are the same. The purpose: to protect and advance the good image of the employer. The technique: news management.

In one form or another, news management is probably as old as news. But conscious, full-time, *professional* news management is a relatively recent invention. The first corporate press agent was hired in the 1880s. The first presidential press secretary was hired twenty years later (by Theodore Roosevelt). Today there are more than 100,000 public-relations people working for private companies, plus tens of thousands more in government. The federal government spends more than $400 million a year on public relations and public information. The executive branch alone spends more on publicity and news than the entire combined budgets of the legislative and judicial branches. All together, the cost of federal government PR is more than double the total newsgathering expenses of AP and UPI, the three television networks, and the ten largest American newspapers.[2] News sources, in short, pay more to manage the news than the media pay to collect it.

PRESS RELEASES

By far the most important vehicle for news management is the press release. Preparing such releases and distributing them to the media is the main job of nearly every public-relations person.

Releases are ground out by the bushel. In a single ten-day period, one small country newspaper in Vermont received 149 handouts from 68 different sources, totaling to 950 pages or nearly a quarter of a million words —more than the length of this book. The list included 80 releases from businesses; 16 from philanthropic organizations; 14 from government; 6 from lobbies and pressure groups; 29 from educational institutions; and 4 from political parties.[3] That's for a *small* newspaper. The average metropolitan daily receives well above a hundred releases a day; the average big-city broadcast station gets at least sixty.

Most releases—say around three-fifths—are thrown away. The bulk of the rest are either used as is or rewritten and condensed in the office, usually the latter. Only a few releases (all the staff has time for) are actually investigated by reporters.

Though most releases are never used, those that are used account for an incredible share of the average news hole. In many newspapers more than half the articles printed started as press releases. Some departments are almost entirely dependent on handouts— finance, travel, etc. Even political reporters have time to cover only the most important stories themselves; for much of the day-to-day news of local government they count on the City Hall mimeograph machine. The backbone of every news beat is the press release.

However important releases may be in reporting local news, they are far more vital

---

ENVIRONMENTAL PRESS RELEASES

In 1971, eleven environmental reporters in the San Francisco area agreed to list every press release dealing with the environment that they received over an eight-week period. The total came to more than 1,300 releases. Out of this enormous pile, the reporters kept and filed 268 releases. They wrote stories based on 192 releases—an average of more than 17 release-based stories per reporter.

Where did the releases come from? The largest number, 566, were from government agencies. Next came industry and industrial organizations, with 315 releases; then academic and civic groups, with 234 releases; and finally environmental pressure groups, with 229 releases.

At the same time, 200 locally written stories were traced back to see where the information in them came from. Of the 200 stories, 46 (nearly a quarter) were nothing more than rewritten press releases. Another 28 stories were based on press releases plus additional research by the reporter; 31 more resulted from phone calls to the reporter, personal visits to the newsroom, or other public-relations tactics. Only 95 of the 200 environmental stories—fewer than half—were written without the help of PR people.[4]

on the state, national, and international levels. A Washington correspondent covering the White House spends relatively little time chatting with the president, or even the president's aides. Most of his or her effort is devoted to reading and rewriting White House releases. And reporters covering the "minor" executive departments have even less time for in-person digging and interviewing. Instead, they spend a few hours each morning picking up the day's handouts from the various agencies and offices within their assigned departments. The rest of the day they sort through the stack—throwing out most, rewriting many, following up on maybe one or two.

As for Congress, releases dominate news coverage there too, as this item from the *Washington Post* shows:

> A freshman Senator outslicked his veteran colleagues to pick off the easiest publicity plum available last week. He was Clifford P. Case (R-N.J.), whose reaction comment to the President's decision [to veto the Natural Gas Bill] was the first to hit the Senate press gallery. His prize was a prominent play in the afternoon newspapers.
>
> Behind his speed was the quick thinking and faster legs of Sam Zagoria, Case's administrative assistant. . . .
>
> Zagoria had run off several copies of the Senator's "isn't it grand" statement early Wednesday morning. He then parked himself by the Associated Press teletype in the Senate lobby. When the flash came through, he hightailed it back to the press gallery, one floor above, where eager reporters were waiting to write reaction accounts. Zagoria beat a runner for Sen. William A. Purtell (R-Conn.) by one minute flat.[5]

Governments (as well as private organizations) use press releases to announce new policies and procedures, to publicize plans and accomplishments, to reveal facts and research findings, etc. They may also use releases to influence the course of events. The Defense Department, for example, might issue a release on the "tight nuclear race" between the U.S. and the Soviet Union just as the State Department is planning strategy for arms limitation talks. It seems fair to surmise that at least one purpose of the release is to force the negotiators to adopt a tougher stand.

The danger of press releases is obvious— they put the initial decision as to what is and is not newsworthy in the hands of the source instead of the reporter or editor. Even when the media follow up a release on their own, the questions they ask and those they forget to ask are likely to be determined by what's in the release. And most releases are *not* followed up. The blatant propaganda may be edited out, but the substance is printed— and it is substance that the source, not the reporter, has selected. It is substance designed to help build the image and advance the aims of its source. It is, in short, public relations. But it passes for news.

But before condemning press releases entirely, consider the alternatives. If a newspaper were to quit relying on press releases but continued covering all the news it now covers, it would need at least two or three times as many reporters. That would cost money—and how many of us want to pay fifty or sixty cents for our daily paper? And if a paper stopped covering the news it now gets from releases, we would all be a good deal less informed. The less glamorous arms of the federal government would then operate in almost total secrecy; the plans, promotions, and products of business would come and go without notice; graduations, charity drives, and PTA meetings would be nearly invisible to the community. Press releases inevitably reflect the interests of their source, but what they say is often legitimate news just the same.

Short of an outright ban, what can we do to control press-release abuses? One very sensible suggestion that has often been made is to identify release-based news stories in the same way we now identify wire service stories, with the intials PR (instead of AP or UPI)

LEAKS AND TRIAL BALLOONS

When a top public official wants to try out a new policy without committing the government to it, standard procedure is to release the proposal to the press in secret. In late 1956, for example, the Eisenhower administration begun formulating a new policy toward the Middle East. Secretary of State John Foster Dulles invited a select group of Washington correspondents to his home and *leaked* to these reporters the nature of the change. The story was published, on Dulles's instructions, with the source identified only as a high, unnamed State Department official. This was the *trial balloon*. Dulles now waited to see how the public, other government officials, and foreign governments reacted to the proposal. The response was favorable, so Dulles formally announced the new "Eisenhower Doctrine" for the Middle East. If the feedback had been discouraging, Dulles was free to change the plan or to disavow it entirely. Similarly, in 1971 Henry Kissinger anonymously told reporters that Soviet support of India in its dispute with Pakistan might endanger the U.S.–Soviet détente. Kissinger's goal was to warn Russia without committing himself.

The leak and the trial balloon are accepted tactics of diplomacy, but they are subject to abuses. Politicians can punish critical reporters by leaking exclusive stories to those who are not so critical. Alternatively, they can force a reporter to write a one-sided article by trading exclusive information for the reporter's promise not to interview anyone else on the subject. Both practices are common in Washington today.

At best, leaks and trial balloons are delicate. They enable government officials to say anonymously what they don't dare to say on the record. Beyond doubt they are a useful tool of diplomacy, and beyond doubt they are here to stay. But they may mislead the public. Conscientious reporters participate in them reluctantly and cautiously.

---

in parentheses at the start of the story. This would at least warn readers that what was coming had not been checked out by the newspaper's staff. Another proposal would urge reporters to rely on releases only for routine news, not for controversial public issues.

The biggest problem with press releases is not that they are biased, but that their bias is predominantly in one direction. Most releases come from government, industry, or other big organizations with professional PR staffs. Smaller community groups, representing less established perspectives, are far less likely to have the time or skill to write an acceptable release. If all kinds of people with all kinds of viewpoints had equal skill in public relations, news management would be a much less serious threat. The media would still be manipulated, of course, but at least they would be manipulated by everybody. Currently, they are manipulated only by those who know how.

OTHER TECHNIQUES

Press releases are the most useful weapon in the arsenal of news management, but they are by no means the only one. There are at least four other techniques of interest:

1. Canned news and editorials.
2. Pseudo-events.
3. Junkets and favors.
4. Direct access.

We will discuss each in turn.

1. Canned News and Editorials. In the early 1960s, Rafael Trujillo, dictator of the Dominican Republic, hired a New York press agent named Harry Klemfuss to help build pro-Trujillo sentiment in this country. Klemfuss, in turn, hired the U.S. Press Association, Inc., a company specializing in canned news and editorials. For a fee of only $125, the company mailed the following "news item" to 1,300 dailies and weeklies throughout the country: "Today the Dominican Republic . . . is a bulwark of strength against Communism and has been widely cited as one of the cleanest, healthiest, happiest countries on the globe. Guiding spirit of this fabulous transformation is Generalissimo Trujillo who worked tirelessly. . . ."[6] It is not known how many papers actually carried the story, but Klemfuss and Trujillo considered their money well spent.

Canned articles and editorials are like releases, except that they are carefully designed to be used without editing—hence the term "canned." Many come in the form of mats or plates to be inserted right into the paper; all are in standard newspaper style. Most metropolitan dailies refuse to use canned material. But smaller papers may be desperate for content, and the temptation of a well-written, well-researched, *free* article or editorial is often too great to resist.

For corporations and political pressure groups, canned material offers an opportunity to publish anonymous propaganda.

Among the clients of the U.S. Press Association are the American Cotton Manufacturers Institute, the American Legion, the Bourbon Institute, and the Right to Work Committee. The American Medical Association and the National Association of Manufacturers regularly employ similar services. Typically, a canned article or editorial will be picked up by roughly 200 newspapers. Ben Bagdikian calculates that the cost of placing advertisements in all 200 papers would run at least ten times as much—and the canned stuff is more effective than ads.[7]

The most successful canned articles are fillers and light features, which many editors slip into their papers without even noticing. The North American Precis Syndicate, for example, has done very well with stories like "Candy Through the Ages" (sponsored by the candy industry), "How to Keep Your Dog in Condition" (plugging the use of veterinarians), and "How to Be a Two-Faced Woman" (promoting eyeglasses).[8]

2. Pseudo-Events. The cognac industry of France wanted to introduce the product to the American market with a splash, so in the late 1950s it hired a PR man named Bill Kaduson. On President Eisenhower's 67th birthday in 1957, Kaduson offered several

A FREE WIRE SERVICE

Business Wire is a privately owned, San Francisco-based public-relations wire service. Here's how it operates. Corporations, industry associations, and other groups (including at least one university, Stanford) pay Business Wire to carry their press releases. The company rewrites the releases to resemble standard AP-type wire stories. Then they go out on the wire, to teletypewriters installed—without charge—in the newsrooms of subscribing newspapers, magazines, and broadcast stations.

From the media's standpoint, Business Wire is a free wire service, carrying news of special interest to the business editor. From the customer's standpoint, it is a fast, inexpensive, respectable way to get press releases out to the media.

It works. As of 1971, Business Wire had about 400 customers, and nearly a hundred outlets in many Western states. General Manager Lorry Lokey estimates that the *San Francisco Chronicle,* for example, uses about one-fifth of the stories it gets from the wire. And some Business Wire stories are later picked up by the Associated Press or United Press International.[9]

bottles of 67-year-old cognac as a gift. He insured the bottles for $10,000, then took them to the city room of the *Washington Daily News* for photos. The cognac was poured into a special keg and conveyed to the White House by two uniformed guards, where secret service agents accepted the gift on behalf of Eisenhower. The stunt received newspaper headlines throughout the country.

Kaduson also arranged for French Premier Pierre Mendes-France to be photographed drinking cognac when he visited the United States in 1954. He got a French chef onto the Jack Paar television show to create on camera the world's biggest crepe suzette, sprinkled with a gallon of cognac. Between 1951 and 1957 cognac sales in the U.S. increased from 150,000 to 400,000 cases a year. Bill Kaduson claimed much of the credit.[10]

The interesting thing about Kaduson's antics is that they took place solely to gain the attention of the mass media. In Daniel Boorstin's terms, they were not real events at all, but rather "pseudo-events," performed in order to be reported.[11] The media are easily manipulated through pseudo-events. By their very nature they feel compelled to cover conventions, demonstrations, dedications, press conferences, stunts, and the like. Anyone who desires news coverage is therefore wise to arrange a convention, a demonstration, a dedication, a press conference, or —like Kaduson and his cognac—a stunt.

The congressional committee hearing is a perfect example of a government-sponsored pseudo-event. Some hearings, of course, aim at obtaining information on proposed legislation. The House impeachment hearings, for example, involved obviously momentous decisions. And although the Senate Watergate hearings were not primarily aimed at legislation, they did uncover vital new information (such as the existence of the White House tapes), and they put the Watergate story on the record, live, for a daytime television audience of 25 million people. But many congressional hearings have a different purpose—to provide publicity for the committee, its members, and its predetermined legislative goals. The 1951 hearings of the Senate Crime Investigating Committee were the first ever to be televised, and they catapulted their chairman, Senator Estes Kefauver, to national fame. The chief witness was Frank Costello, an over-the-hill ex-con, with no real power and little inside information. Kefauver knew that Costello's testimony would have great public impact on TV, despite its limited value as a source of new knowledge. And he was right.[12]

Television is uniquely susceptible to manipulation by means of pseudo-events. The chief advantage of TV over the other media is its ability to reproduce talking pictures. Quite naturally, TV news directors strive constantly to make use of this ability, to come up with effective films or videotapes. But most television news departments are severely understaffed. They can seldom afford to let a reporter and camera operator spend a day or two digging into a story the hard way. It is much, much easier to send the team to cover a ready-made story—a press conference, say, or a demonstration.

A news source who arranges for easy-to-shoot effective footage will always get better coverage from television than a source who fails to do so.

THE DANGERS OF HAIR

The power of a good public-relations expert is incalculable. Throughout the 1920s, PR man Edward L. Bernays promoted the idea that loose or long hair is a health and safety hazard in restaurants, manufacturing plants, and such. As a result, many states passed laws requiring waitresses and female factory workers to wear hair nets at all times. Bernays was working for the Venida hair net people.

"I HAVE HERE IN MY HAND. . . ."

Perhaps the greatest news manager of them all was Senator Joseph McCarthy, the Red-baiting Wisconsin Republican. He began as soon as he reached Washington in 1948, treating reporters to Wisconsin cheese and making himself available night and day for comment on any subject.

McCarthy was a master of the pseudo-event. Often he would call a morning press conference solely to announce an afternoon press conference, thus earning headlines in both editions. His lists of Communists in government service were released only minutes before newspaper deadlines. This insured that he could not be questioned closely, and also made it impossible for the accused to reply in the same edition as they were charged. McCarthy made his most damaging allegations from the Senate floor, where he was protected by law from libel suits. He seldom permitted reporters to examine the "documentary evidence" that he habitually carried in his briefcase and frequently waved in his hand.

By 1952, most of the Washington press corps already knew that McCarthy's claims were often fraudulent and always self-serving. Yet they continued to accord him headlines, day after day. They were caught in the mechanics of the pseudo-event: When a famous Senator accuses someone of Communism it's news—even if the charge is without foundation.

Then came the televised Army-McCarthy hearings of 1954. This time the news management was in the Army's hands, and McCarthy could do nothing to halt the pitiless publicity that brought his career in demagoguery to a quick end.

---

3. Junkets and Favors. From the November 20, 1954, issue of *Editor & Publisher* comes the following article:

> Schenley Distributors, Inc. [threw a party] for the first American importation of Canadian OFS, Original Fine Canadian. It seems that the first shipment was due in New York aboard the SS President Monroe. So a special car on a New Haven Railroad train was arranged to take the press representatives from New York to Boston . . . [followed by] an overnight trip on the Monroe to New York. The letter of invitation said: "I know you will thoroughly enjoy it, for we are prepared with sumptuous cuisine and delightful entertainment." An *E&P* staffer noted: "And with a boat load of whiskey, it sounds like a perfect lost weekend." [13]

The goal of a press junket like this is, of course, to put reporters in a good mood, thus insuring favorable news coverage. Apparently it works, or junkets wouldn't be the tradition they are. Most large corporations and many small ones organize junkets from time to time. So do some philanthropic groups, and others interested in keeping reporters happy. Even the federal government has been known to take journalists on tours of foreign military installations and the like.

News sources generally do their best to make life pleasant for reporters. Customary favors run the gamut from free movie tickets for reviewers to cash "contests" for articles, from banquet invitations to outright bribes. Some of these practices are obnoxious and some are not, but all have the same purpose—to influence the news in the source's favor.

4. Direct Access. Where possible, news sources generally prefer to have their say directly to the public, without "interference" from reporters and editors. Paid advertising is the most obvious example of direct access, but it has disadvantages—it costs money, it gets low readership, and it is distrusted. Advertising may be the best that private companies can manage, but the government can do better.

Before the development of radio, public officials had few means of reaching the public. They could speak personally with small groups, either in their offices or publicly. They could use the postal system. Or they could direct their efforts to reporters and work through the mass-circulation newspapers.

Radio opened up another method. It permitted politicians to address a mass public directly, with no reporters to interpret their words. President Franklin Roosevelt was the first to make use of this medium; his "fireside chats" told millions of listeners how he planned to halt the Depression of the 1930s. Roosevelt had everything he needed to make effective use of radio—a warm voice, an easy manner, and the right to demand free air time whenever he wanted it. In theory, perhaps, a broadcaster can turn the president down, but no broadcaster ever has.

Television, like radio, offers direct access to the public. It is also a far more powerful, ubiquitous, and believable medium. This raises a problem, aptly expressed by *New York Times* editor James Reston: "Thought-ful observers have wondered, ever since the inception of nationwide television, what would happen if a determined president, who had both the will and the ability to use the networks effectively, really set out to exploit television for his political advantage." [14]

Reston believes that the first American president to make this effort was Richard Nixon. Nixon requested air time far more frequently than any of his predecessors. In January of 1970 he became the first chief executive ever to take to the air simply to explain his reasons for vetoing a bill (an appropriation for the Department of Health, Education, and Welfare). Three months later he was on television twice within a ten-day period, discussing the war in Southeast Asia.

There are two dangers here. First, the president's opponents cannot so readily obtain free air time for rebuttal. Only after sharp controversy did the networks offer some time to critics of the war, and critics of the HEW veto were not able to talk back. Perhaps more important, people automatically tend to support the president in times of crisis—and a direct television address gives the impression of crisis. Pollster George Gallup found increased public approval of the president after every major TV speech. "The

---

GOVERNMENT AS PUBLISHER

The Government Printing Office was authorized by Congress in 1860. Today it sells 67 million publications a year. The GPO currently has about 25,000 titles in stock, ranging from a booklet on how to cook fish to the *Congressional Record* and the *Public Papers of the Presidents*. Each of these publications is a chance for the government to speak directly to the reader, without the mass media in the middle.

The government underwrites book publication in more controversial ways as well. Often a federal agency will put a security classification on essential information on some subject. It may then approach a writer and offer to reveal the information to that writer alone in return for permission to edit the finished book. Such books have been published commercially without mention of the fact that they were censored. The United States Information Agency and the Central Intelligence Agency even pay authors and commercial publishers subsidies for political books favorable to the official government position. The books are distributed overseas through USIA libraries. They are sold domestically, however, with no indication of their origin.[15]

public traditionally rallies around the president immediately following a major foreign policy decision," writes Gallup.[16] The effect is heightened when that decision is announced live and in color on national television.

Faced with Watergate and related scandals that refused to disappear, President Nixon in 1973 began a series of television appearances designed to assure the American public of his integrity. At first it seemed possible that this direct appeal to the people might prove as successful as the president's earlier TV shots had been. But as the Watergate story continued to unfold, the president's standing in the polls continued to slip. Even television could not stop the steady decline in public trust.

On April 29, 1974, President Nixon again made use of the television platform. This time he announced that he was making public the edited transcripts of some of the White House tapes, previously subpoenaed by the House Judiciary (impeachment) Committee. In his speech, the president stressed the enormous length of the transcripts; each conversation was bound in a separate volume, creating the desired appearance of great bulk. Then he offered his own careful summary of the transcripts, presumably hoping that the public would accept the summary and ignore the transcripts. It didn't work. The complete one-volume paperback of the transcripts became a nationwide bestseller; huge segments were printed verbatim in many newspapers and even acted out on some TV stations.

Direct access to the public through television is a powerful tool of news management, but there are some things even it cannot accomplish.

We have described four techniques used by news sources to help them control what is said about them in the mass media— canned news and editorials, pseudo-events, junkets and favors, and direct access. Add to these the omnipresent press release, and a picture of the extent of news management in the United States today begins to emerge.

When people talk about biased reporting, they usually mean the reporter's bias. That is a real problem, of course. But the greatest bias in most news stories is not the reporter's bias, but rather the bias of the source. With the help of news management experts, it is usually possible to get your story into the media pretty much the way you want it, regardless of the reporter's views. Government, industry, and other established institutions have ready access to these sorts of experts. The rest of the country hasn't.

Most cases of news management involve public-relations people who want the story told, and

---

SOFT SOAP

Henry Wieland, Jr., the assistant public-relations director of the Soap and Detergent Association, describes the more or less typical PR operation of his organization:

> A typical day's activities involve several inquiries from news media representatives and also several inquiries from the public, usually requesting industry information about product categories or the environment. In addition, we handle dozens of letters daily from the public and the press. We distribute an average of one news release a month, generally to conservation publications, trade papers, and newspaper, radio, and TV reporters who have requested to be on our mailing lists. . . . We rarely schedule press conferences, but at our annual meeting in January of each year we do have a press room visited by scores of reporters.[17]

The 1971 environmental press kit of the Soap and Detergent Association contained thirty-one separate items, including a release on the safety of arsenic in detergents.

told their way. But sometimes the goal of a news source is not publicity, but secrecy. When the government censors a reporter's article, that too is news management. It is news management also when a reporter is forbidden to attend a meeting, examine a record, or interview an official. And it is news management when the media are threatened, bribed, or even politely asked to keep an item to themselves. These practices are associated mainly with government—but private companies and associations have their secrets too.

GOVERNMENT SECRECY

The central premise of the democratic process is that government officials are accountable to the public. That accountability is essentially meaningless unless the public is told what the officials are doing. "The people's right to know" is therefore a cardinal principle of democracy. In practice this means the media's right to know—because only the media are capable of keeping tabs on the government and reporting back to the public.

The concept of government secrecy is thus totally alien to the democratic theory of press-government relations. But the reality is rather different from the theory. Government officials naturally prefer to conduct much of the public's business in private. Often their reasons are self-serving, but at least occasionally government secrecy seems desirable or even necessary. The problem is deciding when secrecy is called for, and when it isn't. In the United States, the government must have a good reason for hiding anything from the public. But what counts as a good reason?

The most frequent answer—and the most frequently abused—is national security. Nearly everyone agrees that wartime information on troop movements, battle plans, and the like should be kept secret. During World War II an American newspaper revealed that U.S. forces had broken the Japanese Navy Code. (The government of Japan

somehow missed the article, and thus failed to change the code.) Certainly the Defense Department should have prevented publication of that fact.

But most cases are not so clear. Troop movements are related to national security all right, but what about troop morale? Which is more important, that the enemy should be misled about the mood of American forces, or that the American people should be fully informed? And how does national security apply to cold wars, to unpopular wars where many people don't consider the "enemy" an enemy, or to internal "wars" against dissident groups? These are not easy questions to answer.

John B. Oakes of the *New York Times* has pointed out that "the natural bureaucratic tendency to hide mistakes or stupidity behind the sheltering cover of 'national security' is almost irresistible." [18] So is the temptation to use national security as an excuse for political expediency. In 1957, Assistant Secretary of Defense Murray Snyder refused to release photographs of the Titan missile—though the missile itself had been sitting on an open launching pad in Boulder, Colorado, for months. Snyder waited until just before the 1958 elections, then handed the press a picture of President Eisenhower viewing the Titan.[19] Was national security behind the delay, or vote-getting?

In the early 1960s, in such cases as the Bay of Pigs invasion and the Cuban missile crisis, the media voluntarily withheld information from the public, believing it was up to the president to determine what constituted a threat to national security. This practice continued in the early years of the Vietnam war. But as the war grew more and more unpopular, reporters began to substitute their own judgment for the government's as to whether or not it was in the public interest to report a particular piece of news. In November, 1967, the government launched an extensive media campaign to reassure the American people about military progress in Vietnam. Two months later, the Tet offensive against South Vietnam shattered what was left of the media's trust in the official version of the war. Thus, when the government decided to bomb Cambodia in 1969, it could hide this fact from the public only by hiding it from the press as well. (See Chapter 17 for a more detailed discussion of these events.) Reporters were no longer willing to keep the government's secrets for it.

In 1971, a former Defense Department consultant named Daniel Ellsberg delivered to the *New York Times* a copy of a forty-seven-volume top-secret report on Vietnam policy-making throughout the 1960s. Despite the report's security rating and the fact that

LOCAL GOVERNMENT SECRECY

City, county, and state authorities are at least as tempted as the federal government to withhold information from the media. But they don't have the excuse of national security. As a result, considerable progress has been made in guaranteeing the people's right to know on the local level.

By 1975, only two states were without either open-record or open-meeting laws. These regulations are binding on every level of government within the state, right down to the neighborhood board of education. They allow some exceptions—for income tax files and personnel hearings, for example—but by and large they insure that a reporter can get access to local news if he or she works at it.

Unfortunately, working at it often means making a fuss, antagonizing local news sources, and going to court. In 1974, the *Home News* in New Brunswick, N.J., discovered that a local police department was withholding details of crimes "under the pretense the victims want it that way." Because readers were asking why a local crime wave had gone unreported, the *Home News* ran a door-to-door survey. It uncovered eleven burglaries over a two-month period; none of the victims said they had asked the police to keep the crimes secret. Confronted with this information, the police admitted at least twenty-five burglaries had occurred in the two months, but still refused to release names and exact addresses of the victims.[20] There the issue was dropped. Papers like the *Home News* rarely bother to go to court for information, and so police departments continue to protect the images of their communities and their own reputations by keeping secrets.

Even when a newspaper does go to court, it doesn't always win. For an investigation of welfare costs, the *Philadelphia Inquirer* sought access to state and city welfare rolls under the Pennsylvania "right to know" law. The state courts ruled against the paper, partly to protect the privacy of welfare recipients, and partly because the *Inquirer* would not be using the information for "noncommercial" and "nonpolitical" purposes as specified in the law. The U.S. Supreme Court upheld the decision.[21]

The philosophy behind the right to know is well-expressed in the preamble to the Ralph M. Brown Act, California's open-meeting law:

The people of the State do not yield their sovereignty to the agencies which serve them. The people, in delegating authority, do not give their public servants the right to decide what is good for the people to know and what is not good for them to know. The people insist on remaining informed so that they may retain control over the instruments they have created.[22]

It's a good philosophy. With perseverance from the media, it could become a reality as well.

its release was unauthorized, the *Times* selected huge segments of it for publication. *Times* editors argued that the report revealed nothing that was dangerous to American national security, but much that was significant in understanding the tragic U.S. involvement in Southeast Asia. In particular, the report made clear how consistently the American government had lied to the American people about the war.

As soon as the first two installments were published in the *Times,* the federal government applied for a temporary injunction to forbid any further installments. When the *Washington Post* began reprinting the report, it too was served with an injunction. Other newspapers were also involved, but it soon became clear that the *Times* and *Post* would serve as the test case. The Nixon administration believed that only the government was entitled to release classified information, and planned to prove the point by forcing the papers to cease publication. This exercise of prior restraint of the press— a technique characteristic of authoritarian dictatorships—was unprecedented in modern American history. The government argued that the circumstances were unprecedented as well; never before had a major American newspaper determined to reveal defense secrets to the entire world. The conflict between freedom of the press and national security seemed unresolvable.

If the report had actually contained vital defense secrets, as the government claimed, the resulting court decision would have been a legal landmark. But a federal district court, a federal circuit court, and finally the U.S. Supreme Court all studied the documents in question, and all were unable to find any important secrets. True, the report would embarrass certain government officials, and even the government itself—but embarrassment is not the same as national security. The Supreme Court dissolved both injunctions, and the "Pentagon Papers" (as they came to be called) were widely reprinted. Even the U.S. Government Printing

Office came out with an almost complete edition.

Having failed to prevent publication of the Pentagon Papers, the Nixon administration sought to make an example of Ellsberg. But the 1973 trial of Ellsberg (and his associate, Anthony J. Russo Jr.) ironically became instead a "trial" of the administration's efforts to keep its secrets secret. The trial revealed that convicted Watergate conspirators G. Gordon Liddy and E. Howard Hunt had broken into the office of Ellsberg's psychiatrist. It also led to the revelation that Ellsberg had been overheard by government investigators when he used the wiretapped telephone line of a former aide to Dr. Henry Kissinger. The wiretap was one of at least seventeen ordered by the Nixon administration, beginning in 1969, to trace and stop leaks of confidential information to the media. Because of these events, the trial judge dismissed the case against Ellsberg. And the media continued building the case against government secrecy.

EXECUTIVE PRIVILEGE

In 1792, a committee of the House of Representatives asked President George Washington to hand over all documents relating to the Indian massacre of Maj. Gen. Arthur St. Clair and his troops. In response, Washington told Congress that the executive branch of government had a right to withhold any information that might injure the public if disclosed. He turned over the documents anyhow, but later presidents used his arguments for withholding them as the basis for a new "legal" principle, now known as the doctrine of executive privilege. It has been used by many presidents since Washington to thwart not only congressional investigations, but inquisitive reporters as well.

In 1946 the concept of executive privilege was formalized into the Administrative Procedure Act. The act provided that all official documents of the federal government were open to the public, with three exceptions:

1. "Any function of the United States requiring secrecy in the public interest."
2. "Any matter relating solely to the internal management of an agency."
3. "Information held confidential for good cause found." [23]

In other words, everything was open to the public except whatever the executive branch wanted to keep secret.

During the Eisenhower administration, the veil of government secrecy was extended even further. In a series of executive orders, Eisenhower established the security classifications of confidential, secret, and top secret, thus forbidding disclosure of defense-related information. He also commanded all executive employees to keep quiet about their internal discussions, debates, and disagreements. So far as Congress and the public were to know, Eisenhower decreed, the executive branch was unanimous on every issue.

Such matters became far removed from national security. In 1959, for example, a reporter for the *Colorado Springs Gazette-Telegraph* was unable to obtain from the Forest Service a list of ranchers with permits to graze in the Pike National Forest. Explained a Forest Service official: "We have to protect the permittees. We consider their dealings with the Forest Service and their use of Forest Service land strictly a private affair between them and the Forest Service." [24]

Executive privilege, remember, helps the president keep information from Congress as well as from the mass media. In 1955, therefore, the House Subcommittee on Government Information was set up to look into the problem. Under Democrat John E. Moss of California, the committee accumulated thirty-one volumes of testimony. In several cases it forced executive departments to reveal information they had been keeping hidden. In many more cases, it simply documented the need for a stronger federal law protecting the people's right to know.

The Moss Subcommittee was instrumental in drafting the 1966 Federal Public Records Law (also known as the Freedom of Information Act). The bill was designed to put a stop to unnecessary government secrecy—but by the time President Lyndon Johnson signed it into law, nine exemptions had been added. The law thus left plenty of loopholes for government officials who wanted to evade public accountability for their actions.

Still, the Freedom of Information Act was a definite step forward. It put the burden of proof on the government to justify each secret, and it empowered any citizen (or reporter) to sue in federal court for release of a public record. Among the documents that were "sprung" under the law in the late 1960s were: Labor Department lists of corporations violating federal safety standards; Interstate Commerce Commission travel vouchers; Renegotiation Board records on excessive corporate profits from defense contracts; and Federal Aviation Agency handbooks.

CORPORATE "NATIONAL SECURITY"

In the early 1960s the federal government began safety tests on various airplanes, carefully crashing the planes and studying the debris. The tests were open to the public, and were frequently filmed by network television crews. Several airlines complained that the crash telecasts were hurting their image, so the government obligingly declared the tests to be secret. [25]

National security? Or good public relations?

VARIATION ON A THEME

The National Aeronautics and Space Administration is as secret-prone as most other federal agencies. Yet it frequently boasts that the American space program—unlike Soviet Russia's—is completely open and aboveboard.

How does NASA resolve the conflict? Easy. It simply floods reporters with mountains of technical facts and figures—too much to understand and much too much to publish or broadcast. NASA aides ("public-relations scientists") are available night and day to help reporters figure out what it all means. At the height of the space program, the job of interpreting the handouts kept the press too busy to look into more controversial aspects of the NASA operation—subcontracting deals, excessive costs, safety problems, etc. Which, of course, is probably what NASA had in mind all along.

In each of these cases, however, someone had to go to court to *force* the government to release the information. The government did not do so willingly. In fact, as consumer advocate Ralph Nader charged in 1970, "Government officials at all levels . . . have violated systematically and routinely both the purpose and the specific provisions" of the Freedom of Information Act.[26]

And usually there was no one sufficiently interested in a particular secret to bother to sue for it. During the first four years of the Freedom of Information Act, only 112 cases were filed under it, and most of those came from persons or organizations outside the mass media. The typical reporter with a deadline to meet is not free to kill a few weeks in a federal courthouse.

The Watergate scandals of 1972–1974 gave new importance to the fight against excessive government secrecy, and new meaning to the doctrine of executive privilege. The key issue was the White House tapes, secretly recorded by President Nixon over a period of several years. As soon as the existence of these tapes was revealed at the Senate Watergate hearings of 1973, it became obvious that they could answer at least some of the questions that had been raised about Watergate and related scandals.

Claiming executive privilege, Nixon refused to give the Watergate grand jury a number of the tapes it requested. A subpoena

was issued, and Federal Judge John J. Sirica ordered the White House to submit the tapes to him. The president appealed the decision, arguing that the confidentiality of presidential discussions should be protected, and that his right of executive privilege was absolute and could not be second-guessed by any judge.

The U.S. Court of Appeals rejected both arguments.[27] The president responded by firing Special Prosecutor Archibald Cox, because Cox refused to give in on his demand for the tapes. Finally, in response to tremendous public pressure, including cries for impeachment, the president gave up the tapes (one of which was missing eighteen crucial minutes).

In 1974, it all happened again. The House Judiciary (impeachment) Committee requested, then subpoenaed, a number of White House tapes. Nixon announced that he was releasing to the public edited transcripts of *some* of the subpoenaed tapes. Still claiming executive privilege, he refused to give up the tapes themselves. That hardly settled the matter. The Judiciary Committee called for more tapes. The new special prosecutor, Leon Jaworski, called for more tapes. The transcripts were printed and dissected in the media, and some of the staunchest Republican newspapers in the country ran editorials calling for a new president.

In mid-May President Nixon, again invoking executive privilege, announced that he would not give up any more White House tapes.

Special Prosecutor Jaworski's fight for the tapes of sixty-four White House conversations reached the Supreme Court as *United States of America v. Richard M. Nixon* and *Richard M. Nixon v. United States of America*. The Court heard oral arguments on July 9, 1974—just as the House Judiciary Committee was moving toward impeachment. A unanimous decision against Nixon was announced on July 24; the president would have to give up the tapes to Judge Sirica for use in Watergate criminal proceedings. Speaking for the Court, Chief Justice Warren E. Burger acknowledged the existence of a doctrine of executive privilege rooted in the Constitution, but held that the application of that doctrine could be limited by the courts. Executive privilege, he declared, "must yield to the demonstrated, specific need for evidence in a pending criminal trial." [28]

On July 27, the House Judiciary Committee voted an article of impeachment charging the president with obstruction of justice. The second article of impeachment, voted on July 29, charged abuse of presidential power. The third, on July 30, concerned the president's refusal to hand over the tapes subpoenaed by the committee. On August 5, Richard Nixon made public the transcripts of three conversations with H. R. Haldeman, all from June 23, 1972. One of the transcripts demonstrated clearly that Nixon had lied about his 1972 involvement in the Watergate cover-up. Faced with the virtual certainty of impeachment and conviction, Richard Nixon resigned on August 9, 1974.

Spurred on by Watergate, Congress passed seventeen amendments to the 1966 Freedom of Information Act, closing many of the loopholes in the original law. One of the key amendments called for judicial review of classified information to determine if the executive branch was justified in withholding it. In October, 1974, President Ford vetoed the package, arguing that judicial review of classified materials would give federal judges "the initial classification decision in sensitive and complex areas where they have no expertise." [29]

Congress overrode the president's veto in November, and the new Freedom of Information Act went into effect in February, 1975. The amended law enables a reporter—or any citizen—to petition a federal court to decide whether "secret" government information should be released. It also provides strict time limits to keep a government agency from sitting for years on a demand for information. Loopholes still exist, but the amended Freedom of Information Act should make government secrecy a lot harder, and access to government information a lot easier.

CORPORATE SECRECY

Except for the government, Americans are free to keep whatever secrets they want to keep. There are limitations on this freedom; corporations, for example, are required to make public their financial statements and the names of their principal stockholders. But if a company wants to say absolutely nothing to the mass media about its activities, it is within its rights.

Some day the United States may decide that large corporations, like governments, should be held accountable to the people. A huge company like General Motors or Exxon obviously has a very substantial impact on the lives of many Americans. The policy decisions of GM's president, for example, probably affect you more than the policy decisions of all but a handful of government officials. At the moment, you not only have no control over those decisions; you have no right even to know what the decisions are. Only the government must have a good reason for hiding information from the public. Corporations may hide—or try to hide—whatever they wish.

To make matters worse, reporters are a lot less persistent about investigating the secrets of industry than they are in pursuing government secrecy. Most journalists believe that politics is the nation's number one news story, and so business reporters are both fewer in number and lower in status than political reporters. And they are much more polite to their sources. While most government reporters would jump at the chance to expose official double-dealing, many business reporters consider this sort of muckraking grossly inappropriate, almost sacrilegious.

When corporate secrets *are* exposed in the media, it is usually because some interest group opposed to the corporation has obtained and leaked the information. In recent years this has happened with greater and greater frequency, as consumer advocates, environmental groups, populist political movements, and the like have discovered how to use public relations to their own advantage. The result is a startling and important change in business reporting. From the very beginning, political reporters could count on opposition forces to supply the information that government officials were hiding. But until recently large corporations had no organized opposition. Today that opposition exists, and it is slowly teaching the media what rocks to look under in their coverage of corporate America.

The move toward aggressive coverage of business is greatly helped by the increasingly public activities of many American corporations. Most big companies today are enmeshed in a complex network of government subsidies, government contracts, and government regulations. Their dealings with government provide ample opportunity for political reporters to get a good look at their policies and actions. Those dealings also require a more active corporate PR strategy than was customary a few decades ago. To win the government concessions they want and defeat the government regulations they fear, companies must present their case to the public via the media. The days when corporate PR departments felt free to respond to every unpleasant question with a tight-lipped "no comment" are almost over. Today they usually offer an answer of some sort, and thus open the door for other sources to offer quite different answers.

Because of these changes, corporate secrecy today often means manipulating the media, not ignoring them. A good example is the way the Transamerica Corporation lined up press support for construction of its massive, pyramid-shaped headquarters in downtown San Francisco.[30]

The company kept plans for the building secret as long as possible. Finally, in January, 1969, Transamerica announced a press conference. The date was chosen to coincide with the annual chamber of commerce banquet. The company planned to make this "the day of the pyramid," and so it was.

GARDEN CLUB NEWS MANAGEMENT

News management can turn up in the most unlikely places. One afternoon in 1964, reporter Alex Dobish of the *Milwaukee Journal* showed up at the Wauwatosa Woman's Club to cover its monthly meeting. The featured speaker was a local attorney, and his topic was "managed news."

No, said club chairwoman Mrs. Cyril Feldhausen, Mr. Dobish could not cover the lecture. "What he says is for us," she vowed, adding that she would "give the papers what is to be said." Before booting Dobish she reminded him that "we are not getting the news from the news media."[31]

Transamerica filled the morning with briefing sessions for key officials and neighborhood groups. Next, the company served lunch to the publishers and general managers of all the city's newspapers and television stations. Then came the afternoon press conference, featuring not only company officials, but the mayor and the president of the chamber of commerce as well. The mayor himself helped pull back the drapes to expose a five-foot model of the building. The model was prominently displayed at the banquet that evening, and the audience of more than a thousand listened while the chamber of commerce president praised the pyramid.

Press coverage was massive and favorable. The pyramid was front-page news in Northern California. Both wire services carried pictures of the model and the story appeared in more than 140 American newspapers. Even more important to Transamerica, both San Francisco papers ran editorials supporting the project.

Despite the press support, various citizen groups and some public officials fought the Transamerica pyramid. Demonstrations were organized by both sides to rally support. John Krizek, Transamerica's public-relations manager, describes the company's response to one anti-pyramid demonstration—a model of effective public relations:

> Our strategy was not to lock ourselves up in our corporate fortress, and thereby lend credence to the charges of corporate arrogance and insensitivity. And we did not want to expose our officers to a dialogue with highly emotional demonstrators, in front of the TV cameras. Therefore it was the public relations manager who greeted the leaders of the demonstration, as they came through the door, followed by the TV cameras. After promising to deliver their petition to the chairman of the board, he led a covey of attractive corporate secretaries out on the sidewalk to serve iced tea to the demonstrators, with the news cameras as witnesses.

Within less than a year, Transamerica convinced the necessary city boards to approve the exact design it wanted. To forestall any possible rebirth of the opposition, Transamerica held the groundbreaking ceremony in absolute secrecy.

The point of this anecdote is that big corporations can't always keep their secrets totally secret any more. No doubt Transamerica would have liked to build its pyramid without a word to anyone—but it couldn't. So it kept quiet about what it thought it could hide successfully, and embedded the rest in a facile, professional publicity campaign. And it won.

In July and August of 1973, seven American corporations faced an even tougher secrecy problem. In the wake of the Watergate scandals, they were forced to admit that they had illegally donated almost half a million dollars to President Nixon's 1972 re-election campaign. They couldn't keep their guilt a secret. What they could do— and did do—is control the announcement in such a way as to insure minimal public impact.

Before making its confession public, each of the seven companies sent a lawyer to the office of the Watergate special prosecutor, Archibald Cox, to formally acknowledge the illegal contribution; and then to the office of the Finance Committee to Re-Elect the President, to ask for the money back. Then each company issued its public statement— almost invariably on a late Friday afternoon.

Why late Friday afternoon? On Fridays, especially during the summer, most newspapers and broadcast news departments operate short-handed after about 5 P.M. Any statement released at that time is certainly too late for the Friday papers, and probably too late for the Friday evening network news. Since these releases were very short, a reporter who wanted to make a substantial story out of one of them would have had to go looking for more information—hard to do on a Friday night or a Saturday with only a skeleton crew in the newsroom.

The result for most of the companies was a short article in Saturday's newspaper and a short story on Saturday's newscast. Saturday papers and news programs, of course, have the smallest audience of the week. And by the time Monday rolled around and people were available for comment, the confessions were old news. This strategy did not prevent the bad publicity entirely, but it did help ease the PR blow, maybe a lot. Prof. Raymond D. Horton of the Columbia University School of Business comments: "If a public official had to admit to this kind of thing, he'd be in a hell of a lot of trouble. What amazes me is that there isn't more of an outcry. They seem to be getting away with it." [32]

Eventually, at least eighteen American corporations were convicted of making illegal contributions to the Nixon campaign, for a total of $2.5 million. (Can you name one of these corporations? See footnote 32.)

COOPERATION AND INTIMIDATION

Keeping secrets from the public is the hardest kind of news management to accomplish. It takes a lot more clout to keep news out of the media than to get news into the media. In fact, the only sure-fire way to prevent newspapers and broadcast stations from revealing a piece of information is to make certain they never find out about it. But sometimes, inevitably, a reporter stumbles onto the secret. What then?

When the British government is anxious to prevent a certain piece of information from appearing in the British media, it uses what is called the D notice system. A D notice is a formal letter circulated confidentially to the media, warning them that some fact is of secret importance to the government and should not be published. The notice is only advisory, but the implication exists that any item covered in a D notice may also be protected under the British Official Secrets Act. Very few D notices are ever ignored, even when they seem to the

media less concerned with national security than with national scandal.

The United States has nothing like the D notice system. But a confidential chat between a reporter and a government official often serves the same purpose, as does a phone call from the president to the publisher. This is called voluntary self-censorship. In wartime it is necessary, and far safer than government-enforced censorship. In peacetime, however, it is a dangerous form of government news management.

President Franklin Roosevelt had a standing request that no pictures be taken of him while in pain from the polio that crippled him for decades. Once, surrounded by dozens of photographers, the president fell full-length on the floor—and not a single picture was snapped. This was very polite of the photographers—but are journalists supposed to be so polite? In May of 1970, a Nixon adviser asked the *New York Times* to skip certain details of the resumption of bombing in North Vietnam, because those details were "embarrassing" to the president.[33] The *Times* printed them anyhow— a blow to politeness, perhaps, but a victory for the people's right to know.

Traditionally, the American media have tended to cooperate with the American government on the matter of keeping secrets, especially when national security was involved. But in recent years—largely because of the government's "credibility gap" in foreign affairs—such cooperation has waned. The *New York Times* dutifully downplayed the planned Bay of Pigs invasion in 1961, and kept the secret of the Cuban missile crisis in 1962. But by 1971 the *Times* was willingly reprinting top-secret government documents supplied by a former Defense Department consultant. We will return to this issue in Chapter 17.

When cooperation fails as a tool of government news management, intimidation may be tried in its stead. On November 3, 1969, President Richard Nixon appeared on national television to explain, in person, his

Vietnam policy. Immediately after the speech, network commentators and their guests began to discuss the president's remarks—analyzing, interpreting, often criticizing.

Ten days later, addressing the Midwest Regional Republican Committee in Des Moines, Vice President Spiro Agnew delivered a stinging attack on network television news. He focused particularly on the "instant analysis" that had followed the Nixon speech, arguing that TV commentators comprised a "tiny and closed fraternity of privileged men." Agnew continued:

> I am not asking for government censorship or any kind of censorship. I am asking whether a form of censorship already exists when the news that forty million Americans receive each night is determined by a handful of men responsible only to their corporate employers and filtered through a handful of commentators who admit to their own set of biases.[34]

On November 20, the vice president delivered his second attack on the media, this time before the Montgomery, Alabama, Chamber of Commerce. Now he concentrated on "fat and irresponsible" newspapers, especially the *New York Times* and the *Washington Post,* both critics of Nixon's war policy. A third onslaught the following May made it crystal clear that Agnew was fighting against "the liberal news media in this country"—media that were helping to make life difficult for the Nixon administration.

There is much truth in what the vice president had to say. That is not the point. The question is, to what extent was President Nixon, through Agnew, trying to cow the media into being less critical of White House policies? And to what extent did he succeed?

Shortly after Agnew's first speech, the Federal Communications Commission asked all three networks to submit transcripts of their commentary on the Nixon Vietnam telecast—clearly implying at least the possibility of government interference. White

House Director of Communications Herbert Klein made the threat even more explicit. "If you look at the problems you have today," Klein said, "and you fail to continue to examine them, you do invite the government to come in. I would not like to see that happen."[35] As for the effectiveness of the attack, many observers noted that television commentary on the president's later war messages tended to be bland and noncommittal. CBS cut out all "instant analysis" for a while, then reinstated it.

Veteran ABC broadcaster Edward P. Morgan called the first Agnew speech "one of the most significant and one of the most sinister . . . I have ever heard made by a public figure." Morgan added: "It is significant because it is a perfect gauge of what this administration is doing. They've been trying to manage the news ever since the campaign."[36]

The Nixon administration's efforts to intimidate the media reached a first-term peak as the 1972 election approached. Vice President Agnew told a Republican rally in Palo Alto, California, that "the pundits of the networks and national publications" are "demagogues" who "pander to the worst instincts of the leftist radical mob." Presidential speechwriter Patrick J. Buchanan declared in a television interview that if the networks continued to "freeze out opposing points of view and opposing information . . . you're going to find something done in the area of antitrust-type action, I would think." Sure enough, the Justice Department moved against the networks, accusing them of having "monopolized and restrained trade in prime-time entertainment programming." Bill Monroe, Washington editor of the NBC "Today" show, called the administration campaign an effort to "maximize government pressure and minimize media independence."[37]

The attacks on the media continued after the election, with the harshest assaults aimed at the *Washington Post*'s Watergate coverage. Nixon allies applied for the licenses of *Post*-owned broadcast stations in Florida, while at the White House the *Post* stories were explicitly denounced as "character assassination" and "the shoddiest type of journalism." [38] But as the Watergate saga unfolded, the tables were turned. By spring, 1973, White House Press Secretary Ron Ziegler was publicly apologizing to the *Post* and declaring the president's previous statements on Watergate·"inoperative." And still the attacks on the media continued. With his own crimes on the verge of exposure, Agnew kept up the battle, and during his October 26 press conference Nixon himself called the network news "outrageous, vicious, distorted." [39]

The liberal leaning of many top journalists is real; so is the threat of powerful media monopolies. But when high government officials publicly attack the mass media, there is more at stake than merely whether or not their criticisms are justified. Even the most valid arguments, from that source, constitute a form of news management—an attempt to intimidate the media.

Intimidation is by no means confined to the White House. It seems most frequent, in fact, in the military. During the postwar occupation of Japan, General Douglas MacArthur branded several reporters as Communists, and demanded the removal of others because they were unfair or overly critical. Some correspondents were threatened or interrogated, and one had his home raided by Army investigators. The harassment continued until only friendly reporters were left.

In 1962, Assistant Secretary of Defense Arthur Sylvester directed all Pentagon employees to file a report on "the substance of each interview and telephone conversation with a media representative . . . before the close of business that day." [40] Sylvester also had Public Information Officers sitting in on many of the interviews—effectively terrorizing both the source and the reporter. Hanson Baldwin of the *New York Times* recalls that his fellow military writers were investigated by the FBI, shadowed in the halls of the Pentagon, and subjected to frequent telephone wiretaps—all on stories without any overtones of national security.[41]

A STAGED ATROCITY?

Late in 1969, the CBS evening news program broadcast a film of a South Vietnamese soldier stabbing to death a North Vietnamese prisoner. The Pentagon asked CBS to turn over the unused portion of the film for study, and CBS refused. At that point Presidential Assistant Clark Mollenhoff went to work. Mollenhoff decided that CBS had staged the entire episode. He passed along his conclusion to syndicated columnists Jack Anderson and Richard Wilson, who then published versions of the Mollenhoff theory.

On May 21, 1970, CBS responded to the attack. In a seven-minute segment incorporating the original film, the network convincingly demonstrated that it was genuine. CBS correspondents even tracked down the South Vietnamese sergeant who had done the stabbing, and put his cheerful confession on the air. The White House was forced to back down.

Walter Cronkite concluded this unprecedented nationwide rebuttal with the following words:

> We broadcast the original story in the belief it told something about the nature of the war in Vietnam. What has happened since then tells something about the government and its relation with news media which carry stories the government finds disagreeable.

In 1970, CBS produced and broadcast a documentary entitled "The Selling of the Pentagon." One of the most admirable (and controversial) programs of the year, the documentary dealt with the public-relations activities of the Defense Department.

The government's response to this exposé of Pentagon news management was more news management. The Defense Department immediately issued a statement claiming that the documentary was biased, that interviews with Pentagon spokesmen were edited out of context to make them appear more damning than they actually were. Some of the specific complaints were indeed justified, but they effectively obscured the main point —that the documentary itself was essentially accurate. When the Defense Department demanded rebuttal time, CBS agreed—and rebutted the rebuttal in the same program. It also rebroadcast the original documentary for those who had missed it the first time.

In the wake of these events, the House Commerce Committee, headed by Harley O. Staggers (D.-W.Va.), decided to investigate the documentary. The committee asked CBS to supply all film used in preparing the program, including film that was not broadcast. Despite a subpoena, CBS President Frank Stanton refused, claiming the protection of freedom of the press. The committee voted 25–13 to cite Stanton for contempt of Congress, but the full House (not anxious to battle a powerful network on a debatable legal point) turned down the recommendation. It is conceivable, of course, that the Staggers Committee actually contemplated some sort of government regulation of broadcast documentaries (though any such regulation would almost certainly be unconstitutional). But most observers agreed that the purpose of the investigation was more probably to intimidate the media, to make broadcasters think twice before planning another documentary critical of the federal government.

Private corporations are also fond of intimidation as a form of news management.

Back in the 1950s, syndicated columnist Ray Tucker wrote a scathing account of airline lobbying for the rights to a new route. The day before the column was scheduled to appear, Pan American Airways sent the following telegram to every newspaper that subscribed to the syndicate: "Pan American understands that you may be planning to publish a column by Ray Tucker containing numerous scurrilous references to Pan American. We feel it our duty to tell you that we believe a number of these statements to be libelous. You may also wish to take into consideration the columnist's obvious bias against the airline that has earned for the United States first place in world air transport." Many papers decided not to carry the column.[42] The threat to withdraw advertising if a certain story is published (see Chapter 5) is another common variety of corporate intimidation.

In the final analysis, the best answer to secrecy is an uncompromising attitude on the part of the mass media. Reporters must be willing to dig, to ask embarrassing questions, to play off one source against another, to follow up unpromising leads. Editors must be willing to back up their reporters, to give them the time and freedom they need in tracking down elusive secrets. And owners must be willing to publish or broadcast what the reporters and editors have found, without bowing to polite requests or overt threats.

It can be done. In the 1960s, while columnist Joseph Alsop was complaining about "total news control" by Defense Secretary Robert McNamara, his brother Stewart Alsop was publishing a detailed story on American defense planning, based on unauthorized interviews with forty senior Pentagon officials.

Notes

1 "Authentic Voice," *Time*, January 27, 1958, pp. 16–20.

2 William L. Rivers, *The Adversaries* (Boston: Beacon Press, 1970), pp. 49–50.

3 Evan Hill, "Handouts to the Country Editor," *Nieman Reports,* July, 1954, pp. 8–9.

4 David B. Sachsman, "Public Relations Influence on Environmental Coverage," Ph.D. Dissertation, Stanford University, Stanford, California, 1973, pp. 50, 88, 275–76.

5 Douglass Cater, *The Fourth Branch of Government* (New York: Vintage Books, 1959), pp. 52–53.

6 Ben H. Bagdikian, "Journalist Meets Propagandist," *Columbia Journalism Review,* Fall, 1963, p. 30.

7 Ben H. Bagdikian, "Behold the Grass-Roots Press, Alas!" *Harper's,* December, 1964, pp. 102–105.

8 Ralph Blizzard, "How to Edit Without Hardly Being an Editor," *Grassroots Editor,* March/April, 1969, pp. 5–6.

9 Conversation between David Sachsman and Lorry Lokey, July 26, 1971.

10 Irwin Ross, *The Image Merchants* (Garden City, N.Y.: Doubleday, 1959), pp. 23–24, 129.

11 Daniel J. Boorstin, *The Image* (New York: Atheneum, 1962).

12 Ivan Doig, "Kefauver Versus Crime: Television Boosts a Senator," *Journalism Quarterly,* Autumn, 1962, p. 490.

13 Wilbur Schramm, *Responsibility in Mass Communication* (New York: Harper & Brothers, 1957), p. 145.

14 *San Francisco Sunday Examiner and Chronicle,* "Sunday Punch," February 1, 1970, p. 3.

15 Rivers, *The Adversaries,* pp. 157–64.

16 George Gallup, "Nixon's Rating After Cambodia," *San Francisco Chronicle,* May 11, 1970, p. 5.

17 Letter from Henry Wieland, Jr. to David Sachsman, July 8, 1971. Reprinted by permission of Henry Wieland, Jr.

18 John B. Oakes, "The Paper Curtain of Washington," *Nieman Reports,* October, 1958, p. 3.

19 Samuel J. Archibald, "Secrecy from Peanuts to Pentagon," Freedom of Information Center Publication No. 20, School of Journalism, University of Missouri, Columbia, Missouri, pp. 1–2.

20 Jerry Laderman, "Police Withhold Burglary News," *New Brunswick* (N.J.) *Home News,* February 27, 1974, p. 46.

21 Warren Weaver Jr., "High Court Dismisses Paper's Plea for Access to Welfare Rolls," *New York Times,* March 19, 1974, p. 13.

22 Ralph M. Brown Act, California Government Code, Sec. 54950.

23 "Press-Endorsed Info Act Restrictive, Frustrating," *Editor & Publisher,* November 12, 1966, p. 11.

24 Archibald, "Secrecy from Peanuts to Pentagon," p. 1.

25 Marvin Alisky, "Safety Test Casts Discouraged," *RTNDA Bulletin,* June, 1964, p. 2.

26 "Government's Urge to Hide Facts," *San Francisco Sunday Examiner and Chronicle,* "This World," April 12, 1970, p. 21.

27 "The Nixon Tapes: Round Two to Cox," *Newsweek,* October 22, 1973, p. 44.

28 Raoul Berger, "Lessons of Watergate," *New York Times,* February 19, 1975, p. 35. Saul Pett, "An American Ordeal," *New Brunswick* (N.J.) *Home News,* April 6, 1975, p. A14.

29 Martin Arnold, "Congress, the Press and Federal Agencies Are Taking Sides for Battle Over Government's Right to Secrecy," *New York Times,* November 15, 1974, p. 15.

30 John Krizek, "How to Build a Pyramid," *Public Relations Journal,* December, 1970, pp. 17–21.

31 Curtis D. MacDougall, *Reporters Report Reporters* (Ames, Iowa: Iowa State University Press, 1968), pp. 95–96.

32 Michael C. Jensen, "The Corporate Political Squeeze," *New York Times,* September 16, 1973, pp. F1–F2. "Corporations: Where the Money Went," *Newsweek,* January 13, 1975, p. 66. The seven companies were: American Airlines, Ashland Oil, Gulf Oil, Goodyear Tire and Rubber, Minnesota Mining and Manufacturing, Phillips Petroleum, and Braniff Airways.

33 Jack Anderson, "A Reminder of McCarthy Era," *San Francisco Chronicle,* May 8, 1970, p. 41.

34 Address of Vice President Spiro T. Agnew before the Midwest Regional Republican Committee, Des Moines, Iowa, November 13, 1969.

35 "Beat the Press, Round Two," *Newsweek,* December 1, 1969, p. 25.

36 "Agnew's Complaint: The Trouble with TV," *Newsweek,* November 24, 1969, p. 89.

37 Potomacus, "The Word from Washington," *Progressive,* July, 1972, p. 10.

38 James McCartney, "The Washington 'Post' and Watergate: How Two Davids Slew Goliath," *Columbia Journalism Review,* July/August, 1973, p. 18.

39 "The President's Complaint," *Newsweek,* November 5, 1973, p. 71.

40 Clark R. Mollenhoff, "News 'Weaponry' and McNamara's Military Muzzle," *Quill,* December, 1962, p. 8.

41 Hanson W. Baldwin, "Managed News, Our Peacetime Censorship," *Atlantic Monthly,* April, 1963, p. 54.

42 Schramm, *Responsibility in Mass Communication,* p. 154.

Suggested Readings

"After the Pentagon Papers—Special Section: The First Amendment on Trial," *Columbia Journalism Review,* September/October, 1971.

BAGDIKIAN, BEN H., "Behold the Grass-Roots Press, Alas!" *Harper's,* December, 1964.

BALDWIN, HANSON W., "Managed News, Our Peacetime Censorship," *Atlantic Monthly,* April, 1963.

BERGER, RAOUL, *Executive Privilege.* Cambridge, Mass.: Harvard University Press, 1974.

BOORSTIN, DANIEL J., *The Image.* New York: Atheneum, 1962.

ROSS, IRWIN, *The Image Merchants.* Garden City, N.Y.: Doubleday, 1959.

"Special Section: Watergate and the Press," *Columbia Journalism Review,* November/December, 1973.

Chapter 7
Government Control

The mass media are so important to society that they are often referred to as "the fourth branch of government." Quite naturally, the other three branches are very interested in what this "fourth branch" is doing. In some countries the government rules the media. In others, including the United States, government control of the media is more relaxed. Nowhere does the government leave the media entirely free to do whatever they wish.

The First Amendment to the United States Constitution reads in part: "Congress shall make no law . . . abridging the freedom of speech or of the press." This is the earliest and most important statement of the relationship between the U.S. government and the mass media. Because it is part of the Constitution, all other laws and government policies must be consistent with it—otherwise they are unconstitutional and therefore illegal.

Freedom of the press is not limited to newspapers and magazines. In a series of judicial decisions, the courts have made it clear that the First Amendment applies also (though somewhat differently) to broadcasting, film, and the other mass media. Nor is it only Congress that must respect press

freedom. The other arms of the federal government are equally bound by the First Amendment. By means of the Fourteenth Amendment, the same restrictions are binding on state and local governments as well.

It is fair, then, to rephrase the First Amendment as follows: "No arm of any government shall do anything . . . abridging the freedom of speech or of the media." That is where we start.

Throughout our history, there have been judges on the Supreme Court who believed that the First Amendment meant exactly what it said: "no law." The most recent representative of this viewpoint was the late Justice Hugo Black, who steadfastly held that anything any government does to regulate the mass media is unconstitutional. Justice Black was in the minority. His colleagues believe that libel laws are needed to protect individuals from unfair attacks, that the FCC is needed to hold broadcasters to the public interest, that antitrust legislation is needed to prevent newspapers from gaining a monopoly. They believe, in other words, that freedom of the press is not absolute, that it has exceptions.

This chapter—one of the longest in the book—is devoted to the exceptions, to the ways our government permits itself to control our mass media. We will start by examining some alternative theories on the proper relationship between government and the media.

THE AUTHORITARIAN THEORY

The printing press was born in the wholly authoritarian environment of fifteenth-century Europe. The Church and local political leaders exercised their waning power with little thought for the will of the people. Infant nation-states flexed their new-found muscles. Absolute monarchies demanded absolute obedience. It was no time for a small printer with a small hand press to insist on freedom.

The first books to be published, Latin Bibles, posed no particular threat to the Establishment. But before long books and pamphlets began to be printed in the vernacular, and a growing middle class soon learned to read them. Here was an obvious danger to the aristocracy—who could tell what seditious or heretical ideas those books and pamphlets might contain? Every government in Europe recognized the urgent need to regulate the press.

A philosophy of regulation quickly · developed. By definition, the ruling classes were right in everything they did and said. Any published statement that supported or benefited the government was therefore "truth." Any statement that questioned or damaged the government obviously had to be "falsehood." Consistently truthful publishers—those who regularly supported the government—were rewarded with permission to print religious texts, commercial newsletters, and other nonpolitical material. Untruthful publishers—dissenters—were denied permission to print anything; many wound up in prison as well. As one scholar has put it, the function of the mass media in the sixteenth century was to "support and advance the policies of government as determined by the political machinery then in operation." [1] This is the authoritarian theory of the press.

Johann Gutenberg and his successors were not government employees. The printing press was invented well before State Socialism, and for the first 400 years of post-Gutenberg history the presses were privately owned. From the very beginning, private ownership was the major problem of the authoritarian theory: How can the government control the media when it doesn't own them?

The earliest answer was licensing. Each printer was required to obtain a "royal patent" or license to print. Usually the license included vast privileges, often a local monopoly. It was understood that if a printer deviated from the government-defined truth, that printer's license would be revoked. Licensing by itself didn't work very well. Unlicensed printers appeared by the hundreds, and even some licensed ones occasionally published anti-government materials, possibly by accident. For a while precensorship was tried—a government censor for each press, reading every word it printed. But the volume of copy soon made precensorship impossible except for emergencies.

By the end of the seventeenth century, the primary tool of authoritarian governments was postcensorship. Printers could publish anything they liked. Eventually the government got around to reading it—and if the government didn't like what it read, that was the end of that printer. Stiff fines, long jail sentences, and occasionally even death were the penalties for a seditious publication. The mere threat of these punishments was enough to keep most printers in line.

The authoritarian theory is not some dead notion dredged up from seventeenth-century history. Many Asian, African, and South American countries today maintain authoritarian controls reminiscent of Henry VIII. A 1966 survey conducted by the Freedom of Information Center found "controlled" press systems in twenty-nine countries, representing nearly 40 percent of the world's population.[2] In the decade that followed the survey, very few countries moved toward increased freedom of the press, but many moved toward increased authoritarianism. In a 1972 survey, the Associated Press reported increased control in Argentina, Panama, and Uruguay.[3] Another AP poll a year later cited Brazil, Cambodia, Chile, Greece, Indonesia, Laos, Lebanon, the Philippines, Rhodesia, Singapore, South Africa, South Korea, South Vietnam, Taiwan, and Uganda

---

CONTROL OF THE WORLD'S PRESS

In 1966, the Freedom of Information Center (a U.S. organization) analyzed government policy toward the press throughout the world, and ranked each country in one of seven categories of press freedom.[4] In the following list, an asterisk (*) is used to identify those countries whose press was generally considered more controlled in 1975 than it was in 1966. In addition, the reader should note that most of the countries in the "unranked" category have relatively tight government control of the media.

Free—High Degree	Free—Moderate Controls	Free—Many Controls
Australia	Austria	Argentina*
Belgium	Bolivia	Brazil*
Canada	Colombia	Ceylon
Costa Rica	Cyprus	Chile*
Denmark	Ecuador*	China (Taiwan)*
Finland	El Salvador	Dominican Republic*
Guatemala*	France	Greece
Netherlands	West Germany	India
Norway	Honduras*	Kenya
Peru*	Ireland	Lebanon*
Philippines*	Israel	Malawi
Sweden	Italy	Mexico
Switzerland	Jamaica	Morocco
United States	Japan	Rhodesia*
Uruguay*	Malaysia	South Africa*
Venezuela	New Zealand	Tanzania
	Panama*	Thailand
	Singapore*	Uganda*
	Turkey	Zambia
	United Kingdom	

Transitional	Unranked (Insufficient Information)	
Burma	Burundi	Niger
Congo	Cent. Afr. Rep.	Paraguay
Ghana	Dahomey	Rwanda
Indonesia*	Guinea	Saudi Arabia
South Korea*	Ivory Coast	Sierra Leone
Laos*	Liberia	Somalia
Nigeria	Libya	Sudan
Pakistan	Malagasy Rep.	Togo
South Vietnam*	Mali	North Vietnam
Yugoslavia	Mongolia	Yemen
	Nicaragua*	

Controlled—Low	Controlled—Medium	Controlled—High
Afghanistan	Cameroon	Albania
Cambodia*	Haiti	Algeria
Iran	Hungary	Bulgaria
Iraq	Senegal	Chad
Jordan	Syria	China (Mainland)
Nepal	U.A.R.	Cuba
Portugal		Czechoslovakia
Spain		Ethiopia
Tunisia		East Germany
		North Korea
		Poland
		Rumania
		U.S.S.R.
		Upper Volta

At a symposium on world press freedom in 1974, it was reported that only 30 of the 138 members of the United Nations had a free press.[5]

---

as examples of a worldwide trend toward tighter government control of the media.[6]

In 1974, Peru's military government took over the nation's major newspapers, while in Guatemala several reporters critical of the government died or disappeared under mysterious circumstances.[7] On the brighter side, a new government replaced the military junta in Greece and relaxed press censorship. And in 1975, the government censors were withdrawn from the composing room of *O Estado de Sao Paulo,* Brazil's most important newspaper. Still, the authoritarian theory of government-press relations was at least as healthy and popular in 1975 as it was in 1675.

THE SOVIET THEORY

The problem of controlling private owners of the media is solved in the Soviet Union and mainland China through state ownership. Newspapers, magazines, and broadcast stations are all owned and operated by the government itself. It is no mere metaphor in Russia to speak of the media as "the fourth branch of government"; it is a simple statement of fact. The chiefs of *Pravda* and *Izvestia,* for example, are high officials in the

Communist Party—rather as if the Vice President ran the *New York Times.*

Under state ownership there is no question of whether the mass media will support or oppose government policy. They are *part* of government policy. The fundamental purpose of the press, states the 1925 Russian Constitution, is "to strengthen the Communist social order." Consider these instructions offered to a broadcasting trainee in the Soviet Union: "The Soviet radio must carry to the widest masses the teachings of Marx-Lenin-Stalin, must raise the cultural-political level of the workers, must daily inform the workers of the success of socialist construction, must spread the word about the class struggle taking place throughout the world." [8]

Professor Fred S. Siebert offers this description of the Soviet theory:

The function of the press is not to aid in the search for truth since the truth has already been determined by the Communist ideology. No tampering with the fundamental Marxist system is tolerated. . . . The stakes are too high and the masses too fickle to trust the future of state policies to such bourgeois concepts as "search for truth," "rational man," and "minority rights." [9]

Accustomed to a media system that is part

of the government, Soviet authorities are naturally inclined to censor American correspondents as well as their own. In preparation for President Nixon's 1974 trip to the Soviet Union, an uncensored satellite relay system was negotiated for the use of Western journalists. But when the time came, ABC's Harry Reasoner and NBC's John Dancy were cut off in mid-sentence as they tried to transmit interviews with dissident Russian physicist Andrei D. Sakharov. Murray Fromson of CBS was interrupted when he tried to report on a jailed Jewish scientist, and Marvin Kalb of CBS was censored when he tried to mention the blocked transmissions. Moscow simply pulled the plug on New York. Richard S. Salant, president of CBS News, commented: "There it is—for everyone to see—what happens when a government controls the news." [10]

Paradoxically enough, the Soviet media are free to criticize the government—not the basic dogmas of Communism, of course, but the actions of specific government agencies and officials. Because the media are part of the government, such criticism is considered to be *self*-criticism, and is therefore acceptable. A few years ago *Pravda* ran an article on factory production shortages, headlined: "Bring Parasites To Account!" Undoubtedly, the article was part of a carefully orchestrated government campaign. Nonetheless, such a story could never have appeared in a country with privately owned media governed by the authoritarian theory.

These, then, are the three essential differences between the authoritarian and Soviet theories of the press: (1) The media are privately owned in the authoritarian theory, state-owned in the Soviet theory; (2) Authoritarian control of the media is negative, while Soviet control is affirmative; (3) The authoritarian theory permits no criticism of the government, while the Soviet theory allows some criticism but forbids the questioning of ideology. You could sum it up this way. In the authoritarian theory, the government decides what the media should not

---

VOICES FROM THE GULAG ARCHIPELAGO

Dissident Russians cannot legally publish their ideas inside or outside the Soviet Union. But that hasn't stopped them. In 1962, the so-called "Phoenix Group" began circulating typewritten manuscripts hand to hand. This was the beginning of the Russian underground *samizdat* (self-publication) press. It culminated by the end of the 1960s in a regularly published underground newspaper, *Current Events,* which survived until 1972.

Many of the Phoenix writers and publishers were caught and sent to insane asylums, forced labor camps, or prisons. Others who smuggled their manuscripts out of the country for publication in the West were similarly punished. But some of the leading dissenters, notably nuclear physicist Andrei D. Sakharov and novelist Aleksandr I. Solzhenitsyn, were protected from such treatment by their worldwide reputations, and were allowed to voice their protests publicly.

By 1973, Soviet officials had had enough. They seized portions of Solzhenitsyn's book *The Gulag Archipelago,* a searing indictment of the vast network of Soviet prisons and detention centers. Solzhenitsyn then decided to publish the book in the West. Two months after it appeared, he was charged with treason and banished from Russia forever—a fate one of his characters had called "spiritual castration." [11]

Throughout the cycles of tolerance and repression, Russian dissent continues. A story is supposedly making the rounds in Moscow about a Russian a hundred years from now who asks a friend, "Who was Brezhnev?"

"Oh," the friend replies, "he was a politician who lived in the time of Solzhenitsyn."

do, and punishes it. In the Soviet theory, the government decides what the media should do, and does it.

THE LIBERTARIAN THEORY

Apples fall from trees because of gravity, not the whim of some dictator or the dogma of some church. One does not need a dictator or a church to understand the law of gravity; one needs only one's own mind. This was the great insight of the scientific Enlightenment of the seventeenth and eighteenth centuries: People are rational beings, and as such they can discover natural laws on their own.

If it's true of natural laws, reasoned the philosophers of the Enlightenment, it should be true of people's laws as well.

> If men were free to inquire about all things, . . . to form opinions on the basis of knowledge and evidence, and to utter their opinions freely, the competition of knowledge and opinion in the market of rational discourse would ultimately banish ignorance and superstition and enable men to shape their conduct and their institutions in conformity with the fundamental and invariable laws of nature and the will of God.[12]

How does this philosophy apply to the mass media? People are rational beings. Offered a choice between truth and falsehood, they will unerringly choose truth—at least in the long run. It follows that the best thing a government can do with the media is to leave them alone, let them publish whatever they want to publish. This is the libertarian theory of the press.

The libertarian theory developed out of the Enlightenment, out of science, but it is doubtful that it would have done so without the parallel development of democracy. Even if a dictatorship accepted the philosophical premise of libertarianism—that the people can tell truth from falsehood—there would be no reason for it to relax its hold on the mass media. Why should an authoritarian regime want the people to know the truth in the first place? *It* does the governing, not they. It is important for the government to know the truth, perhaps—and for the people to know whatever the government feels like telling them, no more, no less.

In a democracy, on the other hand, the people do the governing. If they are to make the right decisions, they must know the truth. James Madison put it this way: "Nothing could be more irrational than to give the people power, and to withhold from them information without which power is abused. A people who mean to be their own governors must arm themselves with power which knowledge gives. A popular government without popular information or the means of acquiring it is but a prologue to a farce or a tragedy, or perhaps both."[13] Thomas Jefferson was more blunt: "If a nation expects to be both ignorant and free it expects what never was and never will be."[14]

It is no coincidence, then, that the growth of libertarian theory in eighteenth-century England was accompanied by the rising power of Parliament over the king. Nor is it accidental that libertarianism achieved its most nearly ideal form in the democracy of nineteenth-century America. Other countries with a libertarian press include Canada, Australia, New Zealand, Sweden, Norway, Denmark, and Israel—all democracies.

The greatest assets of the libertarian theory, one scholar has said, "are its flexibility, its adaptability to change, and above all its confidence in its ability to advance the interests and welfare of human beings by continuing to place its trust in individual self-direction."[15] There is no doubt about the last point. Libertarianism is almost incredibly optimistic about the rationality of the people. The other two points—flexibility and adaptability—are more debatable. It can be persuasively argued, in fact, that the libertarian theory has failed to keep up with social change, that it is now obsolete and should be discarded.

What are the implicit assumptions of the libertarian theory? The most important one, of course, is that the people are capable of telling truth from falsehood, given a choice between the two. Some of the other assumptions include:

1. That there are enough voices in the mass media to insure that the truth will be well represented.

2. That the owners of the mass media are different enough to include all possible candidates for truth.

3. That the mass media are not under the control of some nongovernmental interest group, such as news sources or advertisers.

4. That it is not difficult for those who wish to do so to start their own newspaper, broadcast station, or other mass-media outlet.

All of these premises were more or less satisfied by conditions in the eighteenth and nineteenth centuries. As we have seen in the last several chapters, all of them are considerably less well-satisfied today. The modern mass media are a vital part of Big Business. The number of media voices decreases every year, as the similarity of the remaining voices increases. Media owners are extremely responsive to the wishes of pressure groups. And starting a new mass medium is difficult and costly.

Even the first premise of libertarian theory —that the people can tell truth from falsehood—may be less valid today than it was three hundred years ago. Life and government are far more complex now than they were then. Decisions are harder to make, harder even to understand. It is no longer so obvious that common sense is enough to solve the problems of the world.

THE SOCIAL RESPONSIBILITY THEORY

The social responsibility theory was first articulated in 1947, by the Hutchins Commission Report on a Free and Responsible Press. This important piece of press criticism from scholars in many fields accepted the basic assumption of libertarian theory. It agreed, in other words, that the way to run a democracy is to expose the people to all kinds of information and all kinds of opinions, and then let them decide for themselves. But the Hutchins Commission questioned whether the libertarian theory was working, whether the people were getting enough information and opinions to give them a fair chance of making the right decision. It therefore proposed five "requirements," designed to guarantee that the media include "all important viewpoints, not merely those with which the publisher or operator agrees." [16] According to the Hutchins Commission, the mass media should:

1. Provide a truthful, comprehensive, and intelligent account of the day's events in a context which gives them meaning.

2. Provide a forum for the exchange of comment and criticism.

3. Provide a representative picture of the constituent groups in society.

4. Be responsible for the presentation and clarification of the goals and values of society.

5. Provide full access to the day's intelligence.[17]

The difference between the libertarian and social responsibility theories is subtle, but vitally important. The libertarian theory holds that if each publication and station does whatever it wants, all will work out for the best. The social responsibility theory disagrees. It *urges* the media to do what the libertarian theory *assumes* they will do—provide a free marketplace of ideas. "A new era of public responsibility for the press has arrived," stated the Hutchins Commission. "The variety of sources of news and opinion is limited. The insistence of the citizen's need has increased. . . . We suggest the press look upon itself as performing a public service of a professional kind." [18]

The essence of the social responsibility theory is that the media have an obligation to behave in certain ways. If they meet that obligation voluntarily, fine; otherwise the government may be forced to make them meet it. Theodore Peterson interprets the theory this way:

> Freedom carries concomitant obligations; and the press, which enjoys a privileged position under our government, is obliged to be responsible to society for carrying out certain essential functions of mass communication in contemporary society. To the extent that the press recognizes its responsibilities and makes them the basis of operational policies, the libertarian system will satisfy the needs of society. To the extent that the press does not assume its responsibilities, some other agency must see that the essential functions of mass communication are carried out.[19]

THEORY AND PRACTICE

The four theories of the press are less concerned with what the media should and should not do than with *who decides* what the media should and should not do. Consider the chart at the bottom of the page.

In libertarian theory there is no control over the media. In Soviet theory the state controls everything, while in authoritarian theory the state has only negative controls. In social responsibility theory the "experts" suggest answers; the media carry them out either voluntarily or through state control.

Which theory offers the most freedom? The most obvious answer is the libertarian theory, under which the media are free to do whatever they choose. But that is freedom for the publisher and the broadcaster, not for the private citizen. Soviet philosophers argue that a government-run press is likely to be freer than a press that is controlled by corporations and advertisers, whose special interests seldom mirror those of the general public. Authoritarian theorists assert that the freedom to oppose the government is not freedom, but anarchy. And advocates of social responsibility claim that the people are truly free only when the media are required to inform them properly.

Different theories of the press follow inevitably from different theories of government. Dictators invariably choose the authoritarian model; communism leads naturally to the Soviet model; simple democracies follow the libertarian model; more complex, bureaucratic democracies seem to require the social responsibility model. It is hard to imagine a communist state with a libertarian press, or a democracy with an authoritarian press, or any other mismatched combination of media and government.

Yet it is just as hard to find a pure example of any of the four theories. In practice, everything turns out to be a combination—with one element dominant, perhaps, but with others represented as well. The First Amendment to the U.S. Constitution perfectly embodies the libertarian theory; yet the Constitution itself was debated and passed in secret, and journalists were told only what the Founding Fathers thought they ought to know. This authoritarian strain has persisted throughout the history of our country. Sedition is *the* mass-media crime under authoritarian regimes. It is still a crime in the United States today.

The United States is not, in fact, the most libertarian country in the world as far as freedom of the press is concerned. The lead-

	Who decides what the media should do?	Who decides what the media should not do?	Who enforces these decisions?
Authoritarian theory	The media	The state	The state
Soviet theory	The state	The state	The state
Libertarian theory	The media	The media	The media
Social responsibility theory	The experts	The experts	Ideally the media; if necessary the state

Prior restraint of the press (also called precensorship) is almost a defining characteristic of the authoritarian theory. Nothing could be more basic to the libertarian notion of freedom of the press than the right to publish absolutely anything without prior interference by the government. Once an item has been published, the publisher may be subjected to suit or prosecution—but according to libertarian theory it has to be published first.

Nonetheless, in 1971 the U.S. government successfully obtained a temporary injunction forbidding the *New York Times* and the *Washington Post* to publish further installments of the "Pentagon Papers" (see pp. 149–50). The government justified this almost unprecedented move by arguing that continued publication of the top-secret documents could irreparably damage U.S. national security. The Supreme Court disagreed. It could find no vital secrets in the Pentagon Papers, and therefore permitted the *Times* and the *Post* to continue publishing them. Perhaps the papers can be prosecuted for releasing secret documents after they have done so, the Court said, but they cannot be stopped in advance.

The *Times* and *Post* were never prosecuted, so the legality of that particular kind of postcensorship was not tested. Even the precensorship issue wasn't really settled. The Supreme Court noted in its decision that if the Pentagon Papers had actually contained information dangerous to American national security, then the government might possibly have been entitled to prevent publication. The authoritarian tactic of prior restraint of the press is exceedingly rare in the United States, but the Court was not willing to rule it out entirely.

In a much less publicized case in 1974, a federal district court precensored the media on grounds of national security. At issue was a book, *The CIA and the Cult of Intelligence,* by former CIA agent Victor Marchetti. While an agent, Marchetti had signed agreements promising to get advance clearance for anything he wrote about the agency. The CIA won an injunction supporting its right to review the book before publication, and then insisted on 339 deletions.

Marchetti and his co-author, John D. Marks, went back to court, arguing that the First Amendment prohibits precensorship and also that most of the passages in question were not based on classified information. While the case was pending, the CIA agreed to restore 171 passages, leaving 168 in doubt. The publisher went to press at that point, with the 171 restored passages in boldface, and the 168 disputed ones replaced with the label, "DELETED." Then, in 1974, the judge decided that 141 of the remaining passages were not classified and could be published, leaving 27 forbidden ones.[20]

Though the decision clearly supported the legality of precensorship where national security was involved, the CIA was not satisfied, and decided to appeal the case. The judge's order was stayed pending the appeal, thus keeping all 168 deletions under wraps. In 1975 the appeals court found for the CIA, and sent the case back to the district court judge for further action. Fearing that the judge would now order more than 27 deletions, Marchetti asked the Supreme Court to step into the battle.[21]

ing contender for that title is probably Sweden, the first nation ever to pass a law guaranteeing press freedom from government control. In Sweden, unlike the United States, reporters have a right to look at nearly every government document and attend nearly every government meeting; they have had that right since the 1766 enactment of the "King-in-Council Ordinance Concerning Freedom of Writing and Publishing." Similarly, Swedish journalists may not be compelled to name their confidential sources of information unless that is absolutely essential to reach a judicial decision. In all other cases it is illegal for a Swedish reporter to reveal the names of informants without their permission.[22]

But even Sweden is not perfectly libertarian. The Swedish law forbidding journalists to reveal their sources is as much an expression of social responsibility theory as the U.S. law requiring journalists to reveal theirs when subpoenaed. The two countries apparently disagree on what is best for the society, but they agree that this decision should not be left in the hands of the media. In much the same vein, Sweden has a long history of press councils—voluntary and nongovernmental, but nonetheless a departure from pure libertarianism.

Swedish television, like American television, is privately owned. But while the U.S. government lets its three networks compete but imposes a complex web of regulatory constraints, the Swedish government appoints a majority of the board members of the country's only network, and then leaves it pretty much alone.[23] Which policy gives the broadcast media more freedom? The question is difficult to answer. Certainly neither policy is libertarian.

No government in the world today has a truly libertarian stance toward broadcasting. The very nature of broadcast technology— the limited number of available channels —makes it necessary for the government to hand out licenses. A few governments, like the U.S., leave the stations in private hands but regulate them and set conditions on their keeping the license. Many more govern-

ments, like England, Canada, and Sweden, establish quasi-governmental organizations to run all or some of the broadcast stations in the country. And most governments simply own the broadcast media outright.

In France, for example, broadcasting is a state-owned monopoly. The director of the Office of French Radio and Television (ORTF) is appointed by the government, and serves under the watchful eye of the minister of information. At the start of the French student uprising and general strike of 1968, French television decided not to cover the crisis. Angered by the news management, many journalists joined the strike, and 102 of them were fired. In 1973, ORTF Director Arthur Conte announced that "I can no longer put up with outright political interference that has fallen in an intolerable way on some section heads and journalists." He was dismissed a week later. To avoid political embarrassment, the minister of information was simultaneously shifted to a minor cabinet post.[24]

The French print media, meanwhile, are guaranteed freedom of the press except during national crises. In 1958, when the government fell and Charles de Gaulle came to power, newspapers were censored and some issues were seized. The seizures continued from time to time until 1965, when a court ruled that one newspaper had been seized illegally. Other controls still remain. In 1967 and 1968, several French journalists were convicted and fined for insulting the president in columns and uncomplimentary cartoons.[25]

The rest of this chapter will concentrate on those aspects of press-government relations in the United States that are *not* libertarian. We will find authoritarian elements such as sedition and blasphemy laws, government news management, post office mailing permits, licensing of broadcast stations, etc.; social responsibility elements such as libel and privacy restrictions, antitrust laws, the fairness doctrine and the equal time law, etc.; even Soviet elements such as the Government Printing Office and the U.S. Information Agency. While reading the chapter, it is vital to bear in mind that most countries are much further from libertarianism than the United States. Most governments have no desire to become more libertarian, and most think the U.S. government is crazy for not becoming less libertarian. Even within the United States, there is at least as much sentiment today for more government control of the media as there is for less.

Despite the First Amendment and the heritage of libertarian theory, the United States government exercises many direct controls over mass-media content. Among the most important are: copyright, sedition, obscenity, libel, privacy, free press/fair trial, and advertising regulation. Some of these controls (like copyright) are designed to protect the individual citizen. Others (like sedition) aim at protecting the government itself. Still others (like obscenity) are intended to protect the society as a whole. All limit the freedom of the mass media.

COPYRIGHT

The authors of this book have in front of them at all times a copyright manual prepared by the publisher. It tells us what we may and may not use from the work of others, when we must give credit, and when we must write for permission. Without its help we would undoubtedly violate the law many times.

We begin our discussion of press law with copyright, not because it is the most important example of government control of the media (it isn't), but because it is the most ubiquitous. Every country has some kind of copyright law. In the United States, it is embodied in the Constitution itself—the same Constitution that contains the First Amendment: "The Congress shall have power . . . to promote the Progress of Science and useful Arts by securing for limited Times to Authors and Inventors the exclusive Right to their respective Writings and Discoveries."

Copyright law is an obvious necessity. Without it, no writer or publisher could earn a living, and hence few would bother to try. Yet strictly speaking, copyright law is a violation of the libertarian theory. It is a government-enforced limitation on what the mass media are permitted to publish.

Copyright is a civil, not a criminal, affair. The government doesn't arrest you for it; the owner of the copyright sues you. The amount of money the copyright owner can collect is limited to the amount you profited by stealing the material, plus a little extra to cover the costs of the lawsuit. For newspapers, then, copyright is seldom a serious matter. Very little money is made or lost when one newspaper steals an article from another; unless it becomes a habit, no one is likely to sue. When a national magazine or a college textbook infringes on a copyright, however, the settlement is likely to be several thousand dollars, enough to justify a lawsuit. And when a best-selling novel or a successful movie is involved in copyright litigation, the winner may stand to gain $100,000 or more.

According to American copyright law, a published work is protected for twenty-eight years, and may be renewed for an additional twenty-eight years. The copyright covers the style and organization of the work, but not its ideas or facts. Brief quotations (less than 250 words from a book, less than two lines from a poem) are usually not considered to be copyright violations, even without the author's permission.

A work is automatically copyrighted if it is published with a formal copyright notice on its title page; the copyright may then be registered with the federal government any time in the next twenty-eight years. Unpublished works are copyrighted forever—as long as they carry the notice.

The most recent major revision of the American copyright law was in 1909. That was well before the invention of computers, photocopy machines, and cable television systems. Can a cable system be required to pay a copyright fee for the broadcasts it picks up? Interpreting the old law in 1974, the Supreme Court said no. Can multiple copies of a published article be photocopied and distributed without permission from the copyright owner? In 1975 the Supreme Court deadlocked 4–4 on that issue. Congress started working on an overhaul of the copyright law in 1965. Eventually it will complete the job.

SEDITION

Sedition is by far the oldest crime of the mass media. It consists of saying or writing something that displeases the government, usually because it criticizes the government. In early English common law, the name of the crime was "seditious libel." Besides sedition, it included blasphemy, obscenity, and ordinary libel. Today these three are separate offenses, and so is sedition.

Even when sedition was a kind of libel, it was a very special kind. In ordinary libel, truth is a defense; in seditious libel it wasn't. On the contrary—since true criticisms of the government are more dangerous than false ones, the English courts felt they ought to be more libelous too. This authoritarian tradition was carried to the American colonies, where it was seldom questioned until the trial of John Peter Zenger. Accused of writing and publishing anti-government articles, Zenger defended himself by arguing that the articles were true. The judge ruled that truth was no defense against seditious libel, but the rebellious jury turned in a verdict of not guilty anyhow. By 1798, when the Sedition Act was passed, truth was accepted as a legitimate defense against charges of sedition.

The Sedition Act made it a crime to publish "any false, scandalous and malicious writing" that might bring into disrepute the U.S. government, Congress, or the president. Seven editors were convicted under the act; all were Republicans and opponents of the Federalist Adams administration. When Jefferson took office in 1801, he pardoned all seven and allowed the Sedition Act to lapse.

Exactly a hundred years later, after the assassination of President William McKinley in 1901, sedition reappeared as a crime in the United States. This time the definition was a lot narrower. It was no longer illegal merely to criticize the government. But it was (and still is) illegal to advocate the violent overthrow of the government—the government of the United States, the government of New York, the government of Wisconsin, and the governments of literally thousands of states, counties, cities, and towns.

Sedition statutes are all designed to protect the government from subversive attacks: from anarchists and socialists at the turn of the century, from Germans during World War I, from Germans and Japanese during World War II, from Communists during the 1950s and 1960s.

There is an obvious conflict between any sedition law and the First Amendment. Over the years, the courts have tried to resolve this conflict through compromise, proposing various standards to limit the crime of sedition without eliminating it entirely. In *Schenck v. United States* (1919), for example, Supreme Court Justice Oliver Wendell Holmes offered the "clear and present danger" standard:

> The question in every case is whether the words used are used in such circumstances and are of such a nature as to create a clear and present danger. . . . When a nation is at war many things that might be said in time of peace are such a hindrance to its effort that their utterance will not be endured.[26]

The "clear and present danger" test lasted for nearly forty years, as court after court tried to interpret its meaning. Then, in 1957, the Supreme Court chose another criterion. It is not sedition, the Court said, to advocate the violent overthrow of the government as an abstract principle. That is protected by the First Amendment. Sedition is confined to advocacy of the violent overthrow of the government as an incitement to immediate action.[27]

In recent years there have been very few prosecutions for sedition. The "incitement" standard is too tough, and the government has easier ways of getting rid of revolutionaries—notably the conspiracy laws. But sedi-

BLASPHEMY

Blasphemy is to religion what sedition is to government. There are still blasphemy laws on the books of some fifteen states today, but they are almost never used. They are holdovers from an earlier era, when Americans viewed Christianity as the one true religion. Most of them, possibly all, are unconstitutional by current Supreme Court standards.

tion is still a crime; the law is still on the books.

As a practical matter, mainstream publishers and broadcasters never have to worry much about sedition. They don't customarily advocate the violent overthrow of the government anyhow. Nevertheless, the very existence of a crime called sedition illustrates the authoritarian strain in American press law. Sedition was born in sixteenth-century Europe, where any criticism of the government was a threat to the established order. In a healthy, free society, criticism is no crime.

OBSCENITY

The purpose of copyright law is to protect the individual. The purpose of sedition law is to protect the government. The purpose of obscenity law is to protect the society as a whole—from what, no one is quite sure.

What is obscene? Until 1933, American courts answered this question by quoting the so-called "Hicklin rule," first enunciated by a British judge in 1868. The Hicklin test of obscenity is "whether the tendency of the matter charged as obscene is to deprave and corrupt those whose minds are open to such immoral influences and into whose hands a publication of this sort might fall." [28] Translated into English, this means that if a neurotic child might be affected by some photograph, say, and there's a chance the child might see the photo somewhere, then the photo is obscene.

American judges added to the Hicklin rule the doctrine of "partial obscenity," which holds that if some passages in a book are ob-

scene (by Hicklin standards), then the whole book is obscene.

Then, in 1933, U.S. customs officials refused to allow the importation of James Joyce's book *Ulysses* on grounds of obscenity. The importer took the case to court. The judge threw out both Hicklin and partial obscenity. He insisted on judging the book as a whole, and decided that it did not "lead to sexually impure and lustful thoughts . . . in a person with average sex instincts." [29] In 1957 the Supreme Court finally got around to endorsing this new standard. The case was *United States v. Roth,* and the Court declared that the big question was "whether to the average person, applying contemporary community standards, the dominant theme of the material taken as a whole appeals to prurient interest." [30] This is the "Roth test." It's a long way from the Hicklin rule.

Supreme Court interpretations of the Roth test throughout the 1960s liberalized the standard even further. To be judged obscene, a book or film had to be completely pornographic, utterly without "redeeming social value." Just about anything with a plot or a few moralistic sentences could pass muster.

The Supreme Court reversed directions in 1973. The key case was *Miller v. California,* which involved a mass mailing of sexually explicit brochures. Speaking for the new majority, Chief Justice Warren E. Burger derided the "redeeming social value" standard. He redefined obscene works as those "which, taken as a whole, appeal to the prurient interest in sex, which portray sexual conduct in a patently offensive way, and which, taken as a whole, do not have serious literary, artistic, political, or scientific value." He went on to rule that a state does not have to "conform its obscenity proceedings around a national standard," and that a jury could use its own community standards to decide what constituted "prurient interest" and "patent offensiveness." [31]

Film producers and book publishers immediately complained that local censorship, enforcing local standards, would cripple their industries. Many state and local governments did begin flexing their regulatory muscle in response to the new decision, but most adult movie houses and book stores stayed open. Moreover, the Supreme Court soon backed down, at least a little. An Athens, Georgia, movie theater owner was convicted of obscenity for showing the prize-winning motion picture, *Carnal Knowledge.* The conviction was overturned by the Supreme Court in 1974. Local juries, the Court said, do not have "unbridled discretion in determining what is patently offensive," and *Carnal Knowledge,* for example, "could not as a matter of constitutional law be found to depict sexual conduct in a patently offensive way." [32]

Film producers and book publishers are still complaining, of course. But as of mid-1975, the Supreme Court appears to be saying that it will not uphold obscenity convictions for anything significantly short of hard-core pornography.

Establishment newspapers and radio and television stations seldom have cause to worry about obscenity laws. By custom they blue-pencil or blip out anything that might conceivably be offensive to anyone; their standards of self-censorship are far more severe than even the Hicklin rule. Underground newspapers, racy magazines, and many books and movies operate from a different premise. They try to come as close as possible to the legal limits of obscenity, without crossing the border into arrests and lawsuits. If every case went immediately to the Supreme Court, this would present no special problems; even if the Court moved back toward tighter censorship, the affected media would at least

know where they stood. Unfortunately, it takes money, time, and luck to fight a case that far. In theory, of course, lower courts and local police departments are supposed to follow the Supreme Court's lead. In practice, they are very likely to revert to the Hicklin rule, or even more stringent standards.

Obscenity is not, therefore, the pointless issue it may seem to be. There are novelists, editors, and filmmakers who claim with total sincerity that they cannot say what they want to say without risking prosecution (or at least harassment) for obscenity. The argument is especially sound when applied to the underground newspapers, which use obscenity to help carry a distinct political message. When an underground paper finds its issues banned and its staff jailed on grounds of obscenity, there is often good reason to agree that its political stance has been intentionally stifled.

Under pure libertarian theory there would, of course, be no such thing as an obscenity law. Social responsibility theory would permit obscenity legislation only if content in "bad taste" were somehow harmful to society, and only if the mass media were unwilling to restrain themselves within the bounds of "good taste." Most of the media *do* restrain themselves in this way. Of those that do not, many are apparently trying to convey a viewpoint that cannot be conveyed "tastefully." When the government censors these media, is it following a social responsibility model or an authoritarian one? To put the question another way: If "dirty" words have come to stand for an ideology, then what is the difference between sexual repression and political repression?

LIBEL

Libel law is an incredibly complicated affair, but for beginning journalists it is by far the most important kind of law to learn. And there is no better illustration of how an essentially libertarian government tries to protect the rights of the individual without abridging the rights of the mass media. We must start with some definitions.

Defamation is any statement about an individual which exposes that individual to hatred, contempt, or ridicule; or which causes the individual to be avoided; or which tends to injure the individual in his or her occupation. Libel is essentially written defamation. The distinction between libel and slander (spoken defamation) was written into the law long before radio and TV came along to confuse the issue. As a rule, scripted broadcasts and films are treated as libel, while live radio and TV ad libs fall under the heading of slander. Since the laws and penalties are pretty much the same, we will ignore the distinction and call them all libel.

There are two kinds of libel—civil and criminal. In civil libel the person who was libeled sues the person who did the libeling, and if the plaintiff wins he or she collects money. In criminal libel the government prosecutes the libeler, and if it wins the libeler gets fined or jailed; the person libeled is no more than a witness.

For every case of criminal libel today there are hundreds of cases of civil libel. Criminal libel, in fact, is little more than a holdover from the days of "seditious libel" (see p. 173). But it is still used from time to time, when someone libels a dead person, or a group, or a local government official.

There are two kinds of civil libel too. Some statements are libelous by definition; judges call them libel *per se*. Accusing a person of a crime, for instance, is automatically libel. So is charging someone with immorality, or a contagious disease, or professional incompetence. Other statements are libelous only sometimes, depending on the conditions; they are called libel *per quod*. Suppose, for example, you wrote a gossip column for your school newspaper, and in it accused a fellow student of getting drunk last weekend. Now getting drunk is not the worst thing a college student can do, so the judge might decide that your statement did not constitute libel *per se*. It would then be up to the jury to say whether or not it was libel *per quod*. If your classmate happened to be president of the local temperance union, the jury would probably say that it was; if the classmate was a regular tippler, on the other hand, the jury might well rule that there was no libel at all.

Most libels are committed by mistake. Often a mechanical error is responsible— John Smith of Jones Street is arrested for shoplifting, and a careless typesetter prints it as John Jones of Smith Street, thus libeling the innocent Jones. Or it may be an information error—Smith is picked up for shoplifting, questioned, and released, and a reporter somehow gets the mistaken impression that he was arrested.

Error is not generally a valid defense in libel actions. There are two exceptions, however. If the error is totally free of negligence —if, for example, the reporter checked all possible sources and they all had it wrong— then the person who was libeled has no case. And if the person libeled is a public official or a public figure, then even a negligent libel (unless it is grossly negligent or malicious) doesn't justify a libel suit. But a careless mistake about an ordinary citizen is actionable.

Even though it doesn't usually excuse the libel, honest error is an important point for libel defendants to try to prove. This is because there are two kinds of judgments awarded in libel suits—actual damages and punitive damages. Actual damages are assessed according to how much harm (financial, emotional, or otherwise) the person libeled actually suffered as a result of the libel. They seldom amount to much, especially if the error is corrected quickly. Punitive damages—which is where the big money comes in—are granted only if the libeler is shown to be malicious or grossly incompetent. If the libel is an honest mistake, only actual damages can be collected.

Since error is not usually a defense against a libel suit, what is? There are three traditional defenses: (1) Truth; (2) Privilege; and (3) Fair comment. A fourth defense was "invented" in 1964 and is now extremely important; it is usually called "the *Times* rule."

1. Truth. A libelous statement that is true is still technically a libel, but it is a legal libel. In all but a few states (where lack of malice is also required), proof that the statement is true is enough to win a libel case, regardless of any other factor. Literal truth on every point is not required, only on the important ones. If a newspaper says that John Smith was arrested for shoplifting in Detroit, when he was really arrested for shoplifting in Chicago, the newspaper is still substantially accurate—and Smith loses his libel suit.

2. Privilege. Certain official documents and proceedings are said to be "privileged." This means that the mass media may quote from them without fear of a lawsuit, even if they contain libelous statements. The precise definition of privilege varies from state to state, and it is important to learn the local variation. A police arrest record, a trial, and a Senate speech are all privileged, but an unofficial interview with the police chief, the judge, or the senator is not. Quoting an interview accurately is no defense if the interview happens to include a libel. The person interviewed can be sued—but so can the reporter who copied it down and the publisher who let it be printed. Usually the publisher is the one with the most money, and therefore the one most likely to be sued.

In 1970 the Supreme Court vastly expanded the definition of privilege, ruling that any statement on a public issue made at a public meeting (such as a city council session) is privileged, and may be quoted with impunity.

What is the purpose of the defense of privilege? The authors of the Constitution recognized that legislators would be unable to debate many issues effectively if they had to steer clear of possible libels. So the Constitution includes a clause providing that "for any Speech or Debate in either House, they [senators and representatives] shall not be questioned in any other place." This was quickly expanded to include a variety of other federal, state, and local government officials. How could a judge conduct a trial, or a police officer file an arrest report, if what they said could be held against them in a libel suit?

But the single most important function of the mass media in a democracy is to report on the actions and statements of government officials. Unless governmental privilege were extended to the media, the police report, the trial, and the Senate speech all would be secret. It soon became apparent that the media must be privileged to report everything that government officials are privileged to say. No doubt some individuals are damaged (libeled) in the process. But without the defense of privilege the mass media would be paralyzed.

3. Fair Comment. Statements of opinion that are not malicious and are of legitimate interest to the public are protected against libel charges by the defense of fair comment. A theater review is the most common example. A reviewer who writes that a particular actor gave a rotten, incompetent performance last night cannot be sued for libel. But if the reviewer says the actor was drunk on stage (a statement of fact, not opinion), then a libel suit is possible. Ditto if the reviewer never bothered to attend the play (malice). And a reviewer can certainly be sued for adding that the actor is also a rotten, incompetent golfer (not of legitimate public interest). But as long as the review is simply an honest opinion of the performance, the reviewer is safe from a libel action.

4. The Times Rule. So much for theater reviewers. But what about political reporters? The survival of democracy, after all, depends at least in part on the ability of the mass media to tell the public all there is to know about government officials and political figures. Wouldn't it be a good idea to extend the defense of fair comment to political reporters, leaving them free to give their honest opinions without fear of a libel suit? Perhaps we should go even further. A newspaper or broadcast station that is afraid to say something untrue will hesitate to say a lot of things that *are* true, for fear it might not be able to prove them. If we really want the mass media to offer a free-wheeling discussion of politics and public affairs, perhaps we should exempt these topics from libel actions altogether.

So far no court has gone quite so far. But the Supreme Court started a significant trend in this direction in 1964, with the landmark case of *New York Times v. Sullivan.*

The case centered on a protest advertisement placed in the *Times* by a civil rights group in Montgomery, Alabama. The ad accused the Montgomery police of a "wave of terror" against black activists. L. B. Sullivan, Commissioner of Public Affairs for the city (responsible for the police department), sued the *Times* for libel. He had a strong case. Newspapers are, of course, liable for anything they print, including the ads. This particular ad undoubtedly contained factual errors of a libelous nature; even though Sullivan wasn't named, the ad reflected badly on his department and therefore (to anyone who knew the governmental set-up in Montgomery) on him. An Alabama jury awarded Sullivan $500,000, and the Alabama Supreme Court upheld the verdict.

The U.S. Supreme Court reversed it. In order to insure free debate on issues of public importance, the Court said, critics of public officials must be given more leeway than those who write about private individuals:

> The constitutional guarantees require, we think, a federal rule that prohibits a public official from recovering damages for a defamatory falsehood relating to his official conduct unless he proves that the statement was made with "actual malice"—that is, with knowledge that it was false or with reckless disregard of whether it was false or not.[33]

In other words, a public official cannot hope to win a libel suit except under circumstances where a private citizen could collect punitive as well as actual damages.

Three years later, the Supreme Court extended the *Times* rule still further. Two cases were involved. In one, retired General Edwin A. Walker sued the Associated Press for a dispatch claiming he had led an attack against federal marshals in an attempt to halt the integration of the University of Mississippi. In the other, University of Georgia athletic director Wallace Butts sued the *Saturday Evening Post* for an article charging that he had fixed a Georgia-Alabama football game.

Both articles were clearly libelous. Neither man was a public official. The cases seemed open-and-shut, and so the lower courts thought. The Supreme Court disagreed. Reviewing both decisions at once, the Court ruled that a public figure can win a libel suit only "on a showing of highly unreasonable conduct constituting an extreme departure from the standards of investigation and reporting ordinarily adhered to by responsible publishers."[34] On the basis of this standard, the Court reversed the *Walker* verdict (the AP was under deadline pressure and made an honest error), but upheld the *Butts* decision (the *Post* was blatantly irresponsible).

The "Butts-Walker rule" for public *figures* is a little narrower than the *Times* rule for public *officials*—but both are plenty broad enough to give the mass media a lot of freedom, and people in the public eye a lot of unwanted publicity.

The trend was extended once again in 1971, this time to include private persons involved in matters of public importance. George A. Rosenbloom was a Philadelphia distributor of nudist magazines. When the police arrested Rosenbloom, Metromedia radio station WIP called his business an example of the "smut literature rackets." Rosenbloom was acquitted on the obscenity charge, and he sued Metromedia for libel. By a 5–3 margin, the Supreme Court ruled against Rosenbloom. Justice William J. Brennan put it this way: "[A] libel action, as here, by a private individual against a licensed radio station for a defamatory newscast relating to his involvement in an event of public or general concern may be sustained only upon clear and convincing proof that the defamatory falsehood was published with knowledge that it was false or with reckless disregard of whether it was false or not." [35] Just like a public official, in short, Rosenbloom could not win his libel suit unless he could prove malice or recklessness on the part of the station.

In 1974, the Supreme Court changed directions and abandoned the Rosenbloom precedent. The John Birch Society magazine, *American Opinion,* had called Chicago attorney Elmer Gertz a "communist fronter" after Gertz accepted as his client the family of a youth shot by a policeman. Gertz sued for libel and initially won, but then the court decided that the Rosenbloom precedent applied and therefore dismissed the case. When the appeal reached the Supreme Court, it ordered a new trial.

This time the Court asserted that states should have the right to set their own standards for libel suits brought by private individuals involved in public events. In such a case, the Court now said, it would be improper to assess punitive damages unless the libeler were proved to be malicious or reckless. And it would be improper to assess even actual damages unless the libeler were proved to be negligent. But within these constraints, a state that wanted to award actual damages for a negligent libel against a private individual involved in a public event was free to do so.[36]

It is too soon to tell yet what state courts and legislatures will decide to do in light of the *Gertz* decision. It is clear that when writing about public officials and public figures, journalists are safe from libel suits as long as they are neither malicious nor irresponsible. But when writing about private individuals—even if they are involved in a public issue—journalists have been duly warned to write cautiously.

The purpose of libel law is not to make the job of the media harder, but rather to protect the rights of individuals. Yet the fear of libel suits *does* interfere with the freedom of the media to report and comment on the news. From 1964 until 1974, the Supreme Court worked to lessen this interference—by expanding the notion of privilege, and by invoking special rules for cases involving public officials, public figures, and public events. In 1974 the Court apparently decided that it had gone far enough, perhaps even a little too far. Freedom of the press is crucial to the survival of democracy, but equally crucial are the rights of people falsely accused of wrongdoing by the media. Where do you draw the line?

Any libel law is inconsistent with strict libertarian theory, but libel is no longer the practical barrier to freedom of the press that it once was.

PRIVACY

The right to privacy is a comparative newcomer to the law. It was first suggested by two young Boston lawyers, Samuel Warren and Louis D. Brandeis, in an 1890 article in the *Harvard Law Review.* The authors argued that precedent for privacy law already existed in legal areas like defamation and trespass. They urged the courts to expand the notion to include the right to be left alone by the mass media.

The courts refused, so various state legislatures did the job instead. In 1903 New York passed the first specific privacy law, making it illegal to use the name or picture of any person for advertising purposes without permission. Today, at least thirty-eight states recognize the right to privacy in one form or another.

The law of privacy varies substantially from state to state, but in every state it is just as illegal for a journalist as for anyone else to invade a person's private property without permission. Reporters who trespass or steal personal files in their search for news are operating outside the law. But if someone else takes the papers and gives them to a reporter, and if the papers are legitimately newsworthy, most courts have ruled that the reporter may legally publish them.

What about publishing a person's name, picture, or personal experience? In most states it is an invasion of privacy to publish any of these in an advertisement or fictional story, unless you have the consent of the person involved. But no consent is needed for a news story of legitimate interest to the public. Almost anything about a public official or public figure satisfies this requirement; presidents and such haven't got much right to privacy. But for private individuals, if the story touches on potentially embarrassing topics, the personal details must be newsworthy in their own right. If the names of former mental patients are unnecessarily used in an exposé on hospital conditions, for example, the ex-patients stand a good chance of winning their suit for invasion of privacy.

Assuming that what is published is genuinely newsworthy, there is normally no invasion of privacy unless the story is reckless or malicious—even if it is mistaken. A 1967 Supreme Court case, for example, concerned a *Life* magazine article claiming that a popular melodrama was based on a real kidnapping suffered by James Hill and his family in 1952. Actually, the play was fiction; it did not name the Hills and differed substantially from the ordeal they had suffered. Yet the Court ruled that there was no invasion of privacy, because Hill's experience was newsworthy and *Life*'s error was an honest one.[37]

In 1968, on the other hand, the *Cleveland Plain Dealer* published a feature story about an Appalachian widow and her family, falsely implying that it had interviewed the woman and overstating the extent of her poverty. She sued for invasion of privacy, and in 1975 the case reached the Supreme Court. This time the Court agreed that the story, though newsworthy, was actionable—because the family had been depicted "in a false light through knowing or reckless untruth." [38]

Of course when a state law specifically prohibits a particular sort of invasion of privacy, that usually settles the matter. In 1975, however, the Supreme Court struck down a Georgia law forbidding the media to publish the names of rape victims. The Court decided that "the interests in privacy fade when the information involved already appears on the public record." [39] But the decision was a narrow one, and state laws involving names not on the public record—those of arrested juveniles, for example—are still in force.

So far privacy law has not had much effect on the day-to-day work of the mass media. But one of the most common complaints about the media today is that they unnecessarily invade the privacy of their news sources (see pp. 87–88). As the social responsibility theory becomes more and more dominant, this complaint may find expression in stronger privacy laws.

FREE PRESS/FAIR TRIAL

The First Amendment to the Constitution guarantees freedom of the press. The Sixth Amendment to the Constitution guarantees the right of every defendant to an impartial jury. When the mass media set out to report a sensational trial, the two amendments come into inevitable conflict. Consider the most extreme case in modern history: the assassination of President John F. Kennedy. After the incredible publicity surrounding the assassination, how could you possibly have found an impartial jury to decide the guilt or innocence of Lee Harvey Oswald (accused of shooting Kennedy) or Jack Ruby (accused of shooting Oswald)?

A number of techniques exist within the judicial system for protecting the rights of defendants. Sensational trials can be moved to distant cities where prospective jurors are less likely to have been influenced by press accounts. Police and lawyers can be ordered to restrain their public announcements concerning a particular case. Juries can be locked up during trials and denied access to the media. When even these techniques fail, the defendant can be given a new trial— and if a fair trial is impossible, the defendant can be released.

Most of these techniques have been around for a long time, but they became much more common in the late 1960s. In 1966, the Supreme Court reviewed the case of Dr. Sam Sheppard, convicted of murder in Cleveland twelve years before. The Court ruled that newspaper publicity before and during the trial (headlines such as "Sheppard Must Swing!" were common) had denied Sheppard his right to an impartial jury. Because the judge had failed to insulate the jury from this furor, the Supreme Court threw out the conviction. After the Sheppard case, responsible reporters covered crimes and trials more carefully, and judges made more regular use of the means at their disposal to insure a fair trial.

For our purposes, the important thing about the Sheppard case is that no action whatever was taken against the news media. Everyone agreed that the Cleveland news-papers had been irresponsible, but no one claimed that they had done anything illegal.

In recent years, some judges have tried to cope with the free press/fair trial problem by restricting the mass media. From the day Martin Luther King was assassinated to the day James Earl Ray was convicted of the crime, the media were under judicial supervision. They were forbidden to publish anything that might possibly prejudice Ray's right to a fair trial. The same procedure was followed to protect Sirhan Sirhan, accused of assassinating Robert Kennedy. Literally hundreds of local judges have continued the new trend, even in simple cases of divorce or assault. They back these gag orders with threats to punish offending journalists with contempt of court citations—and occasionally the threats are carried out.

In the 1971 extortion trial of Carmine Persico, for example, New York Judge George Postel first ordered reporters not to publish anything that had not come out at the trial, such as Persico's nickname, "The Snake." Then he threatened contempt citations, and finally he agreed to a defense motion barring the press and public from the courtroom. Postel did not sequester the jury or move the case to another city; instead he ordered what was in effect a secret trial. Eventually, the New York Court of Appeals ruled that the

---

RESTRICTING BRITISH CRIME COVERAGE

American judges who view contempt of court citations as an appropriate way to insure nonprejudicial coverage of crimes and criminal trials often point to the British model. The British media can be held in contempt for publishing anything that might interfere with a fair trial. They may not use information that would not be admissible as evidence, such as past criminal records; they may not mention the existence of a confession (much less publish the details); they may not conduct their own investigations of crimes or publish their findings. Moreover, the British media are forbidden to question the fairness of judges and court proceedings—a restriction that seems to protect the judicial system more than it does the defendant.

Nevertheless, British popular newspapers provide sensational crime coverage in huge quantities. They shoot for maximum shock value and get their stories across without directly violating specific court restrictions.

judge had violated the First Amendment, calling his action "an unwarranted effort to punish and censor the press." [40]

Judicial muzzling of the media is often overturned by higher courts, but judges keep doing it anyway. Often the muzzled media don't bother to appeal; the defendant's right to a fair trial is thus protected, while the people's right to know what happens in the courtroom is abridged. Even if the media do take the case to a higher court, by the time the decision is handed down the original trial—and the public's interest in it—is over.

Another threat to the public's right to know is the increasing use of comprehensive gag rules to prevent all participants in a case from talking to reporters. It is legal and traditional for a judge to order a prosecutor to refrain from discussing the defendant's past criminal record. It is something else again to order all defendants, witnesses, and lawyers not to talk to the press at all. Just such a gag rule was imposed in the 1973 case of the "Camden 28," accused of conspiracy to destroy draft files. The fine line between constitutional and unconstitutional gag rules is still being drawn.

Some judicial restrictions on the press are traditional. Most judges, for example, have always refused to allow photographers and TV cameras in their courtrooms. The American Bar Association endorses this policy, and in 1965 the Supreme Court ruled that because television was permitted in the courtroom, defendant Billie Sol Estes had not received a fair trial. This powerful precedent gives the print media an advantage over broadcasting, and it eliminates the possibility of live TV coverage of an important trial. But barring the courtroom door to cameras interferes with news coverage a lot less than barring the door to all reporters, or ordering everyone involved to say nothing, or threatening to charge the media with contempt of court.

In 1970, commenting on the ongoing murder trial of hippie cultist Charles Manson, President Nixon offhandedly stated that the defendant was "either directly or indirectly guilty." He soon corrected himself, but the papers headlined his error anyhow. Manson himself displayed the headline to his jury, raising the possibility of a mistrial or a reversal on appeal. Question: Should the media have published Nixon's statement? Another question: Should the media be forbidden by the government to publish such statements?

The answer to the first question is probably no, but the answer to the second question may also be no. Responsible reporters do their level best to protect the rights of criminal defendants. The notion that the government should *enforce* this responsibility reflects a move from libertarian theory to social responsibility theory. Perhaps it is a move toward authoritarian theory as well; government control over trial coverage is at least suggestive of the secret, torture-ridden "Star Chamber Courts" of English history.

Yet judges today continue to restrict the press in order to insure fair trials. Perhaps they should be reminded of Justice Tom C. Clark's majority opinion in the Sam Sheppard case:

> The principle that justice cannot survive behind walls of silence has long been reflected in the "Anglo-American distrust for secret trials." A responsible press has always been regarded as the handmaiden of effective judicial administration, especially in the criminal field. . . . The press does not simply publish information about trials but guards against the miscarriage of justice by subjecting the police, prosecutors, and judicial processes to extensive public scrutiny and criticism.[41]

Sometimes the public's right to know is more important than even the integrity of a criminal trial. In 1971, William L. Calley Jr. was convicted of the 1968 murder of twenty-two Vietnamese civilians at My Lai. In 1974, a federal district court ordered Calley's release, partly on the grounds that pretrial publicity had made an unbiased jury impossible.[42] The government appealed, and in

1975 Calley's conviction was reinstated. But suppose the appeals court had agreed with the district court. There are only three theoretical possibilities: Restrict public knowledge of the My Lai massacre, or send Calley to jail without a fair trial, or let him go free. None of them is good, but the third alternative seems far better than the other two.

Similarly, it is quite possible that those responsible for leaking Watergate grand jury information to the press violated the rights of the Watergate defendants. But there is reason to wonder how much we would have learned about Watergate had there been no leaks. And even if the sanctity of later trials was compromised, it was vitally important that the public find out about Watergate.

ADVERTISING

Like everything else in the mass media, advertising is at least theoretically covered by the First Amendment. Nevertheless, the federal government and every state government have laws forbidding deceptive or irresponsible advertising practices. The purpose of these laws is obviously to protect the reader, listener, and viewer. Sensible though they are, they are not consistent with strict libertarian theory.

Regulation of national advertising is mostly in the hands of the Federal Trade Commission, with a little help from the U.S. Postal Service, the Federal Communications Commission (for broadcast ads), and other government agencies. The FTC has five weapons against misleading ads: (1) Letters of compliance, in which the advertiser informally promises to shape up; (2) Stipulations, containing a formal agreement to drop a specific ad; (3) Consent orders, handed down in the middle of a hearing before a verdict is reached; (4) Cease and desist orders, issued after a formal finding of guilty; and (5) Publicity.

None of these weapons works very well, mostly because the FTC takes so long to use them. Advertising messages are by their very nature ephemeral. By the time the FTC gets around to opposing a particular campaign, the campaign has just about run its course. The advertiser already has a new one in the works, perhaps every bit as deceptive as the original. The FTC starts all over again—and never catches up.

Are the mass media free to accept or reject advertising as they wish? The government apparently retains for itself the right to forbid the media to accept advertisements for certain products. Cigarette ads, for example, are no longer permitted on radio or television, and the courts have declared this law constitutional. Similarly, the U.S. Postal Service prohibits some lottery promotions and certain other types of ads from being sent through the mails—which effectively bars them from most newspapers and magazines. But the government uses its power very sparingly. It relies on the media to police their own ads voluntarily. When a fraudulent or misleading advertisement is prosecuted, it is the advertiser, not the publisher or broadcaster, who is brought to trial.

The right to reject advertising is more controversial.[43] Some experts have argued that the media should be required to accept any ad dealing with an issue of public importance, thus insuring that all viewpoints have a chance to be heard (if they have the money to buy the ad). But the courts have consistently held that privately owned print media are entitled to reject any ad they wish. Only print media that are public entities, such as city transit systems or state-owned publications, lack this absolute right to reject advertising.

As for broadcasting, the Federal Communications Commission has occasionally ruled that the fairness doctrine requires stations to accept advertising to balance the opposing ads they have already carried. Before cigarette commercials were outlawed, for example, the FCC forced the broadcasting industry to carry anti-smoking ads. But this application of the fairness doctrine, born in

In 1970, Miles W. Kirkpatrick was appointed head of the Federal Trade Commission. Over the next year he proposed or instituted many innovations designed to help crack down on deceptive advertisers. He encouraged consumer groups to intervene in cases before the Commission. He established industrywide rules prohibiting specific business practices. He began requiring certain industries to send the FTC documented proof of every claim made in every ad they used; this documentation is routinely available not only to FTC staffers but also to citizen groups considering a lawsuit against an advertiser.

Kirkpatrick's most important innovation was probably the use of corrective advertising. When an advertiser is forced or agrees to quit running a particular ad, it may now be required in its new ads to tell the public what happened.[44] In 1971, for example, Profile bread was told to spend one-quarter of its ad budget for the following year on corrective advertising. The result was ads like the following:

> I'd like to clear up any misunderstanding you may have about Profile bread from its advertising or even its name. Does Profile have fewer calories than other breads? No, Profile has about the same per ounce as other breads. To be exact, Profile has seven fewer calories per slice. That's because it's sliced thinner. But eating Profile will not cause you to lose weight. A reduction of seven calories is insignificant. . . ."[45]

Roughly two years after taking office, Kirkpatrick was replaced. Most of the strategies he pioneered remain in the FTC's arsenal. But they do not seem to be used quite so energetically under his successors.

1967, disappeared from use in the early 1970s. And in 1973 the Supreme Court rejected the claims of the Democratic National Committee and Business Executives Move for a Vietnam Peace that they had a constitutional right to buy television time to express their views. Broadcasters, the Court said, have pretty much the same rights as print media publishers to turn down any ad they don't want to carry.

To the extent that the government ever requires the mass media to print or broadcast a specific advertisement, it does so in flagrant violation of the libertarian theory. Of the four theories of the press, several permit the government to tell the media what they must not do. But for the government to tell the media what they must do is characteristic mainly of the Soviet theory. In this sense, the 1973 Supreme Court decision was a victory for libertarianism. But

consider the result. Each publication and station may reject any advertisement with which it disagrees, or which it considers offensive to its audience or to other advertisers. Advocates of certain viewpoints can thus be completely frozen out of the mass media, despite their willingness to pay their own way. Such is the dilemma of an essentially libertarian society, trying to preserve the freedom of the media without endangering the freedom of everyone else.

Not every example of government control over the mass media consists of direct regulation of content. Licensing and antitrust laws, for instance, control who may become a media owner. Government demands for the names of confidential sources threaten the media's ability to investigate controversial news. Postal mailing permits control how the media may be dis-

tributed. These forms of government control have a significant, though indirect, effect on the content of the mass media.

CONFIDENTIALITY

In 1966, an editor of the University of Oregon *Emerald* wrote an article on campus drug use. Shortly thereafter, the editor was subpoenaed by a local grand jury and ordered to reveal the names of the students (the users) she had interviewed. When she refused, she was convicted of contempt of court.

The ability of the mass media to keep their sources of information confidential is often essential to good investigative news coverage. *New York Times* Sunday editor Max Frankel explains why:

> In private dealings with persons who figure in the news, reporters obtain not only on-the-record comments but also confidential judgments and facts that they then use to appraise the accuracy and meaning of other men's words and deeds. Without the access and without such confidential relationships, much important information would have to be gathered by remote means and much could never be subjected to cross-examination. Politicians who weigh their words, officials who fear their superiors, citizens who fear persecution or prosecution would refuse to talk with reporters or admit them to their circles if they felt that confidences would be betrayed at the behest of the Government.[46]

There are many relationships in this country that are considered "privileged"—which means that the government is not permitted to pry into them in search of information. Among these are lawyer-client, doctor-patient, priest-parishioner, and husband-wife; in some states the list also includes social worker-client, accountant-client, and psychologist-patient.

In some foreign countries and in twenty-

five states, the reporter-source relationship is also privileged. New York's statute, for example, protects "journalists and newscasters from charges of contempt in any proceeding brought under state law for refusing or failing to disclose information or sources of information obtained in gathering news for publication." [47] In the federal system and the remaining states, however, a reporter has no more right than the average citizen to withhold information demanded by a court, a grand jury, or a legislative committee.

In early 1970, for example, the Justice Department asked a number of mass media to hand over their unused film, notes, correspondence, memos, and other materials on the Black Panther Party and the Weathermen faction of the Students for a Democratic Society. The government was in the process of preparing cases against members of both groups. It believed that *Time, Newsweek,* CBS, NBC, the *New York Times,* and various other media representatives had information in their files that would be useful to the prosecution. When the media hesitated to comply with the request, the Justice Department went into court and obtained subpoenas for what it wanted.

None of the media gave in willingly—but most gave in. The *New York Times* put up the toughest fight. It editorialized: "Demands by police officials, grand juries or other authorities for blanket access to press files will inevitably dry up essential avenues of information." An even more serious danger, the *Times* noted, is that "the entire process will create the impression that the press operates as an investigative agency for government rather than as an independent force dedicated to the unfettered flow of information to the public." [48]

With the support of his newspaper, *Times* reporter Earl Caldwell took his subpoena to court. (Supporting briefs were submitted by CBS, the Associated Press, *Newsweek,* the

American Civil Liberties Union, and the Reporters' Committee on Freedom of the Press.) Caldwell argued that the First Amendment guarantees reporters the right of confidentiality: "Nothing less than a full and unqualified privilege to newsmen, empowering them to decline to testify as to any information professionally obtained, will truly preserve and protect the newsgathering activities of the media."

Federal District Judge Alfonso J. Zirpoli wasn't willing to go that far. But he did limit the subpoena powers of the government over journalists:

> When the exercise of grand jury power . . . may impinge upon or repress First Amendment rights of freedom of speech, press and association, which centuries of experience have found to be indispensable to the survival of a free society, such power shall not be exercised in a manner likely to do so until there has been a clear showing of compelling and overriding national interest that cannot be served by alternative means.[49]

Caldwell won at least a qualified privilege in the lower courts; Paul Branzburg and Paul Pappas did not. Branzburg, a *Louisville Courier-Journal* reporter, had written an inside story on the drug trade. Pappas had covered the Black Panthers for WTEV-TV in New Bedford, Mass. Both refused to answer grand jury questions, and both faced orders from their state courts to change their minds or go to jail.

The three cases went to the Supreme Court together, and in 1972 the Court ruled 5–4 that the First Amendment did not protect Caldwell, Branzburg, or Pappas. Unless a grand jury is intentionally harassing the media and not acting in good faith, the Court said, reporters must answer its questions. The Court added that Congress or a state legislature could easily extend privilege to reporters by passing a "shield law" if it so desired.[50]

The action immediately shifted to Congress and the various state legislatures. Two kinds of shield laws were introduced and debated. Some granted unqualified privilege to journalists, freeing them from any obligation whatever to reveal information or sources. Others proposed only limited immunity, by requiring officials to demonstrate that the reporter was the only available source of badly needed information. Faced with several competing bills, Congress was unable to decide, and passed none of them. Many state legislatures did likewise, but in at least six states shield laws of one sort or the other were passed.

Meanwhile, some reporters went to jail. The harshest sentence—forty-six days—fell on William Farr. While covering the Charles Manson murder trial, the Los Angeles newsman had obtained a copy of a statement by a witness about the Manson family's murderous plans. The person who gave him the document had probably broken the law, but Farr refused to name his source, and was jailed for contempt of court. After forty-six days he was released pending appeal. The appeals court ruled that the open-ended sentence was illegal, and when Farr was again cited for contempt in 1974, the sentence was five days plus a fine. At the start of 1975, Farr's appeal of the revised contempt citation was still pending.

A brighter note for reporters was sounded in 1973, when a U.S. District Court quashed a group of subpoenas concerning Watergate reporting. As part of a civil suit brought by the Democratic National Committee against the Committee to Re-Elect the President, CREEP had subpoenaed the unpublished notes and records of ten reporters and news executives. Judge Charles R. Richey voided the subpoenas. "This court cannot blind itself," he said, "to the possible chilling effect the enforcement of . . . these subpoenas would have on the press and the public." He added that the courts "must be flexible to some extent," and that the current cases "are all exceptional." Moreover, Judge Richey said, the CREEP lawyers had failed to show that alternative sources of information "have been exhausted or even approached," or that the materials subpoenaed were central to the case.[51]

In effect, Judge Richey granted journalists a qualified privilege on First Amendment grounds. This was essentially the same stance Judge Zirpoli had taken in the Caldwell case, before he was overruled by the Supreme Court. CREEP did not appeal its case to the high court, but judicial protection of the reporter's right of confidentiality remains a chancy thing at best. The real action is still in Congress and the state legislatures, where the push for shield laws continues.

As a matter of journalistic ethics, most reporters protect their confidential sources regardless of the consequences (see pp. 88–90). The argument for a shield law that permits them to do so without going to jail is strong. But the argument is not iron-clad. When the confidential conversation concerns a crime (or when it is itself a crime, as in the Farr case), the government has a legitimate reason for wanting to know the identity of the reporter's informant. Is this less important than encouraging sources to give reporters information by guaranteeing their anonymity? Most journalists think so—but it is easy to see why most prosecutors think otherwise.

When shield laws are expanded to cover confidential information as well as confidential sources, the question gets even more complicated. Most journalistic organizations support an absolute shield law that would protect everything the reporter knows but has not published. They argue convincingly that anything short of absolute privilege might turn the media into investigative arms of the government. But suppose a newspaper has in its files an unpublished photograph of a student rebellion several years back, which shows a particular student throwing (or not throwing) a brick, or a particular policeman beating (or not beating) a student. Should this information be available to the prosecution? To the defense? Proponents of absolute shield laws say no to both questions. We are not so sure.

ANTITRUST

The Sherman Act of 1890 provides that "every contract, combination in the form of a trust or otherwise, or conspiracy, in restraint of trade or commerce among the several states, or with foreign nations, is hereby declared illegal." The Clayton Act of 1914 further outlaws all practices that "tend to lessen competition or to create a monopoly in any line of commerce." These two laws are the basis for all antitrust action in federal courts today.

As we have seen (see Chapter 4), the mass media are by no means immune to the twentieth-century trend toward monopoly. It is not surprising, then, that the Sherman and Clayton Acts have sometimes been invoked against the media—the First Amendment notwithstanding.

The first such case occurred in 1945, when the Supreme Court decided *Associated Press v. United States.* The Justice Department brought suit against the Associated Press, charging that it was a "conspiracy in restraint of trade." At issue were two AP bylaws: One provided that AP members could not sell news to nonmembers, and the other gave each member virtual veto power over the applications of competitors for the service. Together, these two regulations permitted a one-newspaper monopoly of wire news within each city. The Supreme Court agreed that this constituted an illegal news monopoly, and outlawed the two bylaws.

The following are typical of antitrust actions against the mass media since 1945:

• *Lorain Journal Company v. U.S.* A local newspaper refused to accept advertising from any company that advertised on a competing radio station. The court outlawed the practice.

• *Times-Picayune v. U.S.* Two New Orleans newspapers required advertisers to buy ads in both papers or neither. The court permitted the practice so long as it had no deleterious effects on competing media.

- *U.S. v. Kansas City Star.* A morning-evening-Sunday newspaper combination killed its daily competitor by requiring advertisers to buy space in all three at once. The court stopped the practice, and made the company sell its radio and TV outlets.
- *U.S. v. Times Mirror Corporation.* The court refused to allow the *Los Angeles Times* to buy the nearby *San Bernardino Sun,* since the two competed for the same advertising and some of the same readers.
- *U.S. v. Citizen Publishing Company.* The court outlawed a Tucson newspaper joint operating agreement because it involved profit pooling, price fixing, and other monopolistic practices. (Congress later passed a law legalizing such arrangements once again.)

As these five cases indicate, antitrust prosecutions against the mass media have traditionally tended to concentrate on advertising. This is because advertising is more obviously related to "trade" and "commerce" than news or entertainment. To base an antitrust suit on *news* monopoly would weaken the government's case and make First Amendment objections more persuasive.

Yet, as we have seen, it is news monopoly that is the real problem for today's mass media. In recent years, the Federal Communications Commission and the Justice Department have begun to attack monopoly in the media without relying on advertising for their rationale (see pp. 119–21). In 1975, for example, the FCC prohibited all future broadcast acquisitions that would result in common ownership of a newspaper and any kind of broadcast station in the same area. It also ordered existing newspaper-broadcast combinations in sixteen communities without any real competition to sell off one or the other of their properties.[52] And also in 1975, the Justice Department went to court

against three feature syndicates, seeking a ban on exclusive contracts that enable one newspaper in an area to prevent competing papers from subscribing to the same service.[53] The concessions it won may well serve as a model for the industry. Government regulation of media monopoly, in short, seems to be on the upswing, and advertising abuse is no longer a prerequisite for regulatory action.

All this is a real dilemma for libertarian theorists. Even the traditional wishy-washy regulation of media monopoly runs contrary to the First Amendment, though the courts have ruled it legal. Who is the Justice Department, after all, to tell the *Los Angeles Times* it cannot buy the *San Bernardino Sun?* In libertarian theory such interference is evil incarnate. Yet only the government is powerful enough to reverse the trend toward monopoly in the mass media. Is the threat of government control still the greatest danger to freedom of the press, as it was when the First Amendment was written? Or is monopoly now a greater danger? Does the problem of media monopoly justify an increase in government regulation?

PERMITS AND LICENSES

Licensing of communications media is a traditional device used by authoritarian governments to insure control over the news. The licensed publication is permitted to print whatever it likes; if it prints something the government *doesn't* like, it loses its license. Unlicensed publications, of course, are forbidden to print anything at all.

Government licensing of the media has generally been held to be unconstitutional. In 1938, for example, the Supreme Court ruled that a local ordinance requiring all distributors of literature to get permission from the city manager was contrary to the First Amendment. A few years later, the

Court outlawed a local ten-dollar license fee for book-sellers. Today, cities may regulate the street sales of publications only if their regulations have nothing to do with the content of those publications. If the Girl Scouts are allowed to distribute their leaflets on Main Street, then the *Berkeley Barb* is free to distribute as well.

There is one big exception to this principle: broadcasting. Because of the limited number of available broadcast frequencies, the governments of nearly every country in the world—including the United States—have taken on the job of licensing broadcasters. We will return to this exception in a few pages.

A less-known exception is the postal mailing permit. The United States government decided many years ago to encourage the distribution of knowledge by establishing the second-class postage category. In order to qualify for second-class postal privileges, a publication must apply to the U.S. Postal Service for a permit. By deciding which publications "deserve" the permit, the post office can set itself up as a licensing authority very much like the English kings of the sixteenth century.

In 1946, for example, the post office withdrew the second-class permit from *Esquire* magazine because of its "smoking car humor." Loss of the permit would have cost *Esquire* $500,000 a year in extra postage, so the magazine appealed the decision to the Supreme Court. The Court ruled that the Postmaster General had overstepped his authority, that he could not on his own declare a publication to be obscene.[54] Nevertheless, the Postal Service still has the power to revoke the second-class mailing permit for any number of reasons—too much advertising, misleading content, sedition, etc.

No matter what it's called, this is licensing. The government, through the post office, offers publishers a special subsidy to help them distribute their publications. Then the government, again through the post office, takes away the subsidy from publishers of whom it disapproves.

In the early 1970s, faced with mounting deficits, the Postal Service announced a series of increases in the cost of second-class postage, aimed at making printed publications pay their own way. The loss of this hidden federal subsidy hit many publications hard, and a number of magazines complained to Congress that they might have to go out of business if all the planned increases were implemented. Is it wrong for the federal government to underwrite some of the cost of distributing worthy newspapers and magazines? Not unless the government decides which are the worthy ones. When it does that, as in the *Esquire* case, the second-class mailing permit becomes a dangerous form of licensing.

YOU CAN'T BITE THE HAND THAT FEEDS

The United States is not alone in subsidizing publishers with special postal rates. Most nations offer some sort of reduced rate for the print media. Many also subsidize the purchase of newsprint, buy government advertising at high prices, and even help pay for reporters' railroad tickets.

The cost of all these practices is censorship through favoritism. Spain, Portugal, Egypt, Cuba, Indonesia, and Bolivia, to name just a few, have used their economic powers to support those newspapers that supported the government. Papers in favor got plentiful and cheap newsprint and lots of government advertising. Papers out of favor faced financial ruin when the advertising disappeared and the newsprint suddenly became scarce and expensive. Obviously, it paid the publisher to stay in the government's favor.[55]

A much more dangerous form of licensing was suggested in 1970 by Dr. W. Walter Menninger, a psychiatrist and a member of the National Commission on the Causes and Prevention of Violence. Dr. Menninger recommended that individual journalists be licensed by the government, in order to increase public confidence and to weed out "individuals who are totally inept." [56]

Although few government officials took Menninger's suggestion seriously, a law passed by the Alabama legislature in 1973 smacks of licensing. It required journalists who wanted to cover the legislature to turn in a declaration stating their sources of income and the jobs held by members of their families. In a similar vein, some state legislatures have their own committees to "accredit" reporters to the legislature, thus controlling who can use the press facilities (in Congress this is done by a committee of journalists). And of course local governments set their own standards for distributing the press passes that reporters need to get through police and fire lines to cover a story. Underground newspapers often are denied their passes.

Closely related to licensing is restrictive taxation—also a traditional tool of authoritarian regimes. The so-called "Stamp Act" was passed by the English Parliament to impose a heavy tax on colonial printers in America; it was one of the major issues of the American Revolution. Punitive taxation is uncommon in U.S. law, but it is not unknown. In the 1930s, Governor Huey Long of Louisiana put a 2 percent tax on the gross receipts of every large newspaper in the state (all were critical of the Long administration). One paper appealed the tax to the courts, and eventually the Supreme Court declared it unconstitutional.

We have discussed three kinds of government control over the mass media in this section: (1) Invasion of confidential sources and information; (2) Antitrust legislation; and (3) Permits and licenses. None of the three has any *direct* effect on the content of the media. But all three have vast *indirect* effects. Invasion of confidentiality (like government secrecy and news management—see Chapter 6) concerns what the media are able to find out; the other two involve who is able to own the media and make use of media privileges. A government with such powerful indirect tools of control has little need for direct ones.

The authority of the government over radio and television is far greater than government control of the print media. In theory, at least, any broadcast license may be revoked by the government if the station fails to fulfill its obligation to the public. In practice, however, government regulation tends to concentrate on the pettier aspects of broadcasting. Though the fear of government intervention often motivates the behavior of broadcasters, the government has done little to justify that fear.

WHY BROADCASTING?

Government regulation of radio began in 1910, when Congress ratified a treaty providing that ships at sea and shore stations must answer each other's emergency radio messages. Two years later came the Radio Act, another common-sense law. It required private broadcasters to steer clear of the wavelengths used for government transmissions. The Secretary of Commerce was given the job of administering the law. Each station was awarded its own radio "license," which authorized it to broadcast whatever it wanted, wherever it wanted, whenever it wanted, on whatever frequency it wanted—as long as it avoided the government-used wavelengths.

By 1927, there were 733 private radio stations in the country. Most were concentrated in the big cities. They spent much of their time jumping from point to point on the radio dial, trying to avoid interference—but the stronger stations still managed to smother the weaker ones. The situation was intolerable. Radio manufacturers, the National Association of Broadcasters, and the listening public all called on the federal government to do something about it. The air waves belong to the public, they argued. Since the airwaves were a mess, it was the government's job to clean the mess up.

Thus was born the Radio Act of 1927. A five-person Federal Radio Commission was given the power to license broadcasters for three-year periods, allotting each one a specific frequency in a specific location. If there were more license applicants than available frequencies (as there were bound to be), the Commission was to favor those applicants most likely to serve "the public interest, convenience, or necessity." The same standard was to be used in judging whether a licensee deserved to keep the license at the end of the three years. And in case new problems came up, the Commission was empowered to "make such regulations not inconsistent with law as it may deem necessary to prevent interference between stations and to carry out the provisions of this Act."

Seven years later, Congress passed the Communications Act of 1934. Besides radio, the Commission was given authority over telephone, telegraph, and television as well. It was expanded to seven members and renamed the Federal Communications Commission. The other provisions were essentially the same as those of the Radio Act. They are still essentially the same today.

The government began broadcast regulation by popular request, in order to allocate frequencies. But there were more would-be station owners than available wavelengths. At that point the government *could* have assigned licenses by picking numbers out of a hat, or by raffling them off to the highest bidder. But it decided instead to judge program content, to award the license to the most "deserving" applicant, not the luckiest or the richest.

If this sounds like censorship to you, it did to some broadcasters too. The 1927 Radio Act provided:

> Nothing in this Act shall be understood or construed to give the licensing authority the power of censorship . . . and no regulation or condition shall be promulgated or fixed by the licensing authority which shall interfere with the right of free speech by means of radio communications.

The Communications Act of 1934 included a nearly identical provision.

Its meaning was tested in 1931, when the Federal Radio Commission refused to renew the license of station KFKB, because the owner used a daily medical program to plug his own patent medicines. The station took the case to court—and lost. The court ruled:

> In considering the question whether the public interest, convenience, or necessity will be served by a renewal of appellant's license, the commission has merely exercised its undoubted right to take note of appellant's past conduct, which is not censorship.[57]

It is fruitless to debate the point. Licensing has traditionally been a tool of authoritarian governments, which used it as a form of censorship. The power to license a broadcast station is—beyond doubt—the power to control what it broadcasts. Yet licensing of radio and television is inevitable, simply because there are not enough channels to go around. Every libertarian government has faced this dilemma. The only ones that didn't wind up licensing their broadcast stations wound up owning them instead—an even more authoritarian solution.

The First Amendment does apply to broadcasting—but not in the same way it applies to newspapers and magazines. As the Federal Court of Appeals put it in 1966: "A newspaper can be operated at the whim or caprice of its owner; a broadcasting station cannot. After nearly five decades of operation, the broadcasting industry does not seem to have grasped the simple fact that a broadcast license is a public trust subject to termination for breach of duty." [58]

LICENSING

The fundamental power of the Federal Communications Commission is its power to grant and renew broadcast licenses. The standard to be used in this operation is, of course, the "public interest, convenience, and necessity." Over the years, the FCC has expanded this notion to include many different criteria. Pike and Fischer, the chief law digest for communications law, classifies them this way:

1. Fair, efficient, and equitable distribution of facilities.
2. Interference.
3. Financial qualifications.
4. Misrepresentation of facts to the Commission.
5. Difficulties with other government agencies; involvement in civil or criminal litigation.
6. Violation of Communications Act or FCC rules.
7. Delegation of control over programs.
8. Technical service.
9. Facilities subject to assignment.
10. Local ownership.
11. Integration of ownership and management.
12. Participation in civic activities.
13. Diversification of background of persons controlling.
14. Broadcast experience.
15. New station versus expansion of existing service.
16. Sense of public service responsibility.
17. Conflicting interests.
18. Programming.
19. Operating plans.
20. Legal qualifications.
21. Diversification of control of communications media—newspaper affiliation.
22. Diversification—multiple ownership of broadcast facilities.
23. Effect on economic interest of existing station.
24. "Need."
25. Miscellaneous factors.[59]

In deciding between competing applicants for an open frequency, the FCC actually uses these twenty-five criteria. But this happens only on occasion. Most of the desirable frequencies are already taken—which is why the government got into broadcast regulation in the first place. In practice, then, the FCC spends most of its time considering license *renewal* applications. And that's another story entirely.

Between 1934 and 1972, the FCC refused to renew the licenses of a grand total of sixty-two radio and TV stations; it revoked licenses or permits from thirty-four more.[60] That's roughly a hundred No votes over four decades, compared to more than 50,000 licenses that were granted or renewed during the same period. And most of the stations that did lose the precious license lost it by default—they failed to operate the station, refused to stay on the assigned frequency, or transmitted with unauthorized power. It would seem that the average broadcaster has very little to worry about.

The FCC is severely limited in the penalties it is allowed to impose on errant broadcast stations. It can assess a small fine, which for a profitable station is a wrist-slap of no particular importance. It can renew the license for a probationary period of one year, which merely prolongs the agony. Or it can take the license away altogether. The FCC is rather like a judge with only two sentences to choose between: five minutes in jail or the gas chamber. The judge knows the first sentence is too light to be effective, but the other one is far too severe. Loss of the license is the gas chamber for a radio or TV station. Understandably, the FCC imposes that penalty only on the most egregiously irresponsible broadcasters. A station that falsifies its records or tries to bribe the Commission stands a good chance of losing its license. A station that merely does a poor job is reasonably safe.

The prevailing attitude of the FCC, at least through the 1960s, is well illustrated by the WLBT-TV case. In 1964, Dr. Everett Parker of the United Church of Christ led a drive by local blacks to deny the Jackson (Mississippi) station its license renewal, on the grounds that it had made no effort to serve the black population. At first the Commission simply dismissed the complaint, claiming that a citizen group had no standing in a license hearing. Dr. Parker went to court and had the ruling overturned. Then the Commission decided that there wasn't enough proof of discrimination by the station to justify taking away the license. Dr. Parker went to court again, and won the right to still a third hearing. Said Judge Warren Burger:

> The intervenors [Dr. Parker and his colleagues], who were performing a public service under the mandate of this court, were entitled to a more hospitable reception in the performance of that function. As we view the record, the examiner [for the FCC] tended to impede the exploration of the very issues which we would reasonably expect the commission itself would have initiated; an ally was regarded as an opponent.[61]

In an unprecedented move, the court *itself* revoked the license of WLBT. It instructed the FCC to consider the matter from scratch, reviewing all applications for the license— including the original licensee's—as if it had never seen them before. Reluctantly, the Commission obeyed, and in 1971 it temporarily awarded the license to a citizen group, until a new licensee could be found (see pp. 216–17).

The WLBT decision forced broadcast licensees to consider the frightening possibility that they, too, might someday lose their license for poor service to the public, even if they stayed on the right side of all formal FCC regulations. A 1969 Commission deci-

sion to deny the Boston Herald-Traveler Corporation its license renewal for Boston station WHDH-TV had the same effect (this is discussed in the following section on diversity). The FCC was still rubber-stamping nearly everyone's license, but even a couple of exceptions were enough to move the broadcast industry to political action. It began putting pressure on its allies in Congress, the executive branch, and elsewhere.

The National Association of Broadcasters stated its case this way:

> The public's interest lies in the continuance of the station license in the hands of a good operator. Without reasonable assurance that his privilege as a licensee will continue if he gives good performance, the licensee has little incentive to build himself a long-term place in the city of license or to try to improve his facilities. Uncertainty imposes on him very difficult problems in such practical areas as hiring and training people which are—one hopes—long-term commitments.[62]

There is a lot of validity to this argument. But it overlooks the basic question: Should the FCC guarantee a permanent license to every just-barely-adequate broadcaster, or should it try to get the best broadcaster for each station?

The Commission did its best to allay the industry's fears. In 1970, it issued a policy statement claiming that "as a general matter, the renewal process is not an appropriate way to restructure the broadcasting industry." [63] The statement went on to affirm that license holders would retain their licenses as long as their programming remained "substantially attuned to meeting the needs and interests" of their audience. In other words, the FCC explained, applicants for license renewal would first be judged on their own merits. Only if they appeared unworthy would competing applications be considered. Never would the competing applicant be measured against the renewal applicant on an even basis.[64]

Opponents of the policy complained that

CHALLENGING THE WASHINGTON POST

The Washington Post Company owns WPLG-TV in Miami and WJXT-TV in Jacksonville. Both stations offer solid news and public-affairs programming, but in 1973 both were faced with license challenges that carried at least a hint of political motivation.

The group after the Miami station was headed by Cromwell Anderson, a law partner of former Florida Senator George Smathers, a close friend of Richard Nixon. Of the three groups challenging the Jacksonville license, one was led by Fitzhugh Powell, who handled George Wallace's 1972 Florida campaign; the second was directed by George Champion, Jr., the finance chairman of Nixon's 1972 re-election campaign in Florida; and the third was a coalition of local conservative politicians.[65] A few months after Nixon's resignation, the Anderson group withdrew its challenge. But the challenges against the Jacksonville stations continued.

What caused these groups to go after the *Post*'s TV stations? Did their decision have anything to do with the vicious battles between the *Post* and the Nixon administration over Watergate and other issues? Do these challenges suggest a danger in the government's power to license broadcast stations?

---

this was like saying a government official must be impeached before others can run for the office. But the FCC insisted the policy was essential to maintain the stability of the broadcast industry. And broadcasters, of course, were delighted.

But they were still nervous. A 1971 federal court decision overturning parts of the FCC policy statement because it conflicted with the Communications Act added to the fear. So did the more-than-perfunctory renewal hearings conducted for stations KRON in San Francisco, WPIX in New York, KSL in Salt Lake City, and KHJ in Los-Angeles. The political pressure from broadcasters continued, and finally bore fruit. Under the guidance of the Nixon administration, the White House Office of Telecommunications Policy drafted a bill to offer greater protection to current license holders. In 1974 the House and the Senate passed somewhat different versions of this Broadcast License Renewal Act. Both extended the license period from three to five years, but the Senate bill lacked a House provision forbidding the FCC to consider newspaper ownership in license renewal cases. Congress adjourned before the joint conference committee could

agree on a compromise, thus postponing action at least until the 1975 session.

In September of 1974, the FCC added fuel to the flames by deciding not to renew the license of a state government agency that operated eight Alabama educational TV stations. Responding to citizen complaints, the Commission voted 4–2 to take away the license, on grounds of discrimination against blacks in employment and programming. It was the WLBT case all over again, but this time the FCC carried the ball.

It is important to understand the paranoia of the broadcast industry. Broadcasters know that the FCC still renews nearly every license it considers. They know that the Commission hasn't got the staff, the time, or the money to give a typical renewal application searching consideration. They know that the Commission merely rubber-stamps renewals unless a competing applicant or a citizen group stirs up a huge political and legal fuss, and that even then it bends over backwards to favor the current licensee. And they know that all this will continue to be true for the foreseeable future, regardless of whether a new law is passed or not.

But then there are those exceptions, unexpected, seemingly almost random: WLBT . . . WHDH. . . . Lurking in the back of every broadcaster's mind is this fear: Maybe *my* license will be the next exception. However unjustified, this fear makes radio and television somewhat more responsive to the public (and much more responsive to the federal government) than they would otherwise be.

DIVERSITY

Government efforts to encourage diversity of the broadcast media through regulation have already been discussed several times—in Chapter 4 on "Monopoly Control" (see pp. 119–21), and earlier in this chapter as an aspect of antitrust action (see p. 188). Here in outline form are the key events in this area.

1940s   The FCC passes the duopoly rule. No licensee may operate two stations of the same kind in the same community. Each licensee may own a total of only seven AM, seven FM, and seven TV stations (of which no more than five may be VHF).

1956   The FCC turns down an applicant for a new license partly because the applicant already owns an extensive newspaper and broadcast chain.

1968   (1) The FCC proposes a rule that would forbid VHF television station owners to acquire a second station of any kind in the same market area, though they could keep the ones they already owned. (2) The Justice Department asks the FCC to forbid the owner of the only two newspapers in Beaumont, Texas, to buy a TV station in Beaumont. The application is withdrawn before a decision is made. (3) The Justice Department asks the FCC to take broad action against broadcast-newspaper combinations on grounds of antitrust problems.

1969   By a 3–2 vote, the FCC refuses to renew the license of Boston station WHDH-TV,

owned by the *Boston Herald-Traveler*. Though the Commission cites legal irregularities as its main reason for taking away the license, many broadcasters see the decision as a move against newspaper-broadcast combinations.

1970   (1) The FCC adopts the "one to a customer" proposed rule of 1968. (2) The Commission proposes (but does not adopt) a much more stringent rule that would require licensees to get rid of their newspaper holdings and other broadcast stations, essentially limiting each licensee to one broadcast station per market area, period. (3) The FCC rules that the networks must get out of the cable TV business, and that TV stations may not own cable systems in the same community.

1972   The Justice Department files suit against the networks, charging them with an illegal monopoly on the production of prime-time entertainment programs. It asks the court to forbid all network investment in entertainment production.

1974   (1) The networks claim that the 1972 Justice Department suit is in retaliation for refusing to cooperate with the Nixon administration. A federal court dismisses the suit, but Justice files again, asking the court to prevent the networks from investing in programs produced by others, and from using their control over airtime to eliminate competitive producers. (2) The Justice Department petitions the FCC not to renew the license of any station whose ownership of other media allows it to control more than 70 percent of local advertising in a single market. This move, too, is accused of being politically motivated. (3) The House of Representatives votes overwhelmingly to forbid broadcast license revocations on grounds of newspaper ownership, but the Senate does not concur and the bill dies.

1975   The FCC rules that no new broadcast-newspaper combinations in the same community will be permitted. But existing ones may continue if there are competing stations serving the same audience, and only 16 small-city combinations are ordered to get rid of either the station or the paper by 1980.

What can we conclude from this chain of events? The Justice Department seems to be the strongest government advocate for breaking up broadcast monopolies. But its rationale is not the pursuit of program diversity, but rather the prevention of unfair business practices. The House, meanwhile, is apparently willing to protect at least some kinds of broadcast monopoly, though the Senate seems a lot less interested. As for the FCC, it has come a long way since 1968 in its efforts to increase broadcast diversity. It has by no means satisfied the critics of broadcasting, but it hasn't exactly pleased the broadcast industry either. If the Justice Department

keeps pushing it and Congress doesn't clip its wings, the FCC may yet impose fundamental changes on the structure—and thus the content—of broadcasting.

Or it may not. A visible improvement in broadcast diversity probably requires something close to revolutionary change in broadcast structure—the creation of new networks, perhaps, or the weakening of existing ones, or an absolute ban on local cross-media ownership. These are steps the FCC does not yet seem prepared to take. It is tinkering with the system more actively than ever before, but it is still only tinkering.

PROGRAMMING REGULATIONS

The FCC is empowered to look at programming when it considers a license renewal, but

---

NETWORKS AND PRIME TIME

There is one additional anti-monopoly rule worth mentioning, passed by the FCC in 1970. It prohibited television stations in the fifty largest market areas from carrying more than three hours of network programming between 7 P.M. and 11 P.M. (with some exceptions for news and documentaries). The purpose of the regulation was to get *something* besides the network shows onto prime-time TV. Ideally, the Commission said, the rule would encourage more locally produced prime-time programming, and hence add to the diversity on television.

One immediate effect was an end to network plans to consider expanding the early evening news program to an hour. Another was a significant boon for independent television producers and syndicators. They sold their wares, mostly game shows and other light entertainment, to local stations eager to fill their prime-time holes at minimum expense. (Most stations had only a half-hour to fill, since the other half-hour was needed for local news.) Early in 1973, FCC Commissioner Benjamin L. Hooks commented: "I am not satisfied to see that the release of seven hours of prime time has resulted in so many cases of the period being filled with game shows and syndicated, nonlocal programs." [66]

In 1974, the FCC acknowledged the failure and modified the rule, allowing the networks to monopolize all prime time on weekends and all but half an hour on weeknights —on condition that they use the time for news, documentaries, or children's shows. The change was to take effect in September, 1974, but the National Association of Independent Television Producers and Distributors filed suit to block the move, and convinced an appeals court to postpone it until September, 1975. The result of the new rule may be better early-evening programs, or it may be more of the same. Certainly it will not be diversity on television.

---

it seldom bothers. The real strength of the Commission's control over programming is embodied in three specific regulations: the equal-time law, the obscenity provision, and the fairness doctrine.

1. Equal Time. The equal-time law, Section 315 of the Communications Act, requires any station that provides time for a political candidate to provide the same amount of time, on the same terms, for every other candidate for that office. The station needn't provide time for anyone, of course. But if one would-be Senator gets a free half-hour, every other "legally qualified" candidate for that seat is entitled to an equivalent free half-hour. If one candidate for city council buys a prime-time minute, every other city council candidate is entitled to a prime-time minute at the same price. Regularly scheduled newscasts and interviews, on-the-spot stories, and documentaries are exempt. No station may censor or edit the equal-time remarks of a political candidate.

The purpose of the equal-time law is, of course, to make sure that broadcasters do not use their power to influence political campaigns by freezing out one candidate and plugging another. But the law raises almost as many problems as it solves. Suppose there are twenty-seven declared candidates for mayor of some city. A local station may wish to schedule half-hour interviews with the two or three top contenders. It knows that if it does so, the other two dozen (Vegetarian, Prohibitionist, Communist) candidates will all be entitled to a free half-hour apiece. So it drops the interview idea entirely. The Nixon-Kennedy debates of 1960 were a public service of major importance; they took place only because Congress passed a special amendment temporarily suspending the equal-time law. There were no presidential debates in 1964, 1968, and 1972 because Congress (and Presidents Johnson and Nixon) didn't want any, and therefore let the equal-time law stand.

2. Obscenity. Federal law specifically forbids "obscene, indecent, or profane language" in broadcasting. Control of broadcast obscenity is far more stringent than the comparable rules for the print media, presumably because broadcasting reaches into every living room. Many stations have been fined—and several almost lost their licenses—simply for letting a single "dirty word" slip out over the airwaves. Poems and plays that were manifestly legal in print and on stage have suddenly become very illegal when repeated over radio or television.

In 1973, FCC Chairman Dean Burch announced that the Commission would investigate sex-oriented radio talk shows ("topless radio") and alleged obscenity on cable TV public-access channels. "The ultimate irony," he said, "is that the boundaries of the First Amendment may next be tested in the context of the right to broadcast garbage —and don't kid yourselves, it will be tested." [67]

Less than a month later, the FCC fined WGLD-FM in Oak Park, Ill., for broadcasting "obscene and indecent" programming. Although the station had already responded to Burch's threat by banning sex-related subjects from the program in question, "Femme Forum," it paid the $2,000 fine. But two citizen groups petitioned the FCC to reverse its decision, and promised to fight the

---

TORONTO'S SEXY TELEVISION

In September, 1972, CITY-TV in Toronto began broadcasting uncut X-rated movies. Within six months, the regular Friday midnight "Baby Blue Movie" was earning the station's highest Nielsen rating. In response to mild public protest, Chairman Pierre Juneau of the Canadian Radio-Television Commission (Canada's equivalent of the FCC) said simply that his agency has no powers of censorship. [68]

hard-line policy on sex in broadcasting.[69]

As of 1975, the issue was still alive. So was "topless radio" in many of the nation's larger cities, and so were several legal challenges to FCC censorship. Can the Commission require broadcasters to clean up their programs? The long-term trend in obscenity law is toward greater and greater liberalization—but broadcasting is a special case. An earlier FCC directive ordering stations to review song lyrics for language glorifying the use of illegal drugs was tested in the courts, and ruled constitutional. An obscenity test case seems likely to follow the same pattern.

The Commission will probably have a harder time cleaning up public-access TV. Although obscenity laws apply to cable television, the Supreme Court's definition of obscenity is very different from the FCC's limits on over-the-air broadcasters. Cable companies are legally forbidden to censor their public-access channels except to prevent a violation of law; anything short of hard-core pornography would thus seem permissible. While most radio and TV stations today remain extremely leery of four-letter words, public-access cable is sometimes truly topless.

3. Fairness Doctrine. The equal-time and obscenity regulations are laws passed by Congress; the FCC merely administers and interprets them. The fairness doctrine, on the other hand, is entirely the invention of the Commission.

From the very beginning of radio, the government has held that broadcasters must not present only one side of controversial issues. As early as 1929, the FRC revoked a station's license for bias, insisting that "the public interest requires ample play for the free and fair competition of opposing views." [70] Over the years, on a case-by-case basis, this notion has evolved into the fairness doctrine.

Between 1929 and 1941, several stations lost their licenses for "unfair" treatment of controversial issues. And in 1941, radio station WAAB nearly lost its license simply for running editorials on various issues. The FCC finally decided to give the station another chance, but it firmly declared that "the broadcaster cannot be an advocate." [71] These decisions badly frightened most broadcast executives. They not only dropped their editorials; they dropped just about all their controversial programming. As long as they didn't talk about anything important, broadcasters reasoned, they couldn't possibly be unfair about anything important.

This was not what the FCC had intended. In the late 1940s the Commission reconsidered the whole fairness problem, and in 1949 it announced its conclusions. Although it has changed over the years, the fairness doctrine today retains the following major provisions:

1. Licensees must devote a reasonable amount of broadcast time to controversial public issues.

2. In doing so, they must encourage the presentation of all sides of those issues.

3. Licensees are encouraged to editorialize so long as the end result is balanced programming on public controversies.

4. Whenever a licensee broadcasts a specific attack against a person or group, the victim must be offered comparable free time in which to reply. Newscasts, news interviews, and on-the-spot coverage are exempt.

5. Licensees have an "affirmative obligation" to seek out representatives of opposing viewpoints.

6. Those who reply to earlier broadcasts under the fairness doctrine have no obligation to pay for the time; the licensee must provide it without charge.

The fairness doctrine is *not* an attempt to insure that individuals and groups will have access to the broadcast media. Aside from the personal attack provision (no. 4), no one has a right to appear on radio or television. Broadcasters may pick whomever they want to represent "the opposing view." The purpose of the fairness doctrine is to protect listeners and viewers, to insure that they have a chance to hear both sides. It pictures the broadcast audience as a collection of passive sponges, with no viewpoint of their own to present, but in imminent danger of accepting someone else's viewpoint uncritically.

The fairness doctrine has been applied to broadcast advertising as well as to news and editorials. In 1967, the FCC declared that cigarette smoking was in fact a controversial issue. Stations that carried cigarette commercials were therefore obliged to give "a significant amount of time" to anti-smoking messages. Congress later outlawed cigarette commercials entirely, but the issue of fairness in advertising was not dead. Friends of the Earth, an environmental group, asked the FCC to provide time for counter-commercials dealing with the air pollution caused by advertised automobiles. The Commission said

no, but in 1971 a U.S. Circuit Court overturned the decision, ruling that air-polluting cars, like cigarettes, involve a health hazard requiring the application of the fairness doctrine.[72]

But such decisions have had practically no impact, because the FCC and the courts have consistently agreed that a little attention to the opposing viewpoint in a news program or documentary is enough to satisfy the fairness doctrine. In this sense the 1967 cigarette decision was unique—the only time the fairness doctrine has been used to require large numbers of counter-commercials. If you were to complain to the FCC tomorrow about the one-sided message of broadcast advertising on some controversial issue of public importance, the Commission might reluctantly conclude that the fairness doctrine applied.

THE RIGHT OF REPLY?

The equal-time law and the personal attack provision of the fairness doctrine both require broadcasters to provide airtime to certain individuals—candidates whose opponents have been on the air, and people who have been attacked on the air. Supporters of a "right of access" to the media have argued that these provisions should be extended to the print media as well (see pp. 223–24). By way of example, they have sometimes cited an obscure 1913 Florida law requiring newspapers to print the reply of a candidate attacked in the paper "in as conspicuous a place and in the same kind of type as the matter that calls for such reply." [73]

The law was tested in 1972, when the *Miami Herald* accused Pat L. Tornillo, Jr., a candidate for the Florida legislature, of being a "labor czar" who took part in "shakedown statesmanship." Tornillo wrote a reply to the attack, the *Herald* refused to print it, and the case went to court. The Florida Supreme Court declared that the right-of-reply statute "enhances rather than abridges freedom of speech and press," and ruled that the law was constitutional.[74]

In 1974, the U.S. Supreme Court unanimously reversed the decision. Wrote Chief Justice Warren E. Burger: "The choice of material to go into a newspaper, and the decisions made as to limitations on the size of the paper and content and treatment of public issues and public officials—whether fair or unfair—constitutes the exercise of editorial control and judgment." The state, he said, is prevented by the Constitution from interfering with that judgment.[75]

The equal-time law and the fairness doctrine are still constitutional. The courts have repeatedly stressed that this is because the limited number of broadcast frequencies justifies government interference to insure fairness. But as far as the print media are concerned, the right of reply is an unconstitutional concept. And the right of access remains more an ethical theory than a legal one.

But it would probably point out that the stations under attack did mention the other side (the pollution caused by cars, for example) in news from time to time. And it would probably rule that that was sufficient.

In short, the fairness doctrine does not impose on broadcasters anything close to equal time for conflicting points of view. It says simply that a station that gives some attention (or a lot of attention) to one viewpoint on a controversial issue must give at least a little attention to opposing viewpoints—whenever it wants, however it wants, using whatever formats and sources it wants. Opponents of broadcast policy have charged for years that this is just not enough to guar-

antee fairness, or to protect the audience from being misled by unbalanced broadcast content.

Opponents of government regulation, on the other hand, have charged for years that even this much is too much. Does the fairness doctrine violate the First Amendment? Many broadcasters, perhaps most, think so—but the Supreme Court disagrees. In 1969 the Court stated:

> The Congress and the Commission do not violate the First Amendment when they require a radio or television station to give reply time to answer personal attacks and political editorials.[76]

RULES AND MORE RULES

Every year *Broadcasting Yearbook* includes twenty pages or so listing specific FCC regulations pertaining to the broadcast media. We have already covered the important ones. But it is the "unimportant" ones—hundreds and hundreds of them—that keep the FCC always on the mind of every broadcaster. The following is a sample of ten, selected more or less at random.[77]

1. Two television stations operating on the same channel number may not be located less than 155 miles apart.
2. No station may move its main studio across any state or municipal boundary without first receiving a special permit from the FCC.
3. Every station must remain on the air at least two-thirds the number of hours per day that it is permitted to be on the air, except Sundays.
4. FM radio stations in cities of over 100,000 people must not devote more than half of their programming to programs duplicated from an AM station owned by the same company in the same market area.
5. One or more persons holding a valid first-class radio-telephone operator license must be on duty at all times at the transmitting facility of every station.
6. No licensee may sign an exclusive contract with any network forbidding the station to buy and use programs distributed by other networks.
7. Every station must file a detailed financial report and a complete programming log with the FCC every year.
8. Every licensee must announce its call letters and location at least once every hour that it is on the air.
9. Every station must announce the name of the sponsor of every program that is paid for, in whole or in part, by some source outside the station.
10. No class II-D AM radio station may run on less than 0.25 kilowatts or more than 50 kilowatts of power.

Remember, these are only ten rules. We could list hundreds—and a broadcaster must know and obey them all.

Be that as it may, the fairness doctrine (like the equal-time and obscenity regulations) is certainly a violation of libertarian theory. It is undoubtedly the most powerful direct weapon in the government arsenal for controlling broadcast content.

Julian Goodman, then president of NBC, charged in 1972 that the government uses the fairness doctrine to inhibit what broadcast journalists may report. He pointed out that in 1971 the FCC had received more than 1,500 fairness doctrine complaints—each one a possible threat to the journalistic independence of broadcasting.[78] His point was persuasively demonstrated a year later, when the FCC ruled 5–0 that an award-winning NBC documentary, "Pensions: The Broken Promise," violated the fairness doctrine. Accuracy in Media, a largely conservative citizen group, had complained that the documentary concentrated too much on bad pension plans and too little on good ones, and the FCC agreed.

NBC could have ended the matter by broadcasting something complimentary about pension plans, but instead it announced that it would appeal the decision. The government, it contended, had no right to use the fairness doctrine as a basis for second-guessing the news judgment of broadcast journalists. In 1974 a three-judge panel of the Court of Appeals endorsed the NBC position, ruling that when a broadcaster exercises news judgment in good faith, the fairness doctrine does not provide a vehicle for the FCC to substitute its own news judgment instead. The full nine-judge Court of Appeals considered the case in 1975. But the FCC suggested that the conflict was now irrelevant, since Congress had passed a pension reform law and pensions were no longer a controversial issue. The court agreed, and let the panel's decision stand.

There are two dangers implicit in the fairness doctrine. The first is that broadcasters, reluctant to assume the burdens of

---

FAIRNESS AND EXTREMISTS

In theory, the fairness doctrine seems most useful to protect extreme viewpoints from the media monopoly of the middle. But in practice, when extremists on both sides of the political spectrum have asked the FCC to require media attention to their views under the fairness doctrine, the Commission has often been unresponsive. When extremists control a broadcast station, on the other hand, the fairness doctrine may well require them to pay attention to more conventional viewpoints.

In 1970, for example, the FCC refused to renew the license of WXUR, a Media, Pa., radio station owned by the Rev. Carl McIntire's Faith Theological Seminary, because the station preached religion and rightwing politics and refused to air opposing views. The decision affected more than just the WXUR license. McIntire's attacks on liberals in church and state were syndicated to more than 600 stations in a program called "The 20th Century Reformation Hour." After the FCC decision, many stations dropped the program, fearful that the fairness doctrine might be applied to them too.[79]

McIntire appealed to the courts and lost. (Rather than confronting the fairness doctrine issue directly, the courts supported the FCC's further contention that a McIntire aide had misrepresented programming intentions in the license application.) But McIntire refused to be silenced, and in September, 1973, he boarded a World War II minesweeper equipped with a 10,000-watt transmitter and headed for international waters off the coast of New Jersey. After weeks of technical troubles, the pirate preacher (as *Newsweek* called him) came on the air, only to be shut down again—this time by government injunction.[80]

fairness, will avoid some controversies altogether. There is considerable evidence that this has happened; broadcast editorials, for example, still deal mostly with consensus, "apple pie" issues. The second danger is more acute. In the average broadcast day, dozens of opinions on various controversies are either stated or implied. It is the government that gets to decide which ones must be balanced under the fairness doctrine, and which ones are okay as is. The FCC decided that a documentary critical of pension plans was unfair (though the courts later reversed that judgment). Would the FCC have reached the same conclusion about a documentary that whitewashed pension plans? Should a government agency be allowed to make that kind of choice?

In the long run, which is more important: the right of the audience to balanced broadcasting, or the right of the broadcaster to free broadcasting?

CHANGES

The FCC began its career by allocating frequencies in order to eliminate interference. As befits this beginning, the Commission is always very preoccupied with technology. The vast majority of FCC regulations are technical—they concern the height of the transmitter, the precise wavelength of the signal, the number of "dots" per square inch on the TV screen, etc.

Government regulation of broadcast technology is important not only to technicians, but to anyone who cares about the role of broadcasting in American society. Past FCC decisions about which technologies to encourage and which to ignore have largely determined what we hear on the radio and see on TV today. Current decisions will largely determine what we hear and see tomorrow.

In 1945, for example, the FCC was considering two infant technologies—FM radio and television. It decided to encourage TV and let FM sit for a while. As a result, FM made little progress until 1961, when the Commission authorized FM stereophonic broadcasting, a unique service especially attractive to music lovers and hi-fi fans. In 1964, the FCC adopted rules limiting AM-FM simulcasting, thus encouraging separate FM programs specifically aimed at FM audiences. At last, FM began to grow.

Like FM radio, UHF television has been around for several decades. But throughout the 1950s, the FCC chose to concentrate on the VHF channels instead, preferring to build the economic base of the TV industry rather than working for a larger number of less powerful stations. Only after VHF television was firmly entrenched did the Commission adopt a series of rules aimed at encouraging the growth of UHF. These culminated in a 1962 law that required every new television set made in 1964 or later to include a UHF receiver and antenna. Today, most TVs can receive UHF—but VHF had an enormous head start.

Pay television has had to wait even longer than UHF for the FCC's nod. In 1957 the Commission asserted its right to regulate pay TV. Faced with strong opposition from the "free" TV establishment, it adopted a wait-and-see approach that permitted only small, experimental subscription programs. And when the Commission finally authorized regular pay TV service in the late 1960s, its plan included a number of important restrictions. Pay television cannot carry a series program with an interconnected plot, a sports event that has been offered on "free" TV during the previous two years, or a motion picture between two and ten years old. Pay TV is growing despite these limitations—but slowly, painfully, as a specialized medium that does not seriously threaten established broadcasters.

Satellite television is another technology whose time has come belatedly as a result of government policy. In 1962 Congress created Comsat, a semi-public corporation charged with developing satellite communications. AT&T is Comsat's largest stockholder. But AT&T also owns the profitable land lines that connect American TV networks with their local stations. Comsat understandably decided not to develop a domestic satellite television system. Despite proposals and recommendations from a number of companies, foundations, and even government commissions, the FCC made no move to encourage Comsat or anyone else to take action on satellites. The Nixon administration forced the issue in 1969, urging the FCC to give the go-ahead to any company willing to build a domestic satellite system. Pressured by the White House Office of Telecommunications Policy, the Commission formally adopted this "open-sky" approach in 1972, ending the domination of Comsat and finally opening the way for satellite communications in the United States.

FM, UHF, pay TV, and satellites are all important now, and potentially more important in the future. But at least in the short term, the two most promising alternatives to the broadcast establishment are probably noncommercial television and cable television. What is the government's policy toward these two?

Noncommercial Television. In 1952, the FCC reserved 242 television channels for nonprofit educational use. More channels were set aside later. Applicants for these special TV licenses must meet the same FCC regulations as everyone else, with one all-important addition: They are not permitted to carry advertising.

Some noncommercial TV stations are financed by school systems or state governments for specialized educational use, but most are run by nongovernment philanthropies and aimed at the general public. Until 1969, such stations got nearly all their money from foundation grants, corporate donations, and viewer contributions. Aside from providing the licenses, the federal government played essentially no role in noncommercial television.

This started changing in 1967, when Congress created the Corporation for Public Broadcasting (CPB) and told it to help round up money for noncommercial TV. But the money itself still came from outside the government. Then, in 1969, Congress appropriated a $5-million contribution to the operating costs of noncommercial stations, and directed the Corporation for Public Broadcasting to distribute the money.

With federal funding came the beginning of federal control. The CPB board of directors is appointed by the president with the advice and consent of the Senate. Most of its members are bankers, politicians, and industrial leaders, and many are very sensitive and responsive to the wishes of government. The Public Broadcasting Service (PBS), which was set up to create and distribute programs nationwide, is a little more independent; most of its members are the managers of local noncommercial stations.

In the early 1970s, CPB and PBS spent several years battling over the future of noncommercial television. At issue was the question of how centralized public TV was to become—a noncommercial "fourth network" with many national programs produced by PBS, or a collection of unconnected local stations using CPB money to produce their own programs, or something in the middle. Fearing that a noncommercial network might lean to the left in its political reporting, the Nixon administration backed the decentralized approach, and pushed the CPB board to take a hard line. CPB Chairman Thomas B. Curtis resigned in protest, and in 1973 a compromise was negotiated. By then it was clear that the federal government's interest in noncommercial broadcasting extended beyond financial support and into politics.

If noncommercial television is to survive as something more than a source of low-budget educational programs, it needs federal funding. The Ford Foundation, which has generously funded public television, is phasing out its support, and corporations and the public cannot take up the slack. The question is how much federal funding, and on what terms.

Advocates of a strong and independent noncommercial TV system argue for a long-

term funding arrangement that would insulate public broadcasters from year-to-year
political reprisals. Until 1974, the Nixon
administration preferred to stick to one-year
appropriations that kept the stations on a
short leash. But just before he resigned, apparently satisfied that PBS had moderated
its politics, President Nixon announced that
he would support long-range funding. Although the political appointments to CPB
are still a problem, with long-range funding
noncommercial television may gain a measure of stability at last. It might even get
enough money to make a difference.

Cable Television. The technology of
cable television offers almost infinite potential for a revolution in broadcasting. Since
the cable signal is transmitted over wires,
not through the air, the only limit on the
number of channels is the capacity of the
cable. When cable systems carry local channels, the picture quality is usually substantially improved. But cable operations
can also pick up distant channels and bring
them to an audience that was previously out
of range. Cable is ideal for specialized programming aimed at small audiences—not
just city council meetings, but neighborhood
meetings as well. Just by adding a telephone,
a cable system can be turned into a two-way
communication network, permitting such
science-fiction possibilities as home plebi-
scites and shopping by television.

All this is understandably threatening to
traditional broadcasters. In 1966, the FCC
asserted its authority to regulate cable television, and set up a system of rules designed
to lessen the threat. Cable operators were
required to carry the transmissions of all
local stations on request, and those in the
hundred largest markets were forbidden to
bring in distant signals without special FCC
approval. In essence, this limited cable systems in big cities to offering nothing more
than a clearer picture; the channels they
carried for a price were identical to the
channels available over the air for nothing.
In 1970 the Commission began trying to

develop some of the potential of cable, while
still protecting the interests of over-the-air
broadcasters, especially the economically
weak UHF stations. Cable companies with
more than 3,500 subscribers were required to
originate some of their own programming.
The networks were banned from cable
ownership, and owners of TV stations were
forbidden to own cable systems in the same
community. Pay-cable systems were prohibited from carrying programs (like the Super
Bowl) that were not allowed on over-the-air
pay TV. Other rules were proposed that
would permit cable companies to import
distant signals under certain conditions,
while requiring them to provide extra channels for local government, education, and
public access.

In 1972, after heated politicking by broadcasters and cable operators (and a compromise mediated by the White House Office of
Telecommunications Policy), the FCC finally issued a full set of rules. Once again,
the main thrust of the new rules was to develop the potential of cable slowly, with careful attention to the welfare of broadcasters.
Among the chief provisions were:

- Cable systems in major markets must be able
  to handle two-way communications, and must
  carry at least 20 channels, including one each
  for local government, education, and public
  access.

- Cable systems must carry all local noncommercial stations.

- Cable systems in the top hundred markets
  may import two out-of-town signals.

- Local and state governments may continue to
  set their own additional conditions for the
  awarding of cable franchises.

One huge issue remained to be resolved:
compensation to copyright holders for re-
transmission of their programs over cable.
Broadcasters have steadfastly insisted that
they are entitled to payment when a cable
company carries their programs; even cable
operators have sometimes agreed that some
form of compensation was appropriate. The

In 1970 a consumer-oriented research center issued a report exposing abuses in the awarding of municipal cable TV franchises in New Jersey. In response to the report, and the indictment of four Trenton city councilmen for allegedly trying to rig a cable franchise on behalf of TelePrompTer, Inc., a state legislative committee was set up to investigate cable. Although the Trenton officials were acquitted, the committee found enough evidence of corruption and confusion among municipal politicians to recommend a moratorium on the awarding of cable franchises.

The moratorium was enacted in 1971. By the time it was lifted in 1973, the state's Board of Public Utility Commissioners had been given the power to regulate cable in New Jersey and to veto franchises awarded by city governments. But when the incoming governor, Brendan Byrne, reviewed the cable situation, he found it still in a "rather chaotic state." Richard Leone, the incoming state treasurer and an author of the 1970 cable study, said of the PUC system, "We still don't have much of a state operation." He added that municipal officials were still confused, and that state standards were needed for cable TV contracts.[81] By 1975 New Jersey had adopted statewide cable standards. What is the situation in your state?

FCC made it clear that it considered a new copyright law covering cable essential to the success of its 1972 rules. As of mid-1975, Congress had yet to pass such a law.

TOO MUCH GOVERNMENT CONTROL?

No other single entity exercises so much control over the mass media in the United States as the federal government. No other mass medium is so stringently controlled by government as broadcasting. Many of these controls, perhaps most, are inconsistent with the American tradition of libertarian theory, with the spirit of the First Amendment.

Yet anyone who spends much time with the media, including the broadcast media, eventually comes to a puzzling conclusion: The government does not seem to be having much effect.

There is a paradox here. Look at any specific government control over the media, and you are likely to conclude that it is too much and too strong. Then look at the totality of government control, and you are likely to conclude that it is too little and too weak. Perhaps it is neither too much nor too little, but simply misdirected. Somehow the government has managed to inhibit seriously the freedom of the mass media without improving seriously their performance. Perhaps what we need is not *more* government control or *less* government control, but *different* government control.

Notes

1 Frederick S. Siebert, "The Historical Pattern of Press Freedom," *Nieman Reports*, July, 1953, p. 43.

2 Ralph L. Lowenstein, "Press Freedom as a Political Indicator," in *International Communication*, ed. Dietrich Fischer and John C. Merrill (New York: Hastings House, 1970), pp. 134–35.

3 "Survey Shows that Restrictions on News Media in Major Countries in Latin America Have Increased," *New York Times*, October 8, 1972, p. 14.

4 John C. Merrill, Carter R. Bryan, and Marvin Alisky, *The Foreign Press* (Baton Rouge: Louisiana State University Press, 1970), p. 33.

5 "Press Freedom Around the World," *Editor & Publisher*, December 7, 1974, p. 6.

6 "A Further Ebbing of World Press Freedoms Found," *New York Times*, January 6, 1974, p. 18.

7 "Repression Kills Free Press in Latin America,"

New Brunswick (N. J.) *Home News*, August 7, 1974, p. 14 (Washington Post–Los Angeles Times News Service).

8 Fred S. Siebert, Theodore Peterson and Wilbur Schramm, *Four Theories of the Press* (Urbana: University of Illinois Press, 1963), p. 135.

9 Siebert, "The Historical Pattern of Press Freedom," p. 44.

10 "U.S. TV Screens Go Blank as Russians Block News," *New Brunswick* (N. J.) *Home News*, July 3, 1974, p. 2.

11 "The Exile: A Tale of Repression," *Newsweek*, February 25, 1974, p. 36.

12 Carl Becker, *Freedom and Responsibility in the American Way of Life* (New York: Vintage Books, 1945), p. 34.

13 Alvin E. Austin, "Codes, Documents, Declarations Affecting the Press," Department of Journalism, University of North Dakota, August, 1964, p. 55.

14 *Ibid.*, p. 56.

15 Siebert, Peterson, and Schramm, *Four Theories of the Press*, p. 71.

16 *Ibid.*, p. 90.

17 *Ibid.*, pp. 87–92.

18 *A Free and Responsible Press* (Chicago: University of Chicago Press, 1947), p. 92.

19 Siebert, Peterson, and Schramm, *Four Theories of the Press*, p. 74.

20 Lesley Oelsner, "Judge Backs Publishing of C.I.A. Book If 27 of 339 Sought Deletions Are Made," *New York Times*, April 2, 1974, p. 39.

21 Lesley Oelsner, "Supreme Court Gets an Appeal on Censorship of Book About C.I.A.," *New York Times*, March 16, 1975, p. 48.

22 Merrill, Bryan, and Alisky, *The Foreign Press*, pp. 128–29.

23 Merrill, Bryan, and Alisky, *The Foreign Press*, p. 131.

24 Nan Robertson, "2 Ousted in Paris on Radio-TV Issue," *New York Times*, October 24, 1973, p. C5.

25 Merrill, Bryan, and Alisky, *The Foreign Press*, pp. 90–91.

26 *Schenck v. U.S.*, 249 U.S. 47, 39 S.Ct. 247 (1919).

27 *Yates v. U.S.*, 354 U.S. 298, 77 S.Ct. 1064 (1957).

28 *Regina v. Hicklin*, L.R. 3 Q.B. 360, 370 (1868).

29 *U.S. v. One Book Called "Ulysses,"* 5 F. Supp. 182, 184 (S.D.N.Y. 1933).

30 *U.S. v. Roth*, 354 U.S. 476, 77 S.Ct. 1304, 1311 (1957).

31 Harold L. Nelson and Dwight L. Teeter, Jr., *Law of Mass Communications*, 2nd ed. (Mineola, N.Y.: Foundation Press, 1973), pp. 424–28.

32 "Supreme Court Shifts Position on Obscenity,"

New Brunswick (N. J.) *Home News*, June 25, 1974, p. 24 (Associated Press).

33 *New York Times Co. v. Sullivan*, 376 U.S. 254, 279–80, 84 S.Ct. 710 (1964).

34 *Associated Press v. Walker*, and *Curtis Publishing Co. v. Butts*, 388 U.S. 130, 87 S.Ct. 1975 (1967).

35 *Rosenbloom v. Metromedia, Inc.*, 403 U.S. 29, 91 S.Ct. 1811 (1971).

36 "Term 'Private' in Libel Ruling Stumps Attorneys," *Editor & Publisher*, August 31, 1974, p. 15. "10-Year Libel Payments Top the $2 Million Mark," *Editor & Publisher*, November 2, 1974, pp. 11, 27.

37 *Time Inc. v. Hill*, 385 U.S. 374, 87 S.Ct. 534 (1967).

38 Martin Arnold, "Privacy vs. the Press: The Issue Remains," *New York Times*, March 6, 1975, p. 12. Warren Weaver Jr., "Court Backs Invasion-of-Privacy Award," *New York Times*, December 19, 1974, p. 39. I. William Hill, "Newspaper Must Pay Award for Invasion of Privacy," *Editor & Publisher*, December 28, 1974, p. 13.

39 "The Right to Privacy," *Newsweek*, March 17, 1975, p. 66. Arnold, "Privacy vs. the Press," p. 12.

40 Lesley Oelsner, "Court of Appeals Says Postel Erred in Barring Press," *New York Times*, March 23, 1972, p. 1.

41 *Sheppard v. Maxwell*, 384 U.S. 333, 86 S.Ct. 1507 (1966).

42 Jack E. Swift, "Pre-Trial News Culprits in Calley Case Named," *Editor & Publisher*, October 5, 1974, p. 11.

43 Peter M. Sandman, "Who Should Police Environmental Advertising?" *Columbia Journalism Review*, January/February, 1972, pp. 41–47.

44 "Advertising: Mea Culpa, Sort Of," *Newsweek*, September 27, 1971, p. 98.

45 *Ibid.*, p. 98.

46 "Passing Comment," *Columbia Journalism Review*, Spring, 1970, p. 3.

47 Associated Press, May 13, 1970.

48 United Press International, February 4, 1970.

49 "How Much Privilege?" *Newsweek*, April 13, 1970, p. 77.

50 Nelson and Teeter, *Law of Mass Communications*, pp. 354–55.

51 Walter Rugaber, "Court Quashes Subpoenas on Watergate Reporting," *New York Times*, March 22, 1973, pp. 1, 19.

52 I. William Hill, "FCC Bars Cross-Ownership, Breaks-Up Media in 16 Cities," *Editor & Publisher*, February 1, 1975, p. 9.

53 Lenora Williamson, "Syndicate Exclusivity Policy on Trial in Anti-Trust Case," *Editor & Publisher*, February 1, 1975, p. 14.

54 *Hannegan v. Esquire,* 327 U.S. 146, 148–49, 66 S.Ct. 456, 457–58 (1946).

55 Merrill, Bryan, and Alisky, *The Foreign Press,* pp. 28–29.

56 Associated Press, February 5, 1970.

57 *KFKB Broadcasting Association v. FRC,* 47 F.2d. 670, 60 App.D.C. 79 (1931).

58 *Office of Communication of United Church of Christ v. FCC,* 359 F.2d. 994, 1003 (1966).

59 William L. Rivers and Wilbur Schramm, *Responsibility in Mass Communication* (New York: Harper & Row, 1969), pp. 63–64.

60 *Federal Communications Commission Annual Report Fiscal 1972,* pp. 172–73.

61 Marvin Barrett, ed., *Survey of Broadcast Journalism 1968–1969* (New York: Grosset & Dunlap, 1969), p. 32.

62 Vincent T. Wasilewski, "Remarks Before the Federal Communications Bar Association," May 29, 1969, p. 7.

63 "FCC Tries To Keep Up with Technology," *Broadcasting,* December 29, 1969, p. 50.

64 "Test Case," *Newsweek,* September 28, 1970. Marvin Barrett, ed., *Survey of Broadcast Journalism 1969–1970* (New York: Grosset & Dunlap, 1970), p. 70.

65 Nancy Beth Jackson, "The Politics of Revenge," [*MORE*], February, 1974, pp. 5, 7.

66 Albin Krebs, "F.C.C. Aide Scores Prime-Time Rule," *New York Times,* February 2, 1973, p. 63.

67 Albin Krebs, "Burch Scores Fad of 'Topless Radio,'" *New York Times,* March 29, 1973, p. 94.

68 Jay Walz, "Toronto Accepts 'Sexy Television,'" *New York Times,* March 11, 1973, p. 23.

69 Newton Lamson, "Aural Sex and the F.C.C.," [*MORE*], June, 1973, pp. 5–6.

70 *Great Lakes Broadcasting Co.,* 3 F.R.C. 32 (1929).

71 *Mayflower Broadcasting Corp.,* 8 F.C.C. 333 (1941).

72 *Friends of the Earth v. FCC,* 146 U.S.App.D.C. 88, 449 F.2d. 1164 (1971).

73 Tom Wicker, "The Press: Who Shall Edit It?" *New York Times,* January 22, 1974, p. 39.

74 *Ibid.* Arthur S. Miller, "The Right of Reply," *New York Times,* April 24, 1974, p. 41.

75 "Right-to-Reply Demand Rejected," *New Brunswick* (N.J.) *Home News,* June 25, 1974, p. 2 (Associated Press).

76 *Red Lion Broadcasting Co. v. FCC* in Barrett, *Survey of Broadcast Journalism 1968–1969,* p. 39.

77 *1970 Broadcasting Yearbook,* pp. C49–C66.

78 Albin Krebs, "N.B.C. Head Scores F.C.C. Doctrine," *New York Times,* October 12, 1972, p. 95.

79 "The Pirate Preacher," *Newsweek,* September 24, 1973, p. 93.

80 *Ibid.* Donald Janson, "McIntire Gains Support in Radio Station Dispute," *New York Times,* December 3, 1973, p. NJ43.

81 Joseph F. Sullivan, "State Will Enforce Controls on Cable TV," *New York Times,* January 6, 1974, p. NJ1.

Suggested Readings

FRANKLIN, MARC A., *The Dynamics of American Law.* Mineola, N.Y.: Foundation Press, 1968.

A Free and Responsible Press. Chicago: University of Chicago Press, 1947.

FRIENDLY, FRED W., "What's Fair on the Air?" *New York Times Magazine,* March 30, 1975.

GILLMOR, DONALD M., and JEROME A. BARRON, *Mass Communication Law* (2nd ed.). St. Paul, Minn.: West Publishing Co., 1974.

JOHNSON, NICHOLAS, *How To Talk Back to Your Television Set.* New York: Bantam Books, 1970.

LeDUC, DON L., *Cable Television and the FCC: A Crisis in Media Control.* Philadelphia: Temple University Press, 1973.

LEVY, LEONARD W., *Freedom of Speech and Press in Early American History: Legacy of Suppression.* New York: Harper Torchbooks, 1963.

NELSON, HAROLD L., and DWIGHT L. TEETER, JR., *Law of Mass Communications* (2nd ed.). Mineola, N.Y.: Foundation Press, 1973.

PEMBER, DON R., *Privacy and the Press.* Seattle: University of Washington Press, 1972.

POWLEDGE, FRED, *The Nixon Administration and the Press: The Engineering of Restraint.* New York: American Civil Liberties Union, September, 1971.

SIEBERT, FRED S., THEODORE PETERSON, and WILBUR SCHRAMM, *Four Theories of the Press.* Urbana: University of Illinois Press, 1956.

UNGAR, SANFORD J., *The Papers and the Papers.* New York: Dutton, 1972.

Chapter 8
Public Control

A democracy works only if its important institutions are somehow responsive and responsible to the public. The mass media are a vital democratic institution. Since media executives are not elected, other means must be found to guarantee that public opinion will play a role in the determination of media content. But existing channels for public control of the media are weak, and new channels have been slow to develop.

When the Army Corps of Engineers first announced its plan to widen a creek running through a municipal park in a poor section of town, no one thought much about it. But soon it became clear that the operation would almost totally destroy the park. Ms. Green, a local resident, organized a small citizen group that petitioned the Corps to abandon the project. The request was denied. Ms. Green next asked the support of the weekly newspaper in her area, and the metropolitan paper about fifteen miles away. "Bring us a petition with a thousand names and we'll run something," both editors said. "We can't get a thousand names unless the issue is presented in the press," Ms. Green replied. "Sorry," said the editors, "we can't do much on an organization with only a few dozen members." Finally Ms.

Green asked, "Do we have to stage a sit-in and block the bulldozers in order to get any attention?" No one answered.

Mr. Henderson was worried about his two children, aged seven and four. The kids spent nearly four hours a day watching television, and he wasn't pleased about the results. "For one thing," Mr. Henderson explained to the general manager of a local station, "there are too many commercials for junk foods and junky toys. And so many of the programs are violent. I don't want my kids to learn that a fistfight is the best way to solve their problems." The station manager was cordial, but not very helpful. "We just run the shows the networks give us," he explained. "We can't afford to produce very many of our own, and if we cut out the commercials we couldn't afford to produce any shows at all. Why don't you take your children to the park instead?"

Ms. Green and Mr. Henderson are hypothetical, but every day hundreds of real Ms. Greens and Mr. Hendersons across the country discover to their surprise that they are unable to influence the content of the mass media. Control over the flow of information and entertainment is exercised by publishers and reporters, station owners and editors, advertisers and government officials. What about the public?

All successful communication is two-way. In the jargon of communication theorists, the mechanisms that permit two-way communication are called "feedback loops." When we talk about public control of the mass media, then, we are really talking about the ability of the media to accept and deal with feedback. Suppose you are listening to a speech in a large auditorium. There are two kinds of feedback you may wish to give the speaker. First, you may want to influence what is said or the way it is said, asking the speaker to talk louder or explain a point further, perhaps requesting that the discussion move to a different topic. Second, you may want to respond to what the speaker has said, disputing the evidence or conclusions, telling the audience what you think. A good speaker will usually find some way to accommodate both kinds of feedback.

The mass media must also accommodate both kinds of feedback. Mr. Henderson is interested in the first kind; he wants to change what the media say to him and his children. Ms. Green, on the other hand, is concerned with the second kind of feedback; she wants to use the media to say something to her fellow citizens. We will discuss Mr. Henderson's problem in the first half of this chapter, then Ms. Green's in the second half.

MEDIA RESPONSIVENESS TO CONSUMERS

Mr. Henderson is a media consumer. Unlike Ms. Green, he doesn't especially want to get access to the media for his own views. He just wants to have some say about the media content his children are exposed to; he wants fewer commercials and less violence on television.

To what extent are the mass media in this country responsive to the individual media consumer—to Mr. Henderson or to you? The print media traditionally answer this question by saying they know what their readers want, and if they're wrong the readers can always stop buying. Broadcasters have a slightly better answer: the ratings.

The broadcast industry pictures its rating system as a democratic one in which each sampled home (representing tens of thousands throughout the country) has one vote in determining the nation's radio and television content. Arthur C. Nielsen, president of the rating company that bears his name, put it this way to the Oklahoma City Advertising Club in 1966:

> After all, what is a rating? In the final analysis, it is simply a counting of the votes, . . . a system of determining the types of programs that people prefer to watch or hear. Those who attack this concept of counting the votes —or the decisions made in response to the voting results—are saying, in effect: "Never mind what the people want. Give them something else."[1]

But ratings are not the perfect feedback device that Nielsen describes. In most cases, the public can only voice an advisory yes or no vote on the programs presented to it. It cannot suggest new forms of programming via the ratings, nor can it communicate to the programmers *how much* and *why* it likes or dislikes a show. Most ratings simply measure what channel the television is tuned to. They do not determine whether anybody is actually watching, much less whether those who watch are enjoying the program. Finally, the ratings serve a broadcast industry that demands mass audiences of 20 or 30 million for network programs. A mere 5 or 6 million people would constitute far too small a minority to influence broadcast content through the ratings. Mr. Henderson is free to turn off his TV set if he doesn't like children's programming, but he can hardly expect that action to have much impact on the ratings, and thus on broadcast content.

Until quite recently, the American mass media didn't worry much about their responsiveness to consumers. Broadcasters cited the ratings as proof that they were "democratic," while the print media boasted of their infallible instinct for reader interests.

The media's disinterest in feedback from the public applied to news as well as entertainment. To the extent that the news media thought about responsiveness at all, it was responsiveness to the profession, not to the public, that concerned them. The unstated assumption of most reporters and editors was that journalists knew how to serve the public better than the public itself did. It followed that the public would be served best when journalists were free to follow the ethical standards of their profession. The real battle was between professional standards on the one hand, and meddlesome owners, sources, advertisers, and the like on the other hand. In this battle the audience was seen as merely an interested bystander.

As we saw in Chapter 2, professionalism is still a bigger issue in journalism than responsiveness to the public. But this may be changing. Perhaps it was the attacks on the press by former Vice President Spiro Agnew

that did the trick. Perhaps it was the nationwide debate over the role of journalism in uncovering the Watergate scandals. Perhaps it was just the culmination of twenty-five years of rhetoric about the social responsibility of the media. Whatever the cause, the 1970s are witnessing a greater effort than ever before to respond to public doubts and complaints about media practices.

Among the earliest examples is "Let Me Speak to the Manager," a weekly program on Dallas television station WFAA since 1960. The general manager of the station fields questions and challenges from viewers on the operation of the station and on television in general. The show has proved surprisingly popular; it attracts some 250,000 viewers every Saturday evening, beating such competition as "Lassie" and "Green Acres." [3]

This sort of programming is becoming more and more common. So is the use of media ombudspersons, independent troubleshooters within a newspaper or broadcast station who check on the accuracy of stories and answer complaints from the public. One of the earliest and most respected of these is John Herchenroeder of the *Louisville Courier-Journal*, who took the job in 1967 after twenty years as a city editor. At first he received 300 to 400 complaints a year, but now the figure is up to 4,000.[4] Questions pour in not just about news coverage, but about advertising and circulation problems as well. The paper prints Herchenroeder's apologies under the standing headline, "Beg Your Pardon." It also runs his columns explaining in more general terms how the paper works, what the various editors do, and how news decisions get made.[5] Other newspapers with ombudspersons include the *Wilmington* (Del.) *News* and *Journal,* the *Minneapolis Star,* the *Salt Lake City Tribune,* the *Dayton* (Ohio) *Journal Herald,* and the *St. Petersburg* (Fla.) *Times.*

Some newspapers now send out printed forms to people named in the news, asking them if the facts were accurately reported (and the names spelled right). The *Seattle Times* tacks on a question about which news items the reader finds most interesting. The *Enid* (Okla.) *Morning News* asks for news tips and for suggestions to improve the newspaper. The *Omaha World-Herald* runs a column called "Your Newspaper," while the *Miami Herald* has one called "View from the Newsroom"; both try to explain why the papers do what they do.[6] The general manager of New York City's public television station, WNET, has also answered questions from viewers on the air.

These first steps toward responsiveness to the public are largely public-relations efforts to build credibility. But we shouldn't dismiss them as unimportant. They help enormously in getting the reader and viewer to understand the constraints, goals, and practices of journalism—and that understanding is an essential prerequisite to useful dialogue between the media and the public. In his efforts to cut down the violence and commercials in children's television, Mr. Henderson may even get some help from "Ask the Manager" shows, ombudspersons, and the like. At the very least, these developments will help him understand the system that perpetuates the violence and commercials.

PRESS COUNCILS

A more ambitious mechanism for media responsiveness to the public is the press council. Typically, a press council is an appointed, voluntary body of professional journalists, distinguished citizens, ordinary laypeople, or some combination of the three. It investigates complaints from the public about media performance and reports its findings. Usually it has no formal power to enforce its recommendations, just the power of publicity and its own prestige. National press councils of this sort have existed for many years in Denmark, Sweden, West Germany, India, Australia, Chile, Great Britain, and many other countries. In 1973, a National News Council was established in the United States.

The British press council is the principal model for the American experiment. It was first recommended by a royal commission that had been appointed by Parliament in 1946 to explore ways of making the press more accurate. The British media were not wild about the idea, but saw it as inevitable. (The American media would have viewed even the existence of such a government commission as a major threat to their First Amendment freedom.) The British council held its first meeting in 1953. Its members were all journalists and publishers. Not until 1963 were outsiders added to the council. This helped improve its credibility with the public and, paradoxically, also increased its prestige among the newspapers it had to regulate.[7]

Cases before the British press council fall into five categories: regulation of content; privacy and news sources; professional ethics; access to news sources; and sex in the news. In each case, the injured party is asked to try to work things out with the local editor first. If that fails, the council will act as a mediator between the two. Only as a last resort does the council issue a public statement. When that happens the council action is given wide publicity. In a recent three-year period there were only two instances when an offending newspaper failed to publish a council statement critical of its own performance.[8]

A typical council action came when a British newspaper printed the story of a married woman whose ex-lover had committed suicide. The woman had begged the paper to leave her connection to the victim out of the article. When the story was run anyhow, she also committed suicide. The council charged the newspaper with needless invasion of privacy.[9]

The council has also praised the British media when appropriate, and has acted as a buffer against government regulation. These actions have helped it gain credibility and acceptance among publishers. In 1966 the council published a Declaration of Principle, aimed at upgrading British journalism by establishing standards for ethical conduct. Every important newspaper editor in the United Kingdom endorsed the document.

Phillip Levy, who has written extensively about the council, concludes: "In England the Press Council today is a force to be reckoned with. The days when it was described by an irate editor as 'a vague and powerless body' have been left far behind. In a recent report by a government committee it was said to be 'feared, respected and obeyed.' "[10]

Press councils in the United States may eventually repeat the British experience, but at the moment we are far behind. We started even. In 1947 (while Britain's royal commission was still pondering its findings), the nongovernment Commission on Freedom of the Press in this country issued its own report. Among its recommendations was the establishment of a voluntary council to monitor the performance of the media in the United States.

The idea was not well received. Publishers

LENNERT GROLL OF SWEDEN

The Swedish press council was the first national council anywhere in the world. Called the Court of Honor, it was founded in 1916. In 1969 its structure was changed radically, with the appointment of Lennert Groll as national media ombudsman.

A lawyer by training, Groll now handles all inquiries from the public. He screens about 400 complaints a year, investigates the 300 or so that he considers serious, successfully mediates more than 200, and passes on some 80 cases a year to the full council for action. In roughly 60 of these cases the newspaper in question is eventually rebuked by the council. According to the rules of the council, voluntarily accepted by the Swedish media, this means an automatic fine of 1,000 crowns (about $220) for the first offense each year, escalating to a top of 3,000 crowns per rebuke for repeated offenders. One Stockholm paper was fined eleven times in a single year.[11]

Groll tries to avoid the problem of determining news bias, and deals mostly with charges of libel and fraudulence.[12] He also monitors the Swedish press to insure that it is following the Code of Honor of the National Press Club. Says Groll: "The main rules are that names of suspected persons should not be given and that names of persons sentenced to prison terms of two years or less should not be published. . . . It is one of my duties as Press Ombudsman to insure that these rules are followed by newspapers and to bring violations before the press council."[13]

The Code of Honor, the fines, and the council itself are all voluntary, yet they are universally accepted by Sweden's media. Groll is the only one of Sweden's many ombudspersons who is not a government official.

and broadcasters didn't like the thought of meddling laypeople any more than they liked the thought of meddling politicians. A few local editors sprinkled around the country did agree to meet regularly with a group of readers to evaluate the paper; the most notable of these early press councils served the tiny *Littleton* (Colo.) *Independent*. But with rare exceptions the recommendation was met with a deafening silence that lasted nearly twenty years.

The proposal was moved off dead center in 1966, when the Mellett Fund for a Free and Responsible Press (a private foundation) decided to support local press councils around the country. Cooperative papers were hard to find, but eventually publishers agreed to sponsor the councils in Bend, Oregon; Redwood City, California; Cairo and Sparta, Illinois; Seattle, Washington; and St. Louis, Missouri. The councils in Bend and Redwood City, for example, were composed of nine persons each, who met monthly with the papers' executives in the private dining rooms of local restaurants. Much of the time was spent educating the panel members on the operation of a newspaper, but the councils did debate such topics as balance on the editorial page and whether the names of juveniles should be printed in crime stories.[14]

William L. Rivers and William B. Blankenberg, who guided the Bend and Redwood City councils from their base at Stanford University, offer this description of how a press council should work: "The council brings the community's information needs (in addition to its wishes) to the attention of the publisher, who is in no way bound to follow the council's criticisms and suggestions. But he listens to the viewpoints and acts upon those that are feasible. The improvement in his newspaper is perceived by the public, which in turn feeds back its appreciation to the publisher directly and through the council once again." [15] Apart from this dialogue between paper and public, the mere existence of a press council may raise the credibility of a newspaper in the eyes of its readers, while sharpening the sense of responsiveness of the paper's staff.

Despite the totally noncoercive nature of press councils, many publishers—accustomed to exercising their power in private—find them frightening. When the owners of the *Bend Bulletin* and the *Redwood City Tribune* agreed to work with local councils, each received a letter from a high executive of the *Wall Street Journal*. The letter asked: "Why are you giving up your press freedom?" [16]

Even at their best, local councils can confront only local issues, and only those local publishers willing to accept a council. Regional or national councils, on the other hand, might be able to deal with state, national, and international coverage—and they might accumulate enough prestige to force at least limited participation by reluctant media owners.

The first step in this direction was taken in 1971, when a statewide press council was established in Minnesota. Headed by State Supreme Court Associate Justice C. Donald Peterson, the council is composed of nine laypeople and nine representatives of the media. The entire operation is voluntary, and the council's only power is publicity.[17] Issues of substance have been slow to come to the Minnesota council, and its impact cannot be determined yet. But at least the citizens of Minnesota have somewhere to go with their complaints.

Not until 1973 did a truly national press council open its doors for business in the U.S. Funded by $400,000 from the Twentieth Century Fund of New York, the National News Council is headed by William Arthur, a former editor of the now-defunct *Look* magazine. Like its predecessors, the Council can only investigate, offer to mediate, and release its findings. It is wholly voluntary, and has no power other than its own prestige.

So far that prestige is minimal. The *New York Times* has said it will not cooperate with the Council in its investigations.[18] The American Society of Newspaper Editors voted against its formation by a margin of three to one.[19] In an editorial entitled "Who Needs Them?" the *New York Daily News* voiced the most militant opposition:

> [The Council] will, in the foundation's pious words, "promote freedom of the press" by investigating public complaints of unfairness, error, bias or prejudice and publishing their findings.
>
> The latter, we assume, will carry written guarantees that this panel of Paul Prys is itself 100 percent free of bias and prejudice.
>
> We don't care how much the Fund prates its virtuous intentions. This is a sneak attempt at press regulation, a bid for a role as unofficial news censor. . . .[20]

It is much too early to tell whether the Council will ever gain the prestige it needs to work effectively. Certainly it had little impact on the first two major cases it handled. First, the Council offered to investigate the claim by then-President Richard Nixon that the television networks were guilty of biased reporting in their Watergate coverage. But the White House declined to supply specifics on the charge, and the Council's offer to mediate died on the vine.[21] Second, the Mobil Oil Corporation asked the Council to assess the fairness of an ABC-TV documentary entitled "Oil—The Policy Crisis," which the company said contained some twenty-three inaccurate statements. The Council dismissed the complaint, stating that there were "no significantly misleading factual misstatements," and that a program on such a complex issue is bound to omit much that is important.[22]

Even if the National News Council eventually gains the respect of the nation's media, it will probably never be as effective a mechanism for media responsiveness to the public as the British press council. The United States has many, many more news-papers and broadcast stations than Britain. It is doubtful that a single organization could ever police them all.

There are other limitations on the usefulness of the National News Council. For one thing, it is sticking to the emphasis in its title—news—and declines to deal with problems arising from advertising or entertainment in the media. Like most press councils, furthermore, the National News Council is concerned almost exclusively with "offenses," sins of commission, things the media did that they shouldn't have done. It has little to say about the equally important sins of *omission*, the things the media could do to serve the public a little bit better. And finally, the National News Council concentrates on departures from journalistic tradition. It is in the business of exposing wrongdoers, and just isn't prepared for complaints that insist there is something wrong with the tradition itself, with the media system as a whole. The quasi-judicial structure of the press council movement makes these limitations inevitable—but they are serious limitations nonetheless. True responsiveness to the media consumer requires a forum where general proposals for the future get just as serious consideration as specific complaints about the past.

ORGANIZED CONSUMER ACTION

As an individual, there is fairly little that Mr. Henderson—or you—can do to change the content of the media. You can complain to local media executives, and maybe even get your complaint published or read over the air. You can stop reading or watching and wait for the media to notice. Or you can appeal to an ombudsperson or a press council (if you can find one).

When these tactics prove unsuccessful, you have no choice but to organize.

The media can afford to ignore the complaints of a single dissatisfied reader or viewer like Mr. Henderson. But they cannot afford to ignore an active, vocal, organized protest. In this section we will consider four strategies for organized consumer control of the media:

1. Consumer boycotts.
2. The fairness doctrine.
3. License challenges.
4. Negotiation and public pressure.

Before going on, it is important to note that the second and third techniques apply only to broadcasting. Though fairly weak in themselves, these legal strategies become potent when combined with negotiation and public pressure. Consumers thus have a fighting chance to influence broadcast content. When it comes to the print media, on the other hand, only the first and fourth techniques are available. Newspapers and magazines are therefore much less susceptible than broadcasting to organized consumer action.

1. Consumer Boycotts. When one person stops buying a newspaper or stops tuning in a TV station, the paper or station is very unlikely to notice—or care. But when many people do it, the results can be impressive.

The trouble with consumer boycotts is the difficulty of getting people to join. In Richmond, California, for example, there is only one local newspaper, the *Independent*. The paper was notorious for ignoring the needs of Richmond's substantial black population, and in 1968 a subscription cancellation drive was organized. Although it was backed by leaders of the white liberal and black communities, the drive failed miserably. Out of a total circulation of nearly 40,000, the *Independent* lost perhaps a hundred subscribers. Many who agreed with the goals of the boycott were unwilling to cut off their only source of local news by cancelling their subscriptions to the daily.

Though rarely successful, local newspaper boycotts stand a far better chance than national magazine boycotts—simply because it is almost impossible to organize a national cancellation drive. For the same reason, national broadcast boycotts almost never work. And local broadcast boycotts usually fail when viewers return to their favorite programs before their defection has had time to show up in the ratings.

The only mass medium regularly influenced by consumer boycotts is the film industry. For many years the Legion of Decency, for example, rated all new movies on their acceptability for Catholic audiences. The Legion was able to dictate hundreds of alterations in various films, threatening a box-office boycott if the changes were not made. Recently, however, the Legion's power has waned, as American society becomes more permissive on matters of sex.

At best, the consumer boycott is a negative weapon. It can help an organized group fight objectionable media practices, but it cannot help them substitute something better. And because a boycott is such a passive technique, it requires huge numbers of people to work. More aggressive strategies can be effective with fewer participants.

2. The Fairness Doctrine. Strictly speaking, the Federal Communications Commission's fairness doctrine is not a form of public control of the mass media. Rather, it is an example of government control exercised on behalf of the public. The fairness doctrine requires two things of all broadcasters: (1) They must include some discussion of controversial issues in their programming; and (2) When discussing controversies, they must make a reasonable effort to provide a balance of conflicting viewpoints. A viewer or listener who feels that the fairness doctrine has been violated may complain to the station involved, and then to the FCC if the station doesn't offer a satisfactory solution. Though it almost never happens, a station *can* lose its license because of flagrant or continued violations. More likely, the FCC may require the station to cover the neglected viewpoints. And still more likely, the station may cover these viewpoints "voluntarily" in order to avoid an FCC investigation and possible rebuke.

In the mid-1960s, lawyer John Banzhaf founded Action on Smoking and Health (ASH), which contended that cigarette smoking was a controversial issue of public importance, and therefore subject to the fairness doctrine. ASH singled out WCBS-TV in New York for a test case. Banzhaf asked the FCC to order WCBS to broadcast information on the hazards of smoking, to balance its steady diet of cigarette commercials. The FCC agreed in 1967, and the broadcast industry was forced to give millions of dollars worth of free time to such groups as the American Cancer Society. This decision was a prelude to the removal of all cigarette ads from the broadcast media in 1971.

The fairness doctrine is often used as a way of gaining access to the media—that is, as a way of solving Ms. Green's problem instead of Mr. Henderson's. It sometimes works that way. If a station agrees that it has neglected a particular viewpoint, it may decide to remedy the situation by offering free time to the person or group that filed the fairness complaint in the first place. But it doesn't have to; John Banzhaf never made it onto WCBS. As far as the FCC is concerned, the fairness doctrine is designed to protect the media consumer, not the would-be advocate. It doesn't grant you the right to appear on television. Instead, it imposes on the station an obligation to tell you something about all sides in a public controversy.

In the years since the ASH decision, the FCC has taken an increasingly narrow view of the fairness doctrine, especially as applied to advertising. Time and again it has summarily dismissed fairness doctrine complaints similar to Banzhaf's. Sometimes the Commission concludes that the issue isn't controversial or important enough; more often it rules that somewhere in the smorgasbord of content the station has already touched on the opposing view. Actually winning a fairness doctrine case requires an enormous amount of time, energy, money, and luck.

But you don't have to win in order to succeed. Merely mentioning the fairness doctrine to a local station may be enough to convince the station's management that it had better pay more attention to alternative viewpoints. Or the threat of a fairness complaint may persuade the station to cut back the one-sided content on which the objection is based. Of course the fairness doctrine is a limited weapon. It is useful only against broadcasters, and only in response to unbalanced content of a controversial nature. But when you feel that a radio or television station is not telling you the whole story, the fairness doctrine is the best tool you have for making it pay attention to the other side.

3. License Challenges. Every three years a broadcast station is required to apply to the FCC for renewal of its license. In the past, renewal procedures have been simple and straightforward, with no embarrassing questions asked. Most renewals still are. But in recent years a number of citizen groups have made use of license-renewal time to question the performance of established stations—not because they wanted the license themselves, but because they wanted it to go to someone who would meet their needs more responsibly.

The change began in 1964, when black leaders in Jackson, Mississippi, challenged the license of Jackson television station WLBT. Aided by Dr. Everett Parker, head of the Office of Communications of the United Church of Christ, they charged that WLBT had systematically promoted segregationist views in its editorials and news coverage.

The FCC dismissed the challenge, asserting that the public had no "standing" before the Commission—no right, that is, to help decide whether a licensed broadcaster has earned the privilege of keeping the license. The Jackson citizens appealed this decision to the federal courts, and in 1966 the FCC was ordered to hold a hearing and let the blacks testify. It did so, then renewed WLBT's license anyhow, claiming that racial discrimination had not been proved. So Dr. Parker and the citizens of Jackson went back to the courts.

In 1969, appeals court judge Warren Burger (now Chief Justice on the U.S. Supreme Court) announced his decision. The FCC was rebuked for shifting the burden of proof from the licensee to the challenger, and was ordered to consider new applications for the WLBT license. Two years later, the FCC gave a temporary license to an interim group called Communications Improvement, Inc., which immediately integrated its staff and added some black programming. Meanwhile, the Commission considered five competing applications for the original license. In 1974, the FCC was about to award the license to the Dixie National Broadcasting Corporation, when opponents alleged that some officers of Dixie had misled the Commission about their outside business dealings. A group of Jackson blacks also charged that the president of Dixie National was simultaneously a vice president of a racially segregated private school.[23]

The WLBT case did establish that media consumers have a right to challenge a station's license without wanting the license for themselves, and that it is *possible* to get the FCC to take away the license of a station that is ignoring the needs of its audience. But eleven years after the initial complaint, channel 3 in Jackson, Mississippi, was still without a permanent licensee.

As the WLBT case shows, the license-renewal challenge is a powerful weapon for consumer control of the media, but it is not a cure-all. Like the fairness doctrine, it applies only to broadcasting, and only to those cases where the challenging group has a significant grievance against the station. Mr. Henderson must keep in mind that license challenges take even more time, energy, money, and commitment than fairness doctrine complaints. And most challenges still fail. Former FCC Commissioner Kenneth A. Cox warns that "possession is nine points of the law. FCC will not put a license holder out of business if he has even a halfway decent record." [24]

But like a fairness doctrine complaint, a license challenge doesn't have to be legally successful in order to achieve the goals of the challengers. As we shall soon see, many groups have used the threat of license challenges to win important concessions from local stations—without ever actually making it to the FCC.

4. Negotiation and Public Pressure. Complaining publicly to (and about) the media is a much less expensive strategy than legal action. It is also less extreme, and it can be applied to the print media as well as broadcasting. Sometimes it works.

One of the most effective media pressure groups has been the National Organization for Women. NOW meets regularly with editors around the country; it also publishes pamphlets, gives speeches, pickets, and lobbies in a wide variety of ways to change male media managers' attitudes toward women.

In its mimeographed guidelines for editors, NOW asserts that "part of the traditional style of writing about women requires describing them in relation to external and superficial concerns—what they look like, what they are wearing, how their homes are decorated, and what their husbands do for a living. This is related to the common view which perceives women as objects. Our Movement is declaring that women are subjects and that what we think and do is what matters to us, not what we wear." [25]

Specifically, NOW has urged the media to hire more specialists in women's news, and more women generally. It has asked that only females under the age of 16 be termed "girls"; those between 16 and 21 are "young women," and the rest are "women"—not girls, gals, or ladies. The sex of a person in the news, NOW says, should not be stressed unless it is relevant to the story, and more news about women should find its way into the general news sections, instead of the society or women's pages. Code phrases of derision like "Lib Ladies" or "Lib Gals" are out, and NOW doesn't want to hear any more about bra-burning. The honorific "Ms." is encouraged in place of "Miss" or "Mrs."

While pushing for these and other changes, NOW has also lent its support to women's caucuses being formed within the media in various cities around the country. Such groups now exist at *Newsweek, Newsday* (a Long Island newspaper), the *Ladies' Home Journal,* CBS, and elsewhere. Other concerns of NOW are the image of women in advertising (as sex objects, floor-waxers, or bug-eyed consumers); the lack of meaty roles for women in films; sexism in the lyrics of popular songs; and the unwillingness of television programmers to deal with the contemporary, independent woman.[26]

NOW is only one of literally dozens of national and regional groups that are working through public pressure and negotiation for changes in media content. Another very successful group, coincidentally, is Action for Children's Television, which has won major concessions from broadcasters on violence in children's programming and the frequency and content of children's commercials. Mr. Henderson should certainly join ACT.

Of course not all media pressure groups are working the "liberal" side of the street. Some of the most effective local organizations, for example, are those devoted to the battle against sex in the media. In many communities such groups have forced theater owners to promise not to run X-rated movies, newspapers to promise not to advertise them, and TV stations to promise to cut out the sexy parts when the movies are sold to television.

Negotiation and public pressure are strategies that are available to all segments of the public. All you need is the public-relations skill to rally a substantial and active constituency for the changes you are demanding. The media may not be sufficiently responsive yet to individual consumers, but to organized groups of consumers they can be very responsive indeed.

These various techniques for organized consumer control of the media—negotiation and public pressure, license challenges, the fairness doctrine, and boycotts—all work best when the changes demanded can be accomplished without costing the media too much money. Suppose you are part of an environmental group that strongly disapproves of a local manufacturer's advertising campaign, which boasts about pollution-control equipment you consider inadequate. A little organized pressure may well convince local newspapers to ask for changes in the ads. Similar pressure combined with the threat of a fairness doctrine complaint is quite likely to win concessions from local broadcasters. After all, the papers and stations can request the changes you want and still keep the company's ad account. But if your group insists that *any* advertisement from an industrial polluter is socially irresponsible, it will meet much stronger resistance from the media, because such a decision would cost the papers and stations a great deal of money.

CONSUMER CONTROL OR HARASSMENT?

The most successful consumer groups usually combine negotiation and public pressure with the threat of something more. This works best against broadcasting, where the "something more" can be a fairness doctrine complaint or a license-renewal challenge. Most groups don't have the resources to pursue the legal path all the way, and most would probably lose if they did. Broadcasters know that. But they also know that even an ineffective legal challenge would have to be defended against, and this would cost the station enormous amounts of time and money, plus a lot of bad publicity—not to mention the remote danger that the FCC might rule against the station. It is often easier and cheaper to comply with the group's demands, or at least offer a compromise.

For credibility if for no other reason, an active pressure group must occasionally fol-

---

THE MEDIA GADFLIES

The Office of Communications of the United Church of Christ, under Everett C. Parker, has long been a leader in efforts to make the media more responsive to the public. But it is not alone. Other effective national and regional groups include the National Association for Better Broadcasting (in Los Angeles); the National Organization for Women; the Television, Radio and Film Commission of the Methodist Church; the American Council for Better Broadcasting (in Madison, Wisconsin); and the Media Access Project (in Washington, D.C.). The following organizations have also been active and often successful:

Action for Children's Television. Founded by a group of Boston parents in 1968 ACT now has a nationwide following. It has concentrated on improving the quality of children's television, especially on the three networks. The group has forced changes in toy and sugared cereal commercials, has helped reduce the amount of advertising in children's programming, and has kept alive the debate over media violence. ACT is now working for a complete ban on commercials in children's television, and has even sponsored studies by economists to determine the cost to the networks of dumping the ads.

Accuracy in Media. Funded mostly by conservatives and conservative organizations, AIM has successfully used the fairness doctrine and public pressure to force the networks to present more balanced documentaries. Its most famous case concerned the NBC documentary "Pensions: The Broken Promise," aired in 1972. AIM said the program didn't pay enough attention to the positive aspects of pension plans. The FCC supported the claim, but a federal court overturned the FCC decision, and in 1975 AIM was planning an appeal to the Supreme Court. AIM also joined in 1972 with the Catholic United Front, the Way of Faith Fellowship, and other organizations to protest "moral pollution" on television.[27]

The National Citizens Committee for Fairness to the Presidency. This group was born in 1973 to protest news coverage of the Watergate scandals, and died in 1974 when President Richard Nixon resigned from office. During its brief existence, it sponsored a series of full-page newspaper ads around the country, accusing the media of bias against the president. The seventh ad in the series, for example, termed the media "the President's would-be pallbearers," and noted that they were "conglomerates . . . with a gluttonous appetite for POWER AND PROFIT."[28]

The National Citizens Committee for Broadcasting. An umbrella organization based in Washington, the NCCB lends expertise and help to smaller citizen groups around the country engaged in confronting the broadcast industry. Its board is chaired by former FCC Commissioner Nicholas Johnson. In 1974 the group published a hundred-page guidebook called *Demystifying Broadcasting,* designed as a do-it-yourself introduction to the ins and outs of legal challenges against established broadcasters. Its biweekly newsletter, *access,* aims at the same goal.

low through on its legal threats. It is not surprising, then, that in 1972 NOW challenged the license of WABC-TV in New York, "on the grounds of consistent failure to cover serious women's issues and a disparaging portrayal of women's role in society as reflected in overall programming and commercials." [29] The NOW petition to the FCC offered data showing that only 3.6 percent of the station's programming dealt with such issues as women in politics, abortion, child care, and the Equal Rights Amendment. The petition also said that when women won seven of the eight U.S. gold medals in the 1972 Winter Olympics, ABC network coverage gave the women only 40 seconds of air time, and didn't even mention their names. [30] Predictably, NOW never got the FCC to take away the license of WABC-TV. But there is no doubt that since 1972 it has been taken far more seriously as a force for change in the media.

Similarly, in 1969, station KTAL-TV in Texarkana, Texas, received its license renewal only after it signed a thirteen-point contract with local citizen groups, promising to improve its performance.

Twelve local black groups had challenged the license, charging that the station failed to meet the needs of the black community. They agreed to withdraw the challenge on condition that the station sign the contract. Among other points, KTAL-TV is now legally obligated to hire a minimum of two full-time black reporters; to preempt network programs only after consultation with minority groups; to solicit public-service announcements from those groups; and to meet with them once each month to discuss programming plans. [31] The Office of Communications of the United Church of Christ, which assisted the Texarkana groups, reports that the station has kept its promises to the community. [32]

The Council on Radio and Television in Los Angeles used the same combination of legal and public pressure to get KCOP-TV to agree to run more programming for

blacks and chicanos, and to hire more minority group members. [33] To avoid legal protests against its purchase of stations in Philadelphia, New Haven (Conn.), and Fresno (Calif.), Capital Cities Broadcasting had to promise groups in the three cities that it would spend a million dollars on special minority-interest programming. [34] And the New Jersey Coalition for Fair Broadcasting was able to wring commitments of increased news coverage of New Jersey from six New York City television stations—WNBC, WABC, WCBS, WOR, WNEW, and WNET. [35]

Depending on the issue at stake, public pressure can sometimes be combined with economic pressure as well. In 1973, for example, the United States Catholic Conference objected strenuously to two episodes of the CBS program "Maude" that dealt sympathetically with abortion. The Conference not only urged the network and its local affiliates to skip the two programs, but also urged sponsors to drop the show. As a result, Pepsi-Cola and the J. B. Williams Company defected from the advertising line-up, and twenty-five CBS affiliates declined to carry the abortion episodes. [36]

Many of the people who have applauded the success of minority and women's groups in forcing changes in the media deplored the success of the United States Catholic Conference at the same game. But public pressure, legal pressure, and economic pressure are tools of change that are open to groups of every ideology. These strategies are also open to outright rip-off artists. In the early 1970s, someone visited every TV station in a large Midwestern city, promising that for $1,000 each he could protect them against license challenges from black groups. [37] Nobody approves of extortion, but the distinction between legitimate consumer control on the one hand and harassment and intimidation on the other is largely a matter of whose ox is gored.

For a moment at least, consider the plight of the poor broadcaster, urged from every side to meet the needs of an infinity of con-flicting constituencies, threatened with ev-erything from picket lines to lawsuits if the station fails to comply. Little wonder the media sometimes cry out to be left alone to do their job as they think best, without pressure from anyone.

But of course that is not about to happen. As we have seen, the media are controlled by many forces—owners and gatekeepers, ad-vertisers and sources, government officials and professional codes. There is every rea-son why the public—all kinds of publics—should play a role in the pressures and cross-pressures that determine media con-tent.

"PUBLIC" TELEVISION

From its name if nothing else, one might suppose that "public television" was an im-portant enclave of consumer control of the mass media. In truth, the public has no more control over the content of public television that it does over the content of commercial television.

Public television consists of some 240 TV stations around the country that are not permitted to accept commercial advertise-ments. Instead, they are supported—barely—by Congress, corporate donors, private foundations, and the contributions of view-ers. Not surprisingly, public television is responsive less to the will of the people than to the wishes of the government and founda-tion powers that keep it alive.

The board of directors of your local pub-lic television station is almost certainly com-posed of political "heavies" in the commu-nity. This is equally true of national public TV organizations. The first head of the Corporation for Public Broadcasting, which distributes the money to local stations, was Frank Pace, Jr., also chairman of the board of the General Dynamics Corporation. The board of the Public Broadcasting Service, which distributes the programs themselves,

includes Dallas executive Sam E. Wyly; Bos-ton lawyer Thomas I. Atkins; Leonard Woodcock, president of the United Auto-mobile Workers; and others of similar stature.[38]

Another member of the PBS board is Dollie Cole, wife of the president of Gen-eral Motors. In early 1974 she told an inter-viewer that "I joined the board of direc-tors of the Public Broadcasting Service about a year ago so that I could get a show called 'Black Journal' off the air" because she considered it "destructive and racist." She also opposed televising the Senate Watergate hearings on public TV, and voted against appropriating an additional $200,000 to continue that coverage.[39]

Cole's views illustrate the perspective of a powerful conservative bloc in public tele-vision. But there is also strong representa-tion from the liberal establishment, and so far it is the more powerful of the two. "Black Journal" and the Watergate hear-ings both survived the attacks of Dollie Cole.

The point is not whether public TV is controlled by liberal leaders or conservative leaders. The point is that it is not, in any meaningful sense, controlled by the public. Even the most rudimentary mechanism for audience control over broadcasting, the rat-ings, is not an important factor in public television. Except for an occasional spectacu-lar like the Watergate hearings, ratings for prime-time public TV programs rarely get above one or two percent. Such special-interest (or low-interest) programming could never survive on commercial tele-vision.

On this one point, at least, critics from a variety of political perspectives agree. Con-servative radio commentator Jeffrey St. John writes:

A degree of intellectual dishonesty permeates much of the discussion about public broadcast-ing. First, there is the quaint fiction that it truly serves the "public." In reality it serves an

RECEIVER-CONTROLLED COMMUNICATION

All the mass media today are controlled, not by the receiver, but by the sender—the publisher or broadcaster. One new medium, the computer, promises receiver control in the not too distant future. Edwin Parker, a professor of communication at Stanford University, envisions what it could be like:

> Imagine yourself sitting down at the breakfast table with a display screen in front of you. You touch a key and the latest headlines appear on the screen. Not the headlines that were written last night—or even those of six or seven hours ago. But headlines that may have been rewritten and updated five minutes or just 50 microseconds before you see them on the screen. You type another key or poke a light pen at the appropriate headline and the whole story appears on the screen. . . .
>
> Are you interested in something that hasn't made the major headlines? Like a bill on education being considered in Congress. . . . Perhaps there's something you missed yesterday or the day before that's not front-page news today; the computer has it stored for you. You can have the latest information whether it's on today's or yesterday's story. . . .
>
> There's a person in the news you'd like to know more about. Ask your computer for a biographical sketch. You don't understand the economics of the gold market. Request a tutorial program on the subject. You want the comics? Press the right button. Catch up on the strips you missed while you were on vacation. . . .[40]

Dr. Parker's dream is technologically feasible today. Whether it will actually come about is another question.

---

elitist audience of students, academics, intellectuals, professionals and politicians.

Second, its political bias is mirrored in its news and public-affairs programs with a major portion of time devoted to those issues and beliefs held firmly as articles of faith by the liberal and left-wing elite which watches and supports public broadcasting. No programs representing millions whom we have come to regard as "middle America" have been produced. In fact, the values and beliefs of this large segment of working-class Americans have been viciously attacked by public broadcasting on news and public-affairs programs.[41]

The Network Project, a liberal group of communications researchers working out of Columbia University, doesn't dispute the point. Its report on public television notes:

The term "public broadcasting" implies to many people a truly democratic alternative to the commercial television empires—a communications system that is more responsive to the broad range of popular needs and wishes and more accessible to bold ideas and innovations than are the well-established and entrenched commercial networks. Such assumptions could not be further from the truth; those who control "public" broadcasting are as small and, by the unity of their purpose and the exclusiveness of their interests, as private a group as those who manage the commercial television networks.[42]

The issue of public control of the media is raised most often not by consumers, but by would-be sources who feel the media are ignoring them. The notion that unpopular and minority viewpoints have a right of access to the media is increasingly attractive to many media critics, but it has made little legal headway. Meanwhile, existing mechanisms for access are inadequate, and new ones have been slow to develop. Often the only practical option is to start one's own medium, an incredibly expensive alternative unless one is willing to settle for a low-circulation handout or newsletter.

THE "RIGHT" OF ACCESS

The first half of this chapter considered only the obligation of the media to be responsive to the consuming public, to give readers, listeners, and viewers what they want. We turn now to an equally important obligation—to permit the public to talk back. The mass media do not serve merely as a means of molding public opinion; they are also a vital channel for *expressing* public opinion. This is Ms. Green's problem. She wants the media to cover her save-the-park campaign, not so that she can find out about it, but so that others (local residents, the Army Corps of Engineers, etc.) can do so. Without media coverage her campaign is very unlikely to succeed.

The problem of access to the media has been ignored for many years, but it is not being ignored today. Dozens of special-interest groups—ghetto blacks and middle-class whites, young people and senior citizens, radicals and rightists—have come to recognize that access to the media plays a vital role in the fulfillment of their goals. As Hazel Henderson has put it:

> The realization is now dawning on groups espousing . . . new ideas, that in a mass, technologically complex society, freedom of speech is only a technicality if it cannot be hooked up to the amplification system that only the mass media can provide. When our founding fathers talked of freedom of speech, they did not mean freedom to talk to oneself. They meant freedom to talk to the whole community. A mimeograph machine can't get the message across anymore.[43]

In 1967 the *Harvard Law Review* published an article by Jerome A. Barron, entitled "Access to the Press—A New First Amendment Right." The article argued that the entire mass-communications industry "uses the free speech and free press guarantees to avoid opinions instead of acting as a sounding board for their expression."[44] This denial of media access, Barron said, was devastating to the proponents of a new viewpoint, and thus also to the public that might benefit from that viewpoint. Barron therefore urged a new interpretation of the First Amendment, which would recognize the obligation of all the media to afford access to a wide range of opinions, especially unpopular ones. A newspaper publisher, for example, might be required to print at least a representative sample of letters replying to earlier articles or editorials in the paper.

Opposition to the Barron theory stems from an understandable fear of any increased government control of the press. Someone would have to determine, on a day-to-day basis, which representatives of which views were offered time and space. That someone would probably be the government—a cure that many feel would be even worse than the disease. Dennis E. Brown and John C. Merrill of the University of Missouri's Freedom of Information Center assert that Barron's theory will take root "only when our society has proceeded much further along the road toward Orwell's 1984, wherein a paternalistic and omnipotent Power Structure makes our individual decisions for us."[45]

In the late 1960s and early 1970s, the right-of-access notion seemed to be making legal headway. A federal court, for example, ruled that members of the Students for a Democratic Society must be permitted to advertise their antiwar views in New York's public bus and subway stations. And in the "Red Lion" decision upholding the constitutionality of the fairness doctrine, the Supreme Court noted with apparent approval the emerging concept of a right of access, at least for broadcasting. But the trend came to a grinding halt in 1974.

At issue was a seldom-used Florida law requiring every newspaper to publish, without charge, any reply a political candidate submitted in response to criticism in that paper. Pat L. Tornillo, a candidate for the Florida House of Representatives, cited the law when he asked the *Miami Herald* to

In Buenos Aires four men and two women, members of a leftwing group called the People's Revolutionary Army, kidnapped the owner of an Argentine newspaper and held him until his paper printed their political statement. Hector Ricardo Garcia was released unharmed six hours after his paper published a complete rundown on the kidnappers' ideology.[46]

In Paris an armed revolutionary broke into a radio station and forced the announcer to read an anti-government statement over the air. He then threatened to blow up the place with a grenade unless he was granted half an hour on French television. Four hours later he surrendered to police.[47]

In this country, too, skyjackers and political terrorists have sometimes made access to the media a key point in their negotiations with police. Shortly after the kidnapping of Patricia Hearst by the Symbionese Liberation Army (and before her conversion to the SLA cause), Harvard Law Professor Roger Fisher proposed that the attorney general be authorized to offer political kidnappers up to half an hour of television time in exchange for release of their hostages.[48]

---

print his answer to a *Herald* editorial against him. The paper refused, so Tornillo took the case to court. Eventually it reached the U.S. Supreme Court, which declared the Florida law unconstitutional.[49]

For the moment, at least, this decision established that the print media have no legal obligation to provide access to any viewpoint, even one they have opposed in earlier content. In broadcast law, where the First Amendment is interpreted less literally, the right of access has made somewhat greater headway. Persons attacked in a broadcast editorial, for example, are entitled to respond. But even in broadcasting, an individual or group whose viewpoint has been ignored entirely—like Ms. Green—cannot legally insist on the right to express it. At this stage of the law, there is simply no such right.

The concept remains merely an ethical principle, something for responsible publishers and broadcasters (and editors and reporters) to think about as they choose the news. Many media managers today *do* think about it, and try to give fair coverage to those viewpoints they consider important, respectable, or otherwise worthy of the public's attention. Viewpoints that don't pass that test are out of luck.

GETTING ACCESS

The most effective way to get access to the media is to seem newsworthy to the people who control the media. Reporters cover an event—or an opinion—because it is important, unusual, timely, local, interesting, amusing, violent, traditional, etc. An event or opinion that appears to possess several of these characteristics is very likely to be well-covered. An event or opinion that appears to possess none of them is very likely to be ignored. The trick, then, is to embed your viewpoint in a series of events and "pseudo-events" that will oblige the media to cover it, regardless of their own viewpoints.

The craft of doing this effectively is, of course, public relations. Unfortunately, PR skill is very unequally distributed in the American population. Corporations and government agencies employ professional PR people who know how to get their viewpoints into the media. So do political groups, left, center, and right. But most small citizen groups lack these skills. How likely is it that Ms. Green knows how to write a press release, stage a press conference, or use any of the other public-relations techniques discussed in Chapter 6?

Apart from traditional public relations, what can a citizen group do to gain access to the media? There are at least three major access mechanisms available:

1. Letters and talk shows.
2. Advertisements.
3. Legal challenges.

As we shall see, none of the three is really adequate for the job.

1. Letters and Talk Shows. Probably the most common method of expressing one's viewpoint through the media is the letter to the editor. It is also the oldest; the *New York Times* published its first letter in 1851, four days after the newspaper was founded. In 1931 a special page was set aside for the letters. Today the *Times* receives more than 40,000 letters a year, of which 2,000 are printed. Letters are edited for grammar, style, and length, but not for content.

Most newspapers today run around twenty column inches of letters a day, usually on the page opposite the editorial page. With some exceptions, most editors are scrupulously careful to use letters that are critical of the newspaper and its editorial stand.

Numerous researchers have found that letter-writers are able to "blow off steam" [50]

and "get something off their chest" [51] by writing the editor their thoughts. Letter-writers tend to be educationally well above average, definitely not cranks or crackpots. They are usually well-read and highly individualistic; they are also predominantly male, white, and members of business and professional groups.

Letters to the editor are among the best-read parts of the newspaper. Letter-writing is therefore an excellent device for those who write persuasively to communicate with those who read critically. For individuals who are less literate, or who want to reach audiences other than the elite, the letter to the editor is of limited value.

Though radio and television stations do not usually broadcast letters to the station manager, in the past decade many have instituted phone-in "talk shows" instead. These programs give the public an opportunity to converse with moderators and their expert guests on almost any topic of interest. Callers are limited to once every three or four days, and the calls are screened to weed out drunks, young children, and other undesirables. The talk show format has proved to be immensely popular, and it's a cheap way for broadcasters to fill time. The value of the talk show in providing public access to the media is obvious. Its limitations are equally apparent—no caller stays on for more than a minute or two, and most callers never get through at all.

2. Advertisements. During the battle

TOP LETTER-WRITERS

The champion letter-writer in the *New York Times* is Martin Wolfson, an economics teacher at Brooklyn Tech High School in New York. Wolfson writes five or six letters a week to the *Times*, and has had more than 2,000 printed in various publications since 1927.

The all-time champion is Charles Hooper, who lived off a private income in Coeur d'Alene, Idaho, from 1913 to 1941 and wrote letters to newspapers all day, every day. Hooper's goal, which he nearly reached, was to get at least one letter published in every newspaper in the United States. [52]

over Prohibition, both the Brewers Association and the Prohibitionists attempted to lobby public officials by taking out newspaper ads supporting their positions. It wasn't until the mid-1960s, however, that the tactic gained much popularity with private citizens and citizen groups. Then ads began to appear in metropolitan dailies condemning everything from the bombing of North Vietnam to the massacre of baby seals in Canada. Between 1955 and 1960, fewer than two protest advertisements per month were placed in the *New York Times* (ads for political candidates were not counted). By the first years of the Kennedy administration the average was 4.2 protest ads per month, and the first years of the Johnson administration saw the average rise to 5.7 per month. Nonprotest ads that take a stand on some issue have also increased dramatically in number.

The popularity of the protest advertisement does not seem to be based on any conviction that it works. In a study of one anti-war ad placed by a hundred professors at a New England college, J. David Colfax found that only 20 percent of all readers recalled having seen the ad. More than 90 percent disagreed with it, and no readers said they were heeding the ad's call to write Congress and protest the war. On the other hand, more than half the sponsors of the ad admitted that they expected it to have no effect—though 70 percent said they would sponsor another such ad anyhow.[53] If the Colfax study is typical, then access to the media through protest advertising may not be a very useful solution.

But advertising can be a potent tool in the hands of a citizen group that understands its uses. It is least useful, probably, in the case of a hot national issue on which people have already made up their minds. But when the issue is local and little-known, advertising is a good way to generate interest and concern. And when the issue is one for which potential support already exists, advertising is a good way to arouse these supporters to action. In the late 1960s, for example, Friends of the Earth and other environmental groups on the West Coast successfully used newspaper ads to channel the growing environmental concern of the public into concerted action to save particular parks, landscapes, and urban amenities.

The problem is that controversial groups are not always permitted to advertise, even if they have the money to buy the ads. A few newspapers, most broadcast stations, and all three networks have firm policies against controversial advertising. Broadcasters say they are afraid the fairness doctrine would oblige them to carry free answers to a controversial paid ad, so they'd rather not take the ad in the first place. This is true as far as it goes, but there's a more basic reason for closing the airwaves to controversial advertisements. Such ads might shatter the tranquil broadcast environment so crucial to selling toothpaste, detergent, and beer.

In 1970 both the Democratic National Committee and an ad hoc group called Business Executives Move For Vietnam Peace were turned down when they tried to buy airtime from the three networks. The Supreme Court upheld the networks' right to reject the ads.[54] And it isn't just liberal groups that run afoul of this broadcast policy. In 1974 the Mobil Oil Corporation wanted to run an ad on all three TV networks soliciting viewers' opinions on whether Mobil should be allowed to drill for oil and gas beneath the continental shelves. Only NBC would accept the ad. Even after Mobil offered to pay for counter-advertising, thus avoiding the fairness doctrine objection, CBS and ABC said no. According to Walter A. Schwartz, president of ABC Television, the Mobil proposal would "open a Pandora's box" of controversial commercials.[55]

Less controversial ads stand a better chance of acceptance. Sometimes, in fact, they may be accepted without charge. As a service to the community, many broadcast stations and newspapers accept a certain number of free ads each day. Known as "public-service announcements" (PSAs), these ads urge the audience to help prevent forest fires, support the Scouts or the Red Cross, register to vote, drive safely, etc. The media have plenty of PSAs to choose from, and they naturally prefer the noncontroversial ones. Nonetheless, many local and national citizen groups have successfully used PSAs to gain free publicity for their cause. Even if Ms. Green is unable to talk the media into an anti-Corps PSA, she may well persuade them to run one on the value of local parks.

3. Legal Challenges. Fairness doctrine complaints and license-renewal challenges were discussed earlier in this chapter as weapons for consumer control of broadcasting. And that is mainly what they are—methods for influencing the content that radio and television offer you. But sometimes they can be used as tools for access to broadcasting as well.

Suppose you write to a station objecting to the way it has treated a certain issue, and threaten a fairness doctrine complaint unless its performance improves. If the station doesn't want a battle, it may well decide to pay more attention to the neglected viewpoint. Now the station has to find some way of getting that viewpoint into its programming—and there you are, ready to go with your PSA, or your news release, or your scintillating spokesperson ripe for an interview. So the station decides that the easiest way to satisfy its fairness doctrine obligation is to give you some airtime. It doesn't have to decide that way—but it often does.

The license challenge is another legal tactic that often results in access, though again that is not its purpose. Of course if you apply for a station's license and actually get it, then you have all the access you could want—24 hours a day of it. But most license challenges don't aim at getting the license, or even at taking it away from the current licensee; often their goal is simply to force improvements or changes in programming. Once again, the simplest solution for the broadcaster is often to give the challengers some control over what goes on the air. In anyone's language, that's access.

Legal challenges, advertisements, talk shows, and letters to the editor are all techniques that a citizen group should consider carefully when trying to reach the public through the mass media. But they are all limited weapons. Access to the media depends first and foremost on public-relations skill, on the ability to make the media want to cover what you have to say. If a group can persuade the media that it is genuinely newsworthy, the rest comes easy. If it can't, it has tough sledding ahead.

PRINT COMPETITION

Individuals and groups that fail in their efforts to influence existing mass media are sometimes tempted to start their own. Owning your own newspaper or broadcast station is a sure way to guarantee that it runs what you want it to run. But what are the chances of success?

When Daniel C. Birdsell founded the *Hartford* (Conn.) *Telegram* in 1883, he became the fifth newspaper publisher in that city. From the very start he was able to compete successfully with the other four. The first issue of the *Telegram* sold 2,000 copies, as opposed to 10,000 copies a day for the established *Courant* and *Times*. Within months Birdsell's *Telegram* was also considered an "established" newspaper, and a sixth publisher was no doubt preparing to enter the fray.[56]

Modern-day Birdsells are few and far between. Today the outlook for a new publisher in Hartford—or any other American city—is exceedingly glum. The following are some of the more important barriers to starting a new mass-circulation newspaper:

1. *Start-up costs.* Birdsell began the *Telegram* for under $10,000; his press cost him $900. By contrast, when the *Hartford Times* bought a new press in 1959, the price was

more than $1 million. Equipment prices have continued to soar. So has the cost of labor, ink, paper, distribution, and just about everything else. In 1968 the *New York Times* surveyed the afternoon market in that city with an eye to competing with the *Post*. Estimates were that the *Times* would lose $60 million in ten years before the new P.M. paper turned the corner.[57] Even the *Times* decided it couldn't afford that large an investment.

2. *Mass-market demands.* The nineteenth-century newspaper was an individual. It had its own editorial policy, its own style, its own quirks and favorite topics—and its own special readership. By comparison today's daily newspapers are all pretty much alike. It is that much more difficult, then, for a new paper to woo readers from the old ones. And unless a newspaper attracts large numbers of readers, it has nothing to offer advertisers.

3. *Wire-service problems.* A new mass-circulation newspaper cannot survive without a wire service for national and international news. Yet neither the Associated Press nor United Press International is overly cooperative with new publishers. During the Detroit newspaper strike of 1964, Mike Dworkin founded the *Detroit Daily Press* as an interim paper. He recalls his negotiations with UPI: "We were told we had to sign a five-year contract, at close to $2,500 per week, and pay the last year in advance—an amount in excess of $128,000. These were impossible and unrealistic conditions. We told them we did not want the entire package of services. They said all or nothing. We offered to pay them $3,000 per week, payable two weeks in advance, in cash, and again this wasn't for everything. We offered to assume all installation costs. . . . Their answer was 'No.' "[58]

4. *Syndicate problems.* A new publication may also have trouble subscribing to syndicated comics, columnists, and news features. Syndicates often offer their clients exclusive contracts for an entire geographical area. The *Los Angeles Times,* for example,

controls the West Coast from San Diego to Santa Barbara and east to the Colorado River. The *Philadelphia Evening Bulletin* holds territorial rights over Delaware, southern New Jersey, and all of eastern Pennsylvania. Some newspapers buy the rights to syndicated materials they rarely print, just to insure that no competing paper will get them (see pp. 249–50).

5. *Circulation audits.* The Audit Bureau of Circulations refuses to vouch for a newspaper's circulation unless at least half of it is paid. A new paper that wants to give away introductory copies is thus denied the ABC audit—and without ABC figures few advertisers are willing to purchase space.

6. *Other problems.* A host of seemingly petty problems confront the beginning publisher. Delivery people who carry the established paper are often forbidden to sell the new rival. It may take up to fourteen months for the paper to be listed in the local telephone book, perhaps even longer to get an entry in the standard advertising rate books. Established papers buy up the printing equipment of failing newspapers so that cheap, used presses are kept off the market. And if it surmounts all other barriers, the fledgling paper may be faced with a protracted circulation and advertising war designed to force it out of business.

In the face of these problems, successful new mass-circulation daily newspapers are understandably rare. Normally the best a competing paper can hope for is to force an improvement in the established paper before folding itself. In 1957 the *Lima* (Ohio) *News* was sold to Freedom Newspapers, Inc., a very conservative newspaper chain. The staff of the paper decided to quit and start its own in competition. Over the next seven years the new *Lima Citizen* cost the *News* $4 million in a hard-fought circulation and advertising battle. Although the *Citizen* was finally killed off, the *News* had to become a much better newspaper in order to keep its readers.[59]

Despite the risks, the lure of running your own newspaper is a powerful one, and there are always a few expansionist companies or wealthy individuals around who are willing to try. After the *New York Times* decided not to start an afternoon New York paper to compete with the *Post,* millionaire industrialist John M. Shaheen resolved to make the attempt. Shaheen plans to give his paper a strong financial emphasis, competing as much with the morning *Wall Street Journal* as with the *Post.* As of mid-1975, Shaheen was busy hiring a staff, choosing a building, negotiating with unions, subscribing to wire services, and buying his presses. The last item alone has cost in the area of $2 million so far.[60]

Starting a national magazine or a book publishing house is a little easier than starting a daily newspaper—but just a little. Atheneum Publishers is considered something of a miracle because it began in 1959 with only a million dollars—a mere pittance. Even big money is no guarantee of success. The magazine *Careers Today* was capitalized at $10 million when it was founded in 1968. It folded after two issues. Still, several successful new magazines and publishing houses make their mark every year (though hundreds fail). The average year has very few if any successful new mass-circulation daily newspapers.

BROADCAST COMPETITION

Though the economics of print journalism make competition exceedingly difficult, it is at least theoretically possible. In broadcasting this is not always the case. The electronic spectrum has room for only so many radio and so many television stations. Once they are all gone, no amount of money can make space for one more.

Not quite all the stations are gone. The Federal Communications Commission, which is responsible for dividing the spectrum and handing out broadcast licenses, still has hundreds of TV and radio frequencies that are up for grabs. Nearly every one of them, un-

fortunately, has some kind of catch to it. Either the station is reserved for noncommercial use, or it's an unprofitable UHF, or it's located out in the country where there's no audience to hear it, or it already has five competing applications—or, most likely, some potent combination of these and other disadvantages. Certainly there are few commercial AM radio or VHF television licenses in good-sized cities going begging for lack of interest. For those interested in operating such a station, transfer of an existing license is the only way.

The entire question is really an academic one. In practice, only a big business can afford to go into broadcasting. Having to buy an existing station instead of getting an unassigned frequency from the FCC only adds to the start-up cost—which customarily runs in the millions anyhow. Occasionally someone starts a small FM radio station somewhere with just ten or twenty thousand dollars, and runs it exactly the way he or she thinks a station ought to be run. But by and large competing with the established broadcast media is simply out of the question.

There is another way—cable television. The cable TV signal is transmitted through wires instead of through the air. Since the electronic spectrum is not involved, cable TV can handle as many channels as the cable itself has room for. The cables now being installed around the country can carry at least twenty separate programs; some can carry as many as eighty.

The question is what to do with all those channels. Naturally some of them are used to carry the regular over-the-air programming—the three networks, the local independent and noncommercial stations, and often a few signals from out of town. That still leaves plenty of unused channels—which is where the public comes in.

In 1972 the FCC adopted rules requiring every cable system in the hundred largest markets to make available a "public-access channel." New systems must provide the access channel immediately, while older ones have until 1977 to comply. Once the channel is available, local citizens may bring in their own videotapes for broadcast, or sometimes they can tape their programs using the cable company's studios. Everything that isn't commercial or libelous is carried free over the public-access channel on a first-come first-served basis. Some people sing and dance; some make political speeches; some produce documentaries on their favorite cause or organization; some offer to help the blind or deaf or aged; some prepare programs for children or for particular ethnic or interest groups.

At the moment all this programming is on the same channel—a smorgasbord of special-interest shows for (and by) dozens of different groups. This lack of continuity is a major barrier to attracting an audience, especially since the newspaper TV logs usually don't include a listing for the public-access channel. Most of the public-access shows aren't for you, and it's hard to find out when a program that is for you is going to be shown. In response to this problem, some special-interest groups and cable systems have agreed to produce regularly scheduled weekly shows on public access. If you want to go on TV every Wednesday night at eight with "A Student Views the News" (or "The Polish-American Hour" or "Today's Astronomy" or "Your Ecology Center"), the local cable system will probably say yes.

When one public-access channel gets filled up, there is plenty of room on the cable for another, and another, and another. It is even possible to subdivide the cable system geographically, so that only certain sets receive a particular program. The result could be neighborhood television, or block television, or even apartment building television if you want it. But of course there's no profit for a cable system in offering more free access than required by law. Unless a local government negotiates a cable franchise that provides for

---

PUBLIC ACCESS IN READING

In Reading, Pa., channel 5 is the cable system's public-access channel. It carries programs from an incredibly wide range of community groups—the Spanish Civic Center, the Zion Mennonite Church, the John Birch Society, the NAACP, the Ku Klux Klan, the Che-Lumumba-Jackson Collective, the National Organization for Women, etc. It also carries many less ideological shows produced by local residents, such as "This Is Your Life, Dr. Goodwin," a two-part farewell to a retiring black physician. And it is known throughout the country as one of the most successful public-access systems anywhere.

Nearly anyone in Reading may enroll in the system's "video workshop," for three free lessons on how to use a portable TV camera. The system owns four of them, and lends them out without charge to individuals and groups. Whatever comes back goes on channel 5. "The words 'edit' and 'censor' don't exist around here," boasts the cable system's manager, Earl W. Haydt. "We don't give a damn what your story is; we just want you to tell it." The result is an endless series of technically terrible but fresh and varied programs—a sort of extended broadcast bulletin board.

The problem is that nobody watches. Reading's cable system has 32,000 subscribers, 55 percent of the area's television homes. But channel 5 attracts no more than 3 to 5 percent of these subscribers, and often settles for a good deal less. If three people phone in to ask Haydt to run a certain public-access program again, he does. "It is not a mass medium," admits Paul Braun, who teaches the video workshop. "If it is, then it's a failure. But sometimes a show may be designed for just 12 particular people. If you reach the right 12, you're a success." [61]

several public-access channels, most cable systems will stick to the FCC requirements—one channel for systems in the top hundred markets, no channel for systems in the smaller markets.

If the public-access channel isn't enough for you, you can always lease a vacant channel (or part of one) from your local cable system. It won't be free, but it will cost a lot less than time on an over-the-air TV station. To make back the cost, you can sell commercials. Or you can develop a pay-cable arrangement and charge your viewers. Suppose, for example, you think there's a market in your city for live televised plays once a week. Acting as producer, you can hire a local theater group and lease channel 27 every Tuesday night. Then you can try to convince advertisers to sponsor the plays, or viewers to pay you for the privilege of watching. You might even earn a profit.

Any way you look at it, cable television offers enormous potential for public access to the media. But so far it's mostly just potential. The stark fact is that most people want to watch facile, slick, entertaining, technically superb television—which is precisely what the networks already offer. They don't want to watch specialized shows thrown together by amateurs.

As of 1974, roughly half the television homes in the country can get cable TV if they want it. About a quarter of them want it. Thus, only 12 percent of all TV households in the U.S. are cable subscribers. And most of the people who do subscribe use the cable for better reception of the same programs that are offered over the air, or for importation of distant programs that are offered over the air someplace else. The viewing audience of the typical public-access channel at any given time can almost be counted on your fingers and toes.

Proponents of cable predict that eventually everyone will subscribe. We'll use our cable sets, they say, for everything from banking to shopping, from voting to studying. Viable public-access television will come almost automatically. Maybe so. In the meantime, cable offers us a chance to say whatever we want to whoever happens to be watching. Even that isn't to be sneezed at. At last, Ms. Green has a guaranteed forum where she can promote her save-the-park campaign. Perhaps someday she'll have a sizable audience as well.

ALTERNATIVE MEDIA

The best hope for increased access to the media is the development of new communication technologies. Cable may one day put a channel or two within the grasp of every special-interest group. Cheaper and more flexible movie equipment allows independent filmmakers to produce high-quality products, which may eventually find outlets in cable and UHF television as well as neighborhood movie theaters. Time-shared computer terminals (see page 222) may offer individual subscribers an opportunity to televise what they want to say and watch what they want to see. If and when these innovations begin to fulfill their promise, the problem of public control of the media may be greatly alleviated.

But what are we to do while all this is happening?

The most significant technological contribution of the moment is photolithographic printing, also known as offset or cold-type printing. The offset process has reduced the cost of small-scale publishing to a level that is within the reach of nearly everyone. Using equipment like a Varityper, a Justowriter, or even an ordinary electric typewriter, would-be publishers can turn out neat and attractive copy in their basements and their spare time. Joblot printers can produce 5,000 copies of an eight-page offset newsletter for under $200. Some of them print literally dozens of such publications every month.

Offset printing has spurred the growth of weekly newspapers in many communities too small to support a letter-press paper. It has also fostered thousands of "shoppers," mini-papers that are distributed free to area residents, paid for by local advertisers. But the most exciting effect of offset technology is neither of these. It is the special-interest newsletter, the ideological bulletin, and the underground newspaper.

Suppose you are deeply involved in the ecological problems of your local community, devoting most of your leisure time to the fight for cleaner air and water. Naturally you will want to do your best to get the mass media to cover your activities. But your best may not be good enough. So in addition to lobbying the local newspapers and broadcast stations, you may also put out a monthly publication of your own—which you will mail to other environmental activists and potential converts.

Economically, of course, you are in no way competing with the mass media. You do not want, and cannot get, their mass readership and mass-market advertisements. But in a more important sense you *are* competing. You are providing your community with specialized information that the mass media do not provide. Offset printing makes it possible for you to do so on a very low budget.

Many offset publications offer more than merely news too specialized to attract mass-media attention. They offer a completely different way of viewing the world, a unique ideological perspective on issues and events. For their readers they are not just a supplement to the traditional media, but rather a more relevant substitute. Such publications deserve the label "alternative media." The most obvious example is the underground press.

In 1955 the *Village Voice* carved a small niche for itself in the New York City newspaper market with a potpourri of film and theater reviews, hip features, and acid political commentary. Ten years later the *Voice* had a circulation of 56,000 and a respectable profit for the first time. It had become the newspaper of the "Establishment Left"—and in 1966 the anti-Establishment Left was forced to start another publication,

aptly named the *East Village Other*. Said Jack Newfield of the *Voice:* "EVO is for the totally alienated. We're the paper for the partially alienated." [62]

In *The Open Conspiracy,* a book on underground newspapers, Ethel G. Romm defines the underground as a paper with "a peculiar sense of what was news, a mad eye for design, an instinct for the shocking." [63] Others would say that the underground newspaper combines social revolution, sexual titillation, psychedelic exultation, and traditional muckraking into a single tabloid package. By either standard the *Village Voice* no longer qualifies. But there are plenty of others to take its place, from the *Free Press* in Los Angeles to the *Great Speckled Bird* in Atlanta.

The size of the underground press is a matter of considerable debate. Using a fairly narrow definition, Romm counted 111 papers in 1969; others during the same period offered tallies as high as 6,000—not including some 3,000 additional high school underground papers around the country. But even at the height of the underground movement in the late 1960s, no more than 400 or 500 of the papers were really stable. And the subsequent death of many that seemed stable suggests that even this is a generous estimate. In 1972 the Liberation News Service, a sort of underground news and feature syndicate, listed 800 clients, including some (like *Time* magazine) that were hardly underground.

Journalism professors Everette E. Dennis and William L. Rivers have identified three distinct periods in the underground press, as follows:

1. During the *hippie period, 1964–1967,* the papers were primarily known for psychedelic art and essays on drug use, sexual freedom, and Eastern religion.

2. During the *radical period, 1967–1970, the* hippies were politicized and blended with the New Left and other radical political groups. The papers were heavy with articles about such political folk heroes as the Black Panthers and political organizers in a fairly simplistic stance of counter-culture versus the straights.

Underground broadcasting is almost a contradiction in terms. An FCC license implies more respectability than most undergrounds could tolerate. Apart from a few "pirate" stations that broadcast without a license, then, there is no real underground broadcasting in the U.S.

Still, some 400 licensed radio stations, most of them FM, almost deserve the label. Devoted mostly to hard-rock formats, these stations won their audience from the so-called "bubblegum rock" stations by offering longer music cuts and fewer commercials. In many cases they also offer innovative news and public-affairs programming. The stations tend toward irreverent newscasts that try to expose the ridiculous side of prominent political personalities, along with frank discussions of sex, drugs, and politics.[64] Some of them acted out the complete Watergate transcripts on the air, adding the deleted expletives. One station, KPFA in Berkeley, Calif., was the go-between for Patricia Hearst and her parents during the kidnapping/conversion episode in 1974. KPFA is part of the Pacifica Group, the only leftist broadcasting chain in the U.S.

Really underground broadcasting can't be broadcast. Some of it appears instead on the public-access channels of cable TV systems. Since cable systems don't censor the public-access channel, the doors are open for politically and sexually explosive content. What doesn't make it onto cable TV is sometimes shown on college campuses, or passed along for private showings from one underground video group to another.

Such groups now exist in many parts of the United States. Though generally young and politically left, they are less interested in the content of underground television than in the counter-cultural potential of the technology itself. As the editors of *Radical Software* (an underground video periodical) wrote in their first issue: "Only by treating technology as ecology can we cure the split between ourselves and our extensions. We need to get good tools into good hands—not reject all tools because they have been misused to benefit only the few." [65]

Among the groups that have acted on this assumption are the Raindance Corporation, Global Village, and Videofreex in New York City; the Community Service Television Project in Santa Cruz, California; Ant Farm in Sausalito, California; and Video Free America in San Francisco. In 1972 another such group, Top Value Television (TVTV), produced two highly acclaimed videotape documentaries on the Democratic and Republican nominating conventions. TVTV did it for less money than the networks spent on coffee during the conventions.

And then there's Joseph Blanco of Monsey, New York. Blanco has constructed a sort of closed-circuit radio station that uses the electrical grid in his neighborhood to send a weak signal into the surrounding homes. This is known as a carrier-current station; many college radio stations operate on the same principle. The FCC doesn't require a license for carrier-current operations, and doesn't bother them as long as there's no interference with a licensed broadcaster. Blanco is "on the air" Sundays only for nine hours, offering neighborhood news and a community bulletin board. He is aided by a volunteer staff of five.[66]

3. During the *period of internal dissension and new complexity, since 1970,* the issues that once seemed clear-cut are more complicated, many staff splits have occurred, and there have been debates about stance and tactics. Sexism in advertising is under attack, and the style of writing and appearance of the papers is moving closer to conventional standards.[67]

Though stereotyped, these distinctions reflect genuine changes in the underground press. Today the underground movement is splintered but healthy. Some of the psychedelic papers from the "hippie period" have survived, serving what is left of the counterculture plus a sizable audience of tourists and weekend hippies. Others have specialized in sex, period; a raunchy New York publication called *Screw* has made publisher Al Goldstein a wealthy man. The political papers from the "radical period" have also gone their own ways—some sticking with a broad leftist orientation, others purifying and rigidifying their ideologies, still others turning to explicit political organizing instead of news or radical theory. And out of the "period of internal dissension" several additional kinds of underground papers have emerged. These include newspapers of black liberation and women's liberation; newspapers devoted to more specialized issues such as health care, education, prisons, and environmental quality; and newspapers attempting to explore the alternative lifestyles implicit in such developments as communes and cooperatives.

Many observers have noted the impact of underground newspapers on the straight press, but few have pointed out that the influence works both ways. While a number of big-city dailies used to publish "Dr. Hippocrates," an unorthodox medical column that began in the *Berkeley Barb,* equally many underground papers are subscribing to muckraking Washington columnists like Jack Anderson. Many underground papers today also pay serious attention to local investigative reporting of city councils, zoning boards, and the like—the kind of newswriting that mainstream dailies could (but too often don't) run.[68]

Sometimes an underground publication strikes a responsive chord, accumulates a substantial audience, and goes straight. The *Village Voice,* now owned by *New York* magazine, is one example. *Rolling Stone* is another.

Rolling Stone was founded in 1967 by Jann Wenner, an unemployed recent graduate of the University of California. With a $7,500 stake and six volunteer staffers, Wenner devoted his new magazine to rock music, "the energy center of the new culture and youth revolution." [69] The first press run was 40,000 copies, 34,000 of which didn't sell. But Wenner had a formula that caught on, first in the San Francisco area, then nationwide. The magazine has grown to a paid circulation of 300,000, with eighty full-time staffers including such noted writers as Timothy Crouse and Dr. Hunter S. Thompson. The focus on rock has lessened; national politics and youth lifestyles now occupy much of the magazine. In 1973 *Rolling Stone* earned $5 million.[70]

Despite incessant legal harassment (most often on charges of obscenity or peddling without a license), the underground press has been immensely influential. Occasionally an underground paper manages to earn a profit. Occasionally one succeeds in winning a convert or two from the middle class. Occasionally one attracts a readership diverse enough to justify going above-ground. Occasionally one is quoted or imitated by the Establishment press. But none of these is the main goal of the undergrounds. Their goal is to build a cohesive community of like-minded people—the radical, the countercultural, the liberated, whatever. In this they are probably succeeding. Their impact on mainstream American culture is considerable, but largely accidental. Their impact on their own subcultures is huge.

George A. Cavalletto of Liberation News Service put it as simply as it can be put: "As hundreds of new communities develop across the country, they start their own newspapers. The information they want they can't get through the regular press." [71]

The radical young have no monopoly on offset technology. Every serious ideology and special interest has its own publication or publications—from the John Birch Society to the Black Panthers, from the Sierra Club to the lumber lobby. If you are unable to convince the mass media to cover what you think they ought to cover, then you must cover it yourself—and offset helps you do it. An admiring critic of the muckraking *San Francisco Bay Guardian* sums it up: "That's what the First Amendment is all about." [72]

Notes

[1] Arthur C. Nielsen, Jr., "If Not the People . . . Who?" Address to the Oklahoma City Advertising Club, July 20, 1966, p. 5.

[2] Harry J. Skornia, *Television and Society* (New York: McGraw-Hill, 1965), p. 57.

[3] "WFAA's Shapiro Into Syndic with 'Speak To Mgr.' " *Variety*, November 24, 1971, p. 31.

[4] "Setting the Record Straight," *Newsweek*, January 28, 1974, p. 51.

[5] "How Newspapers Hold Themselves Accountable," *Editor & Publisher*, December 1, 1973, p. 16.

[6] *Ibid.*, pp. 16, 28.

[7] Phillip Levy, "British Press Council a Force to Be Reckoned With," *IPI Report*, September/October, 1973, p. 13.

[8] William L. Rivers, "How to Kill a Watchdog," *Progressive*, February, 1973, p. 47.

[9] Helen Nelson, "Watchdog of the British Press," *Saturday Review*, August 8, 1964, p. 42.

[10] Levy, "British Press Council," p. 15.

[11] Hillier Krieghbaum, "Corrections Rise in Sweden's Newspapers with Ombudsman," *Editor & Publisher*, April 28, 1973, p. 42.

[12] "Press Ombudsman Describes Work," *New York Times*, September 23, 1973, p. 49.

[13] Krieghbaum, "Corrections Rise," p. 40.

[14] Donald E. Brignolo, "Community Press Councils," Freedom of Information Center Report No. 217, School of Journalism, University of Missouri, Columbia, Mo., March, 1969, p. 3.

[15] *Ibid.*

[16] William L. Rivers, William B. Blankenberg, Kenneth Starck, and Earl Reeves, *Backtalk* (San Francisco: Canfield Press, 1972), p. 16.

[17] "Minnesota Press Forms a Council," *New York Times*, January 30, 1972, p. 60. "Minnesota Establishes First State Press Council in U.S.," *FoI Digest*, March/April, 1971, p. 1.

[18] "The Times Bars Support to Panel for Monitoring News Media," *New York Times*, January 16, 1973, p. 35.

[19] "Council Is Planned to Monitor the Press," *New York Times*, December 1, 1972, p. 53.

[20] Rivers, "How to Kill," p. 44.

[21] "Biased News," *New York Times*, June 2, 1974, p. 37.

[22] "Mobil Oil Loses on Complaint Against ABC-TV News Show," *New York Times*, May 11, 1974, p. 62.

[23] "F.C.C. Asked to Hold Hearings on Jackson Licenses," *New York Times*, August 17, 1973, p. 62. "Church Group Seeks to Bar TV License," *New York Times*, November 27, 1973, p. 82. "Jackson, Miss., TV License Case Reopened by F.C.C. Review Bd. On Charge of 'Hidden' Information," *Variety*, January 16, 1974, p. 47.

[24] *Access to the Air*, Report on a Conference at the Graduate School of Journalism, Columbia University, New York, N.Y., September 28–29, 1968, p. 25.

[25] "Newspaper Guidelines," National Organization for Women, mimeographed, p. 7.

[26] "Images of Women in the Mass Media," Image of Women Committee, New York Chapter, National Organization for Women, undated.

[27] "Launch Movement to Clean Up 'Moral Pollution' on Home Tubes by Coalition of Conservative Orgs," *Variety*, December 13, 1972, p. 27.

[28] *New York Times*, December 2, 1973, p. 18.

[29] "National Organization for Women Challenges WABC-TV License on Grounds of Blatant Sexism," press release, New York Chapter, National Organization for Women, May 1, 1972, p. 1.

[30] *Ibid.*, p. 3.

[31] Marvin Barrett, ed., *Survey of Broadcast Journalism 1968–69* (New York: Grosset & Dunlap, 1969), pp. 44, 122–24.

[32] Thomas Billings, "Anatomy of a Pressure Group," Freedom of Information Center Report No. 284, School of Journalism, University of Missouri, Columbia, Mo., June 1972, p. 4.

[33] "2 Stations in Pacts on Minority Hiring," *New York Times*, November 24, 1971, p. 71.

[34] Martin Mayer, "The Challengers," *TV Guide*, February 3, 1973, p. 8.

35 "TV Stations Will Air More Jersey News," *New York Times,* October 10, 1972, p. 36.

36 "25 C.B.S. Affiliates Won't Show 'Maude' Episodes on Abortion," *New York Times,* August 14, 1973, p. 67.

37 Mayer, "The Challengers," p. 6.

38 *The Fourth Network* (New York: The Network Project, 102 Earl Hall, Columbia University, 1971), pp. 17–27.

39 "Detroit Blanks Pollution Shows; Wife of G.M.'s Cole Hits PBS," *Variety,* June 19, 1974, p. 31.

40 William L. Rivers and Wilbur Schramm, *Responsibility in Mass Communication* (New York: Harper & Row, 1969), pp. 9–10.

41 Jeffrey St. John, "Does Public TV Have a Future? Should It Have? Nay!" *New York Times,* July 21, 1972, p. 31.

42 *The Fourth Network,* p. 3.

43 Hazel Henderson, "Access to the Media: A Problem in Democracy," *Columbia Journalism Review,* Spring, 1969, p. 6.

44 Jerome A. Barron, "Access to the Press—A New First Amendment Right," *Harvard Law Review,* 1967, pp. 1646–47.

45 Dennis E. Brown and John C. Merrill, "Regulatory Pluralism in the Press," Freedom of Information Center Report No. 005, School of Journalism, University of Missouri, Columbia, Mo., p. 4.

46 "Argentine Rebels Seize a Publisher," *New York Times,* March 9, 1973, p. 12.

47 "Gunman Takes Over Paris Radio Station," *New York Times,* February 10, 1974, p. 7.

48 Roger Fisher, "Preventing Kidnapping," *New York Times,* March 13, 1974, p. 41.

49 "Justices Void Florida Law On Right to Reply in Press," *New York Times,* June 26, 1974, pp. 1, 18.

50 Sidney A. Forsythe, "An Exploratory Study of Letters to the Editor and Their Contributors," *Public Opinion Quarterly,* 1950, p. 144.

51 William D. Tarrant, "Who Writes Letters to the Editor?" *Journalism Quarterly,* Fall, 1957, p. 502.

52 Irving Rosenthal, "Who Writes the 'Letters to the Editor'?" *Saturday Review,* September 13, 1969, pp. 114–16.

53 J. David Colfax, "How Effective Is the Protest Advertisement?" *Journalism Quarterly,* Winter, 1966, pp. 697–702.

54 "Court Backs TV and Radio Refusal of Political Ads," *New York Times,* May 30, 1973, p. 79.

55 "Networks Reject Mobil Equal-Ad Plan," *New York Times,* March 16, 1974, p. 1.

56 Carl E. Lindstrom, *The Fading American Newspaper* (Gloucester. Mass.: Peter Smith, 1964), pp. 82–83.

57 O. Roy Chalk, "The High Cost of a Fresh Voice," *Grassroots Editor,* May/June, 1968, p. 16.

58 Keith Roberts, "Antitrust Problems in the Newspaper Industry," *Harvard Law Review,* 1968, p. 334.

59 John M. Harrison, "How a Town Broke a Newspaper Monopoly," *Columbia Journalism Review,* Winter, 1963, pp. 25–32.

60 "A 4th Newspaper Considered Here," *New York Times,* March 29, 1973, p. 53.

61 Tom Shales, "One Town Tries TV Of, By and For the People," *Washington Post,* March 24, 1974, pp. L1, L5.

62 "Voice of the Partially Alienated," *Time,* November 11, 1966, p. 92.

63 Ethel Grodzins Romm, *The Open Conspiracy* (Harrisburg, Pa.: Stackpole Books, 1970), p. 17.

64 "New Trends Alter Underground Radio," *New York Times,* January 10, 1972, p. 1.

65 "The Alternate Television Movement," *Radical Software,* No. 1, 1970, first page foldout.

66 "A Suburbanite's Radio Station Tries a Mini-Media Approach," *New York Times,* January 6, 1972, p. 75.

67 Everette E. Dennis and William L. Rivers, *Other Voices* (San Francisco: Canfield Press, 1974), pp. 139–40.

68 " 'Underground' Press Coverage Shifts from Rock, Sex and Drugs to Politics," *New York Times,* March 7, 1973, p. 45.

69 Peter A. Janssen, "Rolling Stone's Quest for Respectability," *Columbia Journalism Review,* January/February, 1974, p. 61.

70 *Ibid.,* p. 60.

71 Richard Askin, "The Underground Press: Where It's At," unpublished paper, University of Texas, 1970, p. 1.

72 Personal communication from Wallace Turner to David M. Rubin, April, 1970.

Suggested Readings

BAGDIKIAN, BEN H., "Right of Access: A Modest Proposal," *Columbia Journalism Review,* Spring, 1969.

BARRON, JEROME A., "Access to the Press—A New First Amendment Right," *Harvard Law Review,* 1967.

CHALK, O. ROY, "The High Cost of a Fresh Voice," *Grassroots Editor,* May/June, 1968.

DENNIS, EVERETTE E., and WILLIAM L. RIVERS, *Other Voices*. San Francisco: Canfield Press. 1974.

EPSTEIN, DANIEL, "The Anatomy of 'AIM,'" Freedom of Information Center Report No. 313, School of Journalism, University of Missouri, Columbia, Mo., October, 1973.

HENDERSON, HAZEL, "Access to the Media: A Problem in Democracy," *Columbia Journalism Review,* Spring, 1969.

LEVY, PHILLIP, "British Press Council a Force to Be Reckoned With," *IPI Report,* September/October, 1973.

MAYER, MARTIN, "The Challengers," *TV Guide,* February 3, 1973.

RIVERS, WILLIAM L., "How to Kill a Watchdog," *Progressive,* February, 1973.

RIVERS, WILLIAM L., WILLIAM B. BLANKENBERG, KENNETH STARCK, and EARL REEVES, *Backtalk.* San Francisco: Canfield Press, 1972.

ROMM, ETHEL GRODZINS, *The Open Conspiracy.* Harrisburg, Pa.: Stackpole Books, 1970.

PART III
MEDIA

So far in this book we have discussed the functions and impact of the mass media, their history, and their control by various groups and institutions. By and large, our discussion has treated the media as a whole, not stressing the differences from one medium to another. But those differences are extremely important. It is impossible to understand the mass media without, at some point, considering them one by one.

We have now reached that point. Our discussion will begin with the wire services, feature syndicates, and networks—the "common denominators" that determine much of the content of the major media. Next will come newspapers, traditionally the most prototypic of the media. Then we will turn our attention to two less news-oriented print media, magazines and books. The following chapter is devoted to broadcasting, which has replaced the print media as the public's main source of news and entertainment. After broadcasting, we will look briefly at a more specialized entertainment medium, film. The final chapter in this section will consider two activities closely related to the mass media that are, in the long run, perhaps the most influential of all: advertising and public relations.

We will discuss a grand total of nine different media: wire services, feature syndicates, networks, newspapers, magazines, books, television, radio, and film; plus advertising and public relations. It is important to recognize that these are by no means the only mass media in existence. Consider the following list:

Comic books
Matchbooks
Posters
Buttons
Phonograph records
Record jackets
Tape recordings
Plays
Nightclubs
Lectures
Operas
Concerts
Billboards
Graffiti
Paintings
Sculptures
Museums
Boxtops
Postcards

All of these—and many more—are in some sense mass media.

Some of them are extremely important mass media. You don't have to be under thirty to know that rock music, for example, has replaced everything else as *the* medium of expression and communication for many young people.

The mass media differ from each other in many ways. The most important ways tend to be the most obvious as well. You will find very little to surprise you in the next two pages, but much that is worth keeping in mind as we examine the media one by one. Remember also that only a few of these differences are essential characteristics of the media themselves; most could be otherwise if the people who ran the media wanted them otherwise.

1. Speed. The first medium to find out about an event is almost always the nearest newspaper. The wire services get the story from the paper, and everyone else gets it from the wires. Speed in reaching the public is another matter. Radio is usually first, followed by television. Newspapers come next, then magazines, and finally books.

2. Depth. Depth is inversely proportional to speed. The slowest media, books and movies, are (at least potentially) the deepest. Magazines are next in line. Of the faster media, newspapers are the most likely to treat a subject in depth. Television and the wire services seldom do, and radio almost never does. Advertising could, but doesn't.

3. Breadth. The broadest range of subjects and interests is covered by books and magazines. By comparison, the rest of the media are appallingly narrow.

4. Ubiquity. Virtually every American has access to both a radio receiver and a television set—and spends at least a few hours a day with each. Newspapers reach more than 90 percent of the homes in the country, but seldom get more than a half hour's attention from any reader. Two-thirds of all American

families subscribe to at least one magazine; roughly half of the adult population sees at least one movie a month. By contrast, less than one-tenth of the adult population reads a book a month. Every American, of course, is exposed to advertising on a daily—if not hourly—basis.

5. Permanence. Books are the most permanent of the mass media. Magazines are next, followed by newspapers. Only film companies save films; only ad agencies save ads; only editors save wire-service copy. Almost nobody saves radio and television shows.

6. Locality. Newspapers are the only purely local medium. Radio is mostly local; advertising, public relations, wire services, and television are both local and national. Magazines, books, and movies are almost entirely national.

7. Sensory Involvement. Books appeal only to the eye, usually in black and white and without pictures. In sensory terms, they are the dullest of the mass media. Newspapers have pictures, and magazines have pictures and color—but they are still designed only for the eye. Radio, on the other hand, reaches only the ear. Television and film (and much advertising) appeal to both the eye and the ear, with moving pictures and often in color.

8. Credibility. The print media have traditionally been considered more believable than broadcasting or film. But recent surveys have found that most people believe television more readily than newspapers or magazines. Public relations often masquerades as news and thus gains credibility, while advertising is by far the least credible.

In the Introduction (see pp. 8–11), we listed four functions of the mass media in modern society—to serve the economic system, to entertain, to inform, and to influence. How do the different media compare according to these four criteria?

The "medium" that most directly serves the economic system is of course advertising, with public relations close behind. The rest of the media make their contributions to the economy principally as vehicles for those two. In terms of profits, on the other hand, one can safely say that television is by all counts the most profitable medium. The advertising and PR industries come second, followed by newspapers, magazines, and radio—probably in that order. Book publishing earns a small but steady profit; films alternately earn huge sums and lose huge sums. And the wire services are losing money.

Although the purest entertainment medium is undoubtedly film, television is a close second—and is watched a great deal more. Entertainment is also the principal purpose of most radio stations, and of many magazines and books. Just about every newspaper sugar-coats its information with a heavy dose of entertainment. So do the feature syndicates. Even advertising and public relations try hard to entertain, and often succeed.

The United States, unlike many other countries, has no purely informational mass media. Books probably come closest, since more textbooks are published every year than any other kind of book. Newspapers (which get most of their information from public relations and from the wire services and feature syndicates) are split about evenly, news versus advertising. So are magazines. Though television and radio do less than they should to inform the public, they are the main source of information for most people. Film and advertising are least intended to inform—but even they teach us something about our world and ourselves.

The principal purpose of advertising and public relations is to influence people. Both are remarkably successful. By contrast, newspapers usually confine their efforts at outright influence to the editorial page. Many books (but not most) are written with influence in mind; some magazines and a few films have the same purpose. Television and radio (and the networks) make little if any conscious attempt to influence our society; their influence is of course enormous, but it is unplanned. The wire services are the most objective and least influence-conscious of the mass media.

The purpose of these oversimplified comparisons is to set the stage for the medium-by-medium discussion that follows. As you read the next six chapters, keep in mind the following questions: How is this medium different from the others? Why is it different in those particular ways? What role does it play in the "media mix" of American society? What role should it play? How could the change be accomplished?

Chapter 9
Wires, Syndicates, and Networks

Most of the nonlocal information in the American mass media comes from the wire services and feature syndicates, especially the Associated Press and United Press International. These two services tell us almost everything we know about events in other states and other countries. Working with skeleton staffs at breakneck speeds, the wire services often provide less than adequate coverage—but without them we would have little coverage at all.

"There are," said Mark Twain, "only two forces that can carry light to all corners of the globe—the sun in the heavens and the Associated Press." While we could get along a good deal easier without the Associated Press than without the sun, there are not many newspaper publishers or broadcast station managers who would like to try.

The Associated Press (AP) is one of the two major American wire services. The other one is United Press International (UPI); it is smaller and younger than AP, but almost as influential. Many other countries have their own wire services—Reuters in Britain, Agence France-Presse in France, Tass in the Soviet Union, etc. But AP and UPI are not only the most important wire services in the United States; they are the most important in the world.

Nearly a billion people a day read or hear the news courtesy of the Associated Press. Each day AP churns out roughly three million words, the equivalent of fifteen books the size of this one.[1] UPI produces about the same amount of copy, and reaches nearly as many people. Within the United States, just under 1,300 of the nation's 1,760 or so daily newspapers subscribe to AP. Almost all the remaining 460-odd papers subscribe to UPI, and nearly 400 papers subscribe to them both.[2] In addition, AP serves some 3,400 U.S. broadcast stations, while UPI serves about 2,300—and both are beginning to build up a sizable clientele among cable television systems.[3]

What do the wire services do? By means of electric typewriters and teletypes hooked up to long-distance telephone lines, they disseminate news from everywhere in the world to everywhere in the world. They thus serve as the eyes and ears for thousands of news organizations that cannot afford to send a reporter to another county, much less another continent. Even the largest and most self-sufficient news operations in this country—the *New York Times,* the *Washington Post,*

241

the three networks, etc.—rely on the wire services for much of their day-to-day coverage. The typical daily newspaper or broadcast station simply could not cover nonlocal news without the wire services.

EVERYTHING FOR EVERYBODY

The goal of the wire services is to get the news as quickly as possible, as objectively as possible, and as cheaply as possible. These three characteristics—speed, objectivity, and cost-consciousness—account for both the strengths and the weaknesses of the wires. All three result from the central fact that the wire services must meet the needs of thousands of clients with different schedules and different ideologies, but with a unanimous desire to keep costs down. We will consider each characteristic in turn.

Speed. Every minute of every day, somewhere in the world, a wire-service client has reached its deadline. As a result, wire reporters are always under pressure to get the story now. As one Midwest editor put it: "AP covers the news in a hell of a hurry, and this is what we expect of it." [4] Wire reporters are the last of a dying breed of journalists, immortalized in countless old movies, who sprint for the nearest telephone to dictate a quick, breathless bulletin to the super-calm rewrite specialist back at the office.

Speed has its drawbacks, of course, and one of them is mistakes. On the night of September 30, 1962, the AP office in Atlanta was the focal point for the hottest news story of the day—James Meredith, a Negro, was enrolling at the University of Mississippi. Reporter Van Savell was on the phone from the campus. Retired Army General Edwin A. Walker, he dictated, had just taken command of the violent crowd, and had personally led a charge against federal marshals. Savell's dispatch sped over the AP wire to clients from Manhattan to Manilla. But in the heat of the moment, Savell had made a

---

MORE AND FASTER

The biggest limitation on the speed of the wire services has always been the speed of the teletype machines that reproduce wire copy in the world's newsrooms. But AP has a solution. With its new "DataStream" system, copy will move at 1,050 words per minute, about sixteen times as fast as the old method.

"Faster delivery of copy," says AP, "smoothes out the flow" of news. "Immediate availability of copy enables news editors to effect better assembly of the news, in contrast to standard speed wires which may deliver important sidebars long after the central story has been cleared. In DataStream, even with the same amount of intervening copy, the sidebars reach the desk at almost the same moment as the main lead."[5]

DataStream and similar innovations have two possible effects—they can get the news to the client faster, and they can get more news to the client. The second effect could turn out to be the more important one. Even major AP and UPI stories seldom run over 500 words, and many minor ones don't make the national wire at all—there simply isn't enough time to transmit long stories or lots of stories. With a faster delivery system, the wire services could carry longer stories or more stories or both.

But what would the typical telegraph editor do with it all? Most newspapers and broadcast stations today use less than one-tenth of the news they get over the wires. If AP or UPI decided to send them sixteen times as much, they'd have trouble even reading it all, much less deciding what to use. Probably DataStream won't change the nature of wire news after all—just move it faster.

mistake. General Walker sued for libel and won.

The Supreme Court overturned the decision for an interesting reason. "The dispatch which concerns us," it said, "was news which required immediate dissemination. . . . Considering the necessity for rapid dissemination, nothing in this series of events gives the slightest hint of a severe departure from accepted publishing standards." [6] In other words, the wire services have to work so fast they're bound (and allowed) to make mistakes.

Several years later, on a lonely protest walk through the rural South, Meredith was shot. The wire reporters covering the event didn't dare wait to find out how badly he was hurt; they mistakenly reported that he was dead. Of course they soon filed updated stories correcting the error—but many papers and stations had already used the earlier reports.

AP and UPI struggle valiantly to minimize the number of errors caused by their quest for speed. They avoid errors by relying on established sources of information, by attributing as many statements as possible to witnesses or authorities, and by trying to stay cautious about the distinction between what is known and what is merely supposed or predicted. These tactics can cause problems of their own, as we shall see, but they do work. In the media accuracy sweepstakes, the wire services can cite at least as many success stories as horror stories.

Consider the Attica Prison uprising of 1971, for example. While other media, including the *New York Times,* accepted official claims that most of the violence was perpetrated by the prisoners, the Associated Press carefully reported that it didn't know who was doing the shooting or who was responsible for the death of the hostages.[7] Eventually it was proved that most of the killing was done by the army of police and soldiers sent to break the siege—and AP looked pretty good.

Apart from mistakes, the stress on speed has another drawback—it inevitably results in superficial coverage. During a typical hour-long presidential press conference, AP and UPI may produce as many as five different leads each, continually updating the story to meet their clients' deadlines. Half a dozen reporters are kept busy rewriting the story again and again, devising new leads and adding paragraphs on later questions and answers. The result is an up-to-the-minute report for every client—but no attention at all to what the president isn't saying or what the press isn't asking.

Despite their large and prestigious Washington bureaus, the wire services played almost no role in helping to break the Watergate scandals. Watergate just wasn't the sort of story that lends itself to five updates an hour.

Objectivity. The political biases of wire-service clients run the gamut from the far left to the far right. To keep everybody happy, the wires must have no biases of their own. "We can't crusade because we have papers of every complexion under the sun," notes Wes Gallagher, general manager of AP. "A crusade that pleases one is an anathema to another." [8] Hence the traditional wire-service "cult of objectivity." During the early 1970s, when media credibility was under heavy attack by the government, AP and UPI were seldom criticized.

But objectivity, like speed, has its drawbacks. Often the facts alone are not enough to make the meaning of a story clear. Sometimes the facts are simply misleading. One longtime Washington staffer recalls: "You said what Joe McCarthy said and you couldn't say it was a goddamn lie." [9] This is still a big problem for wire-service reporters. They are encouraged to present both sides of the story whenever possible—but not to tell which side they believe is right. Some client somewhere would be bound to disagree.

The growth of interpretive journalism hasn't bypassed the wire services entirely. AP, for example, has the Washington-based Special Assignment Team and the "Mod

Squad," a group of young investigative reporters. But these are the exceptions. One critic estimates that AP and UPI together employ no more than a hundred reporters who are regularly freed for investigative or interpretive assignments.[10] The rest cover routine stories. They are urged to get the facts as quickly as possible, and report them as succinctly as possible. News analysis takes time and space, both of which are in short supply. And besides, some client somewhere would surely disagree.

To insure their objectivity, the wire services try to attribute every debatable statement to the most authoritative available source. This practice, according to conventional wisdom, makes the statement less likely to be false—and even if it is false, at least the wire service quoted it accurately. The result, of course, is a bias in favor of what reputable people are doing and saying. When covering a demonstration, for example, wire-service reporters rely heavily on the police for information, rather than seeking out the viewpoint of the demonstrators. A typical AP story about a minor disturbance in Chattanooga ran eleven paragraphs; information was attributed to the police and public officials ten times, while the demonstrators were quoted once.[11]

In a sense, objectivity is itself a bias (see pp. 82–87). Typically, reporters who are struggling to be objective refuse to decide for themselves what is important or what is true. They let other people and institutions make the news, and then they cover it. The news that gets covered, then, is the news that is created by someone with enough power to make news. It almost requires an activist reporter to find out what is happening to powerless people. Wire-service reporters—the most objective and hence the most passive of all—cover mostly the powerful.

Cost-Consciousness. The Associated Press was founded in 1848 by six New York newspapers. To this day it remains a newspaper cooperative; broadcast stations may subscribe but may not join. The member papers elect an eighteen-person governing board (currently seventeen men and Katharine Graham of the *Washington Post*), which tells the operating staff what to do. Costs are split up among the member papers and client stations. Like most cooperatives, AP is under heavy pressure to keep those costs low.

United Press International, on the other hand, is a private business. It is the product of a 1958 merger of the United Press (founded by E. W. Scripps in 1907) and the International News Service (founded by William Randolph Hearst in 1909). UPI has no members, only customers.

Since UPI must compete with AP for clients, and since that competition is very fierce, UPI is also forced to cut corners and save money any way it can. "I don't know of two outfits more destructively devoted to the American principle of free-enterprise competition than AP and UPI," said top UPI reporter Louis Cassels in 1969. "Competition in news gathering drives expenses up, and competition in selling drives income down." [12] Today, UPI is losing money, and AP finds it increasingly difficult to break even.

Both AP and UPI have bureaus in more than a hundred U.S. cities and more than fifty foreign ones, as well as part-time "stringers" in more remote areas. If that sounds like a small army of journalists, it is —but the army is too small for the job it must do. The vast majority of wire-service bureaus have only a couple of reporters and editors on duty at any time, and many bureaus have a staff of one reporter-editor, period. This overworked individual seldom ventures out of the office to report the news in person. Instead, he or she reads the early editions of the local newspapers, picks out the major stories, summarizes them in wire-service style, and sends them on their way. The rest of the day is spent rewriting press releases and updating the most important stories by phone. Out of 3,300 AP employees, only a quarter are actually reporters who regularly leave the office to cover events.[13]

Given the nature of the job, it is hardly surprising that the wire services can't hold on to their best reporters. They don't really try. Experienced investigative journalists demand high salaries and a chance to practice their craft. They get neither at AP and UPI, and soon leave for newspaper work or free-lancing.

There are exceptions, of course. The pride of the wire services is their Washington bureaus, with staffs of 150 for AP and 90 for UPI. Even that isn't enough, as Jules Witcover of the Newhouse National News Service explains. Here's how congressional committees are often covered:

> Overworked AP and UPI staffs routinely make collection runs, visiting a number of committee hearings on any given morning, dutifully collecting witness' speech texts, and going back to the House or Senate press gallery to dictate or to grind out several stories. Far from its being digging reporting, it is not even routine reporting. It is skimming. . . .[14]

Both AP and UPI offer a variety of services to their clients. At AP, for example, the most important national and international news is carried on the A wire. The B wire is a secondary national wire that catches the overflow from A and prints the complete text of important speeches and documents. The world service wire is designed to meet the needs of foreign clients. Each region of the U.S. has its own regional wire, while the more populous states have state wires as well. There is a financial wire, a sports wire, a racing wire, a weather wire, a special high-speed wire for the stock prices, and of course the wirephoto for pictures. Additional broadcast wires transmit pretimed five-minute newscasts, ready for a disc jockey to rip and read. And an audio service for radio stations is available with taped newscasts that can be played as needed.[15]

Convenience is the key. The broadcast wires don't contain much news, but they don't require much work from the disc jockey either. Similarly, both AP and UPI offer their major services on perforated tape, geared for automatic typesetting machines. This makes it very inconvenient for the local editor to revise the story—but it saves the local publisher a substantial amount of money.

How much does the client pay for these services? Rates are based on what the individual client decides to subscribe to, and also on where it is located; media in big cities are charged more for the same package of services than media in small towns. The *New York Times,* which subscribes to just about everything AP offers, pays $750,000 a year. A small daily paper that settles for the A wire, one regional wire, and the stock quotations may have an annual bill of less than $5,000.[16]

Whatever the cost, the wire services are a lot cheaper than hiring your own reporters to cover the world. In fact, they're cheaper than hiring your own reporters to cover the city. For most newspapers and broadcast stations, wire-service news is the least expensive news they can get, a lot cheaper than local reporting. They aim to keep it that way. Notes Norman E. Isaacs, longtime editor of the *Louisville Courier-Journal:* "Most small papers don't seem to give a damn about the quality of wire service copy—as long as the price is kept low and they can get it delivered on tapes."[17]

THE POWER OF THE WIRES

Take any issue of your local newspaper and count up the total number of news stories. Then go back and count the number of stories designated "AP," "UPI," or "Combined Services." Add in any stories you find from the supplemental wires (see box). If your newspaper is typical, you will discover that between half and three-quarters of the news in the paper came from the wires. This is the power of the wire services.

AP and UPI have no real competition in the United States. Nobody else covers both the U.S. and the world in enough detail to meet the needs of American media. But there are other sources of nonlocal news, and many newspapers (and some broadcast stations) make substantial use of them.

Some of the nation's most distinguished newspapers—notably the *New York Times,* the *Chicago Daily News,* and the *Washington Post* and *Los Angeles Times* in combination—sell their newsgathering abilities and reputations to papers in other cities. For a fee, they will put a teletype in any client's newsroom, over which they transmit selections from each day's paper. These supplemental services concentrate on political commentary, investigative reporting, and hard news exclusives—content not available from AP or UPI. It is thus possible for newspaper readers in Cleveland or Seattle to encounter a James Reston column from the *New York Times* or a White House exposé from the *Washington Post.*

A number of newspaper chains, including Copley, Gannett, Knight, and Newhouse, offer similar services. They are designed mainly to serve newspapers owned by the chains, but are available for a fee to nonmember papers as well. Both kinds of services are growing. The *New York Times* wire, for example, has 139 clients; the *Chicago Daily News* service has 77, as does the *Washington Post–Los Angeles Times* joint operation; Copley has 42.[18]

Then there are the foreign wire services—Reuters, Agence France-Presse, etc. None of these covers the United States in enough detail to replace AP and UPI, but several of them offer excellent coverage of Europe and the Third World. And their non-American perspective provides a useful alternative, especially on diplomatic and war stories. Though the American media make much less use of foreign wire services than the foreign media make of AP and UPI, a few U.S. papers do subscribe. In addition, several European newspapers, such as the *London Daily Express,* offer their own supplemental wires to U.S. subscribers.

Finally, there are dozens of more specialized services that sell news to subscribing newspapers and broadcast stations—the World Book Service, the Congressional Quarterly Service, the Women's News Service, etc. For almost any social issue or special interest you can name, from gay liberation to stamps and coins, from environmental quality to movie stars, there is a supplemental news service to keep interested clients up to date.

Most of the supplemental services provide only printed copy, which limits their usefulness to radio and television. But a few offer audio or even video packages for broadcast clients. In 1973, radio stations in forty cities signed up to receive hourly five-minute news feeds of black-oriented information from the National Black Network.[19] A company called Television News, Inc. sells film reports on major news events to TV stations, especially those not affiliated with a network.[20] And in 1975, NBC began to provide 24-hour feeds of news, sports, and features to radio stations around the country converting to the "all-news" format. Subscribing stations simply drop in their own local news packages at regular intervals and sell local ads.

The structure of AP and UPI resembles a tree, with crucial news judgments made at every branch. Suppose the mayor of Green Bay, Wisconsin, fires the police chief. First, a wire-service stringer in Green Bay decides whether to file the story with the nearest bureau. If the decision is no, that's it —you'll never know what happened in Green Bay unless you live there. If the decision is yes, then the bureau chief decides whether to transmit the story to the capital bureau in Madison. The capital bureau staff, in turn, decides whether to put it on the state wire, and also whether to telegraph it to the regional office in Chicago. If the story makes it to Chicago, that office decides whether to include it on the regional wire, and also whether to send it on to New York. New York can put the story on the national wire, or transmit it to the other regions for possible use on their regional wires, or kill it. Most wire stories, of course, never make it to New York; of those that do, fewer than half get onto the national wire.

If the Green Bay story is dropped at any stage in this process, it might just as well not have happened as far as the rest of the world is concerned. Conversely, if the story makes the national wire, hundreds of clients are bound to pick it up, and millions of people will become aware of it.

A truly important story, of course, will inevitably find its way to the national wire (unless someone, somewhere along the line thinks otherwise). Then it's up to the local paper or station to decide whether to use the story. But what the story says is still up to the wire services.

The city of Pittsburgh learned this the hard way the year the Pirates won the pennant. On the night of October 17, 1971, Pirate fans celebrated in their city, some of them a bit too boisterously. AP bureau chief Pat Minarcin saw cars overturned, windows smashed, and stores looted. He called it a riot—and so did millions of people around the country who read his story. Pittsburgh Police Superintendent Robert E. Colville disagreed. He accused AP of "gross distor-

tion," and pointed out that UPI had reported only "minor looting" and some horn-blowing. But for all those who read the AP version, Pittsburgh had had a riot.[21]

The wire services exercise their greatest influence on radio. Most radio stations (and some TV stations) subscribe to the AP or UPI broadcast wire, which offers five-minute newscasts that a disc jockey can simply rip off the wire and read on the air. These stations exercise no news judgment at all, except perhaps to decide what local stories to crib from the nearest newspaper. On thousands of radio stations across the country, the hourly news is identical word for word. The wire services wrote it.

Newspaper editors must at least decide which wire stories to run—but the wire services help with that too. Every morning and evening, AP and UPI transmit lists of what they believe are the most important stories of the day. Editors who are afraid to trust their own judgment may put together their newscast or front page from the wire-service lists. Hundreds of editors make use of this service, offering their readers, listeners, and viewers news that is not only written by the wire services, but chosen by the wire services as well.

The wires even help decide what stories local reporters will cover. Every day, each major wire bureau compiles a list of local events scheduled for the next day. This "daybook," as it is called, is transmitted over the wires as a service to editors. Since the daybook is made up entirely of pre-scheduled events, it is dominated by things that wouldn't have happened at all except for the media—press conferences, celebrity appearances, store promotions, and the like. Because of the convenience of advance planning, editors often give these "pseudo-events" (see p. 143) more attention than they would otherwise deserve. Television and radio stations are especially dependent on the daybook; it insures usable film or tape, and efficient use of the limited supply of film crews and engineers. As an added help, the wire services frequently indicate which of

CRIB SHEET FOR EDITORS

Below is a portion of the UPI daybook of events scheduled for Monday, March 11, 1974, in and around New York City, as sent to New York area clients on Sunday, March 10. As you read the list, bear in mind two things—how easy it must have been for New York editors to plan Monday's coverage, and how contrived and PR-inspired many of the items seem to be.

More than 100 businessmen discuss trade with COMECON Countries at East-West Trade Conference, 55th floor, One World Trade Center, 8:30 A.M.

Rep. Barry Goldwater, Jr., R-Ariz., former Secretary of the Interior Stewart Udall and others address 20th Annual Systems Management Conference of American Management Association, Hotel Americana, 9:30 A.M.

The Student Struggle for Soviet Jewry and the Greater New York Conference on Soviet Jewry hold "vigil" to protest treatment of Soviet Jews, United Nations, 43rd Street and First Avenue, 9:30 A.M.

Some 250 landlords demonstrate to protest arrest of Lee Sterling, Executive Director of the American Property Rights Association and seven others, Criminal Court Building, 9:30 A.M.

Rep. Jonathan Bingham, D-NY, is leadoff witness at Interstate Commerce Commission hearings on Northeastern Railroads, Room 305, 26 Federal Plaza, 9:30 A.M.

Deputy Mayor James Cavanagh presents proclamation by Mayor Beame declaring March as Shamrocks Against Dystrophy Month, City Hall Plaza, 10 A.M.

City Council Finance Committee holds a work session on the proposed capital budget, City Hall, 10 A.M.

Aviation High School opens aircraft and equipment presentation and display, King's Plaza, Flatbush Avenue and Avenue U, Brooklyn, 11 A.M.

Antiwar activists David Dellinger and Alan Ginsburg speak at "Radical Spokesmen Defend Daniel Berrigan Against Charges of Anti-Semitism" news conference, Roosevelt Hotel, 11 A.M.

State Human Rights Commissioner Jack Sable hosts news conference to introduce "Human Rights Observance Week," Room 2114, 270 Broadway, 11 A.M.

Public hearing is held against Merrill, Lynch, et al, on alleged $15-million fraud involving sale of Scientific Control Corp. stock, Room 2, Customs Court House, Federal Plaza, 11 A.M.

Various New Jersey prison officials and former inmates discuss New Jersey penal system on "Straight Talk," WOR-TV, 11 A.M.

Suffolk County Executive John Klein holds news conference on energy crisis, Abraham & Strauss Building, Walt Whitman Shopping Center, Rte. 110, Huntington, L.I., noon.

Swimsuit competition in Greater New York's Miss New York Beauty Pageant is held, Act I Restaurant, 15th floor, Allied Chemical Building, Times Square, noon.

"Pentagon Papers" defense attorney Leonard Boudin speaks on "Ellsberg, Watergate and Impeachment," Brooklyn College Student Center, Campus Road North and East 27th Street, Brooklyn, noon.

Rep. James Symington, D-Mo., speaks on Watergate at American Paper Institute luncheon, Waldorf Astoria Hotel, 12:30 P.M.

Celanese Corp. feminists hold news conference, Suite 1610, 30 East 42nd St., 2 P.M.

Nutritionist Dr. Myron Winick discusses "Nutrition and Mental Development," Downstate Medical Center, first floor, Basic Sciences Building, 450 Clarkson Ave., Brooklyn, 4 P.M.

Rep. Hugh Carey, D-Brooklyn, and Rep. Ogden Reid, D-Westchester, speak at Lexington Democratic Club, 173 East 83rd St., 7:30 P.M.

WNYC Radio broadcasts live concert by Light Fantastic Players, 8 P.M.

New Castle, New York Supervisor Richard E. Burns is guest on "Meet the Mayors," WOR-TV, 9:30 P.M.

Doctors and health officials hold panel on "Hot Line to Health—Cancer" program, WNET-TV, 9:30 P.M.

City College President Robert E. Marshak is guest on "New York Report," WOR-TV, 10 P.M.

the listed pseudo-events they won't bother to cover, so local papers and stations can be sure to be there themselves.

AP and UPI, then, are not merely the nonlocal eyes and ears of the news business. They are the mouth too. They don't just decide what stories to cover and how to cover them. By putting or not putting a particular story on a particular wire, they determine who gets it. By including or not including the story in the predigested broadcast wire and the day's list of important news, they influence who uses it. And by means of the daybook, they even have a say in what the local media will do with their own reporters. In all, they are beyond doubt the most powerful media institutions in the country, the common denominators of American news.

FEATURE SYNDICATES

If it wants to, a newspaper can easily fill all its nonadvertising space with wire-service copy, plus a dash of local reporting. But a steady diet of hard news is unappetizing to today's newspaper readers. They want columns, comics, puzzles, recipes, and the like as well. Most papers buy this material from outside sources known as feature syndicates.

The first feature syndicates were organized during the Civil War, but they were small-time affairs until the 1880s, when Samuel S. McClure got into the act. McClure signed contracts with some of the most famous writers of the day, including Robert Louis Stevenson, Rudyard Kipling, Jack London, and Sir Arthur Conan Doyle, and sold their serialized work to newspapers at a bargain price. McClure's rationale for syndication makes as much sense now as it did then:

> A dozen, or twenty, or fifty newspapers—selected so as to avoid conflict in circulation—can thus secure a story for a sum which will be very small for each paper but which will in the aggregate be sufficiently large to secure the best work by the best authors.[22]

The 1974 *Editor & Publisher Yearbook* lists more than 350 feature syndicates. Some are tiny and offer the work of only one individual. Others, such as King Features, North American Newspaper Alliance, and Newspaper Enterprise Association, are huge. The United Feature Syndicate, one of the biggest, offers seven different puzzles and word games; twenty-three comics (including "Peanuts"); four editorial cartoonists; twelve political columnists (including Jack Anderson, Marquis Childs, Victor Lasky, and Martin F. Nolan); nine humorists; and specialized columnists on business, television, consumer affairs, health, food, beauty, decorating, sewing, fashion, astrology, and a host of other topics.[23]

Big or little, nearly all the feature syndicates follow McClure's model. They offer newspapers exclusive local rights to a particular comic or column, in exchange for a fee that may range from $5 a week or less to $150 a week or more, depending on the popularity of the feature and the circulation of the paper. The combined fees from newspapers all over the country are split by the author and the syndicate. If the feature is popular, both earn substantial incomes—while each subscribing paper gets a local monopoly at a fraction of the cost of hiring its own staff.

Comics are the mainstays of most syndicates, their biggest moneymakers and their most attractive offerings. But don't underestimate the substantive value of the feature syndicates to American journalism. They offer readers a higher caliber of political commentary, humor, advice, and specialized reporting than the staffs of most local papers could possibly produce. And they do it at a price that makes even the most cost-conscious publisher smile.

Yet there are two objections often raised about the use of syndicated features. The first concerns the exclusive nature of the feature franchise. Exclusivity is crucial to the success of most syndicates. It is an incentive to newspapers to sign up the best and most popular features before the competition gets hold of them. Often the only visible difference between two newspapers in the same city or neighboring cities is the different comics and columnists they carry. But sometimes the competition goes too far. Many wealthy papers habitually buy the rights to scores of features—more than they could possibly use—simply to guarantee that competing papers won't get them. The *San Francisco Chronicle,* for example, owns the San Francisco Bay Area rights to Jack Anderson, the muckraking Washington political columnist. When *Chronicle* editors decide to skip an Anderson column, as they often do, the entire Bay Area must do without. In 1975 the Justice Department went to court in opposition to exclusive feature-syndicate contracts that offer a wide geographical monopoly. The concessions it won from the *Boston Globe* and three syndicates may well serve as a model for the industry.

The second objection to the feature syndicates is more basic. Most syndicated features are light entertainment, the frosting on the newspaper cake. Even the serious columns deal with national and international issues, not the local problems and concerns of readers. When a newspaper replaces a local commentator with a syndicated national one, it lessens its ability to help readers deal with events close to home. And when a newspaper replaces hard news (local or otherwise) with a syndicated comic or a column on astrology, it lessens its ability to inform its readers about events that affect their lives. Because syndicated features are both cheap and popular, publishers are tempted to go overboard. One critic estimates that between 20 and 35 percent of the nonadvertising space in the average newspaper is devoted to syndicated material.[24] That is probably too much of a good thing.

The feature syndicates have at least one advantage over the wire services—diversity. To some extent, of course, nationally syndicated features contribute to the standardization of media content—the same column or comic may appear in Los Angeles and New York. Duluth and Miami. But at least there are lots of columns and comics to choose from, and papers in the same area necessarily make different choices. AP and UPI, on the other hand, are the only available full-scale American wire services. If newspapers and newscasts in this country all seem pretty much the same, the blame and the credit go principally to the wire services. When the wires do a good job, so do the nation's news media. When the wires do a bad job, it is literally impossible for the media to do a good one.

What the wire services are to news, the networks are to broadcast entertainment. The vast majority of what Americans watch on television each evening comes to us courtesy of three companies— CBS, NBC, and ABC. Network control over television programming developed inevitably, because it benefits everyone. Stations earn higher profits, advertisers gain easier access to a national market, and viewers get better (or at least more expensive) programs. But many critics fear the overwhelming power of the networks, regret network-imposed standardization, and wish for greater diversity in American broadcasting.

HOW IT WORKS

A network is a collection of broadcast stations tied to a programming source through a series of cables and microwave relay stations. This hook-up permits the programming source to send the same show to all its affiliated stations at the same time. The three major U.S. networks are all headquartered within a six-block area of New York City. The typical network-affiliated television station relies on CBS, NBC, or ABC for about 80 percent of its content.

In most television markets, one station is affiliated with each network. The two companies sign a contract in which the network promises to offer all its programs to the affiliated station first; in return, the affiliate promises to base most of its programming on that network's offerings. The network cannot force its affiliate to accept a particular program, so as an incentive it pays the station a fee for each program it carries. At first glance this may seem a little backwards; you might expect that the station would pay the network for the privilege of using its programs. Not so. The network pays to insure that as many stations as possible will carry a given program (give the program "clearance"), so that the ads within that program will reach the largest possible audience.

This is necessary because the networks earn nearly all their profits by keeping the revenue from national advertising. Only the local ad revenue goes to the stations—and the networks kindly leave a couple of ad minutes in each program open for the affiliated stations to fill with these local ads.

The business of the networks, then, is to sell the combined audience of local stations across the country to advertisers interested in a national market. To keep the advertisers happy, each network needs an affiliate in every major city and as many minor ones as possible. To keep the affiliates happy, each network needs popular programming that will successfully attract local viewers and thus local advertisers. The number of stations affiliated with each network varies some from year to year. In 1974 NBC was the leader with 219 stations, CBS had 191, and ABC had 168. All three networks were earning huge profits.

For a local station, the choice is a simple one. If it accepts a network affiliation, it gains two new sources of income—the fees paid by the network for each program given clearance, and the local advertising lured by a chance to "sponsor" a popular network show. At the same time, the station solves its problem of what to do with 16 to 20 empty hours of airtime a day. Of course the *potential* profit is higher without a network affiliation—but only if the station can manage to produce local programs that outdraw the network shows, and only if it can find enough local advertisers to fill all those min-

utes of ad time. It is a rare station indeed that meets these requirements. The vast majority find it more profitable to turn on the network spigot.

Nearly all independent stations—those without a network affiliation—are independent by necessity, not by choice. Since there are only three television networks, in a city with more than three commercial TV stations the rest have to be independent. As a rule, independent stations carry only a little more local programming than the network affiliates. Instead of the network shows, they run old movies, reruns of former network programs that are no longer being produced, and whatever else they can buy cheaply enough from the TV syndicates.

Like the print media's feature syndicates, broadcast syndicates sell their shows to stations around the country, offering the same incentive of exclusive local rights. Besides reruns and old movies, the syndicates have some original material for sale. Entertainers like Mike Douglas, Merv Griffin, and Lawrence Welk, who do not have their own network shows, are widely syndicated instead. Network affiliates can buy syndicated programs too; they use them to fill the hours when the network offers nothing, or to replace the least popular network programs (if they can sell enough local ads to pay for the show). But for the network affiliates, syndicates are just a minor alternative programming source; syndicates are the lifeblood of the independent stations.

Though it is not a perfect match, most network affiliates are VHF stations, while most independents are on the newer UHF band. In fiscal 1972, according to the FCC, 366 of 453 reporting VHF stations earned a profit, but only 47 of 149 reporting UHF stations did.[25] It is virtually impossible for a VHF station affiliated with a network *not* to make a healthy profit.

Besides the network affiliates and independents, there is a third category of broadcast stations—those owned and operated by the networks themselves. Like any other corporation, a network is entitled to apply for a broadcast license. It is limited only by the FCC rules that restrict each licensee to a maximum of seven AM radio stations; seven FM radio stations; and seven TV stations, no more than five of which can be VHF. All three of the networks own their full complement of VHF television stations, and they own them in the biggest markets—New York, Los Angeles, Chicago, San Francisco, Cleveland, etc. This is no coincidence. The networks were among the first to recognize the profit potential of television, and they moved early to secure the most attractive licenses. Among broadcasters, these stations are referred to as "o-and-o's"; that is, stations owned and operated by a network. Naturally, they carry the full network line-up, thus guaranteeing each network an audience in the largest markets.

Occasionally a network and one of its affiliates (not an o-and-o) will come to a parting of the ways, generally because the station is turning down too many network shows.

NEWS AND DOCUMENTARIES

In addition to entertainment, the networks provide their affiliates with national news, documentaries, and other public-affairs programming. The news itself is sometimes a moneymaker, but the rest of the public-affairs programs almost always operate in the red. The networks produce these programs to build prestige and to keep the FCC happy; the affiliates take them (reluctantly) for the same reasons. If all three networks dropped their documentary and public-affairs departments tomorrow, most local stations would not be especially disappointed.

In the meantime, the networks have a stranglehold on national TV news and documentaries. Almost without exception, CBS, NBC, and ABC produce all their own public-affairs programs, on the ground that they can't adequately evaluate the work of outsiders. As a result, only three sources produce nearly all the nonlocal public-affairs shows on TV.

In 1968 the Westinghouse Broadcasting Company, which owns stations in Boston, Philadelphia, Baltimore, Pittsburgh, and San Francisco, established an Urban America Documentary Unit. Over the next five years, the unit produced twenty documentaries, many of which won awards for journalistic excellence. But they never found much of a market outside the Westinghouse stations. In New York, for example, the unit often ended up "selling" the shows to educational station WNET for one dollar. At the end of 1973 Westinghouse killed the unit.

Dick Hubert, executive producer for the unit, offered this explanation for the Westinghouse failure:

> First, stations are only interested in documentaries in order to win "brownie points" with the Federal Communications Commission, especially before license-renewal time. . . .
>
> Second, documentaries on social, political, economic and cultural issues are audience losers. Bigger audiences can be earned with game shows. Besides, documentaries are often controversial, and broadcasters generally don't like getting involved in controversy.
>
> Third, many local stations and for that matter the networks, too, are unwilling to purchase news programming from outside sources because, they say, "We can't vouch for the accuracy or editorial independence of such sources." Of course, if that standard were observed by the print media, I would not be able to publish this article in The Times, Seymour Hersh could never have broken his My Lai story via the Dispatch News Service and there would not be any newspaper syndicates distributing columnists' and reporters' stories.[26]

In 1971, for example, CBS abandoned KO-LO-TV in Reno, Nevada, because the station ran a popular local show instead of the network's "Gomer Pyle" reruns.[27] But this is a rare event. Affiliates frequently refuse to clear such low-rated public-service programs as "Meet the Press" or "Face the Nation." Documentaries often run into trouble, late-night talk shows are sometimes replaced with a more profitable non-network movie, and the occasional controversial episode of a network series may be denied clearance. But affiliates almost always clear the popular game shows, soap operas, and prime-time dramas and comedies.

If they hesitate, a veiled threat from the network is usually enough to keep them in line. Networks need affiliates, but they don't desperately need any particular one. A station, on the other hand, is seldom in a position to shop for another network; if it loses the one it has, it will probably be forced to go independent, and will sacrifice a lot of profit in the process.

The network system dominates American television because it works. It offers local stations the maximum possible profit with the minimum possible risk. It offers advertisers the greatest convenience in reaching whatever audiences they want to reach, local or national. And it offers viewers the most elaborate, most expensive, most standardized entertainment in the world. Almost anywhere you may be in the United States, tonight and every night, you can watch the same national shows starring the same national personalities. Almost anywhere you may be, you will find that the three strongest stations in town are carrying whatever CBS, NBC, and ABC have offered them. Most broadcasters, advertisers, and viewers can't imagine a better system.

HOW IT GOT THAT WAY

In 1923, the Eveready Battery Company produced a musical variety show to promote its products. This was only three years after the first full-scale radio station went on the air, and only one year after the first radio advertisement was broadcast. The "Eveready Hour" was fairly expensive to produce, and since the company was already selling its products nationwide, it naturally wanted to distribute the program as widely as possible. So in 1924 it bought time simultaneously on more than a dozen stations that AT&T had already begun to link into a primitive network.

Eveready thus became broadcasting's first national advertiser, and in so doing gave the network notion a big push forward. Others liked the idea too. Station owners liked it because it reduced their programming burden. Listeners liked it because national programs could afford a bigger budget than local ones, and thus attracted bigger stars. By 1929, there were three profitable radio networks in the U.S. Two were owned by the National Broadcasting Company (NBC), the third by the Columbia Broadcasting System (CBS). ABC wasn't founded until 1943, when the FCC forced NBC to sell the weaker of its two networks. Probably because of its late start, ABC is still the least profitable of the three.

Throughout the 1930s and 1940s, the networks dominated radio, and radio dominated home entertainment. Families gathered punctually around the radio set each evening to listen together to shows like "Amos 'n' Andy" and the "Maxwell House Showboat," and to stars like Eddie Cantor, Fred Allen, Ed Wynn, and Bob Hope. But by the early 1950s, television had begun to steal radio's audience, and with it the interest of sponsors. In January of 1949, for example, the Bob Hope radio show had a healthy 23.8 rating; by 1951 it was down to 12.7, and by 1953 it stood at a sickly 5.4—not enough to interest a national advertiser.[28] The networks adapted quickly to the new situation. They moved their best performers and shows to TV. They applied for the choicest television licenses themselves. And they encouraged their radio affiliates to apply for the rest.

Even at the height of network radio, there were plenty of non-network stations. They weren't as profitable as the network affiliates, but they survived. When the networks turned their primary attention to television, radio as a whole became a good deal less profitable, but non-network radio got a shot in the arm. Today, the networks confine their interest in radio to the handful of o-and-o's, plus the hourly news feed. The vast majority of radio stations are not affiliated with a network, and get their news from the wire services instead. Even those that are network affiliates do most of their own non-news programming.

Television was (and is) a different story. The TV spectrum has room for many fewer stations than the radio band. Before cable and UHF came on the scene, it was a rare city that had more than three commercial TV stations—and all three were of course affiliated with one or another network.

From the very beginning, television was dominated by the "Eveready Hour" model. Sponsors conceived and produced the programs as well as the commercials; the networks acted principally as conduits, disseminating the programs and ads to local stations around the country, which in turn disseminated them to viewers. The networks did produce some programs themselves, but most big advertisers preferred to run their own shows, and the networks were just as happy to stay in the networking business, not the programming business. After all, network and sponsor had the same goal—attracting the largest possible audience. And if a sponsor did come up with a show that the network thought would bomb so badly that it might endanger the rest of the night's schedule, it could always raise its price or simply refuse to carry the program.

Then came the quiz show scandal of 1959. The immensely popular "$64,000 Question" and "$64,000 Challenge" turned out to be rigged by their sponsors. The networks denied knowing anything about the issue, saying the advertisers had sole responsibility for the programs. A Senate committee investigated the scandal, and the contrite network bosses promised that in the future the networks would oversee program production themselves. Since then, advertisers have had a lot less power over program content, and networks a lot more.

PROGRAMMING AND THE NETWORKS

Today, neither the networks nor the sponsors produce most television programs. Instead, they come from independent producers, who put together a series "package," and then try to sell it to one of the networks.

But the networks still maintain a heavy (and, some say, heavy-handed) economic interest in program production. Network-owned facilities, for example, are often rented to the producers of programs to be carried by that network. In the 1972 season, ten of the twenty-three CBS prime-time entertainment series were filmed at CBS studios. In addition, the networks produce many of their own specials and made-for-TV movies.[29] Finally, all three networks habitually put up the money to finance the "pilots" of new series in which they are interested.

In 1972, the Justice Department filed suit under the Sherman Antitrust Act to force the networks out of program production. The networks complained that such a decision might well put program production back in the hands of sponsors [30]—possibly leading to the sorts of abuses that culminated in the 1959 quiz-show scandals. The suit was modified in 1974, and is still pending in the courts.

Even if the Justice Department wins its case (or if the FCC adopts a similar ruling itself), the networks will surely remain a strong force in national television programming. Independent producers know the rules of the game. They know what types of shows the networks are likely to purchase for distribution. They know which plot lines are

"SHERIFF WHO?"

The impact of the networks on virtually every step in the development of a new series can be seen from the experience of Lee Rich, who almost—but not quite—sold NBC a comic western.

Rich approached all three networks with his concept. Neither CBS nor ABC expressed much interest, but two NBC vice presidents saw some promise in Rich's fifteen-page presentation. Entitled "Sheriff Who?", the series would feature a Texas town whose resident villain bumps off a different guest sheriff in each episode. NBC offered to put up $7,000 for the cost of writing a script for the pilot, with a pledge of more if it liked the script.

Three months later Rich came back with his script. NBC was impressed, and a deal was made to produce the pilot. The network advanced $125,000 to pay for the pilot, and agreed that if the show did become a series it would pay $75,000 for each episode, plus $16,500 for each rerun. As part of the agreement, NBC was to receive a 45 percent ownership in the series.

Armed with his advance, Rich hired a star, supporting actors, a director, camera crews, and the rest of the staff. He also rented a western street from CBS for the shooting. Some eight months after the idea for "Sheriff Who?" was first presented to the network, a half-hour pilot show was delivered to NBC.

Rich screened the pilot for various groups of NBC executives, most of whom said it was the funniest show they had seen in years. The most important viewer, however, was Don Durgin, president of the network. He also liked it, but felt it might be a bit too violent in spots. Rich, who by this time had spent nearly a year on the project and desperately wanted to get it on the air for the next season, said the violence could be cut out. He left the print with Durgin, and settled down for two more weeks of nail-biting. NBC, meanwhile, compared the show with all the other pilots it had commissioned, and showed it to various potential advertisers to get their reactions.

Finally, NBC made its decision: "I think it's a great pilot, but it's too original." And: "It's never been done before, I'm afraid the public isn't ready for it." The answer was no. Rich tried CBS and ABC again; both said they liked the pilot, but their fall schedules were already locked up and it was too late to change.

Rich was out of customers. "Sheriff Who?" was dead.[31]

---

acceptable, and which are not. Above all, they know that the market for their wares is very slim—the networks or a few scattered independents and syndicates, period. Without any direct financial interest whatever, the three networks could still dictate the content of TV programming.

So what are the rules of the game? What standards do network executives use to determine which series pilots to buy and which to let die?

The most important rule is to aim at the "lowest common denominator" of the viewing audience. The networks, remember, earn their profits almost entirely from national advertising. And what national advertisers appreciate most about television is its efficiency, its ability to reach huge numbers of people—not just a few hundred thousand or even a few million, but up to 50 million at once. Network ad rates are determined by the size of the audience; the more people who are watching a particular show, the more an advertiser will pay for 30 seconds in the middle of it. So the networks naturally strive for the biggest possible audience. They therefore pick programs with the broadest possible appeal—nothing too highbrow or too lowbrow, too controversial or too boring, nothing too anything.

What do rich people and poor people, dumb people and smart people, tired people and alert people, white people and black people, urban people and suburban people all have in common? Whatever it is, that's what the networks want to appeal to in every program. In their search for the lowest common denominator of American television viewers, the networks have so far come up with game shows, situation comedies, melodramas, and sports. They are quite willing to substitute something else, once they're convinced that just about everyone will enjoy watching it.

Suppose a national advertiser doesn't want this sort of huge, random audience, but rather prefers a smaller and more homogeneous collection of viewers. To some small extent, such "demographic selection" is possible even on network TV. Sports events are aimed mostly at men, afternoon soap operas at women; children and their grandparents like westerns the best, while the generation in the middle prefers police shows; "Rhoda" is popular in urban areas, "Marcus Welby, M. D." in suburbia. But if the advertiser's demographic choices are any narrower than that, network television inevitably fails. By their very nature, the networks are a poor medium for selling, say, computers—too many people are bound to be watching who don't buy computers. An ad in a data-processing magazine would be a much wiser choice.

Despite these realities, national advertisers occasionally want to sponsor a "highbrow" program aimed at an elite audience. If it's a once-in-a-while special, a network will readily agree; it has to do that sort of thing from time to time anyhow to keep the FCC happy. But a highbrow *series* will provoke nothing but frowns from network executives, even if the sponsors are lined up and ready to go. Why? For one thing, the smaller audience for such a program will force a lower

advertising rate, while production costs remain as high as ever, and profits therefore decrease. Second, local ad minutes for the unpopular program will be hard to sell, which will greatly displease the network's affiliates. And third, viewers may well dislike the show so much that they'll actually get up and switch channels, killing the network's ratings for the rest of the night as well.

The lowest common denominator strategy thus reigns supreme. No program with a potential audience of fewer than ten million viewers can make it onto the networks in prime time.

Even within this framework, network programmers hate to experiment. Instead of guessing at what sort of show might attract a large audience, they use the successes of this season as a guide for planning next season. A hit program about doctors this year insures half a dozen doctor programs next year. When it was first proposed, "All In The Family" was bounced from network to network until it finally found a home. But once it earned a high rating—bigots liked it too—a flock of imitators were hustled into the network line-ups.

Next to choosing new programs and renewing old ones, the networks' biggest headache is deciding what goes where in the schedule. The three networks compete, mostly with each other, for the largest share of the viewing audience. Each network tries to attract a third or more of all the people watching TV at any given moment. If a particular show is chosen by only a quarter of the viewers, it's doomed. Scheduling obviously plays a crucial role in this competition.

The main rule used to guide scheduling decisions is "the theory of the least objectionable program." [32] Network officials are convinced that most of the television audience is there to watch television, rather than any specific program. We are addicted to the medium, not its message. It is a rare viewer, the networks reason, who carefully selects an evening's TV diet—first that drama on CBS, then to ABC for that comedy, then to

NBC for that movie, etc. Instead, the typical viewer just turns on the set and watches—until something comes on that he or she doesn't like. Then the viewer reluctantly switches channels, settles back, and watches some more—until another objectionable program turns up. The goal of scheduling, then, is to have the least objectionable programs, especially in the early evening when viewers are picking the night's channel.

In order to steal a portion of the audience from the opposition, a network may try another strategy—counter-programming. If CBS and NBC are both running comedies in a particular time slot, for example, ABC may schedule a western or detective series. If both competitors are showing programs aimed at the older generation, ABC may counter with something for young marrieds. But counter-programming is never allowed to interfere with the "least objectionable program" principle. Stealing new viewers is nice, but keeping your own is essential. Thus, every program must have mass appeal.

STANDARDIZATION

CBS, NBC, and ABC control American television. It's as simple as that. By giving local stations, national advertisers, and the vast majority of viewers exactly what they want, the three networks have achieved unchallenged dominion over the most powerful mass medium yet discovered.

The power of the networks over television is far greater than the power of the wire services and feature syndicates over newspapers. It is probably true that few American newspapers could survive without the wires and syndicates. But at least each paper receives more wire copy than it can use, and is therefore forced to make choices; it can subscribe to both wire services if it wants; it has thousands of syndicated features to choose among. Once a TV station has negotiated a network affiliation, the bulk of its programming decisions are permanently out of its hands.

There are as many criticisms of network performance as there are critics, and lots of them are justified. The networks incorporate too much violence in their shows. They carry too many commercials, especially during children's programs. They are dominated by a white, male, urban, liberal perspective. They don't hire enough women and minorities. But none of these failings—nor the dozens of others that could be listed—result from the peculiar nature of networks. Most local programming is just as violent, just as commercial, and just as white, male, urban, and liberal. Reducing the influence of the networks would not automatically cure all the evils of television.

What would it cure? Maybe nothing. If the networks were somehow abolished tomorrow, would local station owners feel any less compelled to make every program attract the biggest possible audience? Would they simply purchase network-type shows from independent producers and syndicates, or would they follow the example of radio and cultivate more specialized audiences? Would the result be greater diversity or just more of the same? Nobody knows. It seems reasonable to predict that a host of independent stations would offer a wider range of programming than three carbon-copy networks—but maybe not.

At a minimum, any lessening in network influence would reassure those who fear the sheer fact of network power, who worry that the minds of millions of Americans are molded every day by a handful of executives in New York.

Of course we'd lose something in the process. It is hard to imagine a more efficient system than the network system for bringing skillfully produced information and entertainment into millions of homes across thousands of miles. The networks help establish the common goals, habits, perceptions, attitudes, and experiences that unite the country. They confer celebrity and status, and they take it away. They are the principal source of current information for many, and the principal leisure-time activity for most. They are nearly indispensable to hundreds of companies that depend on them for selling goods and services. They have the power to confront government and industry when they want to, and the wealth to support unprofitable programming when they need to. They offer us escapist entertainment of incredibly high quality, plus a modest dose of news and public affairs—and except for the cost of the receiver and the hidden cost of advertising, they do it for free.

So far, efforts to weaken the networks have not met with resounding success. In 1970, for example, the FCC imposed its prime-time access rule, requiring each local station to make its own programming decision—without network help—for one prime-time hour a night. Most stations already handled half an hour a night themselves, for local news. The Commission hoped they would use the other half-hour for documentaries or local-interest shows, something that would add a little diversity to evening television.

They didn't. Half an hour per station per night in the top fifty television markets amounted to 1,050 half-hours a week. A 1973 survey of a typical week found 427 game shows, 110 action-adventure series, 97 situation comedies, 76 musical variety shows, etc. Only 154 of the half-hours were filled with news or documentaries. Moreover, the vast majority of the programs were nonlocal. They came from syndicated producers, broadcast chains, or off-network reruns; very few stations did their own programming.[33] In 1974 the FCC acknowledged its failure and offered to give half an hour on weeknights and the full hour on weekends back to the networks, if they would use the time for children's shows, news, or documentaries.

The power of the three networks could be diluted at least a little by creating a fourth. The White House Office of Telecommunications Policy announced in 1974 that up to eighty-three new VHF television stations could be squeezed into the spectrum in the top hundred markets.[34] If licensed, these stations could conceivably be knit into a fourth network. But don't hold your breath. Dozens of corporations and consulting firms have investigated the feasibility of a commercial fourth network. Most have decided, as the Rand Corporation did in 1974, that the prospects "are not very bright." [35] A noncommercial network of public television stations seemed likely in the early 1970s, but President Nixon quickly scuttled the idea (see pp. 327–29). The three existing networks would naturally fight the creation of a fourth, and that alone should be enough to stop it.

The best hope for diminishing network power is undoubtedly alternative technologies, and the most promising of these is probably cable TV. Cable can increase the number of channels available in any community from ten or so to eighty. The result, in theory, should be audience segmentation, with each special-interest audience watching its own shows, possibly on its own channel. Since the networks need a mass audience to survive, cable could spell their doom, much as the growth of specialized magazines killed *Life* and *Look*.

Before any of this happens, however, cable operators must figure out what to program that will entice viewers away from the networks. So far, cable programming has been vastly inferior to the network offerings, and many cable companies produce no local programming at all. Most viewers, especially in metropolitan areas, haven't bothered to buy the cable service. Until they do, cable will pose no real threat to the networks.

For the foreseeable future, then, the networks will remain a strong force for standardization in television content—a force stretching from New York City into virtually every home in America.

The wire services, feature syndicates, and networks combine to form the backbone of the news and entertainment business in the United States. There is hardly a newspaper or broadcast station in the country that can manage without at least one of them. They are our truly national mass media.

Notes

1 Fred Powledge, "New York—The Associated Press, according to official sources, may have problems communicating with its own people, but it is not out of touch with reality, as some critics have charged. . . ." *New York*, November 15, 1971, p. 55.

2 Edward J. Trayes, "News/Feature Services by Circulation Group Use," *Journalism Quarterly*, Spring, 1972, p. 135.

3 "Media Executives to Hear Kissinger," *New York Times*, April 22, 1973, p. 64.

4 A. Kent MacDougall, "Grinding It Out, AP, UPI Fight Fiercely for Front Page Space," *Wall Street Journal*, January 28, 1969, pp. 1, 16.

5 *AP Log*, August 12, 1974, pp. 1, 4.

6 *Associated Press v. Walker*, 388 U.S. 130, 87 S.Ct. 1975 (1967).

7 Powledge, "New York—The Associated Press," p. 56.

8 MacDougall, "Grinding It Out," pp. 1, 16.

9 Jules Witcover, "Washington: The Workhorse Wire Services," *Columbia Journalism Review*, Summer, 1969, p. 10.

10 Madeline Nelson, draft article for [*MORE*] on the Associated Press.

11 Powledge, "New York—The Associated Press," p. 56.

12 MacDougall, "Grinding It Out," pp. 1, 16.

13 Powledge, "New York—The Associated Press," p. 56.

14 Witcover, "Washington: The Workhorse Wire Services," p. 11.

15 "AP Will Supply News for Radio," *New York Times*, June 1, 1974, p. 59.

16 Nelson, draft article.

17 MacDougall, "Grinding It Out," pp. 1, 16.

18 Trayes, "News/Feature Services," p. 135.

19 "National Black Network Goes Into Operation," *New York Times*, July 3, 1973, p. 53.

20 "Television News Services Agree on Domestic Sale," *New York Times*, May 31, 1974, p. 23.

21 "What Riot?" *Newsweek*, November 1, 1971, p. 82.

22 Ben H. Bagdikian, "Journalism's Wholesalers," *Columbia Journalism Review*, Fall, 1965, p. 28.

23 *Editor & Publisher Yearbook*, 1974, p. 541.

24 Bagdikian, "Journalism's Wholesalers," p. 28.

25 *Federal Communications Commission Annual Report Fiscal 1972*, pp. 182–83.

26 Dick Hubert, "Why 'Group W' Couldn't Sell Television Documentaries," *New York Times*, June 9, 1974, section 2, pp. 1, 15.

27 "KOLO-TV Quits CBS in Program Hassle; Reno Link Goes to KTVN," *Variety*, December 15, 1971, p. 31.

28 Erik Barnouw, *The Golden Web* (New York: Oxford University Press, 1968), p. 288.

29 Kenneth H. Bacon, "TV Network Production of Own Programs Would Be Barred by Rule FCC Is Drafting," *Wall Street Journal*, December 3, 1973, p. 2.

30 "Trust Suits Filed to Restrict Role of TV Networks," *New York Times*, April 15, 1972, pp. 1, 14. *Variety*, April 19, 1972, p. 39.

31 Lee Rich, "Sheriff Who?" in John D. Stevens and William E. Porter, eds., *The Rest of the Elephant: Perspectives on the Mass Media* (Englewood Cliffs, N.J.: Prentice-Hall, 1973), pp. 89–101.

32 Paul Klein, "The Men Who Run TV Aren't That Stupid . . . They Know Us Better Than You Think," *New York*, January 25, 1971, pp. 20–29.

33 *Variety*, December 26, 1973, p. 24.

34 OTP Sees Up To 83 VHF's As Drop-Ins," *Variety*, May 22, 1974, p. 46.

35 "4th TV Network Soon Is Doubted," *New York Times*, January 7, 1974, p. 63.

Suggested Readings

BAGDIKIAN, BEN H., "Journalism's Wholesalers," *Columbia Journalism Review*, Fall, 1965.

CAPPON, RÉNE J., "New York (AP)—" *APME News*, January, 1972.

DIAMOND, EDWIN, "Goodnight, Walter, John, David, Harry, and You, Too, Howard," *New York*, July 23, 1973.

EPSTEIN, EDWARD J., *News From Nowhere*. New York: Vintage Books, 1974.

KLEIN, PAUL, "The Men Who Run TV Aren't That Stupid . . . They Know Us Better Than You Think," *New York*, January 25, 1971.

MACDOUGALL, A. KENT, "Grinding It Out, AP, UPI Fight Fiercely for Front Page Space," *Wall Street Journal*, January 28, 1969.

POWLEDGE, FRED, "New York—The Associated Press, according to official sources, may have problems communicating with its own people, but it is not out of touch with reality, as some critics have charged," *New York*, November 15, 1971.

WITCOVER, JULES, "Washington: The Workhorse Wire Services," *Columbia Journalism Review*, Summer, 1969.

Chapter 10
Newspapers

The newspaper is the oldest and traditionally the most important source of current information. Even today, the average daily paper contains far more news than is available on television or elsewhere. But most of that news is not read, and the newspaper appears to be growing less influential every year. This is a source of profound dissatisfaction for many publishers and reporters, and a possible threat to American society.

A newspaper is an unbound, printed publication, issued at regular intervals, which presents information in words, often supplemented with pictures.

Don't memorize that definition. It is accurate, but not very useful. Perhaps more useful is this rough breakdown of the content of a typical daily newspaper:

60% Advertising
15% Wire-service news (state, national, and international)
10% Syndicated features and columns
10% Sports, society, and other specialized departments
5% Local hard news

The breakdown tells you some important things about newspapers: that more than half of their content isn't news at all, but advertising; that almost half of the remainder is really features and specialized departments; that the bulk of what's left is written by wire-service reporters dozens, hundreds, or thousands of miles away; that only a tiny fraction of each paper is local hard news.

That is what a newspaper is. What should it be? Most observers agree that the main function of the daily newspaper is to tell readers what's happening in the world, the country, the state, and the city. It should strive to report significant political and social developments, to include news of special relevance to particular groups of readers, to scrutinize the actions of local government, and to act as a forum for various community viewpoints.

Students of journalism and political science are agreed that this is the role of the daily newspaper. Readers, reporters, and publishers, however, have somewhat different notions of the purpose of the paper. And it is their views (not ours) that control what actually happens.

THE NEWSPAPER READER

Newspaper reading is a firmly entrenched American habit. A 1972 survey found that 77 percent of American adults regularly read at least one paper, averaging 4.3 "reading sessions" during a five-day week.[1] The habit may be dropping off slightly; in 1970, for the first time in modern history, there were more households in the U.S. than newspaper subscriptions.[2] Nonetheless, more people read a paper every day than drink coffee, or drive a car, or go to work.

But what do they read? What percentage of the audience reads each kind of news? The following list shows one typical, if somewhat outdated, set of findings.[3]

Picture pages	74.3%
Comic pages	42.6
Front page	34.3
Solid news-feature pages	24.0
Editorial pages	23.1
Amusement	21.3
Split news-advertising pages	18.2
Solid advertising pages	15.7
Society and women's pages	15.5
Sports pages	13.9
Financial pages	5.4

The readership pattern is clear. Most people turn to the least taxing, most entertaining sections first, glance at the front page, and then stop. Nearly twice as many read the comics as the editorials. Almost as many read solid ad pages as inside news pages. It is figures like these that feed the cynicism of journalists, that prompted one city editor of the 1920s to say: "You and I aren't hired to make the world a better place to live in, or to fight and die for noble causes, or even to tell the truth about this particular main street. We're hired to feed human animals the kind of mental garbage they want. We don't have to eat it. I don't read our paper for instruction or even for fun. I just read it for errors and to see if we're handing out regularly what the boobs like for breakfast."[4]

The statement is exaggerated. Newspaper readers aren't boobs. They are, in fact, considerably higher in education and income than nonreaders. And a study conducted in 1965 by the *Louisville Courier-Journal* found that more than 90 percent of "influential decision-makers" in the Louisville area were regular readers of the paper.[5] The newspaper audience is, relatively, an elite audience.

Elite or not, most newspaper readers are not very interested in news. When a strike deprives them of their daily paper, what do they miss most? They miss the ads, the "news" of supermarket sales, apartments for rent, and new movies in town. And they miss the service announcements; weddings go uncongratulated, funerals unmourned, and the weather unprepared for. Above all, they miss the habit of reading the paper. But newspaper *news* they can do without—there's always television.

Television is, in fact, the preferred source of news for most Americans today. In 1959, Roper Research Associates asked a sample of Americans where they got their news. Newspapers were mentioned by 57 percent of the respondents; television by 51 percent; radio by 34 percent; and magazines by 8 percent (multiple answers were accepted). In 1972, Roper repeated the survey. This time, 64 percent mentioned television; newspapers were down to 50 percent, radio to 21 percent, and magazines to 6 percent.

The decline in newspaper credibility at the expense of television is even more dramatic. When Roper asked its sample which medium is most believable, this is what it found.[6]

	1959	1972
Television	29%	48%
Newspapers	32	21
Magazines	10	10
Radio	12	8
No answer	17	13

Students of journalism believe that the newspaper is the best available daily source of news. But many newspaper readers prefer to get their news from television. They rely on the paper for entertainment and service, for comics, crosswords, and classifieds.

THE NEWSPAPER REPORTER

For reporters, newspapering is first and foremost a job. Traditionally, it has been a job that didn't pay very well. Newspaper reporters still earn less than their on-the-air colleagues in television, and less than many of the backshop employees who set the paper into type and print it. But the income of newspaper reporters more than doubled between 1960 and 1974, and it's still rising fast.

In 1974, starting salaries for reporters at the 162 unionized papers in the country ranged from $358.80 a week for the *New York Times* to $104.50 a week for the *San Antonio Light*. Most metropolitan dailies paid their starting reporters between $150 and $200 a week. The union minimums for veteran reporters (with two to six years' experience) ranged as high as the *Washington Post*'s $423.25, and as low as the *Monessen Valley* (Pa.) *Independent*'s $175—with most papers paying between $200 and $300. Copy boys and copy girls today start at $110 to $160 a week—about what a veteran reporter earned in 1960.[7]

The minimum salaries at nonunion papers are generally lower, but not much lower; these papers must remain competitive or they'll lose their best reporters to the union shops. And of course every paper, union or nonunion, pays at least a few of its reporters more than the minimum. A top, prize-winning reporter at a top, prize-winning newspaper may earn as much as $30,000 a year.

But how many prize-winning reporters are there, and how many prize-winning papers? An undistinguished reporter at a mediocre small-city newspaper may earn as little as $8,000 a year—and most reporters are closer to the $8,000 figure than to the $30,000 one.

Besides the pay, newspaper reporters must learn to live with low status, terrible hours,

and insecurity (every time a newspaper folds, a roomful of reporters starts looking for work). They must also put up with the whims of publishers, the anger of news sources and would-be sources, and the tedium of covering press conference after press conference after press conference.

Why do they stay? Many don't. One typical study traced the careers of thirty-five outstanding journalism students. Only nineteen of them (just over half) went into newspaper work after graduating. Ten years later, only eight of them were still holding down newspaper jobs. The rest had left for public relations, advertising, broadcasting, insurance, or whatever.[8]

What's left after this winnowing process is the typical newspaper reporter. He is a male in his late forties and earns $12,000 to $15,000 a year. He's been in the newspaper business for half his life, and though he doesn't find it especially exciting any more, he doesn't intend to leave either. He has a college diploma, a wife, and a mortgage. He believes in the mystique of journalism, and will occasionally remark that he has "ink in his veins." But he is a little resentful of the younger reporters, men and women who expect to take the world by storm, and he is secretly pleased whenever one of them quits and takes a job in public relations.

The experienced reporter is something of a cynic. He has seen the worst in life and been unable to report it, or has reported it and been unable to change it. Theodore Dreiser put it this way:

> One can always talk to a newspaper man, I think, with the full confidence that one is talking to a man who is at least free of moralistic mush. Nearly everything in connection with those trashy romances of justice, truth, mercy, patriotism, public profession of all sorts, is already and forever gone if they have been in the business for any length of time.[9]

The cynicism of the journalist is largely the result of frustration—the frustration of a would-be participant forced to play the

In the ideology of most newspaper reporters, nothing is more sacrosanct than the claim that they are not trying to advance any particular social goal. In 1973, while many observers were congratulating or condemning the media for pursuing the Watergate scandals, political reporter Richard Reeves offered the following demurrer:

> I am a reporter. In twenty minutes, with a telephone and typewriter, I can write a coherent and substantially accurate 700-word story of a subway accident or the fall of a government. With a rumor, two facts, and an inch-high stack of clippings, I can put together a scandalous account of what's being done with your tax dollar. I can fake my way through a probing conversation with a foreign minister or a mobster. I have knocked on strange doors at 4 A.M. to say, "I'm sorry your son was just killed, do you have a picture of him and could you tell me what kind of kid he was?" I am, according to the New York Newspaper Guild, worth a minimum of $365 a week.
>
> I love it, even if I know it's a kind of prolonged adolescence. That doesn't mean I don't take it seriously—I do, I think it's very, very important, but I'm glad it's fun. . . .
>
> I just wanted to cover good stories, write them well, give the people kind enough to read them a sense of what's going on. I want to be accurate, fair, perceptive and, when I'm lucky, incisive. If I'm interested in influence, it's influence with other reporters. More than anything I want the respect of the men and women in my peer group. . . .
>
> I have met few editors and fewer reporters with ambitions greater than getting better stories—getting stories, not Presidents, whatever the incumbent thinks.[10]

What Reeves says is accurate, but it is misleading nonetheless. It is true that most reporters have no particular policy goals behind their journalism, no hidden bias for which they write consistent propaganda. But it is also true that most reporters have strong opinions about the events and issues they cover, and a strong desire that their coverage should influence the way decisions are made. Yes, reporters set out to get the Watergate story, not to get President Nixon. But as the Watergate saga unfolded, reporters came to expect that the story itself would "get" the president—and their faith in journalism would have been profoundly shaken if it had not done so.

It is no accident that the period immediately after Watergate witnessed a substantial increase in the number of college journalism majors around the country.[11] These novice reporters, attracted to journalism for its power, will also try to cover the news fairly. And they will expect governments to fall, policies to change, and readers to be aroused as a result of their coverage.

Richard Reeves, by the way, is a "New Journalist" and political columnist; for an example of his very personal, very opinionated approach to the news, see page 272. The typical newspaper reporter works under much stricter constraints than those confronting Reeves. Such a reporter may find newspaper work somewhat less satisfying than Reeves does. When governments don't fall, policies don't change, and readers are not aroused, the result may be disillusionment and cynicism.

role of an observer. What city hall reporter has not wished to be a LaGuardia? What education writer a Dewey? What sports columnist a Mays? Many journalists pick newspaper work, it seems to us, in order to change the world. They soon discover that they *can't* change the world, that the most they can do is to report the world-changing decisions of others. And so the activist reporter becomes a passive writer of articles. After work he or she adjourns to the neighborhood bar to tell other reporters what the mayor *should* have done.

Perhaps this is an exaggerated view of newspaper work. No doubt there are reporters around who exult with editor Walter Humphrey that "every human activity is on my beat and I am interested in everything that happens in the world, for everything is my concern." [12] No doubt there are other reporters who simply do their job, and do it well, with a minimum of frustration or cynicism. But the typical reporter, we maintain, is a disillusioned idealist.

THE NEWSPAPER PUBLISHER

For publishers the newspaper is a business, and like all business executives the publisher wants the paper to earn a profit. By and large, it does.

Newspaper financial statements are hard to come by. Publishers are constantly pleading that the wolf is halfway in the newsroom door, and treat any inquiry into profits as a direct assault on freedom of the press. The *New York Times* is one of the few newspapers in the country that publicly report their profits. In 1973, The New York Times Company earned $17.6 million in net profit on revenues of $356 million. The *Times* itself accounted for only 60 percent of these earnings; the rest came from newspapers in Florida, broadcast stations in Tennessee and New York, various magazines, several paper mills, etc. [13]

According to 1973 data prepared by Kidder, Peabody & Co., the typical small-city newspaper with a 35,000 circulation has total revenues of about $3.5 million, 71 percent from advertising and 29 percent from circulation. Expenses come to about $2.7 million, leaving roughly $800,000 a year in profit. For a metropolitan paper with a circulation of 250,000 or so, revenues amount to about $21.5 million a year, 84 percent from advertising and 16 percent from circu-

lation. Expenses are $16.5 million, leaving an annual profit of about $5 million. [14] The American Newspaper Publishers Association predicts that total newspaper advertising revenue will rise from just over $7 billion in 1973 to more than $10 billion a year by 1980. [15] If so, newspaper profits should rise also.

All this is not meant to imply that starting a new newspaper is a safe investment. It isn't. The initial capital requirements are huge, and it takes years to establish a new paper to the point where it attracts enough readers and advertisers to earn a profit. But those fortunate enough to own one of the 1,760-odd dailies already established in the country are—on the whole—earning a better than adequate income.

The profitability of today's newspaper is reflected in the difficulty and cost of buying one. Only two or three metropolitan papers change hands each year; most of the available action is in the 5,000 to 50,000 circulation range. A few decades ago, you could have bought the Athens, Georgia, daily paper (circ. 7,000) for a mere $50,000. The asking price in the mid-1960s was $1.7 million. And the 400,000-circulation *Cleveland Plain Dealer* was sold to the Newhouse chain in 1968 for a cool $51 million.

Occasionally, of course, a newspaper loses money. The Cowles chain dropped nearly $2.2 million on the *Suffolk Sun* before giving up in 1969. But on the whole, an existing newspaper is a good, safe, solid investment— even if it costs a fortune to buy. The *Dubuque* (Iowa) *Telegraph Herald,* for example, is a family-owned paper that earns more than a million dollars a year on a gross of $4.5 million—a very nice return indeed. Bill Woodward, the head of the family that owns the paper, is approached at least once a month with a purchase offer from a chain or conglomerate. But he is not interested in selling. In fact, he would like to start his own chain with some of the *Telegraph Herald* profits. [16]

There are, unfortunately, a few dark

clouds hanging over this rosy economic picture. A major short-term problem is the uncertain availability of newsprint at a reasonable price, possibly at any price. A more fundamental issue is the threat of competition from new media. Publishers have nightmares about some science-fiction combination of cable television and computers that could turn the traditional newspaper into a technological relic almost overnight. But the real worry for the next decade or two is neither of these. It is the battle over automation.

The oldest of the mass media, newspapering is also the most old-fashioned. As long as the profits were satisfactory, many publishers were content to leave it that way. In an age dedicated to speed, cleanliness, and efficiency, there was a certain thumb-your-nose pleasure in slow, dirty, inefficient newspaper work.

A little of that feeling survives today, but not much. Only twenty years ago, the typical publisher owned a newspaper, period. Today, that publisher may own four papers, or forty—plus a couple of TV stations, a cable system, and maybe some real estate on the side. The heads of conglomerates and media chains are seldom very attracted to the ink-in-your-veins traditions of journalism. Their god is profit. The owners of smaller newspapers, meanwhile, are faced with steadily rising costs; for them streamlining may be a matter of survival.

Why, then, have so few newspapers (and most of those small ones) made real progress toward automation in the last decade? The answer is organized labor. Computerized typesetting, for example, would render instantly obsolete thousands of backshop employees who now operate the linotype machines. The linotype process, essentially unchanged since it was patented in 1885, sets the reporter's words in metal for use on the printing press. Punched tape and computers can do the job much cheaper over the long run, with many fewer employees. Understandably, the various locals of the typographical union have steadfastly opposed the change.

In May, 1974, following a precedent set in San Francisco the previous year, the *New York Times* and the *New York Daily News* reached an important agreement with the typographers. In return for lifetime job security for all backshop personnel, the union agreed to give the two papers a free hand to automate as they saw fit. In essence, the

EUROPEAN PAPERS IN TROUBLE

While newspaper profits in the United States are holding up, at least so far, the situation for Europe's press is not so healthy.

The British papers are suffering from the same ills that distress American publishers—rising newsprint and labor costs, frequent strikes by backshop employees fearful of automation, competition from television for ad revenues, etc. But they're suffering more. Total losses for Britain's evening newspapers are now estimated at $46 million a year. One major chain, Beaverbrook Newspapers, recently had to close three papers in Glasgow. Still other papers are talking merger or negotiating joint operating agreements. In London, meanwhile, hard-pressed publishers are increasingly reluctant to send reporters abroad for on-the-spot coverage.[17]

Things are even worse in the rest of Europe. In Italy, despite a system of government subsidies, every single newspaper in 1974 was in the red. In France, only the dailies *Le Monde* and *Le Figaro* were making money, and their circulation was heading down too; between 1960 and 1970 twelve dailies folded in France. Even the strong West German newspapers have felt the decline.[18]

union was willing to die out slowly so that its current members could be assured of their jobs for as long as they wanted them.[19]

Automation, when it comes, will inevitably lead to more profitable newspapers. Whether it leads to better newspapers will depend on whether the additional profits are invested in the editorial side of the operation. Some reporters may regret the change from romantic chaos to smooth efficiency, but if the editorial budget is fattened as a result they will be quickly consoled. Most readers won't notice the difference. The choice itself, of course, will be up to the publishers, who make most of the major decisions about their newspapers.

THE NEWSPAPER

The content of a newspaper is the product of the conflicting goals of the reader (to be entertained), the reporter (to change the world), and the publisher (to make money). In this conflict the reporter usually loses. For one thing, the reader and the publisher have most of the power; for another, their goals are highly compatible. The reporter represents a minority viewpoint.

Consider, for example, the syndicated feature. Syndicated material—comic strips, advice columns, and the like—makes up as much as one-third the editorial content of many daily newspapers. Why? Because it's cheap; a cost-conscious publisher can use the syndicates to fill 35 percent of the paper's news hole for only 10 percent of its editorial budget. And because it's entertaining, which is what the public wants.

The decline of the newspaper editorial is another perfect example of the publisher-reader coalition at work. Until the Penny Press era the unsigned editorials were the most important part of most newspapers. But today's readers find the editorial page too heavy for their taste. That's okay with most publishers. They use the edit page to praise the weather, pontificate on the latest news from Afghanistan, and urge everyone to vote in the next election. There are very few newspapers left in the country that regularly publish strong editorials on local controversies, thus risking the reader's anger.

A third example is the growing ascendancy of advertising over news copy. In 1941, the average newspaper was 52 percent news, 48 percent advertising. Today a respectable ratio is 60 percent advertising and 40 per-

---

THE NEWSPAPER: 1970 VERSUS 1950

To find out how newspapers have changed in the past two decades, Ben H. Bagdikian studied 153 daily papers as they were in 1950, and again as they were in 1970.

The average paper, he found, gained in size from 34 to 54 pages. Most of this increase—in fact, 83 percent of it—was advertising; the papers added thirteen columns of ads for every three columns of news. Still, the amount of news in the papers did rise.

But what kind of news? Pictures and art increased by 63 percent. The sports section went from half a page to three or four pages a day. The financial news increased from practically nothing to several pages a day. Fashion, food, and real estate all went up. So did the editorial page and columns. Hard news of local, national, and international affairs changed very little.

Bagdikian also found the 1970 papers to be tighter and cleaner in make-up than the 1950 ones. And he judged that there were fewer lead stories stressing violence, sex, and the bizarre in 1970 than in 1950.[20] These last two findings may represent victories for the reporter. The rest of the study seems to show the coalition of publishers and readers at work—economics and entertainment prospering at the expense of news.

cent news. (In all fairness, the size of the typical newspaper has also increased, leaving a bigger news hole by absolute measures than ever before.) Reporters and editors fight for every column-inch of news they can get. But publishers prefer to print ads. And readers often would just as soon read ads.

The growth of newspaper monopolies is a fourth example—and an enormously important one (see Chapter 4). Publishers are always pleased to own the only newspaper in town; without competition, costs are lower and ad revenues higher. As long as the survivor picks up the dead paper's comics and columns, readers seldom object to the loss of a newspaper.

The result: merger after merger, ending in monopoly after monopoly. In 1910, there were 689 American cities with competing daily newspapers. By 1930, the figure was down to 288; by 1960, it was down to 61. In 1974, Chicago was the only city in the country with two competing newspapers in the morning, and two more in the afternoon (two companies owned all four papers). Then *Chicago Today* folded, and there were no cities left with four competing dailies. The vast majority of Americans today live in communities without effective newspaper competition.

When newspaper competition dies, part of the challenge of newspapering dies too.

Most reporters swear that newspaper quality declines as a result. Management claims the opposite. Without competitive pressure, publishers argue, a paper is free to stress accuracy and balance instead of speed and sensationalism.

The debate is hard to resolve. One researcher studied the *Tri-City Herald* in Washington during periods of monopoly and of competition. He found that sensational copy filled 30 percent of the paper's news hole during its competitive era, but only 22 percent when it was a monopoly. On the other hand, the *Herald* devoted more space to local news when faced with competition (51 percent of the news hole) than it did with no competition (41 percent).[21] Monopoly, in other words, improved the paper in some ways, but hurt it in others.

Another study found that competitive newspapers tended to have a larger news hole than monopoly papers. They also allowed more space for letters to the editor and wrote more editorials on local subjects. The differences, however, were very small.[22]

A third study focused on competing dailies in Pottstown, Pa. Author Stanley Bigman compared the two papers on many characteristics, and concluded that they were identical. Because the two publishers were so similar in social class and political ideology, Bigman asserted, the town would lose nothing if it lost one of the papers.[23]

THE ENDOWED NEWSPAPER

Press critic A. J. Liebling was fond of comparing the job of running a newspaper with that of running a university. He reasoned that newspapers, like universities, should be endowed, thus freeing the publisher from the effort to please readers and advertisers.

"The hardest trick, of course, would be getting the chief donor of the endowment (perhaps a repentant tabloid publisher) to a) croak, or b) sign a legally binding agreement never to stick his face in the editorial rooms." The best kind of endowment for a newspaper, Liebling continued, "would be one made up of several large and many small or medium-sized gifts."

"Personally," he added, "I would rather leave my money for a newspaper than for a cathedral, a gymnasium, or even a home for street-walkers with fallen arches, but I have seldom been able to assemble more than $4.17 at one time."[24]

The central lesson of Bigman's study is that it's the publisher, not the reporter, who controls newspaper quality. No doubt a conscientious reporter does a better job if he or she has another paper to compete with. But competition or no competition, the publisher has the ultimate power. The *Louisville Courier-Journal* and the *Atlanta Constitution* are monopoly newspapers, yet they are excellent newspapers. The *Detroit News* and the *Cleveland Press* have competition, but they do a poor job anyhow. Perhaps the competitive publisher has to make a greater effort to keep readers happy—but pleasing readers doesn't necessarily make for a better newspaper.

One person can change the face of a newspaper. In 1960, the *Los Angeles Times* was "best represented by a middle-aged lady in a mink shrug on her way to a Republican tea." [25] It had three reporters in its Washington bureau, a total news staff of 220, and an annual editorial budget of $3 million. Then Otis Chandler took over as publisher. By the 1970s, the *Times* had 18 reporters in Washington, a news staff of more than 500, and an operating budget of $12 million a year. And it was one of the most aggressive, respected (and profitable) newspapers in America. Under Colonel William Rockhill Nelson, on the other hand, the *Kansas City Star* was once ranked among the top papers in the country. Today it is just another big-city daily.

Publishers control their newspapers. And, as Bigman points out, most publishers are very much alike—conservative, well-to-do businessmen, confirmed members of the Establishment. Their newspapers reflect their values, and the values of their friends. Editor H. Lang Rogers of the *Joplin* (Missouri) *Globe* comments that the average publisher tries "to mold his newspaper around the comments, desires, and complaints of his country club buddies." [26] The result may be a newspaper responsive only to the upper classes, not to the entire community.

"Country-club journalism" is nothing new. William Allen White had this to say about it back in 1939:

> If he is a smart go-getting up-and-coming publisher in a town of 100,000 to 1,000,000 people, the publisher associates on terms of equality with the bankers, the merchant princes, the manufacturers, and the investing brokers. His friends unconsciously color his opinion. If he lives with them on any kind of social terms in the City club or the Country club or the Yacht club or the Racquet club, he must more or less merge his views into the common views of the other capitalists. . . .
>
> So it often happens, alas too often, that a newspaper publisher, reflecting this uncon-

---

GOOD-BYE TO GOOD NEWS

A complaint that newspaper editors hear from the public again and again is this one: "Why do you print so much bad news? Why don't you ever print anything good?"

Rather than fall back on the usual response—that good news is seldom a change from the ordinary or expected, and thus is not news at all—Californian Bill Bailey decided to start his own weekly tabloid, *The Good News Paper*. Bailey printed only the listings for stocks that went up. He frequently reported that five million college students had not participated in a particular campus demonstration, or that more than 200 million citizens did not use illegal drugs.

Bailey's paper attracted readers in fifty states and ten foreign countries, and he managed to survive for some sixteen months. In April, 1972, he went broke. True to its credo, the paper did not print a notice of its own death. That was left to the carriers of "bad" news in the rest of the profession.[27]

---

scious class arrogance of the consciously rich, thinks he is printing news when he is doctoring it innocently enough. He thinks he is purveying the truth when much that he offers seems poison to hundreds of thousands of his readers who don't move in his social and economic stratosphere. . . .[28]

Country-club journalism is less of a problem today than it was in White's time. Today's publishers are more interested in money than in power, so they keep their biases in check. Today's readers are more interested in entertainment than in news, so they barely notice the biases that are left. Once again the publisher and the reader are getting along fine, and only the reporter is left out in the cold.

THE REPORTER FIGHTS BACK

In the last section we discussed five characteristics of newspapers that are approved (or at least tolerated) by most publishers and readers, but bitterly resented by many reporters:

1. The growth of syndicated features.
2. The decline of the editorial.
3. The supremacy of advertising over news.
4. The trend toward newspaper monopoly.
5. Country-club journalism.

The inability of reporters to halt any of these developments has contributed substantially to newsroom cynicism, and has helped spur the growth of the "reporter power" movement in the U.S. (see pp. 80–81).

Even though reporters lose most of their battles with the publisher-reader coalition, they are bound to win a few. Two such victories have had a significant effect on the quality of today's newspaper—specialized reporting and interpretive reporting.

Specialized reporting is not a recent invention. The *New York Sun* had its own police reporter back in the 1830s. But except for a few areas (sports, society, busi-

ness), specialization didn't begin to take hold until the 1950s. A study of fifty-two metropolitan dailies revealed that in 1945 only ten of them had specialized education writers. By 1955 there were twenty-three such writers; by 1960 the number was up to forty. In 1966, only three of the fifty-two papers still had no education reporter on their staffs.[29]

In 1974 the *Milwaukee Journal* (a better-than-average metropolitan daily) listed the following specialized departments and beats: art, auto, aviation, boating, business/financial, education, environment, farm, fashion, food, garden, home furnishings, labor, medicine, men's, motion pictures, music, outdoor, politics, radio/television, real estate, religion, science, society, sports, theater, travel, urban affairs, women's. In addition, a number of the paper's "general assignment" reporters consistently covered certain areas—city hall, police, etc.

Publishers dislike specialized reporting because it costs more than the all-purpose sort. Specialized reporters need more training, command higher salaries, and grind out fewer words to fit between the ads. Readers don't seem to care much either way. Specialized reporting has grown only because reporters and editors have insisted that specialization is essential to good journalism.

There is little doubt that specialized reporters can do a better job than those on general assignment. A specialist gets to know both the subject and the sources, and develops the background necessary to interpret the story for readers.

But specialization is of little value unless reporters are free to include their expertise in their articles. The traditional who/what/where/when/how/why kind of journalism allows almost no leeway for this sort of interpretation. A complicated political or economic story written in the traditional style can be almost completely incomprehensible. It is not enough for reporters to understand the issues they are writing about; they must be permitted to explain the issues in a way that readers can follow, comprehend, and enjoy.

Hence the rebirth of interpretive reporting. Newspapers in the eighteenth and nineteenth centuries habitually interpreted the news for their readers. But then came the wire services, and just-the-facts objectivity became a hallmark of good journalism. That standard lasted until the Depression of the 1930s, when reporters discovered that neither they nor their readers could make sense of New Deal legislation without plenty of background explanation. At first, interpretation was saved for really big or really complicated stories. But by the mid-1960s, interpretive news articles were becoming more and more common—and more and more outspoken—every day.

The boundary between hard news and interpretive reporting is difficult to define. And there's another boundary that's even harder to draw—between interpretive reporting and a still more subjective, more personal kind of writing that proponents have hailed as the New Journalism. By way of example, consider the six excerpts that follow. The first five are from the *Philadelphia Inquirer* of August 10, 1974, the morning after President Richard Nixon resigned under fire and Gerald Ford was sworn in as the next president. The sixth excerpt also concerns this transition, but represents a kind of writing that the *Inquirer* and most other establishment newspapers would consider unacceptable.

1. Hard News Story. The lead story on the front page, under the byline of Clark Hoyt of the *Inquirer* Washington Bureau, begins:

> Washington—Gerald Rudolph Ford, declaring that "our long national nightmare is over," was sworn in Friday as 38th President of the United States.
>
> As Richard Nixon flew across the continent and into history after a tear-choked White House farewell, Ford, 61, took the oath of office in a simple, moving ceremony presided over by Chief Justice Warren Burger.

> In a short, eloquent address to the overflow crowd of more than 300 in the White House's East Room and a national television audience, the new President called for healing and reconciliation. . . .

Hoyt's article follows the traditional summary lead pattern, with the who, what, where, when, and why of the story packed into the first few paragraphs. Less important information comes later. A majority of newspaper articles are written according to this formula; they are the meat and potatoes, if not the relish, of the business. Hard news writers are expected to work quickly, to write clearly and dispassionately, to get their facts straight, and to keep their opinions totally out of the story. Because of the importance of this particular event, Hoyt was allowed slightly more latitude than is usual in hard news; phrases like "moving ceremony" and "eloquent address" would probably be cut from an article on a less monumental topic.

2. News Feature. "Portrait Removed in U.S. Offices," by Dominic Sama of the *Inquirer* staff, begins on the lefthand side of the front page, below the fold:

> When President Richard M. Nixon's resignation became effective at noon Friday, his framed picture was stripped from the walls in thousands of Federal offices, but there was nothing to take its place.
>
> "I know it's a ritualistic thing to do during an election, but the significance of it escapes me at the moment," said a postal worker at the Media Post Office in Delaware County.
>
> "Mr. Nixon's picture has been removed, but I'm quite sure no one had the foresight to have a picture of President Gerald Ford printed. . . ."

News features are intended to throw additional light on a hard news event (in which case they are often called "sidebars"), or to deal with less weighty topics. Sama is expected to be not only accurate, but entertaining as well, and he is permitted greater stylistic freedom than Hoyt in organizing and writing his article. Such techniques as humor, suspense, and irony are appropriate. But language must remain within the conventional boundaries of the newspaper, and Sama's own views are still no part of the story.

3. News Analysis. "All-New Ballgame In Politics," by Loye Miller, Jr. of the *Inquirer* Washington Bureau, begins below the fold on page one:

> Washington—With the departure of Richard M. Nixon, it looks like a brand new ballgame in American politics.
>
> From Maine to California, Republicans who were fearfully anticipating that Watergate would bring down massive defeat on the GOP next November are taking new hope.
>
> Their new optimism may prove ill founded, but there is widespread belief that the Nixon resignation will remove the Watergate monkey from the backs of Republican candidates. . . .

Also called an interpretive story, the news analysis helps the reader deal with complex issues by explaining their origin and likely impact. Such stories almost always appear as companions to major hard-news articles. Miller is expected to bring his professional knowledge and judgment to bear on the issue; the reader must thus judge the story in the context of Miller's special expertise. Unlike Hoyt and Sama, Miller is entitled to draw conclusions—but they must be based on the facts (which he also reports) and his interpretations of them. He is not to be a cheerleader for any particular ideology, and he is expected to modify his conclusions when new facts arise. Like Sama, he has some freedom in language and organization, but is still bound by the conventions of the paper.

4. Signed Column. Appearing on the editorial page is this column by William Raspberry of the *Washington Post* syndicated service:

> Mr. Nixon finally was driven to confess at least a little of what we knew all along. . . .

> The system works: That is the lesson of Watergate. The system works. . . .
>
> The thing that keeps haunting me is how much the vindication of the system is the result of two freak accidents: Frank Wills' discovery of the Watergate burglars and the President's decision to bug his own office. . . .
>
> If he hadn't tape recorded himself and his fellow conspirators, or if he had taken the tapes to the furnace room as soon as their existence became public knowledge, we would have suspected much but known very little, and Mr. Nixon would still be firmly in charge of the government. . . .

The column is a personal statement by the individual who writes it, and readership is limited to those who care what he or she thinks. Readers come to know the personal bias of each columnist—liberal, conservative, hawk, dove, or whatever—and pick the people they want to read. Raspberry, like all columnists, filters facts from hard news and features through his own particular ideology, and emerges with the sort of thought-provoking synthesis that would seldom be permitted on the news pages. Style, language, and organization are all up to the individual columnist, and vary from the conventional to the counter-cultural.

5. Editorial. Appearing on the lefthand side of the editorial page, this statement from the *Inquirer*'s management carries the headline, "It's President Ford Now—And He Begins Well":

> . . . Gerald Ford has never been known as an orator, and he described his own remarks following his inauguration as "just a little straight talk among friends."
>
> But there was eloquence in the simplicity with which he spoke, and after too long a period in which it has been a scarce commodity at the highest level of our government straight talk is welcome.
>
> The shattered trust of the American people in our political process will not be restored overnight, but Mr. Ford has made a prompt and persuasive beginning. . . .

The hard news, general-assignment tradition in American journalism has led to many deficiencies. One of the most serious is a tendency to forget to follow up developing stories. A politician makes a promise, duly reported, but no one reports when the promise isn't kept. Police get good coverage when they arrest a suspect, but no one covers the suspect's release the following week. Reporters fight to interview a scientist with a promising new cure for cancer, but no one fights for a story on later progress in the research.

The *New York Times* took a small step toward correcting this problem in early 1974, when it inaugurated a popular weekly feature called "Follow-Up on the News." *Times* copy editor Lee Dembart keeps a notebook full of stories that are left hanging in mid-air, and one at a time he gets back to them. Dembart has run items on forty-one astronauts who never got into space, on what happened to Alcatraz Island after it was opened to the public, on progress toward a proposed tunnel linking France and England, etc. The best part, he says, is confronting politicians with their campaign promises. "I ask them, 'What happened to that. . . ?' And you can almost feel them squirm. It's a lot of fun." [30]

And it's useful to readers, too. This is one new feature that may well catch on at other papers.

The editorial is usually unsigned; it is where the newspaper speaks—with one voice —to its readers. Good editorials have a strong point of view, and attempt to persuade the reader that they are right, based on facts, logic, and sometimes even emotion. Of course the paper should have covered the same topic in its news columns, so that readers can make up their own minds whether to accept or reject the paper's position. Language and style are entirely up to the editorial writer, but traditionally tend to be dignified, perhaps even pompous.

6. New Journalism. Here is a sixth approach to the same subject. This one most definitely did not appear in the *Inquirer,* but rather in the May 6, 1974, issue of *New York* magazine. The author is political reporter Richard Reeves:

I have seen the future and it scares the hell out of me.

I have seen Gerald Rudolph Ford in Troy, Michigan, bringing up busing sixteen times in a seventeen-minute press conference when none

of the questions were about busing. . . . I have heard him at Harvard talking about "that great Russian writer" because he can't pronounce Solzhenitsyn. . . . I have seen him, from a chartered airplane, playing golf in the Xanadu isolation of the guarded Annenberg fortress in Palm Springs—choosing to spend his time with the rich, the trying-to-get-rich, and a personal staff that can most charitably be described as being in over their collective heads. . . .

Even more than the typical columnist, Reeves is a very visible part of his article. He uses the forbidden "I," and a richness of language that would make a newspaper copy editor blanch. Much of what he writes is fact (hypoed a bit to involve the reader). Much is opinion. Sometimes it is hard to tell which is which. But for those readers who have come to trust Reeves, this style of reporting has many rewards—it is entertaining; it successfully communicates mood as well as information; it can cut through the pomposity and doubletalk to the core of the matter. Of course for readers who don't trust Reeves, this sort of journalism is totally unreliable. And for readers who don't know whom to trust, who tend to trust everything they read in the papers, the New Journalism is a dizzying, disorienting, and potentially misleading experience.

The New Journalism isn't new. The colonial press was intensely personal; so was the Penny Press in the 1830s and the Yellow Press in the 1890s. It can be argued, in fact, that newspaper "objectivity" was nothing but a passing fad that is already on its way out. Perhaps by 1980 newspaper reporters will write as personally and subjectively as newspaper publishers and editors wrote in the early history of American journalism.

But probably not. Both publishers and readers object to the New Journalism, because they fear it will open the door to biased reporting, and because newspaper reporters tend to be more liberal than their readers, and far more liberal than their publishers. H. Lang Rogers of the *Joplin* (Missouri) *Globe* puts the objection this way: "We find fewer of the young journalists with the basic honesty and integrity to seek to write entirely objectively and to bend over backwards to keep their own beliefs from slanting their writings." [31]

The problem of biased reporters is a serious one, as former Vice President Spiro T. Agnew pointed out in 1969 (see pp. 107–8). Heavily personal newswriting in the style of Richard Reeves probably shouldn't become the mainstay of daily journalism. But somewhere between this New Journalism and just-the-facts objectivity lies the future of newspapers: interpretive reporting. In their efforts to do something broadcasting can't do, publishers are getting used to it. In their rediscovered pleasure at the art of expository writing, readers are getting used to it. And the best of the new crop of young reporters are insisting on it.

The typical publisher, after all, wants only to make money. The typical reader wants only to be entertained. But reporters—especially the under-30 reporters—want to change the world. Perhaps we should give them a chance to try.

The process of creating a newspaper is a good reflection of the paper's character. That process is, of course, different for different papers, and the process differs even for different stories in the same paper. But always it is hurried, harried, and demanding. Many of the developing trends in newspaper work are changes in the way the paper is produced. They will inevitably result in a different kind of paper.

PROCESS AND TECHNOLOGY

The typical reporter on a typical newspaper may spend the morning covering a fire in a downtown jewelry store—good for fifteen inches on an inside page. That afternoon he or she may sit in on a zoning board hearing, trying to summarize a complex dispute in three or four paragraphs to be buried among the classified ads. Late in the afternoon the reporter may put in some overtime preparing a feature on the opening of a suburban carnival. All three stories will be skimmed quickly by an assistant city editor, and then inserted into the paper.

Occasionally the reporter is assigned a more important story—perhaps a local strike. As each deadline approaches (the paper has several different editions), the reporter dictates the article by phone to a rewrite specialist in the newsroom, who revises the story as he or she writes. A copy boy or copy girl rips each page out of the typewriter and brings it to the city editor. The city editor checks it over, adds a few paragraphs of background, and hands it to a copy editor, who corrects the style and grammar and then writes a headline. The page is shot through a pneumatic tube to the composing room, where a linotypist is assigned the job of setting it in type. By the time the reporter has finished dictating, the first few paragraphs of the story may have already been set. Since the city editor has decided to put the strike on the front page, the managing editor will read the story over before the order is given to start the presses.

If newspapers lavished this much care on every story, they would be a lot better than they are. Unfortunately, nobody can spare the time. Most newspaper pages are part news and part advertising. Each day the advertising department "dummies" its ads into the paper. It tells each editor—city, state, telegraph, sports, business, etc.—exactly how much space is left for news. The editor makes the assignments, then devotes most of the day to the three or four top stories. The routine articles are left to subordinates—or to chance. More often than not, they appear in the newspaper almost exactly as they came off the teletype machine or the reporter's typewriter.

The process of researching, writing, and editing a news story has changed little in the past few decades, but the process of getting the story into print has changed enor-mously. New technologies have transformed the look of newspaper backshops and of newspapers themselves; now they are beginning to affect the work of reporters and editors as well.

Rapidly becoming obsolete is the manual "hot type" system with a linotype machine at its center. In this traditional set-up, a piece of newspaper copy is first sent to the linotype operator, who sets the story in strips of hot, molten lead. As each separate line of type is added to the previous one, the story takes shape on a metal tray or galley. The type is then taken from the galleys and fastened into page forms, which tightly hold hundreds of individual lines together to make up a page of the newspaper. The page form then goes to a stereotyper, who turns the unwieldy columns of lead into a curved plate that fits onto the printing press.

In a "cold type" operation, by contrast, the linotype machine is replaced by a much cheaper device resembling an ordinary type-writer. When the story comes out of this machine, it is carefully cut up and pasted

---

THE REST OF THE STAFF

The vast majority of a newspaper staff is made up of neither reporters nor their bosses. Consider the following:

The advertising department, which sells the ads that fill 60 percent of the paper.

The circulation department, made up of hundreds of executives, secretaries, truck drivers, and delivery people.

The dispatch department, which turns scrawled-out display advertising into printer-ready copy.

The linotypists, scores of them, who set all of the news and many of the ads in type (other ads are set by hand).

The make-up staff, which arranges the type into pages and somehow makes it fit.

The photographers and photoengravers, who illustrate the news and then prepare the illustrations for printing.

The rim staff, or copy editors, who write every headline; check every article for grammar, spelling, and accuracy; then check it again for printer's errors.

The stereotypers, who convert the flat beds of type into curved plates for high-speed printing.

The pressroom staff, which operates the presses that turn out the finished newspapers.

The telephone operators; the receptionists; the classified ad department; the equipment main-tenance people; the janitors; the librarians; the cafeteria workers; the suppliers of ink and paper; the elevator operators; and many, many more.

Without the help of all these people, reporters and editors would be powerless.

---

into a "dummy," along with all the other stories, headlines, and ads that belong on that page. The dummy goes to a photo-engraver, who takes a picture of the entire page, and the stereotypers make their plate out of that. The cold-type system is neater and cleaner than hot type, and since it uses simpler equipment and fewer (and less highly trained) employees, it's a lot cheaper.

Both cold-type and hot-type operations can be further improved by the use of an automated system instead of a manual one. The story is first transformed into punched holes in a piece of tape, with each letter and symbol represented by a different combination of holes. The tape is then fed into a composing machine (for cold type) or an automatic linotype machine (for hot type). Guided by a computer memory, these machines translate the punches into words and paragraphs. There are two advantages here. First, automated systems require fewer back-shop employees than manual ones, and thus save the publisher money despite the initial cost of the new equipment. Second, automated systems are faster; they can produce 150 lines of copy a minute, while manual systems poke along at about 30 lines a minute. The biggest savings come from wire copy, which can be transmitted in the form of already punched tapes.

Union contracts with the many backshop employees whose jobs are threatened by cold type and automation have slowed the adoption of both technologies. But many smaller, nonunion papers have already abandoned the manual hot-type system, and the major metropolitan dailies are not far behind.

Even these innovations will soon be old-fashioned. Computers don't have to use punched tape; they can be taught to "read" the words themselves, right from the reporter's typewriter. The *Oakland Tribune* was the first metropolitan paper on the West Coast to convert to this "optical scanning" system. Karen Emerson, a veteran reporter in the *Tribune*'s Sunday department, describes the transition:

At the same time the aged linotype machines were being moved out of the composing room, brand new IBM Selectric II typewriters began appearing in the editorial department. This was in late 1972. At first we were using the machines only as we would have used our old manual typewriters. Then yellow copy paper gave way to a new kind of paper—white, square, and with red lines printed on it to mark borders.

At first we typed our stories on this new paper, made corrections in pencil and added -30- at the end, just as before. Slowly we became acquainted with the touch of the new machines. It was just about this time that a member of the production department began making rounds, first teaching the columnists how to use the special codes which "tell" the computer what type size and face are desired and at what measure it is to be set. Columnists began turning out the first copy to be scanned by the newly installed OCR (Optical Character Recognition) scanner.

By February 1973, each member of the editorial staff was coding and preparing copy for the scanner. Everyone had received a half-hour indoctrination with the production expert and a thick booklet with all coding information in it for quick referral. We were soon remembering that a single letter mistake could be omitted by a special symbol on one key. A black, felt-tip pen would delete whole words and no other correction would be necessary. And if an entire line of typing was not wanted, three special characters at the end of the line deleted the whole line. Our typing repertoire began including these symbols as a matter of course. . . .

Today, a reporter rushes to his typewriter, rolls in special high quality 20-pound bond paper with pre-attached carbons, and types out a coded story with a special carbon ribbon. Corrections are inserted with special coded keys by both reporter and editor. The copy desk adds a byline and headline (all coded with special numbers), and the story, which is pre-numbered at the top of the copy, is sent to the composing room.

Here it is set on the OCR scanner, which

reads the story at 110 characters per second and sends the appropriate impulses to the computer, which justifies the copy, hyphenates it and stores it in a memory bank until needed. The minute the story is complete in the computer, a Versatec copy is sent to the editorial department in which it originated, and another copy is sent to the Versatec machine in the composing room. . . .

In order to have the story set in cold type, it is necessary only to "call out" the story number on an I/O (Input/Output) typewriter which is in direct contact with the computer. When this occurs, an impulse is sent to a Fototronic TXT and the story is ejected as photographic copy, ready to be pasted onto a page form.

It is only a matter of minutes from the time copy reaches the OCR scanner that a finished piece of copy is available for proofreading. It is possible to make corrections even faster directly into the computer by "calling out" the story on a Video Display Terminal. This terminal (which resembles a television screen) displays the entire story. By means of a "cursor" corrections can be made directly into the computer.[32]

All this fancy technology is frightening—at first. Says Emerson: "Our first inevitable rejection of anything new is past. Now it is as easy as using normal copy paper, and a lot tidier. The tools of our trade are now as up-to-date as the news we print." [33] The next step for the *Tribune* will be "pagination," a system that permits editors to put together the whole newspaper automatically from pages displayed on a screen in the newsroom.

Computers have other uses as well—such as storing information where reporters (and others) can get at it easily. In 1969, the *New York Times* announced the start of the Times Information Bank. According to *Times* vice president Ivan Veit, this computerized information retrieval system permits "instantaneous accessibility of a gigantic store of background information on virtually every subject of human research and inquiry." [34]

The ultimate impact of computer technology might be the placing of a computer terminal in every home. Such a "home console" could make all the conventional mass media obsolete overnight. Readers could simply sit down at their terminals and request whatever they felt like—the latest news from South Africa, a rerun of last year's World Series, or the past three weeks of Dick Tracy. Should this actually happen, the newspaper industry will have to reorganize itself for the task of gathering news for the computer.

In the meantime, computer technology means better-looking newspapers, more late-breaking news in each issue, no jobs for linotypists—and higher profits for publishers. How those profits will be used remains to be seen. Technological advances can give us better newspapers, but they don't inevitably have to.

THE FUTURE

In the process of describing today's newspaper, we have already depicted some of the trends of the future, such as increasing specialization, monopolies, more personal and interpretive journalism, and new technologies. There are at least four other trends of importance:

1. Suburban newspapers.
2. Weekly newspapers.
3. Magazine-style layout.
4. New information sources.

We will consider these one at a time.

1. Suburban Newspapers. The migration of the middle class out of the central cities and into the surrounding suburbs has occasioned as much interest and concern by newspaper owners as by sociologists and urban planners. Metropolitan publishers watch uneasily as their traditional base for circulation and advertising—middle-class people and the stores that serve them—leaves town in ever-increasing numbers.

Big-city papers have tried to adapt to this

development by beefing up their suburban coverage. In New York, for example, both the *Times* and the *Daily News* have added special New Jersey sections. The *Philadelphia Inquirer* is focusing more on news of southern New Jersey and Delaware; the *St. Louis Post-Dispatch* publishes a supplement for outlying St. Charles County; the *Washington Post* and *Star-News* are spending more time and energy covering Maryland and Virginia. Some publishers have gone even further, physically leaving the cities whose names grace their mastheads. The *Post-Dispatch,* for example, has shifted two-thirds of its publishing facilities to the suburbs.[35]

This shift in emphasis comes, of course, at the expense of the people left in the inner city. The problems of urban people and urban government are no less urgent than they were a decade ago, but the effort to cultivate suburban readers and advertisers inevitably diminishes newspaper attention to those problems. It may not help the papers that much either. A suburban commuter may well continue reading a metropolitan paper along with the local one, but a suburban shopping center will usually confine its advertising to the local paper. The big beneficiaries of the flight to the suburbs, then, have been the suburban newspapers.

To protect their investments, many metropolitan publishers have taken to starting or buying their own suburban papers. In 1966, for example, Field Enterprises, publisher of the *Daily News* and *Sun-Times* in Chicago, founded a series of brand-new papers in the Chicago suburbs. The tactic failed because an existing chain of Chicago suburban weeklies, owned by the Paddock Corporation, fought off the new competition by improving its own product.[36] Buying a suburban paper often proves more profitable. The *New York Times* now derives a substantial percentage of its income from suburban newspapers in Florida.

Suburban papers vary tremendously in quality. Some hardly deserve to be called newspapers. Consider, for example, the *Van Nuys* (Calif.) *News and Green Sheet,* delivered free to 250,000 homes every Tuesday, Thursday, Friday, and Sunday. The paper generally runs 300 pages or more a week, up to 166 pages in a single issue—about four times as much as the average daily newspaper. Its content: page after page of ads from neighborhood stores and shopping centers, with just a sprinkling of local news and photographs.[37] Publications like the *News and Green Sheet* are called, appropriately enough, "shoppers." Whether mailed or hand-delivered, they usually earn handsome profits for their publishers.

On the other end of the scale, some suburban newspapers carry almost as much national and international news as their big-city cousins, justifying the claim that readers don't really need to buy another paper as well. *Newsday* on Long Island is often cited as one of the best newspapers to profit from the middle-class flight to the suburbs; its prize-winning staff frequently outdoes even the nearby *New York Times.*

But it doesn't take a superlative suburban newspaper to compete effectively with the metropolitan press. Many big cities today are surrounded by suburbs whose run-of-the-mill dailies outdraw the metro papers in local circulation. Suburbanites presumably buy the home-town paper for its local news and local ads. But if they find that the paper satisfies their appetite for national and international news as well, the metropolitan newspaper may soon seem superfluous.

2. Weekly Newspapers. In 1973, according to the National Newspaper Association, there were 7,641 weekly, semi-weekly, and tri-weekly newspapers in the U.S., more than four times the number of dailies. True, the list of weeklies is shorter today than the 1963 all-time high of 8,158. But it's on its way back up; there were 88 more weeklies in 1973 than in 1972. Perhaps more important, weekly circulation is climbing rapidly, up 9 percent in 1973 to a total of nearly 35 million copies.[38]

The typical small-town weekly is no longer a mom-and-pop operation, published on an antique press held together with spit and baling wire. That kind of weekly still exists too, but it is quickly giving way to more up-to-date competition. Consider, for example, the *Windsor-Hights Herald* (circulation 4,490), part of a seven-paper New Jersey chain of weeklies owned by the *Princeton Packet*. It's printed in an ultra-modern, air-conditioned plant, utilizing the most sophisticated electronic typesetting equipment. And most of its reporters are college graduates.[39]

Some weekly papers do an extraordinary job of local coverage. The *Naples* (Fla.) *Star,* for example, exposed the environmental destruction of mangrove-laden Black Island by a company owned in part by a powerful state senator.[40] The *Lexington Park* (Md.) *Enterprise* opened up almost an entire issue to a debate on whether an oil refinery should be built on the outskirts of town.[41] And the *Jefferson Reporter* in Kentucky printed a much-applauded 46-page Bicentennial Issue on the state's heritage, and a 43-page "Progress 1973" issue that examined what the community might be like in the year 2000.[42]

Despite salaries that seldom climb above $130 a week, weeklies offer an excellent opportunity for young journalists to sink their teeth into important stories, take pictures, do layout, and learn the newspaper business. Many weeklies employ just two or three reporters, plus the editor/owner. One staffer can have a significant impact.

The greatest virtue of the small-town weekly is summed up by Sam Dillon, who publishes one in Venice, Florida: "I think we're closer to the people, to the grass roots than the dailies," he says. "If somebody has a bone to pick with me then they can walk right in the door and here I am." [43] Try that with the publisher of a metropolitan daily some time.

The urban weekly, meanwhile, is growing every bit as fast as the small-town and suburban paper. Today, the typical big city supports several neighborhood weeklies (plus underground papers—see pp. 231–35). As just one example of what these papers can do,

the *Home Reporter and Sunset News* in Brooklyn waged a campaign against the Pennsylvania Railroad for not properly protecting the high-voltage lines in one of its yards, leading to the electrocution of eight children. The resulting community outrage forced the railroad to spend $200,000 to eliminate the danger.[44]

Many urban weeklies specialize in neighborhood news of bowling leagues, high school dances, and the like. But many others are anything but bland. The outspoken, muckraking metro weekly has become a feature of many cities. Such papers are havens for dissatisfied readers and reporters.

The *Detroit Inner City Voice,* for example, bills itself as "The Voice of Revolution" in the black ghetto. "It's funny," says assistant editor James Williams, "but when we started we wanted to have an objective paper with a hard militant editorial page. It didn't take us long to realize that that wouldn't work. People just don't read the editorial page in the paper. You have to put your editorials everywhere—in every article so they'll see it."[45] Williams and his colleagues are trying to tell the truth about the ghetto, which they believe the white press ignores or distorts. Their main problem—which they share with all anti-Establishment papers—is finding enough advertising to survive.

The *Pittsburgh Point* and the *San Francisco Bay Guardian* are examples of white urban weeklies. Both are latter-day muckrakers. They delight in exposing sacred cows —public utilities, grand juries, real estate developers, draft boards, and the like. Any story the established dailies won't touch is their kind of story. "We're not just accepted" by readers, says *Point* editor Charles Robb. "We're seized upon as a beacon of light. The paper has become important to them." [46]

3. Magazine-Style Layout. The typical newspaper ten years ago was already loaded with features and interpretive news stories. Although its content more closely resembled a magazine than a newspaper of fifty years ago, its layout was still modeled on the old "hard news" concept. There were eight columns on a page, and type usually was set in single columns, giving the paper a "vertical" look. Banner headlines were used to grab the reader's attention even if there was no big story to justify the fuss. As many as a dozen articles were squeezed onto the front page, scattergun fashion. Photos were most often one-column "mug shots" or splashy space-wasters.

In the early 1960s, the *New York Herald Tribune* (possibly influenced by the weekly *National Observer*) pioneered the move toward magazine-style newspaper layout—horizontal, simple, and neat. Stories were laid out in blocks, no more than four or five to the page. Headlines were lighter and more varied, with bold type saved for the truly important stories. White space, centered heads, and unusual column widths were used to suit the look of an article to its subject matter. In the last ten years, many newspapers have adopted these techniques, often moving to a six-column format. Almost certainly these are the newspaper design principles of the 1980s.

Photos, drawings, and color may be extensively used by the newspaper of the future to heighten the visual appeal of the page. The editors will no longer be forced to throw the front page together as they go along; instead, a layout specialist will be hired to design it each day. The inside pages, meanwhile, may become compartmentalized, like those of the weekly newsmagazines—Washington news on one page, police news on another, education news on a third. All in all, the newspaper of 1985 should be a great deal easier and more pleasant to read than that of 1975.

4. New Information Sources. Historically, newspapers have relied almost exclusively on four information sources: wire services, feature syndicates, press releases, and reporters. To a large extent that is still the case today—but it will not be tomorrow. Newspapers can be expected to make increasing use of the following sources:

1. Special-interest magazines.
2. Underground papers and news services.
3. Scientists, politicians, and other outside experts.
4. Books and libraries.
5. University research findings.
6. The newspaper's own morgue.

This expansion of horizons is essential if the newspaper is to meet the challenge of the new media. Newspapers must keep pace with the expanding consciousness of the American reader, or the American reader will find something else to read.

The typical daily newspaper in the mid-1970s is mildly entertaining—though not as

---

KEEPING UP WITH THE TUBE

The sports department of the *Miami Herald* has contrived a unique way to compete with live television broadcasts of sporting events. One staffer covers the game, while another watches it on TV. Afterwards, the two work out the best approach for the story, trying to come up with an angle that the sportscasters missed. Sometimes this means a special post-game interview; sometimes it involves a lengthy explanation of the fine points of a rule or a play. In any event, Miami fans get something in the *Herald* that wasn't on TV.[47]

Slowly but surely, the newspaper industry is shaping a new role for itself, in the face of up-to-the-second radio and TV coverage. Some day it may be standard practice for a news editor to monitor the newscasts, in a conscious effort to offer readers something they cannot get elsewhere.

entertaining as television. It is reasonably informative—though not as informative as many magazines. And it is a superlative vehicle for local advertising. Will that be a sufficient rationale for a mass medium in the 1980s?

Notes

1 "Readers of Papers Surveyed," *New York Times,* November 22, 1972, p. 46.

2 Leo Bogart, "Urban Papers Under Pressure," *Columbia Journalism Review,* September/October, 1974, p. 37.

3 Charles E. Swanson, "What They Read in 130 Daily Newspapers," *Journalism Quarterly,* Fall, 1955, p. 414.

4 "Sell the Papers!" *Harper's Monthly,* June, 1925, p. 5.

5 Chilton R. Bush, *News Research for Better Newspapers* (New York: American Newspaper Publishers Association Foundation, 1967), II, p. 18.

6 "What People Think of Television and Other Mass Media 1959–1972," Television Information Office, New York, May, 1973 (pamphlet).

7 American Newspaper Guild, "Collective Bargaining Manual 1," June, 1974.

8 Chilton R. Bush, *News Research for Better Newspapers* (New York: American Newspaper Publishers Association Foundation, 1968), III, pp. 80–82.

9 Theodore Dreiser, *A Book About Myself* (New York: Boni and Liveright, 1922), p. 396.

10 Richard Reeves, "A Media Monster—Who, Me?" *New York,* November 26, 1973, pp. 37–38.

11 William A. Sievert, "Watergate Floods the J-Schools," *Chronicle of Higher Education,* September 3, 1974.

12 Alvin E. Austin, "Codes, Documents, Declarations Affecting the Press," Department of Journalism, University of North Dakota, August, 1964, p. 17.

13 Sheldon Zalaznick, "The Evolution of a Pleasant Young Man," *New York,* May 6, 1974, pp. 30, 32–33.

14 John H. Colburn, "Economics of the Press," in *Proceedings: Education for Newspaper Journalists in the Seventies and Beyond* (Washington: American Newspaper Publishers Association Foundation, mimeo, 1973).

15 "Advertising: The Name Is News," *New York Times,* April 25, 1973, p. 55.

16 Ben H. Bagdikian, "The Little Old Lady of Dubuque," *New York Times Magazine,* February 3, 1974, pp. 14, 35.

17 Tony Brenna, "Grim Situation Faces Newspapers in Gt. Britain," *Editor & Publisher,* March 30, 1974, p. 52D.

18 "Many Newspapers in Europe on Verge of Going Bankrupt," *Editor & Publisher,* July 13, 1974, p. 18.

19 "Coast Papers Get Automation Pact," *New York Times,* January 21, 1973, p. 46. "Kheel Gives Details on Innovative Pact of Papers and Union," *New York Times,* May 25, 1974, p. 1. "City Papers on Threshold of Future As Result of 11-Year Automation Pact," *New York Times,* July 29, 1974, p. 12.

20 Ben H. Bagdikian, "Fat Newspapers and Slim Coverage," *Columbia Journalism Review,* September/October, 1973, pp. 15–20.

21 Galen Rarick and Barrie Hartman, "The Effects of Competition on One Daily Newspaper's Content," *Journalism Quarterly,* Autumn, 1966, pp. 461–62.

22 Raymond B. Nixon and Robert L. Jones, "The Content of Non-Competitive vs. Competitive Newspapers," *Journalism Quarterly,* Summer, 1956, pp. 299–306.

23 Stanley K. Bigman, "Rivals in Conformity: A Study of Two Competing Dailies," *Journalism Quarterly,* June, 1948, pp. 130–31.

24 A. J. Liebling, *The Press* (New York: Ballantine Books, 1961), p. 23.

25 John Corry, "The Los Angeles *Times,*" *Harper's Magazine,* December, 1969, pp. 75–81.

26 "Newspapers Blamed for Loss of Image," *Editor & Publisher,* April 5, 1969, p. 12.

27 *New York Times,* April 5, 1972, p. 52.

28 George L. Bird and Frederic E. Merwin, eds., *The Press and Society* (Englewood Cliffs, N.J.: Prentice-Hall, 1951), p. 74.

29 Charles T. Duncan, "The 'Education Beat' on 52 Major Newspapers," *Journalism Quarterly,* Summer, 1966, pp. 336–38.

30 Carla Marie Rupp, "Reporter Likes Writing '30' on Unfinished News Stories," *Editor & Publisher,* May 11, 1974, p. 11. "Follow-Up on the News," *New York Times,* February 24, 1974, p. 31.

31 "Newspapers Blamed for Loss of Image," p. 12.

32 Letter from Karen Emerson to David M. Rubin, August 6, 1974. Reprinted by permission.

33 *Ibid.*

34 "New York Times Develops Public Information Bank," *Editor & Publisher,* April 5, 1969, p. 9.

35 "Big-City Newspapers Stepping Up Their Coverage of News in Suburbs," *New York Times,* April 23, 1973, p. 36.

36 Carl M. Larson, "The Struggle of Paddock Pub-

lications Versus Field Enterprises, Inc.," *Journalism Quarterly,* Winter, 1971, pp. 700–706, 713.

37 Carroll W. Parcher, "Anatomy of the Suburban Newspaper Phenomenon," *ASNE Bulletin,* April 1, 1964, p. 4.

38 *Editor & Publisher,* March 16, 1974, p. 7.

39 Bill D. Ross, "Small-Town Weeklies of All Kinds Thriving," *New York Times,* September 23, 1973, p. NJ101.

40 Joseph Plummer, "Florida Weeklies Come On Strong," *Floridian,* May 26, 1974, pp. 20–23.

41 Margaret Cronin Fisk, "Weekly Editor—How to Serve Readers Without Taking Sides," *Editor & Publisher,* December 15, 1973, p. 15.

42 Philly Murtha, "Weekly Editor—Kentucky Weekly Features Bicentennial," *Editor & Publisher,* February 16, 1974, p. 18.

43 Plummer, "Florida Weeklies Come On Strong," p. 23.

44 Jack Deacy, "What the Big Dailies Don't Tell You About What's Going On in the City," *New York,* May 24, 1971, p. 42.

45 Roger M. Williams, "The Irrepressible Weeklies," *Columbia Journalism Review,* Summer, 1968, p. 31.

46 *Ibid.,* p. 33.

47 John Hohenberg, "The New Foreign Correspondence," *Saturday Review,* January 11, 1969, pp. 115–16.

Suggested Readings

ARGYRIS, CHRIS, *Behind The Front Page.* San Francisco: Jossey-Bass Publishers, 1974.

BABB, LAURA LONGLEY, ed., *Of the Press, By the Press, For the Press (and Others, Too).* New York: Dell, 1974.

BAGDIKIAN, BEN H., "Fat Newspapers and Slim Coverage," *Columbia Journalism Review,* September/October, 1973.

————, "The Little Old Lady of Dubuque," *New York Times Magazine,* February 3, 1974.

BOGART, LEO, "Urban Papers Under Pressure," *Columbia Journalism Review,* September/October, 1974.

CORRY, JOHN, "The Los Angeles *Times,*" *Harper's Magazine,* December, 1969.

DEACY, JACK, "What the Big Dailies Don't Tell You About What's Going On in the City," *New York,* May 24, 1971.

DENNIS, EVERETTE E., and WILLIAM L. RIVERS, *Other Voices: The New Journalism in America.* San Francisco: Canfield Press, 1974.

FURGURSON, ERNEST B., "Fire on the Mountain," *[MORE],* October, 1974.

LIEBLING, A. J., *The Press.* New York: Ballantine Books, 1961.

QUIMBY, THOMAS H. E., *Waste Newspapers.* Washington: Resources for the Future, 1973.

TALESE, GAY, *The Kingdom and the Power.* New York: World Publishing Co., 1969.

WILLIAMS, ROGER M., "The Irrepressible Weeklies," *Columbia Journalism Review,* Summer, 1968.

WOLFE, TOM, *The New Journalism.* New York: Harper & Row, 1973.

Chapter 11
Magazines and Books

The typical magazine of the past was a potpourri of features and fiction, aimed at a general audience. Television has now usurped that role, and successful magazines today are highly specialized. They are run by an editor and staff who know precisely who their readers and advertisers are. While some of these specialized magazines can still claim "mass" circulations, the future of the magazine industry clearly lies in providing a unique service to specialized audiences.

Caskie Stinnett, former editor of *Holiday* magazine, tells this story which he says "sums up the magazine business today." Stinnett was on a travel junket to Portugal with a number of other writers, including *Holiday* contributor Marc Connelly. At a reception for the mayor of Lisbon the visiting journalists were asked to stand and identify their magazines. Connelly announced that he represented *Popular Wading*, a journal for enthusiasts of shallow-water sports. It specialized, said Connelly, in medical articles, particularly the ravages of "immersion foot."

Comments Stinnett: "It was hilarious, and we were all howling. But you know, I don't think anyone would laugh today. In fact, I'll almost bet that somewhere out there, you could find a special-audience magazine for waders." [1]

GENERAL MAGAZINES

The term "magazine" comes from the French word *magasin,* meaning "storehouse." The earliest magazines were literally storehouses of sketches, poems, essays, and assorted other content. Their incredible diversity led journalism historian Frank Luther Mott to offer this definition of the magazine: "A bound pamphlet issued more or less regularly and containing a variety of reading matter." [2]

For more than two hundred years, the most general magazines were invariably the most popular, and the most profitable. The mass-circulation leaders in the late 1800s were the *Saturday Evening Post, Collier's, Leslie's,* and *Harper's Weekly. Collier's* and the *Post* continued into the twentieth century, and were joined by *McCall's, Life, Look,* and the *Reader's Digest.* All these magazines earned substantial profits from subscriptions and newsstand sales. Except for the *Digest,* they earned even more from advertising.

In 1929, the nation's 365 leading magazines had an average circulation of 94,836. By 1950, the 567 top magazines were averaging 223,581 readers apiece.[3] Magazine circulation—and magazine revenue—was at an all-time high.

Then came television. TV did comparatively little damage to the public's appetite for general magazines. But it devastated their appeal to advertisers. The largest magazines could offer a readership of merely a few million; a run-of-the-mill network series offered tens of millions of viewers. And television ads cost less too. In 1970, a minute of time on NBC's "Laugh-In" (with 17 million viewers) sold for $3.82 per thousand households. A full-page four-color ad in *Look* (with 7 million readers) ran $7.16 per thousand households. Nearly three times as many people watched NFL football as read *Life* magazine—yet both ads sold for the same amount, $64,200. Naturally, advertisers preferred "Laugh-In" to *Look,* NFL football to *Life.*

The mass magazines responded to the challenge of television by trying to build TV-size circulations. In the dozen years after 1950, both *McCall's* and *Look* doubled their readership. In 1960, the *Saturday Evening Post, Life, Look,* and the *Reader's Digest* proudly noted that a single ad in each of the four magazines would reach every other American 2.3 times.[4]

The technique for building circulation

DEATH OF THE POST

For 72 years the *Saturday Evening Post* was the flagship of the Curtis Publishing Company empire. It had a circulation of 6.8 million satisfied readers in 1968. Then it folded.

When Martin Ackerman became president of Curtis in 1968, the *Post* was deep in debt. Advertisers, it seems, simply were not interested in the *Post*'s rural readership and middle-American appeal. Ackerman's battle plan was simple and straightforward: stop fighting for circulation, cut back to three million readers, and turn the *Post* into "a high-class magazine for a class audience." The subscribers to be retained were those living in designated Nielsen A and B counties. These are television rating terms for the most affluent counties in America—the ones advertisers are most eager to reach.

Of the *Post*'s 6.8 million subscribers, 4.5 million lived in the Nielsen A and B areas. Ackerman instructed his computer to drop not only the 2.3 million C and D area people, but 1.5 million from the B areas as well—leaving him with a circulation of three million big spenders. *Life* agreed to purchase the extra B subscriptions. But no one was interested in the small-town C and D folks. Form letters went out, telling subscribers that the *Post* no longer wanted them. Among those so informed were Arkansas Governor Winthrop Rockefeller, former *Post* editor Ben Hibbs, and small-town boy Martin Ackerman.

In an effort to impress Madison Avenue, Ackerman spent a lot of money advertising the "new" *Post.* He prepared four dummy issues of the magazine to show off the planned "classy" approach. But advertisers were unconvinced. They doubted the magazine could slough off its rural image so easily. The *Post* earned millions of enemies in 1968, but very few new advertisers. It continued to lose upwards of $400,000 a month. Ackerman finally admitted defeat, and the *Saturday Evening Post* folded.

At the very end, a prosperous rock-and-roll group offered to buy the *Post* for $250,000 and turn it into a pop music magazine. The offer was refused.[5] Instead, the *Post* emerged under new management as a magazine for nostalgia fans. The lesson was clear: Pop music magazines and nostalgia magazines may have a future in this country. General-interest magazines don't.

was simple: offer cut-rate subscriptions at a price so low that it would be silly not to subscribe. Newsstand sales, naturally, declined. During World War II, *Life* and *Look* sold 55 percent of their copies at the newsstand price. By the mid-1960s, the number of newsstand sales had dropped to less than 10 percent. As the subscription price went down, production and distribution costs rose steadily. Some time in the late 1950s the two passed each other. It was now possible to subscribe to a magazine for less than the cost of printing it. Advertisers, of course, were expected to make up the difference.

They didn't. Take *Life* for example. In 1969, the magazine sold for an average of 12 cents per copy. But it cost 41 cents per copy to edit, print, and distribute. For *Life* to break even, advertisers had to cough up the remaining 29 cents per copy. At the start of 1970, ad revenues amounted to only 27 cents per copy. Every week *Life* was actually losing two cents on each copy sold.[6]

Over the next three years the situation went from bad to worse. Because of its low circulation rates, *Life* was forced to charge very high advertising rates—more than twice as much per household as TV (or *TV Guide*). Advertisers were unwilling to pay the premium, and so gross ad revenue dropped from its high of nearly $170 million in 1966 to $91 million in 1971.[7] Meanwhile, production and distribution costs were skyrocketing. Newsprint was a particularly big expense for the oversized magazine, and scheduled postal rate hikes would raise the cost of mailing by as much as 170 percent in five years.[8]

On December 29, 1972, *Life* published its last weekly issue. It will be remembered for such series as "The Picture History of Western Man," "The World's Great Religions," and "The World We Live In." The journalistic style it pioneered—a combination of tight writing and huge, effective photographs —set it apart from other magazines and exerted a tremendous influence on two generations of Americans. But *Life* could not compete with television.

It has taken nearly twenty years for the magazine industry to learn that it cannot beat television at the numbers game. In the process, such giants as *Life, Collier's, Coronet, Women's Home Companion, Look,* and the *Saturday Evening Post* have died. But magazines offer advertisers something that neither television nor any other medium can provide: a specialized national audience.

SPECIALIZED MAGAZINES

The special-interest magazine is nothing new. When film stars first captured the public's imagination, *Photoplay* was founded to cater to that interest. A new hobby in the 1930s gave rise to *Model Railroader;* a labor shortage in the 1940s led to *Jobs;* a sudden craze of the 1950s gave birth to *Skin Diver.* But the number of specialized magazines has increased dramatically in the past decade. *Writer's Market* is an annual magazine directory for free-lance writers; the 1973 edition listed 4,978 publications, including:

26 Animal magazines
10 Art magazines
14 Astrology and psychic magazines
41 Automotive and motorcycle magazines
12 Aviation magazines
12 Black magazines
37 Business and finance magazines
14 Confession magazines
11 Consumer service magazines

Writer's Market, of course, covers only the major magazines that regularly commission free-lance articles. The 1973 edition of the *Standard Periodical Directory* lists more than 62,000 periodicals in the U.S.—including 2,702 college and alumni publications, 2,274 corporate house organs, 2,105 religious magazines, 1,959 education journals, etc. Name any special interest and you will likely find a magazine devoted to it—even wading.

The specialized magazine is a perfect vehicle for advertising. It offers advertisers a chance at a hand-picked audience. Suppose, for example, that you were a manufacturer of low-calorie foods. If you could afford it, you'd probably advertise on television and in the newspapers. But despite the higher cost per thousand readers, you certainly wouldn't miss a chance to take out an ad in *Weight Watchers Magazine*. The average reader of that publication is far more likely to be interested in your product (and hence your ad) than the average newspaper reader or TV viewer.

Some magazines earn so much money from advertising that they don't even need to sell copies; they give them away instead. This is most common among trade journals. A magazine for plastics manufacturers, for example, is well-advised to send a free copy to every plastics manufacturer in the country. That makes it a superlative advertising vehicle for companies that produce the sorts of supplies and equipment plastics manufacturers use. Aside from trade publications, free-circulation magazines include the *American Legion Magazine, Scouting, Today's Education, Signature* (for Diner's Club members), *TWA Ambassador,* and *Nation's Business.*

MS. MAKES MONEY

A publication devoted to the concerns of 52 percent of the American people shouldn't really be called a "special-interest magazine." But Ms. isn't for all women, only for those who want to read a monthly about feminist issues and feminist culture. When the magazine was founded in 1971, many male publishers predicted it wouldn't find enough readers of that sort to survive. They were wrong.

In early 1971, explains feminist writer Jane O'Reilly, "some women writers, editors and activists began to meet with Gloria Steinem [a leading feminist and an editor of Ms.] to discuss some Working Truths we all shared. The media consistently distort and trivialize the women's movement. Women need a magazine which addresses itself directly to the way they are actually living and the things they really care about. Women need a publication which will put them in touch with each other about the great changes going on. The magazine must be controlled and created by women." [9]

Support came slowly—but it came. Katherine Graham, publisher of the *Washington Post,* invested $20,000 to start the ball rolling. Warner Communications offered $1 million in exchange for 25 percent of the stock; the women who run the magazine accepted the financing but retained a majority interest. By September of 1973, after only sixteen monthly issues, Ms. had built a paid circulation of 350,000, with a phenomenal subscription renewal rate of 70 percent. Readers were bombarding its offices in New York City with hundreds of telephone calls a day, a thousand letters a week, and 1,500 unsolicited manuscripts a month.[10] Ms. had become not just a successful magazine, but a national clearinghouse for feminist information.

Ms. readers are relatively high in education and income, and are thus very attractive to advertisers—even though the magazine refuses all ads that portray a clichéd or belittling stereotype of women. In October, 1972, Ms. earned $47,600 in ad revenue; one year later the month's figure was $99,000.[11] The magazine's success has financed a nonprofit feminist foundation and several very profitable sidelines, including Ms. tee shirts, a record and TV show entitled "Free to Be . . . You and Me," and an anthology of the best Ms. articles.[12]

Free-circulation magazines almost always have a "controlled" readership; only certain people are permitted to receive them. Sometimes the readership is made up of members of an organization. Sometimes it is a captive audience like airplane passengers. But usually the major common ground of a free magazine's readers is that they are a ready market for some specialized group of advertisers. Sometimes the editorial content of such a magazine is quite weak. It is read for its ads.

But specialized magazines don't appeal to advertisers alone. They attract readers as well—readers who are willing to pay high subscription prices for just the right magazine. Martin Gross, then editor and publisher of the *Intellectual Digest,* predicted in 1970 that in the next few years "you'll see more and more magazines supported almost totally by circulation. This has to come with the trend toward specialized reading and a stronger reader commitment." [13]

There are thus two ways for a specialized magazine to earn a profit. By offering advertisers just the right market for their products and services, it can justify high advertising rates. By offering readers editorial content that is tailored to match their interests, it can justify high subscription rates. Many of the most successful specialized magazines are able to make money from both advertisers and readers.

One advertising executive summarized the trend in 1970: "Don't look at it like a mass medium. Look at it like a medium that is catering to special interests. I think there is a whole new way to use print that we are not using today. And I think that's the challenge of the Seventies." [14]

SURVIVAL IN THE SEVENTIES

The death of *Life* proved that general magazines cannot compete with television as an advertising vehicle for mass audiences. What can mass-circulation magazines do,

then, to survive and prosper in an age of magazine specialization?

First of all, they can specialize too. The *Reader's Digest* covers dozens of topics in each issue, but its treatment and style are designed with the busy business executive in mind. Similarly, *Playboy* is aimed at young, urban males with money to spend; *Seventeen* appeals to teenage girls with fashion on their minds; *TV Guide* combines a list of the week's shows with behind-the-scenes articles and interviews. *Family Circle, Woman's Day, Cosmopolitan, Ms.,* and *Playgirl* are all magazines expressly for women, but they are for different sorts of women. Each magazine attempts to carve out its own unique appeal. Instead of trying to be minimally interesting to just about everyone, it struggles to be absolutely essential to a particular group. The appropriate readers will thus pay more for the magazine, and the appropriate advertisers will pay more to reach those readers. None of these magazines is as specialized as, say, *Field and Stream* or *Coin World*. But all are a good deal more specialized than *Life*—which is why they are still alive.

Some are immensely profitable. Consider, for example, *Sunset,* which offers recipes, gardening help, and the like to more than a million West Coast households. From 1969 to 1975, *Sunset* has averaged more than 200 pages per issue, with more regional advertising in its four editions than any other major magazine. In 1972, and again in 1974, the company grossed about $25 million,[15] more than 10 percent of which was profit. The *New Yorker* is a very different magazine—urbane, sophisticated, strictly Eastern. With a circulation of less than half a million, it showed a net profit of $1.3 million in 1973. Comments one Madison Avenue executive: "Their salesmen do not see you, they grant you an audience; their advertising departments do not sell advertising, they accept it." [16]

Mass-circulation magazines can specialize in another way as well—by dividing their readers into demographic categories and selling ads by the category. To attract advertisers of luxury products, for example, *McCall's* and *Better Homes and Gardens* publish special zip-coded editions for high-income areas. *Time* has a college student edition, a doctor's edition, an educator's edition, etc., for advertisers interested in reaching these particular audiences. When the *Reader's Digest* started its special edition for readers earning more than $15,000 a year, it charged $11.25 per thousand copies for an ad, versus $3.33 per thousand for the *Digest's* regular edition. Editorial content in these demographic editions is usually identical; only the ads are different.

This tactic can earn a mass magazine a good deal of extra income. But in the long run, it does nothing to rid the magazine of its unwealthy, unspecialized readers—the ones advertisers would rather reach on television, not in print. The only real solution is to force these readers to pay the full cost of the magazine. And so cut-rate subscriptions have pretty much disappeared, and annual subscription costs have soared. Inevitably the less rich and less interested readers drop their subscriptions. This leaves the publisher with a smaller number of readers who are paying more for the magazine, and who—since they have more money—are more attractive to advertisers as well.

For many comparatively general magazines, the move away from cut-rate subscriptions has meant a move away from subscriptions altogether. As the gap between

THE COST OF MAILING

Though general magazines may manage to trade their subscriptions for over-the-counter sales, specialized publications can't. Newsstands and supermarkets value their shelf space too highly to handle a magazine with only a dozen interested readers in town. Such a magazine *must* use the mails.

In the past, the government has always indirectly subsidized the magazine and newspaper industries by means of the inexpensive second-class mailing rate. But since its reorganization in 1971, the U.S. Postal Service has tried to reduce its deficit by making all mailers—including magazines—pay the real cost of delivery. In 1972, the Postal Service proposed a series of rate hikes that would nearly double the postage bills of many magazines over a five-year period. For example, *Newsweek* would face a jump from $6.2 million to $11.7 million;[17] the cost to *Saturday Review/World* would rise from $500,000 to $980,000.[18]

In response, many magazines reduced their page size or switched to a lighter paper (since second-class rates are based on weight). Many more joined an industrywide lobbying campaign to convince Congress that it should roll back the proposed increases. Particular attention was focused on the plight of the money-losing political journals, such as the *New Republic* and *National Review,* which might not be able to survive the new rates. In some quarters the death of *Life* was attributed to the increase, though postage was only a small part of that magazine's problems.

In 1974, Congress agreed to spread the increase out over a greater number of years than the Postal Service had proposed. That lessened the immediate burden, but not the long-term problem. The days of bargain postal rates are over for the magazine industry. Government subsidies are on their way out, and subscribers will have to take up the financial slack. So far no major magazine has been put out of business by the Postal Service alone. But many small magazines are hurting, and no one knows how many publications may never start because of the higher cost of mail distribution.

the subscription price and the newsstand price has narrowed, more and more readers have chosen to buy their favorite magazines —when they feel like it—at the store. For such magazines as *TV Guide,* the *Reader's Digest, Family Circle,* and *Woman's Day,* supermarket and drugstore sales have proved even more successful than newsstands. The stores like this trend because the commissions are high—four cents, for example, on each fifteen-cent *TV Guide.*[19] And the publishers like it because they save on overhead and simplify distribution. In 1974, roughly 60 percent of all retail magazine sales were at chain stores.[20]

As postal rates continue to climb, magazine circulation will inevitably move from the mails to the chain-store racks. Highly specialized magazines will still have to rely on mail subscriptions, but the more general ones may well abandon the postal system just as they have abandoned the cut-rate subscription. The change is striking. In 1972, only 4 percent of *Life*'s readers paid the cover price at the newsstands; in 1973, 80 percent of *Playboy*'s readers did precisely that.[21]

THE EDITOR

Once upon a time, a strong-willed would-be editor started a newspaper. Today, he or she is far more likely to start a magazine.

Why? For one thing, the magazine industry is extremely fluid. Of the twenty most profitable magazines in 1927, half were gone by 1950. Of the top twenty magazines in 1962, fifteen were not yet founded in 1920.[22] It is possible, in other words, to start a magazine today and be an instant success tomorrow. Even more important, the specialization of magazines allows plenty of running room for editors with unusual ideas. One newspaper is pretty much like another; it has to try to appeal to all the readers in town. A magazine, on the other hand, can

aim at attracting a small, devoted readership of people who think like the editor.

Magazines, notes Clay Felker (himself editor of the highly successful *New York* magazine), are "peculiarly and stubbornly personal products." [23] *Time, Life,* and *Fortune* were the vision of Henry R. Luce. *Playboy* is Hugh Hefner. Arnold Gingrich guided *Esquire* to popularity; Helen Gurley Brown made a winner of *Cosmopolitan;* Robert Peterson did the same with *Hot Rod.* It is hard to think of a successful magazine that is not the reflection of one person. Historian James Playsted Wood writes:

> A strong editor, even a strongly wrongheaded editor, has usually meant a strong and influential magazine; whereas intelligent editors of moderate means and no firm opinions have often produced colorless and comparatively ineffective magazines.[24]

Perhaps, as Roland E. Wolseley claims, this is no longer true of many comparatively general magazines, whose voices tend to be "institutional rather than individual." [25] But most of the outstanding specialized magazines—the ones that attract and hold readers who are willing to pay for what they get—are the work of a single mind.

They almost have to be. The typical magazine staff is much, much smaller than its readers imagine. Take *Wastes Engineering,* for example, a successful monthly for the sanitation industry. It has one editor, one associate editor, one managing editor, one editorial assistant, and one part-time editorial consultant. It also has an eighteen-person editorial advisory board to read and comment on articles—but they work only a few hours a month. Obviously the editor of *Wastes Engineering* has a chance to give personal attention to every word in the magazine.

Magazines are written by staff writers, free-lance writers, or some combination of the two. Staff writers, of course, work on salary. Free-lancers are paid by the article, at rates ranging from $20 an article all the way up to $3,000 an article. While there are perhaps 25,000 writers in the country who consider themselves free-lancers, most work only part-time. Fewer than 300 of them earn $10,000 a year or more from their writing.[26] The same hard core of a few dozen free-lancers does 90 percent of the writing in all the top-paying publications.

Each article begins with an assignment. Free-lancers usually think up their own topics, then "query" various magazines to see who's interested. Staff writers, of course, are often told what to write. Either way, one editor is always responsible for approving the topic, the research approach, and the finished manuscript. On most magazines the top editor does this for every article. Some of the larger and more decentralized magazines have department editors for the job. *Better Homes and Gardens,* for example, has twelve of them: residential building, foods, furnishings and decorations, gardens and landscaping, kitchens and equipment, money management, family cars, home entertainment, family health, travel, sewing and crafts, and education.

Once a manuscript is approved, it goes to a copy editor for the finishing touches. At the same time, a copy is sent to the art department, which begins work on drawings, photographs, and other illustrations. The art director and the managing editor rough out an approximate layout, then tell the production editor to prepare the article for the printer. The printer sends back galley proofs. A proofreader checks these for errors, while the production editor cuts and pastes them into a "dummy" of the magazine. The printer uses the dummies to prepare a set of page proofs, a one-color version of the magazine. After final adjustments are made on the page proofs, color proofs are prepared and checked. Finally, the magazine is okayed for printing.

All this takes time. When necessary (as for a weekly magazine), the entire process is squeezed into a single week of frenzied activity. The average monthly, though, takes about ninety days to process an article from accepted manuscript to printed copies. And still the activity can be frenzied.

THE NEWSMAGAZINES

The most influential magazines in the United States are probably the three newsweeklies: *Time, Newsweek,* and *U.S. News and World Report.* For 7.5 million readers, these three magazines are a vital source of news. They share three important characteristics: (1) Brevity—the week's news is compressed into as few pages as possible; (2) Subjectivity—fact, opinion, and colorful adjectives are blended together into a slick, highly readable puree; and (3) Group journalism—dozens of researchers, writers, and editors collaborate on each major article.

The oldest and most successful of the three newsweeklies is *Time,* founded by Henry R. Luce in 1922. In his biography of Luce, John Kobler describes the preparation of a single *Time* cover story. The following narrative is adapted from Kobler's account.[27]

On November 1, 1963, South Vietnam's General Duong Van Minh staged a successful *coup d'état* against President Ngo Dinh Diem and his regime. It was a Friday morning. *Time* managing editor Otto Fuerbringer immediately decided to substitute the coup for the planned cover story on Calvin Gross, superintendent of the New York City public schools.

The previous Tuesday, the senior foreign news editor had begun the week by selecting a dozen stories for his section, based on suggestions from 260 correspondents in 30 bureaus. Writer Edward Hughes was assigned two of them—one on Italian politics, the other on an army coup in Dahomey. He was also assigned a research assistant for each article. The researchers (there were 78 of them) quickly began combing *Time*'s mas-

The success of American newsmagazines has spawned a raft of imitators around the world—*Tiempo* in Mexico, *Akis* in Turkey, *L'Express* in France, *Shukan Asahi* in Japan, *Elseviers Weekblad* in the Netherlands, *Link* in India, etc. Probably the most controversial of the world's newsmagazines is *Der Spiegel*, published in Hamburg, West Germany, by Rudolf Augstein.

Founded in 1946 under a different title, *Der Spiegel* is obviously patterned after *Time*; it uses the same format, the same editorial style, and the same departmentalized structure. But its content is a great deal spicier, "deliberately aggressive" in the words of one former editor.[28] This aggressiveness is one source of *Der Spiegel*'s success, but it's also a source of frequent controversy. In 1962, for example, the magazine accused West German Defense Minister Franz Josef Strauss of inefficiency, and published some allegedly classified documents to bolster the charge. In retaliation, the government raided the magazine's office and arrested publisher Augstein on suspicion of treason. The public outcry that followed led to Strauss's resignation. And *Der Spiegel* continued its editorial policy of picking a fight whenever possible.

sive files on 225,000 individuals and 100,000 subjects. In addition, Hughes asked them to interview certain local sources by phone. *Time*'s foreign bureau chiefs, meanwhile, were busy questioning sources at the scene, and cabling their findings to Hughes.

On Thursday Hughes was handed two new assignments, U.S. troop withdrawal from West Germany and sabotage in South Africa. The Italian story was just about done; the Dahomey piece was given to another writer. In three hours, Hughes whipped off the short sabotage article (it never ran) and went home, saving Germany for Friday.

But on Friday, with 36 hours till press time, Fuerbringer ordered Hughes to drop everything and do the cover story on the Vietnam coup. Working with him was Margaret Boeth. Boeth spent the day in the *Time* Vietnam files. She put together a folder on recent Vietnamese political history, the biographies of the coup principals, and other relevant information—circling the most important items as she went along.

An unending series of cables began to pour into the *Time* offices in New York. A Saigon correspondent (who had witnessed the coup flat on his belly on a rooftop) sent in a 10,000-word dispatch. Reporters in Hong Kong interviewed Vietnamese who had fled the country in the wake of the coup. The Los Angeles bureau forwarded the comments of the touring Madame Nhu, while the Washington bureau described the reaction at the White House. A picture editor assembled a portfolio of appropriate photographs, from which Fuerbringer chose seven to illustrate the text. A staff cartographer prepared a map of Saigon showing the main events of the coup. At a cost of $7,000 the cover portrait of Calvin Gross was dumped, and by 10:30 that evening the Chicago printing plant (one of six around the country) had already engraved the new cover of General Minh.

As Hughes began to write, Fuerbringer and the foreign news editor bombarded him with suggestions—quotes to use, points to emphasize, phrases to work in. Hughes worked until midnight Friday; a rented *Time* Cadillac took him home.

Saturday morning he was back at his desk. New developments had to be worked in (Diem had been assassinated overnight). So did new suggestions from Fuerbringer and others. It was 8:30 Saturday night when Hughes ripped the last page of copy from his typewriter.

Now Margaret Boeth got back to work. She

methodically checked Hughes' article against her files, putting a dot over each word to show that it had been verified. Some items she couldn't verify, and questions were phoned or cabled to correspondents on the scene. Boeth argued with Hughes over the color of a Vietnamese cathedral, the source of a quote, the number of Buddhist monks who had burned themselves to death. The two debated whether or not the streets of Saigon were really "tree-lined" as Hughes had claimed. Once these battles were settled, the copy went to the foreign news editor, and then to Fuerbringer. Both requested insertions, deletions, and further checking before they would initial the article.

At 12:30 A.M. Sunday, the corrected story was given to a copy reader, who checked it for infractions of grammar, syntax, and "*Time* style." Then back to the foreign news editor for a final look before going to the printer. Hughes followed the story to the printer, indicating where cuts could be made to fit the available space. At dawn on Monday, the Chicago plant confirmed that the article was ready to go. Hughes went home.

Tuesday morning the magazine was on the stands, and Hughes attended the weekly assignment conference. He was given two stories. . . .

IMPACT

There is no doubt that magazines have far less impact on American society than either broadcasting or newspapers. It wasn't always that way. Throughout the eighteenth and nineteenth centuries, magazines were the nation's most important entertainment medium. Nearly all the great American authors published their novels in serial form first. And the muckraking magazines of the early twentieth century did much to revolutionize our system of government. The January, 1903 issue of *McClure's,* for example, contained three articles of lasting importance: Ida Tarbell on "The History of the Standard Oil Company," Lincoln Steffens on "The Shame of Minneapolis," and Ray Stannard Baker on "The Right to Work." These articles dealt with serious issues—monopoly, corruption, labor.

Today, the market for magazine fiction is reduced to three or four major publications and a host of tiny literary quarterlies. As for muckraking, that kind of writing can now be found most frequently in unprofitable magazines with small circulations and little influence on the general public.

Yet magazines are not unimportant. They offer three unique services:

First, magazines are the only mass medium that is both timely and permanent, quick and deep. Television and newspapers take only hours to report a story, but they can report it only briefly. And neither is customarily saved or savored. Books, of course, offer the maximum depth and permanence—but books take years to produce and seldom circulate more than a few thousand copies. Magazines are the ideal compromise.

Second, magazines are national. So is television, of course—but television is sketchy, impermanent, and devoted almost entirely to light entertainment. The "American perspective" on everything from theater to politics to underarm deodorants is molded largely by magazines. When a serious writer wants to say something, and wants to say it to the whole country, he or she says it in a magazine.

Third, magazines are specialized. If you want to know what's on television, you read *TV Guide.* If you want to know what explorers and anthropologists are doing, you read the *National Geographic.* If you want help repairing your car or building a stereo, you read *Popular Mechanics.* If you want to know where it's at in rock music, you read *Rolling Stone.* It is only in magazines that writers and advertisers can reach precisely those readers most interested in what they have to say.

The demise of magazines has been predicted many times—in the 1910s with the automobile, in the 1920s with radio, in the 1930s with movies, in the 1950s with television. Each time the prediction proved wrong. Magazines have changed greatly over the years, but they have survived, even flourished. They will continue to change, and survive, and flourish.

As a mass medium, the book is a failure. Once they finish their schooling, most Americans have very little to do with books. And when they do read a book, they almost always choose a mass-market paperback, the lightest of light entertainment. Except for fiction, it is relatively easy to get a book published, and thus exercise some influence over the "reading public." But the general public remains untouched.

BREAKDOWN

The book is the basis for our system of education and the repository of our culture. It is through books that the young learn what they have to learn and the wise teach what they have to teach. To those who are literate, books offer a permanent record of the best and worst in American civilization—and all other civilizations.

The offer is often ignored. The average American reads very few books after leaving school. And the books that do get read have very little to say (except by example) about American civilization or any other. Of course there are books that have changed the world—Harriet Beecher Stowe's *Uncle Tom's Cabin,* for example, or Charles Darwin's *Origin of the Species.* But they did it indirectly. Fewer people have read these two since they were published than the number who watched network television last night. In the long run, books may well be the most important of the mass media. But in the everyday life of the average citizen, they are by far the least influential.

The best way to understand book publishing is to look at the kinds of books that are published every year. The following table shows the 1973 total sales volume for each kind of book produced in the U.S.[29]

Educational Books

Primary and secondary textbooks	$ 547,900,000
College textbooks	392,200,000
Standardized textbooks	28,800,000
University press books	42,600,000
Subscription reference books	262,200,000
Technical and scientific books	138,400,000
Business and professional books	206,200,000
Medical books	60,800,000

General Books

Mass-market paperbacks	$ 285,900,000
Trade paperbacks	86,700,000
Book-club books	262,400,000
Mail-order books	221,200,000
Religious books	124,700,000
Juvenile books	108,600,000
Trade hardbacks	264,800,000
Other books	164,200,000
Total	$3,197,600,000

Some of these categories deserve amplification.

Educational Books. It is obvious from the table that educational books—especially textbooks—are one of the biggest segments of the book publishing industry. Educational books account for more than half of total sales dollars. Textbooks alone account for more than 30 percent of total sales. Of course textbooks and other educational books have always been an important part of the publishing business, but they came to dominate the business in the 1950s and 1960s, as war babies reached school age and higher education expanded enormously. In the mid-1970s their dominance started a slow decline, mirroring the slowdown in college enrollment and the efforts of public school systems to save money wherever possible. But for the foreseeable future, educational publishing will remain a mainstay of the industry.

Needless to say, textbooks are read only by students. University press books and reference books circulate mostly to libraries and specialists. Technical, scientific, business, professional, and medical books are reserved for specialists in these various fields. If you are interested in the effects of books on the average American adult, you must forget about this category.

Paperbacks. Much has been written about the "paperback revolution," and most of it is wrong. For one thing, paperbacks are not a recent invention. As early as 1840, many newspapers earned money on the side by printing paperback "extras" of popular novels. Hardcover publishers did the same thing in the 1870s, specializing in pirated editions of the English classics. They soon ran out of classics, and the International Copyright Law of 1891 put most of the paperback publishers out of business.

They started again in the 1930s. By this time the economics of the industry were clear. Cheap paper-bound books could earn money only if they were published and sold in enormous quantities. In 1939, Robert F. deGraff decided to market his Pocket Book series through newsstands and chain stores instead of bookstores. That year he published thirty-four titles in all, selling 1,508,000 copies. The mass-market paperback was born.

The main difference between mass-market paperbacks and "trade" paperbacks is quantity. Trade paperbacks are printed in lots of ten or twenty thousand. They are usually about the same size as hardcover books, and are sold mostly through the nation's 800 full-fledged bookstores and 8,000 variety and stationery stores with substantial book departments. The average price for a trade paperback is now at least three dollars. Mass-market paperbacks, on the other hand, are printed in lots of 200,000 or more. They are usually pocket-size, and are designed to sell for $1.50 or so in drugstores and supermarkets—a total of nearly 100,000 outlets throughout the United States.

In 1973, mass-market paperbacks accounted for $285,900,000 in book sales. This represented a jump of more than 13 percent over the 1972 figure, the greatest increase for any category of books. Trade paperbacks showed a total 1973 volume of $86,700,000—up a respectable 8.9 percent over the 1972 figure. As hardcover books get more and more expensive, paperbacks—especially mass-market paperbacks—will probably continue to grow in importance.

But remember, mass-market paperbacks are cheap. They sell a lot of copies, but don't earn all that much money per copy. By the time a publisher is through buying reprint rights and paying wholesalers and distributors, a book has to sell a lot of copies to earn anything at all. Less than 9 percent of total book sales in 1973 came from mass-market paperbacks; less than 3 percent came from trade paperbacks. The percentage of total profits falling into these two categories was smaller still. Contrary to popular opinion, paperbacks do not dominate the book business—at least not from the publisher's point of view.

The reader's point of view is another story. Textbooks aside, more than two-fifths of all the books in the country are paperbacks. The average nonstudent seldom if ever reads a hardcover book.

Book-Club Books. The Book-of-the-Month Club was founded in 1926. Members were notified of each month's selection a few weeks in advance; they had the option of turning it down or buying it by default. In some fifty years of operation, the system hasn't changed a bit. The only difference is the number of clubs. Today one may join travel book clubs, mystery book clubs, psychology book clubs, feminism book clubs, environment book clubs, and even pornographic book clubs. The 1973 gross income of all the clubs was $262 million, up more than 9 percent from the year before.

Publishers initially feared that book clubs would hurt bookstore sales. They had the same fear about paperbacks—but neither has proved justified. Cass Canfield of Harper & Row notes that "club mail-order operations have created hundreds of thousands of new book-buyers in areas where booksellers are scarce or nonexistent." [30]

Trade Hardbacks. When most people hear the word "book," they immediately think of the trade hardback—the kind of book you find in libraries and bookstores. Most of the nearly 40,000 new titles published in the United States every year are trade hardbacks. Aside from some 3,000 to 4,000 novels, most trade hardbacks are devoted to information—agriculture, art, biography, business, etc.

Trade hardbacks offer a wealth of culture, information, and entertainment to those who read them. Very few people read them. Fewer than 5 percent of all trade hardbacks sell more than 5,000 copies before they go out of print. Americans buy fewer than 50 million hardcover trade books a year. That's less than one book for every four people in the country.

PUBLISHERS

Despite the limited appetite of most readers, book publishing is a profitable industry. In the period from 1963 to 1973, that industry set some enviable records. Total sales rose from $1.7 billion to nearly $3.2 billion. The total number of books in print

---

THE MAKING OF A BESTSELLER

Blockbuster bestsellers are important to publishers not just for the profits they earn but also for the prestige they bring. In order to attract the sorts of authors whose books are likely to sell well, publishers need a reputation for knowing how to turn a run-of-the-mill good book into a bestseller. The formula for accomplishing this task is complex, elusive, and ever-changing. But it can be done.

One book for which it *was* done is *Jaws,* a first novel by Peter Benchley about a great white shark that terrorizes a small Long Island town. The book is fun to read. But Doubleday, its publisher, built it into a million-dollar 1974 bestseller through skill and promotion. In an article in the *New York Times Sunday Magazine,* veteran free-lance journalist Ted Morgan described how.[31]

Tom Congdon, then a Doubleday senior editor, had admired some magazine pieces by Benchley and invited him to lunch to discuss possible book ideas. Congdon asked him if he had considered writing fiction. Benchley, an expert on the habits of sharks, said he had been toying with the idea of a story about a shark that attacks a resort town. Congdon liked the idea because it combined two important elements of a bestseller—the public's fascination with the mysterious (in this case, sharks) and the concept of a community trying to cope with disaster. He asked Benchley to prepare a one-page outline.

Congdon whipped up some enthusiasm for the project at Doubleday, and wrangled permission to give Benchley a $1,000 advance on the first four chapters. When the chapters came, Congdon was a little disappointed. He and others at Doubleday liked the shark scenes and the sense of menace in the opening pages, but they thought that Benchley's characters were weak and his plot was too predictable. Scores of suggestions were made for tinkering with the incomplete novel. Unlike many authors in similar positions, Benchley willingly accepted most of them.

Nine months after that first lunch, Doubleday offered Benchley a $7,500 advance on the book.

Once the manuscript was completed, the search for a title began. Some 237 different ones were tried, including *The Summer of the Shark* and *The Jaws of the Leviathan.* Benchley himself suggested *Jaws*—simple and powerful and frightening, and attractive on a book jacket. The jacket was also troublesome; should they put a shark on the cover, or just a pair of jaws, or a shark plus a swimmer, or a shark plus a town, or (and selling well enough to stay in print) climbed from 163,000 to 398,000. The number of new books each year increased by 49 percent to 39,591 titles in 1973, while the selling price of the average new book went up 42 percent.[32] Many of the "name" publishing houses—Macmillan, Random House, Doubleday, Simon & Schuster, etc.—acquired new subsidiaries or were themselves acquired by profit-seeking conglomerates. The price of their stocks and the size of their operations soared. It was a good decade.

This sort of glamor came as something of a surprise to the publishing business, which has traditionally been extremely conservative. Bestsellers are the flashy part of the business, but they're also the chancy part. Twenty companies said no to Thomas Wolfe before an editor at Scribner's saw potential in *Look Homeward, Angel*. No one believed that Jacques-Yves Cousteau's *The Silent World* or George Plimpton's *Paper Lion* would earn millions. For every bestseller that made it, there's a potential bestseller that flopped despite heavy promotion. One balances the other, and bestsellers wind up responsible

---

what? Doubleday wanted to be sure readers would know that the book was about a menacing monster of a fish, not dentistry or deep-sea fishing.

Meanwhile, the subsidiary rights department at Doubleday sent the manuscript out to paperback publishers for bids. Bantam was the first to respond, bidding $200,000 (of which Benchley would get half) for the paperback rights. This was more than Doubleday had expected, but instead of accepting the offer, it sent the manuscript around to some other paperback houses, and then held an "auction." Bantam was given a chance to top the highest bid, which it did—paying $575,000 for the rights. With that as a start, Doubleday was able to get $150,000 more for the movie rights, plus $85,000 from book clubs.

Even before *Jaws* was published, in other words, Benchley and Doubleday were guaranteed a successful book. But it was still important to make the hardcover edition a bestseller—to keep the paperback and movie people happy, to make Benchley a "name" so that his second and third books would also succeed, and of course to make some extra money from hardcover sales. To this end, Congdon worked to convince Doubleday's sales staff of the marketability of the book. This was essential and by no means automatic. Doubleday publishes 700 trade books a year, and a salesperson can push only so many titles at the bookstores.

To aid in the effort, Doubleday publicists mentioned the book enthusiastically to reviewers over lunch. (Congdon thought about sending a free shark's tooth to each reviewer, but the teeth proved too scarce.) Blurbs—admiring quotes about the book—were secured from other Doubleday authors for use in the advertising campaign, on which Doubleday spent more than $50,000—a huge sum for a book. Benchley toured the country plugging *Jaws* in every city, and was fortunate enough to get an invitation to NBC's "Today" show, a prime showcase for authors.

It all paid off. *Jaws* quickly sold 40,000 of its first 75,000 copies and landed on the *New York Times* bestseller list, where it remained for many weeks. Benchley estimated that his total earnings from the book would come to more than $600,000, enough to permit him to write for many years without worrying about money. He quickly began work on his second novel for Doubleday.

Benchley's second book will certainly get the sort of bestseller build-up that worked so well for his first. But next time it may not work. Each book is a gamble and the public's fancy is notoriously fickle. Expert promotion does not guarantee a blockbuster. But as Peter Benchley would be glad to tell you, it helps.

---

for only a small part of publishing profits. Most of the money is made on textbooks, children's books, reference books, and run-of-the-mill trade books and paperbacks. The income of a publishing company is determined largely by its "backlist"—the number of books that achieve small but steady sales year after year.

The "typical book," remember, is a trade hardback. An editor reads the manuscript and guesses that it might sell 5,000 copies or so, at $7 a copy. Adding up the expenses of printing, distribution, and overhead, the editor calculates that 5,000 sales will mean a net of $8,000 or so. On the basis of these figures, the publisher offers the author a contract—a 10 percent royalty, say, with a guaranteed advance of $3,000. A year or two later (publishers work slowly) the book comes out. If it sells the expected 5,000 copies, the author earns back the $3,000 advance plus an additional $500 in royalties; the company keeps the remaining $4,500 as its profit. If the book sells only 2,000 copies (to most of the bigger libraries and all of the author's good friends), the author gets to keep the advance and the publisher loses a few thousand dollars. And if by some miracle the book sells a few hundred thousand copies, the author gets rich and the publisher gets richer. But miracles don't happen often. Most books either earn a few thousand dollars or lose a few thousand dollars. It's a slow way to get rich.

In a sense, 1963 to 1972 was a miracle decade. The audience for textbooks, reference books, and mass-market paperbacks was expanding so fast that even run-of-the-mill books were earning better than run-of-the-mill profits.

That decade is over. In 1973 and 1974, profit margins got thinner and thinner as inflation forced up the price of materials and labor. In the space of a year, the cost of manufacturing a book at William Morrow & Co. rose from $1.45 to $2.03.[33] Paper was the biggest villain; depending on the quality of paper used, the price shot up between 35 and 80 percent in one year. The ordinary stock used for most novels went from 18 cents a pound in January of 1974 to 29 cents a pound in November.[34]

In response, publishers have had to raise their prices too. In 1961, Joseph Heller's first novel, *Catch-22,* was priced at $5.95. His second novel, *Something Happened,* was published in 1974 at a price of $10. It is no longer unusual for an ordinary biography to carry a $12.95 price tag, and $17.50 is now an acceptable price for a major work of nonfiction.

With prices that high, publishers are assuming that people will buy and read more selectively. So they have begun plans to trim their lists of new titles. Macmillan was among the first to announce a sharp cutback in the number of titles it planned to publish in 1975 and 1976. Experts predict that new authors, and authors with mediocre sales records, will now have a harder time finding publishers. Advances to authors and promotional budgets are also expected to decline. Fiction will be the hardest hit. A book on how to ski, the history of sea shell collecting, or the sinking of the Titanic is pretty much assured at least a few thousand sales to libraries and devoted fans of the topic. A novel by an unknown author, on the other hand, has no guaranteed audience at all.

As trade hardbacks and textbooks decline because of the price squeeze, the paperback arm of the industry may take on greater prominence. Until recently, paperback houses exerted little influence on the course of publishing. They merely reprinted cheap editions of successful hardback books, with only a smattering of original titles in their lists—mainly pulpy gothics, westerns, and romances. But at $1.50 or even $3.00, a paperback is a lot more palatable than the $8.95 hardback edition of the same book, and so the paperback houses are beginning to flex their muscles. Instead of just buying the reprint rights to a bestseller (or what they hope will become a bestseller), some paperback publishers are now signing contracts with their own authors. The $2-million offer to former President Richard Nixon for his memoirs came not from an established hardback publisher, but from Warner Paperback Library, which will sell the hardcover rights to the highest bidder. William Peter Blatty's *The Exorcist* was originally signed by Bantam Books, a paperback publisher.[35] Avon Books, another paperback house, has built up a stable of authors whose books don't appear in hardcover at all.[36]

Book publishing is simultaneously a tight-knit monopoly and a wide-open field. Ninety percent of all book titles are published by the 350 biggest companies, and a mere two dozen publishers account for two-thirds of the nation's books. But there are 6,500 publishing houses in the country. Most of them have just one or two editors, hire joblot printers to produce their books, and publish only a few titles a year. The big companies inevitably earn most of the money, because they publish most of the books. But anyone can compete with them.

In the 1960s, small-scale publishers often competed through the use of jazzy promotional campaigns, taking advantage of the stodginess of mainstream publishers in a time of rapidly expanding markets. In the 1970s, competition is likely to take another form: low-budget production of the cheapest possible books. Both big companies and small ones will be cutting corners. Traditionally low salaries in publishing will remain low. Traditionally low advances to authors—which soared in the 1960s—will come down to reasonable levels. Fewer books will be published and fewer titles will be kept in print. Books with substantial merit but little sales appeal will be relegated to the university presses, while books with little merit but substantial sales appeal will be snapped up quickly. New authors, especially new novelists, will have more trouble finding a publisher, and established ones will have to settle for less flashy promotion and a stricter budget.

Publishing expert Eliot Fremont-Smith sees it this way: "Book publishing survived the Great Depression better than many industries in part because its operations (number of titles published, number of people employed) were modest—in fact, tiny by today's standards. It is still a small industry; yet it has become geared to ever-expanding and increasingly affluent markets. Hard times, if they come, will cause some noisy crunching and stripping, in more ways than one." [37]

Notes

1 "The Hot Magazines Aim at Special Targets," *Business Week,* May 2, 1970, p. 64.

2 Roland E. Wolseley, *The Magazine World* (Englewood Cliffs, N.J.: Prentice-Hall, 1951), p. 8.

3 Theodore Peterson, *Magazines in the Twentieth Century* (Urbana, Ill.: University of Illinois Press, 1964), p. 59.

4 *Ibid.,* pp. 60–61.

5 Otto Friedrich, "I am Marty Ackerman. I am Thirty-Six Years Old and I am Very Rich. I hope to Make the Curtis Publishing Company Rich Again," *Harper's Magazine,* December, 1969, pp. 95–118.

6 "The Hot Magazines Aim at Special Targets," p. 68.

7 "Advertising: Life Magazine's Post-Mortem," *New York Times,* December 11, 1972, p. 67.

8 "Dated Publishing Strategy Linked to Downfall of Life," *New York Times,* December 9, 1972, p. 16.

9 Jane O'Reilly, "Whatever Happened to 'Ms.'?" *New York,* June 26, 1972, p. 39.

10 "Ms. Magazine, a Success After 16 Issues, Now Tries Other Business Ventures," *New York Times,* September 21, 1973, p. 38.

11 *Ibid.*

12 "The Ms. Biz," *Newsweek,* October 15, 1973, p. 70.

13 "The Hot Magazines Aim at Special Targets," p. 72.

14 *Ibid.,* p. 74.

15 "Laurence William Lane Jr. of Sunset. Rising in the West," *Nation's Business,* January, 1973, pp. 34–38.

16 Lewis Anthony Dexter and David Manning White, eds., *People, Society, and Mass Communications* (New York: The Free Press, 1964), p. 259.

17 Charles Marler, "Magazines and Postal Rates," Freedom of Information Center Report No. 306, School of Journalism, University of Missouri at Columbia, July, 1973, p. 6.

18 "Advertising: Reprieve on Rates," *New York Times,* June 21, 1974, p. 57.

19 "Magazines Fight It Out at the Checkout Counter," *Business Week,* March 30, 1974, p. 64.

20 "Advertising: New Magazine Tack," *New York Times,* September 4, 1974, p. 64.

21 "There's New Life in the Mass Magazines," *Business Week,* October 13, 1973, p. 86.

22 John Tebbel, "Magazines—New, Changing, Growing," *Saturday Review,* February 8, 1969, p. 55.

23 Clay S. Felker, "Life Cycles in the Age of Magazines," *Antioch Review,* Spring, 1969, p. 7.

24 James Playsted Wood, *Magazines in the United States* (New York: Ronald Press, 1956), p. 36.

25 Roland E. Wolseley, *Understanding Magazines* (Ames, Iowa: Iowa State University Press, 1965), p. 203.

26 Warren G. Bovee, *The Editor and Writer Relationship* (Milwaukee: Marquette University Press, 1965), p. 9.

27 John Kobler, *Luce, His Time, Life, and Fortune* (Garden City, N.Y.: Doubleday, 1968), pp. 189–201.

28 John C. Merrill, Carter R. Bryan, and Marvin Alisky, *The Foreign Press* (Baton Rouge: Louisiana State University Press, 1970), p. 142.

29 "Annual Statistics," *Publishers Weekly,* July 22, 1974, p. 43.

30 Cass Canfield, *The Publishing Experience* (Philadelphia: University of Pennsylvania Press, 1969), p. 60.

31 Ted Morgan, "Sharks," *New York Times Magazine,* April 21, 1974, pp. 10–11, 85–96.

32 John P. Dessauer, "Too Many Books," *Publishers Weekly,* September 30, 1974, p. 24.

33 "Books: A Sad Story," *Newsweek,* October 28, 1974, p. 87.

34 Eliot Fremont-Smith, "Book Prices: The Burst of the Bubble," *New York,* November 11, 1974, p. 111.

35 "Paperback Houses Test Clout," *New York Times,* October 22, 1974, p. 46.

36 Richard R. Lingeman, "Original Fiction Boom in Paperback," *New York Times Book Review,* October 13, 1974, p. 40.

37 Fremont-Smith, "Book Prices: The Burst of the Bubble," p. 111.

Suggested Readings

FELKER, CLAY S., "Life Cycles in the Age of Magazines," *Antioch Review,* Spring, 1969.

FRIEDRICH, OTTO, "I am Marty Ackerman. I am Thirty-Six Years Old and I am Very Rich. I Hope to Make the Curtis Publishing Company Rich Again," *Harper's Magazine,* December, 1969.

"The Hot Magazines Aim at Special Targets," *Business Week,* May 2, 1970.

KOBLER, JOHN, *Luce, His Time, Life, and Fortune.* Garden City, N.Y.: Doubleday, 1968.

MARLER, CHARLES, "Magazines and Postal Rates," Freedom of Information Center Report No. 306, School of Journalism, University of Missouri at Columbia, July, 1973.

MORGAN, TED, "Sharks," *New York Times Magazine,* April 21, 1974.

PETERSON, THEODORE, *Magazines in the Twentieth Century.* Urbana, Ill.: University of Illinois Press, 1964.

STEIN, ROBERT, " 'What Am I Bid for Lyndon Johnson?' Or How the Literary Auction Works," *New York,* August 30, 1971.

SWANBERG, W. A., *Luce and His Empire.* New York: Charles Scribner's Sons, 1972.

TEBBEL, JOHN, *A History of Book Publishing in the United States.* New York: R. R. Bowker, 1972 [vol. 1].

Chapter 12
Broadcasting

Television is by far the most powerful and ubiquitous of the mass media. Yet it is used almost exclusively for entertainment. TV programming has been attacked by some as a degradation of American culture. Others assert that it is a dangerous corrupter of the nation's morals. More moderate critics claim that it is, at best, a waste of the viewer's time and the medium's potential.

Television is everywhere. There are, at present, more than 66 million American homes with at least one TV set.[1] That's nearly all the homes in the country. More families own televisions than bathtubs.

And they use them more. The average in 1973 was 6⅓ hours of TV viewing time per home per day—that's more than 44 hours a week, more than 2,300 hours a year.[2] The average American spends 3½ hours a day sitting in front of a television screen. Some of that time we are doing other things as well—eating, reading, or talking. But 15 hours a week are devoted *exclusively* to TV.[3] In a single day, 65 percent of the U.S. population is exposed to television; in a week, 87

percent of the population can be found watching the tube.[4]

In 1972 there were just over a quarter of a billion television sets in the world. Thirty percent of them—81 million sets—were in the U.S. That's roughly 400 sets for every thousand people. The Soviet Union was second with 31 million sets; then came Japan with 22 million; then England and West Germany with 16 million each.[5]

Radio is almost as pervasive. There are half again as many radio sets in America as people. Nearly every American owns at least one, and has it turned on an average of 2½ hours in each day. Three-quarters of the population listen to the radio at some time in a typical day; more than 90 percent tune in some time in an average week.[6] Unlike television viewing, radio listening is usually a secondary activity. The typical radio listener is busy driving or dancing. The typical TV viewer is staring at the tube.

Any activity that takes up so much of the time of so many people is bound to exert a tremendous influence on society. Harry J. Boyle of the Canadian Radio-Television Commission was not exaggerating when he stated that "the license to broadcast is almost the heaviest obligation society can allow individuals to bear." [7]

ENTERTAINMENT

How do broadcasters respond to this obligation? As we have emphasized before, they respond with entertainment—hour after hour after hour of entertainment. They respond with soap operas and situation comedies, with westerns and detective thrillers, with sporting events and music. The vast majority of all radio and television content is meant strictly to entertain.

Americans are so accustomed to the entertainment role of broadcasting that it is necessary to stress what should be an obvious fact: Television and radio are not *inherently* entertainment media. In the developing countries of Asia, Africa, and South America, broadcasting is used almost exclusively for education and information. Even in Western Europe, news and public affairs fill a substantial part of the broadcast day. American broadcasting is entertainment-centered because American broadcasters want it that way. They want it that way because they believe (rightly or wrongly) that that is what the public and the advertisers want. But broadcast advertising isn't inevitable either; there are many countries without it. And it is at least possible to give the public what someone decrees it should want instead of what it does want.

We are not arguing that American broadcasting should be turned into a government-controlled educational monopoly—though that has been argued. In the face of the daily grind of living, Americans need to relax and unwind. Broadcast entertainment serves this need admirably. But there *are* alternatives to the American system of broadcasting.

Most observers have long been critical of broadcasting's emphasis on entertainment. In 1961, former FCC Commissioner Newton Minow told the National Association of Broadcasters: "When television is bad, nothing is worse. I invite you to sit down in front of your television set when your station goes on the air and stay there without [anything] to distract you—and keep your eyes glued to that set until the station signs off. I can assure you that you will observe a vast wasteland." [8] Robert M. Hutchins of the Center for the Study of Democratic Institutions made the point even more stringently:

> We have triumphantly invented, perfected, and distributed to the humblest cottage throughout the land one of the greatest technical marvels in history, television, and have used it for what? To bring Coney Island into every home. It is as though movable type had been devoted exclusively since Gutenberg's time to the publication of comic books. [9]

Read these two quotations carefully. Minow and Hutchins are criticizing more than just the *fact* of broadcast entertainment. They are criticizing the *quality* of that entertainment. Although there are some entertainment shows on television (symphony concerts and Shakespearean dramas, for example) that simply do not fit Minow's image of a vast wasteland or Hutchins' analogy to comic books, the majority of TV programming does fit.

Judging the quality of entertainment is a thorny problem. Broadcast executives assert that the proper standard is ratings. If people watch a show then they must like it, and if they like it then by definition it must be good entertainment. Critics of television are not satisfied with this standard. They judge programming according to their own criteria—ideological, esthetic, or moralistic. The ideological critics argue that broadcast entertainment is destroying American values. The esthetic critics claim that it is degrading American culture. And the moralistic critics insist that it is corrupting American morals. Let us examine each argument in turn.

SPORTS ON THE TUBE

Once upon a time spectator sports were something you journeyed to the stadium or arena to see. Today you stay home and watch them on TV. At least two professional football games are televised in major markets every Sunday during the season, with a third on Monday night. One or two college games are on the tube every Saturday from early September through Thanksgiving. And major-league baseball now offers two nationally televised games each week, plus broadcasts of local teams.

Television has affected sports in other ways as well:

Tennis. Balls are now yellow instead of white, and competitors must wear snappy colors and matching outfits for doubles play. To insure that singles matches don't last too long, sets tied at six games each are ended with a tie-breaker thirteenth game. For the same reason, the traditional five-set match is down to three. There is even talk that tennis balls will be made heavier, to slow down the game and make it more visible for television.

Baseball. The World Series and the All-Star Game are now routinely scheduled at night to catch the prime-time audience. In 1973, to give the game more viewer appeal, the American League adopted the designated-hitter rule, so that the pitcher need never come to bat. Next in line may be the designated runner and the designated fielder.

Boxing. Ruined by overexposure on television in the 1950s, boxing is now a single-event sport—the world heavyweight title bout. It is scheduled entirely for the convenience of closed-circuit television and home TV. The 1974 fight between George Foreman and Muhammad Ali, for example, was held in Zaire at 3 A.M.—which just happens to be 10 P.M. in New York.

Football. Two new leagues, the AFL and the WFL, were started to compete with the NFL for a share of the TV jackpot—leading to astronomical player salaries and less talented teams. Notre Dame and Georgia Tech opened their 1974 seasons on September 9—the earliest date in history—to accommodate ABC, which wanted to broadcast a game that Monday night. Officials are permitted to call timeouts throughout most of the game to fit in commercials, thus dragging out the average contest to three hours.

In all professional sports, television has helped force elaborate playoff systems that guarantee dozens of "big" games after the season, which can be sold to advertisers at fat rates. Cameras and commentators have turned up in post-game locker rooms and baseball bullpens. And the most famous figure in sports today may well be ABC's caustic commentator Howard Cosell, who never played a professional sport.

Television controls many aspects of athletics because it pays the bills. In 1974, the three networks spent $74 million for the rights to football games alone. The sports world is hooked on television; much of it would collapse without TV.

ENTERTAINMENT AND VALUES

To say that American broadcasting is mostly entertainment is not to say that it has little or no effect on American society. No doubt our country would be different without televised moon landings and election results, assassinations and battles. But it would also be different without TV coverage of the World Series and the Academy Awards. Westerns, soap operas, and the rest of television entertainment teach us things. They reflect and reinforce certain characteristic national traits—competition and aggression, materialism and racism, humor and openness, faith and ambition. It is as entertainers that the broadcast media have their greatest impact on American society. And that in itself says something about the American character.

As we pointed out in the Introduction (see pp. 15–18), the mass media are far better at reinforcing existing values than at inculcating new ones. In this sense the impact of all the media, including broadcast entertainment, is inherently conservative. Yet values do change, and TV plays an important role in that change, by mirroring the world as seen through the eyes of the people who write for TV.

For example, much of what people know about the practices of doctors, lawyers, detectives, soldiers, social workers, and teachers comes from observing their behavior in television dramas. How accurate are these stereotypes, and what is their impact?

Robert Daley, a former deputy police commissioner in New York City, spent a week watching "The Streets of San Francisco," "Adam-12," "The Rookies," "Ironside," "Police Surgeon," and all the other cop shows. In just two episodes of "Madigan," which he had been told was one of the more accurate TV representations of police work, Daley found the following errors:

- Madigan worked alone. Daley says no detective works alone because it is too dangerous.

- Madigan was assigned a partner who had passed directly from a university course in social psychology to a detective's job. Daley says no one is made a detective on the spot; all must work their way up through police ranks.

- Madigan was told over the police radio where to meet an informer. Daley says such transmissions are almost always conducted in code.

- Madigan failed to frisk a suspect properly for weapons. Daley says this habit would soon earn a real detective a bullet in the gut.

- Madigan recovered $1,000 stolen from a guest at a dinner party and returned the money. Daley says the rules of evidence would require a detective to turn the money in to the police department's property clerk.

Daley has a few questions for television's writers and producers. "Are our police departments important to us?" he asks. "If they are, is it not important that we know who our policemen are and how they conduct themselves? Should we really go on watching actors impersonating the way other actors have always impersonated policemen? Are we in the process of fabricating a police myth via TV that will last for decades to come?" [10]

From quite different perspectives, other viewers have criticized TV police shows for encouraging disrespect for the civil liberties of suspects, for downplaying the realities of racism and corruption in police departments, and for glorifying violence and punishment as solutions to social problems. The same sorts of objections can be raised about television's portrayal of patient care by physicians, courtroom procedure, teacher-student interactions, etc.

Of course the values and information in television entertainment often serve the public instead of misleading it. Every time a TV soap opera features a cancer case, thousands of viewers go for checkups, and dozens of cancers are diagnosed and treated. Many experts in family planning claim that the liberalization in public attitudes toward abortion is a direct result of television programs in which sympathetic characters considered, obtained, or advocated abortions. And just as TV entertainment has often reinforced the stereotype of witless, dependent women, so too TV entertainment is at last beginning to reflect the existence of women who work, think, and control their own lives.

None of this is planned or intentional. The values and information embedded in broadcast entertainment are the values and information in the heads of the people who write and produce the shows—generally white, male, middle-class, urban, liberal people. Without especially trying, these people are constantly bombarding the rest of the country with *their* sense of reality. Little wonder both the radical left and the police brass are displeased with programs like "Madigan."

There are two kinds of ideological critics of television entertainment—those on the extremes complaining about TV's constant reinforcement of middle-American values, and those in the middle complaining about TV's occasional reflection of less conventional values. The first group has a much better case, since television is most powerful and most insidious when it is affirming the biases of its audience. But it's a hard case to argue effectively. How do you convince people that television is doing them an injustice by subtly and constantly telling them they're right? Feminists, rightists, leftists, environmentalists, and other advocates of a different sort of society than we now have are seldom successful in their efforts to lessen the constant reinforcement of the status quo in TV entertainment.

When a change does begin to take place in society, TV writers are among the first to notice. They quickly pick up the new value, and build it into their work. This greatly broadens the movement and hastens the transition. But until a new viewpoint is common and acceptable in liberal New York and Hollywood circles, it is unlikely to find its way onto television.

Even then, the new perspective is likely to be attacked as extremist by critics with more traditional values. And this attack is likely to be successful, since it is easier to arouse people about efforts to change them than about efforts to keep them the same. Broadcasters fear controversy, and controversy is defined as any expression of a value not shared by the audience. Those television abortions that did so much to change public attitudes toward family planning were broadcast only after bitter ideological battles; some weren't broadcast at all.

Political controversy is especially sensitive. Most of the political action centers on news and documentaries, but broadcast entertainment is not immune. This was highlighted in the spring of 1973, when nearly forty CBS affiliates forced the network to postpone presentation of David Rabe's play "Sticks and Bones." The station managers were nervous about putting on the air a play about a Vietnam veteran, blinded in the war, whose unsympathetic parents finally drive him to suicide. They felt that the play, which had had a long run on Broadway, would be particularly offensive if aired during the return of U.S. POWs from Vietnam.[11] When CBS finally ran the show some four months later, during television's summer doldrums, many local affiliates still decided not to carry it.

MASS CULTURE

Some time in the not too distant future, one of the networks may announce a new half-hour series called "Hawthorne Place," based loosely on Nathaniel Hawthorne's novel *The Scarlet Letter*. It will be billed as a sort of Calvinist "Peyton Place," with the role of the fallen woman, Hester Prynne, played by Joey Heatherton. In keeping with the All-American spirit of the show, its theme song will be drawn from the works of Aaron Copland, arranged for jazz sextet.

Guardians of the sacred flame of Culture will no doubt greet "Hawthorne Place"—if they stoop to greet it at all—with cries of dismay. The mass media, they will say, are again raping and debasing our culture in pursuit of profit. In the face of such irreverence it is impossible to be a serious artist or critic in America. The series is just one more proof of the old saying that everything television touches turns to tripe. That's what they'll say.

What is culture? Edward A. Shils supplies this definition: "Superior or refined culture is distinguished by the seriousness of its subject matter, i.e., the centrality of the problems with which it deals, the acute penetration and coherence of its perceptions, the subtlety and wealth of its expressed feeling." [12] This is High Culture. Twentieth-century examples include the music of Stravinsky and Berg, the novels of Conrad and Hesse, the paintings of Picasso and Wyeth, and like works of esthetic and intellectual refinement. High Culture has traditionally been the province of the upper classes.

Before the Industrial Revolution, the only competitor with High Culture was Folk Art —the culture of the common people. Folk Art, says critic Dwight Macdonald, was "the people's own institution, their private little garden walled off from the great formal park of their masters' High Culture." [13] It was expressed in craftsmanship, dance, music, and poetry.

Then came the Industrial Revolution, the burgeoning middle class, and the mass media. With them came Mass Culture—also known as Masscult, Low Culture, Pop Culture, and *Kitsch* (the German word for mass culture). Unlike Folk Art, Mass Culture borrows from the basic content of High Culture. But unlike High Culture, it is designed

to be popular, to "sell" to a mass audience. Alexis de Tocqueville described the difference as long ago as 1835:

> In aristocratic ages the object of the arts is . . . to manufacture as well as possible, not with the greatest speed or at the lowest cost. . . . In democracies there is always a multitude of persons whose wants are above their means and who are very willing to take up with imperfect satisfaction rather than abandon the object of their desires altogether. . . .
>
> In aristocracies a few great pictures are produced; in democratic countries a vast number of insignificant ones. In the former statues are raised of bronze; in the latter, they are modeled in plaster.[14]

America is by all counts the world's greatest producer of Mass Culture. And television is by all counts America's greatest producer.

Broadcasting is a mass medium in the literal sense of the word. In order to attract advertisers, networks must attract an audience of millions, not thousands or even hun-

---

CULTURAL IMPERIALISM

Among many other products, the United States exports television programs. American TV shows, especially westerns and detective series, are staples in many foreign broadcast schedules. Much of what people in other countries learn about the U.S. comes from our television entertainment programs.

For the countries on the receiving end, this practice has two unfortunate effects. First, it discourages the development of their own broadcast programming industries. And second, it bombards them with an endless barrage of American popular culture, resulting in a sort of "cultural imperialism" that can overwhelm or distort their own customs and standards.

One country that has been concerned about this for some time is Canada. In response, the Canadian Radio and Television Commission has adopted a series of rules requiring Canadian broadcasters to carry more Canadian programming. For example, at least 30 percent of all records played by AM radio stations in Canada must be Canadian-made. Television programming must be at least 40 percent Canadian, and under consideration is a proposal requiring nearly all commercials to be for Canadian products.

In the five years since the radio content rule was adopted, the Canadian recording industry has grown by 50 percent, offering many new jobs to Canadian musicians, composers, agents, managers, engineers, etc.[15] Similar growth is predicted for the Canadian film, broadcast production, and advertising industries. And perhaps a truly Canadian culture is beginning to emerge from under the blanket of American TV programs.

dreds of thousands. There is no conspiracy at work here. If broadcasters were convinced that the public appetite for ballet was enormous, they would gladly program hour after hour of ballet. But since there is almost no demand for televised ballet, there is almost no ballet on television. Of course it is hard to generate a massive demand for ballet when most people have never *seen* one. Television could probably teach the public to enjoy ballet in the same way it has taught the public to enjoy doctor shows and situation comedies. But broadcasters are not in the business of breaking vicious circles. As long as viewers are satisfied with Mass Culture, there is no reason to bother training them to appreciate High Culture.

Critics like Dwight Macdonald not only deplore the public's satisfaction with Masscult. They fear it. Macdonald puts the point this way: "Bad stuff drives out the good, since it is more easily understood and enjoyed. . . . When to this ease of consumption is added *Kitsch*'s ease of production because of its standardized nature, its prolific growth is easy to understand. It threatens High Culture by its sheer pervasiveness, its brutal, overwhelming *quantity*." [16]

Macdonald fears that television may destroy High Culture in America. Shils is more optimistic:

> There is much ridicule of *Kitsch*, and it *is* ridiculous. Yet it represents aesthetic sensibility and aesthetic aspiration, untutored, rude, and deformed. The very growth of *Kitsch*, and of the demand which has generated the industry for the production of *Kitsch*, is an indication of a crude aesthetic awakening in classes which previously accepted what was handed down to them or who had practically no aesthetic expression and reception.[17]

Only history can settle this dispute. Perhaps broadcasting will kill American High Culture. Perhaps it will create a new audience for that culture.

Whatever the eventual effects of broadcasting on High Culture, there is no doubt that the culture in today's broadcasting is

anything but high. Despite their pompous elitism, Macdonald and Shils are right. So are Minow and Hutchins. Television is a vast wasteland, an endless succession of electronic comic books. Maybe that's all for the best, and maybe it isn't. But certainly it is what's happening.

BROADCAST CORRUPTION

Sex, profanity, violence . . . Our children are in danger! Such is the cry of many critics of the broadcast media.

While the fight against Mass Culture is confined to a few universities and literary magazines, the fight against broadcast corruption is out in the open—in Congress, in the FCC, in outraged letters to networks and stations. Broadcasters have more or less ignored their esthetic critics. But they have been forced to make major concessions to their moralistic ones.

Sex. The battle over sex in the mass media has traditionally centered on books, magazines, and movies, not broadcasting. The reason for this is not that sex was accepted in broadcasting, but rather that before the 1970s sex was nonexistent in broadcasting. At least forthright sexuality was nonexistent; a leering sort of "sexiness" was okay.

Thus, television advertisers have always implied all sorts of sexual advantages to their products, but late-night talk shows used to supply handkerchiefs to women whose clothes might otherwise show a hint of cleavage. TV serials have always relied on sex as the principal motivation of many characters, but when CBS broadcast the movie *Elmer Gantry* it cut out the scenes between Gantry and a prostitute. Off-color insinuations have always been a staple of TV comedy routines, but the costumes for a female "genie" in a popular series in the 1960s were carefully designed to cover her navel.

By the early 1970s, this approach to sex seemed to be changing. Prime-time network TV programs changed very little; they became more tolerant of sexual innuendo and humor but no more tolerant of open sexuality. On the fringes of the industry, however, the change seemed more real. Cable TV public-access channels began experimenting with nudity and explicit sex. Closed-circuit TV systems in hotels tried running X-rated movies. And in Los Angeles, "topless radio" was born and briefly flourished.

The format was introduced in 1972 by radio personality Bill Ballance, then of station KGBS in Los Angeles. His program, "Feminine Forum," encouraged listeners (most of them women) to phone in and recount some of their most intimate experiences with human sexuality. Protected by the anonymity of radio, many of the callers were quite explicit, revealing a range of language, imagery, and experience not often heard on the airwaves. The program was soon syndicated in thirty other markets.

In January, 1973, the FCC received 3,362 complaints about broadcast "obscenity," especially topless radio.[18] It responded quickly on several fronts. A small FM station in Oak Park, Illinois, was fined $2,000 for the "indecent language" in its program "Femme Forum." [19] FCC Chairman Dean Burch warned the National Association of Broadcasters at its annual convention that stations would have to clean up "this new breed of air pollution" before the Commission cleaned it up for them.[20] And the FCC announced a wide-ranging probe into the "topless" format to determine what federal laws such programs might be violating.[21]

This was more than enough pressure to whip most radio station managers into line. KGBS in Los Angeles, WHN in New York, and other stations across the country dropped their sexually oriented talk shows.[22] Except for a few cable TV operations in the biggest cities, frank sexuality is once again nonexistent in American broadcasting.

Profanity. The moralists have also won their battle against profanity. In January of 1970, the Walter Cronkite news show aired the expression "goddamn" three times. First Joseph Yablonski Jr., the son of a murdered labor leader, declared that "the federal government doesn't give us a goddamn

bit of help anywhere along the line." Then a Chicago black, commenting on home mortgage problems, complained that his house was "a goddamn cracker box," and that "the goddamn foundation is cracking."

The government made no attempt to prosecute CBS for these minor infractions. But the public reaction was instantaneous. The Bible Belt was outraged, viewers everywhere objected, and station managers around the country called network headquarters in New York to protest. Cronkite later defended the Yablonski goddamn: "Our policy is to permit such language only when it seems essential to the development of the character or nature of the news." He apologized for the other two.[23]

Violence. American TV has been exceedingly violent almost since the birth of the medium. In a single week of Los Angeles television in 1960, there were 144 murders, 11 murder attempts, 13 kidnappings, 7 torture scenes, 4 lynchings, and hundreds upon hundreds of fights.[24] According to communications researcher George Gerbner, more than three-quarters of all network dramatic shows from 1967 to 1971 contained elements of violence.[25] Nor was the mayhem limited to prime time. The average Saturday morning cartoon hour in 1967 included three times as many violent episodes as the average adult dramatic hour. By 1969 there was a violent episode every two minutes in Saturday morning's cartoon programming.[26]

While violence is obviously good for the ratings, politicians, parents, and behavioral scientists have often wondered how good it is for the impressionable minds of young people. Dozens of studies throughout the 1960s produced mixed results. Generally, they tended to confirm that children learn techniques of violence from the media and imitate those techniques in their play. But on the crucial question of whether this imitation actually makes children more violent the studies were inconclusive. Broadcasters found plenty of ammunition in the data with which to fight off any effort to change the content of TV programs.

Then, in the late 1960s, the Senate Subcommittee on Communications, chaired by John O. Pastore (D.-R.I.), began investigating television violence. In an effort to stave off congressional interference, the networks declared 1969 "the year of anti-violence." The superhero cartoons were eliminated, and so was most of the on-camera killing in adult programs. Commented TV critic John Stanley, "It was the year that if you shot anybody on 'Bonanza' he was only wounded. (If you shot him off-camera, it didn't matter —he could live or die.)" [27]

Despite this progress, the Pastore Committee decided to commission a thorough study of television violence. Appointed in 1969, the Surgeon General's Scientific Advisory Committee on Television and Social Behavior emerged in 1972 with a report entitled *Television and Growing Up: The Impact of Televised Violence*. The report concluded that violence on television can be dangerous.

Media violence seems to have two kinds of effects on children (and possibly on adults). The Surgeon General's Committee called them "imitation" and "instigation."

Imitation is the effect that had already been documented in the 1960s. Children do copy the styles of violence they see on TV— and not only when they're playing. In Los Angeles in the 1950s, for example, a 7-year-old was caught sprinkling ground glass into his family's stew in hopes that the method would work as well as it had on television. Two Chicago boys tried to extort $500 from a neighbor through a bomb threat, a scheme they had watched succeed on TV.[28] And in 1972, after the movie *West Side Story* was televised, children at P.S. 108 in New York's East Harlem spent their play time dividing into gangs of Jets and Sharks, threatening "rumbles," and pulling knives on each other.[29] TV probably didn't create these children's aggressive feelings, but it did teach them more destructive ways to express those feelings. Thanks to television, just about every American youngster knows how to shoot a gun. For an angry child, shooting at baby sister may be the emotional equivalent of yelling at her—but if the gun is real and loaded, the effect on baby sister can be tragic.

Closely related to imitation is the media's ability to teach the audience that violence is an acceptable, even a fashionable way to cope with problems. This is a difficult effect to prove; violence is so thoroughly embedded in our culture that it is hard to isolate the influence of the media. But experimenters have found that children exposed to violent films are more likely to view violence as a solution to their own conflicts than children exposed to films depicting other ways of handling the situation. And of course a small child who has not yet learned to distinguish fact from fantasy may well assume that violence in life will have as few consequences as it has in a "Roadrunner" cartoon.

If imitation is dangerous, instigation is doubly so. Under some circumstances, media violence can actually arouse aggressive feelings (or good feelings about aggression), and thus directly stimulate violent behavior.

AS AMERICAN AS APPLE PIE

If there is one characteristic that clearly identifies a dramatic program as made in the United States, it is the presence of violence in the plot development. Nobody is sure why, but American television is enormously more violent than TV in most other countries.

A British Broadcasting Corporation study released in 1972 found that American TV programs shown in Britain, such as "Mannix," "The Untouchables," and "I Spy," had twice as many incidents of violence as comparable British productions.[30] Television in Israel has less than one-sixth the violence of American television, while a content analysis of Swedish television turned up so little violence that it was "meaningless" to keep a detailed accounting of it.[31]

One 1971 experiment paired preschool children who watched the same amount of TV at home, monitoring the extent of aggression in their play. Then one member of each pair was exposed to a violent Saturday-morning cartoon, while the other watched a nonviolent program. A second play session followed. The researchers found that "the two groups had departed significantly from one another in terms of the frequency of interpersonal aggression. In fact, for every pair, the child who observed aggressive television programming had become more aggressive than his mate who watched neutral fare." [32]

A 1961 study demonstrated the combined effects of imitation and instigation. Children were shown a film of a boy named Rocky throwing a ball at his playmate Johnny, hitting him with a baton, shooting darts at him, and finally carrying off a bunch of his toys in a sack. After watching the film, many children tended to act aggressively—in Rocky's style. One girl went so far as to ask the experimenter, "Do you have a sack here?" [33]

Soon after the committee report was published, NBC President Julian Goodman said that "the time for action has come" to reduce television violence. His counterpart at ABC, Elton Rule, added: "Now that we are reasonably certain that televised violence can increase aggressive tendencies in some children, we will have to manage our program planning accordingly." [34] And so the networks replaced some of their violent cartoon shows with nonviolent children's programs. They even toned down the violence in adult programming another notch or two.

Opponents of television violence kept up the pressure, and in 1975 the networks announced another concession. They declared the early evening period from 8 to 9 to be "family viewing time," and pledged to remove from that time slot all programs containing violence (or sex) unsuitable for children. Young people who watch TV after 9 will have to take care of themselves.

So will young people who watch local day-time programming. While the violence in network children's shows really has decreased since 1969, the violence in local children's shows has not. Many stations, in fact, are still using reruns of pre-1969 network superhero cartoons. In 1973, the National Association for Better Broadcasting, joined by Action for Children's Television and several other citizen groups, pressured Los Angeles station KTTV into barring forty-two violent cartoon series, and prefacing eighty-one noncartoon series with a "caution to parents" if it used them. The groups had threatened to challenge the station's license unless it agreed. [35] This sort of organized political action may be what it takes to force local broadcasters to stop peddling violence to children.

Most of the research on media violence, by the way, has concentrated on the sort of violence the media like best—sanitized. Some psychologists have suggested that this may be the most dangerous sort of violence of all, because it stresses the action and ignores the evil results. Though it is unhealthy to watch a private eye beating up a suspect on TV, perhaps it would be healthy to contemplate the victim's bleeding face. If so, American television is very unhealthy indeed. It still has a great deal of violence, but very little pain or suffering.

The broadcast media have incredible potential for the dissemination of news and information. To some extent this potential is realized; certainly broadcast news has contributed greatly to the political awareness of the American public. But the nonentertainment programming on radio and television is often disappointing. In some ways broadcast news is limited by the nature of the medium; in most ways it is limited only by the policies of broadcasters.

TELEVISION NEWS

Television is an entertainment medium. The typical TV station offers perhaps four hours of nonentertainment programming a

ADVERTISING AND CHILDREN

Aside from violence, the aspect of TV that upsets parents the most is advertising. One study found that 79 percent of American mothers believed television commercials were misleading their children, and 90 percent thought there were too many ads in children's programs.[36] The most resented ads were those for junk foods, sugary cereals, flavored vitamins, and dangerous toys. Several citizen groups exist to combat such commercials; among the most successful are Action for Children's Television and the Council on Children, Media and Merchandising.

Many other countries have already acted on these issues. In 1973, the Canadian Broadcasting Corporation agreed to drop all commercials from shows aimed at children age 12 or younger.[37] Independent Canadian stations cut the number of advertising minutes in children's shows from 12 an hour to 8.[38] And in Australia, the Broadcasting Control Board set up strict rules for children's advertising on TV. Child actors in the ads must be well-mannered and respectful of their parents; children may not be urged to pressure their parents to buy a particular product; personalities and characters from children's programs may not endorse products; and no ad may imply that a product makes its owner superior to peers, or that the lack of a product could lead to ridicule.[39]

Broadcasters in the U.S. are not enthusiastic about such changes, because they earn a lot of money from commercials on children's programs—$75 million in 1970 alone. Yet there have been some victories for parents. In 1972, the National Association of Broadcasters reduced the recommended number of ad minutes per hour in Saturday- and Sunday-morning programming from 16 to 12, and cut the recommended number of commercial interruptions in half.[40] The NAB also ruled that children's show hosts should no longer deliver commercials.

Citizen groups kept up the pressure, and in 1974 they were joined by the Federal Trade Commission. FTC Chairman Lewis A. Engman called for tighter federal controls on premium offers, on commercials that exploit children's anxieties or their "propensity to confuse reality and fantasy," on the use of hero figures, on advertisements for dangerous toys, on children's vitamin commercials, etc.[41] Engman added:

> The advertiser who chooses a child audience as a target for his selling message is subject not only to the standards of truthful advertising; he is, in my judgment, also bound to deal in complete fairness with his young viewers.[42]

It was impossible to miss the handwriting on the wall. The NAB quickly enacted a number of voluntary reforms, including the elimination of vitamin ads and further cutbacks in the recommended number of ad minutes per hour, down to 10 on weekends and 14 during the week. It also promised additional cuts in the years ahead, to 9½ minutes per hour on weekends and 12 on weekdays by 1976. These changes came just in time. In October, 1974, the Federal Communications Commission finished its four-year study of children's television. The FCC endorsed the NAB's new voluntary standards, adding only a policy statement against program hosts endorsing products.

Citizen groups are still not satisfied. Several have urged a total ban on children's TV advertising, and most continue to push for stronger regulations. Thanks to their efforts, children's advertising on television has already improved significantly.

day—roughly 20 percent of the total. Only half of the four hours is devoted to news: 90 minutes at dinner time and 30 in the late evening. A little of the remainder is used for documentaries. Most of it goes to "Today"-type features and to religious and agricultural programming in the early morning.

The late evening news is usually a rehash and condensation of the early evening news. And the early evening news is at least a third advertising, sports, and weather. The average TV viewer is lucky to be offered as much as 60 minutes a day of hard news.

Nevertheless, television news is incredibly powerful. As we have seen (see page 261), the American public relies more on television for its news than on any other medium. There are more people watching the network newscasts every night than there are reading all the front pages of all the newspapers in America. No newspaper reporter in the country even approaches Walter Cronkite in influence.

The chief virtue of television news is almost universally acknowledged: In a thoroughly professional manner it touches on the principal points of the dozen or so most important events each day, plus a few light features and 90-second "in-depth" backgrounders. The chief drawback of television news is equally obvious: Sixty minutes a day isn't much time to do justice to the problems of the world, country, state, and city, and so TV news inevitably becomes little more than a headline service. News on television is a handy guide to what's happening, but a poor guide to why it's happening or what the viewer should do about it.

If the preceding paragraph had been written a decade ago, not a word would have been different. Television news hasn't changed much. The format of the three network news shows, for example, has been essentially the same since 1963, when they moved from fifteen minutes to half an hour. An anchorman (who's been around for more than a decade himself) reads the story, or introduces a film clip narrated by a correspondent in the field. Hard news starts the show;

a light feature or a brief commentary by a resident pundit ends it. The only visible change in recent years has been the addition of billboards at the beginning of the program to tell the viewer what is coming up.

In the early 1970s there was talk of expanding the network news to an hour, but the idea was dropped when the FCC ordered local stations to run more non-network shows in prime time. With the revision of the prime-time access rule, the plans for an hour show may be revived—or they may not. Meanwhile, the hottest thing in network news is a new camera called the Minicam, which can beam pictures live from a remote location via microwaves.[43] This promises even greater speed and immediacy in television news coverage—but no greater depth.

Perhaps because of the stale format, the audience for network news is not growing. Except for brief spurts in 1968 (assassinations and riots) and 1973 (Watergate), the audience has been static since 1966. Roughly 45 million viewers a day—35 percent of all TV households—watch the three network news broadcasts.[44]

Why don't the networks experiment more in search of a better news format? They have too much invested in the current format, and in the popularity of such TV personalities as Walter Cronkite and John Chancellor. In 1972, NBC News alone shot more than 4,000 miles of film, employed a hundred people just to edit it, and used on the air one foot of film for every ten shot. Its bill for film was $1.9 million; for travel, $600,000; for telex and cable, $450,000; for telephones, $951,000.[45] The *weekly* budget for the NBC nightly news is $200,000.[46]

The stakes are high in local news as well. An increase of a single rating point (1 percent of the television audience) is worth $500,000 a year in additional ad revenue in a city the size of New York or Los Angeles. In a market like St. Louis or Baltimore, 1 percent of the news audience is worth $125,000 a year to advertisers. Moreover, market researchers have established that many viewers of the early-evening local news stick to the same channel all evening.[47] A good rating for the local news thus leads to a good rating for the whole prime-time schedule—and many extra dollars in advertising. Understandably, there is a great deal of pressure on news directors to pull in the viewers.

Most local news operations start with a lot less viewer loyalty to particular formats and personalities than is the case for the network shows. They are therefore free to experiment more in pursuit of a ratings advantage. Hour-long local news programs are now common and getting more so, and some stations have gone to 90 minutes or even a full two hours of local news. In order to fill up so much time, the programs have come to resemble magazines more than newspapers, dominated by soft features, consumer services, interviews, and cultural news. Less than half an hour of the two-hour WNBC local show in New York is devoted to hard news coverage.

Most of the local experimentation takes the form of trying to entertain the audience. Techniques that have proved useful include: (1) Hiring anchormen and anchorwomen with distinct (but soothing) on-the-air personalities that viewers can relate to; (2) Stressing violent crime, sex, and human-interest stories; (3) Encouraging the news team to tell jokes and liven up their presentations; (4) Crowding huge numbers of very short stories into the program; (5) Replacing "talking head" stories that are read in the studio with more action film; and (6) Promoting the news team heavily through advertising and personal appearances. Several consulting firms now earn good money surveying the local news audience for their clients and peddling advice on how to handle the news so as to raise the ratings.

Does any of this improve the quality of TV news? It does if you define quality in terms of ratings—and that is precisely how the broadcast industry defines quality. Television executives are rarely former reporters. Most often they are promoted out of the sales department; occasionally they come from the entertainment side. They control the activities of the nation's most important

journalists, but they are not interested in journalism. Nor are they interested in power, though they possess all too much of it. What interests them is profit.

TV VERSUS NEWSPAPERS

Television and radio news differ from newspaper news in scores of ways. Some of these differences are inevitable results of the nature of broadcasting—but most of them are not.

1. Sensory Involvement. The power of television rests in its capacity to combine voices and moving pictures. Yet that very capacity often turns out to be a disadvantage. TV reporters are trained to think in terms of good film footage. They avoid at all costs the "stand-upper" or the "talking head"—a reporter simply reading the story without audiovisual aids. The assumption that the viewer wants to see action may or may not be justified, but it is nearly universal. The parallel assumption in radio is that voice actualities are a must. "Get the s.o.b. on the phone" is the motto of most radio news departments.

But how do you get good films or tapes on the new city budget? Or on the president's decision to veto a housing act? Or on the discovery of a new treatment for arthritis? Because of its preoccupation with audiovisuals, broadcasting is forced to underplay such stories as these. At best, the newscaster will emphasize some filmable aspect of the event —the political repercussions of the decision instead of the decision itself. Many important stories never get covered on TV because they cannot be effectively photographed.

2. Pseudo-events. Broadcasting's undying allegiance to film footage encourages it to concentrate on pseudo-events (see pp. 143–44). Press conferences, grand openings, conventions, and such may not offer much real news—but they guarantee decent footage. By the time a station has covered all these ready-made stories, it has very little time or staff left for anything else.

Newspapers report events. Television and radio, by and large, report staged interviews about events. Michael Arlen of the *New Yorker* carries this to its logical extreme:

> I have this picture of the last great interview: The polar icecaps are melting. The San Andreas Fault has swallowed up half of California. Tonga has dropped the big egg on Mauritius. The cities of the plain are leveled. We switch from Walter Cronkite in End-of-the-World Central to Buzz Joplin, who is standing on a piece of rock south of the Galapagos with the last man on earth, the water rising now just above their chins. Joplin strains himself on tiptoe, lifts his microphone out of the water, and, with a last desperate gallant effort—the culmination of all his years as a TV newsman—places it in front of the survivor's mouth. "How do you feel, sir?" he asks. "I mean, being the last man on earth and so forth. Would you give us your personal reaction?"

> The last survivor adopts that helpless vacant look, the water already beginning to trickle into his mouth. "Well, Buzz," he says, gazing wildly into the middle distance, "I feel real good." [48]

3. Speed. Television and radio can get the news to the public much faster than newspapers. The bulk of your evening newspaper is written in the morning; the evening newscast includes stories that won't be printed until tomorrow morning. This makes broadcasting the ideal vehicle for spot news. Radio is far superior to television in this respect, because TV executives are reluctant to interrupt profitable entertainment programming with a news bulletin. After all, who sponsors a news bulletin?

4. Time Limitations. TV news is usually limited—by choice, not necessity—to half an hour at a time. There is room for perhaps twenty stories at the most, some of which will get no more than thirty seconds. If you were to set the text of a half-hour newscast in type, it would fill less than half of a newspaper front page.

On big news days, a newspaper can add a few pages to make room. Television can't—

a highly profitable show is scheduled right after the news. It takes a major cataclysm (an election or an assassination) to make a TV station add more news. When it does so, it loses money.

5. Indexability. Newspapers can be indexed. For reporters, this means they can be clipped, filed, and used later as background for a story. For readers, it means they can be browsed through. Nobody reads a newspaper cover to cover. You turn to the sections that interest you, check the headlines, and read only what you want.

None of this is possible in broadcasting. Radio and TV newscasts can be taped and stored, but they cannot be indexed for easy access. Unless a station builds a morgue of newspaper clippings (and very few do), it starts fresh with every story. As for the viewers, they have no choice but to watch the show "cover to cover." That's great for advertisers—it takes effort to skip the commercials. But it is a giant barrier to lengthening the newscast. How many people will sit through ninety minutes of news just to hear the three or four stories they're interested in?

6. Impermanence. Newspapers can be saved. You can read them at your leisure, clip them, show them to your friends, or post them on your wall. But unless you own a home videotape machine, broadcasting is a now-or-never proposition. The impermanence of broadcast news probably contributes to its frivolity. Why kill yourself researching a story that will be dead and gone thirty seconds after it starts?

7. Intrusiveness. Broadcasting is intrusive. Even a tape-recorder makes many news sources self-conscious and careful. A camera, a microphone, and a bunch of klieg lights are much, much worse. The appearance of a TV crew alters the nature of any event, from a press conference to a riot. In comparison with broadcasters, print reporters are almost invisible.

Part of the intrusiveness of broadcasting is the fame of many broadcast journalists. Few people know what James Reston looks like —but everyone can recognize Walter Cronkite. "During the 1964 campaign," recalls Robert MacNeil, "David Brinkley went to a shopping center in California to watch Nelson Rockefeller on the stump. There was a sizable crowd around Rockefeller but, when Brinkley was spotted, it melted and massed around the bigger attraction, the TV commentator." [49] The same thing can happen to a local "star" newscaster.

8. Competition. One thing you can safely say about radio and TV news: Both are highly competitive. A typical big city today has only two newspapers, but it has three or four television stations and dozens of radio stations. Newscasts get ratings like everything else on TV, and thousands of dollars may ride on the results. Competition may not always produce a better newscast, but it does keep reporters on their toes.

9. Generalism. Except for the weather and sports people, broadcasting has very few news specialists. The typical station is too poor and understaffed to afford a labor writer or a science reporter. The broadcast journalist covers everything.

10. Local News. Most television stations are located in big cities—but their signals reach dozens of smaller cities and towns. The local news of these smaller communities is almost never covered on TV. If you live more than twenty miles from the nearest TV station, you will have to subscribe to a newspaper to get any local news. And for national and international news you will be relying on the networks and the wire services. Very few local stations cover anything but their own cities.

We have detailed ten major differences between broadcast news and newspaper news—mostly to the disadvantage of broadcasting. Some of these differences are inevitable; others can be changed. It is up to broadcasters—and viewers—to determine whether they ought to be changed, and if so how they ought to be changed.

It is probably unfair to judge television news by the same standards applied to newspapers. The media *are* different. Certainly television does a better job of covering the news than radio or movie newsreels did before it. Moreover, two of the most traditional criteria for judging newspapers are speed and accuracy. Television is far superior to the print media on the former, and at least their equal on the latter.

Where television falls down is on the traditional criterion of comprehensiveness and the relatively recent criterion of interpretation. The first failing is almost inevitable, given the technical limitations of the medium. And the second is improving. Network TV now does a good job of reporting *and* interpreting the major national and international stories of the day. In the process, unfortunately, the minor stories get reduced to headlines—or are eliminated entirely. And most local TV news operations give their cities only token attention.

RADIO NEWS

Throughout the 1940s, radio was the most important news medium in America. It nurtured such renowned journalists as Edward R. Murrow, William L. Shirer, and H. V. Kaltenborn, who covered World War II with honor and distinction. Then came television. In 1951, for the first time, the networks earned more money from TV than from radio. In 1952, for the first time, A. C. Nielsen reported that there were more TV sets than radio sets in use every evening. And by 1956 radio's share of the advertising dollar was down to a meager 5.7 percent.

Today, radio ranks third in entertainment (behind television and movies), and third in news (behind television and newspapers). In order to survive, radio stations have been forced to adopt one or another formula—usually music. Today's radio programming is designed for background, not for concentration:

Radio is the one medium that cannot seize

the eye. It is therefore the one mass medium that can serve an active audience: getting up, bathing, eating, doing housework, shopping, commuting, picnicking, camping, cooking, going to bed. Radio became a symbol of the competitive determination of the mass media to occupy any remaining fragment of audience attention. Radio's role became that of a constant companion.[50]

Formula radio may well have saved the medium from near-extinction.

But it had a devastating effect on news quality. The typical radio station styles its news coverage to fit its formula. A hard rock station will adopt a frantic pace, with wire service teletypes pecking away in the background. A classical music station will present a sedate, underplayed, two-minute report every hour. Both newscasts are prepared and read by disc jockeys, not trained journalists.

The typical radio station subscribes to only one wire service—the special UPI or AP broadcast wire, which moves the news in neat five-minute packages, ready to read. Every hour the disc jockey rips the copy from the wire and reads it over the air. Local news is pirated from local papers. Larger metropolitan stations may have a news staff of four or five reporters. But even there the emphasis is on the headlines, the notable and quotable. Even the four major radio networks (ABC, CBS, NBC, and Mutual) carry little more than headlines and features.

As of June, 1974, there were 4,409 AM radio stations and 3,231 FM radio stations in the United States.[51] In entertainment programming they are reasonably diverse. In news programming they are incredibly similar. Melvin Mencher of the Columbia University School of Journalism made these observations on a cross-country auto trip:

A station in a town thirty miles ahead came in, and for the fifth time that day I heard the same state news that had been ripped from the wires most of the day. The first item was the number of traffic fatalities in the state for the

year, with a description of the latest death; next an endless rundown on bids on state highway construction; then the weather—temperature, wind velocity, barometric readings for every section of the state.

It was like this from Canada through the midwest into the southwest. Local stations sounded alike. Traffic accidents, arrests, judicial actions, deaths—courtesy of the local mortuary—statements by the mayor, the governor, a senator. All of it from the record, as dry and as concealing as dust on the highway. . . .[52]

Despite this performance, radio news is an important source of information for many people. A 1974 survey conducted by the Opinion Research Corporation for CBS Radio found that 57 percent of the adults in the country get their first news in the morning from radio; 19 percent tune in the TV instead, and only 18 percent read a newspaper before they have heard or seen the news.[53]

The best available radio news comes from the handful of big-city stations that have adopted an all-news format—notably WINS in New York, KYW in Philadelphia, and the CBS-owned stations in Chicago, Boston, New York, and San Francisco. Even these stations don't carry all that much news. They generally run news in one-hour cycles, repeating the old stories and adding a few new ones each hour. With only three or four reporters on duty at any time, all-news radio stations rely heavily on the wire services, special audio services, local newspapers, and such pseudo-events as press conferences and airport arrivals. But at least a quick, up-to-date rundown on the news is available when you want it. And during elections, disasters, important government hearings, and the like, all-news radio often offers the most comprehensive news to be found anywhere.

LIVE COVERAGE AND DOCUMENTARIES

The strongest moments in television are its on-the-spot reports of important events.

The Kefauver crime investigation . . . the Army-McCarthy hearings . . . the assassination and funeral of President Kennedy . . . the first man on the moon . . . the Nixon resignation. These are the programs one remembers and talks about for years afterward.

The power of television was first widely recognized in 1951, with the Kefauver Crime Investigation Committee hearings in New York. *Daily News* reporter Lowell Limpus described the public's response to the televised hearings:

> They're still trying to figure out just how many people dropped everything to camp in front of the TV screens for an entire week or more. They packed bar-rooms and restaurants to watch Virginia Hill. Suburban housewives entertained swarms of neighbors who studied Frank Costello with bated breath. Big department stores set up TV sets for customers who wouldn't buy anything while former Mayor O'Dwyer was on the stand.[54]

The televised Army-McCarthy hearings a couple of years later are widely credited with having put a stop to the demagogic career of Senator Joe McCarthy. The public was able to judge the man and his methods for itself. In four years, newspapers had not been able to demolish McCarthy. Television did it in a few weeks.

Why does television make so little use of its unique ability to cover important events as they happen? Because television is a commercial medium, and extended live coverage loses money.

Ordinary documentaries also lose money —even the ones that are prepared in advance and don't have to preempt scheduled shows. TV stations run them because they are prestige-builders, and because they earn credit in the eyes of the FCC. Most stations use as few documentaries as they think they can get away with.

Television excels in noncontroversial documentaries. Underwater photography, African wildlife, the treasures of our art museums—these and hundreds of similar topics have been magnificently handled by one or another network in the last few years. Controversial documentaries are something else. Almost always, they turn out wishy-washy.

Part of this is the government's fault. The fairness doctrine requires broadcasters to present every side of any controversy they touch at all. Though the fairness doctrine says nothing about presenting all sides "equally" in the same program, many broadcast executives are afraid to produce a hard-hitting documentary. Robert MacNeil tells the story of an NBC documentary on gun control. The first version examined the problem in some detail, then closed with strong support for gun-control legislation. After viewing this version, NBC executives ordered that an interview with Frank Orth (head of the National Rifle Association) be added at the end to "balance" the presentation. MacNeil feels that what was finally aired had no guts, no spirit, and no point of view.[55]

Any topic that's worth a documentary is bound to involve some powerful people and institutions. If the documentary is hard-hitting, someone is likely to resent it—and television doesn't like to make enemies. The fairness doctrine is sometimes a reason for avoiding controversy; more often it is an excuse. In the late 1960s, CBS planned a program on the role of organized religion in the war on poverty. The producers found that many Protestant churches were reluctant to accept federal anti-poverty money for fear they might endanger the traditional separation of church and state. At the request of several Protestant groups the documentary was canceled. How did these groups know what CBS was up to? CBS had asked them—routinely—if they had any objections to the proposed documentary.[56]

The attitude of many television executives toward documentaries was well expressed by Richard Behrendt, program manager of KRON-TV in San Francisco. A documentary, complained Behrendt, "takes

TV coverage of the Watergate scandals demonstrated once again that television is best when it is live and spontaneous.

For the first year of its unfolding, Watergate was the sort of story television journalism inevitably botches. It was complex, and TV news does not have the time for complexity. It involved leaks and anonymous sources, and such people do not like to be captured on film. It required dogged persistence to unravel, and television correspondents seldom have that luxury. At one point NBC's Carl Stern scooped the print media on the fact that presidential counsel John Dean had cautioned dirty-trickster Donald Segretti not to discuss his campaign manipulations—but the story never got on the air because it would have required too much explanation.[57] As ABC News vice president William Sheean put it: "This kind of story is not our strength."[58] Throughout 1972 and the first half of 1973, the newspapers and newsmagazines essentially owned the Watergate story.

Television came into its own when the focus shifted to public events—the Senate Watergate Committee hearings under Sam Ervin in the summer of 1973, then a year later the House impeachment inquiry under Peter Rodino, the resignation of President Nixon and the swearing in of President Ford. The ratings companies estimated that 70 million Americans watched some portion of the impeachment debates on TV.[59] More than 45 million U.S. TV sets were tuned in when President Nixon announced his resignation on August 8, 1974.[60]

In a survey of television news directors, 72 percent said Watergate coverage was a reason for new hope and self-respect among journalists. Seventeen percent noted a decrease in complaints from viewers about news bias, as the tragic Watergate conclusion vindicated the accuracy of the past two years of news reporting. In addition, 31 percent said their news budgets had been increased as a result of Watergate; 15 percent had more money for investigative reporting, and 14 percent had more money for documentaries.[61]

Characteristically, when television was at its best it was losing money. Many advertisers don't want to "sponsor" an event as controversial as an impeachment hearing, and TV journalists are understandably reluctant to cut away for ads during such a hearing. For economic reasons, the three networks rotated daytime coverage of the Ervin Committee hearings, and decided not to broadcast the last few days of the hearings at all. They carried the six-day House impeachment inquiry in full—at a loss of $3.4 million.[62] A three-hour NBC special the night of the Nixon resignation cost the network $900,000 in canceled ads.[63]

Free from advertising worries, public television taped both proceedings in full and replayed them each night. Noncommercial TV devoted more than 250 prime-time hours to the Ervin hearings alone, earning its largest audience to date and greatly increasing its popularity, visibility, and fund-raising potential.[64] In the process, the American public learned not only about the Watergate cover-up but also about the principles and realities of due process, executive privilege, and separation of powers—and about how the American system of government responds to the crisis of corruption in high places. Television proved once again how powerful a force it can be when its energies are focused on a single event, when it is not preoccupied with cartoons, situation comedies, and earning money.

up a great deal of time and money . . . and may hold people up to ridicule." [65]

When television does undertake a controversial documentary, the results can be magnificent. Undoubtedly one of broadcasting's finest moments in 1970 was the CBS documentary "The Selling of the Pentagon." The power of this exposé of Defense Department news management is indicated by the magnitude of the response it produced. The government protested bitterly; the Pentagon demanded and received rebuttal time; a congressional committee investigated the documentary for bias (see p. 159) and ordered CBS to turn over its unused film so that its editing procedure could be examined. CBS refused this last demand, and eventually the storm blew over. But it did have an effect. Soon afterward, CBS circulated a long memo to its staff on how to edit questions and answers together on film.

CBS undoubtedly knew in advance that "The Selling of the Pentagon" would stir up a hornet's nest of denials and recriminations. In broadcasting the show, and rebroadcasting it in the midst of the furor, the network showed great (and unaccustomed) courage.

EDITORIALS

In 1941, the Federal Communications Commission outlawed broadcast editorials, ruling that "the broadcaster cannot be an advocate." The Commission changed its mind in 1949, but few stations even today take much advantage of the opportunity to editorialize. In 1972, fewer than half of the TV stations in the country and fewer than 60 percent of the radio stations ran even a single editorial. Only about 10 percent of the stations said they editorialized every day—standard practice on even the poorest newspapers. In Canada, by contrast, 45 percent of the radio stations and 36 percent of the TV stations editorialize daily.[66]

When broadcasters do editorialize, they usually stick to noncontroversial topics: "Support Your Local Red Cross" and such. Why? The history of FCC disapproval is part of the answer. So is current government regulation. The fairness doctrine encourages a "yes, but on the other hand" approach in editorials. And the personal attack rule requires stations to give free time to any individual or group criticized in their editorials. Broadcasters who endorse a political candidate must give free time to all opponents. These are significant hindrances to a strong editorial policy, but they are not the real reason most broadcasters lack such a policy. The real reason is much simpler. Strong editorials make enemies, and broadcasters will do nearly anything to avoid making enemies.

NEWS, POWER, AND PROFIT

Television is a medium with unparalleled capacity to inform and influence its audience. It combines sound, pictures, and motion in the intimacy and convenience of one's own living room. Paying attention to television is a national habit. If the people who control our nation's TV news and documentaries wanted to use their power to shape our awareness of certain issues or manipulate our attitudes toward certain policies, they might very well succeed in their goal.

The skilled intercutting of words and pictures can heighten the emotional impact of a story far beyond the ability of the print media. Witness the 1968 Democratic convention in Chicago. On the audio, Mayor Richard Daley denied the existence of police violence; on the video, that violence filled the screen. Many observers felt the combination was unfair and misleading. Many others felt it was an example of superb journalism. Certainly it was powerful. A *New Yorker* critic observed:

> It seems to me quite likely that television will bring forth, sooner or later . . . a man so

skilled at manipulating and juxtaposing, in strong individual style, innumerable fragments of visual and aural reality into a sequential mosaic that he will carry forward the present state of instantaneous electronic-image montage to an altogether new level. It will be an extraordinarily compelling and dangerous journalistic art form.[67]

The power of television is demonstrated by the power of its opponents. TV journalists have been attacked from all sides. The Nixon administration accused them of being tools of a liberal Eastern clique. Black radicals and young people accused them of being tools of the Establishment. Everyone senses the power of television—and would dearly love to control it.

The people who do control it are not intentionally the tools of any ideology. Rather, they are the tools of corporations whose only serious goal is profit. Fortunately or unfortunately, television fritters away its power in exchange for money.

Local station owners have the option of using or not using each network program. This is called giving the show "clearance." And nonentertainment programming has always had significant clearance problems. In 1968, for example, ABC received clearance from 217 affiliates for the entertainment series "Bewitched"—but only 124 clearances for its evening news. NBC had 222 clearances for "Bonanza"—but only 171 for its documentary "NBC White Paper." [68] Many of the stations that do give clearance to network documentaries tape them for use on Sunday mornings or at other outlandish hours. The average station turns down nearly 30 percent of network news and public-affairs programs, scheduling old movies or series reruns instead.

How do you maximize profit in nonentertainment programming? You make the news light-hearted and action-packed. You keep live coverage infrequent, and documentaries noncontroversial. And you don't editorialize much. Whatever kind of nonentertainment programming we look at—news, live cover-

age, documentaries, or editorials—the conclusion is the same: incredible potential, seldom fulfilled. Perhaps the greatest public service the broadcast media can be expected to perform is to make viewers aware that there is much more to be known than they can ever learn from radio and television.

The quality of broadcast programming is determined by the structure of the broadcast industry. It is determined, in other words, by the power of the networks, by the impotence of the government, and by the overwhelming need to satisfy a mass audience and thus attract advertisers. If broadcasting is to change for the better, its structure must change first. Technological developments make this possible, but political factors make it unlikely.

MONEY

Television is one of the most profitable businesses in the United States. Precise figures are hard to come by, but some TV stations return a profit of nearly 100 percent annually on their tangible investment. FCC figures for 1973 show that eighteen stations had profits in excess of $5 million, while twenty-five more earned between $3 million and $5 million. The three networks reported a combined total profit of $185 million.[69] No wonder television is sometimes called "a license to print money."

Of course it depends on the kind of television. In 1973, 88 percent of the network-affiliated VHF stations in the country earned a profit, while only 66 percent of the independent VHF stations operated in the black. For UHF stations the figures were much lower: 54 percent of the network-affiliated stations earned money, and only 30 percent of the independent ones.[70]

Radio is also a risky proposition. No big-city TV station with a network affiliation loses money—but some network radio stations do. Still, most major radio outlets earn tidy if unexciting profits.

Broadcasters earn all their money from advertising. Local broadcast advertising rates range from $2,000 a minute down to $10 a minute or even less. Network rates go as high as $100,000 a minute, sometimes higher. Ad rates are calculated in terms of the cost for every thousand viewers or listeners. Radio, naturally, costs less than television. Afternoons are cheaper than evenings, the shows rich people watch cost more than the shows poor people watch, and the most popular programs are naturally the most expensive.

The goal of nearly all broadcasters is to earn money. They can satisfy that goal only by attracting advertisers. And on network television at least, they can attract advertisers only by achieving a mass audience, an audience measured in millions and tens of millions. And how do you capture a mass audience? By programming light entertainment.

It wasn't always that way. In the mid-1930s, half the shows on CBS radio were unsponsored. Listeners were offered drama from the Mercury Theater, music from the New York Philharmonic, news from the Capitol Cloakroom, and information from the American School of the Air. In 1936, CBS presented 311 public-service broadcasts from 27 countries—opera from Moscow, Palm Sunday services from Jerusalem, the 400th anniversary of the death of Erasmus from Rotterdam. NBC, meanwhile, organized the NBC Symphony Orchestra under Arturo Toscanini, and commissioned a series of original operas by American composers. Early television was similarly blessed.

Very little of this remains. Except in emergencies, no program today goes unsponsored. And the sponsor demands two things of the show: that it bore no one, and that it offend no one. Inevitably it won't excite anyone very much either—but that doesn't bother the sponsor. The goal of most sponsors is millions and millions of listless, uncritical viewers. Broadcasters do their best to give them what they want.

WHERE DOES IT GO?

Where does television spend its money? The average half-hour episode of a network TV series costs more than $100,000 to make. Below is a breakdown of where the money went for one such episode.[71]

Story	$ 7,500	Make-up	$ 500
Executive producer	8,000	Production sound	1,000
Producer	7,000	Transportation	1,000
Director	3,000	Dailies	4,000
Performers	27,000	Editing	4,000
Union benefits	500	Music	1,500
Production staff	2,000	Post-production sound	2,000
Camera	2,500	Stock film	500
Set design	1,500	Titles	500
Set construction	2,000	Opticals	1,000
Set operation	2,000	Lab processing	3,000
Electrical	2,500	Testing	1,000
Special effects	500	Administrative	1,500
Set dressing	1,500	Promotion	2,000
Props	1,000	Facilities	15,000
Wardrobe	1,000		
		TOTAL	$108,000

NETWORKS

There are three commercial television networks in the United States: CBS, NBC, and ABC. All three operate radio networks as well; the only other radio network of any size is Mutual.

As we saw in Chapter 9 (see pp. 250–58), the main job of a network is to produce or purchase programming—roughly 100 hours of programming a week. For each program the network must find an advertiser or group of advertisers to foot the bill. Then the network offers the show to local TV stations around the country. It doesn't sell them the program. On the contrary, it pays them to carry it, and even lets them insert some of their own local commercials in the middle.

The network set-up works to everyone's advantage, so naturally it dominates the industry. The vast majority of the commercial television stations in the country are affiliated with one or another network. If there are two stations in town, one is bound to be CBS and the other NBC. If there are three stations, the third will settle for the less profitable ABC affiliation. Only if there are four or more stations in a city will there ever be an "independent."

The independents have it rough. Few can afford to produce more than five or six hours a day of their own programming. The rest they have to buy. Independent stations are the principal customers of the syndicates and independent producers. They buy old movies and serial reruns by the thousands. Occasionally they are allowed to use a network show which the local affiliate has turned down.

As of June 30, 1974, there were 706 commercial TV stations in the United States. Of these, 219 were affiliated with NBC, 191 with CBS, and 168 with ABC. Only 128 stations had no network affiliation. All but a handful of these were UHFs, and many were in financial difficulties.

Network control does its part to help keep television a *mass* medium. Occasionally a local advertiser might be found who was willing to sponsor a minority-interest program, an opera for example. It is much, much harder to find a national advertiser who is willing to do so. And even if one existed, the sponsors of adjacent programs would complain bitterly. An opera would turn off so many viewers that many would actually switch to another channel.

GOVERNMENT

Government regulation of broadcasting is discussed in detail elsewhere in this book (see pp. 190–205). What is important to stress here is government *nonregulation* of broadcasting. In the morass of hearings and proposed rules and policy statements that characterize the relationship between government and the broadcast media in the United States, it is easy to lose track of the following basics.

Licensing. Between 1934 and 1972, while more than 50,000 broadcast licenses were granted or renewed, only a hundred or so stations lost their license. And most of these ran afoul of some clear-cut law or policy— they transmitted on the wrong frequency, went off the air entirely, lied to the FCC in their license application, or committed some such obvious infraction. Both critics and defenders of traditional broadcasting tend to view the occasional license revocation as a sign of radical change just around the corner; the critics applaud and the defenders appeal to Congress for protection from the FCC. But the fact is that the Commission has never used the license-renewal process as a vehicle for wholesale reform of the broadcast industry. And it probably never will.

Diversity. In recent years the government has talked a lot about the evils of broadcast monopoly. But government action has been much less extreme than government rhetoric. The FCC, for example, proposed a rule that would take away the licenses of all stations owned by local newspapers; but it wound up listing only sixteen small-city combinations as sufficiently monopolistic to require action —and said it would entertain requests for waivers from those sixteen. Similarly, the Justice Department filed suit to stop the networks from producing their own shows; but if precedent is any guide, the suit will eventually be dropped or settled amicably. What has the government actually accomplished in this area?—a limit on the number of stations any company can own; a rule requiring stations to get a little of their prime-time programming from non-network sources; a freeze on the growth of cross-media monopolies in the same city; and some fairly strict rules to keep broadcasters out of the cable TV business. Three identical national networks still control American television and use it to sell mass audiences to corporate advertisers. Nothing the government has done seems likely to change that basic fact.

Programming. The equal-time law assures mainstream politicians an even break. The obscenity laws guarantee that even bluenoses can safely watch television. The fairness doctrine provides a vehicle for making the most grossly one-sided stations pay a little attention to reasonably common viewpoints they have ignored. The rest is talk. The FCC frequently asks stations how much local news they run, how violent their entertainment shows are, how many programs they carry for minority audiences, etc. But it seldom does anything with the answers.

The government has two truly important effects on the nature of broadcasting. First, by setting policy for new broadcast technologies (such as FM and UHF in the past, cable and satellites in the present and future), the government can help determine whether these technologies become a force for change or just a new piece of the traditional industry. Second, the very existence of a government regulatory mechanism, however seldom it is used, keeps broadcasters nervous and thus provides citizen groups with a pressure point in their battles for local reform. Aside from these two impacts, the government has done little, and is doing little, to alter the structure and content of broadcasting.

None of this is necessarily bad. A good argument can be made that licenses shouldn't be revoked just because a bureaucrat thinks someone else would do a better job, that broadcast monopolies should be left powerful enough to take on any institution (including the government) in relative safety, that censorship of programming is not the government's business. In a libertarian society it isn't easy to decide what, if anything, we would want the government to do about broadcasting. The point is that whatever we want, the government is in fact doing very little. For better or for worse, what broadcasters offer you on TV tonight will not bear a heavy burden of government interference.

THE PUBLIC

Broadcasters reply to every criticism of programming with the statement that they are only giving the public what it wants. Are they? The question is hard to answer.

Any survey of public attitudes toward television is likely to reveal the same sorts of criticisms we have been talking about in this chapter. A 1970 Louis Harris poll, for example, found that viewers wanted to see more news, documentaries, and educational programs—and less rock music, game shows, soap operas, and mysteries.[72] Is this a true reflection of public opinion, or does it reflect what the public thinks it should think? Probably the latter. There has seldom been a documentary with a higher rating than the average game show.

College graduates are the most caustic critics of television programming, and they watch TV at least one-third less than the national average. But when a college grad does tune in, he or she skips the "quality" programs and settles for the same light entertainment everyone else is watching.[73]

Consider two studies from 1969. The first one found that only 10 percent of the population said there was ever a time when they wanted to watch television but could find nothing on that they cared to watch.[74] The second one found that the total television audience was declining for the first time. Between 1968 and 1969, thirty-six of the top fifty markets showed drops in the number of viewers.[75] Put the two studies together and they yield an important conclusion. Those who customarily watch TV are happy with what they see. Those who are unhappy with TV simply aren't watching. Television cannot expand its audience beyond current levels unless it appeals to this latter group.

Will broadcasters voluntarily diversify their programming in order to attract the unhappy minority? Not likely. They're doing very nicely, thank you, with the happy majority. They aim to keep it that way.

CHANGES

Back in 1959, FCC Chairman John Doerfer apologized for broadcasting in the following words: "It is an infant industry and it is going through growing pains, the same as the printing press had to do over a period of years. It is a stage." [76]

Broadcasting hasn't changed much since then. Perhaps it is still an infant. Perhaps it

is a retarded adolescent. In any case, it often seems unchanging and unchangeable.

If broadcasting ever does change, it will be because technological developments forced it to do so. There are at least six technologies with this capacity:

1. Cable TV.
2. Pay TV.
3. Video playback.
4. FM and UHF.
5. Noncommercial broadcasting.
6. Satellite TV.

We will discuss each in turn.

1. Cable TV. Cable television is a system for transmitting the TV signal via a wire or cable, instead of over the air. It was first developed in the mid-1930s. For more than a decade, cable was used mainly to connect stations into networks. By the 1950s it was used also to improve TV reception in rural areas, mountainous terrain, and skyscraper cities. The subscriber usually paid a hook-up fee of $10 and a monthly rate of $5, in return for a guaranteed perfect picture. The broadcast industry was delighted.

Then, early in the 1960s, a few cable operators began to import signals from other

---

"DEAR FCC . . ."

In 1972 the Federal Communications Commission received more than 22,000 letters of complaint about some aspect of broadcasting, plus nearly 23,000 letters of comment. The topics that provoked the most anger included obscene language (2,141 letters), cancellation of a program (1,891), fairness doctrine abuses (1,617), the equal-time law (1,383), distortion or suppression of news (1,311), and criticisms of specific programs (1,274). The Commission received only 1,060 communications in connection with license-renewal applications (less than one per station)—663 were favorable to the station in question, and 397 were opposed.

The single largest category of letters—6,599—were those laudatory of station performance.[77]

The FCC keeps a letter file for every station, which it reviews at license-renewal time. A thick file full of critical letters may be enough to provoke a second look at the station's performance, though of course it is unlikely to lead to denial of the license. The best approach is probably to send the letter directly to the station, with a copy to the FCC. Ever fearful of even the remote possibility of government action, broadcasters take a complaint letter much more seriously when they know the FCC has a copy.

cities for their clients. Suddenly local broadcasters were no longer delighted; the cable outfits threatened to steal part of their audience. And distant broadcasters complained that the cable companies were using their programs without payment.

Enter the FCC. In 1965, under pressure from the broadcast industry, the Commission declared that it had the right to regulate cable TV. A year later it established a complete set of highly restrictive rules. Among other things, cable systems in the top hundred markets were forbidden to import distant signals unless they could prove that no damage would be done to existing stations.

The proponents of cable quickly organized their own lobbying effort. They pointed out the incredible advantages of the new medium:

- Cable can easily carry 20 channels; technically, its capacity extends as high as 84 channels. Yet cable "stations" take up no space on the overcrowded electromagnetic spectrum.
- Cable can "broadcast" as selectively as needed. Specialized news and advertising can be programmed for each city, town, neighborhood, or block—even for particular racial or political groups.
- Cable picture quality is uniformly excellent, especially in color.
- Cable is far cheaper than over-the-air broadcasting, sometimes running as little as $5 an hour for an entire channel. This is well within the grasp of school systems, local political candidates, and even ordinary citizens wishing to communicate with their neighbors.
- Cable paves the way for a two-way communications network. It can transmit a facsimile newspaper or a library reference service. It can replace the post office and the telephone. The possibilities are endless.

This is not just propaganda: The possibilities *are* endless. Once an entire country is wired for two-way telecommunications, anything is feasible—from instant political referendums to stay-at-home shopping centers. It all starts with cable.

In early 1972, the FCC adopted a more permissive series of rules governing cable development (see pp. 204–5). The new regulations required the larger cable systems to produce some of their own programming; made all cable operations set aside channels for city government, education, and public access; and permitted cable companies in the top hundred markets to import two distant signals apiece. Cable's boosters predicted that the new rules would quickly force cable to realize some of its potential, to take its place as an important medium of communication.

In the next three years very little happened, and in 1975 the goal of a "wired nation" seemed as far away as ever. Cable operators were unable to convince city dwellers that their service was worth from $6 to $10 a month. The government channels were unused; the programs on the public-access channels were amateurish and uninteresting to middle-class viewers; the programs originated by the cable systems themselves were mostly old movies and sporting events. In 1974, 8 million homes were on cable, about 12 percent of the viewing audience—but only a quarter of these were in the top hundred metropolitan areas.[78] In Manhattan, the two existing cable companies were able to attract only 120,000 subscribers between them, less than 20 percent of the potential; both were losing money.[79] In Boston and Kansas City, public officials decided not to permit any cable development at all for the time being. In Dayton and Birmingham, San Antonio and Newark, owners of cable franchises refused to build the systems until (and unless) they could figure out a way to make them earn a profit.[80]

Says one executive of a large cable company: "Cable bombed in the cities, and we will be a long time recovering from it. We not only oversold ourselves and made ridiculous promises to the cities, we underestimated the cost of wiring the urban communities and also the kinds of services the urban consumer would require."[81]

To attract subscribers in areas where the over-the-air picture is acceptable, cable companies will have to offer programming that is not available from the networks and independent stations. As of mid-1974, only 658 of the nation's 3,100 cable systems were originating their own shows. In some of the smaller cities and towns, cable-originated programs managed to attract small but devoted special-interest audiences.[82] But it is in the big cities that cable programming is most important, since cable's ability to import distant signals is less attractive in a metropolis served by a full range of local stations. And in the big cities, apart from covering sports events that may be blacked out on local over-the-air channels, cable programming has offered little to lure subscribers (or advertisers). The biggest excitement generated so far has come from sex and nudity on some public-access channels—and that may quickly disappear once the government figures out how to censor public-access cable without running afoul of the First Amendment.

The future of cable is not clear. Some critics have suggested that instead of concentrating on entertainment services to home customers, cable systems in the cities should stress services to business, such as linking banks or hospitals.[83] In early 1974, the White House Office of Telecommunications Policy (OTP) issued a report on cable's future, urging that it be lightly regulated by government and allowed to develop as the marketplace demands. The report envisioned cable operating more or less as a public utility, with cable owners leasing channels to all comers—to the networks for additional entertainment shows; to church, labor, and citizen groups; to businesses for commercial uses; etc. Rates for leasing a channel would be standardized and published.

The OTP report also urged the FCC to back off its regulations forbidding cable ownership by broadcasters. While acknowledging the danger of any media monopoly, the report warned that broadcasters would surely oppose the development of cable if they could not share in the action.[84]

At the moment, there isn't much action to share. Not too long ago, cable started out as a mom-and-pop industry, but it soon became clear that the profit potential, if any, was long-term and very speculative. Cable is now dominated by a few giants. The ten largest cable firms serve nearly half of all subscribers.[85] The names to watch are Tele-PrompTer, Viacom, Warner Cable Corp., American Television and Communications, Cox Cable Communications, and a few others. These are the companies that will become rich and powerful if cable ever gets off the ground. And these are the companies that will go bankrupt or cost their parent corporations a bundle if cable continues going nowhere.

Alfred R. Stern, chairman of Warner Cable, sums up the current status of cable this way: "We have hit a plateau, as other developing industries have done before us. Everyone in the cable business is treading water until we find the services that will make people in the cities want cable. We need help from others. We can't do it ourselves. We're not a real communications industry at the moment." [86]

2. Pay TV. Pay television earns its profits directly from the viewer, not through advertising. It is therefore immune to the "mass market" syndrome; any show can be profitable if those who want to see it are willing to pay enough for the privilege. Broadcasters and theater owners are apparently convinced of the potential of this new medium. For the last twenty-five years they have waged an aggressive and never-ending battle against it.

Until the early 1970s, pay TV went nowhere. The FCC helped retard its development by authorizing only small-scale experiments until UHF got off the ground. But even the experiments were discouraging; most people just didn't want to pay a monthly fee or drop coins into a box on top of the set for the privilege of watching more movies and sports on television.

The catalyst for pay TV growth was cable. In order to attract more subscribers, some urban cable systems decided to sweeten the pot by offering pay TV as part of the package. By early 1974 there were forty-six combined pay-cable systems in operation, with some 60,000 customers paying extra for the pay TV option.[87] A study by Kenneth Penchos of the Stanford Research Institute predicts that by 1985 pay-cable will be a multibillion-dollar industry, with subscribers in 30 percent of all U.S. television homes. The futures of cable and pay TV, according to Penchos, are inextricably tied; neither can succeed without the other.[88]

Pay-cable lobbyists are now working hard to reverse the various FCC rules that keep pay TV in check. Movies are available for pay TV only during the first two years of release or after ten years, not in between. Series are forbidden. And sporting events that have been carried by regular broadcast stations can't be run on pay TV for at least two years. An FCC investigation of the entire pay television industry is underway to determine if these rules should be abandoned or altered.

Over-the-air broadcasters are lobbying too. They have retained the PR firm of Hill & Knowlton to help convince viewers that pay TV will eventually take away their favorite programs. The National Association of Broadcasters has given its member stations kits with anti-pay bumper stickers, buttons, fact sheets, and a model speech entitled "The Day Free TV Died." [89]

Ralph M. Baruch, head of the pay-cable committee of the National Cable Television Association, says it is "ludicrous" to imagine that "this small animal called pay-cable could kick or crush the wealthy and profitable elephant of conventional television." He predicts that even if pay-cable achieved 2.5 million subscribers by 1980, it would take away less than 0.3 percent of the over-the-air television audience.[90]

In the short term, at least, pay TV has a limited future. At best, it will provide easier access to first-run movies and sports events for those who can pay the price. At worst, it will go nowhere for another twenty-five years.

3. Video Playback. Some day in the not

too distant future you may be able to walk into a department store and buy a color television set equipped with a playback unit. This will enable you to record programs off the air for future viewing, or to play prerecorded video disks or tapes available at the same store for rent or purchase.

Devices of this sort are already on the market and are selling at the rate of more than 100,000 a year to schools, government agencies, and corporations. But they are still too expensive to be popular for home use. And none of the half-dozen available systems is compatible with any of the others; once you commit yourself to a disk unit from one company, you can't use it to play tapes or cartridges from another. In any case, the number of prerecorded programs for sale (on any system) is still very small. These problems will have to be solved before the video playback industry can begin catching up to past projections of $1.2 billion in annual sales by 1975.[91]

Even if the problems are solved, the industry may collapse. In 1973 the company that was furthest advanced in the video cassette field—Cartridge Television, Inc.—declared bankruptcy, costing its parent corporation a reported $48 million.[92]

Like pay TV, video playback is not dependent on advertising. In theory, something akin to the phonograph record industry should develop: prerecorded sports, films, and entertainment for a mass audience; prerecorded operas, ballets, and educational materials for more specialized audiences. But it is still an open question whether the American consumer wants this new medium enough to pay for it.

4. FM and UHF. Frequency modulation (FM) radio is a different area of the spectrum from ordinary amplitude modulation (AM) radio. Ultrahigh frequency (UHF) television is a different area of the spectrum from ordinary very high frequency (VHF) television. The technical differences are unimportant here. What is important is that FM doubles the size of the radio band, while UHF sextuples the space for television stations. By providing for many more stations, both FM and UHF make it possible to diversify broadcast programming.

Neither is a new invention. Both, in fact, date back before World War II. But for several decades the FCC actively opposed their development, preferring to nurse along the infant AM and VHF media. It wasn't until the 1960s that the Commission changed its mind. In 1961 it permitted FM stations to broadcast in stereo, opening up a new market of music buffs and hi-fi nuts. In 1962 it persuaded Congress to require UHF receivers on all new television sets in interstate commerce. And in 1964 it put strict limits on FM simulcasting, forcing the stations to develop their own programs.

These moves made FM and UHF economically feasible. AM broadcasters who had kept their FM properties inactive began to see the possibility of profit. Companies that had been unable to find an available VHF station began to apply for UHF licenses. By June, 1974, there were 2,547 commercial FM radio stations and 192 commercial UHF television stations on the air.

Neither medium, overall, is profitable yet, but both are getting close. In 1972, FM as a whole lost $12.7 million, $2.3 million less than it lost in 1971. Out of 590 independent FM stations (those not tied to a sister AM station), 224 showed a profit, an increase of 42 stations over 1971.[93] One clear success story is KIOI in San Francisco, which was started on a $6,000 investment in 1957; the owner has turned down a $3.5-million offer for the station.[94] UHF, meanwhile, lost $7.7 million in 1973—compared to $15.9 million in 1972, $32.7 million in 1971, and $45.5 million in 1970.[95] Both media expect to earn overall profits well before 1980.

According to a 1974 survey, 33 percent of all American adults said they listened to FM some time during the week; 67 percent said they listened to AM. In 1973, by contrast, only 28 percent listened to FM, while 72 percent listened to AM.[96] The trend from AM to FM is clear. More than 90 percent of American homes had an FM receiver in 1973, up 5 percent from 1972.[97] The same thing is happening to UHF. In 1973, 86 percent of U.S. television households had a set capable of receiving UHF, up 6 percent since 1971.[98]

Two additional developments support the rosy prognosis. More and more automobile buyers are taking the FM radio option in their cars, which will help listenership during the drive-time periods when ad rates are highest. (A bill that would require all new car radio sets to receive both AM and FM was passed by the Senate in 1974, but died in the House.) The big spur for UHF now is cable television. Since cable systems are required to carry all stations in their market, it is just as easy for a cable subscriber to tune in a UHF station as a VHF station. And in a cable system the two stations get equally good reception. In a community served by cable, UHF and VHF can compete on an even basis.

What are FM and UHF doing with their new profits? They are looking for an audience that is not satisfied with the competition. For FM this means special-interest programming—acid rock, classical music, or jazz; radical or rightist political commentary; whatever isn't available on AM. For UHF it means taking a network affiliation if there's one available, otherwise concentrating on local sports, old reruns and movies, and syndicated interview and variety shows. The key for non-network UHF stations is counterprogramming—running something different from what is on the networks at the same time. Says Gene Jacobson of KHTV in Houston: "When they [the networks] go for adults, we go for kids, and in prime time when we all go for adults we play features and counter them as much as we can."[99]

One of the most successful UHF operations is the Spanish International Communications Corp., with stations in Los Angeles; Miami; San Antonio; Paterson, N.J.; and

Hanford, Calif. Sales Director William D. Stiles explains the company's strategy:

> We're dealing with a fraction of the market. Ours is not so much a UHF-vs.-VHF sell as a Spanish-vs.-English sell. But we *are* part of a segmentation trend. Instead of trying to be all things to all people, we're all things to a small segment of the population.[100]

Critics of FM and UHF complain that they are not as different from AM and VHF as they ought to be. The stations have to earn money to survive, and that means they have to come up with something that will attract advertisers and audiences. Too many FM stations carry the same sorts of music as their AM counterparts; too many UHF stations settle for old reruns of former network series. But the most successful FM and UHF stations are the ones that counter-program the opposition, that *do* offer something at least a little different. The diversity offered by FM and UHF is not ideal, but it helps.

5. Noncommercial Broadcasting. As of June, 1974, there were 918 noncommercial broadcast stations in the country; 684 of them were radio stations, 143 were UHF television stations, and 91 were VHF television stations. These stations are operated by colleges and universities, state and local governments, and various nonprofit civic groups. Some are strictly educational. Others go far beyond the classroom to program political, social, and cultural events of interest. Whatever their content, none of the 918 stations accepts advertising. They are supported entirely by donations from individuals and grants from companies, foundations, and governments.

From the beginnings of public television in 1951, its main source of support (about $150 million through 1975) was the Ford Foundation. In early 1974, Ford announced that over the next several years it would slowly pull out. "The business of a foundation," explained a Ford executive, "is to try to start new things in the high-risk businesses.

No foundation is doing its job if it stays with one project forever." [101]

The federal government is expected to take up the slack. Shortly before resigning, President Nixon announced his support for a long-term funding plan that would give noncommercial stations $70 million in 1976, escalating to $100 million in 1980. The stations would be expected to raise $2.50 from other sources for every dollar contributed by the government.[102] As of mid-1975, President Ford had not yet committed himself on this issue, and of course no one knew if Congress would go along. But even assuming the greatest possible support, noncommercial broadcasting will still be dirt poor, as it has always been.

The big issue in noncommercial television is, of course, politics (see pp. 203–4). President Nixon withheld his support for any kind of long-term funding until he had largely won two major battles: putting a stop to "creeping liberalism" in public television's news coverage, and halting the growth of the Public Broadcasting Service (PBS) as a possible fourth network. Nixon wanted a decentralized collection of local nonprofit stations that paid little or no attention to national politics. Before leaving office, he got what he wanted.

A compromise negotiated in 1973 between PBS and the government-appointed Corporation for Public Broadcasting set up a "marketplace cooperative" for noncommercial broadcasting. The money is doled out to local stations, which can use it to produce their own programs or, if they wish, to pay a share of the production costs of some other station's program, thus earning the right to broadcast it when it's done.[103] This cooperative arrangement is quite different from the set-up in the early 1970s, when PBS had its own budget to produce national shows (such as the Ervin Committee hearings on Watergate) that were then available to local stations without charge.

The predictable result was a quick drop in the amount of national programming, especially political programming. In the first year of the new arrangement, fewer than 16 percent of the programs coming out of the Washington PBS production center dealt with public affairs.[105] And many special-interest programs, such as "WNET Opera Theater," were canceled because too few stations wanted to pay their share of the cost. Commented one critic:

> The presumption—indeed, the pious resolution—of public TV was that there should be a place for opera, ballet, serious drama, public affairs documentaries. When representatives of 246 public TV stations get together to vote their hearts and pocketbooks, and only 10 of them want "WNET Opera Theater," and, as a result, "Opera Theater" is apparently dead, the time has come to ask if there's much significant difference between the public TV people and the commercial network people.[106]

The opposing argument, of course, is that public television was never meant to provide a more convenient cultural life for the rich and well-educated (see pp. 221–22). But neither was it meant to duplicate the network shows. In 1969, John Macy, then head of the Corporation for Public Broadcasting, stated:

> Our aim is not to compete with the commercial networks in mass audience, with sustained viewing, but rather to provide a diversity of viewing choice and, hopefully, to offer something that is going to be meaningful, stimulating, and entertaining to the people who view it.[107]

The question that noncommercial broadcasting has never been able to answer convincingly is this: What does "quality programming" mean for a mass audience that is quite satisfied with commercial offerings? Traditional educational broadcasters have an answer that makes sense; they reach millions of people in and out of schools who are watching or listening for information, not entertainment. The newer children's programs, such as "Sesame Street" and "Mister Rogers' Neighborhood," have an equally sound rationale; kids enjoy the shows at least as much as the network ones, and parents and educators like them a lot more.

An argument could be made that political documentaries were a kind of programming with at least the potential for mass appeal, but this particular alternative to network entertainment is anathema to the government that pays the bills. Some stations have tried special-interest shows for minority cultural, ethnic, or interest groups, but the result is usually a low rating and a collective yawn that neither raises money from the public nor justifies money from the government. What is left besides high-brow culture for elites, or a pale, underfinanced imitation of the networks?

Noncommercial broadcasting has unlimited potential. The frequencies are allotted and the stations are on the air. Now three huge problems must be solved—where to get the money, how to achieve freedom from government control, and what to do with the money and freedom once they're gained.

6. Satellite TV. In 1962, AT&T launched the first experimental communications satellite. Later that year, Congress created Comsat, a semi-public corporation charged with developing communications satellites. Intelsat, an international consortium with the same purpose, was organized in 1964. AT&T is the largest single stockholder of Comsat, and the most influential member of Intelsat.

AT&T, you should recognize, is also the company that owns the land lines connecting TV stations into networks. It earns a substantial percentage of its profits from those lines. Quite naturally, then, AT&T was not too enthusiastic about communications satellites—which do the job more cheaply. As a consequence, satellite development in the U.S. was very slow, and tended to be restricted to international transmissions of news and special events.

In 1972, prompted by the White House Office of Telecommunications Policy, the FCC finally broke the AT&T monopoly and adopted an "open-sky" rule. A number of companies immediately began plans to put up their own satellites, including Western Union, RCA, General Telephone and Electronics, and even AT&T. In 1974 Western Union launched the first two U.S. commercial communications satellites. Each one

---

INTERNATIONAL SATELLITE PROPAGANDA?

An interesting international political debate is shaping up over the possible use of satellites for communication from the government or broadcast industry of one country to the people of another. Satellites are already used extensively for international broadcasting, courtesy of Intelsat, but the procedure is carefully controlled: Foreign correspondents can beam their reports back to their own stations; networks can transmit live overseas programs to the home office; a station in one country can agree by prearrangement to pick up a signal from a station in another country. But what would happen if NBC decided to use satellites to carry its shows directly to TV sets in the Soviet Union, or if a Soviet-made broadcast suddenly turned up on channel 4 in the U.S.?

Concerned about such possibilities, the Soviet government has asked the United Nations to establish the principle that no country may beam TV programs into another without the consent of the recipient country. The U.S. opposes the agreement on the grounds that it would contradict the libertarian notion of a free marketplace of ideas.[108] One critic is Dr. Frank Stanton, former vice chairman of CBS, who said the Russian proposal "would make censorship a principle of international law." According to Stanton, "You don't negotiate free speech."[109]

can carry more than a thousand telephone conversations, or about a dozen color TV programs.[110]

The satellites will have many uses besides broadcasting—they can transmit telephone or telegraph messages, beam data from one computer to another, etc. Within broadcasting, their most immediate use will be to cut the cost to the networks of transmitting their shows to distant local stations. The monthly cost of a radio land line between New York and San Francisco is $2,298—versus $1,700 by satellite. A three-hour football game on color TV can reach Alaska for $3,500 via domestic satellite, as opposed to $5,000 via Intelsat and even more via land lines.[111]

In theory, satellites could eventually eliminate the need for local stations entirely, except for local programming. Network to satellite to home transmission is technologically feasible today—not just for the three existing networks, but for thirty new networks or more, enough for every kind of minority programming. No one in power is seriously considering this alternative.

Science writer Arthur C. Clarke and scholar Wilbur Schramm are among those who have seen the real potential of satellites. Writes Clarke:

> The Electronic Blackboard would be of enormous educational value. . . . It would teach medicine, agriculture, sanitation and simple manufacturing techniques even to primitive peoples. Later, specially-taped programs could teach writing to preliterate populations; ultimately the Blackboard could act as the village newspaper and information center. The social value of such a device can hardly be overestimated; it would change the political and cultural patterns of the whole world.[112]

And Schramm:

> The likelihood is that governments, businesses and industrial concerns will have more data than ever before on which to base decisions and less time in which to make them. . . . It is likely that satellite communications will tend to speed up diplomacy just as it will speed up other relationships involving discussions, data handling and decision making.[113]

All this is within our grasp today. If we never get there, it will be for political and economic reasons, not technological ones.

This is by now a familiar story. We have looked at six technologies with the potential to change broadcasting in meaningful ways —cable TV, pay TV, video playback, FM and UHF, noncommercial broadcasting, and satellite TV. In time, one or several of these may revolutionize the broadcast industry. But traditional broadcasting has a powerful hold on American society, and is not about to let go voluntarily. In structure and in content, radio and television in 1976 are little different from radio and television in 1966. And 1986 may well bring more of the same.

Notes

[1] *1974 Broadcasting Yearbook,* p. 12.

[2] *Ibid.*

[3] "The Harris Poll," *San Francisco Examiner,* January 19, 1970, p. 50.

[4] *1968 Broadcasting Yearbook,* p. 22.

[5] "World TV Set Census 251-Mil.; U.S. Has 30%," *Variety,* April 12, 1972, p. 1.

[6] *1968 Broadcasting Yearbook,* pp. 22, 24.

[7] *San Francisco Chronicle,* May 9, 1970.

[8] Newton N. Minow, *Equal Time, the Private Broadcaster and the Public Interest* (New York: Atheneum, 1964), ch. 1.

[9] Gary A. Steiner, *The People Look at Television* (New York: Alfred A. Knopf, 1963), p. 235.

[10] Robert Daley, "Police Report on TV Cop Shows," *New York Times Magazine,* November 19, 1972, pp. 39, 84–106.

[11] "Papp's 'Sticks and Bones' Put Off by C.B.S.," *New York Times,* March 7, 1973, p. 87. " 'Sticks' Nixed By 38 CBS-TV Affils; Many Delaying It," *Variety,* July 25, 1973, p. 21.

[12] Norman Jacobs, ed., *Culture for the Millions* (New York: Van Nostrand Reinhold, 1961), p. 508.

[13] Bernard Rosenberg and David Manning White, eds., *Mass Culture: The Popular Arts in America* (New York: The Free Press, 1957), p. 60.

14 Alexis de Tocqueville, *Democracy in America* (New York: Vintage Books, 1945), II, pp. 50–54.

15 "Canada Pressing Airwave Control," *New York Times,* September 15, 1974, p. 20.

16 Rosenberg and White, *Mass Culture,* p. 61.

17 Jacobs, *Culture for the Millions,* p. 510.

18 "Obscenities Boxscore," *Variety,* March 7, 1973, p. 36.

19 " 'Topless Radio' Shows Draw Fine from F.C.C.," *New York Times,* April 14, 1973, p. 94.

20 "Burch Scores Fad of 'Topless Radio,' " *New York Times,* March 19, 1973, p. 94.

21 "F.C.C. Will Study 'Obscene' Shows on Radio and TV," *New York Times,* March 28, 1973, pp. 1, 37.

22 "Storer Drops Sex Talk From KGBS and WHN," *Variety,* April 4, 1973, p. 42.

23 Dwight Newton, "How Permissive Can TV Get?" *San Francisco Sunday Examiner and Chronicle,* February 1, 1970, p. B5.

24 Robert M. Liebert, John M. Neale, and Emily S. Davidson, *The Early Window: Effects of Television on Children and Youth* (Elmsford, N.Y.: Pergamon Press, 1973), p. 23.

25 *Ibid.,* p. 25.

26 *Ibid.,* p. 24.

27 John Stanley, "The Year Many a Villain Was Worded to Death," *San Francisco Sunday Examiner and Chronicle, Datebook,* January 4, 1970, p. 12.

28 Liebert, Neale, and Davidson, *The Early Window,* pp. 2–3.

29 "Was 'West Side Story' Bad for East Harlem?" *New York Times,* April 2, 1972, p. D15.

30 "B.B.C. Study Finds U.S. Fare Twice as Violent as British TV," *New York Times,* January 27, 1972, p. 75.

31 Liebert, Neale, and Davidson, *The Early Window,* p. 28.

32 F. B. Steuer, J. M. Applefield, and R. Smith, "Televised Aggression and the Interpersonal Aggression of Preschool Children," *Journal of Experimental Child Psychology,* 11, 1971, 442–47.

33 A. Bandura, D. Ross, and S. A. Ross, "Transmission of Aggression through Imitation of Aggressive Models," *Journal of Abnormal and Social Psychology,* 63, 1961, 575–82.

34 Liebert, Neale, and Davidson, *The Early Window,* p. 154.

35 "KTTV Yields to Arm-Twisting By NABB on Kidvid Violence," *Variety,* October 3, 1973, p. 20.

36 "Advertising: Views of Children," *New York Times,* April 3, 1974, p. 69.

37 " 'Wrath of McGrath' Pays Off; Drive by M.P. Cues CBC Ban on Kidvid Blurbs; Asks Govt. to Take Up Money Slack," *Variety,* June 27, 1973, p. 43.

38 "Canada to Trim Kidvid Blurbs," *Variety,* September 19, 1973, p. 2.

39 "Aussie Guidelines in Kidvid," *Variety,* July 25, 1973, p. 27.

40 "N.A.B. TV Board Votes a 25% Cut in Ads for Children," *New York Times,* January 22, 1972, p. 59.

41 "Caveat Vendor," *Newsweek,* June 17, 1974, p. 69.

42 "Children's TV Premiums Illegal, F.T.C. Head Says," *New York Times,* June 4, 1974, pp. 1, 75.

43 Edwin Diamond, "Goodnight, Walter, John, David, Harry, and You, Too, Howard," *New York,* July 23, 1973, p. 32.

44 "TV News Viewing In 5-Month Drop," *New York Times,* June 8, 1974, p. 63.

45 "Count-Up for NBC News," *Variety,* May 2, 1973, pp. 63–64.

46 Edward Jay Epstein, "Onward and Upward With The Arts: The Selection of Reality," *New Yorker,* March 3, 1973, pp. 63–64.

47 "Livelier and Longer TV News Spurs Hunt for Talent," *New York Times,* April 22, 1974, pp. 37, 71.

48 Michael J. Arlen, *Living-Room War* (New York: Viking Press, 1969), pp. 194–95.

49 Robert MacNeil, "The News On TV And How It Is Unmade," *Harper's Magazine,* October, 1968, p. 75.

50 Richard L. Worsnop, "Competing Media," *Editorial Research Reports,* II, No. 3, July 18, 1969, 542.

51 *Broadcasting,* August 12, 1974, p. 39.

52 Melvin Mencher, "The Roving Listener," *Columbia Journalism Review,* Fall, 1966, pp. 45–46.

53 Opinion Research Corporation, "U.S. Public's Usual First Source of News in the Morning," Study II, May, 1974.

54 Lowell Limpus, "Television News Comes of Age," *Nieman Reports,* July, 1951, p. 11.

55 Robert MacNeil, *The People Machine* (New York: Harper & Row, 1968), ch. 11.

56 Richard Severo, "What's News at CBS?" *New Republic,* March 12, 1966, p. 33.

57 "Watergate on Camera," *Newsweek,* May 28, 1973, p. 113.

58 *Ibid.*

59 "Nixon's Days in Court Are TV's, Too; Impeachment Coverage Makes History," *Broadcasting,* August 5, 1974, p. 18.

60 "Almost 47-Mil U.S. Homes Saw Nixon-Ford Switch," *Variety,* August 28, 1974, p. 2.

61 "Watergate Spurs Journalism on TV," *New York Times*, December 9, 1973, p. 51.

62 "Nixon's Days in Court," p. 18.

63 "Record TV Audience Attends Nixon Resignation," *Broadcasting*, August 12, 1974, p. 6.

64 "Watergate Spurs Journalism on TV," p. 51.

65 "FCC's KRON-TV Quiz: 2 Views," *Variety*, April 22, 1970, p. 35.

66 *1973 Broadcasting Yearbook*, p. 33.

67 Thomas Whiteside, "Corridor of Mirrors," *Columbia Journalism Review*, Winter, 1968–69, p. 54.

68 Marvin Barrett, ed., *Survey of Broadcast Journalism 1968–69* (New York: Grosset & Dunlap, 1969), p. 14.

69 "Television's 1973 'Operation Moneybag,'" *Variety*, September 4, 1974, pp. 39, 53.

70 *Ibid.*

71 "Where The Money Goes For 100G Half Hour," *Variety*, September 12, 1973, p. 47.

72 "The Harris Poll," *San Francisco Examiner*, January 19, 1970, p. 50.

73 Steiner, *The People Look at Television*, pp. 159–60, 168, 202.

74 John P. Robinson, "Television and Leisure Time: Yesterday, Today, and (maybe) Tomorrow," *Public Opinion Quarterly*, Summer, 1969, pp. 219–20.

75 "The Mystery of the Missing Audience," *Broadcasting*, February 9, 1970, p. 19.

76 Meyer Weinberg, *TV in America* (New York: Ballantine Books, 1962), p. i.

77 *Federal Communications Commission Annual Report Fiscal 1972*, pp. 170–71.

78 "Cable TV, Overextended, Is in Retreat in Cities," *New York Times*, March 9, 1974, pp. 1, 59.

79 David M. Rubin, "Short Circuit in the Wired Nation, [MORE], September, 1973, pp. 16–18.

80 "Cable TV, Overextended," pp. 1, 59.

81 *Ibid.*

82 "Cable Systems Unveil Range of Ways to Meet Challenge of Local Origination," *Broadcasting*, June 3, 1974, pp. 26–28.

83 Rubin, "Short Circuit in the Wired Nation," p. 18.

84 "Press Freedom for Cable TV Is Urged in Whitehead Report," *New York Times*, January 17, 1974, pp. 1, 78.

85 "NCTA Figures Reflect Cable's Emphasis on Subscribers," *Broadcasting*, July 8, 1974, p. 27.

86 "Cable TV, Overextended," p. 59.

87 "Pay Television Reaches 12% Penetration on Cable Systems Where It's Offered," *Broadcasting*, April 29, 1974, p. 25.

88 "Latest from Stanford: Pay Is the Way to Riches for Cable," *Broadcasting*, April 22, 1974, p. 32.

89 "Networks Sound Alarm to Stem Growth of Pay-TV," *New York Times*, May 23, 1974, p. 83.

90 *Ibid.*

91 Gene Smith, "Disks Pass Tapes in Video Derby," *New York Times*, March 18, 1973, sec. 3, pp. 1, 9.

92 "Cartridge TV's Debacle, $48-Mil Avco Loss," *Variety*, July 4, 1973, p. 1.

93 "Onward and Upward in FM Penetration," *Broadcasting*, July 1, 1974, p. 28.

94 "The FM Boom," *Newsweek*, May 22, 1972, p. 57.

95 "Television's 1973 'Operation Moneybag,'" pp. 39, 53. Rufus Crater, "UHF: Out of the Traffic and Heading for the Open Road," *Broadcasting*, June 10, 1974, p. 35.

96 "Radio Listening Is Stable, But FM Climbs, AM Drops," *Variety*, May 22, 1974, p. 52.

97 "Onward and Upward in FM Penetration," p. 28.

98 "UHF Penetration 86%," *Variety*, February 6, 1974, p. 2.

99 Crater, "UHF: Out of the Traffic," p. 38.

100 *Ibid.*, pp. 37–38.

101 "Ford Fund Will End Its Aid to Public TV; Gave $150-Million," *New York Times*, January 24, 1974, pp. 1, 74.

102 "President Shifts on Public TV And Sanctions Long-Range Aid," *New York Times*, July 17, 1974, pp. 1, 73.

103 "Ford Fund Will End Its Aid," p. 74.

104 "After 50 Years, BBC Facing Change," *Variety*, November 1, 1972, pp. 35, 40.

105 "Climate of Crisis Worsening for Public TV," *New York Times*, July 11, 1974, p. 63.

106 "Maybe Money Is the Name of the Programming Game in Public TV, Too," *New York Times*, July 28, 1974, sec. 2, p. 13.

107 "Future of Non-Commercial TV," *U.S. News and World Report*, December 8, 1969, pp. 94–97.

108 "U.S. Opposes Soviet Draft of a Satellite TV Treaty," *New York Times*, October 13, 1972, p. 2.

109 "Stanton Hits Proposed Curb on TV Satellite Use," *New York Times*, October 5, 1972, p. 94.

110 "Westar Opens Drive to Cut U.S. Communications Costs," *New York Times*, April 15, 1974, pp. 1, 22.

111 "New Satellite Linked Up by RCA to Join Alaska With 'Lower 48,'" *New York Times*, January 9, 1974, p. 48.

112 Edward M. Kimbrell, "Communication Satellites II," *Freedom of Information Center Report No. 245*, Columbia, Mo., July, 1970, p. 7.

113 *Ibid.*

Suggested Readings

ARLEN, MICHAEL J., *Living-Room War*. New York: Viking Press, 1969.

BARRETT, MARVIN, ed., *Survey of Broadcast Journalism*. New York: Grosset & Dunlap, 1969, 1970, 1971, 1972.

BOWER, ROBERT T., *Television and the Public*. New York: Holt, Rinehart and Winston, 1973.

BROWN, LES, *Television—The Business Behind the Box*. New York: Harcourt Brace Jovanovich, 1971.

CRATER, RUFUS, "UHF: Out of the Traffic and Heading for the Open Road," *Broadcasting*, June 10, 1974.

EPSTEIN, EDWARD J., *News From Nowhere*. New York: Vintage Books, 1974.

JACOBS, NORMAN, ed., *Culture for the Millions*. New York: Van Nostrand Reinhold, 1961.

JOHNSON, NICHOLAS, and JOHN JAY DYSTAL, "A Day in the Life: The Federal Communications Commission," *Yale Law Journal*, 82, July, 1973.

LIEBERT, ROBERT M., JOHN M. NEALE, and EMILY S. DAVIDSON, *The Early Window: Effects of Television on Children and Youth*. Elmsford, N.Y.: Pergamon Press, 1973.

MACNEIL, ROBERT, *The People Machine*. New York: Harper & Row, 1968.

MELODY, WILLIAM, *Children's Television: The Economics of Exploitation*. New Haven: Yale University Press, 1973.

On The Cable: The Television of Abundance. New York: McGraw-Hill, 1971.

RUBIN, DAVID M., "Short Circuit in the Wired Nation," [*MORE*], September, 1973.

SCHILLER, HERBERT I., *Mass Communications and American Empire*. New York: Augustus M. Kelley, 1969.

SKORNIA, HARRY J., *Television and Society*. New York: McGraw-Hill, 1965.

———, *Television and the News*. Palo Alto, Calif.: Pacific Books, 1968.

STEINER, GARY A., *The People Look at Television*. New York: Alfred A. Knopf, 1963.

SURGEON GENERAL'S SCIENTIFIC ADVISORY COMMITTEE ON TELEVISION AND SOCIAL BEHAVIOR, *Television and Growing Up: The Impact of Televised Violence*. Washington, D.C.: U.S. Government Printing Office, 1972.

WHITESIDE, THOMAS, "Corridor of Mirrors," *Columbia Journalism Review*, Winter, 1968–69.

Chapter 13
Film

Feature films are no longer the immensely profitable mass medium they once were. Television put a stop to that. But the film industry today is—surprisingly—alive and well. It earns its bread and butter from television, but even at movie theaters it is doing all right, thanks to modest budgets, independent filmmakers, and the continuing interest of young people in the movies.

In 1947, more than 85 million people in the U.S. visited a movie theater each week. By the mid-1950s, the movie audience had dropped to about 45 million per week. And by 1971, weekly movie attendance was down around 18 million. Many factors contributed to the decline, but television was by far the most important. The recent history of the film industry is the history of its response to television.

At first, the major Hollywood studios responded to the competition of TV by producing fewer but more spectacular feature films. Movie theaters moved to the suburbs with the expanding middle class, and rocking-chair seats, wide screens, and stereophonic sound created a film experience that could not be duplicated on the home television set. Throughout the 1950s and well into the 1960s, Hollywood operated on the desperate assumption that big-budget blockbusters would save it from television.

Occasionally the tactic worked. *The Ten Commandments* (1956) and *Ben-Hur* (1959) grossed $40 million each in domestic theaters, did well on the international market, and were eventually sold to television. *The Sound of Music* (1965), which cost $7.6 million to produce, was the biggest moneymaker of the 1960s, grossing $72 million in the United States and Canada and perhaps as much as $60 million more internationally. *Doctor Zhivago* (1965), *Funny Girl* (1968), and *2001: A Space Odyssey* (1968) were other big pictures that made money.

But the losers outnumbered the winners. A more typical spectacular was *Doctor Doolittle,* on which Twentieth Century Fox took a loss of $18 million. The end of the 1960s saw a string of such blockbuster flops, including *Sweet Charity, Star, Ice Station Zebra,* and *Chitty Chitty Bang Bang.* The failure of so many spectaculars led to some spectacular failures; in 1969 five of the major studios reported net losses totaling $110 million. In the 1960s and early 1970s, a number of Hollywood studios were forced to fold or merge, while others drastically curtailed their activities. Magazine articles on the "death of Hollywood" were plentiful.

Rising costs were part of the problem. "I wish *The Sound of Music* had never been made," remarked one studio production chief. "The industry lost sight of reality and thought that budgets didn't require a ceiling."[1] Star performers were demanding as much as a million dollars a film, and the studios paid the price, unable to believe that an Elizabeth Taylor or a Julie Andrews no longer guaranteed a hit. Many films in the 1960s cost as much as $20 million to make. To earn a profit after the movie theater owners have taken their percentage off the top, a $20-million motion picture must gross about $50 million in box-office receipts. Most movies simply didn't earn that much.

Even a $20-million spectacular, of course, can make money if enough people want to see it. The big mistake of the film industry was to underestimate the public's satisfaction with television. The Hollywood studios of the 1960s were like two-headed monsters with no communication between the heads. One part was busy producing big-budget films for theatrical distribution. The other part was busy selling old movies (and some not-so-old ones) to television, and producing TV programs for the networks. Even while they were selling their souls to television, the studios steadfastly misjudged the success of the electronic medium.

Today, theatrical films and made-for-TV movies comprise roughly half of all prime-time network programming, while the products of the film studios fill as much as 80 percent of the airtime on non-network stations. Movie magnates should have seen this coming. They should have realized that faced with the choice of a movie on TV (for free) or a movie in town (at $3 a seat), most Americans would rather stay home in their easy chairs. Instead, the major studios ignored their own increasing contributions to the success of television, pointed to the *Sound of Music* bonanza, and plunged full

steam ahead into the disasters of the late 1960s.

ART AND THE YOUTH MARKET

Throughout the 1960s and early 1970s, the Motion Picture Association of America commissioned a series of surveys to find out what sorts of people were still going to the movies. The findings were consistent:[2]

1. Nearly two-thirds of all moviegoers are under 25.
2. Nearly half are between 12 and 20.
3. Roughly a third are under 15.
4. Adults over 50 seldom go.

Despite these facts, the major studios for years paid very little attention to teenagers and young adults. Instead, they aimed their films at a middle-class, middle-aged "family" audience—hoping that if box-office receipts didn't justify that emphasis, sales to television and foreign markets would.

In the late 1950s and early 1960s, the studios did try to attract the youth market with a series of beach-party and Elvis Presley movies. But these films were several years behind the musical pulse of America's teenagers. In choosing between a Presley movie and a Beatles record, young people bought the record—and had their own beach party.

It took Hollywood until the late 1960s to figure out how to appeal to young people. But even before this was accomplished, college and precollege students made up an increasingly large percentage of the movie-going audience. Why?

For one thing, movies were an essential part of the American dating game. While many middle-aged people came to think of films as an unnecessary inconvenience and expense, the younger generation saw them as an escape from the prying eyes of parents and other adults, as a place to be "alone" with a friend or a date.

But the enthusiasm that young people

At least one film company understood early that there was money to be earned from the youth market. Since its founding in 1954, American International Pictures has never had a losing year. Concentrating on cheap movies and always staying one jump ahead of its young audience, AIP has consistently earned solid profits—$931,400 (on sales of $32.5 million) in 1974. AIP alumni include such now-famous actors, writers, and directors as Peter Fonda, Dennis Hopper, Willard Huyck, Jack Nicholson, Bruce Dern, Martin Scorsese, John Milius, and Woody Allen.

At the beginning, AIP decided to specialize in horror films for the teenage audience at the nation's growing number of drive-in theaters. While the major studios were making big-budget features like *The Robe,* AIP produced black-and-white cheapies such as *The Beast with 1,000,000 Eyes* (made in eight days for $35,000) and *I Was a Teenage Werewolf* (a $123,000 film that grossed $2 million). Between 1954 and 1960, not one AIP movie lost money.

Faced with imitators, and sensing that its audience would no longer buy black-and-white double features, AIP went to color in 1960, and upped its typical budget to $400,000. Edgar Allan Poe stories were in the public domain and Hollywood horror stars were underpriced, so the company released *The Fall of the House of Usher* starring Vincent Price. A string of seven more Poe films followed.

The company continued to demonstrate an uncanny ability to read its young audience's interests in advance. In the mid-1960s, it switched to motorcycle movies, scoring a huge success in 1968 with *Wild in the Streets* (featuring Christopher Jones as a young president who puts his mother in a concentration camp). By the 1970s, AIP was busy making movies about black supermen and superwomen (*Slaughter, Foxy Brown*), as well as a special line of black horror films (*Blacula*). When Kung Fu became the rage, AIP distributed at least a dozen films with titles like *Shanghai Killers* and *Deep Thrust;* by the time the fad was over, AIP had long since moved on to other things.

Horror films continued to be AIP's meat and potatoes until disappointing returns on *The Bat People* and Vincent Price's *Madhouse* forced the company to reexamine the genre in 1974. "What we call 'Horror' and they call 'Suspense' is all over TV," concluded AIP head Samuel Z. Arkoff. "You cannot sell what is being given away."

Given his track record, Arkoff's prescription for success is worth listening to: "There's no way to sell the young today that's as clearcut as in the past. I don't think our audience is the same audience any more for any two different pictures. Each picture must be attractive to some segment of youth, to some part of the audience under 30."[3] As long as AIP keeps aiming cheap movies at specific young audiences, and keeps finding its target, it will continue to answer its critics (who call AIP films "trash") by quoting its box-office statistics.

---

have shown for film goes beyond the pleasures of popcorn and a dark room. Huge numbers of Americans, most of them under 30 and almost all of them under 40, now take movies seriously as an art form. Writing in 1966, film critic Stanley Kauffmann put it this way:

[T]here exists a Film Generation: the first generation that has matured in a culture in which the film has been of accepted serious relevance, however that seriousness is defined. Before 1935 films were proportionately more popular than they are now, but for the huge majority of film-goers they represented a regular weekly or semiweekly bath of escapism. Such an escapist audience still exists in large number, but another audience, most of them born since 1935, exists along with it. This group, this Film Generation, is certainly not exclusively grim, but it is essentially serious. Even its appreciations of sheer entertainment films reflect an over-all serious view.[4]

Kauffmann went on to list five reasons for the emergence of a film generation. First, in an age of technology, film is a heavily technological enterprise, yet it uses that technology to celebrate the human being. Second, film offers a new opportunity to apply artistic sensibility to the world of physical details; "it manages to make poetry out of doorknobs, breakfasts, furniture." Third, the film form is especially appropriate for dealing with many of the pressing issues of modern times, especially the relationship between inner states (tension, doubt, apathy) and external reality. Fourth, a film is instantly available to the entire world without translation, vividly recreating foreign settings and situations. And fifth, film is a young medium whose potential has not yet been explored, much less exhausted.[5]

While Hollywood was very slow to appreciate the artistic potential of movies, European filmmakers were not. The innovative films of the European masters—Truffaut, Godard, Fellini, Antonioni, etc.—were imported to the U.S. and shown through an informal network of small "art" movie theaters. The audience, of course, was mostly college students and recent graduates.

Some of the young people in the audience were also amateur filmmakers themselves. And a few of them were good enough, and dedicated enough, to try to carve out a career in motion pictures. But Hollywood was not necessarily their goal. "It was frustrating," one young filmmaker explained. "For one reason or another, the industry was unresponsive to personal films. The industry was controlled and dominated by a business industrial mentality."[6] Some of these young filmmakers sought jobs with the major studios anyway. Others joined independent film companies—and a few founded their own.

The success of *The Graduate* and *Bonnie and Clyde* in 1968 shook the big studios badly. Both movies were produced on incredibly low budgets by Hollywood standards, and both earned phenomenal profits. Speaking personally to the under-30 audience, *The Graduate* told the sentimental story of a young man's struggle with the adult establishment; it grossed $43 million in the domestic market alone. Independently produced by its star, Warren Beatty, *Bonnie and Clyde* celebrated random violence as a kind of cultural revolution against stodgy values and lifestyles; it grossed $22 million in U.S. theaters.

A year later came *Midnight Cowboy, Easy Rider,* and *Alice's Restaurant.* All three earned huge profits. And Hollywood began to get the message—big-budget films were dangerous, and the movies that returned the highest percentage profits were independent, low-budget productions aimed specifically at a young audience.

Strangely enough, it was the independent filmmakers who helped sustain the Hollywood studios during this crucial period. Even a low-budget movie can easily cost a couple of million dollars to produce. Success requires not just filmmaking skill, but also expertise in financing and distribution. More often than not, the independents wound up depending on Hollywood for these services—and when their films proved successful, the big studios reaped much of the profit. If filmmaker Haskell Wexler could bring in *Medium Cool* for under a million dollars for Paramount release, why should Paramount risk over $20 million on a possible bomb like *Paint Your Wagon?* It shouldn't. By the end of the 1960s, the major studios were in the bankrolling business, betting on independent low-budget productions and the American youth market.

In 1970, the Hollywood studios produced a number of "youth movies" of their own. Most of them failed at the box office; young people sensed the attempt to exploit their ideological and artistic leanings and stayed away in droves. In the same year, Robert Altman's *M*A*S*H* was an immense success. Twentieth Century Fox was able to capitalize on that success by turning the film into a highly rated—and highly profitable—television series. The studios learned several lessons from the year's experience. First, aiming a movie at young people doesn't guarantee a profit. Second, youth movies are most likely to succeed when the power and money are handed over to a filmmaker (young or old) who understands and sympathizes with the young audience. And third, a movie that appeals to young people may appeal to older moviegoers and television viewers as well.

Thus Hollywood derived its formula for success in the seventies: Find a creative filmmaker, give him or her a tight budget and a lot of artistic independence, and hope that the result will have box-office appeal to both young people and their elders.

As the 1970s progressed, the formula proved itself. In 1971, for example, Warner Brothers spent a mere $1.5 million on *Summer of '42,* and grossed $18 million in return. Elliot Witt, treasurer of M.C.A. Inc. (the talent agency that owns Universal Pictures), explained his company's 1973 strategy this way: "We hope we can average $2 million a film [in expenses] on our 15 to 17 pictures a year. This year we have *American Graffiti* at less than $1 million." [7] *American Graffiti,* of course, turned out to be a bonanza. Naturally, not every low-budget movie has a happy ending at the box office. But Hollywood has yet to come up with anything better.

Notice that the very concept of a "youth

THE NEW FILMMAKERS

The catchwords of the new filmmakers are independence and artistic control. They want to do their *own* movies, without interference from anyone. In search of this kind of autonomy, many of them become "hyphenates"—producer-writer-directors, or even producer-writer-director-actors. John Milius, for example, worked for American International Pictures before he made his mark as a big-time film writer (*Jeremiah Johnson, Life and Times of Judge Roy Bean*). But Milius wanted to be a director as well. So he went back to AIP. "Milius got $300,000 from First Artists for *Life and Times of Judge Roy Bean,* says AIP's Samuel Z. Arkoff, "because they wouldn't let him direct. So we came to him with the idea for *Dillinger* and got him—as a writer and director—for a fraction of his usual price." [8]

Whenever possible, most hyphenates would rather eliminate all contact with the major studios, except for financing and distribution. Many form their own companies. Typical is Robert Altman (*M*A*S*H, McCabe and Mrs. Miller, Thieves Like Us, California Split*), who says he became a producer-writer-director to avoid the "group think and group opinion" that prevails at the studios. "Everything I decide to make originates in my own Westwood office," Altman maintains. He doesn't even use studio editing facilities. "When you're around a studio, you're easily persuaded into making a 'type' of picture that seems to be the current fad. I don't want those attitudes to rub off on me." [9]

When a low-budget movie earns big money today, one of the new filmmakers is usually behind the success. Following the European model, they make films that reflect their own personalities—or at least their own personal predictions of what the theater andience will buy.

movie" has taken on a new meaning in the Hollywood formula. In the late 1960s, it meant a movie whose revolutionary content or counter-cultural tone or artistic style appealed only to young people. But since 1971, it has meant a movie aimed simultaneously at young people and the middle-aged, with a youngish (under 50) filmmaker at the helm. The youth subculture and mainstream American culture moved closer together in the early 1970s, at least on the surface. Young people are still the principal audience for feature films. But with only occasional exceptions, the movies they choose

THE INTERNATIONAL MARKET AND THE FOREIGN FILM

In 1955, the American film industry dominated the international market, with 70 percent of worldwide box-office receipts. But as other nations developed their own filmmaking potential, the figure went down. In 1960, twenty-six countries produced twenty or more feature films; the U.S. was responsible for 211 movies, Europe for 823, and Asian filmmakers for an incredible 1,479. By 1964, U.S. productions were bringing in only 55 percent of the world's movie receipts.

That was still a lot of money, and a lot of influence. To protect their share of the international market, and reduce costs at the same time, many American filmmakers went abroad. U.S. producers, using U.S. and international stars and cheap local extras and technicians, made "foreign" movies—and sometimes even collected low-interest loans from local governments trying to promote their own film industries. Today, many American movie companies have significant investments in overseas production, distribution, and exhibition; American films earn roughly half their revenues overseas. And in many countries around the world, American-made movies still play a major role.

While Hollywood was busy insuring an international market for its movies, foreign films began a parallel invasion of American movie theaters. In 1960, nearly forty foreign-language features played New York's first-run theaters, and an "art" theater circuit relying heavily on foreign films stretched across the nation. Film buffs in the 1960s lined up for Brigitte Bardot's latest unveiling, and tasted the innovative work of such masters as Truffaut, Godard, Fellini, Antonioni, Bergman, and Kurasawa. It was a film experience very different from Doris Day and Rock Hudson movies, and it nurtured a new generation of serious American filmgoers and filmmakers.

By the late 1960s, the new generation of filmgoers was large enough to interest more commercial theaters, and a number of American filmmakers were producing complex, perceptive, personal movies. As the American audience for artistically sophisticated and sexually explicit films grew larger, and found satisfaction in distinctly American products, the "art" theater circuit and the demand for foreign movies began to disappear. In 1972, every major American distributor turned down Bergman's *Cries and Whispers,* and a tiny company, New World Pictures, picked it up for less than $150,000. In the first nine months of 1973, New York's first-run theaters offered only eighteen foreign-language movies—about half the number offered a decade earlier. Many foreign films that would have been eagerly booked in the 1960s today play only the film festivals.

In 1975, the tide may be turning again. As the tastes of the American youth market come closer and closer to those of the general audience—and as filmmakers try to please both with the same movie—a smaller, more "cultural" audience may find once again that its needs are not being met by American films.

are the same ones their parents pick—for a night on the town now or an evening's television several years later.

The runaway best-seller of 1971, for example, was *Love Story.* Though produced on a relatively low budget and devoted to the romance of two college students, *Love Story* can hardly be said to have pandered to the youth cult. It pandered to a much broader interest in sophisticated soap opera. The biggest hit of 1972 was *The Godfather,* directed by a brilliant young filmmaker named Francis Ford Coppola. Produced for $6.2 million, *The Godfather* grossed $82 million in its first nine months. Its almost sympathetic portrait of the Mafia appealed to a cross-section of American, including the all-important youth market. *The Sting* and *The Exorcist,* 1974's top two films, followed the same pattern; students were not the only ones who appreciated the former's nostalgic tribute to the craft of the confidence artist and the latter's sophisticated evocation of terror. And in 1975, *Jaws* scared everyone.

To complicate the matter even more, some successful movies of the early 1970s don't seem to be tied even indirectly to the youth market. These included *Airport* and *Patton* in 1970, *Cabaret* and *The Poseidon Adventure* in 1972, etc. By any definition these must be called general-interest movies. They differ from their predecessors of the 1960s only in the size of their budgets. Because Twentieth Century Fox was unwilling to invest more than $2 million in *The Poseidon Adventure,* producer Irwin Allen had to raise the rest of his $4-million budget himself. *Poseidon* made back that much and a lot more at the box office, and in 1974 ABC paid $3 million for the right to show the movie—just once—on television.

The general-audience movie, in other words, is still very much alive, though the spectacular is probably dead. Hollywood continues to gamble on feature films for just about everybody. But with a tight rein on the budget, it's betting less.

Also very much alive are movies aimed at the pre-teen market. Even during Hollywood's blackest days, producers at the Disney studios whistled while they worked, turning out an endless stream of medium-budget features for children. Number five on the 1974 best-seller list was *Herbie Rides Again,* Robert Stevenson's sequel about a flying Volkswagen.

Where, then, do feature films stand as of the mid-1970s? Independent filmmakers are still riding high, accepting financial help but not artistic interference from the Hollywood studios. But the movies they produce with Hollywood's money no longer appeal only to students and intellectuals. Stanley Kauffmann's "Film Generation" is now watching pretty much the same movies as everyone else.

The profits of the big Hollywood studios depend on how successfully they can deal with two external groups—independent filmmakers and television. But Hollywood also faces challenges from the public, including charges of discrimination and stereotyping from minorities and women, and charges of pornography from moralists and the courts. While the manufacturers of feature films try to cope with these pressures, another film industry flourishes unnoticed, busily producing shorts, documentaries, and informational films for education and industry.

DEALING WITH THE INDEPENDENTS

Independent film production is not a recent invention. United Artists was founded in 1919 to distribute independently produced movies. Throughout the 1950s and 1960s, many actors (Burt Lancaster, Kirk Douglas, Frank Sinatra), directors (Alfred Hitchcock, William Wyler, Otto Preminger), producers (Sam Spiegel), and writers (Joseph Mankiewicz, Richard Brooks) put together their own films without studio help. Among the independently produced movies of this period are *On the Waterfront, Around the World in Eighty Days, The Apartment, The Hustler, Guess Who's Coming to Dinner, David and Lisa,* and of course *The Graduate, Bonnie and Clyde,* and *Easy Rider.*

But until the late 1960s, the big studios still produced most of their own films; independently made movies weren't rare, but they weren't customary either. They didn't become customary until the studios committed themselves to big-budget spectaculars, and wound up in financial hot water. Then Hollywood switched its emphasis from production to financing and distribution, and the 1970s became the decade of the independents.

The simplest relationship between a studio and an independent filmmaker is direct and total financial support from the very beginning. But usually the support comes later, and the big question in the movie business today is how much later. Universal Pictures, for example, likes to take credit for *American Graffiti,* but the film was produced by Francis Ford Coppola and directed by George Lucas—neither of whom was an employee of Universal. Lucas commissioned the script, and Coppola sold the package (Lucas plus script) to Universal. As studio-filmmaker relationships go today, this was a comparatively early deal. By the time the movie was cast and actual shooting began, Universal was already committed, and it was Universal's money that Lucas and Coppola were spending.

This sort of arrangement ties up a lot of studio cash, and inevitably leads to significant studio influence over budget, casting, shooting, and editing. Since many studios are short on money, and many independent filmmakers prefer a greater degree of artistic independence, a number of alternatives have arisen.

One of the most common is the "negative pickup deal." Here the studio agrees in advance to buy the film and distribute it, but no money changes hands until after the shooting is done and the negative is com-

pleted. With this kind of guarantee from a studio, the filmmaker usually has no trouble financing the production costs elsewhere. Robert Altman explains the negative pickup deal for *California Split*: "Columbia read the script, approved the cast and approved me. Then we formed our own company, Won World Productions, and went to the bank ourselves. The executives at Columbia don't know what they're going to get until they see the final picture." [10]

Another variation is co-financing. When a studio is unwilling to invest more than a given amount of money in a particular motion picture, it asks the filmmaker to raise the rest of the budget somewhere else. *Lady Sings the Blues,* for example, was co-financed by Paramount and Motown Records; Motown later bought out Paramount and took complete control of the production.

All of these arrangements involve some sort of advance commitment from a Hollywood studio—financing, or partial financing, or at least a pledge to distribute the movie when it's done. But many 1970s films have been privately financed and produced without any studio guarantee at all. *Serpico,* for example, was funded entirely by Italian producer Dino de Laurentiis. And the budget for *Mean Streets*—a mere $480,000—came from the Cleveland friends and neighbors of producer Jonathan Taplin. The Martin Scorsese script had been rejected by most of the major studios, and Warner Brothers agreed to distribute the film only after viewing the finished product.

Working without a studio guarantee is a big risk for filmmakers and investors both. Movies produced under these circumstances often die if they cannot find an interested studio willing to work on distribution. You've almost certainly never heard of John Frankenheimer's *Impossible Object,* a $1.8-million film produced in Europe in 1972. As of late 1974, the movie still had no American distributor.

Even if an independently produced movie does find a distributor, there's no guarantee the company will push the picture when it doesn't have a big financial stake in it. *Billy Jack,* independently produced by writer-actor Tom Laughlin and co-star Delores Taylor, was released by Warner in 1971. The studio didn't bother to promote the film very hard, and it soon returned to the shelf, a certified box-office failure. This typical story became very untypical when Laughlin and Taylor sued Warner Brothers over its handling of the picture. In a 1973 settlement, Warner agreed to re-release the film, using some highly unorthodox marketing techniques. A $500,000 advertising campaign, three-quarters of it on television, paved the way for the Southern California reopening. Sixty-two theaters grossed $1.2 million the first week, and nationwide *Billy Jack* grossed at least $26 million in re-release.[11] A sequel followed in 1974, and was also a financial success.

The second release of *Billy Jack* was unorthodox in another way as well. Instead of splitting the gross with theater owners in the usual fashion, Warner, Laughlin, and Taylor rented the theaters at a flat rate, and kept all the box-office receipts themselves. This technique is called "four-walling," and is very attractive to theater owners, since it guarantees them a small but steady profit. It's not a new idea, and it is sometimes an immensely profitable one. Pacific International Enterprises made *American Wilderness* for $28,000 in 1969; by 1974, the film had grossed $11.5 million through four-walling, and was still going strong.

But the major studios have been very reluctant to try four-walling with unspecialized feature films; it seemed safer in case of a box-office failure to split the loss with the theater owners. The success of *Billy Jack* may lead other studios to experiment with four-walling. More important, it may provide a chance for independent filmmakers to distribute their movies at their own risk without studio support.

For the major studios, then, the big issue in the movie business today is how, when, and to what extent to support independent filmmakers. For the independents, the big issue is how much studio support to accept, and how to function without the support they don't want or can't get. The way this studio-filmmaker relationship is resolved will have a lot to do with the sorts of movies you watch for the rest of the decade.

DEALING WITH TELEVISION

Feature filmmaking is a highly speculative business. An independent director or producer may manage a string of seven or eight hits, with only a couple of flops along the way, and wind up very far ahead of the game. But a major studio has to involve itself in at least twenty or thirty movies a year just to keep its employees and equipment busy. The result may be huge profits one year and huge losses the next. The modest but steady earnings that most investors seek come only over the long haul, if then. It's an ulcer-producing business.

To pay the rent during the inevitable bad years, the studios rely on television. The sale of a feature film to TV can bring millions, and almost every movie is sold within a few years after its theater run. Television money is just icing on the cake for a box-office hit, but for the average movie it often spells the difference between red ink and black. If for some reason the nation's TV stations and networks ever decided to abandon their habit of running theatrical movies from the past, the film industry as we know it today would promptly die.

Besides selling old movies to television, the Hollywood studios also produce their own made-for-TV films. In 1973, for example, Universal Studios turned out more than eighty full-length motion pictures, an industry record. But over two-thirds of them never saw the inside of an American movie theater. They were sold directly to television, which had commissioned them in the first place. These TV movies are often run interchangeably with old theatrical films; they are also used for one-of-a-kind "specials" and for feature-length series programs such as "Columbo."

Finally, Hollywood is heavily involved in the production of ordinary half-hour and one-hour television series. In 1974, Universal alone supplied the networks with thirteen hours of prime-time programming a week. Strangely enough, these network sales are not very profitable. The big money comes after the networks have finished running a successful series, when the studio can begin selling it overseas and syndicating it to non-network stations. Of course an unsuccessful series that is canceled after one season will probably never be syndicated or sold on the international market. The TV series business is thus almost as speculative as the feature film business.

This was especially true in 1974. Hit hard by inflation, the major studios reported that most of the programs they produced for television were being sold to the networks below cost. Edward A. Montanus, vice president of MGM-TV, noted that only 9 percent of all TV series last four years or longer—yet a four-year backlog of reruns, he said, is essential for syndication. "There's an opportunity to hit the jackpot," Montanus concluded, "but it's such high risk speculation that sensible companies may not want to get involved with it." [12]

Though even television production is a risky business, it's a lot less risky than theatrical movies, and the studios absolutely depend on it for their bread and butter. The extent of the TV takeover can be seen clearly in the report of the Screen Actors Guild on its members' 1971 earnings. Thirty percent of the $114,300,000 total came from television filmmakers, 51 percent from the producers of TV commercials, and only 18 percent from the budgets of theatrical movies.

Because the movie business—even the television movie business—is so speculative, most of the companies that keep at it are in other, safer businesses as well. Walt Disney Productions, one of the most successful movie studios, nevertheless makes most of its money from Disneyland and Disneyworld. Universal is a part of M.C.A. Inc., which is deeply into real estate, retailing, a talent agency, recording companies, and a savings and loan association. United Artists is a subsidiary of the Transamerica Corporation, an insurance and financial giant; Gulf & Western, an industrial leader, owns Paramount. Nearly every Hollywood studio today is the most speculative arm of an otherwise stable conglomerate.

STEREOTYPING: BLACKS AND WOMEN

In Edwin S. Porter's 1903 film production of *Uncle Tom's Cabin,* a white actor in blackface played Uncle Tom. Eleven years later, Sam Lucas became the first black to perform a leading role in a major motion picture; he starred in William Robert Daly's *Uncle Tom's Cabin,* the fourth film version of that classic. With the coming of talking pictures, the number of parts for blacks greatly increased. *Hearts in Dixie* and *Hallelujah,* both released in 1929, were the first two in a long line of all-black spectacles, including such films as *Green Pastures* in 1936 and *Porgy and Bess* in 1959.

Although they employed black performers, these movies were produced and directed by whites for studios owned by whites, and the audience they tried to attract was predominantly white. Lincoln Motion Pictures was founded in 1916 to produce films that were by blacks and for blacks. Other black companies joined in the competition, and by the late 1920s the nation's 700 movie theaters in black neighborhoods were offering a steady diet of black-made films. The switch to talking pictures, the impact of the big Hollywood studios, and the hardships of the Depression forced most of these companies out of business. A few independent filmmakers continued making movies explicitly for a black audience—but nearly all the filmmakers themselves were white. By the end of World War II Hollywood was too strong for these independent competitors, and they too were forced to fold. Black moviegoers were left with no choice but to watch whatever the big studios produced.

The 1950s and 1960s were the era of Sidney Poitier, whose portrayals of integrationist heroes were acceptable to both blacks and whites. But as early as 1958, some segments of the black community had become disenchanted with the Poitier image. Black film historian Donald Bogle reports that ghetto theater audiences jeered when Poitier saved Tony Curtis in *The Defiant Ones*.[13]

While mainstream moviegoers watched Poitier triumph again and again, patrons of the "art" movie theaters were offered a less upbeat picture of the black experience. This white liberal audience applauded films such as John Cassavetes' *Shadows* (1961), Frederick Wiseman's *The Cool World* (1963), Sam Weston and Larry Peerce's *One Potato, Two Potato* (1964), and Michael Roemer's *Nothing But a Man* (1964). Though the work of whites, these movies at least tried to deal seriously with race relations and the real world of black Americans. They paved the way for watered-down Hollywood treatments of the same themes, such as *A Patch of Blue* in 1965 and *Guess Who's Coming to Dinner* (starring Sidney Poitier) in 1967.

Photographer and author Gordon Parks was the first black to direct a major movie for a Hollywood studio. *The Learning Tree,* based on Parks' autobiographical novel, was released in 1969. That year saw several other black films, including *Uptight, Slaves, The Lost Man,* and *Putney Swope.* These movies criticized the white establishment, often militantly. Perhaps more important, most of them featured black artists behind the scenes as well as before the cameras.

In the 1970s filmmakers rediscovered the black audience. While Ossie Davis' *Cotton Comes to Harlem* (1970) was designed to please both white and black moviegoers, Melvin Van Peeble's *Sweet Sweetback's Badasssss Song* (1971) was aimed explicitly at blacks. Twelve percent of the American movie audience is black, and *Sweetback* proved that an independent black filmmaker could gross more than $10 million by serving that audience. Gordon Parks' *Shaft* (1971), an MGM release, also scored at black theaters. Advertised as "Hotter than Bond, Cooler than Bullitt," *Shaft* grossed $13 million, and demonstrated that Hollywood could make money bankrolling movies by and for blacks.

The result was an avalanche of black films. Among those released in 1972 were *Super Fly, Sounder, Buck and the Preacher, Slaughter, The Legend of Nigger Charley, Lady Sings the Blues, Melinda, Trouble Man, Blacula,* and *Blackenstein.* Some of these movies appealed to both black and white audiences, but most were strictly black. *Super Fly,* directed by Gordon Parks, Jr., was independently financed by a group of black business executives; it told the story of a ghetto cocaine dealer who beat the system, with plenty of raw violence and sex along the way.

Many critics, both white and black, don't think very much of films like *Super Fly* that glorify black criminals. They even have a name for the trend—"blaxploitation." Junius Green, president of the Hollywood branch of the NAACP, complains that "these films are taking our money while feeding us a forced diet of violence, murder, drugs and rape." But Gordon Parks (who directed *Shaft* and whose son directed *Super Fly*) responds: "The most important thing to me is that young blacks can now, if they work hard enough, enter an industry that has been closed to them for so long." [14]

Parks might well have added that violence, murder, drugs and rape are the backbone of many successful white films as well. After decades of having to settle for movies made by and for whites, black audiences are now able to watch the work of black filmmakers—good and bad, violent and non-violent.

Women in the movies face their own problems. Hollywood has always treated women from a male point of view. Three female stereotypes were prominent—sex object, earth mother, and amusing idiot. There were exceptions of course, films that depicted women as real, complex people with goals and problems and abilities. For the most part, however, women in film were interesting not for what they did, but for what men did because of them.

At least there *were* women in film. Six of the top ten box-office stars in 1934 were women—Janet Gaynor, Joan Crawford, Mae West, Marie Dressler, Norma Shearer, and Shirley Temple. In 1974, Barbra Streisand was the only woman in the top ten. Today,

the ratio of men's roles to women's roles is an incredible twelve to one. Famous film couples have always been an integral part of the movie business—Spencer Tracy and Katherine Hepburn, Rock Hudson and Doris Day, etc. In the 1970s the most popular movie couple was Paul Newman and Robert Redford.

And the roles that are left for women are as stereotyped as ever—the sex object is now "liberated," the earth mother has become a "victim," and the amusing idiot is going strong. "I'm sick and tired of seeing women being empty-headed," says Marsha Mason, who played the trampy mother in *Cinderella Liberty*. "In the scripts I get," notes actor Susan Anspach, "the woman is either a neurotic, a slut, a whore or somebody's daughter. Or else there are the feminist

---

GLORIFYING VIOLENCE

"The way to get a picture started at United Artists or MGM," commented an executive at another studio, "is to go and say you can make an 'action-adventurer' for $1,200,-000."[15] Violence has always been an accepted part of the movie business, but it has never been rawer—or more profitable—than in the 1970s. Despite mounting evidence that media violence can be harmful (see pp. 306–8), many American filmmakers not only utilize violence; they celebrate it.

Under the old Motion Picture Production Code, films were forced to punish their criminals. But after the code collapsed in 1966, movie crooks were at last allowed to get away with the loot. Some filmmakers used their new freedom to explore the realities of a violent society, but many chose to glorify murder and mayhem instead. In the 1970s, Hollywood has celebrated the skills and lifestyles of professional assassins (*The Mechanic*), overzealous cops (*Dirty Harry, The French Connection*), narcotics peddlers (*Super Fly*), and of course the Mafia (*The Godfather, Godfather II*).[16]

An especially popular—and dangerous—theme was the pleasure of violent revenge, which provided the motivation of *High Plains Drifter, The Cowboys,* and most notoriously *Death Wish,* a 1974 release. Many audiences roared with delight whenever Charles Bronson, as an architect-turned-vigilante, slaughtered a mugger. "If we had more people like Bronson, we would have less crime," one satisfied moviegoer told the *New York Times*. Another said, "I think what Bronson did is right—no one else is doing *anything*." The critics jumped on *Death Wish* for glorifying crime and violence, but Bronson replied simply: "We don't make movies for critics, since they don't pay to see them anyhow."[17]

Not surprisingly, the revenge theme appealed as much to anti-establishment audiences as to establishment ones. *The Trial of Billy Jack* billed itself as a pacifist movie, but its youthful audience broke into applause whenever Billy Jack used his karate to destroy an authority figure.

films about women who hate men. There's never just a real person with real drives—sexual drives and life drives." [18] In this age of the "action-adventure" film, the movie industry generally ignores the interests and needs of women.

It's not surprising. As recently as 1974, there were only 148 women in the 2,976-member Screen Writers Guild, 23 women in the 2,366-member Directors Guild, and 8 women in the 3,068-member Producers Guild. Small wonder female movie characters are still stereotyped.

SEX AND SUCH

The film revolution of the late 1960s and early 1970s depended very heavily on the freedom of the movie business to say and show whatever it pleased. *Midnight Cowboy* featured a male prostitute, and the huge financial success of *I Am Curious (Yellow)* was directly attributable to its explicit sex scenes. In an era when even an establishment star like Richard Burton can portray a homosexual without repercussions, movie taboos have all but disappeared.

In 1952, the U.S. Supreme Court ruled that movies are protected by the First Amendment. Films could be censored and banned, but only under specific laws within constitutional limitations. Throughout the 1950s and 1960s these limitations expanded. By the end of the 1960s, just about anything could safely be displayed on the screen, as long as the film had some "redeeming social value." Some local governments continued to harass "dirty" movies, but they were seldom able to stop them.

Under pressure from citizen groups like the Legion of Decency, the Motion Picture Producers and Distributors of America had long ago passed the Motion Picture Code. This "voluntary code of self-regulation" prohibited sex, vulgarity, obscenity, and profanity, as well as certain controversial topics. It didn't begin to relax until the mid-1950s. *The Man with the Golden Arm* was refused an MPPDA seal because it depicted narcotics addiction. The film received such praise from the critics that in 1956 the code was amended to allow discussion of drugs. By 1961, the code also permitted "restrained, discreet treatment of sexual aberration in movies." [19]

Foreign filmmakers and American independents ignored even the liberalized code. And the filmgoing public (mostly young people) seemed unconcerned that their favorite movies sometimes lacked the MPPDA seal. The major studios, desperate for a piece of the action, were forced to adopt a new code. In 1968, the Production Code and Rating Administration was established by the Motion Picture Association of America. This board took on the job of assigning each movie one of four classifications. The 1970 revised ratings are:

G   All ages admitted. General audiences.

PG   All ages admitted. Parental guidance suggested.

R   Restricted. Under 17 requires accompanying parent or adult guardian.

X   No one under 17 admitted.

In effect, the rating system took the film industry off the self-censorship hook. Henceforth, the industry would simply announce which movies were "clean" and which were "dirty." The rest was up to the public.

But the rating system had some strange side-effects. At the beginning, several studios actually tried for an X rating, as a come-on for fans of "adult" fare. Hard-core movies, meanwhile, came out in the open; encouraged by increasingly permissive Supreme Court decisions, they proudly rated themselves XXX. Then the reaction set in. Local governments and civic groups began putting pressure on theater owners to carry only G and PG movies. In 1970, 47 percent of the members of the National Association of Theater Owners had a standing policy of no X-rated films. [20]

While the porno factories continued to crank out ultra-frank sex films (like *Deep Throat* and *The Devil in Miss Jones*) for the growing number of theaters specializing in hard-core fare, mainstream film producers started censoring their own movies. Many struggled desperately for an R instead of an X, or a PG instead of an R, trying to insure that the films would be acceptable to most theater owners, and that the all-important teenage audience would be allowed in. To accommodate these needs, the code administration relaxed its standards. In 1969 *Midnight Cowboy* was rated X; in 1970 it was re-rated R.

The rating system has not brought about the death of censorship. Nor has it matured over the past few years. There is something incredibly childish about judging the morality of a movie on the basis of what parts of the body show in reel 3. Despite increasing evidence that film sexuality is harmless, while film violence is at least potentially dangerous (see pp. 306–8), the ratings continue to tolerate the latter and brood puritanically on the former. (At the end of 1974, the code administration awarded its first X for extreme violence to *The Street Fighter*.)

Still, the film industry was freer in the late 1960s and early 1970s than ever before. The courts and the rating system share the credit.

The Supreme Court changed directions in 1973. Replacing the "utterly without redeeming social value" formula with a less limited definition of obscenity, it ruled that local juries may decide for themselves what does and does not conform to community standards of acceptability (see pp. 174–75).[21] Filmmakers feared that the decision would bury the industry in a landslide of local censorship cases. In fact, many state and local governments did try using their new regulatory muscles, but despite the increase in anti-obscenity activity, most hard-core movie theaters remained open.

In Athens, Georgia, however, a theater owner was convicted of obscenity for exhibiting *Carnal Knowledge,* a prize-winning film that seemed pretty tame to more urban moviegoers. The case reached the Supreme Court in 1974, and the local decision was reversed. Juries, the Court said, do not have "unbridled discretion in determining what is patently offensive."[22] The Supreme Court thus notified state and local governments that it would not uphold obscenity convictions for anything significantly less than hard-core pornography.

THE REST OF THE BUSINESS

To most people, "film" means entertainment, movies shown in movie theaters. Yet fewer than 200 feature films are produced in the United States each year. By contrast, more than 13,000 nonfictional and nontheatrical films are produced in the U.S. annually. This figure does not include TV programs or commercials. It does include documentaries, as well as educational and industrial movies. We will consider each of these categories separately.

Documentaries. Six years before 1903 audiences gasped at the dramatic action of the first American film story, *The Great Train Robbery,* they watched the equally dramatic action of the Corbett-Fitzsimmons boxing match, the first American film documentary. But as feature films got longer and longer, fiction soon came to dominate the movie industry. Some full-length documentaries were produced—*Nanook of the North,* for example, was a hit in the 1920s—but the motion picture industry never really supported feature-length theatrical documentaries. Instead, by the 1930s newsreels and other kinds of nonfiction "shorts" regularly accompanied the feature presentations.

While many excellent documentaries were made during and after the Depression, including *The Plow That Broke the Plains* (1936), *The River* (1937), and *Louisiana Story* (1948), most full-length nonfiction films did not reach mass audiences when they were first released. Except for World War II, when many war documentaries were shown in theaters across the nation, the feature-length documentary remained a minor and highly specialized medium. Until television.

Television gave documentary films the financial support and mass exposure they had been denied by the movie industry. NBC's "White Paper" series has presented documentaries on topics ranging from "The Death of Stalin" to "The Blue-Collar Trap." On CBS, "Hunger in America" and "The Selling of the Pentagon" became matters of national debate. Many more people watched the ABC debut of "The Undersea World of Jacques Cousteau" than had seen Cousteau's award-winning theater release, *The Silent World,* a decade before. Of course television documentaries are sometimes trivial or flimsy (see pp. 314–17), but then movie documentaries were not all masterpieces either. At least on TV a documentary has a fighting chance at a substantial audience.

Although *Woodstock* in 1970 demonstrated that a rock-music documentary could gross $14.5 million on the theater circuit, most documentarists today either settle for a small, select audience or work for television. Frederick Wiseman, probably the greatest living documentary filmmaker in the U.S., made the switch to TV in 1971. In the 1960s, Wiseman's films had sensitively explored the horrors of a prison for the criminally insane (*Titicut Follies*), the regimentation of the educational system (*High School*), the successes and failures of emergency medical treatment (*Hospital*), and other American institutions. His work won critical acclaim and many awards, but very few theater bookings. Wiseman's "Basic Training" made its debut in 1971 on more than 200 public television stations, linked by the Public Broadcasting Service. "The reason for doing all these films," he explained, "is to share what you learn with other people." [23] Through television, Wise-

man and other documentarists share their learning with millions.

While television saved the film documentary from obscurity, it destroyed the film newsreel. Newsreels had always played second banana to the feature films they accompanied, but they did provide theater audiences with information and opinion that could be obtained in no other way. Always visually exciting and often emotionally moving, newsreels attempted to offer a sweeping interpretive review of the week's news. The champion of this genre, *March of Time,* tried to make sense of the bewildering events of the thirties and forties for millions of Americans.

Television began replacing the newsreel in the early 1950s. Nightly newscasts featured film footage that would not be available to theater audiences until the following week. Their emphasis was on spot news and action. Edward R. Murrow's "See It Now" program took up the slack, eclipsing all earlier attempts at visual interpretive journalism. With newscasts offering the most current film, and Murrow providing the most effective interpretation, there was no need for newsreels. By the mid-1950s, newsreels had virtually disappeared. They were not reborn when "See It Now" died.

Educational and Industrial Movies. The largest category of nonfiction films is the educational and industrial movie. Producers of such nontheatrical motion pictures include government agencies, schools and colleges, religious groups, and corporations—over a thousand nontheatrical film companies, including independents and those housed within other organizations. The films are collected and distributed by some 2,600 American film libraries. Their total budget is more than a billion dollars a year.

Educational and industrial filmmaking developed outside the theatrical film experience. Experimentation began in 1923 with the invention of the 16-millimeter projector, but the first real test came during World

War II. The army soon discovered that soldiers learned a skill much faster if they first saw it demonstrated on the movie screen. Perhaps more important, military training films could incorporate a morale-building dimension that was very influential in molding the attitudes of recruits. Although changing deeply held opinions through film proved extremely difficult, creating brand-new attitudes of the desired sorts turned out to be fairly easy—easier through movies than through any other available mass medium. As an essential part of the war effort, the U.S. military requisitioned some 400,000 16-millimeter projectors.

After the war, civilian institutions adopted the military model. Schools established audiovisual libraries, industrial concerns created movie production departments, and every special-interest group struggled to tell its story on film.

Today, an institutional movie about dairy farms in Wisconsin or careers in banking, the promise of nuclear power or the joys of motor-boating, stands a good chance of reaching an audience of millions. Depending on its topic, such a film may be accepted by movie theaters as a short, run by TV stations as a documentary, borrowed by clubs as an entertainment, used by schools as an educational aid—or even all four of these. Of course there are many strictly educational films that don't try to grind any particular ax; these are usually sold or rented to their users. But the biggest-budget institutional films are often the ones that are distributed free. Their goal is to create a favorable image of the organization or issue discussed—in other words to indoctrinate the viewer. Film has proved itself an ideal medium for this purpose.

Even entertainment films are an indoctrination of sorts. Many theatrical movies deal explicitly with the fundamental concerns of their audience. Their handling of themes such as alienation, violence, race, and sex is sometimes insightful and honest, sometimes not. But regardless of the quality of a particular movie, it inevitably has some small effect on how moviegoers see themselves, their neighbors, and their world.

The mainstays of the motion picture industry today are educational and industrial films, movies made expressly for television, and old movies sold to TV after they have finished their theater run. Theatrical feature films are the most glamorous and most speculative part of the business, but they are not what keeps it alive.

Notes

1 "The Old Hollywood: They Lost It at the Movies," *Newsweek*, February 2, 1970, p. 66.

2 Theodore Peterson, Jay W. Jensen, and William L. Rivers, *The Mass Media and Modern Society* (New York: Holt, Rinehart and Winston, 1965), p. 128. Richard F. Shepard, "Effect of TV on Movie-going Is Examined," *New York Times*, November 24, 1971, p. 20.

3 Aljean Harmetz, "The Dime-Store Way to Make Movies—and Money," *New York Times Magazine*, August 4, 1974, pp. 32–33.

4 Stanley Kauffmann, "The Film Generation: Celebration and Concern," in William M. Hammel, ed., *The Popular Arts in America* (New York: Harcourt Brace Jovanovich, 1972), pp. 45–46.

5 *Ibid.*, pp. 46–49.

6 Richard Houdek, "The New Hollywood," *Performing Arts*, January, 1970, p. 6.

7 Robert A. Wright, "Hollywood's Happy Ending: A Profitable Twist," *New York Times*, November 4, 1973, p. F3.

8 Harmetz, "The Dime-Store Way," p. 32.

9 Paul Gardner, "Hyphenates Seek Unified Film Approach," *New York Times*, February 25, 1974, p. 19.

10 Stephen Farber, "So You Make a Movie—Will the Public Ever See It?" *New York Times*, February 24, 1974, p. D14.

11 "New Moves for Movies," *Newsweek*, September 2, 1974, p. 60.

12 Les Brown, "Economic Crisis Besets Producers of TV Series," *New York Times*, October 17, 1974, p. 82.

13 Donald Bogle, *Toms, Coons, Mullatoes, Mammies, and Bucks* (New York: Viking Press, 1973), p. 182.

14 "Black Movie Boom—Good or Bad?" *New York Times*, December 17, 1972, p. D3.

15 Aljean Harmetz, "How Do You Pick a Winner in Hollywood? You Don't," *New York Times,* April 29, 1973, p. D11.

16 Stephen Farber, "Isn't It Enough to Show Murder —Must We Celebrate It?" *New York Times,* October 21, 1973, p. D13.

17 Judy Klemesrud, "What Do They See in 'Death Wish'?" *New York Times,* September 1, 1974, pp. D1, D9.

18 Maureen Orth, "How to Succeed: Fail, Lose, Die," *Newsweek,* March 4, 1974, pp. 50–51.

19 Harold L. Nelson and Dwight L. Teeter, *Law of Mass Communications,* 2nd. ed. (Mineola, N.Y.: Foundation Press, 1973), pp. 444–45.

20 Vincent Canby, "Will a Censor Get the Teeny-bopper?" *San Francisco Sunday Examiner and Chronicle, Datebook,* March 29, 1970, p. 30.

21 Nelson and Teeter, *Law of Mass Communications,* pp. 424–28.

22 "Supreme Court Shifts Position on Obscenity," *New Brunswick* (N.J.) *Home News,* June 25, 1974, p. 24 (Associated Press).

23 "Public Documents," *Newsweek,* October 4, 1971, p. 99.

Suggested Readings

BOGLE, DONALD, *Toms, Coons, Mullatoes, Mammies, and Bucks.* New York: Viking Press, 1973.

BREITROSE, HENRY S., "Film as Communication," in Ithiel de Sola Pool, Wilbur Schramm, Frederick W. Frey, Nathan Maccoby, and Edwin B. Parker, eds., *Handbook of Communication.* Chicago: Rand McNally, 1973.

FARBER, STEPHEN, and ESTELLE CHANGAS, "Putting the Hex on 'R' and 'X,'" *New York Times,* April 9, 1972, sec. 2, p. 1.

KAUFFMANN, STANLEY, "The Film Generation: Celebration and Concern," in William M. Hammel, ed., *The Popular Arts in America.* New York: Harcourt Brace Jovanovich, 1972.

KNIGHT, ARTHUR, *The Liveliest Art.* New York: Mentor Books, 1957.

UNESCO, "Global Overview of Film Situation," in Heinz-Dietrich Fischer and John C. Merrill, eds., *International Communication.* New York: Hastings House, 1970.

Chapter 14
Advertising
and
Public Relations

Advertising is the all-important connection be-tween the mass media and the world of com-merce. Without advertising, neither the media nor the commercial establishment could survive in the form we know them today. By molding the behavior and attitudes of individuals, ad-vertising also helps shape the character of Amer-ican society itself. This enormous power is firmly in the hands of advertising's practitioners, who have devoted far more effort to increasing the effectiveness of their craft than they have to deal-ing with its ethical implications.

In 1954 the net profits of Revlon, Inc., a cosmetics company, stood at $1,297,826. In 1955 CBS introduced a new TV quiz pro-gram, "The $64,000 Question." Revlon spon-sored the show, as well as its twin, "The $64,000 Challenge." Both programs were on the air until 1958, when evidence began emerging that the programs were rigged (see p. 136). During those four years, Revlon's net profits rose to $3,655,950 in 1955, $8,375,502 in 1956, and $9,688,307 in 1958. When a Sen-ate committee asked Martin Revson, owner of Revlon, whether his phenomenal success was due to sponsoring the two shows, he answered musingly: "It helped. It helped." [1]

In 1963 the Clark Oil and Refining Com-pany spent its entire $1.6-million advertising budget on television. Until then, Clark had limped along with annual earnings of $1.5 million or so. The first year following the TV campaign, the company earned $2.1 mil-lion. It committed itself permanently to tele-vision—and in 1969 Clark Oil earned $13.0 million. Said one Clark executive: "That's really advertising power." [2]

ADVERTISING AND BUSINESS

American institutions—mostly profit-mak-ing institutions—spend more than $25 billion a year on advertising, about two-thirds of it in the mass media. This figure represents the raw cost of buying time or space in the media, plus the cost of comparable cam-paigns through billboards, direct mailings, etc. It does not include the salaries of many of the 400,000 Americans now employed in advertising, and it leaves out a lot of "inci-dental" expenses such as market research, commercial production, and the like. With these items included, the actual cost of ad-vertising is closer to $40 billion a year—$200 for every man, woman, and child in the country.

What does the advertiser get in return? Increased sales, of course. The "success stories" of Revlon and Clark are two of thousands that could be told. Frederick R. Gamble, former president of the American Association of Advertising Agencies, puts it this way:

> Advertising is the counterpart in distribution of the machine in production. By the use of machines, our production of goods and services has been multiplied. By the use of the mass media, advertising multiplies the selling effort. . . . Reaching many people rapidly at low cost, advertising speeds up sales, turns prospects into customers in large numbers and at high speed. Hence, in a mass-production and high-consumption economy, advertising has the greatest opportunity and the greatest responsibility for finding customers.[3]

The purpose of most advertising, then, is to induce the buyer to purchase something that the seller has to sell—a product, a service, a political candidate, or whatever. A successful ad is an ad that sells.

Advertising can boost sales in two ways: by winning a bigger share of the market, or by increasing the size of the market itself (perhaps creating the market to start with). The first technique may be called competitive advertising; it says "Buy our brand of aspirin instead of the brand you're using now." The second is noncompetitive advertising; it says simply "Buy more aspirin." Most ads are a combination. They urge the consumer to switch brands and to buy more.

Business competition is not limited to advertising, of course. A manufacturer or a store may compete by cutting its prices, improving its products, or offering superior service. It is not hard to find examples of ads that are essentially "informational"—telling the public about a genuine competitive edge. But these tactics have limited value. Aspirin is aspirin. It is nearly impossible to make a better aspirin. And price-cutting may lose

more in profits than it gains in sales; how many people would switch brands to save a nickel? Competitive ads for aspirin—and many other products—have no real differences to talk about. The competition is not in the products, but in the ads themselves. Meyer Weinberg describes the big-money television advertisers this way:

> Having eschewed competition by cutting prices, the Top Fifty instead go all out to attract the consumer's attention by amusement or entertainment. There is no other way of driving consumers to prefer one substantially identical item over another. Thus advertising agencies specialize in the manufacture of spurious individuality. . . .[4]

So much for competitive advertising. If the only way a manufacturer could earn a dollar was by stealing it from some other manufacturer, America's gross national product would be at a permanent standstill. Fortunately or unfortunately, this is not the case. Industry grows by creating new consumer needs. Wigs, cigarettes, electric washers, power lawnmowers, toiletries, fur coats, and aluminum cans are not really essential to life, liberty, and the pursuit of happiness. But manufacturers have convinced us that they are. They did it with advertising.

Consider the TV ad budgets of the top twenty television advertisers in 1973:[5]

Procter and Gamble	$220,870,400
General Foods	113,534,100
American Home Products	108,422,000
Bristol-Myers	91,320,800
Colgate-Palmolive	77,689,200
Sterling Drug	71,887,000
General Motors	68,366,500
Ford Motor	64,670,200
Lever Brothers	63,694,300
Sears Roebuck	58,394,100
Gillette	54,664,700
General Mills	53,798,500
Warner-Lambert Pharmaceutical	50,487,200

Nabisco	43,634,900
S. C. Johnson & Son	41,999,700
Chrysler	39,963,500
Coca-Cola	38,182,600
Heublein	36,068,200
Miles Laboratories	35,967,900
McDonald's	35,959,400

Aside from wealth, what do these twenty corporations have in common? Most of them manufacture nonessential goods. The needs they serve are, in the words of John Kenneth Galbraith, "psychological in origin and hence admirably subject to management by appeal to the psyche." Galbraith goes further. "The individual serves the industrial system," he says, "by consuming its products. On no other matter, religious, political, or moral, is he so elaborately and expensively instructed." [6]

The overarching goal of all advertising is to get the consumer to consume. Communications researcher Dallas Smythe recalls an ad in the *New York Times* which filled an entire page with the message: "Buy Something." Smythe comments: "The popular culture's imperative—'Buy Something'—is the most important educational influence in North America today." [7] Erich Fromm sums it all up in a phrase. The typical American, he says, is no longer *Homo sapiens,* but *Homo consumens*—Man the consumer. [8]

America is the wealthiest nation in the world. It is also the most wealth-conscious, the most materialistic. Advertising deserves some of the credit and much of the blame.

ADVERTISING
AND THE MEDIA

If big business as we know it couldn't exist without advertising, neither could the mass media. Newspapers, magazines, television, and radio compete for every advertising dollar. As of 1973, newspapers had 30.7 percent of the total. Television had 18.1 percent;

magazines (and specialized business and farm papers) had 10.2 percent; and radio had 6.5 percent. The other 34.5 percent went to direct mail, billboards, and the like. [9] This division of the spoils is not a constant. The development of radio ate significantly into the percentage shared by newspapers and magazines. The development of television did a lot of damage to radio and magazines.

But as long as advertising continues to grow, there is plenty of money to go around. In 1941, the total cost of all advertising was less than $2 billion. Today, that figure is over $25 billion. A minute of time on network radio may now cost up to $8,000. A full-page ad in a major newspaper may run as high as $10,000. A full page in a national magazine may sell for more than $60,000. And a minute on network television may go for a phenomenal $100,000 or more. Advertisers willingly pay the going rates, and all four media are earning good money.

The influence of advertising over media content has already been discussed in considerable detail (see Chapter 5). Direct threats and outright bribes are not unknown, but they are far less common than tacit "mutual understandings." The mass media, after all, are completely dependent on advertisers for their profits. They don't have to be threatened or bribed to keep the advertisers happy. It comes naturally.

None of this is inevitable. Take British television, for example. There are two networks, one commercial and the other government-sponsored. On the noncommercial network, no ads are permitted. On the commercial network, advertisers have only one choice—which station to give the ad to. Station managers schedule the ads as they please, and no commercials are permitted in the middle of a program. Unable to choose their show (much less to produce it), British advertisers have next to no influence on British programming.

The American mass media do not just adjust their content to meet the needs of individual advertisers. They also adjust their

Most European countries strictly regulate television advertising. West Germany, for example, has three TV stations, all operated by public broadcasting corporations. One permits no advertising at all, while the other two allow commercials only under rigid restrictions. On ZDF, for instance, ads are run together in blocks, totaling no more than 20 minutes a day; all commercials must appear before 8 P.M. on weekdays, and never on Sundays.

To beat these restrictions, advertisers try to sneak their messages onto the air. In a 1974 soccer game between Hamburg and Frankfurt, the players wore ads for Remington shavers and Campari aperitifs on their uniforms. The station outwitted the sneak advertisers by carefully avoiding close-up shots. But when companies started putting their ads on movable billboards in the soccer stadiums, towing them in mid-game to wherever the action was, German television was stymied. It had no choice but to cancel the broadcasts of a few weekend soccer games. "We are not trying to be purists about this," explained a TV official, "but we felt we had to put a stop to the excesses at least." [10]

---

attitudes to promote the interests of the business community as a whole. In an essay entitled "Mass Communication, Popular Taste and Organized Social Action," sociologists Paul Lazarsfeld and Robert Merton put the case this way:

> Since the mass media are supported by great business concerns geared into the current social and economic system, the media contribute to the maintenance of that system. This contribution is not found merely in the effective advertisement of the sponsor's product. It arises, rather, from the typical presence in magazine stories, radio programs and newspaper columns of some element of confirmation, some element of approval of the present structure of society. . . .
>
> Since our commercially sponsored mass media promote a largely unthinking allegiance to our social structure, they cannot be relied upon to work for changes, even minor changes, in that structure. . . . Social objectives are consistently surrendered by the commercialized media when they clash with economic gains.[11]

The point here is not that reporters, or the staff of entertainment programs, or even publishers and station managers take orders from advertisers. As a rule they don't. As a rule they don't have to—and that is precisely the point.

The mass media in the United States are an industry. The product of that industry—the only thing it has to sell—is your attention. And that industry's sole customer is of course the advertising business. When necessary, most of the media are prepared to carry content that may offend a particular advertiser. This maintains not only the self-respect of the media but also their public credibility—and thus it serves the long-term interests of advertisers as well. Media definitions of what is newsworthy and what is entertaining insure that the problem doesn't come up very often.

The vast majority of media content provides an ideal vehicle for advertising, not because the media are struggling to make it so, but because it has always been so. The concept of an anti-business commercial television station or an anti-business daily newspaper is almost a contradiction in terms. The mass media *are* businesses. The standards of journalism and the customs of entertainment have developed in that context, and are consistent with that reality.

ADVERTISING
AND THE PUBLIC

Several effects of advertising on the American public are already implied in what we have said about the impact of advertising on business and the media. Advertising creates and maintains an economic system that offers us a rich and bewildering choice of nearly identical consumer goods. Each time we make that choice, we do so largely on the basis of the thousands of ads we have seen and heard. Our selection is inevitably influenced by which ads have been repeated most frequently; which products have been tied most successfully to our innermost needs for status, security, sexuality, and the like; which endorsements by actors or athletes we have found most convincing; and a variety of other factors that have nothing to do with the quality of the product. Our response to the irrationality of this system of influences is typically a world-weary cynicism that makes us distrust all efforts to alter our attitudes or actions—yet we continue to buy.

Those of us who can, in fact, continue to buy more, and more, and more. For middle-class Americans, advertising creates an environment of compulsive consumption. For poor Americans, advertising produces a justified resentment at being excluded from the world of consumership. For all Americans, advertising inculcates a firm conviction that the quality of our lives depends on the things we buy. Inextricably tied to this system, the mass media consistently reinforce it, paying little or no attention to alternative value systems that might undermine America's culture of consumption.

There is much to admire in all this. The United States does have the highest material standard of living in the world. Our level of consumption is the envy of the vast majority of the world's people. Even the most adamant counter-cultural critics of American materialism might well be reluctant to give up their stereo systems and record collections—and it is doubtful that they would have stereo systems and record collections without advertising.

It is important to bear in mind that advertising not only sells us products; it also sells us ideas and images. Number 23 on the list of television's top advertisers is the American Telephone and Telegraph Company, which spent $31,889,400 on TV commercials in 1973. AT&T is a regulated monopoly; it has no competition in the telephone business. Some of its advertising urged people to make more calls, or use the yellow pages, or rent fancier phones. But many AT&T commercials were institutional advertisements. Their goal was to create a favorable public image of the company, to sell the idea that AT&T is a well-run, public-spirited organization. AT&T's institutional advertising is considered a legitimate business expense, so state regulatory agencies set the phone rates high enough to cover the cost. You pay to have the phone company tell you how terrific it is.

ITALY'S SOFT SELL

One of the most popular shows on prime-time Italian television is called "Carosello." Every night after the 8:30 news, twenty million viewers watch the five 135-second playlets that comprise "Carosello"—eleven straight minutes of commercials.

"Carosello" ads are strictly soft-sell. Midway through a typical commercial, the audience usually has no idea what product is being pushed, and viewers are sometimes left guessing even at the end. Was it a commercial for the heroine's car or for her camera? Some of the world's top filmmakers (such as Claude Lelouch and Richard Lester) have produced mini-dramas and mini-comedies for "Carosello." As one program executive puts it: "We have managed to turn advertising into art." [12]

Institutional advertising is not limited to AT&T and other regulated monopolies. Most large corporations devote a significant part of their advertising budgets to institutional ads. A good public image pays off not just in sales, but in public support for the company when it comes into conflict with other companies or with the government. Institutional advertising is also useful for selling a particular point of view on issues of public policy. In 1974, for example, the oil industry spent tens of millions of dollars on energy advertising, designed to convince people that they should support financial incentives for oil exploration and the elimination of burdensome environmental safeguards.

The distinction between product advertising and institutional advertising is by no means airtight. Many institutional ads help sell a company's products, and many product ads help build its image. Even more important, product advertising often has a substantial impact on our attitudes and values, not just toward the product or the company, but toward every aspect of American society. Consider a snowmobile advertisement, for example. The goal of the ad may be to sell us a particular brand of snowmobile, but in the process the ad also tells us that snowmobiling is a safe, satisfying, red-blooded American sport, just the thing for someone who loves nature and the outdoors. Even if we have no intention of buying a snowmobile, the ad leaves us with a better image of snowmobiling. And when conservationists propose new restrictions on snowmobiles in order to protect the wilderness they sometimes destroy, we are that much less likely to support the proposals.

Government regulatory agencies and industry self-regulation groups seldom concern themselves with the impact of truthful advertising on social values. Their chief interest is the possibility that the ads might be fraudulent or misleading (see pp. 359–62). Advertising professionals often tell the story of an ill-fated TV commercial for a toy submachine gun. The commercial featured a trigger-happy child standing on a hill and cheerfully mowing down hundreds of toy soldiers. When the National Association of Broadcasters refused to pass the ad, the agency assumed at first that it was cracking down on super-violent advertising. Not so. The NAB's objection was that young viewers might be misled into believing that the toy soldiers (and the hill?) came with the gun.

Though regulators seldom worry about the noncommercial effects of advertising, other groups have begun to consider the problem more seriously. Among the most irate—and with considerable justice—is the feminist movement.

American advertising has traditionally treated women as sex objects. This isn't an arbitrary insult, but simply a good sales technique. Advertisers know that overtly sexy women help sell products to men, who enjoy the association, and even to women, who have been persuaded (largely by advertising itself) that it's a good thing to be a sex object. An air-travel slump in the early 1970s, for example, prompted National Airlines to run a series of ads featuring attractive stewardesses who urged the would-be passenger to "Fly Me." Continental Airlines responded with its own equally attractive women, who promised that "We'll really move our tail for you." Feminist groups pushed for a boycott against both companies, and a TV producer in Los Angeles—one of the very few women in the business—called the ads a "ridiculous attempt to portray women flight attendants as sexy, fun-promising amateur call girls." [13]

When they are not sex objects, women portrayed in advertising are usually drudges. Professor Caryl Rivers writes:

> The housewives in TV commercials stalk dirt, dust and stale air. . . . The Lysol lady sticks her nose in the sink and sniffs. . . . The women in the Joy commercials get their dishes so clean guests can see their faces in them. . . . The message is clear. Failure to perform a menial personal service properly brings rejection and the withdrawal of love and approval. Success at her assigned task brings her both

approval and sex. . . . I like to think I am immune. . . . But I still wish my floors were shinier.[14]

Although television advertising often seems to be an endless succession of sex objects and drudges, only 32 percent of the performers in TV commercials are women, according to research by women in the Screen Actors Guild. Even more significant, the same study found that only 7 percent of the off-camera voices in TV commercials are women.[15] Off-camera voices, of course, are the authority figures who tell the viewer what to do.

The advertising industry is not single-handedly responsible for the sexism in American society. Advertising merely uses that sexism to sell products. The ads will change when the society changes. In fact, spurred by the growth in women's consciousness and the lobbying of the feminist movement, the ads are beginning to change. For years, *Redbook* magazine advertised itself as "The Magazine for Young Mamas." In 1974, it coined a new slogan: "The Magazine of the New Management." Describing its readers as "the millions of young women who are now emerging from homebody to somebody," one 1975 *Redbook* advertisement declared: "Married or not, working or not, women run their own lives. They're the New Management." [16] At the same time, an increasing number of television ads portray women who hold down jobs, buy insurance, keep bank accounts, and otherwise lead independent and responsible lives.

Advertisers are as willing to be anti-sexist as they are to be sexist, as long as it won't cut down on sales. The only goal of product advertising is that we buy what they're selling. But the effects of product advertising go far beyond that. When advertisers ground their sales pitch in sexism, they reinforce the sexism in American culture. The same may be said for elitism, competitiveness, status-seeking, violence, sexual insecurity, and many other facets of our lives that advertisers prey on to make us buy. Consumption is not the only American value maintained by advertising.

Who pays for all this commercial and social indoctrination? You do. The cost of advertising is passed on to the consumer in the form of increased prices. A bar of soap that sells for 35¢ might cost only 31¢ if Procter and Gamble didn't spend $220 million a year on television advertising. In the early 1960s, Harry Skornia computed the cost of TV advertising alone to a family with a disposable income of $5,000. The annual "tax" for free TV, he found, was $53. It broke down this way.[17]

Cosmetics and toiletries	$12.00
Patent medicines and drugs	10.00
Car	10.00
Food	6.00
Cigarettes	5.00
Gasoline, oil, tires	3.00
Soaps and detergents	3.00
Other	4.00
	$53.00

A similar calculation today would yield a higher figure. Advertising in radio, newspapers, and magazines, of course, add to the total.

You get something for your money. By increasing the demand for consumer goods, advertising makes possible the economies of mass production and mass distribution—economies that are in part passed on to the consumer. Most economists today agree that advertising earns back more than its cost—especially when you throw in the value of the media.

Economically, then, advertising is a pretty good deal. Skornia's $53 isn't that much to pay for a year's supply of television and an overwhelming choice of products. Which leaves only one question unanswered: What do you think of the kinds of media that advertising gives you, the kinds of products that it offers you, and the kinds of values that it inculcates in you?

ADVERTISING PROFESSIONALS

Advertising professionals face their greatest challenge when introducing a new kind of product, creating a need that does not already exist. Enzyme soaps are a typical case. Developed in the late 1960s, enzyme soaps do essentially the same job as standard detergents, perhaps a little more effectively. But without exception, the companies that manufacture enzyme cleaners also make detergents, and bleaches to boot. Their goal, of course, is to sell the new product while maintaining the sales records of the old ones. How, then, did the Brand X Detergent Company introduce Enzyme X?

The company's first move was to hire a New York advertising agency, one of the big ones geared for national campaigns. Brand X was a major account, so an agency vice president was assigned the job of account executive. Like most account executives, he was a white male with an M.B.A. from a prestigious university. He had been catapulted to the vice presidency at the age of 38 by several phenomenally successful campaigns. He was earning in excess of $50,000 a year, and was already planning to quit and start his own agency, perhaps with Brand X as his first big client.

The job of an account executive is to act as liaison between the client and the agency's creative people. In this case, the executive planned to make use of the following departments: research, copy, art, layout, production, and media. Selecting one or two people from each department, the account executive put together a planning group that would stay with the account from start to finish.

It was a psychologist from the research department who pointed out the obvious: "We cannot base our advertisements on the superiority of enzymes over detergents, because our client manufactures detergents as well. We must therefore urge the consumers to add the enzyme product to the detergent and bleach they already use, in order to obtain an even cleaner wash than before." Everyone

agreed that this appeal was essentially irrational (what is "cleaner than clean"?), but everyone agreed that it could work. The research department verified that many women are emotionally attached to their old detergents and will not give them up—but will cheerfully dump an extra ingredient into their wash if convinced that it will give them the cleanest clothes on the block.

Convincing them was, of course, the job of the copy, art, and layout departments. The media department, meanwhile, tentatively decided to stress national women's magazines and daytime TV soap operas. Work began on four different magazine ads and three television commercials, each in 60-second, 40-second, 30-second, and 10-second versions. Since the agency's movie production facilities were already working to capacity, an independent filmmaker was called in to help.

Throughout this period, the account executive was in constant contact with the Brand X advertising department. He obtained their approval for each ad and each commercial. He also got their permission to test-market the product in a dozen communities, trying out various appeals to see how they worked.

According to the research department, these tests produced one unexpected result. Housewives, it seems, were not only willing to add Enzyme X to their wash; they were also willing to use it as a pre-soak before washing. New commercials were designed to stress this additional function.

Now the media department went into action. Using data from the Audit Bureau of Circulations, the media people began deciding which ads to place in which newspapers and magazines, when and how often. Their main criteria were total circulation and total cost—how many readers per dollar could they reach in each publication. But it wasn't that simple. The "enzyme-buying public" was obviously easier to reach in some magazines than in others; even newspapers vary in the number of women readers they attract. Quality and minority-group magazines required different ads from the mass magazines. There were back covers to be considered, and special editions, and regional magazines, and dozens of other factors.

But choosing the print media was child's play compared with placing broadcast commercials. The main tool here was the ratings, prepared by the A. C. Nielsen Company and the American Research Bureau. Broadcasters live and die by the Nielsen and ARB rating reports, simply because advertisers swear by them. In this case, the main candidates for commercials were the daytime network soap operas. Each show was carefully examined in terms of its cost per thousand viewers, its credibility as an advertising vehicle, its popularity with the sorts of people who might buy enzymes, and so forth. Consideration was also given to the possibility of commissioning and sponsoring a special program, but this was rejected. In the end, spot commercials were placed in seven different network serials.

The media department had plenty of help deciding where to place its ads—from the space and time sales representatives in the advertising department of each newspaper, magazine, and broadcast station and network. In theory, this is a cut-and-dried process. The media have their ad rates; the client pays the full rate; the agency remits 85 percent of it and keeps the other 15 percent as its commission. In reality, there's a lot of room for wheeling and dealing—to get the client a lower price and the agency a higher commission.

Media commissions account for about three-quarters of the income of most advertising agencies. The other quarter comes from surveys, production, and similar "expenses," for which the client pays a premium. After covering its own expenses, the average ad agency has a net profit of only 4 percent of the gross. Madison Avenue is not a cheap address, and advertising executives are well paid.

How did the enzyme campaign work out? Like many advertising campaigns, it was a success. Housewives obediently began adding enzyme products to their wash, or using them as pre-soaks; the more impressionable housewives did both. Enzyme X became a big moneymaker for the Brand X Detergent Company. After a year or two, the company (and nearly all its competitors) decided to add enzymes to its detergent as well. Properly advertised, this gimmick helped to boost detergent sales without damaging the sales of nondetergent enzymes. By 1971, the cooperative American housewife did her wash in the following manner: first an enzyme pre-soak, then an enzyme detergent supplemented with more of the pre-soak and with bleach. Her clothes were cleaner than cleaner than clean, her self-image was ever more closely tied to the washbasket, and detergent-caused eutrophication had become a serious water-pollution problem.

Such is the power of advertising.

ETHICS AND REGULATION

The first advertising agencies were founded in the 1840s. By 1860 there were thirty of them. As intermediaries between the advertisers and the publications, they were in an ideal position to cheat both—inflating prices, demanding kickbacks, and so on.

These abuses didn't improve until 1869, when George P. Rowell began publishing the *American Newspaper Directory,* an accurate listing of newspaper circulations and ad rates. Also in 1869, the N. W. Ayer & Son agency was founded to buy space for advertisers on a straight commission basis. Thereafter, it was not so easy for ad agencies to manipulate publishers and advertisers.

But manipulating the public was something else. Many ads at the turn of the century—especially those for patent medicines—were grossly misleading, often outright falsehoods. The public put up with them for a few decades, then began to complain. Several of the more ethical agencies joined in the campaign against misleading advertising. The Better Business Bureau was founded in

1913, the Audit Bureau of Circulations in 1914. The Association of Advertising Clubs developed a model "truth in advertising" law. It was championed by the trade journal *Printers' Ink,* and was soon adopted by several states.

The federal government entered the scene in 1914, when the Federal Trade Commission Act empowered the FTC to regulate false advertising. But the Commission's responsibility was limited to ads that could be shown to constitute unfair competition—that is, false advertising that hurt the sales of more truthful competitors. The Wheeler-Lea Amendment of 1938 broadened the FTC's mandate to include all false advertising regardless of its effects on competition, especially in the food, drug, and cosmetics industries. Still, the Commission was required to prove that an ad was fraudulent before it could take action against the advertiser.

Some forty years later, this emphasis on consumer fraud is still characteristic of the FTC. Acknowledging that advertisers know how to mislead without lying, the Commission now considers what an ad implies as well as what it says. But the Commission seldom looks beyond content to judge the effects of an advertisement. Many ads today are designed to appeal to unconscious needs and irrational desires; they succeed, at least in part, through psychological manipulation that has nothing to do with the product. The FTC offers little protection from such ads. Nor does it pay much attention to the impact of advertising on social values. Except for children's advertising and a few other special cases, any ad that makes no false or misleading claims is safe from the FTC.

This limitation is probably appropriate. Dangerous though advertising may be, it would probably be even more dangerous to have a government agency deciding which advertisements to ban on grounds of their psychological or sociological impact. But it is a limitation nonetheless.

In dealing with false advertising, the FTC is most effective against marginal operators whose ads are clearly fraudulent. It success-fully challenges many such ads every year, and thus helps insure that advertising does not return to the "patent medicine" standards of the turn of the century. The Commission's record against mainstream advertisers is a good deal less impressive. Many observers have claimed—and some still claim—that this is because the FTC is too subservient to the advertising industry. But even an aggressive FTC would find it difficult to surmount the legal delaying tactics that major advertisers readily employ. It typically takes years for the FTC to collect evidence against a particular advertisement and then push the case through the courts. By then the ad has long since been junked and a new one put in its place.

In the early 1970s, the FTC devised two novel strategies for coping with this time problem (see p. 184). First, it began collecting data from advertisers on the facts behind ad claims on a routine, industry-by-industry basis, thus speeding the process of gathering evidence. Second, it began requiring companies not only to stop running their false ads but also to admit in their new ads that the earlier claims were indeed false. Aided by these and other innovations, the Commission won several important victories against such major advertisers as Profile Bread.

No doubt there is still room for improvement in the Federal Trade Commission's policing of false advertising. But at least in the past few years the FTC has done a reasonably adequate job in that department. Now, who should police the other sorts of advertising abuses—the ads that manipulate psychological weaknesses and mold social values?

The industry position on this "hidden persuaders" approach to advertising is that it doesn't exist. Advertising executives insist that their job is merely to tell people about the goods and services they have for sale. Of course they present this information in the most effective possible light; that's the American way. But there's nothing underhanded, they say, about using sex to sell shaving cream, or athletes to sell aspirin, or compulsive overconsumption to sell just about everything.

The advertising industry does have a self-regulatory apparatus of sorts. Its linchpin is the National Advertising Division of the Council of Better Business Bureaus, which investigates consumer complaints and urges advertisers to abide by its findings. An advertiser who disagrees may appeal to a five-member panel of the National Advertising Review Board. If the NARB decides against an advertiser, the offending ad is almost always withdrawn. This process weeds out the most blatantly dishonest ads—*if* the ad is nationally distributed, and *if* the complaint is vigorously pursued, and *if* the advertiser doesn't switch to a different campaign before a decision is reached, and *if* the problem is a misstatement of fact. That's a lot of ifs.

The mass media, meanwhile, have an almost ironclad right to reject advertising for any reason at all—or for no reason at all. They use this right sparingly, of course. Somewhere in the advertising department of most newspapers and magazines is a person responsible for glancing at every ad submitted and deciding which ones to accept. Ads that might offend large numbers of readers—such as those for X-rated movies—are frequently rejected. So are ads that clearly violate a Better Business Bureau standard of honesty or accuracy. And that's about it. Rarely does a newspaper or magazine reject an advertisement that is neither offensive nor fraudulent, merely because it tries to manipulate the needs and values of its readers.

The same standards prevail in broadcasting. Both the Radio and the Television Codes contain guidelines on advertising. Broadcasters are urged to reject a commercial whenever they "doubt the integrity of the advertiser, the truth of the advertising representations, or the compliance of the advertiser with the spirit and purpose of all applicable legal requirements." They are also supposed to turn down an ad if they have "good reason to believe [it] would be objectionable to a substantial and responsible segment of the community." [18] In practice, broadcasters apply the first standard only when the dishonesty is blatant, but they are very hard-nosed about the second. Many stations refuse commercials for liquors, suppositories, condoms, fortune-tellers, X-rated movies, and controversial ideas of all sorts, in order to avoid offending any group of listeners or viewers. But for years the broadcast industry ignored the lethal danger of cigarettes. Broadcasters cut out tobacco ads only when Congress forced them to—and they complained bitterly every step of the way.

The reluctance of the media to censor advertising is justifiable, not just on economic grounds, but also on grounds of the right of access (see pp. 223–24). Libertarians would be among the first to complain if the media started rejecting huge numbers of ads simply because publishers and station managers disapproved of their message. There is no danger that this will happen. Like the advertising industry itself, the mass media worry about advertising only when it is patently fraudulent or offensive to vocal segments of the public.

The best hope for dealing with advertising abuses other than fraudulence, in other words, is a vocal public that insists that such abuses be dealt with. In recent years a variety of citizen groups have begun exerting this sort of pressure, forcing the advertising industry, the mass media, and even the government to begin considering the social effects of advertising.

The area in which the greatest progress has been made is children's advertising (see p. 309). In the late 1960s, groups such as Action for Children's Television began pressuring the Federal Trade Commission, the Federal Communications Commission, the National Association of Broadcasters, the National Advertising Review Board, and every other relevant agency and organization to do something about children's commercials. By the 1970s they were getting results:

- In 1970 the FCC began a four-year study of the problem.
- In 1972 the NAB reduced its recommended maximum number of minutes per hour for children's commercials.
- In May, 1974, the NARB announced it would devise new standards for children's commercials and monitor the networks for offenders.
- In June, 1974, FTC Chairman Lewis A. Engman proposed a series of strict regulations on children's advertising.
- In summer, 1974, the NAB further reduced the quantity of children's commercials, and devised its own new guidelines in response to Engman's proposed regulations.
- In October, 1974, the FCC ended its four-year study by supporting the NAB's new voluntary guidelines.

Left to themselves, the government, the advertising industry, and the mass media would all prefer to police only blatantly dishonest advertising, ignoring more subtle abuses. It is unlikely they will be permitted this luxury any longer.

To sell their products and services, institutions use paid advertising. But when they want to sell themselves, they turn mostly to public relations. Public relations may be defined as the planned effort to create and maintain a favorable climate of opinion through communications, especially through free publicity in the mass media. Although it became a "science" only in the twentieth century, public relations has been a practical art in the U.S. for more than 300 years. Most of what we know about the actions and interests of corporate America we have learned from the nation's PR professionals.

PR AND THE MEDIA

In 1641, Harvard College sent three preachers to England on a "begging mission." At their request, a fund-raising brochure, *New England's First Fruits,* was prepared by the elders of the Massachusetts Bay Colony —the first public-relations pamphlet written in the New World. Press releases, pseudo-events, and the rest of the PR arsenal followed soon after. Though the first professional public-relations firm wasn't founded until 1904, the techniques were already well-established before the American Revolution.

The difference between advertising and public relations is one of methods, not goals. Martin Mayer puts it this way:

> Advertising, whatever its faults, is a relatively open business; its messages appear in paid space or on bought time, and everybody can recognize it as special pleading. Public relations works behind the scenes. . . . The advertising man must know how many people he can reach *with* the media, the public relations man must know how many people he can reach *within* the media.[19]

This is a valid distinction, but advertising and public relations are often so intertwined that it is hard to tell where one leaves off and the other begins. When political candidates, for instance, put themselves in the hands of the professionals (as most of them do now), they hire not only advertising specialists to write their commercials, but also public-relations specialists to write their speeches. The two kinds of specialists work together to build a consistent (if unreal) image of the candidate they work for.

If anything, public relations is a broader field than advertising. Every politician employs a full-time press secretary even after the election, though there may be no further need for an ad agency. Government departments don't advertise much, but they employ literally thousands of professional PR people. And every college and every corporation has its own "public-information office" or "public-relations department."

Whatever their title and whoever their employer, public-relations people have just one job: through communications, to build in various publics the sorts of attitudes their client wants those publics to have. The job may include a company newsletter for employees, a speaker service for civic groups, a lobbying effort for Congress, and a variety of other specialized approaches. But the main thrust of most public-relations efforts is to reach the general public through the mass media.

PR techniques for influencing the media run the gamut from handouts to junkets, from press conferences to bribes. These techniques are discussed in detail in Chapter 6. That chapter was entitled "Source Control" to stress the fundamental purpose of public relations—PR is what sources do to control the content of the media.

How much control do they actually exercise? By way of example, consider a 1971 study of news coverage of environmental issues in the San Francisco Bay Area. David B. Sachsman asked reporters and editors from twenty-five Bay Area media where they got their information for the 474 local environmental news stories they carried over a twelve-day period. He received answers for 200 of the stories. The breakdown was as follows:

Rewritten press releases	46
Business Wire	3
News film from PR people	2
Telephone or personal contact with PR people	26
Press releases plus additional reporting	28
No public-relations influence	95

In other words, 51 of the 200 stories were based entirely on PR material; the "reporter" did no reporting at all. Another 54 stories came as the result of an initial PR push—a phone call, a personal visit, or a press release —followed by some additional work on the reporter's part. Only 95 stories, less than half, were initiated by the reporter without significant public-relations input.[20]

Sachsman also asked eleven specialized environmental reporters to keep track of what they did with every press release they received over an eight-week period. The reporters logged an impressive total of 1,347

environmental releases. They wrote news stories based on 192 of them, and saved an additional 268 releases for possible later use.[21]

It is clear from these figures that distributing an environmental press release by no means guarantees the desired news story. PR people must compete with each other and with other sources of news (such as the wire services) for the limited space and time available in the media. On the other hand, the figures also demonstrate that PR exercises a very substantial influence over environmental news coverage in the San Francisco Bay Area. Sachsman concludes:

> The easy way for a Bay Area medium to cover the environment is to rely on information supplied by public relations. . . . It is reasonable to estimate that about 40 percent of the environmental content of the Bay Area media comes from public relations practitioners, and that about 20 percent of the environmental content consists of rewritten press releases. When a newsman uses a press release to help him investigate a story, he should not be accused of abandoning his job to the public relations man, but when he simply rewrites a press release or uses a PR wire story or film . . . it is the PR man who is really covering the story.[22]

Many other studies of public-relations influence have reached similar conclusions. During a one-month period in 1973, for example, a group of Pentagon reporters produced 155 news stories. Of these, 47 were based primarily on the words of Pentagon information officers. And 42 more reported the statements of high-ranking Defense Department officials at events engineered by the Pentagon's public-information office, such as press conferences, arranged interviews, and congressional appearances.[23] Military public relations, in short, dominated well over half the Pentagon news stories published during this typical month.

Writing in 1962, Professor Scott M. Cutlip estimated that roughly 35 percent of the news in the average newspaper came from public-relations sources. He contended further that as the content of news became more complex, making it increasingly difficult for reporters to understand fully what they were writing about, the percentage would increase.[24] A fair estimate of how much of today's news is directly inspired by public relations would probably run between 40 and 50 percent.

Journalists are understandably ambivalent about this extensive PR influence. Most reporters are keenly aware of the fact that public-relations people have an axe to grind. They don't especially enjoy rewriting press releases day after day. They'd much rather investigate and write their own stories.

But a reporter's time and expertise are both extremely limited, and without public relations many stories would never get reported at all. The most efficient way to cover a minor event (such as a corporate promotion or a garden club meeting) is to publish the releases submitted by the participants. The most efficient way to cover a

---

GUIDE FOR PUBLICITY HEADS

Public relations doesn't always involve a professional trying to manipulate public opinion; often it is an amateur merely trying to publicize a community event. Many newspapers, especially suburban ones, rely heavily on this sort of amateur PR for their coverage of groups that aren't important or controversial enough to merit a reporter's attention. To help local organizations get their story into the paper, editors often run workshops on how to write and submit press releases. Many also publish guidelines for publicity heads. The following is the "Guide for Publicity Chairmen" provided by the *Somerset Spectator*, a suburban New Jersey weekly.[25]

1. The deadline for all copy is Monday noon each week (except on holidays when an earlier deadline may be announced in the paper). We would appreciate your timing all publicity to appear in area newspapers on the same day.

2. Releases should be mailed to the *Spectator*, P. O. Box 336, Somerset, N.J. 08873, dropped in the mailbox in the downstairs lobby at 900 Hamilton Street or submitted at our office in Room 11 (second floor) on Mondays between the hours of 9 A.M. and 12 noon.

3. Releases should be typed, *double-spaced* (to permit editing between lines, if necessary) and should contain the name and telephone number of the person who can be contacted for additional information. Carbons are acceptable if they are truly legible.

4. We prefer that you take photographs of most club events. Polaroids are fine as long as they are clear and sharp. All photographs should be black and white. Be sure to include complete information for a caption on a separate sheet of paper attached to the back of the photograph with a piece of tape. If something special is coming up, please give us a few weeks notice and we will try to send a photographer.

5. Please check and double check the spelling of all names in your releases. Always include first names (not *Mr. Jones* or *Mrs. Smith*). We prefer that women, married or not, be referred to simply as Marilyn Jones.

6. News items that are submitted on time will automatically be included in "Week at a Glance" or you may submit items specifically for the weekly calendar. The deadline for each month's "Looking Ahead" is announced under the column on page 3 (around the middle of each month for the subsequent month).

7. Since our readers do not want to read the same news more than once, please submit only one release about a particular event unless you have new information. The date, however, can be announced in advance (see no. 6 above).

8. Let us know well in advance about any event or activity you think might make an interesting feature story.

technical issue (such as an air-pollution ruling or the introduction of a new missile) is to publish the expert statements supplied by the agencies. The most efficient way to cover a public controversy (such as a zoning dispute or a close vote in Congress) is to publish the conflicting PR claims of both sides. Public-relations professionals report the routine stories for the media, and help them report the important ones. Few journalists relish their dependence on PR, but nearly all agree that there is simply no other way to get their business done on time.

PR AND THE PUBLIC

Since the media depend largely on public relations for news, the public inevitably does too. Of course reporters decide which press releases to publish, which PR people to talk with, which questions to ask, which answers to include, and which stories to investigate more thoroughly and report more interpretively. Nonetheless, any point of view that does not have expert PR help faces an uphill battle for favorable coverage in the media. And any point of view that is blessed with a superlative PR apparatus has an almost unbeatable advantage.

It is customary to blame every example of biased news coverage on the news media themselves. We tend to say that this newspaper was biased against labor in that strike, that this broadcast station was biased in favor of that candidate in the election, etc. Sometimes the bias is just that, an intentional or unintentional distortion on the part of the media. But most of the bias in the news is not the bias of the reporter, but rather the bias of the sources who knew best how to meet the needs of the reporter. Imbalances in news coverage, in other words, usually result from imbalances in public-relations skill; the reporter is as much a victim as the rest of us.

Not that reporters should be let off the hook entirely. We have a right to insist that the media work especially hard to cover those viewpoints that are not represented by effective PR professionals, and that they struggle to lessen the influence of those viewpoints whose PR is especially expert. But all that takes time, and time is the media's scarcest commodity. As long as reporters continue to rely heavily on public relations, the groups that achieve the most favorable coverage will be the groups that employ the most effective PR people.

It is in this sense that public relations must be viewed as a potent social force, as a mass medium in its own right. How much do you know about, say, the Bell Telephone system? And where did you learn what you know? You learned a little of it from personal experience and conversations with friends. You learned a great deal more from those charming and impressive AT&T ads. And you learned by far the most from the efforts of the Bell PR department. Those efforts range from the little "newsletter" that comes with your bill every month to upbeat newspaper articles about Bell's work in minority recruiting. They range from Bell-sponsored science films distributed free to primary schools to cute magazine fillers about the adventures of a long-distance operator. They range from widely publicized grants to educational TV stations to county-fair exhibits of telephone technology.

There is nothing dishonest about all this. Public-relations people seldom lie. They don't even have to distort the truth all that often. They simply distract the public's attention from disagreeable facts and concentrate its attention on agreeable ones—agreeable to the client, that is. Bell Telephone really does impressive things technologically; it is generous in its support of education; it doubtless has thousands of courteous, helpful operators who love people. But Bell Telephone is other things as well—things you seldom hear about unless an opponent of Bell starts generating its own PR.

The success of a PR campaign is measured in two ways. First, it must be covered by the media; the more news stories a campaign generates, the more successful it is. Second, it must contribute to a favorable climate of public opinion; if sales go up and friendly letters pour in, the campaign is truly successful. As a fairly typical success, consider the story of Lucky Breweries, a West Coast beer company. Lucky's PR expert, Bert Casey, calls it the story of the company's decision to "live and exploit its sense of corporate public responsibility." [26]

Lucky was one of the first companies to discover the public-relations potential of the nation's rising concern about the quality of the environment. In 1969, Casey began publicizing the company's efforts at environmental cleanup. The results were good, and by September, 1970, Lucky had developed a workable bottle-recycling program in Seattle. With Casey's help, the program received wide press coverage; sales started climbing, and Lucky immediately began recycling efforts in other areas. By mid-June, 1971, the company had redeemed more than ten million containers. As a result of its recycling program, Lucky sales were up as much as 20 percent in some areas, and the company had accumulated literally thousands of letters of congratulations in its files.

Casey's biggest coup was undoubtedly his glasphalt campaign. There is nothing fake about glasphalt. A mixture of asphalt and glass chips, it is a paving material with substantial promise. Though making glasphalt out of old bottles isn't nearly as good for the environment as refilling the bottles and using them again, it's a lot better than tossing them into the garbage.

On May 20, 1971, Lucky Breweries paved its first glasphalt parking lot. About forty journalists were there for the occasion. They watched the paving, attended a press conference, received a Lucky press kit, and left with the story Lucky wanted them to have. They were there, of course, because Casey got them there—by mailing 120 invitations to West Coast media and telephoning reminders to dozens of editors.

The story was a natural. It tied the growing public interest in recycling to the novel idea of paving a parking lot with broken glass. Lucky would have considered the campaign a success even if the story had been confined to those newspapers and broadcast stations that sent their own reporters. But Casey was after wider coverage than that. He hired the Business Wire (a public-relations wire service) to telegraph his press release to

---

THE LITTLE RED SCHOOLHOUSE HAS A PR EXPERT

Public-relations professionals have worked for industry and government for many years. Today, they are also employed extensively by such institutions as hospitals, charities, and school systems.

A 1971 survey of 417 New Jersey school districts found that 214 of them—over half—had at least a part-time PR person on their staff. Twenty-tour had full-time public-relations experts—such as Amy Fisher of the East Brunswick schools.

Fisher is responsible for all the school system's publications, including a bimonthly newsletter that is mailed to every resident of the district, a school information guide, a brochure for new residents, the annual superintendent's report, etc. She also writes materials for budget and bond referendums, and a synopsis of each school board meeting. She conducts public-opinion polls and acts as a liaison between the school board and the PTA. And whenever the East Brunswick school system has something to announce to the community, Amy Fisher writes the press release.[27]

every subscriber. And as soon as the paving was over and the reporters were gone, the big push came. Casey explains:

> We selected two photos to be released in a saturation mailing. These were produced overnight, pasted to captions, stuffed along with the news release and mailed May 21 to 2,250 radio stations, television stations, daily newspapers and weekly newspapers in the west. Additionally, we released a 120-second television film clip to 35 western stations.[28]

The results were predictable. The glasphalt story moved on both the AP and the UPI wire. In the San Francisco area (where the event took place), the story appeared in all the metropolitan papers and most of the suburban dailies; it was on most of the area's TV stations and many of its larger radio stations. Overall, more than a hundred newspapers ran a glasphalt story, and twenty television stations used Casey's film clip.

The total cost of the glasphalt campaign was $4,000—a drop in the bucket in Lucky's 1971 PR budget of $150,000. Yet the campaign brought the company more favorable publicity than it could have purchased with $100,000 in advertising. On the strength of glasphalt and several similar successes, Casey soon went into business as Bert Casey & Company, an independent public-relations consulting firm with one major client, Lucky Breweries.

There is nothing unusual about Lucky Breweries and Bell Telephone. Every company, union, government, charity, and political movement uses the same techniques. Much of what we know about our world comes to us (free of charge) courtesy of the nation's 100,000 public-relations professionals.

Back in 1906, PR pioneer Ivy Lee sent the following "Declaration of Principles" to newspaper publishers:

> This is not a secret news bureau. All our work is done in the open. We aim to supply news. This is not an advertising agency; if you think any of our matter ought properly to go to your business office, do not use it. Our matter is accurate. Further details of any subject will be supplied promptly, and any editor will be assisted most cheerfully in verifying directly any statement of fact. . . . In brief, our plan is frankly and openly, on behalf of business concerns and public institutions, to supply to the press and public of the United States prompt and accurate information concerning subjects which it is of value and interest to the public to know about.[29]

This declaration is, in effect, a public-relations handout on behalf of public relations. It forms the basis for the Public Relations Code of the Public Relations Society of America.

Despite these principles, PR is dangerous. Publicists do not often lie, but telling half the truth is an integral part of their business, and stretching the truth is not uncommon. Moreover, they do it in secret; their work does not carry the unspoken *caveat emptor* of paid advertising. And finally, public relations is almost completely unregulated by the government.

In the first part of this chapter, we stated that the principal danger of advertising is its ability to manipulate our needs and values to make us buy whatever the advertisers are selling. PR people, fortunately, seldom employ the psychological traps characteristic of so much modern advertising. The principal danger of public relations is its ability to supply the media with one-sided information that masquerades as objective news.

Advertising and public relations have been around too long to be eliminated now. The media and the industrial establishment depend on them. Society as we know it could not exist without them. But when you make a list of mass media and related institutions, do not forget to include advertising and PR. And if your list is in order of influence on American civilization, do not forget to put them at the top.

Notes

1 Meyer Weinberg, *TV in America* (New York: Ballantine Books, 1962), pp. 46–47.

2 Lawrence B. Christopher, "Clark Oil Finds Out TV Really Works," *Broadcasting*, March 2, 1970, pp. 42–44.

3 Theodore Peterson, Jay W. Jensen, and William L. Rivers, *The Mass Media and Modern Society* (New York: Holt, Rinehart and Winston, 1965), p. 191.

4 Weinberg, *TV in America*, p. 194.

5 "Leading TV Advertisers," *The Official Associated Press Almanac 1975* (Maplewood, N.J.: Hammond Almanac, 1974), p. 767.

6 John Kenneth Galbraith, *The New Industrial State* (Boston: Houghton Mifflin, 1967), pp. 37–38, 201.

7 Dallas Smythe, "Five Myths of Consumership," *Nation*, January 20, 1969, p. 82.

8 Erich Fromm, *Escape from Freedom* (New York: Farrar & Rinehart, 1941).

9 *Information Please Almanac 1975* (New York: Information Please Almanac, 1974), p. 80.

10 Craig R. Whitney, "Germans Upset about TV Commercials," *New York Times*, September 22, 1974, p. 20.

11 Bernard Rosenberg and David Manning White, eds., *Mass Culture: The Popular Arts in America* (New York: The Free Press, 1957), pp. 465–66.

12 "The Art of Selling," *Newsweek*, December 20, 1971, p. 85.

13 "Airlines' Sexy Ads May Cause 'Spontaneous Lack of Enthusiasm,'" *New Brunswick* (N.J.) *Home News*, June 30, 1974, p. A8 (Associated Press).

14 Caryl Rivers, "How to Be Spotless, Sexy, and Loved," *New York Times*, April 28, 1974, p. D15.

15 Philip H. Dougherty, "Female Role in TV Spots Studied," *New York Times*, November 14, 1974, p. 82.

16 Philip H. Dougherty, "Redbook's Approach to Women," *New York Times*, December 9, 1974, p. 60.

17 Harry J. Skornia, *Television and Society* (New York: McGraw-Hill, 1965), p. 96.

18 Radio and Television Codes.

19 Peterson, Jensen, and Rivers, *Mass Media and Modern Society*, p. 191.

20 David B. Sachsman, *Public Relations Influence on Environmental Coverage* (Ph.D. dissertation, Stanford University, 1973), pp. 276–80.

21 *Ibid.*, pp. 50, 275.

22 *Ibid.*, pp. 278–79.

23 Brit Hume and Mark McIntyre, "Polishing Up the Brass," [*MORE*], May, 1973, p. 6.

24 Scott M. Cutlip, "Third of Newspapers' Content PR-Inspired," *Editor & Publisher*, May 26, 1962, p. 68.

25 "Guide for Publicity Chairmen," *Somerset* (N.J.) *Spectator*, December 30, 1971, p. 4.

26 Sachsman, *Public Relations Influence on Environmental Coverage*, pp. 256–59.

27 Louise Saul, "School Boards Turning to Public Relations Experts to Keep the Parents Informed," *New York Times*, September 1, 1974, p. NJ11.

28 Sachsman, *Public Relations Influence on Environmental Coverage*, pp. 256–59.

29 Sherman Morse, "An Awakening in Wall Street," *American Magazine*, September, 1906, p. 460.

Suggested Readings

COHEN, DOROTHY, *Advertising*. New York: John Wiley & Sons, 1972.

CUTLIP, SCOTT M., and ALLEN H. CENTER, *Effective Public Relations* (4th ed.). Englewood Cliffs, N.J.: Prentice-Hall, Inc., 1971.

DELLA FEMINA, JERRY, *From Those Wonderful Folks Who Gave You Pearl Harbor*. New York: Pocket Books, 1970.

LOIS, GEORGE, with BILL PITTS, *George, Be Careful*. New York: Saturday Review Press, 1972.

MANDELL, MAURICE I., *Advertising* (2nd ed.). Englewood Cliffs, N.J.: Prentice-Hall, Inc., 1974.

McGINNISS, JOE, *The Selling of the President 1968*. New York: Trident Press, 1969.

PACKARD, VANCE, *The Hidden Persuaders*. New York: Pocket Books, 1957.

RUBIN, DAVID M., "Anatomy of a Snow Job," [*More*], March, 1974.

SIMON, JULIAN L., *Issues in the Economics of Advertising*. Urbana, Ill.: University of Illinois Press, 1970.

PART IV
COVERAGE

We come now to the last section of the book, "Coverage." In earlier sections we talked about the functions and effects of the media. We detailed their history. We traced the patterns of media control by various groups and individuals, from governments to publishers. We examined each medium in turn to see what made it unique. Now, finally, it is time to turn to content. In a sense, the first three-quarters of the book was intended to show why the media perform the way they do. This section is intended to evaluate the performance itself.

Some 360 pages ago, we listed four functions of the mass media—to serve the economic system, to inform, to entertain, and to influence. It should be obvious by now that the authors consider the second of these functions by far the most important. In the chapters that follow, therefore, we will be interested in only one question: How well do the mass media inform the public?

Before evaluating the quality of news coverage, it is essential to consider standards of evaluation. Nothing is good or bad in itself; it is good or bad with respect to some standard. The following are the most important of the many standards that have been pro-

posed and used by the media and media critics.

1. Profitability. The American mass media are, for the most part, privately owned and privately financed. Unless they earn a profit, they will fail. And a newspaper or broadcast station in imminent danger of failure is unlikely to spend much money improving its news operation. A mass medium that earns a lot of money may still do a poor job of covering the news. But one that loses money almost always does a poor job.

2. Audience Satisfaction. Like profitability, audience satisfaction is a necessary but not a sufficient condition for media quality. If nobody reads a newspaper article it can accomplish nothing—but many articles are well read and still accomplish nothing.

3. Accuracy. An inaccurate news story is always, without exception, a poor news story. Most editors and reporters know this, and strive mightily to spell the names right, even if they do not fully understand what their sources are saying.

4. Objectivity. Nearly all responsible journalists aim at objectivity, and quite often they fail. Words have connotations as well as denotations; they imply more than they say. As long as reporters must work with words, complete objectivity is impossible. And even an "objective" reporter must decide whom to interview, what to ask, and which facts to include in the story. Fairness is a reasonable standard to ask of journalists. Literal objectivity is not.

5. Advocacy. Underground editors and other committed journalists often complain that where one side is right and the other is wrong, objectivity is a false god. Was objectivity a good thing in the 1950s, when it forced the media to be "fair" to the self-serving allegations of the leader of that decade's anti-communist witch hunt, Senator Joseph McCarthy? Journalists whose goal is advocacy, who wish to convince their readers of some point of view, have little use for objectivity.

6. Unusualness. Most editors urge their reporters to find stories that are distinctive, dramatic, or in some way unusual. If overused, this standard becomes more a definition of sensationalism than of news. If the media ignore what is typical and stress what is weird, they inevitably present us with a weird picture of the world. Nonetheless, "man bites dog" is still a bigger story than "dog bites man."

7. Relevance. Relevant news is important news. What kinds of stories are most relevant?—those that are local, timely, and directly useful to the audience. This standard, too, is sometimes overemphasized. The most local, timely, and useful stories around, after all, are the supermarket ads.

8. Completeness. The *New York Times* is the most complete newspaper in the country. But not for everything—it is weak in sports, business, and editorial cartoons. And is the most complete medium always the best medium? A three-hour TV news show is hardly three times as good as a one-hour show, especially if you're waiting for a particular story. When we demand completeness, what we are really asking for is a sample of the news that is adequately large and appropriately varied. We are talking about selection.

9. Independence. However a medium selects its news, its judgments should be its own, and should not be influenced by outside pressures. If a newspaper kills a story because a big advertiser insists on it, then it is a poor newspaper—not because it killed the story (maybe it didn't deserve to run), but because it deferred to the wishes of an advertiser. Independence is absolutely essential for good journalism.

10. Propriety. The mass media have an obligation to keep within the bounds of propriety and good taste. But what are those bounds? Some business executives think it's in poor taste to report declining sales figures. Some revolutionaries think it's in good taste to report do-it-yourself bomb-making techniques. Most editors disagree—on both counts.

11. Comprehensibility. As the world grows more complicated, it becomes less and less adequate for reporters to stick to the bare facts in their reporting. The facts of Vietnam, the facts of inflation, the facts of racial unrest, are not the entire story of these events. Interpretation is essential to put the facts into a meaningful context, to make them comprehensible to the reader or viewer.

12. Uniqueness. Democracy is predicated on the assumption that all kinds of news and opinions are available to the public, competing in the free market of ideas. The trouble with this assumption is that most of the media today are not ideological competitors. They all say pretty much the same things, and that isn't healthy. We therefore propose the standard of uniqueness. Any mass medium that is significantly different from its competitors is in this sense "better" than one that is undifferentiated. New York City is better off with both the *Times* and the *Daily News* than it would be with two papers like the *Times*. Offbeat media should be cherished.

We have listed a dozen standards. We could list a hundred, but this isn't the place for it. The point to be stressed here is that judgments of quality are meaningless without explicit criteria. Go ahead and criticize the mass media; you're as qualified as anyone else. But first make sure you know what your standards are.

Chapter 15
Coverage
of
Government

According to the libertarian theory of press-government relations, the media serve the public best when they act as aggressive watchdogs over government activities. But when this adversary relationship is achieved in practice, it often leads to repression by the government and resentment by the public. It is very difficult to achieve in any case. The most thoroughly covered government official in the world is undoubtedly the president of the United States. Yet news coverage of the president is more a product of White House news management than of aggressive, independent reporting.

The heroic, hard-drinking "typical" journalist of movie fame had a lot of flaws. But in at least one way this stereotype captured an American ideal. The movie reporter's attitude toward government officials was always magnificently suspicious and uncompromising. Inevitably, our hero wound up the third reel with a crusading exposé on the abuse of public trust by a public official —and to hell with the repercussions.

This movie stereotype is solidly grounded in historical reality. "The United States had a press before it had a foreign policy," notes *New York Times* editor James Reston. "The American press was telling the country and

the world where to get off before there was a State Department. . . . In their more amiable moods, [early American journalists] no doubt conceded that the press should serve the country, but they insisted that the best way to serve it was to criticize its every act and thought, and something of this pugnacious spirit has persisted until now." [1]

THE ADVERSARY RELATIONSHIP

Critic and scholar William L. Rivers has a name for this attitude. He calls it "the adversary relationship," and he considers it the basis for all good coverage of government. [2] Every government official, Rivers explains, has a job to do—passing laws, running a federal agency, or whatever. Reporters also have a job to do—informing the public about everything that goes on, including what goes on within the government. Sometimes the reporter's job and the official's job coincide; they work together and everybody is happy. But sometimes their jobs come into conflict. Either the official wants to publish something that the reporter considers inaccurate or unnewsworthy, or the reporter wants to publish something that the official would prefer to keep secret. That's when the adversary relationship comes into play.

If the reporter goes along with the official's view on what should and should not be printed, then he or she is not a good reporter. A journalist who consistently complies with the wishes of government officials has abdicated the responsibility of the media to act as the public's watchdog in Washington or at City Hall. A good reporter, by definition, does not take official statements at face value, refuses to protect the image of office-holders, persists in asking embarrassing questions, and fights for the answers. A good reporter, in short, is an adversary.

The adversary relationship doesn't mean simply that reporters and government officials should get mad at each other occasionally. It means that they should both respect the inevitability—even the desirability—of conflict. Officials often have good reasons for hiding or distorting the truth, at least temporarily. Journalists have good reasons for seeking the truth and releasing it to the public. For the adversary relationship to function properly, each must accept as valid the goals of the other, and the conflict that results.

It is worth stressing that the adversary relationship is a peculiarly American notion of the proper attitude of the media vis-à-vis the government. Throughout most of the world and most of history, the job of the media has been to publish whatever the government wants published. A good reporter in seventeenth-century England or twentieth-century Russia is defined as a reporter who gets the official line right and repeats it effectively.

Only in libertarian societies are the mass media a sort of "fourth branch of government," assigned the task of checking up on the other three branches. And only in a democracy must a good reporter be a hard-headed, two-fisted uncompromising skeptic—

the kind of person you might make a movie about.

Journalism professors have been talking about the concept of an adversary relationship for decades. Between 1969 and 1974, lots of other people started talking about it too—and not always with approval. A series of bloody battles between the Nixon administration and the media during this period led many observers to question the value of an adversary press. The media's longstanding dislike for Richard Nixon, they charged, was producing exaggerated and sensational coverage of the illegal burglary, wiretapping, and cover-up activities now known as Watergate. And Richard Nixon's longstanding dislike for the media, they added, was largely responsible for the very abuses that eventually led to the president's downfall.

For the first time in recent history, Americans had a president who announced to his subordinates that the press is the enemy, meant it, and acted upon it. And for the first time in recent history, it seemed that the press really was the enemy, successfully hounding the nation's chief executive out of office. If this is what the adversary relationship is all about, many Americans concluded, then it is the wrong model for press-government relations in the United States.

President Nixon hated the news media for their joyful readiness to attack and criticize him. His strategies for halting the flow of media hostility were varied and imaginative—instructing Vice President Agnew to whip up public opposition to the liberal press; initiating FBI investigations and tax audits of critical journalists; taking the *New York Times* and the *Washington Post* to court over their publication of the Pentagon Papers; issuing subpoenas to compel reporters to reveal confidential sources and information; barring aggressive journalists from access to White House information sources; etc. Obviously most of these strategies failed in their central purpose; the media continued to attack the president. Nonetheless, they had at least a potential "chilling effect" on the media's exercise of their First Amendment freedoms (see pp. 156–58). And they may well have paved the way for the Watergate cover-up.

When Watergate came, the president and the media were already at war. The following exchange came during a televised press conference in the midst of the Watergate scandals:

Dan Rather, CBS: "Mr. President, I want to state this question with due respect to your office, but also as directly as possible. . . ."

President Nixon: "That would be unusual." [3]

First Amendment expert Harry Kalven believes that the media should treat the government as an adversary, but that the government must not fight back by criticizing the media. "There is no way the government can operate in this area as a polite critic," he says, "and a less-than-polite critic is bound to produce a chilling effect upon those being criticized. . . . The Constitution really does intend to guarantee one-way tension, through a one-way adversary system." [4]

Despite Kalven's argument, it seems unrealistic to expect a president to welcome an adversary press. In any battle between president and press, the Constitution protects the press much more than the president. But when the media use that protection to attack the president, the president will inevitably fight back with secrecy, harassment, news management, and any other available weapon. Not every president will resort to illegal tactics, as Richard Nixon did. But the temptation will always be there. That, too, is part of the adversary relationship.

Another danger of the adversary relationship is the ever-present possibility that in a battle between the press and the government, the people may wind up on the government's side, and may strip the media of their cherished freedoms. Political scientist Ithiel de Sola Pool expresses this fear most cogently:

No nation will indefinitely tolerate a freedom of the press that serves to divide the country and to open the floodgates of criticism against the freely chosen government that leads it. The notion among some newsmen that the press can be at one with the people in combat with the common enemy, the government, is a self-destructive delusion. More often in a democracy the government is the true expression of the nation's feelings. The press may be surprised at who is St. George and who is the dragon. . . . If the press is the government's enemy, it is the free press that will end up being destroyed.[5]

The events of the Nixon years provide some support for this analysis. Vice President Agnew's early attacks on the media, for example, struck a responsive chord in many Americans. As the Watergate revelations began to dominate the news, the issue of government credibility slowly replaced the issue of media credibility in the public consciousness. But a poll of California residents in May, 1974, found that 51 percent of them felt there had been too much Watergate coverage, while only 11 percent felt there had been too little. And 31 percent believed the coverage had been unfair and biased against the president.[6]

Even after Nixon resigned, some people viewed his demise as a media plot. "Congratulations," wrote one woman to the *New York Times,* "on the wonderful hatchet job you did on Richard Nixon! You staged a beautiful crucifixion all the way." [7] Franklin B. Smith, editorial-page editor of the *Burlington Free Press* in Vermont, summarized this viewpoint:

The platitudes about "shooting the messenger of bad news" simply are not relevant here. The publication of news, good or bad, is the essential purpose of the American press, but news leaks, speculations and analyses are masquerades that are demonstrably lethal. . . .

Now, the tragedy having reached its culmination, the press must search its collective soul and ask whether the cause of responsible freedom might better have been served by a dedication to the basic purposes of news gathering and news dissemination.

The role of the press ought to be that of a spectator, alert and concerned, and not that of a participant, intruding and partisan.[8]

Overall, the Watergate scandals probably increased public respect for the media more than they diminished it (see p 316). But despite the vindication of the media's charges against Nixon, the fear remains in the minds of many Americans—if the media can destroy a president, then they can destroy anyone.

But remember that it took two years of sustained coverage, an aroused Congress and public, an honest special prosecutor, an incredible collection of incriminating tapes, and a dozen participants-turned-witnesses to topple the only president ever to resign from that office. Though the Watergate experience does demonstrate the power of the media, it also demonstrates the almost inexhaustible news-management resources of the government. The wonder is not so much that Nixon was finally forced to resign; the wonder is that he almost got away with it.

The mass media's violent hostility to President Nixon during his final years does pose a danger, but it is not the danger that the media may destroy any president who comes along. Rather, it is the danger that the media may adopt a Watergate standard of consistent opposition as their new definition of the adversary relationship between press and government. If that happens, the public may well turn on its media, and the government certainly will.

After Watergate, journalists tried to justify their treatment of Nixon by means of two contradictory strategies. First, they were unusually kind to President Ford in the early weeks of his administration (before he pardoned his predecessor), as if to say "we don't attack everybody." And second, they were unusually harsh in their coverage of other government officials (Nelson Rockefeller when he was proposed for the vice presidency; Wilbur Mills when he became publicly involved with a striptease dancer), as if to say "it wasn't just Nixon."

But as the Ford administration abandoned Richard Nixon's preoccupation with the press and turned its attention to energy, inflation and recession, Southeast Asia, etc., the media slowly returned to their pre-Nixon stance—wary and skeptical, but not automatically hostile. By 1975, it seemed that a sort of balance had been re-established in the adversary relationship between media and government.

BARRIERS TO ADVERSARITY

The problem of too much adversarity surfaced during the Nixon administration for the first time in generations. The more usual problem in news coverage of the government, even today, is too little adversarity. In the real world, as opposed to movies and theories, the adversary relationship has a tough time surviving. Many of the reasons for this will come up later in the chapter, but we will list some of the more important ones now.

1. Friendship. Most government reporters are specialists; they cover the Justice Department or City Hall or the Pentagon full-time. Specialization has many advantages, but one big disadvantage: Reporters are likely to become close personal friends of their news sources. "The more you go out to dinner," said Drew Pearson, "the more friends you make and the more you diminish the number of people you can write about without qualms of conscience or rebukes from your wife."[9] Friendly reporters seldom write embarrassing articles about their friends.

2. Sympathy. Closely related to friendship is the sympathy that often develops between reporters and their major sources. It is good to understand the official's point of view, but if the reporter understands it too well for too long, he or she may come to accept it. It is for this reason that most New York newspapers impose a mid-season shuffle on the reporters who cover the Yankees and the Mets. Such a shuffle would do wonders for Washington coverage.

3. Dependence. Government reporters depend on their sources for everything from front-page scoops to last-paragraph quotes. They are understandably reluctant to do anything to offend them. For years the Senate press corps overlooked the growing financial fortunes of Bobby Baker, a $19,000-a-year Senate employee. It was an outsider who got wind of the story, pursued it, and turned it into a national scandal. The Senate regulars viewed Baker as a vital source of information; they viewed the exposé as a nuisance.

4. Alliance. Many a reporter starts out covering a government agency and winds up working for it—unofficially. Washington is full of such part-time officials. They draft bills, guide press conferences, suggest handouts, and otherwise join in the process of governing. Their reporting, of course, suffers.

5. Complexity. There was a time when most reporters understood (or thought they understood) most news. No longer. Today a government reporter must deal with more than politics. Political writers must discuss the intricacies of space flight, inflation, the arms race, air pollution, and hundreds of similar topics. To make sense of these issues, they rely heavily on the help of government experts. It is hard to be aggressive and independent in covering a story you don't understand to start with.

6. Secrecy. Government secrecy has already been discussed in considerable detail (see Chapter 6). All we need say here is that a reporter who tries to dig for the truth is very likely to run into an endless series of classified documents and closemouthed sources.

7. News Management. A large fraction of the public-relations people in the country are employed by government. Their job (see Chapter 6 and Chapter 14) is to manage the news in the best interests of their employer. A PR staff is like a dam. The reporter who uses it as an information source saves a lot of time and effort. But it is the PR people who manage the flow of news; they can drown the reporter with facts or make the reporter die of thirst. And behind the dam, they may be hiding the dirtiest water of all.

THE PRESIDENT AND THE PRESS

The American president is the most public of chief executives. His every action, word, and gesture is scrutinized, reported, and discussed by hundreds of journalists. This total lack of privacy must be a personal annoyance to the president, as well as interfering with his political and diplomatic flexibility. But it is also very valuable to him. To the extent that the president can influence what is written about him, he thereby influences public opinion. The president needs the press—and uses the press—to help him rally support for his programs, opposition for his enemies, and respect for his office. The history of president-press relations is the history of presidential efforts to control the media.

For the first eighty years of American history, presidents controlled the press by sponsoring their own newspapers. President John Adams offered the official Federalist party line in the *Gazette of the United States.* President Thomas Jefferson did the same for the Republicans in the *National Intelligencer.* Each administration supported its party papers with government advertising and joblot printing contracts. Opposition papers had to scrounge for private funds.

This state of affairs continued until 1860, when President-elect Lincoln refused to establish an official newspaper. Instead, he utilized the Government Printing Office, thus ending the use of printing contracts as hidden subsidies. Suddenly the president was on his own in his relations with reporters. During the Civil War, Henry Villard of the Associated Press became the first reporter assigned to cover the president full-time. A few years later, in the wake of Lincoln's assassination, Andrew Johnson became the first president to be formally interviewed by an independent, unaligned reporter.

After the Civil War, Congress grew in importance and the presidency declined. Press relations were casual. One reporter won a five-dollar bet by ringing up President Grover Cleveland on the new telephone to ask if there was any news. Cleveland reportedly answered the phone himself, and told the reporter he could safely go to bed.

In the 1880s, public interest in the president began to rise again. The stage was set for a president who could capitalize on that interest to wrest control of the government from Congress. That president was Theodore Roosevelt.

Roosevelt was the first president to realize that he could manipulate the media to mold the public. He set up permanent White House quarters for the press. He permitted several reporters to interview him every day while he was being shaved. He ordered his secretary, William Loeb Jr., to act as press liaison. He invented the tactic of releasing news on Sunday to take advantage of the wide-open Monday-morning front page. Comments Elmer E. Cornwell Jr.: "T.R. did not just provide bully entertainment for an enthralled public, but dramatized the potential of the office for affecting the course of public policy by means of a dynamic relationship with the electorate via the mass media." [10]

Roosevelt knew how to take the press off the scent of an embarrassing story.

When T.R. backed a Panamanian revolution against Colombia in an effort to get the Canal Zone, the opposition press began to growl. So the president immediately ordered all military officers in Washington to get out and run in the park as part of a physical fitness program. The hilarious misadventures of pot-bellied generals and admirals kept the press corps busy for a week—by which time it had forgotten all about the Canal Zone.

Presidential press relations after Roosevelt are characterized by three tactics: the press conference, the press secretary, and direct use of the broadcast media.

THE PRESS CONFERENCE

The presidential press conference was invented by Woodrow Wilson as a way of giving every reporter a chance and still leaving time in the day for other matters. At first it worked out very well for everybody. Wilson's press conferences were scheduled twice a week and were open to all accredited reporters.

Franklin Roosevelt made great use of Wilson's invention, holding over 900 press conferences in his thirteen years in office. Unlike Wilson, F.D.R. refused to be quoted directly. But he was unfailingly frank and open with reporters, often devoting an entire conference to a single topic. At this point, the press conference was still a convenience for both the reporter and the president.

Then came Truman. Faced with an increasingly huge press corps, including more and more foreign journalists, Truman gradually abandoned Roosevelt's easygoing press conference style. He stopped trying to explain the thinking behind his decisions, stopped concentrating on a single topic in each conference, and stopped chatting informally with reporters before and after. Everything became much more formal. A reporter would rise, ask a question, and sit;

the president would carefully recite his answer, then turn to the next reporter.

The crowning blow came in 1951, when Truman began taping his press conferences for release to radio. Forced to weigh every word for its possible effects, Truman made the conferences even less lively, less useful than before. He ignored the information needs of the press and public, and concentrated on making a good performance. The press conference was becoming a tool of news management.

Two new wrinkles were added in the Eisenhower years. First, Ike began using the first few minutes of each half-hour conference to read a prepared statement, encouraging reporters to stress that statement in their articles. Second, Eisenhower had his press secretary, James Hagerty, arrange for friendly reporters to ask the questions the president wanted to answer. Both the prepared statement and the planted question have since become press conference staples.

The Kennedy administration was the first to permit live television broadcasts of press conferences, and this too has become standard procedure. Television has reduced the reporter to a participant in a stage show. It is not unusual to see newspaper journalists at press conferences not bothering to take notes; many readers will see the thing on TV anyhow, and a complete transcript will be available minutes after the end. It is also quite common for reporters to ask pointless questions (or sit next to someone who asks intelligent ones) simply in order to be seen on TV by their editors.

Woodrow Wilson scheduled his press conferences regularly, but no president since Truman has felt obliged to do so. Truman, by the way, averaged forty press conferences a year, less than half of Roosevelt's average of eighty-three. Eisenhower averaged twenty-four a year; Kennedy, twenty-one; and Johnson, twenty-five. Then came Richard Nixon, the most reclusive of all the presidents of this generation. Through June 1, 1973, he held a total of thirty-four press conferences—an average of eight per year. For the next year, until his resignation in August, 1974, he avoided the press almost completely.

In the first year of his administration, Gerald Ford tried to revive the press conference as a useful way to communicate with the press and the public. He had his press secretary, Ron Nessen, state that press conferences would be more frequent in the future; and in fact he held seventeen press conferences in his first twelve months, and granted about two dozen exclusive interviews with correspondents. He permitted several reporters to ask follow-up questions when they were not fully satisfied with his first answer. And he tried to project a mood of cordiality that contrasted starkly with the bitterness of Nixon's last few encounters with the press.

Nonetheless, press conferences today are scheduled at the president's pleasure, and are conducted according to the president's rules. The ingredients are now pretty well standardized: a big room, hundreds of reporters, dozens of cameras and microphones, a prepared statement, several planted questions with prepared answers, and perhaps four or five spontaneous questions with little discussion or follow-up. It's not surprising that Tom Wicker of the *New York Times* calls the press conference "more an instrument of Presidential power than a useful tool of the press." [11]

THE PRESS SECRETARY

While President Wilson conducted his twice-weekly press conferences, Joseph P. Tumulty (Wilson's advisor) held daily briefings for reporters. From that time on, presidents came to rely more and more on their press secretaries.

So did reporters. From 1933 to 1945, President Roosevelt's press secretaries were never once quoted in the media. Truman's press secretaries were quoted only once. But James Hagerty, Eisenhower's press secretary, was named hundreds of times as a source of news about the president.[12] And the names of later press secretaries—Pierre Salinger, George Christian, Bill Moyers, Ron Ziegler, Ron Nessen—were as well known to the public as those of the more prominent Senators and cabinet officials.

As the number of presidential press conferences has declined, the importance of the press secretary has soared. The average White House correspondent writes at least a story a day. Yet most reporters count themselves lucky if they actually get to talk to the president once a month. The bulk of the news about the president therefore comes, not from the president, but from his press secretary.

Press secretaries have a tricky job. They dare not antagonize the press corps or justify charges of a "credibility gap." So they try to be genuinely useful. They answer factual questions, help set up interviews with presidential assistants, and even use their influence to get important stories released on time. But their first allegiance is, of course, to the president.

The most talented press secretary of our time was probably James Hagerty. One of his favorite tricks was to release good news from the White House, bad news from anyplace else. A State Department triumph, for example, would always be announced by the president himself; a State Department flop would be announced by the State Department.

Hagerty always held back a few middling stories—the appointment of a new ambassador, say—for the inevitable day when Eisenhower would take off on a golfing trip. Russell Baker explains the ploy:

If editors demanded a Presidential story a day, it follows that reporters will be found to satisfy them one way or another. On days when there is no news, they will poke around darkened rooms, look under the carpet, or start staring at the west wall and adding two and two in news stories. When that sort of thing

happens, the White House is in trouble. Hagerty prevented this by seeing to it that there was rarely a newsless day. If there was no news, he made a little.[13]

There is nothing especially evil about these techniques. Most reporters understand that a press secretary's job includes more than a little news management. Good press secretaries, like Hagerty, are able to maintain their reputation for integrity even when protecting their boss's interests.

But Richard Nixon's press secretary, Ron Ziegler, proved incapable of balancing his loyalties to the president against his obligations to the press. A former advertising executive with no prior news experience, Ziegler misled reporters for nearly two years on the involvement of the White House in Watergate. His deteriorating relationship with the media culminated on April 17, 1973, when events forced him to admit that everything he had said about Watergate (including his attacks on the reporters who covered it) was "inoperative." The word instantly became a part of the American vocabulary of satire.

The decline of the presidential press secretary as a respected source of news was not entirely Ziegler's fault. He was forced to play point man for an administration whose firm policy was to provide as little information as possible to the press and public. Alan Otten, Washington bureau chief for the *Wall Street Journal,* was one of many reporters who complained that the Nixon White House was "probably the most closed administration since I've been in Washington, and that goes over 25 years. Maybe it's part of a continuing trend and we'll be saying this about each succeeding administration. I rather doubt it."[14] Just about every journalist in Washington resented the unavailability of information at the White House. As press secretary, Ziegler bore the brunt of that resentment.

While some press secretaries have had broad authority to answer questions based on

WHY WOODWARD AND BERNSTEIN?

The two journalistic sleuths who did the most to unravel the mysteries of Watergate were Bob Woodward and Carl Bernstein, both young *Washington Post* reporters whose regular beats were not the White House or even the federal government. Woodward had done some investigative pieces on police corruption and unsanitary Washington restaurants; Bernstein had written on rock music and covered the local courts and city hall. For lack of anyone else, they were assigned to cover the odd break-in at the Democratic National Committee headquarters in the Watergate complex on Saturday, June 17, 1972.[15]

With very little help from the rest of the Washington press corps, and almost none at all from the White House press corps, the two reporters bit by bit established the relationship between the seven burglars and the Oval Office. Why did dozens of White House reporters ignore the biggest news story of the decade that was right under their noses? How did two neophyte journalists succeed where seasoned veterans failed? The answers explain much about the deficiencies of presidential news coverage.

First, White House correspondents are responsible for covering the endless flood of presidential news releases, statements, and speechs, leaving little time for investigation. President Nixon was typical in this regard. He generated roughly 500,000 words a year in his speeches, statements, messages to Congress, press conferences, and interviews. Nor was it unusual that in the seven weeks before the 1972 election, when Watergate was just beginning to heat up, Nixon made forty-one speeches; issued eighteen statements, eighteen proclamations, and twelve declarations; announced eight resignations and thirty-four appointments; and sent ten messages to Congress.[16] That didn't leave White House reporters much time for Watergate.

Second, the White House press corps feels duty-bound to travel with the president wherever he goes, killing substantial periods of time in airplanes and hotel lobbies. This is sometimes called the "assassination mentality"—no one wants to miss out on *that* story.

Third, the White House press corps is no exception to the rule that reporters eventually come to identify with their sources. Many White House journalists simply couldn't believe that a president would have anything to do with breaking and entering, wiretapping, or obstruction of justice. They were reluctant to face the emerging pattern in the miscellaneous pieces of Watergate information that slowly unfolded.

Fourth, White House reporters are accustomed to dealing with top-level sources. Woodward and Bernstein got most of their information from low-level officials far from the public eye—from secretaries and clerks, from anonymous bureaucrats, from Hugh Sloan, Jr., treasurer of the Committee to Re-Elect the President, etc. The White House press corps, meanwhile, tried to get answers from the big guns, such as Nixon aides H. R. Haldeman and John Ehrlichman. Even before Watergate, these people were pretty inaccessible; R. W. Apple, chief political writer of the *New York Times,* once spent the day calling seventeen White House officials, and was never called back by any of them.[17] After Watergate, Nixon's top aides were virtually invisible—and so White House reporters had nobody to ask.

Finally, many White House correspondents were afraid of the president's power to make their jobs impossible. When the *Washington Post* refused to let up on the Watergate story, its longtime society columnist was dropped from the press pool for three

White House social events.[18] And several exclusive presidential "scoops" found their way to the *Post*'s competitor, Garnett D. Horner of the *Washington Star-News*. Horner and his paper were not rocking the boat with Watergate stories.[19] Since they were not assigned to the White House on a daily basis, Woodward and Bernstein cared little about these reprisals. But for the White House press corps, the pressure to conform was strong.

Bill Moyers, presidential press secretary under Lyndon Johnson, sums up the situation this way: "The White House press corps is more stenographic than entrepreneurial in its approach to news gathering. Too many of them are sheep. Sheep with short attention spans. They move on to tomorrow's story without pausing to investigate today's." [20]

---

their own knowledge, Ziegler was kept on a very short leash. There was much that he did not know, and much more that he was not permitted to say. In the face of increasingly aggressive questions about Watergate, Ziegler had to resort to "stonewalling." Washington reporter Bob Walters lists the following favorite Ziegler stonewalling techniques: the broad and meaningless statement; the I'll-try-to-find-out ploy; the I-stand-on-my-previous-answer answer; the I-wouldn't-join-you-in-the-gutter response; the wild goose chase; the no comment; the carefully constructed deception; and when all else failed, the lie.[21] Eventually, Ziegler's briefings became as useless as Nixon's press conferences.[22]

Only time and honesty can repair the damage done by Ziegler to the job of presidential press secretary. Sensitive to the low estate of his position, President Ford's first press secretary, Jerald terHorst, resigned the post after holding it for only a month. He had not been informed that his boss planned to pardon Richard Nixon (a move he personally opposed), and had mistakenly told reporters there would be no pardon. A former Washington correspondent for the *Detroit News,* terHorst now writes a nationally syndicated political column.

It remained for President Ford's second choice as press secretary, broadcast journalist Ron Nessen, to restore the job to its former position of respect. He made a good start, reminding reporters that while he was a Ron, he was not a Ziegler.

LIVE AND IN COLOR

Franklin Roosevelt was the first president to demand a chunk of broadcast time to speak directly to the public without a reporter in the middle. Roosevelt averaged only two or three radio "fireside chats" a year—yet their effect on public confidence and support was substantial.

By the Eisenhower years, television was available for the same purpose. Yet both Eisenhower and Kennedy used TV only for emergencies, such as the Cuban missile crisis of 1962. Presidents Johnson and Nixon adopted a different approach. Both resorted to television regularly to circumvent the questions and interpretations of the press corps. Nixon, for example, took to the air twenty-five times in his first twenty-two months in office. In January, 1970, he became the first president ever to deliver a routine veto message (an HEW appropriations bill) live and in color. In January, 1972, Nixon starred in four television specials—first an exclusive interview with Dan Rather on CBS, then a speech on troop withdrawals from Vietnam, then his State of the Union address, and finally a new peace proposal (see pp. 145–47).

Historian Clinton Rossiter claims that immeasurable power has flowed from Congress to the president because of the latter's ability to reach people directly via television.[23] Certainly no other government official can command such use of the public airwaves. In the summer of 1970, several antiwar members of Congress sought a remedy to this presidential TV appearances, so does the Federal Communications Commission for reply time to the president under the fairness doctrine. The networks granted the time voluntarily before the FCC could act—leaving the issue unresolved.

If Congress has grounds for griping about presidential TV appearances, so does the press corps. When the president goes directly to the public, he runs the show. It is hard for a reporter to be an adversary when he or she isn't even there.

Broadcast news executives are increasingly sensitive to the charge that presidents use TV to manipulate public opinion. But they feel they have no choice in the matter. In October, 1974, all three networks decided not to carry a speech by President Ford in Kansas City, on the topic of inflation. The president had addressed the nation (via TV) on economic matters some weeks earlier, and the networks doubted that the Kansas City address would add very much. Then the White House formally requested that they carry the speech live. So they did. The president of ABC News, William Sheehan, ex-

plained: "Historically, any time a president flat-out asks for air time, he'll get it. That's what the party out of power always complains about, but when the president wants to speak to the nation there's no way we can deny him the air." [24]

PRESIDENTIAL COVERAGE

The president of the United States receives more attention from more reporters than any other person in the world. More than thirty news organizations cover the president's activities on a daily basis, and hundreds more pop up regularly at the White House when something of special interest is brewing. Hordes of journalists hungry for a story surround the president and his family at every public appearance, from the ski slopes to the church pews. And when the president does not appear in public, these same reporters bombard his representatives with demands for news of his actions, policies, thoughts, feelings, and moods.

Thus, presidents may safely take the quantity of their news coverage for granted, and concentrate on its quality. For a president,

---

QUESTION PERIOD

Four days a week, from 2:30 to 3:30, the British House of Commons comes alive. Every important government official, including the prime minister, is expected to be on hand to answer whatever questions the members of Parliament may care to ask.

The rules are quite formal. Questions must be submitted in writing at least two days in advance, to give the officials a chance to prepare. A member is limited to three questions, plus "supplementaries" or follow-ups. Members may not make speeches, ask hypothetical questions, slander individuals, or raise broad policy issues that cannot be answered quickly. Aside from that, anything goes.

It is an appealing system. On the very day Sir Anthony Eden ordered the Suez invasion in 1956, he had to stand for questions about the policy. An American president, by contrast, would have been unavailable for comment, or at best would have appeared on television with a prepared speech. It seems strange to us to have members of Parliament performing the adversary function that in this country is reserved for journalists. But the system works. The debate is lively and informative—and widely reported in the press. Parliament gets more unmanaged information out of the prime minister in a week than American reporters can extract from the president in a month.

of course, good news coverage is favorable news coverage. To see if that is what they're getting, most presidents maintain a lively interest in the content of the media. John F. Kennedy was an avid newspaper reader. Lyndon B. Johnson's office was equipped with wire-service teletypes and three TV sets, so he could watch all the networks at once. Richard M. Nixon had his staff prepare a daily twenty-five-page summary of what the media said about him the previous day.[25] Gerald Ford received a similar daily report, which was also circulated to 150 officials within his administration.[26]

In addition to monitoring the news, presidents control it, usually with success. More often than not, it is the president himself who decides what is to be covered and what is to be hidden or ignored. Through press conferences, press secretaries, and television appearances, the president is in an ideal position to manage the news. Within these constraints, the president receives superlative news coverage. Almost every item on his daily schedule is turned into a news story of some sort. There is very little that the American public does not know about its president—except what he does not want it to know.

On the subject of Watergate, Richard Nixon was the exception. Every president has fought battles with the media—that's what the adversary relationship is all about. But Nixon and the media were genuine enemies, and engaged in the fiercest press-government fights of modern times. With the help of Congress, the judiciary, and the Watergate tapes, the media won—barely (see pp. 372–75).

But usually, presidential news management is both more benign and more successful. In the conflict between media and government, the president typically wins most—but not all—of the battles.

In whatever time it can spare from presidential coverage, the Washington press corps must also report on Congress, the Supreme Court, and the federal executive agencies. All three tend to get lost in the shuffle. The less flamboyant members of Congress are ignored; Supreme Court coverage is plagued by a pointless quest for speed; the executive agencies are reported mainly by means of press releases. Outside Washington, meanwhile, state government coverage suffers from inadequate media attention, while civic boosterism hinders aggressive reporting of local government.

THE WASHINGTON PRESS CORPS

Washington D.C. is the news capital of the world, a Mecca for every ambitious political journalist. At this moment, there are more than 2,000 full-time reporters at work in Washington—the largest, most talented, and most experienced press corps anywhere.

It wasn't always that way. The first Washington correspondent reached the city in 1822. He was Nathaniel Carter of the *New York Statesman and Evening Advertiser,* and his job was to supply readers with "the latest intelligence of every description which can be obtained at the seat of government." [27] Carter was soon joined by others, but it wasn't until the Civil War that Washington became a really important source of news. By 1867 there were forty-nine correspondents listed in the Congressional Press Galleries.

As the government grew, so did the press corps. And so did the importance of news from Washington. Elmer E. Cornwell Jr. has analyzed six weeks worth of front pages from two newspapers (the *New York Times* and the *Providence Journal*) for every year from 1885 to 1957. Cornwell's sample for 1885 yielded 447 column inches of news about Congress and the president. By 1909 the figure had increased to 508 column inches. By 1925, it was up to 1,235. And in 1933, the height of the Depression, it reached an incredible 1,914 column inches.[28] Today's figure is probably somewhat lower—but not much. Two thousand reporters can cover a lot of news.

The size of the Washington press corps is a mixed blessing. Public officials couldn't grant personal interviews to 2,000 journalists even if they wanted to. Instead, they resort to mass press conferences—with batteries of microphones, shouted questions, and very little dialogue. In this impersonal, hurried environment, news management is much, much easier.

Even 2,000 reporters may not be enough. The vast majority of American newspapers and broadcast stations have no representative in Washington. Only thirty-one TV stations (4 percent of the total) and forty-six radio stations (1 percent of the total) employ Washington correspondents of their own.[29] Of course the three networks, the nation's top newspapers, the larger chains, and the major newsmagazines all have creditable Washington staffs. The *New York Times,* for example, has thirty-three reporters, six editors, and two columnists in the capital. And 28 percent of the daily newspapers in the country have at least a part-time stringer in Washington. But most of the American media depend on two main sources for their news of the federal government: the Associated Press and United Press International.

AP, with roughly 150 reporters, and UPI, with about 90, do their best to staff every executive department, subcommittee hearing, and diplomatic reception in Washington. Not surprisingly, they fail—there is simply too much to cover. The major events of the day get reported well enough, but the minor ones are rewritten from press releases or ignored entirely. In 1959, AP had six reporters assigned to the Senate and five to the House of Representatives. But only one staffer was available to cover the Treasury Department, the Commerce Department, and the Federal Reserve Board. Inevitably, that reporter missed a lot of stories, and seldom had time to dig beneath the surface of any. "When I went to Washington," recalls a former AP bureau chief, "I had seventeen men. When I left I had seventy-seven. And the whole time I was there, I was one man short." [30]

Besides covering the news for those media without their own Washington correspondents, the wire services also backstop the media that have their own reporters. A newspaper with one or two Washington staffers wants more for its investment than a duplication of the wires. Consider for example the work of Lee Catterall, who is a one-man Washington bureau for eleven Wyoming daily newspapers, including the *Cody Enterprise* and the *Jackson Hole News.* Catterall focuses on the implications for Wyoming of federal legislation and court decisions, and keeps abreast of the activities of the state's two Senators and one Representative. He pays particular attention to government decisions affecting oil shale, cattle ranching, and other special interests of Wyoming residents. He also provides his clients with a weekly column and a summary of the votes of the Wyoming delegation.[31] For obvious reasons, Catterall spends very little time at the Treasury Department, the Commerce Department, or the Federal Reserve Board. That kind of news is left to the wires.

What is the Washington press corps? It is scores of reporters hanging around the White House press room, and one visit a year to the Federal Maritime Administration. It is CBS at a news conference, UPI rewriting a handout, *Newsweek* looking for color, and the *Los Angeles Times* on the trail of an exposé. It is a newspaper stringer interviewing a hometown business executive who has been invited to testify before a congressional committee about the threat of cotton imports. It is an industrial lobbyist masquerading as a reporter for a trade magazine. It is a freelance photographer trying to sell a photo essay on the president's dog. It is a syndicated columnist telling the country what it ought to think about Pakistan. It is a Pakistani reporter telling the people back home what they ought to think about Washington. It is a documentary film crew recording the nightlife at a fashionable party.

It is 2,000 journalists covering the news capital of the world—doing the best job they can, a better job than we have any right to expect, but still in many respects an inadequate job.

CONGRESS AND THE PRESS

The United States has only one president —but it has 535 members of Congress. This simple fact has several important implications. For one thing, it makes it extremely difficult for a Senator or Representative to manage the news as the president does. For another, it puts every member of Congress in competition with every other member of Congress for the limited amount of available publicity. And members of Congress *need* publicity. They need it to get re-elected in their districts; they need it to gain stature as possible candidates for higher office; they need it to bring their views to the attention of the president and the party leaders. The Capitol Hill reporter, unlike the White House correspondent, is operating in a buyer's market for news.

This is not to say that Senators and Representatives have no use for public-relations people. Nearly every member of Congress, in fact, has a press secretary of one sort or another. But it's a different job. The president's press secretary tries to manage the news. A congressional press secretary struggles merely to get into the news. One Senator summed it up this way: "Remember, there is only one evil thing the press can do to you—it may not mention you." [32]

Strangely enough, this congressional desire for more personal publicity may well be a mistake. About 400 journalists now cover the congressional beat in Washington. Since there are 535 members of Congress, and since most Capitol reporters concentrate on the Hill's major bills and superstar personalities, most members are seldom mentioned in the news. Aside from the superstars, the ones who do get mentioned are those whose districts include a newspaper or broadcast station with its own Washington correspondent.

Here, then, is a statistic that should make Congressmen and Congresswomen think twice about the value of publicity: Of the sixty new members elected to the House in 1972, fifty-seven came from districts whose local media had their own reporters in Washington. [33]

Incumbent legislators, in other words, may stand a much better chance of re-election if there is no hometown journalist stalking their tracks, reporting their votes, and analyzing their activities.

Favorable mention in the national media, of course, is another matter entirely. Members of Congress are so desperate for this latter sort of media attention that they often tailor their activities to the apparent preferences of reporters. James Reston comments:

> The influence of reporters on the conduct of individual members of the House and Senate, particularly the House, is much greater than is generally realized. For example, if reporters tend to play up the spectacular charges or statements of extremists on Capitol Hill and to play down or ignore the careful, analytical speeches of the more moderate and responsible members—as, unfortunately, they do most of the time—this inevitably has its influence on many other members, particularly new members. . . . [T]he new Congressman often draws the obvious conclusion and begins spouting nonsense to attract attention. [34]

The days when reporters were unwelcome on Capitol Hill are long gone. The House of Representatives opened its doors to journalists in 1789; the Senate followed suit in 1795. There were occasional squabbles in the early 1800s, but by 1841 the right of reporters to roam freely through the Capitol was well established.

Except for some slight discrimination against the underground press, any legitimate reporter from any country may apply for a congressional press card. Once admitted, the reporter is treated like visiting royalty. The press gallery hovers directly over the presiding officer's desk in both Houses, providing a box-seat view of the proceedings. Wire-service reporters have special muted telephones within the chambers themselves. Pages are available for journalists who wish to summon legislators from their seats for interviews or off-the-record consultations. And few members of Congress ignore such a summons.

Behind the press gallery, reporters have an extensive suite of rooms for work and relaxation, with staff assistants whose salaries are paid by the government. Every possible piece of equipment—from typewriters to reference books to swank leather couches—is provided for the convenience of the press. Symbolic of the easy access of reporters to congressional news is a sign over one of the elevators in the House wing of the Capitol. It reads: "Reserved for Members and the Press." [35]

Broadcasters are more limited than the print media in their coverage of Congress. Only on special occasions, such as a State of the Union address, are cameras permitted on the floor. In late 1974, however, a Joint Committee on Congressional Operations recommended elimination of the ban on broadcasting. The committee reasoned that Congress needed the additional publicity to compete effectively with the president. As one committee member put it: "We are convinced that Congress is not getting through loud and clear today. We are convinced that the American people should have more opportunities to see—and ultimately to understand—how Congress carries out the responsibilities assigned to it under our Constitution." [36]

By the time this book is published, the committee's recommendation may well have been passed. But some legislators have resolved to fight the change, fearing that the publicity would do more harm than good. Senator Jesse Helms (R.-N.C.), himself a former broadcast executive, spoke for the opposition: "It is not difficult to envision members scrambling to the floor to get before cameras in order to impress the voters back home instead of persuading other members, producing much oration and little debate. What is more, oratory would become the chief, if not the only, criterion of legislative ability, to the disadvantage of those members who contribute their valuable skills and knowledge in countless other ways." [37]

In a sense, this debate over the televising of floor sessions illustrates a fundamental paradox in congressional attitudes toward news. On the one hand, members of Congress are starved for publicity. They are tired of being ignored by the media, and they're inclined to believe that any increase in coverage would be a change for the better. On the other hand, Senators and Representatives are accustomed to their clubbish privacy. Many are afraid that the public might disapprove of such congressional traditions as political compromise and reciprocal backscratching. They fear that increased coverage would aid the careers of the grandstanders in Congress, while damaging the re-election chances of its more flexible deal-makers.

At the moment, the deal-makers get little or no coverage (unless the local media send a reporter to Washington)—which at least leaves them free to continue making deals. The grandstanders, meanwhile, monopolize the news.

The Capitol press corps spends most of its time covering the main show—close votes on important bills, public hearings on controversial issues, political maneuvers by presidential hopefuls, etc. These journalists are covering the institution of Congress, not its members. They stress quotable quotes from congressional leaders on opposite sides of whatever legislative choice is currently up for debate. The impression they create is that of a serious body of sober ideologues, moving ponderously but wisely to resolve the major issues of the day. Legislators of less than superstar magnitude are seldom mentioned in these news reports—but they benefit nonetheless from the overall public image of congressional respectability.

Coverage of Congress as an institution, in

other words, is overwhelmingly favorable. Capitol reporters know that the picture they paint of Congress is incomplete and distorted—but they go on painting it anyhow. There are several categories of congressional news that are seldom adequately covered:

1. The content of important laws that are passed without controversy.
2. The activities of lobbyists and their influence on congressional action.
3. The continual hypocrisies of many members of Congress, who *say* one thing in their speeches to keep the constituents happy, but *do* something else entirely when it comes time to vote.
4. The serious, noninflammatory policy speeches of the less famous members of Congress, especially in the House.
5. The personal peccadilloes of legislators—arrests, sexual assaults, drunkenness, marital problems, etc.

6. The political compromises, mutual favors, log-rolling, and similar practices that enable members of Congress to live and work with each other over the long haul.

Some of these omissions can be attributed to broad media problems that have nothing to do with Congress—the emphasis on action and controversy instead of underlying issues, for example. But many of the failures of the Capitol press corps are a direct result of the peculiar relationship that develops between members of Congress and reporters. It is a relationship characterized by mutual dependence and mutual esteem.

After a few years on the Hill, congressional correspondents are likely to develop close friendships with their main news sources. They joke together, party together, literally live together day in and day out. They may even work together—the reporter helping the member draft a bill, then following

CONGRESSIONAL COMMITTEES

Like the rest of the government, Congress uses two main styles of news management—publicity and secrecy. Congressional committees demonstrate both.

When a committee of Congress schedules a series of public hearings, the show is usually staged with the media in mind. In theory, congressional investigations are supposed to collect information for use in the legislative process. In practice, publicity is the main purpose of many investigations. The late Senator Joseph McCarthy built his reputation as a fearsome hunter of communists primarily through his activities as chairman of the Senate Permanent Investigating Subcommittee. A more recent example was the Senate Watergate hearings of 1973, chaired by Sam Ervin (D.-N.C.). Ostensibly set up to gather material that would help in the drafting of a campaign reform bill, the Watergate hearings revealed additional information, eroded public support for President Nixon, and thus paved the way for an impeachment vote in the House Judiciary Committee. It also made an instant folk hero of Senator Ervin.

The real work of Congress, meanwhile, is accomplished in the working sessions of congressional committees. This is where bills are written and political deals are consummated. More often than not, congressional conflicts are compromised and the final decisions are made in committee, long before the floor show begins. Traditionally, these committee sessions have been closed to the media. In 1973, however, the House voted 370–27 to open all committee meetings to the press, unless a committee votes to keep a particular meeting closed.[38] The Senate considered a similar change, but decided instead to stick with its current rule, which keeps committee meetings closed unless the committee votes to open them.[39]

through with the necessary publicity. Not surprisingly, veteran congressional reporters eventually start thinking like members.

The Capitol press corps does a fine job of covering the sensational but nonadversary side of Congress. No really big bill gets passed or defeated without an endless series of articles on who intends to vote which way for what reasons. The political jockeying of Republicans and Democrats is dutifully reported nearly every day. The opinions and activities of congressional leaders are followed almost as closely as those of the president himself.

But when all is said and done, the public learns little about Congress that Congress doesn't want it to learn. To be sure, most Senators and Representatives would like to see more coverage of Congress as an institution, more stories narrating the stately progress of legislation and detailing the sage thoughts of legislators. And they'd appreciate seeing their names in print more often too. But if this increased attention would mean more national exposés on congressional hypocrisy, compromise, and subservience to special interests, or more local reports on the public and private lives of individual legislators, then they'd just as soon do without.

When members of Congress want to say something to the people back home, they can use their free postal franking privilege to mail a "newsletter" to every constituent, or at least a press release to every newspaper. Or they can use the $500,000 congressional broadcast studios to prepare a tape for hometown radio and TV stations. When they want to reach a national audience, they can try introducing a controversial bill, or giving an inflammatory floor speech, or issuing a carefully timed comment on the actions of some more newsworthy personage. These techniques may not provide enough publicity to satisfy the ambitions of some Congressmen and Congresswomen, but at least it's all "good" publicity, controlled by the members themselves.

THE SUPREME COURT

On Supreme Court decision days, at precisely 10 A.M., the Court goes into session, the week's opinions are read aloud, and printed copies are distributed. By noon it's all over until the next decision day.

There are few news beats more clearly defined than this one. Reporters are not allowed to interview the Justices. They write their stories from court-supplied background material, briefs, and the printed opinions, period. This is such a difficult assignment that no more than thirty-five or forty journalists appear regularly enough to rate term passes. The vast majority of the print and broadcast media rely exclusively on the wire services for their Court news.

The hallmark of wire-service reporting is speed. On decision day, AP has three reporters assigned to the Court. One sits in the courtroom, collects the written opinions, and shoots them via pneumatic tube to the press room below. The other two have the job of wading through thousands of words of legal jargon. They must identify the case, determine the decision, pinpoint the majority and minority opinions, select the quotes, and fill in the background—all in a matter of minutes. As always, AP tries frantically to beat UPI with the first bulletin. If a dissenting opinion gets muddled in the process, that's only to be expected.

There are some kinds of news for which speed is a sensible goal—but it is doubtful that the Supreme Court is one of them. Most cases are pending for years before the Court reaches a decision; one would think the public could wait a few minutes more to find out what the decision was. It takes a trained lawyer hours of careful checking to figure out the significance of a judicial opinion. Wire-service reporters do the job in minutes.

Not surprisingly, they often make mistakes. In 1962, AP reported that the Supreme Court had ruled that "a state or city may not interfere in any fashion with peaceful racial integration demonstrations in public places of business." This was simply wrong. The Court had actually decided that any city that officially supported segregation could not prosecute Negroes for seeking service in privately owned stores. The decision applied only to those areas where segregation was official policy.[40] Such errors and misinterpretations are quite frequent.

AP General Manager Wes Gallagher has proposed that the Supreme Court lock its doors on decision day—with the press corps inside. Half an hour or so later, the doors would be opened, and everyone would be released at the same time. So far the Court has refused to go along. The wire services would like to be forced to spend some time studying the decisions. But neither is willing to do so voluntarily, and let the other get the story on the teletype first.

The Supreme Court does not manage the news. It employs only one press officer, who discusses the impact of various decisions with reporters if they ask. If coverage of the Court is inadequate—and it is—the media have mostly themselves to blame.

THE EXECUTIVE AGENCIES

More than 90 percent of the federal bureaucracy in Washington is made up of the personnel of executive agencies—from the State Department and the Defense Department all the way down to the Food and Drug Administration and the Civil Aeronautics Board. The job of these agencies is to put into operation the policies dictated by the president and Congress.

An overwhelming amount of news is generated each day by the executive agencies. Reporting that news aggressively and independently would be a hard job for the entire Washington press corps. And the entire Washington press corps isn't available. Except for the Pentagon and the State Department, agency assignments are the least glamorous of all. The media count on the wire services for just about all their agency news. And the wire services count on a handful of overworked reporters.

In staffing terms alone, the press is beaten before it begins. A UPI reporter, say, assigned to cover the Departments of Labor, Commerce, and Agriculture, may get as many as forty handouts a day from the three departments. There is barely enough time to rewrite a quarter of the releases— if no time is wasted on additional research. Every telephone call to get more information on one story means ignoring another story entirely. A really careful look at one story means forgetting the whole rest of the day's events.

A second impediment to investigative coverage is the attitude of most civil servants toward the press. While Congress and the president seek out publicity, most agency employees wouldn't mind if they never saw their names in print. They are polite and friendly with reporters, but suspicious and closemouthed. In 1970, consumer affairs writer Trudy Lieberman of the *Detroit Free Press* asked the Agriculture Department for the names of those manufacturers whose hot dogs exceeded the government limit of 30 percent fat. It took many weeks (and the combined efforts of Herb Klein, the American Society of Newspaper Editors, the Freedom of Information Center, and a formal appeal) to pry the list loose.[41]

Occasionally disgruntled civil servants will tell reporters (often anonymously) about some agency action of which they disapprove. And even more occasionally a stubborn journalist will dig to the bottom of an agency story. But only the most important executive departments receive investigative coverage more than once or twice a year. The typical executive agency seldom gets even routine coverage.

According to one researcher, 22 percent of all news coming out of Washington can be traced to handouts from the executive agencies.[42] That still leaves hundreds of handouts that are never made into news stories at all. As for investigative reporting, journalists covering the agencies simply haven't got the time.

CONVENTIONS OF GOVERNMENT REPORTING

When a news source agrees to talk to a reporter, it is the source, not the reporter, who decides the rules of the game. And in official Washington, the rules are often aimed at protecting the source. Hence the government tradition of interviews that are not entirely on the record. Top Washington officials, including the president and his cabinet, use such interviews to float "trial ballons" that they can later deny if it becomes convenient to do so. Lower-level officials, such as the bureaucrats in the executive agencies, use such interviews to "leak" information that might cost them their jobs if published with their names attached.

Over the years, a number of interview conventions have developed in Washington to cover these sorts of situations. Reporters who want to keep their sources must obey the conventions. In a 1972 survey, the Associated Press Managing Editors listed seven of them, as follows.[43]

On the record. This is the most open (and still the most common) of the categories. The reporter may quote the source verbatim and by name, with no restrictions.

Check quotes. As the label implies, this convention still permits reporters to quote their source by name, but they must check their quotations with the interviewee before publishing them. Such a restriction is typically imposed by sources of technical information, but it is available to anyone who distrusts the reporter's memory or wants a second chance to withdraw or modify earlier statements.

Not for direct quotation. Interviews in this category may be attributed to their source, but must be paraphrased instead of quoted. Before television, many presidents

held "not for direct quotation" press conferences; if their statements backfired they could always claim that wasn't quite what they meant. Lesser officials still resort to this convention for the same reason.

Not for attribution. This convention permits the reporter to quote the source directly, but not by name. Instead, the remarks must be attributed to "a reliable official," or "a State Department representative," or "persons close to the president," or whatever. The "not for attribution" interview is an ideal way to launch a trial balloon or a leak (see p. 142). Those in the know can usually figure out who was talking, but the general public can't, and the source can always claim it must have been somebody else.

Background. The typical background interview is a combination of "not for direct quotation" and "not for attribution." The reporter must paraphrase what was said, and attribute it to "a Pentagon official" or whatever. This leaves the source free to insist that the reporter misunderstood, or that it must have been someone else talking, or both.

Deep background. Journalists reporting on a "deep backgrounder" may not quote the source; they can't even imply that there is a source. They must use the information essentially on their own authority. This convention provides the greatest safety for low-level government employees who want to attack a decision without losing their jobs, and for high-level ones who want to test public reaction to an undeclared policy.

Off the record. This is the convention of greatest secrecy. Reporters at "off the record" briefings may not publish what they hear, even anonymously. Officials use this device to keep journalists up to date on developing stories. They also use it to plug leaks. One reporter emerged from an exclusive interview with President Theodore Roosevelt and told his colleagues: "I've just seen the President. He told me everything I knew already, and all that I was preparing to write

—but he pledged me to secrecy on every fact I had, and now I can't write the blooming story." [44]

These interview ground rules aren't confined to Washington; they have been widely copied by local and state governments as well, and even by nongovernment sources. But the precise meaning of each convention varies from city to city, from year to year, and from official to official. Many reporters and sources use the word "background" loosely to cover everything from "not for attribution" to "deep background." A reporter who isn't sure what the ground rules are for a particular interview simply has to ask in advance—or assume that everything is on the record and risk a battle if the source was assuming something quite different.

The value of the interview conventions is obvious. They offer the conscientious government official a middle ground between complete openness and complete secrecy. It is fair to say that many important stories would never reach the public at all if it were not for these conventions.

Their danger is just as obvious. Alfred Friendly, former managing editor of the *Washington Post,* points out that backgrounders are useful "when a person of considerable importance or delicate position is discussing a matter in circumstances in which his name cannot be used for reasons of public policy or personal vulnerability." Fair enough. But Friendly adds that backgrounders are also used "by persons who want to sink a knife or do a job without risking their own position or facing the consequences to themselves." [45]

James Reston of the *New York Times* offers a similarly qualified defense:

It leaves room for honest dissenters. It is the refuge of conscience. It can be used for good or evil: to disclose the murders of My Lai, the secret bombings of Cambodia, the cover-up of Watergate. Or it can be used to disrupt elec-

---

BACKGROUND BY KISSINGER

One of the things for which Secretary of State Henry Kissinger is justly famous—at least among the media—is his fondness for backgrounders. The lengths to which the press has gone to protect his identity (not very successfully) are comic in their intricacy. This attribution, for example, appeared in a *New York Times* story of December 15, 1974: "A high American official who often briefs reporters on major foreign-policy issues said, aboard the President's plane during the flight here. . . ." [46]

Kissinger was also at the center of the most serious backgrounding controversy to date. In late 1971, he briefed the reporters chosen to travel with him (known as the "pool") on the conflict between India and Pakistan over Bangladesh. He said that if the Soviet Union did not restrain the Indians, "the entire United States–Soviet relationship might well be re-examined" and "a new look might have to be taken at the President's summitry plans." These were strong words, and Kissinger made it clear they were not to be used with his name.

A *Washington Post* reporter who was not part of the pool, and therefore not directly pledged to adhere to the interview agreement, published the statements and attributed them to Kissinger. The *Post* might well have questioned the propriety of the top U.S. foreign-policy official challenging the Russians on a not-for-attribution basis. But the White House was furious at the *Post* for its breach of journalistic etiquette. [47]

So were the other reporters. Shortly thereafter, in an obvious rebuke to the *Post,* the White House Correspondents Association called on all its members to respect the rules of anonymous briefings. [48]

tions, to vilify and destroy the political op-position. It is a powerful, ambitious, and some-times dangerous instrument. . . . When Wash-ington and Paris get into an awkward argu-ment over policy and consultation, Secretary of State Kissinger can either call a press con-ference and denounce the French, or both sides can "inspire" articles that make their points clear, and still leave room for maneuver.[49]

Whatever their misgivings, reporters usu-ally honor the interview conventions meticu-lously. If they did not, they would have a great deal less political news to report.

STATE GOVERNMENT

In many ways, news coverage of state gov-ernment is like coverage of Congress. Accord-ing to a Rutgers University seminar of leading state legislators, statehouse reporters tend to focus on the superficial side of gov-ernment, the obviously "big" stories. They are unduly attracted to the antics of public-ity-minded celebrities.[50]

Moreover, state government reporters are even more likely than congressional corre-spondents to begin thinking like their sources. Most state capitals are small towns, physically and emotionally. Officials and re-porters work together and play together; they eat at the same restaurants, drink at the same bars, and live in the same hotels. The following admission from an Oregon reporter is probably typical of the views of most state-house journalists:

> I wouldn't report it if a member were drunk all session . . . so long as he was doing a good job for the state. I wouldn't report it, I mean, unless . . . somebody else would, so it would become general knowledge anyway. Or if I knew a legislator was getting his liquor from the dog-race lobbyists, I wouldn't write that up. . . . I'd have to tell all the good about him—all the good things he's done—if I told the bad.[51]

In the past, access to information has been a major problem in the coverage of state government. This excuse is no longer ade-quate. By 1974, all but two states had "free-dom of information" laws guaranteeing re-porters the right to look at official documents, attend official meetings, or both.[52] Nearly half the states permit journalists to sit in on legislative committee hearings. And at least fourteen states allow live broadcasts of legis-lative sessions. The press corps knows most of what's going on in state government. If the public seldom finds out, reporters have only themselves to blame.

Cozying up to news sources is a big piece of the problem—but it is not the biggest piece. The fundamental reason for poor cov-erage of state government is simply that no one wants to pay for good coverage of state government. As John Burns put it in his book *The Sometime Governments,* "The media generally do not value state govern-ment news very highly. Such news usually ranks a poor third behind national and local news."[53] Editors send their best political reporters to Washington or to city hall. They often staff the statehouse with cynical old-timers who couldn't make it and inex-perienced youngsters who have yet to try.

And not too many of those. The *New York Times,* for example, has 33 journalists in Washington—but only four in Albany. The entire Albany press corps (not counting the local media) is made up of fewer than forty reporters, representing twenty-three different news organizations. They cover the governor, the state legislature, and a $9.4-billion bureaucracy of state agencies and commissions. The typical statehouse reporter in Albany files an average of four to five stories a day. Reporters generally check in about ten in the morning and often work till midnight.[54] That sort of overtime is es-sential just to stay on top of the routine news—and besides, what else is there to do in Albany? Says one *New York Times* staffer: "Our Albany bureau is a vale of tears to pass through en route to someplace else."[55]

In Albany and many other state capitals, understaffed and inexperienced statehouse bureaus try to cover the activities of state governments that are often equally under-staffed and inexperienced. The turnover rate among state legislators may go as high as 35 percent every two years. Since most state governments don't run their legislative committees on the seniority system, reporters must cultivate a new crop of key sources after every election. And unlike Washington, the state capital is unlikely to have a cadre of skilled, outspoken bureaucrats to supply essential leaks and background information.

The only adequately staffed offices in many state capitals may well be the PR offices. New York's Senate majority leader employs six public-relations specialists, with combined salaries of $145,000.[56] Given the media's skimpy investment in state government coverage, that's news management overkill.

Yet the statehouse reporter can have an important effect on legislation. Because so many bills are introduced—5,000 a year in New York—those singled out for special attention by the media are almost sure to gain a better than average hearing. A bill to prohibit cigarette smoking in public places was going nowhere in Albany until a reporter from CBS radio in New York City picked it up and mentioned it on the air. Only then did the appropriate committee decide to hold hearings on the bill.[57]

State government coverage combines the worst aspects of coverage of Congress and of the federal executive agencies. As with Congress, reporters are reluctant to offend their sources. As with the executive agencies, reporters are too busy to look into anything carefully. So exposés are rare, and even routine reporting is spotty.

LOCAL GOVERNMENT

In the summer of 1969, the *Cincinnati Enquirer* ran a series of articles entitled "The Movers and the Shakers." The series outlined precisely who ran the city and why,

and was highly critical of many of the Republican friends of *Enquirer* publisher Francis Dale. What turned Dale into an anti-Establishment muckraker? It seems he was annoyed at his country-club cronies for refusing to back him as the Republican candidate for governor of Ohio. He authorized the series to get even.[58]

Some such ulterior motive is often at the root of what little hard-hitting local journalism there is.

On the whole, the mass media are not particularly interested in municipal government. One typical study of daily newspapers in Iowa found that several papers allotted more space to the Drew Pearson column every day than they gave to city hall. Very little local government news ever made the front page, and such important offices as city clerk, city attorney, city treasurer, and city engineer were almost completely ignored. Even the editorials on local issues were devoid of facts.[59]

That was in 1950—but media inattention to municipal government hasn't changed much since then. A typical 1972 study, for example, considered newspaper coverage of community development issues. Two of the papers analyzed were the *Kansas City Times,* which ran 53 column inches of sports for every 10 inches of community development news, and the *Manhattan* (Kansas) *Mercury,* which printed an incredible 100 inches of sports for every 8 inches of community development.[60] Sports, by the way, has its own easy-to-find section of the paper. City government news is usually mixed in with the hold-ups, PTA meetings, and traffic accidents.

The only municipal agency that almost always gets enough attention from the press is the police department. Many would say crime news gets too much attention, or at least the wrong kind (see Chapter 16). But at least it's covered. The rest of the city government goes begging.

Bad though it is, newspaper coverage of city hall is exemplary compared to the job done by the rest of the media. The wire services, which backstop everyone else in

Washington and the state capital, are almost useless on the local level. As a rule they are content to rewrite the front page of the best paper in town.

And the broadcast media are content to rewrite the wire services. Few if any stations have a large enough staff to cover city hall on a regular basis. They show up—cameras, microphones, and all—for scheduled press conferences, period. Even in cities that permit TV cameras in city council meetings and the like, it takes a major controversy to attract the interest of broadcasters. Except for educational stations, televising a routine meeting is out of the question. Even sending a crew for a few minutes of news footage is a rare investment of time and personnel.

In 1968, the newspapers of San Francisco went out on strike. During the blackout, only three or four reporters showed up each morning for Mayor Joseph Alioto's press briefing. And *they* were from the struck newspapers! Despite the strike, nobody from the city's radio and TV stations attended the conference on a regular basis. Hadley Roff, Alioto's press secretary at the time, notes that "the electronic media continued to act simply in response to our alarms. When we told them something big was coming up, they responded. Otherwise, nothing." [61]

When municipal government is covered, the coverage is often unbearably dull. Stuart A. Dunham of the *Camden* (N.J.) *Courier-Post* describes it as "a vast gray monotony, lit only occasionally by a spark of interest." News about city hall, he says, is inevitably written "in the terms of procedure and in the language of city ordinances." [62] Readers naturally shy away from such articles—and editors respond by cutting down the size of the city hall bureau.

LOCAL ADVERSARITY

What is lacking in local government coverage (aside from enthusiastic reporters with enough space to tell the story right) is a sense of the adversary relationship. A study of eighty-eight newspapers in Minnesota revealed the startling fact that most editors saw themselves as promoters of civic virtue. Few thought they ought to serve as "watchdogs" over government, and only two discussed the regular reporting of local controversy. Most wanted to put their best foot forward—and the best foot of their communities. [63]

In 1961, Robert Judd investigated the attitudes of West Coast reporters toward government officials. The reporters, he found, were content to act as "passive gatekeepers" between the officials and their editors. They emphatically denied the existence—or desirability—of any sort of adversary relationship. [64] No doubt the officials were in complete agreement.

Civic boosterism is the name of the game. In 1968, *McCall's* magazine ran an article on the quality of American drinking water. The article named 102 cities whose water supplies were rated as only "provisionally approved" by the U.S. Public Health Service. For newspapers in those cities, it was a big story. Eighty percent of the papers covered it, and half of them ran two or more articles on the subject.

But how did they cover it? Only one paper in five approached the Public Health Service for comment. Only one in five discussed the matter with local water-pollution experts. And a grand total of two reporters got in touch with the *McCall's* author for clarification.

Four-fifths of the papers built their articles around the reactions of local waterworks officials—the sources least likely to admit a problem. The *Topeka* (Kansas) *Daily Capital* was typical of this approach. It left unchallenged this statement from the local superintendent of utilities: "For this guy to pick on our water supply, I am inclined to think he doesn't know what is going on. . . . I just can't see how some guy can come out and say something like this. This is the same water I drink, that I give my wife and kids—

Newspapers and broadcast stations are, of course, businesses, avidly seeking to make a profit. This goal can easily conflict with hard-hitting coverage of local government and local problems—especially when the topic is urban growth.

The economic future of a news medium is intertwined with the future of the community it serves. As population increases, newspaper circulation and broadcast ratings go up. As more business and industry is attracted to the area, advertising goes up. Thus every medium's self-interest dictates that it adopt a civic-booster "chamber of commerce" attitude and promote the growth of the community.

In the 1960s, San Jose, California, grew from a sleepy orchard town to a major metropolitan area. The two San Jose newspapers—the *Mercury* and the *News,* both owned by the Ridder chain—profited enormously from this boom. The papers became so committed to the "growth for growth's sake" philosophy that they provided consistently biased coverage of such topics as airport expansion and mass-transit construction. If you knew whether a particular policy would make San Jose grow bigger or not, you could reliably guess whether the *Mercury* and *News* were promoting it or ignoring it.

The activities of the papers' executives and editors provide some indication of their commitment to economic expansion:

- A yearly "Progress Issue" was used by the city government to recruit new industry to the San Jose area.
- The business manager of the papers was a member of the Greater San Jose Chamber of Commerce, working with representatives of such corporations as the Pacific Gas and Electric Company, Bank of America, and General Electric.
- The real estate editor was a member of the Greeters Committee of the San Jose Real Estate Board.
- The business and financial editor was an honorary member of the Board of Realty.
- The city hall reporter became an administrative assistant to the growth-oriented mayor.
- The papers' general manager was airport development chairman for the Chamber of Commerce, and a member of numerous special committees devoted to making San Jose grow.

Reporters at the two papers quickly became aware of the extracurricular interests of their editors and executives. Self-censorship took over, and stories dealing with zoning, planning, environmental deterioration, and the like often took on a pro-growth slant. Only occasionally was top-down censorship required.[65]

---

even my dog." The vast majority of the papers responded to the *McCall's* article as an insult to their cities. They set out to discredit the article—not to examine the issue.[66]

The prevalence of this my-city-right-or-wrong attitude makes the occasional instances of local investigative reporting all the more impressive. In 1974, for example, an award-winning team of *Philadelphia Inquirer* reporters, Donald L. Barlett and James B. Steele, published a series of articles exposing serious inequities in Philadelphia's criminal court system. The series relied heavily on an innovative computer analysis of each judge's sentencing record, combined with more traditional journalistic legwork. It led to the eventual defeat of Philadelphia's district attorney.[67]

Chicago Today, an afternoon tabloid that folded in 1974, published two searing exposés before it died. The first led to the indictment and conviction of former Governor Otto Kerner, on charges that he had bought stock in an Illinois race track at bargain prices and sold it at a huge profit, in return for giving the track the racing dates it wanted. The second revealed that Chicago Mayor Richard Daley had ordered the city to award valuable insurance contracts to the firm that employed his son.[68]

Broadcasting is also responsible for some bold investigative reporting from time to time. WLPG-TV in Miami filmed a political fixer meeting secretly with city officials. KOMO-TV in Seattle revealed the detrimental effects of the Alaska oil pipeline on Puget Sound. WCVB-TV in Boston forced the removal of a Bicentennial Commission director for lack of progress and planning. WLS-TV in Chicago successfully exposed scandalous conditions in local nursing homes.[69]

Weekly newspapers provide some of the most daring coverage of local government.

One such paper is the *Mountain Eagle,* published in the Whitesburg, Kentucky, area by Tom Gish. Gish has taken on the school board, the coal companies, the electric power utilities, and the state, county, and local police—often all at once. In retaliation, his printing plant was burned to the ground by an arsonist in August of 1974. Gish continued to print out of his home, changing the paper's motto from "The Mountain Eagle: It Screams" to "The Mountain Eagle: It Still Screams." [70]

But these are all exceptions. For every Tom Gish, there are dozens of publishers and reporters who skim the surface of municipal government, reporting only what local officials want reported—and not too much of that.

Throughout most of the world, the mass

A MAVERICK GOES UNDER

To find the adversary relationship in a local context, you have to look at the mavericks —underground papers, urban weeklies, and an occasional courageous editor.

Gene Wirges of the *Morrilton* (Arkansas) *Democrat* was such an editor. In the fall of 1960, Wirges noticed that local candidates supported by the Conway County Democratic "machine" always won their races on the strength of the absentee ballots. In one typical election, a reform school board candidate led the "live" votes by a margin of 200 to 132—but the absentee votes went 143 to 9 for the machine candidate, making him a winner. Wirges suspected fraud. He began looking closely at the Conway County government, and he published what he found. An otherwise placid weekly, the *Democrat* became an investigative tiger.

Harassment began in June of 1961. First the prosecuting attorney announced that charges would be filed against Wirges for double-mortgaging his paper. Wirges was able to prove his innocence. Then the state government charged that he was $600 behind in his unemployment insurance payments. A deputy sheriff immediately posted a notice that the paper would be sold at public auction to cover the debt. Wirges got in touch with the state employment office, and the auction was postponed. Next, the machine organized an advertiser boycott of the *Democrat,* and urged the paper's reporters to resign. Wirges did without advertisers and reporters.

What finally nailed him were two libel suits, brought by members of the machine, and tried before a machine judge. The county clerk sued for $100,000 and was awarded $75,000. A county judge sued for $200,000 and was awarded the full $200,000.

Both verdicts would probably have been overturned by a higher court, but Wirges couldn't afford the appeals. On November 26, 1963, the *Democrat* was sold to pay the libel judgments.[71]

media are considered essentially a tool of the government. The United States is nearly unique in the role it assigns to the media: not only to tell the public what government officials are saying but also to tell the public what government officials are doing—even if the officials would rather the public didn't know. The media in America are expected to inform the people so that the people can select and instruct the officials.

Perhaps this is too much to expect. Limited by news management, friendship with sources, civic boosterism, understaffing, and other factors, it is hard enough for the media to do an adequate job of routine reporting. Independent and aggressive journalism often is out of the question. The American media investigate their government more thoroughly than the media of any other country in the world. But too frequently, even in the U.S., the public's watchdog winds up thumping its tail to the government's music.

The most important political role of the mass media, at least in theory, is to provide the information on which public opinion is based. But through news of polls, the media also report—and misreport—public opinion itself. And when it comes time for the public to act out its opinions in an election, the media pay more attention to political maneuvers and preference trends than to the issues on which informed votes are presumed to rest. Americans can often learn more about the policy stances of the candidates from campaign advertising than from campaign news.

PUBLIC OPINION

In a televised news conference on December 2, 1974, President Gerald Ford stated that he did not favor a stiff new tax on gasoline as a way of reducing American consumption of imported oil from the Middle East. The president justified his position by noting that more than 80 percent of the American people, according to a recent public-opinion poll, opposed such a tax. It would

be unwise, said Ford, to flout the wishes of so large a majority.

This sort of deference to "the will of the people" is not a uniquely American phenomenon. As leader of the Second Empire of France, Napoleon III commissioned weekly public-opinion reports from agents all over the country. In 1866 he was thinking about intervening on the side of Austria in the Austro-Prussian war. But his sources told him that most French citizens wanted peace, so Napoleon decided to stay out of the conflict. Four years later, having disposed of Austria, Prussia went to war against France, leading to the defeat of Napoleon III and the downfall of the Second Empire.[72]

Despite such overseas precedents, the American government undoubtedly pays more attention to public opinion than any other government in the world. It always has. Back in 1837, European visitor Harriet Martinu wrote that "the worship of Opinion is, at this day, the established religion of the United States." [73] Many visitors since have made the same observation.

What is public opinion? Political scientist V. O. Key, Jr. offers this definition: "Public opinion may simply be taken to mean opinion held by private persons which governments find it prudent to heed. Governments may be impelled toward action or inaction by such opinion; in other instances they may ignore it, perhaps at their peril; they may attempt to alter it; or they may divert or pacify it." [74] Note that Key doesn't claim that governments always obey public opinion, only that they always "heed" it. After threatening rationing and a variety of even less palatable policies, President Ford eventually did propose a new excise tax on imported gasoline. By that time he had engineered enough public support for the move to make it politically acceptable.

American politicians almost invariably justify their actions on the basis of public opinion. They may do their best first to manipulate the public so that it supports their views. But when politicians cannot change the public's opinion, they generally change their own, or at least keep very quiet about it. It is extremely rare for an American political figure to declare: "Most people disagree, but *I* believe thus-and-such!"

Of course public opinion doesn't always mean everybody's opinion. On any given issue, some people are more interested and more powerful than others. Inevitably, their opinion counts more. Lester Markel comments that "public opinion in a democracy is a collective viewpoint powerful enough, if the power is exerted, to influence public policy. It may be the viewpoint of a majority of the people, or, in the absence of an effective majority, the viewpoint of an effective minority." [75] The government officials responsible for American policy toward imported textiles, for example, are no doubt very responsive to public opinion on the issue—which turns out to be the opinion of textile manufacturers, textile wholesalers, textile retailers, and textile unions.

Although the "public opinion" of interested minorities dominates many government decisions, it is important not to underestimate the power—at least the potential power—of majority opinion. Especially in this post-Watergate era of suspicion, no government official wants to be accused of subservience to special interests. When mass public opinion is successfully mobilized on behalf of one side of an issue, it stands a very good chance indeed of defeating entrenched powers on the other side. The problem, of course, is that it is very difficult to mobilize mass public opinion. Most of us care very little about most issues. And most of us know very little about most issues, except what the entrenched powers have told us through their public-relations efforts.

Two other factors add significantly to the importance of mass public opinion in the United States. The first is public-opinion polling, a relatively new science (and media fad) that gives government officials more information than they ever had before about what the rest of us are thinking. The second

is voting, an opportunity for every adult American, interested and uninterested, informed and uninformed, to take a stand on the public issues of the moment. Since the rest of this chapter is devoted to mass-media coverage of polls and elections, and since polls and elections contribute enormously to the importance of mass public opinion, it is appropriate to start with this question: What do we know about mass public opinion in the United States?

First of all, we know that it is often egregiously uninformed. In 1965, 73 percent of a national sample failed a CBS News test on current events, judged according to tenth-grade standards. A month after the presidential nominating conventions of 1968, 28 percent of the public could not name the Democratic nominee for vice president, Edmund Muskie, and 33 percent couldn't name his Republican counterpart, Spiro Agnew.[76] In 1970, a California Congressman easily won re-election to his tenth consecutive term; a poll taken just before the election revealed that after eighteen years fewer than half the voters knew his name. A 1973 survey showed that only 39 percent of Americans could name both U.S. Senators from their home state, and only 46 percent could name their Representative. Even more startling, only 62 percent knew that Congress was composed of two chambers, the Senate and the House of Representatives.[77]

Psychologists tell us that public opinion, especially when it's strong, is often based on emotion rather than facts. Moreover, people's opinions are very hard to change. We tend to interpret new realities in terms of old values without re-examining the values—and whatever doesn't fit we simply forget. Walter Lippmann, one of the most perceptive observers of the political process in the twentieth century, argued that most people consistently make decisions based on their comfortable stereotypes of the world, not on the world itself. Lippmann didn't blame the public for these flaws in public opinion, but he did worry about their implications:

The environment with which our public opinions deal is refracted in many ways, by censorship and privacy at the source, by physical and social barriers at the other end, by scanty attention, by the poverty of language, by distraction, by unconscious constellations of feeling, by wear and tear, violence, monotony. These limitations upon our access to that environment combine with the obscurity and complexity of the facts themselves to thwart clearness and justice of perception, to substitute misleading fictions for workable ideas, and to deprive us of adequate checks upon those who consciously strive to mislead.[78]

Public opinion has a myriad of sources. We learn our opinions from our parents and early childhood experiences, from primary schooling and religious training, from friends and college courses, from traveling and other influences. The mass media play a particularly vital role. It is through the media that Americans acquire the current information they need to test old opinions and form new ones. If the American public is uninterested in many important issues, and uninformed on those issues, psychology cannot take all the blame. Some of it belongs to the media, whose job it is to interest and inform us.

POLLS AND THE MEDIA

Several decades ago, President Woodrow Wilson voiced the following heartfelt complaint about his job: "I do not know what the people are thinking about; I have the most imperfect means of finding out, yet I must act as if I knew. I'm not put here to do what I please." [79] If Wilson were president today, he would be an avid reader of public-opinion polls.

Most of us alternately deplore and applaud the reliance of government officials on poll results. When the results differ from our own opinions, we complain that our officials ought to think for themselves more, or at least listen to the people (like us) who really understand the issue. When the results support our views, we congratulate the officials for finally acknowledging the will of the public.

However we feel about it, the fact is that government officials are greatly influenced by public-opinion polls. And here is a more disquieting fact: The public is greatly influenced by public-opinion polls. People like to be in the majority when they can; on issues where they have no firm opinion of their own, they are quite willing to adopt the viewpoint of their neighbors. How poll results are reported in the media is therefore an issue of some importance.

The biggest controversy over polls used to concern the size and representativeness of the sample. Many people still doubt that a survey of just a few thousand citizens can accurately reflect the opinions of millions of others who have never even met a pollster. This was a genuine problem in the 1920s and 1930s, the early years of polling. Today, pollsters know how to select a large enough random sample to serve as a cross-section of Americans. Particularly with the various "weighting" techniques now used to insure that minority groups are properly represented, sampling just isn't a big problem any more.

The choice of questions is. In fact, it's three problems. First, most poll questions are too simple. They typically state a very complicated issue in oversimplified terms, then insist on a one-dimensional yes-or-no answer —no essays allowed. Second, many poll questions are biased. It makes a big difference whether you ask people if they support "unilateral troop withdrawal" (sounds bad) or if they think "the U.S. should make the first move toward peace" (sounds good). By carelessly phrasing their questions, pollsters can predetermine the answers. Third, some poll questions are so poorly phrased that *any* answer is meaningless. Take this question from a 1973 Gallup Poll: "Do you think President Nixon should be impeached and compelled to leave the Presidency, or not?" It is possible to answer either half of this question yes, and the other half no—except that Gallup won't let you. Such a question may actually mislead people into thinking that impeachment (indictment in the House of Representatives) is the same as removal of the president (conviction in the Senate or resignation).

To help readers and viewers cope with such dilemmas, the American Association for Public Opinion Research offers its code of disclosure standards. The code requires pollsters to identify the sponsoring group, give the exact wording of the question, describe the nature and size of the sample, discuss how far off the results might be (the sampling error), state the date of the polling interviews, etc.[80] But of course not all media present this information with every poll. When it is presented, it may not be read. And how many readers would understand its implications for the credibility of the poll?

Because most polls are conducted with the news media in mind, they have to be kept simple. Sophisticated analyses and follow-up questions might clutter the article and turn off the reader. Thus when the pollsters discovered that more people thought President Nixon was guilty of wrongdoing in the Watergate affair than wanted him impeached, they simply reported that intriguing fact. They didn't ask—or even guess—why people who felt Nixon was guilty were nonetheless satisfied to see him continue as president.[81]

By the questions they ask, polls can actually create a public opinion where none existed before. Following up on a proposal by Boston Mayor Kevin White, the Harris Poll asked people whether they thought a special presidential election should be held in 1974, if Congress and the Supreme Court approved. Many respondents answered yes. Undoubtedly most of them had never heard the idea before, much less pondered it seriously. Thus Harris was not really measuring public opinion, but rather engaging in a sort of market research for White's sugges-

tion. And when the results were published in the media, Harris was not so much reporting public opinion as promoting that suggestion.

Similarly, pollsters can change the fortunes of political candidates merely by matching them up—or failing to match them up—against other candidates in the early stages of the campaign. At the start of George McGovern's presidential nomination bid in 1972, most polling experts assumed he had little chance of success. So they didn't bother to include his name in the preference polls. As a result, McGovern's staff complained, people tended to conclude that he was a frivolous candidate, or at best a hopeless one—and his campaign had trouble getting off the ground until the primaries proved the pollsters wrong.

Election time is when the polls are most prominent, and a candidate is likely to attribute all sorts of gains and losses to their influence. Trailing far behind in the polls, it is said, can hurt fund-raising; running far ahead can make the staff lethargic and overconfident; closing fast near election day can produce a bandwagon effect and a final victory spurt; leading substantially near election day can induce supporters to stay home and not vote at all. Much of this post-election assessment of the effects of the polls is little more than a reading of tea leaves. We really don't know what the effects are.

But certainly there are effects, sometimes visible and far-reaching ones. In 1972, going into the New Hampshire primary, the polls showed Edmund Muskie with a wide lead for the Democratic presidential nomination. He won the primary, but not by as much as the polls had predicted. Political reporters then interpreted the outcome as a Muskie setback, and asked the Senator why he had not done as well as the polls had said. Muskie was understandably peeved.[82] When he failed to live up to the polls in succeeding primaries as well, reporters made that failure the main theme of their coverage. Clearly, reporters were viewing the polls as the most important fact of Muskie's campaign. When the polls turned out to be wrong, the candidate, not the pollsters, suffered.

PICKING THE CANDIDATES

Long before a political campaign begins, the media are busy picking the candidates, acting as a combination "handicapper" and "scout." Some politicians are ignored or rejected. Others are identified for the public as political "comers."

Political satirist Russell Baker calls the media "The **Great Mentioner**." It was The Great Mentioner that first suggested George Romney as an ideal Republican presidential candidate for 1968. And it was The Great Mentioner that ruled Romney out of the race after he claimed he had been "brainwashed" by the U.S. military in Vietnam. Similarly, the presidential aspirations of Senator Edward Kennedy have risen and fallen twice as The Great Mentioner gave or withheld approval.

News coverage of a presidential campaign begins almost as soon as the previous one ends. Three years before the election, the national political press corps starts reporting the feints and maneuvers of the likely candidates, scouting for presidential timber. By the time the first state primaries roll around, the country has long since been buried in campaign news.

Then come the two nominating conventions, when the politicians get to choose among the candidates the media have anointed. The conventions are television's Roman circus. In 1972, CBS sent 500 staffers; NBC and ABC sent 450 apiece. The combined convention budgets of the three networks came to $20 million.[83] Only a third of this sum is recouped through commercials—but the networks take the loss willingly to pyramid the prestige of their entire news operations. The average TV viewer spends a total of fifteen hours watching the two con-

ventions—a very impressive hunk of time.

It's as impressive to the politicians as it is to the networks. Convention time is the politicians' greatest single opportunity to attract the attention and approval of the voters. Not surprisingly, they gear the spectacle to meet the needs of television. They put their best foot forward—and the foot has pancake make-up on it.

The planning is minute and precise, leaving nothing to chance. During the 1972 Republican convention in Miami Beach, the BBC somehow got hold of the party's "outline" for one night's events. Actor John Wayne was instructed to accept cheers and applause; football player Bart Starr was told to "nod" at youngsters presenting the colors; twelve minutes were budgeted for a spontaneous "Nixon Now" demonstration.[84]

One critic comments:

Actually, television is in a trap at a political convention. If it agreed just to point its cameras at the surface of events in the hall, the politicians would press their opportunity to put on a self-serving show. When television plunges in to try to find such real news as subsurface deals and dissent, its legions stir up commotion, and the coverage is often illusory anyway. The real decision-making is almost always hidden from the cameras. What we see for the most part is television covering the public version of private arrangements.[85]

There is little doubt that this criticism is accurate. And yet, television convention watchers do get occasional glimpses of the realities of politics. And when the party machine breaks down, as it did in 1968 at the Democratic convention in Chicago, the glimpses are likely to be more than occasional. The selection of presidential candidates is not a wholly public procedure, and probably it never will be. But it is a great deal more public than the selection of state and local candidates—largely because there are few state and local conventions covered by television.

COVERING THE CAMPAIGN

The mass media are not the most important influence on voting decision. Family background, economic status, geographical location, and other demographic factors are far better predictors of an individual's vote than what he or she reads in the papers or sees on TV. But most elections are decided by a small "swing vote" which is able to overcome demographics and change its mind during the campaign. And swing voters are greatly influenced by the media.

Even the average voter may be significantly affected by media content. A 1969 study found that 70 percent of American adults make regular use of television for information on candidates and campaigns; 50 percent use newspapers and 25 percent turn to magazines.[86] An earlier study, completed in 1960, revealed that four-fifths of all Americans learned more about national election campaigns from newspapers and television than from interpersonal conversation.[87] It is still quite likely that most Americans are more influenced by their friends than by the media when it comes to political opinions and attitudes (see pp. 3–4), but political information appears to come largely from the media.

Traditionally, the media have been as unfair in election coverage as they thought they could get away with. In 1952, for example, several researchers found that newspapers that supported Eisenhower on their editorial page tended to give him more and better coverage on their news pages as well. Papers that supported Stevenson were equally biased in favor of their candidate. Since there were many more Republican than Democratic papers, this raised a serious ethical problem.

The problem is much less serious today. Guido H. Stempel III studied campaign coverage in fifteen metropolitan dailies for 1960 and 1964, and found that both parties were given roughly equal news space.[88] The same was true in 1968; even third-party candidate George Wallace was treated

---

EDITORIAL ENDORSEMENTS

Though election news today is usually fairly unbiased, editorial endorsements, of course, are not. Nor are they evenly distributed; Republican candidates still have a near-monopoly on newspaper endorsements. In 1972, for example, 71 percent of the daily papers in the country endorsed Nixon. Only 5 percent endorsed McGovern, and the rest endorsed no one.

Endorsements are enormously influential in small, relatively unpublicized elections. Between 1948 and 1962, California newspapers endorsed the winning candidate in local elections 84 percent of the time. They picked the winning state senator 65 percent of the time, and the winning state assembly candidate 63 percent of the time.[89] A more recent study of mayoral and city council endorsements by ten large Texas newspapers found that in 88 percent of the campaigns, the endorsed candidate won the election. The endorsed candidate also received a 9–7 edge in news coverage, and purchased about twice as many column inches of advertising space.[90]

In national elections, on the other hand, most observers believe that editorial endorsements matter little. Today, television is by far the most important source of national election news—and the vast majority of TV stations don't endorse any candidate at all. But this conventional wisdom is questioned by a recent study of the effects of newspaper endorsements on the 1972 presidential campaign. The study found that independent voters who read a newspaper that endorsed McGovern were twice as likely to vote for him as independents who read a paper endorsing Nixon.[91]

---

fairly.[92] And a content analysis of 1972 campaign coverage in the three networks, the *Philadelphia Inquirer,* the *Philadelphia Evening Bulletin,* and the *New York Times* showed the same even-handed pattern. In fact, the three newspapers gave more space to the candidate they didn't endorse than to the one they did.[93] Obviously, professional news judgment was determining coverage, not the prerogatives of ownership.

Of course there are still some publishers left who let their editorial bias show on their news pages, especially during a hotly contested election. Campaign coverage is probably less fair in the smaller papers than in the bigger ones, and less fair in local races than in national ones. But bias is no longer the biggest problem in campaign coverage.

Most election news today is pretty fair.

Unfortunately, it is also pretty poor. Rarely does a newspaper article or a television program undertake to compare the qualifications of the candidates or their views on the issues of the campaign. Broadcasters claim that the equal-time law (see p. 197) makes this difficult or impossible to do. Newspapers have no such excuse; many simply don't bother.

The same problems that limit the effectiveness of the White House press corps in its coverage of the president also constrain the reporters who handle presidential campaigns. Obliged to cover the candidate minute by minute, reporters see thousands of trees and miss the forest. They hear the same speeches over and over again, ask the same questions,

---

THE CAMPAIGN TRAIL

The conditions of campaign coverage haven't changed much in the last century or two. The following is a tongue-in-cheek excerpt from "Rules of the Road," written by a group of reporters and found among the papers of William Jennings Bryan after the election of 1896.[94]

Working Hours. Nature requiring a certain amount of rest for the recuperation of the faculties, twenty-one hours is fixed as a working day for members of this party. To insure the enforcement of this regulation the Associated Correspondents agree that no record shall be made of speech, reception, bon-fire, salute, or any other occurrence between the hours of 1:30 A.M. and 4:30 A.M. No walking delegate shall have power to abrogate this regulation.

Home Offices. Home offices shall be treated with the consideration due their isolated position, and a chain of communication shall be kept up which will insure hearing from the cashier once in a while. Inquiries from news editors regarding lost dispatches, reminders that the Sunday paper goes to press yesterday afternoon, and requests to interview Bryan on the charge that he robbed his grandmother's orchard, shall be answered by letter the day after the election.

Creature Comforts. All members of this party shall be entitled to three triangular meals a day, subject to appetites of local reception committeemen. Sandwiches from railway eating houses shall be used as mortars for the cannon from which salutes are fired. Campaign cigars shall be smoked only on the open prairies.

Straw Votes. To discourage the straw vote fiend, the poll of the correspondents shall be reported as follows:

To supporters of Bryan—				
McKinley and Hobart	.	.	.	16
Bryan and Sewall	.	.	.	1
To supporters of McKinley—				
Bryan and Sewall	.	.	.	16
McKinley and Hobart	.	.	.	1

read the same polls, see the same babies kissed. Halfway through the campaign they are so exhausted that it's all they can do to file a story of any sort. But their employers are paying a small fortune so they can parade around the country in the wake of the candidate, so they must file every day, even if nothing important has happened. And they must concentrate on what the candidate did and said, period. Any attempt at interpretation or evaluation of the candidate's positions almost guarantees a charge of political bias.

In 1972 one reporter, Hunter Thompson of *Rolling Stone* magazine, earned a national reputation with his free-wheeling stories on the meaning and direction of the campaign. Readers appreciated Thompson's behind-the-scenes interpretations, and reporters envied his journalistic freedom. Thompson's tendency to mix fact, opinion, and imagination without telling the reader which is which represents a potentially dangerous style of political journalism. But at least he tried to explain where the campaign was going, and why. Most election reporting merely tells us that the campaign is still going.

Instead of examining the underlying issues, the media cover election campaigns the way they cover sporting events. Candidate X gains a few points by attracting the support of a certain labor union. Candidate Y recovers by claiming X is soft on the crime issue, and pulls ahead with an aggressive speech at a Rotary luncheon. Candidate X gets back into the game by swimming in a polluted river to dramatize devotion to the environment. And so on, right up to election day. The media dutifully report charges and counter-charges, proposals and counter-proposals, pseudo-events and more pseudo-events. The public learns more about the imaginations of the competing campaign managers than it does about the qualifications and intentions of the candidates.

It is almost as if the newspaper reader and the television viewer were not voters at all, but rather disinterested observers of the political process. The media offer us an incredibly detailed blow-by-blow account of the campaign. They keep up right up to the minute on who's winning and how. But they tell us almost nothing about who ought to win, about how the world might change if one candidate won instead of the other. As amateur political scientists, we can learn a lot from the media. As voters, we seldom learn enough.

POLITICAL ADVERTISING

For many people the main source of "news" about political candidates is not the news at all. It is political advertising, especially television advertising. This use of broadcasting is a fairly recent development. The following chart shows the total amount of money spent on radio and TV time in each presidential campaign since 1952.

1952	$ 6,100,000
1956	9,500,000
1960	13,700,000
1964	34,600,000
1968	58,900,000
1972	59,600,000

These figures do not include production costs, or state and local races, or newspaper and magazine advertising.

The typical political ad is a 30-second or one-minute TV spot inserted between two popular entertainment programs. It is designed and produced by a professional advertising agency. Candidates retain a veto power, but they don't use it very often if they want to win. After all, in the business of packaging and marketing products the ad agencies are pros. The candidates are merely the products, and act accordingly. They do what they're told.

A classic case of political advertising was the 1966 re-election bid of New York Governor (later Vice President) Nelson Rockefeller. The incumbent, Rockefeller was extremely unpopular with the electorate, and early polls indicated that literally any Democrat could defeat him. Frank D. O'Connor was picked for the job.

Rocky won the election (by 400,000 votes) on the strength of a massive media campaign. He spent well over $2 million on television ads alone. On WNBC in New York City, Rockefeller ran 208 commercials at a cost of $237,000; O'Connor bought 23 ads on this station, spending only $41,000. It was that way throughout the state. In the rural city of Watertown, the Rockefeller campaign spent $3,067 on 99 TV spots; O'Connor spent $1,307 on a mere 18 spots.

Jack Tinker & Partners (of Alka-Seltzer fame) designed the commercials. Rockefeller's face and voice were seldom used. A typical early ad featured a talking fish in an underwater news interview. The reporter asks the fish about the governor's Pure Waters Program. The fish says that things are still pretty smelly, but thanks to Rocky they're getting better. "I would say, uh, next to a fish. . . . I'd say he's the best gov. . . ."

Later the campaign took a nasty turn. One script read: "Frank O'Connor, the man who led the fight against the New York State Thruway, is running for governor. Get in your car. Drive down to the polls, and vote." Actually, O'Connor had fought for a free thruway against Rockefeller's plan for a toll-road. But the O'Connor campaign lacked the money to clear up the record.[95]

Campaigns such as the Rockefeller-O'Connor race raise two important questions. First, what does it mean for democracy when only the wealthiest candidates (or those with wealthy supporters) are able to mount an effective, "modern" campaign? And second, what does it mean for democracy when political candidates are sold to the public like Alka-Seltzer?

Of course there is another side to the argument. Political advertising does give the candidates a chance to address the public directly on the issues. This circumvents both the failure of many citizens to pay attention to political news and the tendency of the media to stress who will win instead of who should win. Better thirty slick seconds on Candidate X's opinions about racism or inflation than no information at all. In addition, it is said with some justice that television advertising is the only way an unknown candidate can reach the public and defeat a well-established incumbent. In 1970, John Tunney successfully challenged George Murphy for a California Senate seat largely on the strength of his ads. And in Pennsylvania, a complete unknown named Milton Shapp spent four years, two campaigns, and millions of dollars advertising his way to the governor's mansion.

But 1970 was also the year when the tide began to turn—away from political advertising. *The Selling of the President,* a cynical account by Joe McGinnis of the 1968 Nixon campaign, had become a surprise best-seller. In Illinois, incumbent Ralph Smith outspent his opponent Adlai Stevenson III two to one, but lost nonetheless. In Arkansas, Governor Winthrop Rockefeller was defeated for re-election by unknown Dale Bumpers, who ran his campaign on a considerably smaller budget. And in Florida, Democrat Lawton Chiles won a Senate seat by walking up and down the state in the old-time political fashion. Chiles spent only $30,000 on media advertising, a fraction of his opponent's expenditures.[96]

The new trend continued in 1972. In the Florida Democratic primary, for example, the two candidates who shared 60 percent of the vote, Hubert Humphrey and George Wallace, spent only 20 percent of the money. And the three candidates who spent the most finished third, fourth, and fifth—including the two most photogenic, New York Mayor John Lindsay and Maine Senator Edmund Muskie.[97] Noting these results, media expert David L. Garth was moved to comment: "The media is [sic] highly overrated in importance, and with a large number of candidates it's even less important."[98]

As of 1974, these appeared to be the main

trends in political advertising: (1) A de-emphasis on television; (2) An effort to avoid staged situations, sophisticated or clever approaches, and other signs of slickness; (3) A heavy stress on the personal integrity and ability of the candidate, rather than issues; and (4) A reliance on quickly made videotape commercials, so that the candidate's message can be fresh, new, and responsive to what the opponent is saying.[99]

Where is political advertising going now? The Watergate scandals generated a public mood of suspicion that should insure low-key, you-can-trust-me advertising for at least a few years. And the quantity of political advertising can't increase much beyond the present level. A 1972 law put a fairly low ceiling on how much money political candidates can spend, on advertising or anything else. Candidates for the House and Senate, for example, are limited to ten cents per eligible voter or $50,000, whichever is greater.

Presidential campaigns are similarly restricted on a state-by-state basis.

In the immediate future, then, look for political advertising that is modest in both budget and style. But as the Watergate hangover wears off, politicians may go back to the slickness of the late 1960s—or they may move on to something new. One prediction is a sure bet. As long as the media continue to do an inadequate job of campaign reporting, political ads in one form or another will play an important role on the election scene.

ELECTION NIGHT

The broadcast media devote an incredible amount of money and time to election-night coverage. The networks let out all the stops, hiring every computer programmer and news analyst in sight. Local broadcasters do the same thing on a smaller scale. No expense is spared to make sure that viewers are told

---

CAMPAIGNING IN BRITAIN

Despite the shared political heritage of Britain and the United States, politicking in Britain is vastly different from the American experience. The 1974 British elections provide a case in point.

As soon as Parliament was dissolved and an election called, all broadcast political advertising immediately ceased, as required by British law. Instead, the two major parties, Labour and Conservative, were given five free TV appearances each, while the minority Liberal Party got three. That was it—no extra time may be purchased during a campaign.

Extra time wasn't really needed, since the British media devoted extraordinary attention to the campaign. Both the BBC and the Independent Broadcasting Authority allocated all their public-affairs time to the election. For three days Radio London offered four minutes of free time to each of 300 parliamentary candidates.

The three prospective prime ministers—Harold Wilson, Edward Heath, and Jeremy Thorpe—held daily press conferences at their London headquarters. This effectively limited campaigning to day trips throughout Britain. Thus reporters (and candidates) did not have to undergo the wearying experience of months on the road, American style.

The whole campaign, from the dissolution of Parliament to election day, took three weeks. The average parliamentary candidate was permitted to spend only $4,000—and most spent less. The entire cost for all 1,800 candidates, including Wilson, Heath, and Thorpe, was a mere $5.5 million. [100]

who won and who lost at the earliest possible second. A great deal of network prestige rides on the question of which one makes the important predictions first.

There is little to criticize in this election-night performance. Voters are provided with accurate, detailed, up-to-the-minute information. Only Michael Arlen of the *New Yorker* has found grounds for complaint:

> I do feel considerable sympathy, though, for campaign workers who slave like navvies for months and months, are finally assembled in the ballroom of the Hotel Van Meter with their hopeful smiles and their new hairdos and all those ribbons and paper cups, and are then told by Walter Cronkite twenty minutes after they get there that on the basis of 167 votes in the Upper Lompoc District their candidate has just fallen in the dust and everything is over.[101]

Of the thousands upon thousands of news stories about national and local government, the best-covered story of them all may well be election night. This in itself tells us something important about the mass media. They are at their best with the concrete details of a dramatic competition, where they can impartially record the battle and impartially announce the winner. No story involves less news management than the results of an election. No story is less influenced by friendships with news sources, or by civic booster-ism. No story, in short, makes so few demands for independence, integrity, and the adversary relationship. That is why the media do such a good job with election results.

Notes

[1] Laura Longley Babb, ed., *Of the Press, By the Press, For the Press (And Others, Too)* (New York: Dell, 1974), p. 117.

[2] William L. Rivers, *The Adversaries* (Boston: Beacon Press, 1970).

[3] Aaron Latham, "The Reporter the President Hates," *New York*, January 21, 1974, p. 34.

[4] Harry S. Ashmore, *Fear in the Air. Broadcasting and the First Amendment: The Anatomy of a Constitutional Crisis* (New York: W. W. Norton, 1973), p. 59.

[5] William L. Rivers and Michael Nyhan, eds., *Aspen Notebook on Government and the Media* (New York: Praeger, 1973), p. 16.

[6] "California Poll," *Time*, June 17, 1974, p. 42.

[7] Edith Baumann, letter to the editor, *New York Times*, August 13, 1974, p. 34.

[8] Franklin B. Smith, "The Press as Villain of the Piece," *New York Times*, August 13, 1974, p. 35.

[9] Leo C. Rosten, *The Washington Correspondents* (New York: Harcourt, Brace and Company, 1937), p. 249.

[10] Elmer E. Cornwell Jr., *Presidential Leadership of Public Opinion* (Bloomington, Ind.: Indiana University Press, 1965), p. 14.

[11] James E. Pollard, "The Kennedy Administration and the Press," *Journalism Quarterly*, Winter, 1964, p. 14.

[12] Cornwell, *Presidential Leadership*, p. 220.

[13] William L. Rivers, *The Opinionmakers* (Boston: Beacon Press, 1965), p. 144.

[14] Lewis W. Wolfson and James McCartney, eds., *The Press Covers Government: The Nixon Years from 1969 to Watergate* (Washington, D.C.: American University Department of Communication, 1973), p. 7.

[15] Carl Bernstein and Bob Woodward, *All the President's Men* (New York: Simon and Schuster, 1974).

[16] "Mum's the Word at White House These Days," *Miami Herald*, January 14, 1973, p. 5K.

[17] Charles Peters, "Why the White House Press Didn't Get the Watergate Story," *Washington Monthly*, July/August, 1973, p. 14.

[18] "White House Disputes a Report of Washington Post 'Exclusion,'" *New York Times*, December 19, 1972, p. 30.

[19] "Horner's Corner," *Newsweek*, December 25, 1972, pp. 51–52.

[20] Peters, "Why the White House Press," p. 8.

[21] Robert Walters, "What Did Ziegler Say, and When Did He Say It?" *Columbia Journalism Review*, September/October, 1974, pp. 30–35.

[22] Courtney R. Sheldon, "The White House and the Press: (Almost) Everybody Out of the Pool," *Mass Comm Review*, August, 1973, p. 6.

[23] Clinton Rossiter, *The American Presidency* (New York: Harcourt Brace Jovanovich, 1956), p. 114.

[24] "TV Networks, in a Shift, Air Ford at His Request," *New York Times*, October 16, 1974, p. 20.

[25] "Mum's the Word at White House These Days," p. 5K.

[26] "Ford Getting Daily Reports on the Media," *New York Times*, November 24, 1974, p. 26.

27 Douglass Cater, *The Fourth Branch of Government* (New York: Vintage Books, 1959), p. 78.

28 Elmer E. Cornwell Jr., "Presidential News: The Expanding Public Image," *Journalism Quarterly,* Summer, 1959, p. 278.

29 *Parade,* October 7, 1973, p. 2.

30 Rivers, *The Opinionmakers,* pp. 22–23.

31 "Lee Catterall—Wyoming's 1-Man Washington Bureau," *Editor & Publisher,* December 15, 1973, pp. 35–36.

32 "Politicians and the Press," *Saturday Evening Post,* August 18, 1923, p. 76.

33 Ben H. Bagdikian, "Congress and the Media: Partners in Propaganda," *Columbia Journalism Review,* January/February, 1974, p. 7.

34 James Reston, *The Artillery of the Press* (New York: Harper Colophon Books, 1966), p. 73.

35 George Barnes Galloway, *The Legislative Process in Congress* (New York: Crowell, 1953), p. 222.

36 "Congress Report Asks TV Coverage," *New York Times,* October 20, 1974, p. 38.

37 *Ibid.*

38 "House Restricts Secret Meetings of Its Own Panels," *New York Times,* March 8, 1973, p. 1.

39 "Senate, 47 to 38, Retains a Limit on Open Hearings," *New York Times,* March 7, 1973, p. 1.

40 Wallace Carroll, "Essence, Not Angle," *Columbia Journalism Review,* Summer, 1965, p. 5.

41 *Archibald Newsletter,* Freedom of Information Center, Columbia, Mo., no. 5, August, 1970, pp. 2–3.

42 Edward M. Glick, "Press-Government Relationships," *Journalism Quarterly,* Spring, 1966, pp. 53–54.

43 Courtney Sheldon, "A Vote of No Confidence for Background Briefings," *APME News,* June, 1972, p. 3.

44 "Politicians and the Press," p. 72.

45 Alfred Friendly, "Attribution of News," *Nieman Reports,* July, 1958, p. 12.

46 "U.S. and France: Two Views on Oil," *New York Times,* December 15, 1974, p. 3.

47 Tom Wicker, "Background Blues," *New York Times,* December 16, 1971, p. 35.

48 "White House Newsmen's Group Affirms 'Backgrounder' Rules," *New York Times,* January 4, 1972, p. 28.

49 James Reston, "In Defense of Leaks," *New York Times,* June 21, 1974, p. 37.

50 Tom Littlewood, "The Trials of Statehouse Journalism," *Saturday Review,* December 10, 1966, p. 82.

51 John F. Valleau, "Oregon Legislative Reporting: The Newsmen and Their Methods," *Journalism Quarterly,* Spring, 1952, p. 167.

52 John B. Adams, "State Open Meeting Laws: An Overview," Freedom of Information Foundation Series, No. 3, July, 1974, pp. 6–10.

53 Ralph Whitehead, Jr. and Howard M. Ziff, "Statehouse Coverage: Lobbyists Outlast Journalists," *Columbia Journalism Review,* January/February, 1974, p. 11.

54 Thomas Collins, "For the Press, a Lonely Outpost," *Newsday,* March 6, 1974, pp. 5A, 15A.

55 Whitehead and Ziff, "Statehouse Coverage," pp. 11–12.

56 "Publicity Posts Grow in Albany," *New York Times,* February 2, 1973, p. 13.

57 Collins, "For the Press, a Lonely Outpost," p. 15A.

58 Rivers, *The Adversaries,* p. 120.

59 Bernard Stern, "Local Government News," *Journalism Quarterly,* Spring, 1950, pp. 152–54.

60 Sandra Williams Ernst, "Baseball or Brickbats: A Content Analysis of Community Development," *Journalism Quarterly,* Spring, 1972, pp. 86–90.

61 David M. Rubin, "Politics and a Newspaper Strike," unpublished paper, Stanford University Department of Communication, March 17, 1968, p. 6.

62 Stuart A. Dunham, "Local News Coverage: A Vast, Gray, Dull Monotony," *ASNE Bulletin,* May, 1966, p. 3.

63 Clarice N. Olien, George A. Donohue, and Phillip J. Tichenor, "The Community Editor's Power and the Reporting of Conflict," *Journalism Quarterly,* Summer, 1968, p. 250.

64 Robert P. Judd, "The Newspaper Reporter in a Suburban City," *Journalism Quarterly,* Winter, 1961, pp. 40–42.

65 David W. Jones, "The Press and the Growth Establishment," in David M. Rubin and David P. Sachs, eds., *Mass Media and the Environment* (New York: Praeger Special Studies, 1973), pp. 191–247.

66 David M. Rubin and Stephen Landers, "National Exposure and Local Cover-Up: A Case Study," *Columbia Journalism Review,* Summer, 1969, pp. 17–22.

67 "The Inquirer's Inquirers," *Newsweek,* December 30, 1974, p. 55.

68 Gary Cummings, "The Last 'Front Page,'" *Columbia Journalism Review,* November/December, 1974, pp. 46–47.

69 "TV and the Local Watergates," *Variety,* May 23, 1973, p. 42.

70 "An Eagle That Just Won't Stop Screaming," *New York Times,* August 25, 1974, p. 47.

71 Roy Reed, "How to Lynch a Newspaper," *Atlantic,* November, 1964, pp. 59–63. Ben H. Bagdikian, "Death in Silence," *Columbia Journalism Review,* Spring, 1964, pp. 36–37.

72 Paul F. Lazarsfeld, "Public Opinion and the

Classical Tradition," in Charles S. Steinberg, ed., *Mass Media and Communication* (New York: Hastings House, 1966), pp. 79–93.

73 Seymour Martin Lipset, *The First New Nation* (Garden City, N.Y.: Anchor Books, 1967), p. 123.

74 Lester Markel, *What You Don't Know Can Hurt You* (New York: Quadrangle, 1972), pp. 8–9.

75 *Ibid.*, p. 9.

76 *Ibid.*, p. 31.

77 "39% of Americans in Poll Named Their 2 Senators," *New York Times,* December 3, 1973, p. 34.

78 Walter Lippmann, *Public Opinion* (New York: Free Press Paperbacks, 1965), pp. 48–49.

79 Markel, *What You Don't Know Can Hurt You,* p. 19.

80 *Ibid.*, p. 17.

81 Ralph Whitehead, Jr., "Poll Watching: Do We Really Know How the Public Feels about Impeachment?" *Columbia Journalism Review,* March/April, 1974, p. 4.

82 Timothy Crouse, *The Boys on the Bus* (New York: Random House, 1972), pp. 45–46.

83 "Conventions Costing TV $20-Million," *New York Times,* February 6, 1972, p. 75.

84 "Unexpected 'Preview' Provides a Jolt To a Hitherto Predictable Convention," *New York Times,* August 23, 1972, p. 26.

85 Charles McDowell, Jr., "Carnival of Excess: TV at the Conventions," *Atlantic Monthly,* July, 1968, p. 43.

86 Serena Wade and Wilbur Schramm, "The Mass Media as Sources of Public Affairs, Science and Health Knowledge," *Public Opinion Quarterly,* Summer, 1969, p. 198.

87 Dan Nimmo, *The Political Persuaders* (Englewood Cliffs, N.J.: Prentice-Hall, 1970), p. 113.

88 Guido H. Stempel III, "The Prestige Press in Two Presidential Elections," *Journalism Quarterly,* Winter, 1965, p. 21.

89 James E. Gregg, "Newspaper Editorial Endorsements and California Elections, 1948–62," *Journalism Quarterly,* Autumn, 1965, pp. 532–38.

90 Jack Sean McClenghan, "Effect of Endorsements in Texas Local Elections," *Journalism Quarterly,* Summer, 1973, pp. 363–66.

91 John P. Robinson, "The Press as King-Maker: What Surveys from Last Five Campaigns Show," *Journalism Quarterly,* Winter, 1974, pp. 587–94, 606.

92 Guido H. Stempel III, "The Prestige Press Meets the Third Party Challenge," *Journalism Quarterly,* Winter, 1969, p. 701.

93 Robert G. Meadow, "Cross Media Comparison of Coverage of the 1972 Presidential Campaign," *Journalism Quarterly,* Autumn, 1973, pp. 482–88.

94 Ralph M. Goldman, "Stumping the Country: 'Rules of the Road,' 1896," *Journalism Quarterly,* Summer, 1952, pp. 303–306.

95 James M. Perry, *The New Politics* (New York: Clarkson N. Potter, 1968), pp. 107–37.

96 "Punctured Image," *Newsweek,* November 16, 1970, p. 77.

97 "Media Investment a Loser in Florida," *New York Times,* March 18, 1972, p. 16.

98 "Expert Says Media Role Is Overrated," *New York Times,* April 10, 1972, p. 30.

99 Tony Schwartz, *The Responsive Chord* (New York: Anchor Books, 1974), pp. 88, 102–103.

100 Penn Kimball, "British Elections: The Old Boys on the Bus," *Columbia Journalism Review,* May/June, 1974, pp. 28–32. "Campaigning in Britain Requires Less Time and Money Than in U.S.," *New York Times,* February 18, 1974, p. 3.

101 Michael J. Arlen, *Living-Room War* (New York: Viking Press, 1969), p. 19.

Suggested Readings

BAGDIKIAN, BEN H., "Congress and the Media: Partners in Propaganda," *Columbia Journalism Review,* January/February, 1974.

BERNSTEIN, CARL, and BOB WOODWARD, *All The President's Men.* New York: Simon & Schuster, 1974.

CATER, DOUGLASS, *The Fourth Branch of Government.* New York: Vintage Books, 1959.

CORNWELL, ELMER E., JR., *Presidential Leadership of Public Opinion.* Bloomington, Ind.: Indiana University Press, 1965.

CROUSE, TIMOTHY, *The Boys on the Bus.* New York: Random House, 1972.

"Has the Press Done a Job on Nixon?" *Columbia Journalism Review,* January/February, 1974.

HUME, BRIT, and MARK MCINTYRE, "Polishing Up the Brass," [*More*], May, 1973.

KIMBALL, PENN, "British Elections: The Old Boys on the Bus," *Columbia Journalism Review,* May/June, 1974.

LUMPP, JAMES A., and CHARLES H. MARLER, "Washington Reporting Examined," Freedom of Information Center Report No. 309, School of Journalism, University of Missouri at Columbia, August, 1973.

MARBUT, F. B., *News from the Capital: The Story of Washington Reporting.* Carbondale and Edwardsville, Ill.: Southern Illinois Press, 1971.

McDowell, Charles, Jr., "Carnival of Excess: TV at the Conventions," *Atlantic Monthly,* July, 1968.

McGinniss, Joe, *The Selling of the President 1968.* New York: Trident Press, 1969.

Morris, Roger, "Henry Kissinger and the Media: A Separate Peace," *Columbia Journalism Review,* May/June, 1974. See also reply from A. M. Rosenthal, July/August, 1974.

Moynihan, Daniel P., "The Presidency and the Press," *Commentary,* March, 1971.

Nimmo, Dan, *The Political Persuaders.* Englewood Cliffs, N.J.: Prentice-Hall, Inc., 1970.

Peters, Charles, "Why the White House Press Didn't Get the Watergate Story," *Washington Monthly,* July/August, 1973.

Reed, Roy, "How to Lynch a Newspaper," *Atlantic,* November, 1964.

Rivers, William L., *The Opinionmakers.* Boston: Beacon Press, 1965.

———, *The Adversaries.* Boston: Beacon Press, 1970.

Rubin, David M., and Stephen Landers, "National Exposure and Local Cover-Up: A Case Study," *Columbia Journalism Review,* Summer, 1969.

Sigal, Leon V., *The Organization and Politics of Newsmaking.* Lexington, Mass.: D. C. Heath, 1973.

Thompson, Hunter S., *Fear and Loathing: On the Campaign Trail '72.* New York: Popular Library, 1973.

Walters, Robert, "What Did Ziegler Say, and When Did He Say It?" *Columbia Journalism Review,* September/October, 1974.

Whitehead, Ralph, Jr., "Poll Watching: Do We Really Know How the Public Feels about Impeachment?" *Columbia Journalism Review,* March/April, 1974.

Whitehead, Ralph, Jr., and Howard M. Ziff, "Statehouse Coverage: Lobbyists Outlast Journalists," *Columbia Journalism Review,* January/February, 1974.

Wolfson, Lewis W., and James McCartney, eds., *The Press Covers Government: The Nixon Years from 1969 to Watergate.* Washington, D.C.: American University Department of Communication, 1973.

Chapter 16
Coverage of Violence and Crime

The favorite topic of the mass media, bar none, is violence—violent crimes, riots and civil disturbances, terrorism and revolution. News coverage of ordinary "crime in the streets" tends to be sensational and overemphasized, in contrast to habitually scanty coverage of the American system of justice. Riots, on the other hand, deserve the attention they are given—but much more attention needs to be paid to the issues and grievances that underlie the violence. With the rise of terrorism, meanwhile, U.S. reporters face a new and difficult problem: Is terrorism merely a particularly repugnant sort of crime, or is it a trend with important political meanings that must be analyzed?

America has always been profoundly interested in violence and lawlessness—a holdover, perhaps, from its revolutionary and frontier beginnings. Nowhere is this preoccupation more clearly reflected than in the content of the nation's mass media.

Much of the crime and violence in the media is fictional. Radio and television have grown rich on the exploits of western and detective heroes, on shows like "The Shadow," "The Lone Ranger," "Gunsmoke," and "The Untouchables." The film industry, paperback books, and comic books are equally dependent on crime, preferably laced with sex and torture. And a whole genre of American magazines is devoted to tales of triple murders and the like.

The news media also know a subject that will "sell" when they see one—and violent crime is the biggest seller of them all. It always has been. The first specialized reporter in American journalism, hired in 1833, covered the police beat. The most typical article in the Yellow Press at the turn of the century was the crime story, with headlines like "Death Rides the Blast," "Love and Cold Poison," "Screaming for Mercy," and "Baptized in Blood." The tabloid papers of the 1920s followed the same tradition. They are still at it today. So are many standard-size newspapers, though their headlines may be smaller. Even the *New York Times* cannot resist a juicy murder now and then.

In 1954, Cleveland police announced that osteopath Sam Sheppard was being held on charges of bludgeoning his pretty wife Marilyn to death. The wire services played the story big, and newspapers across the country gave it smash display. Herbert H. Krauch of the *Los Angeles Herald & Express* (2,000 miles from Cleveland) exulted: "It's been a long time since there's been a murder trial this good." [1]

CRIME IN THE STREETS

The average American newspaper or broadcast station may or may not cover a new city ordinance or a school bond issue. But a bank robbery, a mugging, or (gulp—hold the presses) a rape/murder is sure to get extensive play.

Why? The main reason, of course, is that editors firmly believe that crime news sells newspapers and news programs. They are probably right. In 1956, two sisters were raped and murdered in Chicago, boosting newspaper circulation by 50,000 copies. A year later, a rapist ran amuck in San Francisco, and circulation shot up by a similar margin.[2] No school bond issue ever accomplished that.

But why is the media audience so preoccupied with violent crime in the first place? The easy answer is that Americans are bored and crave excitement. There is probably some truth to this charge, but social scientists have repeatedly found that the public's interest in crime is grounded less in excitement than in fear. Crime in the streets is a genuine and serious problem in American cities and suburbs. And the fear of crime is stark, widespread, and very, very real.

The mass media did not create the fear of crime. But by catering to that fear, they perpetuate, exaggerate, and distort it. The prototypic black, teenaged mugger of middle-class white women is not a figment of the media's imagination, but he is a great deal less common than the media imply. Most crimes committed by blacks are committed against blacks, and many violent crimes take place between people who know each other. Yet the media underplay crimes against blacks and crimes arising from family quarrels, and grossly overplay street crimes against the white middle class. They thus increase

the fear that justifies the coverage that increases the fear—and so the cycle continues, apparently forever.

Apart from the public's insatiable interest, there is another reason for lavishing time and space on crime news: It is ridiculously easy to cover. A reporter sits at a desk in the police station, listens to the police radio, and chats with various friends on the force. Every once in a while the reporter telephones the smaller police stations in the area, and asks the desk sergeant to check the blotter. Just before deadline, the reporter calls the newsroom and dictates any gruesome facts to a rewrite specialist, who puts them into paragraphs.

This technique for handling crime news results in several abuses. Since the reporter works hand in glove with the police, crime stories almost invariably favor the official point of view. On a minor story, the reporter is unlikely to meet the accused at all; the suspect's protestations of innocence or charges of police brutality therefore go unreported. Moreover, a journalist whose research is confined to the police blotter will never learn much about the underlying causes of crime, or even the motives for a particular crime. Many criminal acts today are a reflection of social unrest, of racial discrimination or political repression, of poverty, joblessness, and systematic exclusion from "the good life." Such factors are far too seldom adequately covered by the media.

The blood-and-guts approach to crime news and the dependence on police sources also result in far greater coverage of arrests than of trials. News of an arrest is both absorbing and easy to get. News of a trial requires a lot more work on the reporter's part, and is interesting to the audience only if the case is especially important or especially juicy. And when a suspect is acquitted or charges are dropped, that's hardly news at all.

While many media continue to rely on the police blotter for crime news, others are beginning to cover more important aspects of crime. Some papers and stations have explained how people can protect themselves against burglaries, muggings, and rapes. Some have discussed the growth of neighborhood crime-prevention groups. Some have examined crimes against the poor in inner-city ghettos and high-rise low-income developments. Some have looked seriously at white-collar crime. Some have focused attention on organized crime and its ties to corruption in government. Some have even analyzed the sociology of crime, the relationship between criminal violence and intolerable social conditions.

Not all crime news, in other words, is a waste of time and space. The assassination of President Kennedy was a "crime" story, but few would argue that it didn't deserve the intensive coverage it received. The same may be said for the alleged crimes of Jack Ruby, Sacco and Vanzetti, Lt. William Calley Jr., Charles Manson, John Dillinger, and Richard Nixon. As we shall see later in this chapter, riots and terrorism are other crime stories of genuine importance to the public.

But as currently reported, most crime news *is* a waste of time and space. It may even be harmful. As early as 1801, observers were already protesting the excesses of media sensationalism:

> Some of the shocking articles in the paper raise simple, very simple wonder; some terror; and some horror and disgust. . . . Do they not shock tender minds and addle shallow brains? They make a thousand old maids and ten thousand booby boys afraid to go to bed alone.[3]

Much has been written about the effects of media violence on the American psyche (see pp. 306–8). It is hard to assess how much damage, if any, crime news actually does. But certainly it does little good. Unexplained and uninterpreted, a mugging just isn't as important to the community as a school bond issue.

THE SYSTEM OF JUSTICE

In contrast to their incessant attention to crime itself, the daily media have little to say about the American system of justice. Each criminal act is treated as an isolated event that begins at the moment of violence and ends at the moment of arrest. How society deals with the criminal is a matter of little interest to the mass media.

Consider the police department. Though most crime news is obtained from police sources, the police department itself is seldom adequately covered. Are police officers poorly trained? Are they underpaid and overworked? How many are on the take, and why? How many despise poor people, or black people, or all people not in uniform, and how does this affect their treatment of suspects and witnesses? What are the policies and practices of your local police department concerning the harassment of suspected criminals, the use of guns and violence, the reporting of corrupt officers, etc.? How much stress is put by the police on white-collar crime and organized crime, as opposed to pornography, marijuana, and similar offenses? Why do so many noncriminals hate the police? The media rarely raise these sorts of questions.

Why? For one thing, these are difficult issues to cover. They require aggressive investigative reporting, which takes a lot more time and skill than copying the police blotter. Perhaps more important, police reporters understand, admire, and depend on their police sources. They are not generally enthusiastic about the idea of provoking a scandal. And so it takes a renegade cop, an independent commission, or the accidental shooting of a bystander to force the media to examine the police as an institution.

When the police are finished with a crime, the courts are ready to begin. We have al-

Crime news raises a number of specialized ethical issues that reporters and editors must attempt to solve. Four of the thorniest problems are the names of juvenile offenders, the race of suspects, the names of witnesses and victims, and the pressure to ignore some crime news altogether.

Juveniles. Some editors argue that young people are more likely to "go straight" if they are not publicly identified as criminals. They therefore withhold the names of juvenile offenders. Other editors believe that readers have a right to know the names of criminals in their midst, and that the embarrassment of publicity may actually aid in their redemption. Government officials also disagree on this point. In some states all juvenile records are confidential. Other states leave it up to the editor, and still others let the judge decide in each individual case.

Race. Until the 1960s, it was customary for the media to include the race of minority suspects in crime stories. Today this practice is frowned upon, sometimes on the grounds that race is irrelevant, and sometimes on the grounds that its relevance, though genuine, is subject to misinterpretation by a fearful white middle class. In 1970 the *San Francisco Examiner* editorialized:

> Crimes are committed by individuals, not races. Race is not an inherent factor in criminal tendencies. This is basically why we adopted several years ago the practice of omitting race from crime stories unless race has pertinence.
>
> If a crime is racial in nature we say so and identify the principals by race. If a criminal is at large and the printing of his race will aid in catching him, we print it.[4]

Of course most newspapers still give the names and addresses of suspects, making a tentative racial identification possible if the reader wants to work at it. And fearful white readers can and possibly do assume that most unidentified criminals are black. It might do more good for the media to publicize the fact that crimes against whites are usually committed by whites.

Names. The mass media seldom publish the names of rape victims, but aside from that the media are diverse and inconsistent in their policies on using the names of victims and witnesses. The *St. Louis Post-Dispatch* is one of the few newspapers in the country with formal guidelines in this area. Unless the victim asks to be identified, the paper omits the name in all cases where publicity might embarrass or degrade the victim, such as sex crimes. Burglary victims, however, are always identified by name and block number. Except in major cases, witnesses aren't identified at all.[5] Other media have decided these questions differently, and most simply haven't decided them.

Blackouts. The pressure to withhold crime news comes from many different sources, and with many different justifications—spectacular crimes spawn a raft of imitators; criminals thrive on the notoriety given their handiwork; too much crime news creates a mood of fear and a bad image of the community. The media are sometimes persuaded by these arguments, sometimes not. In 1974, the *Daily Freeman-Journal* in Webster City, Iowa, revealed that it had joined with radio station KQWC in a three-month moratorium on local news stories about vandalism. Despite the blackout, the paper reported, vandalism had increased. It concluded: "An uninformed public often harbors a false sense of self-security. The outcome of the past three months is proof of that."[6]

ready noted that court reporting is a lot less extensive than police reporting, because trial news takes more work to cover and is less interesting to the audience. And that's routine court reporting, the sort that merely reconstructs the crime itself in the words of witnesses and attorneys. Investigative court reporting is rarer still.

In recent years the media have slowly come to grips with the conflict between complete reporting of crime news and the defendant's right to a fair trial (see pp. 180–83). Despite many setbacks and exceptions, reporters today are more careful than they used to be about trying not to prejudice their audience against a suspect or defendant. Perhaps as a result of this caution, the once-common practice of independent journalistic detective work is now almost defunct. In the 1970s, newspapers and broadcast stations seldom dig up their own witnesses and evidence to challenge the prosecution's interpretation of a crime.

When the courts are honest and capable, this new journalistic restraint protects the innocent. When the courts are corrupt or incompetent, it protects the judicial system instead. The media audience, unfortunately, is unlikely to find out which is the case, because reporting of the courts as an institution is almost nonexistent. How much do judges differ in the sentences they mete out for the same offense? Which judges are senile, or arbitrary, or consistently overruled on appeal? How long does the average defendant languish in jail before trial, and what staffing needs are responsible for the delay? How adequate are the prosecutors and public defenders, the parole officers and other agents of the judicial system? How are juries chosen, and what sorts of people wind up on them? Why are so many cases settled by an agreement to plead guilty to a lesser charge? And when was the last time you read a news story on these topics in the paper, or saw one on television?

For an example of what court reporting could be like, consider the career of Selwyn

Raab, one of the best court reporters in the United States today.

In 1964, the New York City police accused George Whitmore, Jr. of attempting to rape Elba Borrero, a practical nurse. The police announced that under questioning the young Brooklyn black had confessed to three murders as well—but Whitmore said the confessions had been beaten out of him. Raab's investigation proved that on the day of two of the murders, Whitmore had been 150 miles from the scene. Eventually a drug addict confessed to the two murders. Whitmore's trial on the third murder charge ended in a hung jury, but he was convicted of assaulting Borrero.

On the Borrero case, Raab found a secret FBI lab report that disproved the prosecution's claim that the button Borrero had torn from her assailant had come from Whitmore's coat. Raab kept digging. Finally, in 1972, he helped locate Borrero's sister-in-law, who said that Borrero had first identified her attacker from a police mug shot—at a time when no mug shots of Whitmore existed. Faced with this new evidence, the Brooklyn prosecutor asked that the conviction be set aside, and in 1973 Whitmore was released.[7] After helping to clear Whitmore, Raab moved from WNET, New York's public TV station, to the *New York Times,* where he was instrumental in uncovering new evidence in the controversial Rubin "Hurricane" Carter case.[8]

Raab also offers *Times* readers unusual in-depth examinations of the courts as an institution. In 1975, for example, he reported that eight out of ten New York City homicide cases are settled by plea-bargaining, and that most defendants who agree to plead guilty to a lesser charge are released on probation or given short sentences. An amateur sociologist as well as a detective, Raab is a model of what court reporting could be but seldom is.

The final step in the criminal justice system is the prison. Traditionally, prisons have received no news coverage at all. The 1971

Attica prison revolt stimulated some reporters to take a look at prison conditions in their own communities. In New Jersey, for example, a reporter took a job as a Trenton State Prison guard and wrote a horror story about the corruption he found.[9] But most of the media will wait for a local prison uprising before they get around to investigating the problem.

The typical big-city paper, after all, has several police reporters to cover current crimes, perhaps one court reporter to rehash old crimes, and no prison reporter to find out what happened to the criminals.

COVERING A RIOT

It was Sunday, July 23, 1967. The *Detroit Free Press* had only a skeleton staff in the office when reports of looting and arson in the black section of town began filtering in. Police reporter Red Griffith told the newsroom the demonstrations had begun with a police raid the night before. Griffith also reported that the violence was spreading rapidly—despite police claims that it was under control. One *Free Press* reporter had already been struck by a bottle and sent to the hospital.

The deadline for Monday morning's first edition was fast approaching. Tom De Lisle, the youngest reporter on the staff, was toying with the lead for his rundown on the worst damage areas. "Can I call it a riot?" he asked assistant city editor Wayne King. Determined not to contribute to the trouble, King said no. Shortly afterward, Michigan Governor George Romney called out the national guard, making the riot condition official. Even so, the word "riot" appeared only three times on the front page of Monday morning's paper.[10]

This was only the first of thousands of journalistic decisions that faced the *Free Press* during the next four days of uncontrolled violence. The paper acquitted itself well, and its coverage of Detroit's unrest has

since been hailed as a model for American journalism.

"The truth, the whole truth, and nothing but the truth" isn't a bad motto for the mass media—but it is a very difficult motto to live up to in covering a riot. Nine times out of ten, the media get their first word of a civil disturbance from one of two sources: the police radio or the wire services. Both are more concerned with speed than with accuracy. And both are notoriously unreliable in a crisis, mixing fact and rumor in about equal proportion.

In Tampa, Florida, for example, a deputy sheriff died in the early stages of a disturbance. AP and UPI immediately bulletined the news that he had been killed by rioters. Half an hour later reporters discovered that the man had suffered a heart attack.[11] In 1969, the Third World Liberation Front organized a student strike on the Berkeley campus of the University of California. Mike Culbert, editor of the *Berkeley Gazette*, notes that "the wire services didn't know what was going on. The early leads in the first days of the strike were atrocious. At one point AP was taking down my *speculation* on what was happening and moving it as the early lead."[12]

Not that newspapers and broadcast stations have a much better record on riot rumors. During the Watts riot of 1965, radio station KTLA sent a reporter aloft in a helicopter. In the space of a few hours he told his audience that the Shrine Auditorium was on fire, that communists were directing the uprising, and that the Minute Men were about to invade the ghetto. All were unsubstantiated rumors, and all turned out to be false. The reporter hedged his statements with phrases like "police believe" and "it is thought that" —but few listeners noticed the qualifiers.[13]

KTLA and Watts are not unique. Riot rumors were almost a media staple in the late 1960s. In Detroit, a radio station reported a rumor that blacks were planning to invade the suburbs that night. In Cincinnati, newspapers reported that a group of white youths had a bazooka in their possession. The invasion never materialized, and the bazooka turned out to be inoperable. A false rumor that police had killed a black cab driver in Newark helped trigger a riot in that city, and an unfounded report of the killing of a 7-year-old boy fanned a disturbance in Plainfield, New Jersey.

As the media have grown more experienced with civil disruption, they have become more cautious about publishing unproved rumors. Some editors and broadcasters have gone even further. They habitually withhold the established facts of explosive incidents, in the hope that those incidents will not escalate into full-fledged riots.

News blackouts of this sort have a long history in the South. In the early 1960s, one Southern city established an interracial commission to desegregate its lunch counters. An agreement was negotiated, the media kept mum, and the sit-ins proceeded without violence. Says one member of the commission: "I am convinced that if these matters had received normal news treatment, the alarm would have sounded among the Ku Klux Klan and the redneck types, and that they would have been there with their baseball bats and ax handles; extremists among the Negroes would have responded in kind." [14]

The blackout argument seemed most persuasive during the summer of 1967, when a rash of urban riots appeared to be feeding on each other's publicity. Detroit might not have happened, it was said, if the fury of Newark had not been reported so fully in the media. Editors in some cities negotiated secret agreements to keep quiet about their own ghetto unrest. More often than not, these agreements failed in their goal of giving incipient riots a chance to cool down. Presumably, all or most of them are no longer in effect.

It may be true that early publicity about a minor incident can help it grow to major proportions. People hearing on the radio about a scuffle a few blocks away may head on down to see what's going on, and pretty soon it isn't a scuffle any more; it's a riot. On the other hand, people need to know if the streets are blocked or dangerous; some of those planning to drive or walk through the area of a disturbance may choose another route if they are told what is happening. Furthermore, a news blackout sets a very dangerous precedent. Word-of-mouth rumors are likely to be even less accurate than the mass media. And if serious grievances have festered to the point of a riot, the public has a right to know about it.

Otis Chandler of the *Los Angeles Times* has written of "the social value of truth; whether or not truth hurts, whether or not truth is inflammatory." [15] When the media

---

CREATING THE NEWS

It is hard for the media to cover a riot without affecting its course in one way or another. Marked press cars, tape recorders, spotlights, and cameras all act as lightning rods for the sparks of a disturbance. They attract onlookers and alter the behavior of participants. Both rioters and police have been known to "perform" for the press.

Perhaps the media can't help influencing the news—but they don't have to manufacture it. During the Newark riot, a New York newspaper photographer was witnessed urging and finally convincing a young Negro boy to throw a rock for the benefit of the camera. In Chicago a few years later, a TV camera crew was observed leading two female "hippies" into an area filled with national guardsmen. As the camera started rolling, one of the young women cried on cue: "Don't beat me! Don't beat me!" Virtually all the media have rules against this sort of thing, but rules tend to be forgotten during a riot.

refuse to publish the facts of civil disruption, they do the public as much damage as when they rush to publish unfounded rumors. Truth is what's needed—the whole truth and nothing but the truth.

BALANCE AND BACKGROUND

"The whole truth" about a riot includes a lot more than what happened and how much damage was done. In particular, it includes the "background" of the riot. Why did a group of people suddenly explode? What were their grievances, and how legitimate were they? What could the community have done to attack the underlying issues and prevent the outburst? What can the community do now to keep the same thing from happening again?

Ideally, of course, these questions should be discussed by the media long before any riot. Every civil disturbance is proof that some problem has gone unattended, and usually this means the media have failed to expose the problem for the community to see. The riot itself is a desperate form of communication. When people are able to air their grievances effectively in a peaceful manner, they do not riot.

Once the riot begins, it is up to the media to make up for lost time and begin reporting the issues. It shouldn't take a riot to make editors aware of this responsibility, but sometimes it does. The very least we can expect is decent coverage of the underlying issues during and after the explosion.

Quite often we don't even get that. The reporters and editors who work for the establishment media are predominantly white and middle-class. Their principal audience is also white and middle-class. And so coverage of the riots of the 1960s reflected white middle-class fear of blacks and black rage. Stories about ghetto riots, the Black Panthers, and similar topics stressed the impending destruction of (white middle-class) civilization at the hands of angry blacks. This was not just a racial matter. Antiwar demonstrators and young radicals also seemed to threaten the fabric of American society. The media's way of coping with that threat was to concentrate on violent acts, rather than the issues behind the violence.

Much the same pattern was repeated in the 1970s. In the early years of the decade, reporters covered the culmination of the antiwar movement, the Attica prison uprising, the Native American occupation of Wounded Knee, and dozens of similar inci-

OVERKILL

Important though civil disturbances are, it is doubtful that they deserve as much coverage as they receive. In late 1968 and early 1969, San Francisco State College was the scene of a major student rebellion. The *San Francisco Chronicle*'s file on the story, some staffers jokingly claim, is thicker than its morgue for World War II. In one three-week period, the *Chronicle* carried 1,531 column inches on the events at S.F. State. The Vietnam war, by contrast, was allotted only 388 inches.[16]

If the *Chronicle* had devoted all that space to exploring the issues behind student unrest, we would have no complaint. But as always, the stress was on action. A good demonstration is almost as effective as a good murder for selling newspapers, but who wants to read a list of grievances or demands? Bloody heads add spice to a TV news show, but who wants to watch films of students picketing peacefully? San Francisco's media had hold of a top-notch story. No one dared to drop it and give the competition an edge. And so, spurred on by the competitive ethic, reporters in San Francisco worked hard to keep the story aloft, and to make it as action-packed as possible.

dents. The media were also confronted with political terrorism—bombings and airplane hijackings, the Weather Underground and the Symbionese Liberation Army. Seeing their society threatened, many reporters downplayed the issues and stressed the violence.

The problem is partly a matter of sources. In the middle of a full-scale riot, it is hard enough for a reporter to figure out who speaks for the police. And the reporter *knows* the police, has worked closely with them for years, and has built up a relationship of mutual trust and cooperation. By contrast, the reporter is likely to have no sources at all (let alone cooperative ones) among the rioters —the blacks, students, radicals, or whatever. So the reporter relies heavily on police sources, and the story turns out like a play-by-play account of a ball game: all action and no motivation.

And no inaction either. The media, like the police, are interested primarily in what's happening. They don't much care why, and they don't much care how limited the action is. A single incident of violence in a long, peaceful demonstration is fated to be the only incident that makes the evening news. "By focusing on a handful of violent activ-

ists," admits Frank Stanton of CBS, "we may give the impression that that's the way it is all over. This is the danger in all kinds of demonstrations. Our tendency is to try to go where the action is." [17]

Professor Nathan Blumberg of the University of Montana uses the adjective "orthodox" to describe the attitude of the media toward civil disturbances and peaceful protest demonstrations. He gives as an example the 1968 antiwar march on the Pentagon. The smallest crowd estimates came from police and military sources, and these were the ones the media used. Students and hippies were a minority among the demonstrators, yet the media made it seem that they were the only people there. The army claimed that it was the demonstrators themselves who fired tear gas into the crowd, and the media let the lie go unchallenged until days after the event.

In nearly every demonstration or civil disturbance (Chicago in 1968 was an obvious exception), the "orthodox" media rely on official sources for most of their information. They stress action and violence, and ignore the underlying issues. "Perhaps it is too much to expect," Blumberg concludes, "that a press with an undeniable stake in the economic and political system would report

LEARNING TO USE THE MEDIA

The plight of the American Indian was dramatized in 1972 by a week-long takeover of the Bureau of Indian Affairs in Washington. Although the publicity was generally unfavorable, there was plenty of it—the grievances of Native Americans received little coverage, but at least the public became aware of the fact that there *were* grievances. Coverage of the seventy-one-day armed occupation of Wounded Knee, South Dakota, was even more extensive. Again the news was generally less than favorable, concentrating on violent incidents instead of fundamental issues. But it was clear that American Indians were not happy with their lot, and at least a few people started asking why.[18]

The 1975 occupation of a deserted Roman Catholic novitiate in Wisconsin demonstrated that militant Indians had learned still more about using the media. The armed Menominee Indians staged their takeover shortly after the New Year began, thus taking advantage of the slow holiday news period. The month-long occupation was much less violent than Wounded Knee. It ended in an agreement to deed the novitiate to the Menominee Nation, and produced a good deal of favorable publicity for the Native American cause.

fairly on those who are fundamentally dissatisfied with the status quo." [19]

COVERING TERRORISM

In the early 1960s, the mass media began learning how to cover demonstrations and protest marches. In the middle 1960s, they had to start all over again, learning how to cover ghetto riots. In the late 1960s and early 1970s, it was campus rebellions, antiwar movements, Indian occupations, and the like. As we have seen, the media didn't—and don't—do a very good job of covering these events and the issues behind them. But at least the problem is a familiar one, and in time reporters may find ways to avoid the traditional, orthodox, police-beat approach to coverage. Political terrorism, on the other hand, is a brand-new problem for most American reporters (except those who have dealt with the Ku Klux Klan). It raises in the starkest possible terms the familiar dilemma of action versus issues. Once again the media are painfully learning the ropes.

Early in 1974, American intelligence experts noted that 432 major acts of international political terrorism had occurred in the previous six years. The list included 235 bombings, 94 hijackings, and 57 kidnappings. Uncounted millions of dollars were lost in property damage and ransom payments, and there were 196 deaths and 300 injuries.[20] Terrorism continued to climb in 1974 and 1975, not just in places like Belfast and Jerusalem, but in New York and Washington as well.

News coverage of foreign terrorism typically depends on the politics of the terrorists and the politics of the country whose media are doing the coverage. In countries where the viewpoint of the terrorists is unpopular, political bombings and kidnappings are treated as shocking and spectacular crimes, period. In countries where the ideology of the terrorists is more acceptable,

the same events are treated as regrettably extreme ways of making a political statement.

Consider, for example, news coverage of the Palestinian guerrilla movement. Terrorism has played an important role in Palestinian strategy for decades. But in 1970, fearful that they were being frozen out of Arab decision-making, activists in the Palestinian movement stepped up their terrorist activities and aimed at worldwide publicity. They hijacked planes in Europe, killed Israeli Olympic athletes in Munich, staged spectacular massacres inside Israel, and in a variety of other violent ways demonstrated their dedication to the Palestinian cause. As a result, Europe, the Third World, and above all the Arab nations began to take the Palestinians seriously. Reporters begged the guerrilla leaders for interviews, hailed them as Arab independence fighters, and reported their grievances in detail.

In 1974, largely because of this publicity, Yasir Arafat of the Palestinian Liberation Organization was invited to address the United Nations General Assembly. One Palestinian offered this comment on the success of the terrorist strategy: "We had been forgotten by the world, and we vowed never to be forgotten again. I believe we have kept that vow." [21]

Apart from the underground press, most American newspapers and broadcast stations did not join in the worldwide enthusiasm for the PLO. Coverage of Palestinian terrorism in the U.S. press was shocked and disapproving; it oversimplified the politics of the Middle East and tended to treat the bombings, hijackings, and massacres simply as crimes. But in 1973, the tone of U.S. coverage began to change. Interviews with terrorist leaders and analyses of their ideology became more common. A list of the twenty-five most intriguing people of 1974, published in *People* magazine, included Yasir Arafat—but no mention of PLO terrorism.[22]

The reasons for the change, of course, were the 1973 Middle East war, the oil crisis, and the rapprochement between the United States and the Arab world that they precipitated. As some Americans began taking the Arab nations and the Palestinian political viewpoint more seriously, a crime story became a political story.

By way of contrast, the American mass media covered terrorism in Northern Ireland as a political story from the very beginning. The struggle was viewed not just as a succession of bombings and shootings, but as a genuine civil war, and so the positions of both Catholics and Protestants were carefully examined. Before 1973, in other words, the American press generally treated Arab guerrillas as criminals and Irish guerrillas as revolutionaries. After 1973, it generally treated them both as revolutionaries.

What about American revolutionary terrorists? Small groups of militant American radicals used bombs as a political weapon beginning in the late 1960s. Between 1969 and January of 1975, the Weather Underground claimed responsibility for twenty bombings, including explosions at the Capitol (1971), the Pentagon (1972), and the State Department (1975). Predictably, the underground press treated the terrorists as a legitimate revolutionary movement. Adopting the "orthodox" approach to domestic terrorism, the Establishment press did not.

Soon after the State Department bombing in 1975, the *New York Times* published an eloquent editorial on terrorism here and abroad. Its title embodies its theme: "The Violence Plague."

Like a dread plague in medieval times that moved relentlessly and invisibly from one walled town to another and that walls were powerless to keep out, terrorist violence breaks out today in one great city after another and sophisticated security systems are powerless to prevent it. Within days a bomb goes off in the State Department in Washington, there is a murderous explosion at Fraunces Tavern in New York, planes are shot up and hostages seized in an airport in Paris. No city—Stockholm or Rome, Birmingham or Buenos Aires —is immune, and in the least favored, such as Belfast, violence has become endemic. . . .

The political senselessness and moral nihilism of these terrorist acts may be clues to their essential nature. The fanatics are rebels against —not only a particular grievance or injustice— but against the modern world itself.[23]

The dominant tone of this editorial, and of most American news coverage of domestic terrorism, is fear—fear that a tiny band of crazies is capable of terrorizing the entire world. If the terrorists are not common criminals, then they must be lunatics and fanatics. If their actions have any significance beyond the police beat, then it must be a psychological and sociological significance—understanding their "moral nihilism" and their rebellion "against the modern world itself."

This sort of coverage must be immensely frustrating to domestic terrorists, who certainly view themselves as serious political revolutionaries. Ironically, it is also resented by police authorities, who claim that massive media attention to terrorism encourages a chain reaction of still more terrorism. Of course the police aren't asking the media to give more space to the political ideology of the terrorists. They are asking the media to downplay the details of the terrorism itself, which they believe stimulate unstable people to try their own hand at the craft.

Implicit in this position is the view that most terrorism isn't really political after all. Like any spectacular crime, the police say, a bombing, kidnapping, or hijacking spawns a flurry of imitators, motivated by nothing more than a twisted need for notoriety. In July of 1974, as the House Judiciary Committee debated presidential impeachment charges before millions of television viewers, a bomb threat came into the Capitol switchboard. While the hearing room was cleared and searched, the networks reported the threat to their viewers. In the next several days, according to FBI Director Clarence Kelley, there were seven telephoned bomb threats against the committee, "all apparently generated by the instant, nationwide exposure given the initial threat." [24] Perhaps that first threat was political, but what about the other seven?

Not every airplane hijacked to Cuba in the late 1960s and early 1970s was a sign of American revolutionary consciousness. Not every bombing and bomb threat in the early and middle 1970s was the work of dedicated ideologues. Not every abduction of a wealthy American in the wake of the celebrated Patricia Hearst kidnapping was an attempt to win converts to the radical cause. Some terrorists *are* nothing more than common criminals or lunatics, riding the coattails of a revolutionary fringe they neither endorse nor understand.

The question is, which ones? When terrorism really is political, the media owe it to their audience to explore the story fully, reporting not only the event but also the ideology behind it. But when terrorism is merely the work of criminals, the media should avoid overplaying its spectacular aspects, and should pay more attention to its inglorious results—the arrests, convictions, and jail terms.

By treating all domestic terrorism as a super-juicy crime story, the media wind up mishandling both types. The "terror" gets more attention than it deserves, and the "ism"—when there is one—gets ignored. Perhaps this is only what we should expect from a media system whose favorite topic, bar none, is violence.

Notes

1 "The Case of Dr. Sam," *Time*, November 22, 1954, p. 88.

2 John Lofton, "Trial by Fury—A Projection of the Public Mood" (mimeo of draft for chapter from *Justice and the Press*), pp. 13–14.

3 *Ibid.*, p. 5.

4 *San Francisco Examiner*, January 11, 1970, p. B2.

5 Gerald B. Healy, "St. Louis P-D to Leave Out Some Crime News Details," *Editor & Publisher*, February 8, 1975, p. 17.

6 "So Much for Conventional Wisdom," *New York Times*, March 3, 1974, p. 13.

7 "Uncaped Crusader," *Newsweek*, April 23, 1973, p. 48.

8 Peter Axthelm, "Hurricane Carter," *Newsweek*, October 7, 1974, p. 75. Selwyn Raab, "Hurricane Carter Denied New Trial on Recantations," *New York Times*, December 12, 1974, p. 1.

9 Carla Marie Rupp, "N.J. Reporter Exposes Corrupt Prison Guards," *Editor & Publisher*, December 21, 1974, p. 14.

10 *Reporting the Detroit Riot* (New York: American Newspaper Publishers Association, 1968), pp. 3–4.

11 *Report of the National Advisory Commission on Civil Disorders* (Kerner Commission) (New York: Bantam Books, 1968), p. 373.

12 William L. Rivers and David M. Rubin, *A Region's Press: Anatomy of Newspapers in the San Francisco Bay Area* (Berkeley, Calif.: Institute of Governmental Studies, University of California at Berkeley, 1971), p. 125.

13 William L. Rivers, "Jim Crow Journalism," *Seminar*, March, 1968, p. 16.

14 *Ibid.*, p. 12.

15 Otis Chandler, "The Greater Responsibility," *Seminar*, March, 1968, p. 7.

16 Rivers and Rubin, *A Region's Press*, pp. 112–13, 164.

17 Letter from CBS President Frank Stanton to Pennsylvania Senator Hugh Scott, August 9, 1967, p. 3.

18 "Indians Feel They May Be on the Verge of Some Major Gains," *New Brunswick* (N.J.) *Home News*, January 22, 1975, p. 16 (Washington Post—Los Angeles Times News Service).

19 Nathan B. Blumberg, "A Study of the Orthodox Press: The Reporting of Dissent," *Montana Journalism Review*, 1968, pp. 7–9.

20 "The 'Morality' of Terrorism," *Newsweek*, February 25, 1974, p. 21.

21 *Ibid.*, p. 22.

22 Sol Stern, "Has the Press Abandoned Israel?" [*MORE*], February, 1975, pp. 7–8.

23 "The Violence Plague," *New York Times*, February 2, 1975, p. E14.

24 Clarence Kelley, "Television Is Armed and Dangerous," *TV Guide*, March 8, 1975, p. 6.

Suggested Readings

BLUMBERG, NATHAN B., "A Study of the Orthodox Press: The Reporting of Dissent," *Montana Journalism Review*, 1968.

LANGE, DAVID L., ROBERT K. BAKER, and SANDRA J. BALL, *Mass Media and Violence*. Washington, D.C.: U.S. Government Printing Office, 1969.

Report of the National Advisory Commission on Civil Disorders (Kerner Commission). New York: Bantam Books, 1968.

Reporting the Detroit Riot. New York: American Newspaper Publishers Association, 1968.

WALKER, DANIEL, *Rights in Conflict* (Report of the National Commission on the Causes and Prevention of Violence). New York: New American Library, 1968.

Chapter 17
Coverage of National Security and War

One of the thorniest problems confronting journalists is the conflict between national security and the people's right to know. In the past, this problem was usually confined to wartime—and was easily resolved in favor of national security, through government censorship or voluntary media self-censorship. But in recent years national security issues have arisen more and more frequently, often in connection with undeclared wars or with policies that lacked wide public support. As journalists have become less willing to censor the news, government officials have resorted to prior restraint of the press, lies, and news management instead.

For more than a year, James Reston of the *New York Times* knew that the United States was flying high-altitude spy planes (U-2s) over the Soviet Union. His paper did not report the fact. Then, in 1960, a U-2 was shot down and its pilot captured. President Eisenhower denied everything. The *Times*, which knew the denials were lies, printed them without comment. Only after the president finally admitted the truth did the *Times* finally publish the truth.

Reston defended this judgment in 1966. He agreed that it was contrary to the tradi-

tional journalistic ethic, but he added: "In this time of half-war and half-peace that old principle of publish-and-be-damned, while very romantic, bold and hairy, can often damage the national interest."[1]

No doubt there are times when American military adventures should not be reported by the mass media. Equally clearly, there are times when it is vitally important that those adventures be reported. The problem is telling one from the other.

NATIONAL SECURITY?

Consider two other instances when the *Times* neglected to report what it knew— the Bay of Pigs invasion of 1961 and the Cuban missile crisis of 1962.

Tad Szulc's article on the planned invasion was already dummied into the front page of the *Times*, under a four-column headline. But managing editor Turner Catledge and publisher Orvil Dreyfoos had grave reservations. They feared that the story might give Castro the warning he needed to repel the invasion, thus endangering the lives of the CIA-supported invaders and damaging the national security of the United States. After much heated debate, the article was toned down. References to the CIA and to the "imminence" of the invasion were dropped, and the whole thing was run under a single-column headline. There were no immediate repercussions.

When the invasion took place, it was a total failure, a serious blow to U.S. prestige. A month later President Kennedy confided to Catledge: "If you had printed more about the operation you would have saved us from a colossal mistake."

The Cuban missile crisis was another kettle of fish. The *Times* Washington bureau knew that there were Russian missiles inside Cuba, and that Kennedy was planning to do something about them. The president telephoned Dreyfoos and asked him to hold off on the story. Dreyfoos agreed. The result was a spectacularly successful blockade, a triumph for American diplomacy (which badly needed a triumph). Kennedy generously gave the *Times* part of the credit for that success.[2]

The Cuban crises of 1961 and 1962 illustrate two important points. First, it is extremely difficult for the media to know when they should kill a story for reasons of national security. Kennedy felt that the *Times* made a bad mistake in 1961, but showed extraordinary wisdom in 1962—by doing precisely the same thing. Second, when faced with this sort of dilemma, the media have typically killed the story. With the benefit of hindsight, we can find hundreds of articles that should have been published and weren't. But there are very few cases of published articles that did serious damage to national security.

American journalists have traditionally drawn a hard-and-fast line between wartime and peacetime. When the nation is at war, censorship has been accepted without argument. But in time of peace, reporters have viewed the public's right to know as the paramount consideration in deciding what to publish. An informed public, after all, is a cornerstone of democracy. How then can the truth be detrimental to the national interest?

This once-unquestioned distinction is now permanently muddled. Modern warfare is no longer a matter of clear-cut enemies and established battlefronts. The next formal, declared war the United States fights will probably be the world's last. The conflict in Southeast Asia was a war. The ongoing struggle against the "communist menace" is a war. The battle between Israel and its neighbors in the Middle East is a war. The stockpiling of missiles and atomic bombs is a war. In these terms, the United States has been constantly at war since the 1940s, and will remain at war for the foreseeable future. Does this mean that wartime standards of self-censorship should go forever unopposed?

In 1961, Douglass Cater listed four kinds of stories that should not be reported (even in "peacetime") because of national security:

1. Advance disclosures of the U.S. government's position on issues to be negotiated at the international conference table.

2. Leaks on security matters which include the built-in bias of those who did the leaking.

3. Technical data of little interest to the ordinary reader but of immense value to the "enemy."

4. The clandestine operations of our government, both diplomatic and military.[3]

By and large, the American media abided by these standards until the end of the 1960s. As we shall see later, the fact that they did so contributed significantly to the increasing American involvement in Vietnam.

GOVERNMENT CENSORSHIP

Throughout most of American history, the media seldom faced for themselves the key question of news versus national security—to publish or not to publish. Instead, they allowed the government to make that decision, and to enforce it through censorship.

The history of wartime censorship is as old as the history of war itself. In this country it starts with the Revolution. Loyalist newspapers were persecuted throughout the war, and many were forced to stop publishing altogether. Patriot papers fared just as badly in Tory-held territory.

Soon after the Revolution, troops under the command of Major General Arthur St. Clair were attacked by Indians. A congressional committee convened to study the disaster, and asked President Washington to furnish the relevant documents. Washington replied that the executive branch of government had a right to withhold any information that might injure the public if disclosed. Although Washington did hand over the records, the principle soon took root. Very early in American history, then, the right of the government to withhold information for reasons of national security was asserted. And the difficulty of distinguishing between wartime and peacetime was demonstrated.

Coverage of the War of 1812 was casual, and based mostly on official reports. Censorship was thus unnecessary. Much the same thing was true during the Mexican-American War. News reports were colorful and heavily pro-American, and by the time they were published—often weeks later—they posed little threat to military security. The government felt no need to interfere. But the Civil War was a different story. It was the most heavily and most speedily reported war up to that point in American history, and by far the most divisive.

In July of 1861, the Union Army issued an order forbidding telegraph companies to send reports on military affairs. The goal of this measure was to restrict the communications of spies and to prevent the Confederacy from learning about troop movements and the like through Northern newspapers. For several months the ban was extended to non-military reporting as well, but Congress ob-

jected and the earlier rule was reinstated. Even this was a serious infringement on freedom of the press, but the Supreme Court was in no mood to defend the First Amendment at the expense of the war effort.

In order to transmit news by telegraph, reporters were required to submit their stories for government censorship. In theory only information of military value to the enemy was to be excised, but many field commanders used their censorship powers to eliminate unfavorable publicity as well. Reporters who wrote glowingly about their favorite generals were free to work without restriction. Those who were more critical of military tactics found themselves out in the cold; a few were actually accused of treason.

Critical newspapers were similarly harassed. The federal government temporarily shut down the *New York World,* the *Journal of Commerce,* and the *Chicago Times* for publishing stories deemed detrimental to the war effort. Confederate soldiers dealt even more harshly with the *North Carolina Standard* and other "union-screamers." None of these papers supported the enemy, but any criticism seems perilously close to treason in time of war.

The Spanish-American War was so short and so successful that censorship never got off the ground. Strangely enough, there was need for it. The Yellow Press gleefully printed any news it could find, including news of troop movements and strategy planning. Commented *The Journalist:* "We gave the Spaniards no use for spies, for our yellow journals became themselves the spies of Spain." [4] Sensationalism was at its height; William Randolph Hearst sailed his own yacht to war, and actually captured a few hapless Spanish sailors off the coast of Cuba. High jinks and hoaxes inevitably impeded the war effort, but the confident U.S. military voiced no serious objections. For the press, at least, it was a fun war.

World War I was not fun. Censorship and news management were merciless. Reporters had to be accredited by the Allied forces, and needed special permission to move from one location to another. Every dispatch from the front was ruthlessly censored in the interests of troop morale and domestic enthusiasm, as well as national security.

Back home, meanwhile, the government's Committee on Public Information was organized under George Creel. During the course of the war, the CPI set up standards of voluntary press censorship and issued more than 6,000 press releases, many heavily larded with patriotic propaganda. The press observed the voluntary codes, and many American newspapers printed all 6,000 of Creel's releases.

Just to make sure, the government nationalized the infant radio industry, calling a halt to all wireless experimentation. It also passed the Espionage Act, the Trading-with-the-Enemy Act, and the Sedition Act, all of which limited the kinds of news and opinions the mass media were permitted to publish. The Sedition Act was by far the most expansive of the three. It prohibited "any disloyal, profane, scurrilous, or abusive language about the form of government of the United States, or the Constitution, military or naval forces, flag, or the uniform of the army or navy of the United States." More than seventy-five socialist and German-language publications were prosecuted or threatened under these acts.

But World War I was "the war to end all wars," and very few reporters or editors objected to government censorship. Raymond S. Tompkins comments:

> The censorship irked them and they hated it at first, but gradually they grew used to it and wrote what they could, working up all the "human interest stuff" available and learning quickly that the censors loved it and almost invariably passed it—provided it said nothing about the drinking, stealing and rugged *amours* of the *soldat Américain*. . . .

Dragooned into thinking about and observing the war in terms of what would get printed [the correspondent] went on exuding larger and larger gobs of slush, to the continual delight of the appreciative censor, the supreme satisfaction of his managing editor and the glory of the paper that had sent him.[5]

In World War II, voluntary self-censorship was instituted once again. The government issued codes urging the media to censor their reports of shipping, planes, troops, fortifications, armaments, war production, and even the weather. The program was largely successful. No American paper reported the German submarine blockade of 1942. Radar and the atomic bomb were both developed in absolute secrecy, though there were reporters and editors in the know.

The CPI was revived in the form of the Office of War Information, and once again patriotic press releases filled the media. The same agency examined all communications entering or leaving the United States, and deleted whatever it thought was detrimental to the national interest. In one case this included the word "God-damned" in an Ernie Pyle dispatch. Like its predecessors, World War II had its share of unreported stories.

The Espionage Act was still in force. Though it was used sparingly, America's few pro-Nazi media were soon suppressed.

The Korean conflict was America's first full-fledged undeclared foreign war, and the first generally unpopular war in the twentieth century. The government censors soon became less concerned with national security than with troop morale and military prestige. In 1950, AP's Tom Lambert and UP's Peter Kalischer were forced to return to Tokyo for "reorientation." And the Eighth Army announced that "criticism of Command decisions or of the conduct of Allied soldiers on the battlefield will not be tolerated." [6]

The censorship grew worse after General MacArthur's drive into North Korea brought the Chinese Communists into the war. In the face of intense criticism, MacArthur au-

RADIO IN EUROPE

World War II was radio's finest hour. The entire country thrilled and chilled as Edward R. Murrow and his colleagues reported, live, the air blitz over London, the invasion of France, and other critical events that changed the face of Europe:

> This is Edward Murrow speaking from Vienna. It's now nearly 2:30 in the morning and Herr Hitler has not yet arrived. No one seems to know just when he will get here, but most people expect him sometime after ten o'clock tomorrow morning. . . .
>
> Young storm troopers are riding about the streets, riding about in trucks and vehicles of all sorts, singing and tossing oranges out to the crowd. Nearly every principal building has its armed guard, including the one from which I am speaking. . . . There's a certain air of expectancy about the city, everyone waiting and wondering where and at what time Herr Hitler will arrive.[7]

Murrow was seldom censored by the government. He seldom needed to be. He was a superb reporter and an independent one; after the war he would do more than any other journalist to end the demagogic career of Senator Joseph McCarthy. But like most reporters (and most Americans), he supported the war and did what he could to help.

---

thorized censorship of all dispatches that might injure military morale or embarrass the U.S. government. Only after President Truman removed MacArthur from command was some measure of freedom of the press restored.

Throughout this entire period, from the start of the Revolution to the end of the Korean War, the American media were basically passive in their response to government censorship. Of course there were occasional newspapers that opposed a particular war, and therefore opposed the censorship that accompanied it. And there were frequent skirmishes to keep military censorship from expanding beyond national security to cover the self-interest of battlefield commanders. But on two fundamental points the media and the government agreed: News damaging to the war effort should not be published, and the government should be the one to decide which news is damaging to the war effort.

This happy consensus began its slow collapse during the cold war of the 1950s. It was an undeclared, civilian war of threats and diplomacy, and the traditions of wartime censorship were neither obviously applicable nor obviously irrelevant. The media, by and large, were still willing to adhere to government definitions of national security, but the government was no longer willing to trust the media that far. Military precedents were too shaky, issues were too complex, events were too fast-moving, and the stakes—the ever-present possibility of nuclear holocaust —were too high.

And so, with increasing frequency, the government resorted to lying. At the time of the Cuban missile crisis, Assistant Secretary of Defense Arthur Sylvester, a former reporter himself, explicitly defended this tactic: "It's inherent in government's right, if necessary, to lie to save itself when it's going up into a nuclear war. That seems to me basic—basic." [8]

That right was also assumed by the American government when faced with something less than the threat of nuclear disaster.[9] Politically sophisticated Americans came to expect lies and half-lies from the Departments of Defense and State. So did the media—but they published them nonetheless.

Then came Vietnam.

The story of the U.S. commitment in Southeast Asia begins in the 1950s. By 1961, it was already American policy to camouflage the shortcomings of the Diem regime in South Vietnam. As one U.S. "adviser" put it: "Bad news hurts morale." [10]

He didn't say *whose* morale—and it's a pertinent question, since at that point U.S. officials claimed there were no Americans fighting in Vietnam. When an American aircraft carrier was observed in action on the Saigon River, a U.S. information officer merely said, "I don't see any aircraft carrier." [11] In 1962, the State Department sent a secret cable to Saigon:

> CORRESPONDENTS SHOULD NOT BE TAKEN ON MISSIONS WHOSE NATURE IS SUCH THAT UNDESIRABLE DISPATCHES WOULD BE HIGHLY PROBABLE. . . . WE RECOGNIZE IT NATURAL THAT AMERICAN NEWSMEN WILL CONCENTRATE ON ACTIVITIES OF AMERICANS. IT IS NOT—REPEAT NOT—IN OUR INTEREST, HOWEVER, TO HAVE STORIES INDICATING THAT AMERICANS ARE LEADING AND DIRECTING COMBAT MISSIONS AGAINST VIET CONG.[12]

As the war intensified throughout 1963, this policy could not hold up. A band of young correspondents (Neil Sheehan of UPI, Malcolm Browne of AP, David Halberstam of the *New York Times,* Charles Mohr of *Time*) reported again and again that Americans were indeed fighting in Vietnam—and losing.

Such articles were not popular back home. President Kennedy suggested that the *Times* replace Halberstam. Mme. Ngo Dinh Nhu, in the midst of a good-will tour of the U.S., commented that the reporter "should be barbecued and I would be glad to supply the fluid and the match." [13] The *Times* resisted both proposals, and Halberstam remained in Vietnam. Charles Mohr was not so fortunate. *Time* freely altered the sense of his dis-

patches, and eventually published a special article charging the Saigon press corps with "helping to compound the very confusion that it should be untangling for its readers at home." [14] Mohr immediately quit his job in protest, and later moved to the *Times* himself.

Halberstam and Mohr were part of a small minority. Most of the reporters in Southeast Asia acted more as mail carriers than as journalists. They faithfully delivered to their readers the messages of U.S. diplomatic and military sources. Many depended heavily on the daily government briefings and propaganda sessions—the famous "Five O'Clock Follies." Some never got out into the field at all.

Dependence on official sources was, in fact, the great sin of the media throughout the mid-1960s. Consider the following statements from Defense Secretary Robert McNamara:

1962: "There is no plan for introducing combat forces into South Vietnam."

1963: "We have every reason to believe that [United States military] plans will be successful in 1964."

1964: "Reliance on military pressure upon the North would not be a proper response."

1965: "We have stopped losing the war."

1967: "Substantial progress has been achieved on virtually all fronts—political, economic, and military." [15]

Some of these statements were errors in judgment. Some were probably outright lies. In either case, the vast majority of reporters in Vietnam knew better—but very few of them saw fit to set the record straight.

In November of 1967, the government undertook a supreme effort to reassure the American people about Vietnam. Ambassador Ellsworth Bunker and General William Westmoreland were put on public display. Westmoreland described the situation as "very, very encouraging"; Bunker spoke of "steady progress" and declared that two-thirds of South Vietnam was now under control. A scant two months later came the highly successful Tet offensive against the South.

The media had quoted Westmoreland and Bunker verbatim. They never forgave President Johnson for making them (as well as himself) look foolish. Though the government's "credibility gap" had opened long before, it was only after Tet that the gap was mentioned frequently in the press. From

1968 on, coverage of the war in Southeast Asia grew more and more aggressive, independent, and critical.

To read the American press before Tet, U.S. forces in Vietnam had no deserters, no racial conflict, no drug problem, and no crimes or atrocities. It is a comment on the Saigon press corps that even after Tet, when many "unreportable" stories were beginning to receive coverage, the news of the My Lai

---

TELEVISION IN VIETNAM

Vietnam was television's war—the first time in history parents have watched their sons suffer and die on the six o'clock news. Not that there was much suffering and dying to be seen. In the interests of decency and propriety, the networks managed to present a uniquely antiseptic picture of modern warfare. We saw flag-draped coffins loaded onto helicopters with all due pomp and ceremony—not headless G.I.s in plastic bags. Yet despite the trivialization of violence (and the inevitable oversimplification of issues), television did bring the war home.

Before the Tet offensive, broadcasting (like the rest of the media) docilely accepted the official version of events in Vietnam. On many occasions filmclips that seemed to contradict that version were simply dropped from the nightly news. And documentaries were uniformly patriotic, with perhaps a three-minute interview with Senator Fulbright to acknowledge the existence of "responsible dissent."

All that changed after Tet. The following excerpt from the CBS Evening News of June 27, 1970, is in many ways typical of Vietnam broadcast reporting in the early 1970s. The Cambodian invasion has just ended, a party is underway, and Morely Safer is interviewing a young American soldier on his way out:

> Safer: What was the morale like in the field among the men?
> Soldier: It was pretty bad. These clothes, I've had these clothes on for about 40 days now. We can't get clothes. We can't—mail is slow, it's pretty bad. There were a lot of people killed, and a lot of people were sad. Why this [party] at the end, you know? We're supposed to forget about it, something like that.
> Safer: A lot of men smoking marijuana. Was that common in your outfit?
> Soldier: Pretty common, I'd say. Just about everybody I know smokes marijuana in my outfit. There is nothing else to do.
> Safer: But the beer flows on and the band plays on and the girls are sympathetic and cheerful in that sweet, hometown way. . . . This attempt by the Army to put a nice neat World War II finish to the war in Cambodia makes for very good, very appealing propaganda pictures, but as one tanker asked me as we arrived here back at Katum, who's paying for all those ghosts we left behind? Morely Safer, CBS News, at Katum on the Cambodian border.[16]

If you opposed the war and distrusted the government, this was interpretive reporting at its finest. But even those who supported the war and the government—and deplored Safer's coverage—were forced to admit that at long last television had begun to speak its mind.

massacre first broke as a result of the independent efforts of Seymour Hersh, a freelance writer working out of Washington.

Vietnam was an undeclared war, and so outright censorship played only a minor role. The underground press was free even to support North Vietnam without federal prosecution. Individual correspondents were free to write what they pleased. To be sure, uncritical reporters had an easier time hitching rides to the front, and found their sources more cooperative when they got there. Harassment of the most bitter war critics was common. But on the whole, the government had little use for censorship in Vietnam. It lied instead. It lied to the reporters, and it lied to the public.

And when (as frequently happened) the lies of the authorities were contradicted by events in the field, an embargo was placed on all reporting of those events. The most flagrant embargo came during the invasion of Laos in 1971. For six days, the media were forbidden to report any events taking place on the Laos-Vietnam border. Afterward, the Associated Press wrote:

> The U.S. Command in South Vietnam has placed an embargo on certain news from the northern part of the country. Embargoes are nothing new in Vietnam, but available information indicates the one imposed last week is the strictest yet seen. . . .
>
> In this case, officials informed newsmen of the embargo but prohibited them from mentioning it and did not brief them until later—thus, in effect, placing an embargo on the embargo. . . .[17]

The embargo quite clearly had nothing to do with national security. Its goal was to forestall public protest against widening the war. But the Nixon administration claimed that national security was at stake, and without exception the media went along with the embargo. Though opposed to the war, they were unwilling to second-guess the president on a question of national security. Bay of Pigs all over again.

Later in 1971, a former Defense Department consultant delivered to the *New York Times* a top-secret government report on U.S. Vietnam policy-making throughout the 1960s. The report documented the war's "credibility gap" in fantastic detail, revealing many discrepancies between official policies and official statements. Despite its top-secret status, the *Times* decided to publish the report. A temporary injunction forbidding publication was fought before the Supreme Court, which granted the *Times* the right to publish (see pp. 149–50).

The significance of the Pentagon Papers (as the report came to be called) is twofold. On the one hand, the incident represents an unsuccessful government attempt at precensorship of the press—a hallmark of authoritarian control. Perhaps more important, it represents a decision by the nation's foremost newspaper to reveal the wartime secrets of the government. The *Times* determined to its own satisfaction that the Pentagon Papers contained little or nothing damaging to American national security. Although the Pentagon hotly disputed this conclusion, the *Times* stood firm on its opinion and published the report. The lesson of Bay of Pigs was beginning to take hold.

In January, 1973, after months of private negotiations, an "Agreement on Ending the War and Restoring Peace in Vietnam" was signed in Paris. The Paris accords did not bring peace to Southeast Asia. The wars in Vietnam and Cambodia continued, and the United States continued to supply military aid. But as American soldiers came home, American interest in the war as a war waned. Vietnam became a political story.

By the time the Paris accords were signed, public support for past Vietnam policies was almost nonexistent, and public debate over current Vietnam policies was widespread. Opponents of the war within the government could now be counted on for nearly daily revelations, and the media were free to report these revelations without concern for national security. In July, 1973, for example,

THE ANDERSON PAPERS

In late 1971, India and Pakistan went to war. Presidential adviser Henry Kissinger soon assured the media that the Nixon administration was neutral. He was lying. In the secret councils of government, Kissinger pressed successfully to "tilt" American policy in favor of Pakistan. He sought to transfer arms from Jordan to Pakistan while claiming that the U.S. was not supplying weapons to either side. And an American carrier task force was sent to the Bay of Bengal, not to evacuate Americans but to divert Indian ships and planes.

The truth came out as the war neared its end. Minutes of several secret White House meetings on the subject were leaked to syndicated columnist Jack Anderson, who used them as the basis for a series of columns exposing America's real foreign policy toward the war. On January 5, 1972, Anderson settled the question of his accuracy by releasing some of the secret documents to the wire services and to seventeen newspapers.[18]

Anderson said that at first he was "cautious, even timid" about the story. He did not want to publish U.S. military secrets while the war was still being waged. But he decided after some thought that the secrets in question did not pose a military danger, only a political and diplomatic embarrassment. The documents should not have been classified secret in the first place, Anderson believed. He told his staff: "Let's publish all we can get until the government adopts a sensible policy on classification."[19]

In short, Anderson determined that it should be his responsibility, not the responsibility of the government, to decide whether revealing Kissinger's India-Pakistan policy was a threat to American national security. And unlike the Pentagon Papers, the documents that Anderson revealed were not history. They concerned the current, clandestine foreign policy of the United States government.

---

the Senate Armed Services Committee began an investigation of charges that the U.S. had secretly begun its bombing raids into Cambodia in 1969, when that country was still officially neutral. The media joined Congress in pressuring the Defense Department to reveal the truth—that some 3,500 secret bombing raids had occurred during the fourteen-month period before the United States sent combat troops into Cambodia.

Similarly, in 1975, news coverage of the collapse of the Thieu regime and the evacuation of the last Americans from South Vietnam was characterized by a nearly total disregard for traditional considerations of national security and national self-image. Apparently convinced that there was no legitimate American national interest left in Southeast Asia, the media reported what they saw with total candor, and what they were told with considerable skepticism.

THE INTELLIGENCE APPARATUS

The Central Intelligence Agency was founded after World War II to improve the quality and quantity of information available on the plans of foreign governments. It is the organization that sent U-2 spy planes over the Soviet Union and helped plan the Bay of Pigs invasion of Cuba. For many years it was considered "untouchable" by most American reporters. Throughout the 1950s and 1960s, the media generally accepted the government position that almost any news story about CIA activities would endanger the national security of the United States.

Journalistic skepticism about the CIA grew enormously during the Vietnam conflict, as reporters discovered bits and pieces of various CIA exploits in Southeast Asia. But the story remained untouchable until Watergate. When it was learned that several Watergate

ISRAEL CONTROLS WAR NEWS

Over the long history of Arab-Israeli conflict, most foreign correspondents came to consider Israel a more reliable information source than the Arab countries. But during the first few days of the October, 1973, war, when Israel appeared to be losing, Israeli information was anything but reliable. While the Arabs provided a "barrage of information," Israeli handouts were bland and often false. Israeli leaders, for example, told the Israeli television audience that all but three Egyptian bridges over the Suez Canal had been destroyed—but when viewers turned to the Arab TV channels, they *saw* more than three bridges left standing. Not until the fourth night of the war, as the tide began to turn, did Israel begin to tell the truth.[20]

On the fifth day, Israeli reporters were allowed to go to the front lines, where they joined tank charges on the Golan Heights, missile-boat missions in Egyptian waters, and the Israeli crossing to the west bank of the Suez. When Arab TV stations celebrated the large number of captured Israeli soldiers, Israeli television countered with battle footage —plus hours and hours of extra entertainment programming. Foreign journalists—some 800 of them from more than thirty nations—were permitted to visit the Golan, where Israel had already broken the Syrian offensive, but they were not allowed near the action on the Sinai front. Unable to observe for themselves what was really happening, American journalists had no choice but to report the sharply conflicting information provided by Arab and Israeli government sources.[21]

Both Israel and Egypt practiced strict news censorship throughout the war. Israeli censors, for example, would not permit stories that Defense Minister Moshe Dayan was extremely worried during the early fighting; Egyptian censors refused to allow stories that the Egyptian Third Army had been "encircled."[22] On the whole, Israeli information was most misleading in the early days of the war, when the Arabs were making significant gains. Later, when Israel went on the offensive, Arab information proved undependable. When a country—any country—is at war and losing, accurate information, freedom from censorship, and the free movement of journalists may be too much to expect.

---

burglars had worked for the CIA in the past, and when further investigation raised the possibility that even more direct links existed between Watergate and the CIA, American journalists finally began questioning what really went on behind the closed doors of the secret spy agency.

In September, 1973, a successful coup toppled the government of Marxist President Salvador Allende of Chile. The Nixon administration insisted that the U.S. had played no role in the coup. But in April, 1974, CIA Director William E. Colby told a top-secret congressional hearing that the administration had authorized the CIA to spend more than $8 million between 1970 and 1973 for covert

activities designed to bring down the Allende government (including financial support for the Chilean opposition press). The story was leaked to the *New York Times,* and in September, 1974, the *Times* published it.[23] Ten years earlier the *Times* almost certainly would have sat on the story. But by 1974 the media were deciding for themselves what should and should not be run in the interests of national security—and they were in no mood to protect the CIA.

The *Times* article was written by Seymour Hersh, an investigative reporter who had broken the My Lai massacre story and had provided the *Times* with a number of Watergate exclusives. Now Hersh was on the CIA's trail. In December, 1974, he reported that the CIA had conducted "a massive, illegal domestic intelligence operation during the Nixon administration against the antiwar movement and other dissident groups in the United States."[24] President Ford appointed a commission to look into the agency's activities, and CIA Director Colby released a statement admitting a wide range of domestic efforts against dissenting and antiwar groups.

In March, 1975, the *Washington Star* reported that CIA Director Colby had just briefed President Ford on the extent of the agency's past involvement in plans to assassinate foreign leaders.[25] The possible role of the CIA in political assassination attempts had been perhaps the most untouchable story of the 1960s. Now even that seemed likely to come out.

Is the national security rationale for suppressing news a dead issue, then? The answer is no. For one thing, the government still has plenty of secrets that the media know nothing about. More important, the media still keep the government's secrets on occasion.

By early 1975, the *Los Angeles Times* had discovered that the CIA had contracted secretly with Howard Hughes to raise a sunken Soviet submarine in the Pacific. The attempt had been only partly successful, and most of the sub was still under water. Afraid that the *New York Times* had the story and would publish it, the Los Angeles paper ran an article in early February, but reported that the sub had been recovered in the North Atlantic instead of the Pacific. When the CIA asked the paper to kill the story, it was moved from the front page to the inside.[26]

No less than eleven American news organizations were putting together more extensive sub stories in February and March, but Colby was able to convince them to delay publication until the salvage operation was either completed or dropped. On March 18, Jack Anderson finally decided to break the story. He did so only after determining that the Soviet government already knew, and that

what was involved was "not national security but international etiquette."[27] But for many weeks, most of the nation's prestige news organizations willingly cooperated with the CIA to button up the Soviet sub story. Even in 1975, the national security argument could still be a potent and persuasive one.

But more and more, the media today reserve for themselves the right to decide what to publish and what not to publish in the interests of national security. After two centuries of letting the government make that decision for them, the media are understandably unsure about what standards to use when making it themselves. But the important point is that they *are* making it themselves. The days when government officials could safely take reporters into their confidence, secure in the knowledge that the media would honor their secrets, are over. The media must now fight for what they **know**, and must then decide what—if anything—to hold back.

Notes

1 James Reston, *The Artillery of the Press* (New York: Harper Colophon Books, 1966), pp. 20–21.

2 William McGaffin and Erwin Knoll, *Anything But the Truth* (New York: G. P. Putnam's Sons, 1968), pp. 205–209.

3 Douglass Cater, "News and the Nation's Security," *Montana Journalism Review*, 1961, pp. 2–3.

4 Frank Luther Mott, *American Journalism,* 3rd ed. (New York: Macmillan, 1962), p. 536.

5 Joseph J. Mathews, *Reporting the Wars* (Minneapolis: University of Minnesota Press, 1957), pp. 157–58.

6 Mott, *Amreican Journalism,* p. 853.

7 Erik Barnouw, *The Golden Web* (New York: Oxford University Press, 1968), pp. 77–78.

8 David Wise, *The Politics of Lying* (New York: Vintage Books, 1973), p. 56.

9 Martin Goodman, "Numbers Game," *Columbia Journalism Review,* Summer, 1965, pp. 16–18.

10 Stanley Karnow, "The Newsmen's War in Vietnam," *Nieman Reports,* December, 1963, p. 4.

11 *Ibid.,* p. 6

12 McGaffin and Knoll, *Anything But the Truth,* p. 79.

[13] Gay Talese, *The Kingdom and the Power* (New York: World, 1969), pp. 466–67.

[14] Karnow, "The Newsmen's War in Vietnam," p. 3.

[15] Bruce Ladd, *Crisis in Credibility* (New York: New American Library, 1969), pp. 167–68.

[16] Marvin Barrett, ed., *Survey of Broadcast Journalism 1969–1970* (New York: Grosset & Dunlap, 1970), pp. 145–46.

[17] Associated Press, February 5, 1971.

[18] "A Peek Behind the Scenes," *Newsweek,* January 17, 1972, p. 14. Tom Wicker, "The Anderson Papers," *New York Times,* January 4, 1972, p. 33. Jack Rosenthal, "Anderson Ready for Battle With Government, But Appears Unlikely to Get One," *New York Times,* January 6, 1972, p. 17.

[19] Rosenthal, "Anderson Ready for Battle With Government," p. 17.

[20] Philip Gillon, "Israeli TV Comes of Age," *Hadassah Magazine,* February, 1974, p. 26.

[21] *Ibid.,* pp. 26–27. Terrence Smith, "Israel's Curbs on Press Impair Her Credibility in Current War," *New York Times,* October 17, 1973, p. C15.

[22] Richard M. Smith, "Censorship in the Middle East," *Columbia Journalism Review,* January/February, 1974, pp. 44–46.

[23] Seymour M. Hersh, "C.I.A. Chief Tells House of $8-Million Campaign Against Allende in '70–73," *New York Times,* September 8, 1974, pp. 1, 26.

[24] Seymour M. Hersh, "Huge C.I.A. Operation Reported in U.S. Against Antiwar Forces, Other Dissidents in Nixon Years," *New York Times,* December 22, 1974, p. 1.

[25] "Colby Oral Fill-In to Ford on Assassination Reported," *New York Times,* March 5, 1975, p. 1.

[26] James Phelan, "An Easy Burglary Led to the Disclosure of Hughes-C.I.A. Plan to Salvage Soviet Sub," *New York Times,* March 27, 1975, p. 18. "Salvaging the Sub Story," *Newsweek,* March 31, 1975, p. 66.

[27] "Anderson Says Soviet Knew Submarine Story," *New York Times,* March 26, 1975, p. 13. Phelan, "An Easy Burglary," p. 18.

Suggested Readings

ARLEN, MICHAEL J., *Living-Room War.* New York: Viking Press, 1969.

CATER, DOUGLASS, "News and the Nation's Security," *Montana Journalism Review,* 1961.

EMERY, EDWIN, "The Press in the Vietnam Quagmire," *Journalism Quarterly,* Winter, 1971.

GOULDING, PHIL G., *Confirm or Deny.* New York: Harper & Row, 1970.

LADD, BRUCE, *Crisis in Credibility.* New York: New American Library, 1969.

MARCHETTI, VICTOR L., and JOHN D. MARKS, "Uncovering the CIA," [*MORE*], April, 1974.

MATHEWS, JOSEPH J., *Reporting the Wars.* Minneapolis: University of Minnesota Press, 1957.

McGAFFIN, WILLIAM, and ERWIN KNOLL, *Anything But the Truth.* New York: G. P. Putnam's Sons, 1968.

THE NEW YORK TIMES, *The Pentagon Papers.* New York: Bantam Books, 1971.

NIMMER, M. B., "National Security Secrets vs. Free Speech: The Issues Left Undecided in the Ellsberg Case," *Stanford Law Review,* January, 1974.

RESTON, JAMES, *The Artillery of the Press.* New York: Harper Colophon Books, 1966.

SCHLESINGER, ARTHUR, JR., "The Secrecy Dilemma," *New York Times Magazine,* February 6, 1972.

"Vietnam: What Lessons?" *Columbia Journalism Review,* Winter, 1970–71.

WISE, DAVID, *The Politics of Lying.* New York: Vintage Books, 1973.

As long as there has been an America, there have been racial, ethnic, economic, and sexual groups that the American mass media ignored or mistreated. Chief among these today are blacks. In recent years the media have improved greatly in their coverage of blacks and other oppressed groups, but they still have a long way to go. Public indifference to the plight of minorities is both reflected in and exacerbated by media performance.

In July of 1967, in the middle of a long, hot summer of ghetto riots, President Lyndon B. Johnson appointed the National Advisory Commission on Civil Disorders. Headed by Governor Otto Kerner of Illinois, the commission was charged with the task of determining why blacks were rioting in the streets. Its final report placed a good deal of the blame on the mass media:

The media report and write from the standpoint of a white man's world. The ills of the ghetto, the difficulties of life there, the Negro's burning sense of grievance, are seldom conveyed. Slights and indignities are part of the Negro's daily life, and many of them come from what he now calls "the white press"—a press that repeatedly, if unconsciously, reflects the biases, the paternalism, the indifference of white America.[1]

The Kerner Commission argued forcefully that the media alternately ignore and abuse the black community. White readers are not forced to come to grips with the problems of the ghetto and their own bigotry. Blacks are afforded little opportunity to make known their grievances and lifestyles. Two separate and unequal societies are thus perpetuated, with little communication between them. Unable to make themselves heard in any other way, blacks take to the streets. Uninformed about the realities of ghetto life, whites are surprised. And so are the media, which ought to have known better.

MINORITY MEDIA

Minority groups have always been discriminated against in this country—by American society in general and by the American mass media in particular. Denied access to the majority media, and in many cases unable to understand the language of the majority media, ethnic minorities have traditionally organized their own. Though they could not speak to the WASPs, they could at least speak to each other.

The first foreign-language newspaper in America, the *Philadelphia Zeitung,* was founded in 1732. By 1914, the height of American immigration, there were more than 1,300 foreign-language publications in the country. The German press led the list, followed by the French, Italian, Japanese, Polish, Yiddish, and Scandinavian. War, depression, and assimilation soon took their toll. In 1970, according to *Editor & Publisher,* there were only 232 regularly published foreign-language newspapers in the United States.

The foreign-language media exist for the unassimilated, for ghetto groups that are still not a part of mainstream America. Today, this means primarily the Spanish-speaking—the Puerto Ricans and Cubans in the East, the Mexican-Americans in the West. *El Diario,* for example, is a Spanish-language tabloid daily in New York City, with the biggest circulation of any foreign-language publication in the country.

How is *El Diario* different from other New York City newspapers? One 1968 analysis found the following:

> *El Diario* showed 50% Latin orientation on its front page, 46% on its "important" news pages, 78% in its inside news space, and 75% of its sports space. In addition, *El Diario,* on occasion, added a Latin slant to its coverage of essentially nonethnic news items. . . .
>
> What this means quite simply is that the Puerto Rican butcher, baker and taxi driver in New York City is reading, more often than not, different news than that read by his *New York Daily News*-reading counterpart. He, a member of the minority, is not reading much of the news read by the majority of New York City newspaper readers.[2]

Miami, like New York, supports a thriving

Spanish-language media system, including two daily newspapers (*Diario Las Americas* and *Miami Extra*) and five radio stations. It is also a center for Spanish-language magazine publishing. *Replica,* a newsmagazine that circulates 70,000 copies a week in the U.S. and Latin America, is printed in Miami and New York. *Vanidades,* the biggest women's magazine in Latin America, is printed in Miami as well as several Latin American cities. *Buenhogar,* also a women's magazine, is published in Miami. Many Miami newsstands carry essentially the same publications as newsstands in Mexico City and Santiago de Chile.[3]

Black Americans speak English. Unlike many Mexican-Americans and Puerto Ricans, they can read the white media. But they find so little there of relevance to their lives that they support a second, independent system of black media as well.

The first Negro newspaper in America was *Freedom's Journal,* founded in New York in 1827. More than twenty others, mostly devoted to the slavery issue, were established before the Civil War. Untypical but indicative was the case of one Willie A. Hodges, who in 1847 sought to have his opinions published in the *New York Sun.* He was told that if he wanted to see his ideas in print he would have to print them himself. So he did, in a newspaper he called the *Ram's Horn.*[4]

From 1850 to 1975, nearly 3,000 Negro publications were founded in the United States. Most were short-lived, but some survived for generations, exercising a tremendous influence on the development of the black community. Among the most successful were the *Chicago Defender* (1905), the *New York Amsterdam News* (1909), the *Pittsburgh Courier* (1910), and the *Norfolk Journal and Guide* (1911). Like most black papers, these four emerged from the inner-city ghetto. But they were really national newspapers, available at ghetto newsstands across the country.

Thomas W. Young of the *Journal and*

Guide explains the influence of these papers during the early 1900s:

> By the turn of the century, second-class citizenship had become a hard reality for the Negro. . . . As the grievances against this status began to mount, it was the Negro press that aired them and thus became the chief vocal agency for the protest. These newspapers were more than just protest organs. Because news of Negro progress and aspirations was effectively quarantined by the general press, Negro newspapers became also the chroniclers of contemporary life and activities in their segregated world. . . . Even while waging that battle, many Negro newspapers developed into substantial, successful commercial ventures.[5]

In 1945, the *Pittsburgh Courier* boasted a circulation of 250,000. The *Chicago Defender* (202,000) and the *Baltimore Afro-American* (137,000) were close behind. Whites and blacks alike considered the editors of these papers to be the leaders of the Negro community. Presidents Roosevelt and Truman read the papers almost as faithfully as the typical ghetto black. Gunnar Myrdal could justly comment in his book, *An American Dilemma,* that "the Negro press . . . is rightly characterized as the greatest single power in the Negro race." [6]

Today, there are about 200 black-owned newspapers in the U.S., roughly the same as in 1945. But the *Courier*'s circulation has dropped to around 60,000, and the *Defender* has suffered a similar readership decline. Presidents no longer pay much attention to these newspapers, nor does the black American look to them for leadership.

What happened? Economics are part of the answer. Rising costs have forced most black newspapers to abandon their national editions and curtail even their home editions. Competition is another piece of the problem, especially competition from black-oriented radio stations. But more important than either of these is the failure of the Negro press to keep pace with the black revolution.

John Murphy, publisher of the *Afro-American,* explained: "Newspapers are small businesses and publishers are businessmen. Surely you'd have to describe black publishers as conservatives, I suppose. In earlier years, black newspapers were spearheads of protest. Today we're much more informational." The former publisher of the *Amsterdam News,* C. B. Powell, agreed: "We have not kept up with the black revolution. But you've got to realize that we don't see our role as leaders. We are not out to revolutionize. When the *Amsterdam News* sees issues that are too revolutionary, we speak out against them." [7] In 1971, the *Amsterdam News* and Harlem radio station WLIB were purchased by a group of black business and political leaders, including Manhattan Borough President Percy Sutton. Adopting the red, green, and black colors of black nationalism, the *Amsterdam News* began moving away from its conservative image. One member of the separatist Nation of Islam commented, "It tried to look more black than it really was." [8]

WASSAJA

In 1973, shortly after militant Indians occupied the Washington headquarters of the Bureau of Indian Affairs, the American Indian Historical Society began publishing a twenty-four-page monthly newspaper. Entitled *Wassaja* (Yavapai for "the signal"), the newspaper is consistently critical of the federal government's policies toward Indians. "Communications is the desperate need among Indians," explains Jeanette Costo, head of the society's publication division, the Indian Historical Press. "Indian people around the reservations don't know what's going on, and the BIA occupation brought this out. There were different stories and no one knew what were the facts." [9]

The point is not that the black press has turned suddenly conservative. Rather, most black newspapers have changed very little over the past few decades. They still feature crime and sensationalism on page one, black sports and black society on the inside pages. Meanwhile, the "movement" around them has been changing constantly—from civil rights and freedom someday to Black Power and Freedom Now! Black publishers are at best ambivalent about the change. A young reporter in Chicago comments:

> Look, man, you get tired of brothers and sisters bugging you on the street because your paper isn't with The Movement. You know, one day our paper looks like it might be getting with it and the next day it sounds like the Trib [the highly conservative, white, *Chicago Tribune*].[10]

Little wonder, then, that the best-read black newspaper in the country today is *Muhammad Speaks*, with a circulation of more than 400,000. Together with the *Black Panther* and a number of local anti-Establishment papers, *Muhammad Speaks* stands in the forefront of the revolution. Though some traditional black newspapers like the *Amsterdam News* are moving toward militancy, they still look rather conservative next to *Muhammad Speaks*.

While the national circulations of tradi-tional black newspapers have all but dis-appeared, national black magazines have de-veloped giant readerships. John H. Johnson founded *Ebony,* a black picture magazine similar to *Life,* in 1945. *Ebony* now has a 1,250,000 monthly circulation, and the John-son empire has grown to include *Jet, Tan,* and *Black World.* A black newspaper supple-ment, *Tuesday,* was founded in 1965, and by 1970 had a circulation of more than two million.

In the mid-1960s, most black magazines were as conservative as the traditional black newspapers. Since then, many have been forced to radicalize their content in order to retain their standing in the black com-munity. Still, they tend to shy away from hard political news and commentary, lean-ing instead toward the cultural "Black is Beautiful" side of the revolution. For exam-ple *Essence,* a women's magazine with the slogan "subscribe to blackness," specializes in fiction, fashion, and beauty. Its columns show an awareness and acceptance of black militancy, but they do not generally report or promote it.

Advertising is the lifeblood of the Amer-ican media, and the black press is no excep-tion. For many decades the vast majority of the ads in the black media were for special-ized black-oriented products. But by the 1970s, many mainstream companies had dis-

---

MOTOWN

The rise of Motown is the black media success story of the 1960s and 1970s. Berry Gordy, Jr. founded the Detroit-based record company with an $800 loan. He went on to discover Diana Ross and the Supremes, Martha and the Vandellas, and Stevie Won-der; and with them he created a distinct sound: "Motown." In 1973, Motown Industries had sales of more than $46 million. In 1974 *Black Enterprise* named Motown as the big-gest black-owned and black-managed business in the U.S.

Motown Records is still the heart of the company, but three other divisions are now earning additional profits. Jobete Music publishes music. Multi-Media manages enter-tainers. And Motown Productions put together six television specials between 1968 and 1974. It also produced the "Jackson Five" cartoon series, and *Lady Sings the Blues,* a feature film that earned five Academy Award nominations and grossed over $8.5 mil-lion.[11]

covered the purchasing power of black Americans. In 1972, *Ebony, Jet, Essence, Tuesday,* and *Black Enterprise* (the five biggest black magazines) boasted a combined circulation of more than five million, and a total of 166 pages of advertising per issue.[12]

When white companies want to reach black consumers, are the specialized black media the best place to advertise? Bill Castleberry, president of the largest black advertising agency in the country, thinks the answer is yes—and his agency, Zebra Associates, has $4.1 million in 1974 billings for support. Zebra designs and places black-oriented ads for such manufacturers as Gillette, Schenley, Gulf Oil, and General Foods. Castleberry explains why these companies come to him: "Basically, industry is beginning to fully appreciate that marketing to blacks requires a distinct approach. It is an understanding of the black purchaser's 'predisposition' to a product based on his background, culture and environment that justifies our existence." [13]

But a much larger advertising agency, Young & Rubicam, told its clients in 1972 that advertising in black newspapers and magazines was not worth the cost. While the battle rages, most experts agree that black newspapers get less than their share of the advertising pie. Black radio, on the other hand, does very well.[14]

Black radio is clearly the most successful medium today in speaking to the black community. With rare exceptions, however, that medium does not speak *for* the black community. As many as 530 commercial radio stations in the country program "the soul sound," but no more than about 30 of them are black-owned.[15] Even that figure represents progress; the number of black-owned stations more than doubled from 1965 to 1975. In the typical black-oriented radio station of the 1960s, only the disc jockeys and the janitors were black. Though employment opportunities have improved in recent years, there are still very few black managers with real decision-making power.

New York Times writer Fred Ferretti describes the programming of one black-oriented station:

> A black disc jockey—paid far less than white counterparts on larger stations, and with less chance of advancement—may play an Aretha Franklin record, then in "down home" accents assert that the record undoubtedly "made your liver quiver and your knees freeze." Then he will segue into a frantic plug for a Top Forty rock number before playing the record—deafeningly. On the hour, news will consist of a piece of wire copy ripped from a teletype, and read verbatim by the same disc jockey. Required public service time will be filled mainly by pseudo-evangelist hours. And commercial sponsors will be sought willy-nilly, without sifting the "dollar-down, dollar-a-week forever" entrepreneurs from the non-deceptive advertisers.[16]

It seems almost unnecessary to add that aside from providing an outlet for black music, this sort of programming is of little use to the black community. But there is some reason for hope. The Black National Network (owned and operated by blacks) now offers hourly news feeds to black-oriented radio stations around the country, and in 1974 it began planning the first black wire service.[17]

The real tragedy of the minority media is that they need to exist at all—that the mainstream media have been unable or unwilling to meet the needs of minorities. Almost as tragic is the fact that so many minority media have failed to serve their own communities. The minority media speak to the people, but few speak for them.

COVERING THE REVOLUTION

The history of white coverage of blacks prior to 1954 is brief and undistinguished. From time to time a movie or radio drama would feature a black character (almost always stereotyped as a bumbling, laughable menial). And newspapers and magazines carried their share of hard news about black criminals and features about black athletes. For the most part that was it for the Negro.

Then, in 1954, the Supreme Court announced its school desegregation decision and the modern civil rights movement was born. As far as the white media were concerned, it was a virgin birth—the movement came out of nowhere, with no hint of long-standing grievances. Arthur B. Bertelson of the *St. Louis Post-Dispatch* describes the rude awakening:

> At first, we self-consciously proffered tidbits with a heavy coating of soothing syrup. We dredged up sticky little features about those few Negroes who had made it. . . . In our news columns, God forgive us, we quoted those "leaders" who counseled the Negro community to be patient, that we were all good fellows, that all would be well before they knew it.
>
> When it became obvious that [the civil rights movement] wasn't going to assimilate this kind of pap, some of us began to try a little harder and discovered that what was required was a steady diet of raw—and, more often than not, unpalatable—truth.[18]

The "truth" as served up by the nation's newspapers and TV stations told of blacks valiantly struggling for their freedom from Southern oppressors. Reporters on the so-called "seg beat" were sent south for months at a time. They were horrified by what they saw, and their sense of outrage permeated their stories.

After a burst of gunfire stitched holes in a University of Mississippi doorsill, *Newsweek* reporter Karl Fleming turned to a companion and said, "You know, if I were Meredith, I wouldn't go to school with these bastards." [19] Millions of *Newsweek* readers experienced the same revulsion. So did anyone who watched television or read a newspaper.

From *Brown v. Board of Education* in 1954 to the Watts riot of 1965, the civil rights movement was centered in the South. The Northern media (which means the national media) did a commendable job of covering

that movement. It was an easy story to cover —the heroes and villains clearly identified, the whole mess conveniently far away. Throughout the decade, those very same media managed to ignore completely the festering sores of their own local ghettos. Civil rights reporters invaded Mississippi and Alabama by the hundreds, but only an occasional crime writer bothered to visit Harlem, Watts, or Hough.

The Southern media didn't have it so easy. The violence was in their own back yard; the challenge was to their own way of life. On the whole, they acquitted themselves well. Ted Poston, later a reporter for the *New York Post,* wrote:

> There have always been, and there still are, some fine and courageous Southern papers. As a native Kentuckian, I was reared from my earliest days on the *Louisville Courier-Journal.* As a college student, Pullman porter, and dining-car waiter, I received a valuable adjunct to my education through the *Nashville Tennessean,* the *Atlanta Constitution,* the *St. Louis Post-Dispatch,* and other pillars of liberal journalism in the South.[20]

Ralph E. McGill of the *Constitution* and Harry S. Ashmore of the *Little Rock* (Ark.) *Gazette* both won Pulitzer Prizes for their coverage of Southern racial unrest.

After the Watts riot of 1965, the focus of the story moved north. And the media discovered all over again that black people were big news. Newspapers and broadcast stations moved mountains in a frantic effort to cover the tragic succession of riots, demonstrations, and confrontations that characterized the last half of the 1960s. The job they did was less than perfect (see Chapter 16), but in a casualties-and-damage sense it was better than adequate.[21] By the time other groups— chicanos, Indians, white ethnics, etc.—began asserting their views militantly in the late 1960s and early 1970s, the media had become very skilled at covering minority conflict, and at ignoring minorities when there was no conflict.

To be sure, racial confrontation has not always received fair and ample treatment in the media. Local activist leaders are sometimes ignored by local papers and stations. Peaceful demonstrations are dismissed in a few sentences, or are made to look violent. Police sources are taken at their word, even when directly contradicted by minority witnesses. And events of tremendous significance are downplayed or misplaced. In 1968, three black students were shot and killed by police in Orangeburg, South Carolina. The media barely mentioned the incident. Two years later, when four white students were killed at Kent State University, the story filled front pages for days.

Nevertheless, media coverage of the facts of minority unrest has been magnificent in comparison with coverage of the grievances that underlie that unrest. As the Kerner Commission report stressed again and again: "The Commission's major concern with the news media is not in riot reporting as such, but in the failure to report adequately on race relations and ghetto problems. . . ." [22]

COVERING MINORITY LIFE

There are three criticisms frequently voiced about media coverage (and noncoverage) of black people. First, the media have failed to make clear to white people the problems, frustrations, and tensions of the ghetto. Second, the media frequently exhibit bias or racism in their approach to black news. And third, the media have ignored the everyday life of the black person, the "good news" that comes out of the ghetto.

We have said enough already about the first criticism. As a rule, the media are much better at covering a crisis after it arrives than they are at seeing it on the way. The racial crisis of the 1960s was no exception. As long as the black community kept its suffering and anger to itself, the media were content to leave well enough alone. Only after the inevitable explosion did they suddenly wake to the issue of race. And even then, they con-centrated on the explosion itself, devoting far less time and space to the underlying grievances.

The charge of racism is a hard one to document. In 1968, black militants in Oakland, California, organized a boycott of a white-owned ghetto shopping center. In response, the *Oakland Tribune* printed a cartoon of a gloved hand pointing a pistol at the reader. "What would *you* do in a case like this?" asked the caption. "Think it over carefully because soon you may have to decide whether you want to run a business with a gun to your head or close up shop." Two black reporters resigned in protest, charging *Tribune* publisher William Knowland with racism.[23] At best, the cartoon seems a rather extreme response to the time-honored pressure tactic of a boycott.

Oakland, by the way, is fast becoming a black-majority city, as white middle-class residents flee to the suburbs. The *Tribune* may well flee right along with them, expanding its suburban coverage and cutting down on inner-city reporting. The *Detroit News,* among other papers, has already taken this step. The reasons may well be economic; advertisers are most interested in the wealthy suburbs. But from the viewpoint of the ghetto resident, at least, it looks like racism.

More often than not, racism in the news media is unconscious and indirect, a result of uncomprehending white reporters' failure to understand an unfamiliar culture. Robert E. Smith of *Newsday* offers a few examples: [24]

- The *New York Times,* in an article on President Johnson's farewell to a group of high-ranking black government officials, carefully referred to "the well-dressed Negro officials and their wives."

- Under a photo of two black baseball stars, the *Detroit News* ran the caption: "Here Come de Tigers!"

- An ABC network documentary forgot at least 10 percent of its audience when it had the narrator intone: "We don't know what it's really like to grow up as a black."

THE MOST OPPRESSED MINORITY

There are more than 24 million poor people in the United States. Over 16 million of the poor are white, and almost half of the poor whites live in rural areas. Only 4.3 million poor blacks live in central cities. Anyone who finds these facts surprising has been cheated by the mass media.

When the media imply, as they often do, that poverty is uniquely a problem of urban blacks, they make themselves vulnerable to two serious charges—the charge of racism from the black community, and the charge of indifference from the poor nonblack community.

Why do the media ignore the needs and interests of poor people? The simple, economic answer is that poor people have very little to offer the media in return. Poor people spend more time watching television than the general population, but they buy less—and so TV ads and programs are aimed at the middle class. For the same financial reason, newspapers and magazines try to attract middle-class readers and avoid poor ones. It is true that poor people read fewer newspapers and magazines than the general public, but the difference isn't huge; 75 percent of all low-income families subscribe to a newspaper.[25] Yet there have been many more news stories published about welfare cheats and vandalism in public housing than about how to apply for welfare or housing assistance.

Poor people are the most oppressed minority group in the United States. The media, by and large, cover poverty in a way that confirms the prejudices of their middle-class audience. They do very little to help that audience understand the social impact of poverty in America. And they do almost nothing to help the poor in their struggle for a bigger share of the nation's affluence.

- A *Newsday* article on three black members of a prestigious government committee noted with some wonder that they were "well-educated, articulate, and middle class."

- In the wake of a disturbance, the *Tampa Tribune* headlined the startling fact that "Sunday Night Racial Rioting Had At Least One Negro Hero."

Smith adds that the media often refer to black racism as "reverse discrimination." It is reverse, of course, only from the white point of view. Similarly, a frequent media response to racial unrest is a plea for a "return to normal," which to the black ghetto-dweller presumably means a return to poverty and frustration. On a more trivial level, Smith points out that reporters refer to black athletes by their first names far more often than white athletes. This is, perhaps, a gen-

teel and well-intentioned sort of racism, but it is racism nonetheless.

The third criticism is in many ways the most important. It is almost a prerequisite for white acceptance of blacks that the everyday reality of black living, the good and the bad, be made clear to white people. It is also essential to black self-acceptance (and black pride) that this everyday reality be portrayed by the media. As the Kerner Commission put it: "It would be a contribution of inestimable importance to race relations in the United States simply to treat ordinary news about Negroes as news of other groups is now treated." [26] The Commission went on to specify the need for black content in newspapers, magazines, movies, radio, television, and advertising.

The print media have made the least progress of all. Even today, newspapers seldom carry much in the way of black club news, black society, black engagements and marriages, even black obituaries. And when a black civic group plans a dance, say, or opens a youth club, it is extremely unlikely to get much publicity from the white press. The same goes for magazines. On April 19, 1968, *Life* gave tremendous play to the murder and funeral of Dr. Martin Luther King. The King story featured the only black faces to be found anywhere on the pages of that issue.

The blackout of "good" news about blacks sometimes goes even further. For many years the *Jackson Daily News* Relays were the most publicized track-and-field meet in Mississippi. In 1968, the relays were reluctantly integrated. In 1969, black athletes won many events, but their pictures were not printed in the *Daily News*. In 1970, rather than face the dilemma again, the paper canceled the meet entirely.

Film and broadcasting have a somewhat better record. From *Gone With the Wind* to *Guess Who's Coming to Dinner* was a big step for the movies, and from *Shaft* to *Sounder* and *Lady Sings the Blues* was an even bigger one (see pp. 343–45). The same

change was reflected on television—from black menial to black super-hero to black human being. In 1970, actor Bill Cosby, formerly of "I Spy" (a super-hero show), inaugurated his own comedy series, in which he played an average schmo who just happened to be black. By 1970, also, blacks had begun appearing as journalists in TV news shows, and as consumers in TV commercials. These were major achievements for television.

The early 1970s saw further progress. Flip Wilson starred in a highly successful variety show, and "The Autobiography of Miss Jane Pittman" was acclaimed as one of the finest programs ever seen on TV. Perhaps more important are series programs such as "Sanford and Son," "Good Times," and "The Jeffersons." Though some critics complain the shows are stereotyped, they deal regularly, if superficially, with real economic and social problems, and they all feature characters who are proud to be black. They are enormously popular with black audiences, and earn good ratings with white audiences as well.

COMMUNITY NEWS SERVICE

The Community News Service was established in 1970 to provide consistent coverage of minority affairs in New York City. Staffed mainly by black, Puerto Rican, and other minority journalists (many of whom receive their training on the job and move on to mainstream media), CNS distributes five or six stories a day. Its list of subscribers includes the *New York Times,* the *Daily News, Newsweek,* WCBS-TV, WNBC-TV, and WNET—as well as such specialized media as *New York Age* (a black weekly) and *El Tiempo.*

CNS naturally covers outbreaks of racial hostility, sometimes before the rest of the media discover them. It was the first, for example, to report the occupation of a New York hospital by a militant Puerto Rican group. But a typical batch of CNS stories is likely to stress lifestyles and issues more than such incidents—a conference on early childhood education, a health carnival, an anti-drug rally, a high school sports event, an African culture festival, a special report from the CNS Washington or United Nations correspondent, etc.

As of 1974, just over half of CNS's revenue came from subscribers; the rest was supplied by grants from the Ford Foundation and others. But Ford was planning to end its aid in 1975, and unless CNS can find help elsewhere, this vital source of minority news and important training base for minority reporters may be forced to close its doors.[27]

But change does not come easily. Still living in the 1960s (or perhaps the 1860s) are eight Southern stations that in 1974 refused to carry the ABC network presentation of "The Wedding Band," a play about the marriage of a black woman and a white man. And while light entertainment flourishes, black-oriented public-affairs programs are still few and far between. "Sanford and Son" is no substitute for solid news and documentary coverage of minority issues.

As we have seen, it took a series of violent confrontations to force the media to pay even scanty attention to black grievances and black lifestyles. What about other minority groups?

There are 6.3 million Mexican-Americans in the United States; the more than two million who live in California comprise that state's largest ethnic minority. There have been chicano entertainers and movie stars—

Delores Del Rio and Ramon Novarro, Anthony Quinn and Ricardo Montalban, Trini Lopez and Vikki Carr. But for the most part, the media image of Mexican-Americans has been less than positive. Says TV critic Dwight Newton: "On movie screens, and later television screens, they were pictured as loiterers, loafers, cowhands, revolutionaries, assassins, bad guys." [28] And in the news, of course, they were ignored.

Little wonder, then, that the chicano organization Nosotros (founded by Montalban) objected strenuously to the corn chip advertising campaign featuring the "Frito Bandito." Most stations self-righteously resisted the pressure, but a few agreed to eliminate the ads, and eventually the advertiser abandoned the character.

Since the Los Angeles disruptions of 1970 and 1971, chicanos are beginning to get some serious attention in the news media.

CHALLENGING BROADCASTERS

A minority organization that believes a local broadcast station has failed to serve the needs of minorities is entitled to ask the FCC to take away the station's license. Since the mid-1960s, well over a hundred minority groups have done precisely that. In a couple of cases they actually succeeded in getting the FCC to act. In 1975, for example, the Commission refused to renew the Alabama state government's educational TV license, because the state-run stations had too few black employees and too little black-oriented programming. [29]

But more frequently what minority groups have won is a deal (see pp. 218–21). In response to license-challenge threats from local citizen groups, all but six of Atlanta's twenty-eight radio and TV stations agreed to employ more blacks. WNBC and WABC in New York promised to provide regularly scheduled black-oriented programming. McGraw-Hill pledged to hire more Mexican-Americans at the four television stations it was about to buy, and to run more Mexican-American programming on the stations. When faced with the possibility of a reasonable challenge from an organized minority, most broadcasters would rather make concessions than fight for the license.

Minority protests also take many forms short of the license challenge. Jewish groups have objected to showings of The Merchant of Venice, and a Polish group fought to keep QB VII off the air. The script for a "Marcus Welby, M.D." episode concerning the rape of a 14-year-old boy by an older man was sent to the National Gay Task Force for comment. The group refused to suggest changes, and argued instead that the program should not be shown at all. When ABC decided to modify the script and go ahead, homosexual organizations began putting pressure on local stations. At least two stations in major markets agreed not to carry the episode. [30]

Once again, it took a disruption to capture that attention.

The same familiar sequence of events is beginning to affect the media's treatment of Native Americans. According to movies and television, nineteenth-century Indians were savage warriors, and twentieth-century Indians are incompetent drunks. White storytellers rewrote American history to make Indians the villains, then hired white actors to play the parts. Only after Native American groups began taking over buildings and towns in the 1970s did the media begin taking Indians seriously. In recent years there have been a few thoughtful films about Indian history and Indian reality, occasionally with Indian actors in the major roles. As for news, the demonstrations and confrontations were well-covered, of course. They were the first news about Indians that most white Americans had ever seen. If the black experience is any guide, it will take constant prodding to keep the media from forgetting once again that Native Americans exist.

Whatever minority group you examine, the pattern is the same. American entertainment uses minority groups for comic relief, while American news ignores them. Only when frustration explodes into violence do the media wake up. Then they cover the violence in news, tone down the stereotypes in entertainment, and go back to sleep if they can. It takes constant pressure to keep the media focused on the grievances and lifestyles of American minorities.

WOMEN AND THE MEDIA

Women are the largest "minority" group in the United States. In fact, with something over 50 percent of the population, they are not a minority group at all—but you'd never know that from studying the media.

Since the nineteenth century, there have been specialized mass media in this country that catered to the women's market. Special magazines, special sections of newspapers,

and special daytime TV shows are designed to capture the attention of women—but until the 1970s these media were rarely designed to serve the needs of women (see pp. 466–67).

Women's magazines, for example, have traditionally pictured their audience as fashion-conscious ladies, compulsive housewives, or devoted mothers. These were essentially the only roles for women the magazines were willing to discuss. But with the spectacular success of *Ms.* in the early 1970s (see p. 285), more traditional women's magazines began to change. *Cosmopolitan* now runs articles like "How To Make A Man's Pay," in addition to its usual fare such as "The Poor Girl's Guide to America's Rich Young Men" and "Women, Men and Kinky Sex." [31] And *Redbook,* which used to call itself "The Magazine for Young Mamas," now boasts that it is "The Magazine of the New Management." The changes are less than many feminists want, but at least most women's magazines have stopped putting down women who are employed outside the home. And more and more of the magazines are running occasional articles to meet the practical needs of working women and the intellectual and political interests of women of all sorts.

The women's section of the typical newspaper used to contain no news—only recipes, fashions, beauty and homemaking tips, wedding and engagement announcements, society features, and advice columns. These are still the staples of the section, even though most papers have now changed its name to something like "Family Life" or "Life Styles." But some progress is being made. Many women's sections today run frequent profiles on local women who have thought, said, or done interesting things. This is an important first step, publicly acknowledging that women *do* think, say, and do interesting things. The next step, which a few papers have begun to take, is running serious features on such topics as day care, abortion, divorce, and sex discrimination. And if newspaper women's editors ever begin taking responsibility for hard news stories on these topics, the women's

SEX AND LANGUAGE

A society's language reflects its values and its history. The language of American society is sexist.

In the late 1960s, feminist groups began an all-out assault on sexist language in the media. So far, the campaign has had only modest success. Many editors who willingly acknowledge that sex discrimination is an important social issue balk at changing "Miss" and "Mrs." to "Ms.", or substituting "Congressperson" for "Congressman," or cluttering their sentences with phrases like "he or she" and "his or her." They insist that the media should follow conventional language usage, not try to change or create it. They stand firm for conciseness and against awkwardness. In response, feminists argue that taking the sexism out of language is not just a symbolic achievement, but also a way of raising people's consciousness about the sexism in American society.

In 1974, the McGraw-Hill Book Company came up with a suitable compromise. In sixteen pages of "Guidelines for Equal Treatment of the Sexes in McGraw-Hill Book Company Publications," the publisher suggests changes like the following:

Instead of	Use
the fair sex, the weaker sex	women
lady lawyer, lady doctor	lawyer, doctor
authoress, poetess, usherette	author, poet, usher
libber	feminist, liberationist
mankind, manmade, manpower	human beings, manufactured, workers
the best man for the job	the best person for the job
businessman, salesman, mailman, cameraman, fireman	business executive, sales representative, mail carrier, camera operator, fire fighter
the average American drinks his coffee black	most Americans drink their coffee black, the average American drinks coffee black
chairman	chair, head, coordinator

Essentially, the McGraw-Hill guidelines attempt to keep assumptions about sex out of the language. They don't insist on obtrusively anti-sexist writing, but they do insist on getting rid of obtrusively sexist writing. Thus it is probably acceptable to refer to "Congressman Bob Jones" because we know Jones is a man. But "write your Congressman" should become "write Congress," or "write your Senator and Representative." In McGraw-Hill's view, it is almost always possible to avoid sexism without resorting to awkward phrases like "write your Congressperson."

The guidelines also urge authors to put an end to sexual stereotyping. Books designed for children, for example, should show married women who work outside the home as well as those who don't. Both men and women should be depicted as cooking, cleaning, fixing things, washing the car, etc. Both sexes should be portrayed as sometimes independent, courageous, and decisive; sometimes aggressive and insensitive; sometimes thoughtful, loving, and intuitive; sometimes fearful and illogical.[32]

section will have achieved an important breakthrough.

Daytime television soap operas are still full of traditionally stereotyped women, but they're increasingly full of professional women and serious issues as well. Free-lance writer Beth R. Gutcheon reports:

> There are more women doctors, lawyers, writers, judges, nurses, District Attorneys and corporate executives on daytime television than were ever dreamed of on prime time. . . . There is also more consistent, serious effort to deal sensitively with the red-hot issues of the day, from abortion to homosexuality, than is ever seen on prime time, except in occasional documentaries.[33]

Women's magazines, women's newspaper sections, and daytime television are not all that they should be—but in their treatment of women they are miles ahead of the rest of the media.

Film, for example, is almost totally dominated by a male perspective (see pp. 345–46). Even the list of movie super-stars, which was evenly divided between men and women in the 1930s, today includes mostly men. Molly Haskell sums up the change in the title of her 1974 book, *From Reverence to Rape: The Treatment of Women in the Movies*.[34] She notes that for the most part "the great women's roles of the decade are whores, quasi-whores, jilted mistresses, emotional cripples, drunks. Daffy ingenues, Lolitas, kooks, sex-starved spinsters, psychotics, Icebergs, zombies. . . ."[35] Since very few women are employed as movie producers, directors, or writers, this stereotyping of female film characters is not likely to improve.

Prime-time television, on the other hand, is improving—slightly. It has moved from zany, imbecile housewife Lucille Ball to zany, imbecile public-interest lobbyist Karen Valentine. In all fairness, TV series like "All in the Family" and "Maude" have occasionally dealt with serious women's issues such as breast cancer and abortion. But prime-time TV entertainment has a long way to go.

Advertising has even longer. The National Airlines "Fly Me" stewardesses play amateur prostitutes, while the detergent commercials picture homemakers as work-numbed drudges who need a man in a lab coat to tell them how to get the grease out (see pp. 356–57). Yet even advertising is slowly succumbing to change. A 1974 study found a decline in the number of ads that used women as sex objects,[36] and at least one hairdye commercial now implies that the product will help viewers land a job, not a husband.

The image of women in media entertainment and advertising is a critically important topic, because it will undoubtedly be reflected in society's attitudes toward women ten and twenty years from now. Equally important, and even more important in the short term, is news coverage of issues of special relevance to women. And the media's track record in this area is dismal.

Both in broadcasting and in newspapers, hard news is the almost exclusive province of men. Female reporters and editors handle mostly feature stories. With men firmly in charge of the hard news, one of two things is likely to happen to an event that involves a "women's issue"—abortion, sex discrimination, child care, etc. The story may be given to a female reporter, who will know she's expected to keep it soft and featury. Or it may be covered by a male reporter, who will inevitably accord it the length and treatment that his own socialization and values dictate. Either way, the story is not likely to wind up as a front-page blockbuster.

When the National Organization for Women challenged the license of WABC-TV in 1972 (see pp. 219–20), it stated that the New York station's "Eyewitness News" did not even report the passage of the Equal Rights Amendment by Congress.[37] Most activists in the feminist movement can recall similar lapses on the part of local stations and papers.

In this sense, the response of male reporters to the women's movement is noticeably different from the response of white reporters to the black movement. The mainstream media ignored black people until they started organizing for action—but once the action began the media quickly acknowledged that it was newsworthy. News coverage of black activism hasn't always been accurate, but it has been extensive and serious. The problem has been to get the media to cover the grievances behind the activism, and the lives and lifestyles of the black community. By contrast, the media responded to feminist activism by stepping up their coverage of background issues and lifestyles—but they continue to downplay the activism itself. The media, it seems, take minority movements seriously, but not yet minority lives or minority issues; they are beginning to take women's lives and women's issues seriously, but not yet the women's movement.

EMPLOYMENT

One of the most obvious signs of racism in the media—and one of the most important reasons that racism has survived so long—has been the ludicrously small number of minority reporters. The 1968 Kerner Commission report hit this point hard:

> The journalistic profession has been shockingly backward in seeking out, hiring, training, and promoting Negroes. Fewer than 5 percent of the people employed by the news business in editorial jobs in the United States today are Negroes. Fewer than 1 percent of editors and supervisors are Negroes, and most of them work for Negro-owned organizations. . . . News organizations must employ enough Negroes in positions of significant responsibility to establish an effective link to Negro actions and ideas and to meet legitimate employment expectations.[38]

Spurred on by the commission, the mass media began searching frantically for minority reporters. Not surprisingly, they found few blacks or Hispanics with both the interest and the training; no one had ever bothered to encourage the former or provide the latter. At a California Newspaper Publishers Association convention in the early 1970s, one talented black college junior was extended half a dozen firm job offers, while his white counterparts were informed that money was tight and jobs were scarce. The black student was forced to turn down all his offers; he had already accepted one from a Northern California television station.

This frenzy of recruiting activity raises several questions. First, is it legitimate or is it tokenism? There is reason to suspect the latter. For one thing, the very media that have scurried to hire a black or two have been extremely reluctant to support large-scale journalism training programs for minorities. And they have hesitated to place their minority employees in policy-making positions.

Consider the following incident from the late 1960s. Ben Gilbert, then city editor of the *Washington Post,* received a telephone call from a *New York Times* executive. How many blacks had the *Post* hired, he wanted to know, and where did it find so many? Gilbert told him that the *Post* had twelve, and then asked how many blacks the *Times* employed. "Three," came the response, "but we won't lower our standards."[39]

Tokenism or not, minority employment in the media improved significantly in the early 1970s. According to one study, an astounding 72 percent of all new employees hired by commercial television stations between 1971 and 1974 were members of minority groups. That's an impressive figure, but consider it in the context of two other figures. Roughly 20 percent of America's TV stations have yet to hire their first minority person. And in 1974 minorities still constituted only 9 percent of commercial television's managerial, professional, technical, and sales personnel—a big improvement over 1971's 6 percent, but well below the proportion of minorities in the big cities where many stations are based.[40]

The number of minorities employed by commercial radio, noncommercial broadcasting, and the print media also increased in the early 1970s—but much more slowly.

Media employment of women has improved as well. In 1971, 22 percent of the employees of commercial television stations were women, but only 6 percent of the stations' managers, professionals, technicians, and salespeople were women. Over the next three years, women comprised 58 percent of all newly hired employees. This raised the proportion of women in the higher job classifications to 11 percent in 1974.[41]

Newspapers have hired women for years—but mostly as secretaries and women's-page writers. This, too, is changing. In early 1975 there were more than 20,000 female journalists working for American newspapers, and an increasing number of them reported to the city editor, not the feature editor or the women's editor. Daily newspaper top management in 1975 included some 680 women; an additional 226 women were employed as editors, managing editors, city editors, news editors, or associate editors; and thousands more worked as subeditors in various departments.[42]

No matter which of the mass media you look at, the pattern is pretty much the same. Women and minorities are moving into entry-level professional positions in increasing numbers. In time, if the pressure keeps up, their representation in the media may begin to approach their representation in the audience. It will take even more time, and more pressure, for women and minorities to move into managerial positions. For now and for the immediate future, policy-making in the media is still very much a white, male domain.

And employment of women and minorities is still an issue. The media deserve a lot of credit for their efforts to make up for past employment inequities, but it is important to remember that these efforts came only in the face of pressure—pressure from government agencies and commissions, pressure from citizen groups, and pressure from minority and women's caucuses within the media. By the mid-1970s, many publishers and broadcasters seemed genuinely committed to affirmative action. But it still *takes* affirmative action; equal employment of women and minorities does not come automatically.

In 1974, William Ewald of Pocket Books boasted of the paperback industry's progress in the employment of women. "It's where the action is," he said, "and a lot of young bright women have gone into it because there's a lot of room to swing around in. It's not calcified the way some of the hardcover business is." True enough, but the analysis of Bantam Books Senior Editor Nancy Hardin strikes deep: "It's nice that those women are there, and it's nice that attention is being paid to them, but it would be nicer still if it were just taken for granted that exceptional women had exceptional jobs." [43]

Discrimination in employment is usually considered an issue of social justice. Women and minorities have a legal and moral right to their fair share of jobs in the media. But employment in the media is not only a matter of justice; it is also a matter of coverage. The way the media treat minorities and women in entertainment, advertising, and news is inevitably a product of the sorts of people who work for the media. Black screenwriters, Mexican-American advertising executives, and female reporters are a good deal less likely than their nonminority male counterparts to continue the sorts of coverage problems we have been discussing in this chapter.

What then, should minority and female reporters be doing once they're hired? When the *Washington Post* hired its first black reporter in 1952, it was careful to assign him only nonracial stories, where his presence and copy would stir up no controversy. But during the riots of the late 1960s, many newspapers found that their white reporters were ineffective in the ghetto. When these papers got around to hiring their first black, they naturally assigned him or her to the "civil rights" beat.

Most minority reporters today devote a significant percentage of their time to minority news. Many are glad to do so. But others object to this form of segregation. Says one veteran: "I would want to be hired as a newsman, not as a Negro. . . . I want to feel that if the civil rights problem ended in the morning, I'd still have a job to do. . . . On the job, I try to be a mirror. I talk to somebody and he starts talking about niggers. I don't correct him. I take it down. I just want to be sure I spell it right." [44]

For female reporters the question is especially puzzling. The media have traditionally assigned women to "women's stories"—soft features on food, fashion, and the like. Professional progress for a female reporter has meant moving from the women's section to the front page, where she could cover the same stories as everyone else. But now that newspapers and broadcast stations are slowly beginning to cover the feminist movement and the issues that underlie the movement, should female reporters take over that specialty? Or should they avoid it?

Ideally, of course, minorities and women ought to be covering all kinds of stories, both those that do and those that do not concern race and sex. But ours is not an ideal world. The biggest contribution minority and female journalists can make today is to help their papers and stations do what they should have been doing long ago—covering minorities and women completely, fairly, and sensitively.

Notes

[1] *Report of the National Advisory Commission on Civil Disorders* (Kerner Commission) (New York: Bantam Books, 1968), p. 366.

[2] David Sachsman, "Two New York Newspapers," unpublished paper, Stanford University, 1968, p. 11.

[3] "Miami Gets New Spanish-Language Newspaper," *New York Times*, August 4, 1974, p. 14.

[4] Jack Lyle, ed., *The Black American and the Press* (Los Angeles: Ward Ritchie Press, 1968), p. 3.

[5] Thomas W. Young, "Voice of Protest, Prophet of Change," in Paul L. Fisher and Ralph L. Lowenstein, eds., *Race and the News Media* (New York: Anti-Defamation League of B'nai B'rith, 1967), pp. 127–28.

[6] L. F. Palmer, Jr., "The Black Press in Transition," *Columbia Journalism Review*, Spring, 1970, p. 31.

[7] *Ibid.*, pp. 33–34.

[8] George Goodman, Jr., "Sutton, the Media Man, Stirring Controversy," *New York Times*, October 11, 1972, p. 45.

[9] Wallace Turner, "Paper for Indians Is Issued on Coast," *New York Times*, February 15, 1973, p. 11.

[10] Palmer, "The Black Press in Transition," p. 34.

[11] Robert A. Wright, "The Dominant Color Is Green," *New York Times*, July 7, 1974, p. F3.

[12] "Black Market," *Newsweek*, July 17, 1972, p. 71.

[13] Daniel L. Lionel, "Black-Owned Newspapers Favored by Zebra Agency," *Editor & Publisher*, January 4, 1975, p. 16.

[14] "Black Market," p. 71.

[15] Paul Delaney, "Blacks Start Bid on Cable TV Role," *New York Times*, October 8, 1973, p. 68. Jerry Buck, "Blacks Own Few Radio Stations," *Palo Alto* (Calif.) *Times*, April 8, 1970, p. 21 (Associated Press).

[16] Fred Ferretti, "The White Captivity of Black Radio," *Columbia Journalism Review*, Summer, 1970, p. 35.

[17] Charlayne Hunter, "Blacks to Start a News Service," *New York Times*, October 7, 1974, p. 27.

[18] Arthur B. Bertelson, "Keeper of a Monster," in Fisher and Lowenstein, *Race and the News Media*, pp. 61–62.

[19] Ray Jenkins, "Open Season in Alabama," *Nieman Reports*, March, 1965, p. 8.

[20] Ted Poston, "The American Negro and Newspaper Myths," in Fisher and Lowenstein, *Race and the News Media*, p. 64.

[21] Fisher and Lowenstein, *Race and the News Media*.

[22] *Report of the National Advisory Commission on Civil Disorders*, p. 382.

[23] "Is Oakland There?" *Newsweek*, May 18, 1970, p. 100.

[24] Robert E. Smith, "They Still Write It White," *Columbia Journalism Review*, Spring, 1969, pp. 36–38.

[25] Bradley Greenberg and Brenda Dervin, "Mass Communication Among the Urban Poor," *Public Opinion Quarterly*, Summer, 1970, pp. 224–35.

[26] *Report of the National Advisory Commission on Civil Disorders*, p. 385.

[27] Gerald Astor, *Minorities and the Media* (New York: Ford Foundation, 1974), p. 21. M. L. Stein, "Reporting from the Ghettos," *Saturday Review*, November 13, 1971, p. 95.

[28] Dwight Newton, "A Minority Seldom Seen," *San Francisco Sunday Examiner and Chronicle*, February 14, 1971, p. B4.

[29] "Alabama Educational TV Denied License Renewal," *New York Times*, January 9, 1975, p. 71.

[30] John J. O'Connor, "Pressure Groups Are Increasingly Putting the Heat on TV," *New York Times*, October 6, 1974, p. D19.

[31] Stephanie Harrington, "Ms. Versus Cosmo: Two Faces of the Same Eve," *New York Times Magazine*, August 11, 1974, p. 11.

[32] "Guidelines for Equal Treatment of the Sexes in McGraw-Hill Book Company Publications," New York, 1974 (pamphlet). "'Man!' Memo From a Publisher," *New York Times Magazine*, October 20, 1974, pp. 38, 104–108.

[33] Beth R. Gutcheon, "Look for Cop-Outs on Prime Time, Not on 'Soaps,'" *New York Times*, December 16, 1973, p. D21.

[34] Molly Haskell, *From Reverence to Rape: The Treatment of Women in the Movies* (New York: Holt, Rinehart and Winston, 1974).

[35] Anatole Broyard, "From Star to Satellite," *New York Times*, March 5, 1974, p. 31.

[36] Philip H. Dougherty, "Female Role in TV Spots Studied," *New York Times*, November 14, 1974, p. 82.

[37] George Gent, "Women's Group Challenges WABC-TV's Renewal," *New York Times*, May 2, 1972, p. 87.

[38] *Report of the National Advisory Commission on Civil Disorders*, pp. 384–85.

[39] Jules Witcover, "Washington's White Press Corps," *Columbia Journalism Review*, Winter, 1969–1970, p. 44.

[40] Les Brown, "Women and Minority Groups Increase Again in TV, Study Shows," *New York Times*, December 2, 1974, p. 66. Ralph M. Jennings and David A. Tillyer, *Television Station Employment Practices: The Status of Minorities and Women* (New York: Office of Communications, United Church of Christ, 1973).

[41] Brown, "Women and Minority Groups Increase Again," p. 66.

[42] Robert U. Brown, "New Job Vistas for Women," *Editor & Publisher*, February 1, 1975, p. 32.

[43] Eric Pace, "In the Paperback Field, It's Getting to Be a Women's World," *New York Times*, February 12, 1974, p. 28.

[44] Witcover, "Washington's White Press Corps," p. 46.

Suggested Readings

ASTOR, GERALD, *Minorities and the Media*. New York: Ford Foundation, 1974.

BOGLE, DONALD, *Toms, Coons, Mullatoes, Mammies, and Bucks: An Interpretive History of Blacks in American Films*. New York: Viking Press, 1973.

DUNBAR, ERNEST, "Notes from the Belly of the Whale," [*MORE*], April, 1972.

FEDLER, FRED, "The Media and Minority Groups: A Study of Adequacy of Access," *Journalism Quarterly*, Spring, 1973.

FERRETTI, FRED, "The White Captivity of Black Radio," *Columbia Journalism Review*, Summer, 1970.

FISHER, PAUL L., and RALPH L. LOWENSTEIN, eds., *Race and the News Media*. New York: Anti-Defamation League of B'nai B'rith, 1967.

GREENBERG, BRADLEY, and BRENDA DERVIN, "Mass Communication Among the Urban Poor," *Public Opinion Quarterly*, Summer, 1970.

HASKELL, MOLLY, *From Reverence to Rape: The Treatment of Women in the Movies*. New York: Holt, Rinehart and Winston, 1974.

HOWARD, PAMELA, "Watch Your Language, Men," [*MORE*], February, 1972.

JENNINGS, RALPH M., and DAVID A. TILLYER, *Television Station Employment Practices: The Status of Minorities and Women*. New York: Office of Communications, United Church of Christ, 1973.

LONG, MICHELE L., and RITA J. SIMON, "The Roles and Statuses of Women on Children's and Family TV Programs," *Journalism Quarterly*, Spring, 1974.

LUBLIN, JOANN S., "Discrimination Against Women in Newsrooms: Fact or Fantasy?" *Journalism Quarterly*, Summer, 1972.

LYLE, JACK, ed., *The Black American and the Press*. Los Angeles: Ward Ritchie Press, 1968.

"'Man!' Memo From a Publisher," *New York Times Magazine*, October 20, 1974.

PALMER, L. F., JR., "The Black Press in Transition," *Columbia Journalism Review*, Spring, 1970.

Report of the National Advisory Commission on Civil Disorders (Kerner Commission). New York: Bantam Books, 1968.

SMITH, ROBERT E., "They Still Write It White," *Columbia Journalism Review*, Spring, 1969.

STRAINCHAMPS, ETHEL, ed., *Rooms With No View: A Woman's Guide to the Man's World of the Media*. New York: Harper & Row, 1974.

WITCOVER, JULES, "Washington's White Press Corps," *Columbia Journalism Review*, Winter, 1969–1970.

Chapter 19
Coverage
of
Specialized News

The front pages of American newspapers are filled with news of national and local government, of crime and violence, of wars and racial problems. Little room (and little time) is left for more specialized kinds of news. In areas like foreign affairs, science, environment, consumer protection, education, and labor, only the most sensational stories are likely to reach the public. Often these are not the most important ones.

Different topics become "important" in the mass media for different reasons. Some are well covered because of their obvious and direct impact on the audience—urban riots, for example. Others, such as minor crimes and human-interest features, receive extensive treatment because the audience finds them absorbing, because they are easy to cover, or because they are traditional media staples.

A topic that embodies all these sources of appeal is bound to dominate the news. A battle, for example, is exciting to watch or read about and clearly important to know about; it is a traditional news item and a relatively easy one to report. Battles are likely to be well covered.

The reverse is also true. Topics that are new to the media, or difficult to report, or uninteresting to the audience, usually receive short shrift in our news. Such topics, unfortunately, are often very important.

FOREIGN AFFAIRS

When editors compare notes on audience response, they often disagree on which kinds of news are the most popular—sports, comics, politics, or what. But when it comes to the least popular kind of news, they are unanimous. Foreign affairs takes the palm, hands down.

As evidence of audience apathy, editors may point to any of a number of studies. A typical one, conducted in 1953, found that the average adult read only twelve column inches of foreign news a day, spending roughly 140 seconds doing so. When the readers were asked if they'd like to see more international news in the papers, only 8 percent answered yes. Fourteen percent had no opinion, and 78 percent said definitely not.[1]

Little wonder that most editors have cut their foreign news to the bone. There are exceptions, of course. The *New York Times* gives over 20 percent of its news hole to international affairs, and the *Christian Sci-*

ence Monitor devotes nearly 40 percent of its space to foreign news. But the figure for the average daily paper is less than 8 percent. And the figure for most broadcast news operations is lower still.

Besides public indifference, editors have another good reason for downplaying foreign news: It is difficult and expensive to cover. A good foreign correspondent needs special training in the culture, politics, and language of the country (or more likely the countries) he or she is to cover. But journalists with such training command higher salaries—not to mention the added costs of food, lodging, and "hardship pay" for an American forced to live and work overseas. Just to make matters worse, the host country may impose severe restrictions on where the reporter may travel and whom the reporter may interview. Stories may be censored to the point of uselessness; the reporter may even be kicked out of the country entirely. It seems a lot of trouble to go to for an article that nobody will read anyhow.

War zones aside, there are fewer than 500 full-time American journalists abroad. The wire services have the largest foreign staffs, and supply the vast majority of the international news in the American media. Only a half-dozen newspapers (notably the *New York Times)* have more than one or two reporters overseas. So do the three television networks and a handful of magazines. The typical local newspaper or broadcast station, of course, has no foreign staff at all.

On the whole, American foreign correspondents are topnotch reporters, skilled and experienced in their trade. The swashbuckling loner of movie fame has pretty much disappeared. Leo Bogart notes that the modern overseas reporter "works as part of a bureau team, and . . . is rooted to his station by long residence, an established family life, and a comfortable income." [2]

Nevertheless, 500 reporters spread over an entire world make a thin network. True, they are aided by hundreds of part-timers, freelancers, and foreign nationals working as stringers. But on the other hand, they are heavily concentrated in Western Europe, and spend most of their time reporting the same stories. England, France, and Germany are reasonably well covered. Not so Ethiopia, Finland, and Guyana.

Nearly all the foreign news that reaches the American public falls into one of three categories. In order of importance, these are: the political, the sensational, and the colorful.

Political news is the most common largely because it is the easiest to gather. Government officials are happy to explain their viewpoint, and to supplement the explanation with handouts and other documents (many of them already translated into English). Local newspaper reports, which often reflect official government thinking, are another important source. The opposition stance, of course, is harder to find and more dangerous to report. Many reporters are content to make do without it.

Sensational news is popular with reporters because it is popular with readers. "For the A wire," writes a former AP bureau chief in Colombia, "I file earthquakes, student riots, general strikes, assassination attempts, and plane crashes. These I send 'urgent' if a reasonable number of people have been killed. For the regional and secondary news wires I include items about coffee, oil—Texas is most interested—and banditry." [3]

Colorful news is prized for its human-interest value, though it may give little insight into the people it describes. Typical topics include Japanese geishas and African hitchhikers. Often these items have a strong American angle: "Hot Dogs Big Hit in Iran" or "Bolivians Find New Uses for Saran Wrap."

Often, of course, the categories are combined. When President Nixon visited China in 1972, the story was obviously political. But the media—especially the networks—had made big plans for covering the visit, and there wasn't enough political hard news to fill the allotted time and space. Nor could reporters find anything sensational to cover.

CHAUVINISM

Four-fifths of all U.S. foreign correspondents, according to one study, believe their reports should not be influenced by American foreign policy.[4] This is an admirable stance —but also a somewhat naive one. Reporters are people, and so they inevitably carry a built-in nationalistic bias. So do editors and publishers—and for that matter so do readers. The bias is expressed in the kinds of countries reporters get assigned to, in the kinds of stories they choose to write, and in the kinds of information they include in the stories. There is no more reason to trust an American journalist writing about Cuba than a Cuban journalist writing about America.

In a classic study of the *New York Times,* Walter Lippmann and Charles Merz documented this bias with respect to the Russian Revolution. Most Americans, and hence most American reporters, wanted Bolshevism to fail. Between 1917 and 1919, therefore, the *Times* reported no less than ninety-one times that the new Soviet government was about to fall. The authors termed this "a case of seeing not what was, but what men wished to see." [5] The Lippmann-Merz conclusion is as valid today as it was in 1919.

British journalist Alexander Cockburn argues that Americans overseas must write so as "to confirm existing prejudice, rather than contradict it." His advice to aspiring foreign correspondents on "How To Earn Your Trench Coat" is cynical, stressing the use of clichés:

> The proper adjectival adornment for leaders is a vast and complex subject. If he is one of our dictators then use words like *dynamic, strong man, able.* He *laughs* a great deal, is always *on the move, in a hurry.* He *brushes impatiently aside* questions about franchise and civil liberties: "my people are not yet ready for these amenities you in the West feel free to enjoy. . . ." If, on the other hand, he is one of *their* dictators, then use words like *unstable, brooding, erratic, bloodthirsty, indolent.* He seldom ventures out of his palace unless under *heavy guard.* He is *rumored to be ailing.* Oddly enough he is often *charismatic.* At the moment it is particularly dangerous to use any adjectives about Arab leaders. Stick to general concepts in this case, like *converted to Western ways* or *deeply religious.*[6]

Even if reporters were able to shed their free-world bias, few editors or readers would appreciate the change. A reporter who learned "to float free and almost denationalize himself," writes Christopher Rand, "would be rushed home to be reindoctrinated." [7]

So they resorted to colorful travelogs, generally trivial anecdotes, and often flimsy attempts at interpretation. "One after another," commented *Newsweek*'s Joseph Morgenstern, "the networks' brightest news stars popped up with hundred-year-old egg on their faces." [8]

SCIENCE AND MEDICINE

A survey conducted in 1958 revealed the startling fact that 37 percent of newspaper readers read all the medical news available to them, and 42 percent wanted more. For nonmedical science news both figures stood at 28 percent—considerably higher than the percentages for crime news, national politics, and other "popular" topics.[9]

So what happened? Did editors immediately increase the amount of science and medical news in their papers? They did not. The average newspaper today devotes just under 5 percent of its news hole to science and health. So did the average newspaper in 1958. The average broadcast station allots an even smaller piece of its news time to science and medicine. The weekly newsmagazines do considerably better, but for really complete information you have to read a few specialized publications—*Scientific American, Psychology Today, Popular Science, Science Digest, Today's Health,* etc.

Why have editors ignored what looks like a public mandate for more science news? Money is part of the answer. A skilled science writer must have at least a little training in science; such people are·hard to find and expensive to hire. Most metropolitan papers already have one science writer (as do the wire services, the newsmagazines, and the TV networks). They are reluctant to look for another.

But there is a more fundamental answer. Editors simply don't believe the public really wants more science news. The science that now appears in the papers, they point out, is a very special kind of science: the sensational, the colorful, the halfway-political, plus an occasional monumentally important discovery. Of course the readers like that kind of stuff. But would they really go for the more everyday scientific advances? Most editors think not.

The national space effort was the big science story of the 1960s. It was handled, not as a complex scientific project, nor even as a controversial political one, but rather as an exercise in chauvinism and fantasy. The National Aeronautics and Space Administration was the only available source of information, and its experts literally taught science writers the ABCs of space. NASA's press releases and "information kits" were always voluminous, always enthusiastic, and always careful to conceal any and all problems. The U.S. space effort was the subject of more fan writing and less investigative reporting than the baseball World Series.

Then came the Apollo fire. In January, 1967, three astronauts died during a routine test of their capsule. James A. Skardon wrote in the *Columbia Journalism Review:*

The Apollo fire brought reality with shocking suddenness. It destroyed the fairy-tale aspects of the space program, riddled the carefully contrived NASA success image, and exposed the performance of NASA, its prime contractors, and the press itself to public examination.[10]

Hindsight tells us that Skardon was over-optimistic. The tragic incident was soon forgotten, NASA lived through the scandal, and the public lost interest in space exploration only after the first American set foot on the moon. Mission accomplished.

This show-business approach to science news is more the rule than the exception. When Dr. Christiaan Barnard of Cape Town became the first surgeon to perform a successful heart transplant, the mass media turned him into an instant celebrity. The medical and legal complications of the story were almost ignored, as was the fact that twenty surgical teams around the world were ready to perform the same operation. *Time* gleefully put Dr. Barnard on its cover, and reported that his daughter was a champion water-skier. CBS brought him to America to appear on "Face the Nation," and NBC was shocked to learn that he would not allow it to film the next operation. Instead, NBC paid thousands of dollars for exclusive rights to the life story of Philip Blaiberg, Dr. Barnard's second patient.[11]

Most front-page science and health stories still share this sensational, uncritical approach. But in the 1970s, some observers detected a trend toward more interpretive, more skeptical coverage of the social and ethical implications of science and technology. Gee-whiz science articles began giving way to more balanced examinations of benefits and dangers, discoveries and disagreements. David Perlman of the *San Francisco Chronicle* provided this capsule summary: "Basic science down. Medicine same. Public impact of science way up. Health care politics way up. 'Relevant' science up." [12] In 1974, filmmaker Frederick Wiseman illustrated—and perhaps advanced—the trend with a public television documentary on animal behavior research. Entitled "Primate," the documentary studied one group of scientists as closely as the scientists were studying the apes and monkeys in their experiments. In the process, commented reviewer Chuck Kraemer, Wiseman exposed "their callousness, their obsessiveness, the little games they play with one another and with their funding foundations, and, most revealingly, their peculiarly narrow view of life in general." [13]

The trend is real, but it does not yet constitute a revolution in news about science and medicine. The breast cancer surgeries of Betty Ford and Happy Rockefeller in 1974 provided the hard-news peg the media needed to cover this important disease thoroughly. Medical reporter Jane Brody of the *New York Times* commented that "this was the best thing that could have happened to the women of America." [14] But of course it shouldn't require the illness of famous people to get the media to cover cancer. And even in the spate of stories that accompanied the Ford and Rockefeller surgeries, reporters paid relatively little attention to the raging debate over the extent of surgery required in most breast cancer cases.

While front-page science news moves slowly from sensational enthusiasm to thoughtful interpretation, inside stories usually resort to a light human-interest angle instead. Veteran science writer Frank Carey lists some of the stories he has covered:

> Scientists found that even the mighty dinosaurs had rheumatoid arthritis . . . Researchers came close to isolating the sex-lure chemical by which the female German cockroach calls her boy-friend to a date . . . Proof was established at long last that women are broader in the derriere than men . . . Gout sufferers could take heart in the finding that their ailment apparently is a hallmark of genius . . . Wise men at a famous laboratory ran a six-day cocktail party for mice and found that, as with men, there are "social drinkers" and teetotallers among them, not to mention a few real souses. . . .[15]

While specialists like Carey are busy with these items, many genuinely significant (but unromantic) science stories go unreported.

ENVIRONMENT

In June of 1969, ABC commentator Edward P. Morgan addressed a journalism conference at Stanford University. "In the 1950s," he mused, "reporters covered the cold war in depth, but they missed completely the civil rights movement and the racial crisis of the 1960s. What crisis of the 1970s, I wonder, are the mass media failing to report now?" Morgan then answered his own question: environmental deterioration.

Almost immediately afterwards, the news media suddenly discovered the environment. Maybe it was the Santa Barbara oil spill and the sight of seabirds covered with goo. Perhaps it was the sudden environmental interest of major political figures like Senator Edmund Muskie and President Richard Nixon. Possibly editors across the country finally got fed up with commuter traffic, smog, junkyards, and skyscrapers. Whatever the reasons, there is no doubt that after decades of neglect the subject of the environment was suddenly glamorous.

There are at least six reasons why the media ignored the environment for so long, and why they still do not cover it as well as they might.

1. Until recently there has been no environmental group powerful enough to fight for press coverage. The popular image of the Sierra Club or Audubon Society is that of an ineffectual, fluttery bird-watcher. Only in the 1970s did strong local pressure groups develop, capable of making environmental news and forcing the media to cover it.

2. The short-run economic interests of the media favor unbridled industrial growth and environmental exploitation. On the one hand, advertisers dislike articles on the need for pollution-control (especially if they name the polluters). And on the other hand,

growth—however uncontrolled—means more readers and higher advertising rates. It takes a courageous publisher or broadcaster to bite the hand that feeds.

3. The environmental story is seldom a visible one. Air and water pollution, DDT and mercury poisoning, the population explosion—these are all stories that build up slowly, imperceptibly, from day to day. There is no specific news event, no press conference, no handout on which to hang the story. A reporter cannot interview a lake and ask if it's dying; until the lake is nearly dead, there is seldom *anyone* to interview.

4. For reporters with little background in chemistry, biology, and the like, the environmental story is next to impossible to cover. Without special training, reporters are at the mercy of their sources, who often have good reason to hide the truth. As Roberta Hornig of the *Washington Star* has said, "every story is like taking a college course." [16]

5. Unless it is approached with imagination and flair, an environmental article can be deathly dull—full of facts and figures, chemicals and gadgets, measurements and more measurements. Many editors made it

a policy not to run such stories on their front page—or not to run them at all.

6. Environmental news is inherently interdisciplinary. A good environmental reporter must master not only the scientific technicalities of the beat, but also its political, social, cultural, and economic ramifications. A science writer can't handle it alone; neither can a business writer or a political writer.

In the early 1970s, environmental news coverage was as extensive as one could reasonably expect. Was it effective? Certainly the media succeeded in alerting people to the threat of environmental deterioration, in adding "environment" to the public's list of pressing national problems. But environmental news tended to two unfortunate extremes—doomsday stories about unsolved and apparently unsolvable crises, and upbeat stories about corporate and government successes. The former tended to depress the audience, while the latter tended to persuade the audience that government and industry had the problem solved. Neither tended to encourage active public involvement in environmental issues. And so readers and viewers followed the environmental crisis with

---

ECO-PORNOGRAPHY

The environmental bandwagon has proved as appealing to advertisers as it was to reporters and editors. In 1970, the Standard Oil Company of California claimed that its F-310 gasoline additive would dramatically cut air pollution. The Pacific Gas and Electric Company claimed that its nuclear power plants would provide "a balance of ecology and energy." And Potlatch Forests Inc. claimed that it spent millions to stop its paper plant from polluting the Clearwater River. Literally thousands of ads and commercials have expressed the advertiser's sudden environmental responsibility.

Many of these advertisements are so misleading that Thomas Turner terms them "eco-pornography." [17] The F-310 campaign was questioned by the Federal Trade Commission. The PG&E ads forgot to mention that nuclear power plants cause thermal pollution. And Potlatch proved its concern for the Clearwater River with photos taken upstream of the plant; downstream was an ecological disaster.

Eco-pornography doesn't simply mislead the public; it also exhausts the public's interest in environmental problems. Advertising executive Jerry Mander writes: "People's eyes are already beginning to glaze at the sight of still more jargon about saving the world. It's awfully hard to outshout roughly a billion dollars of advertising money." [18]

interest, but made few if any changes in their own lives.[19]

Then came the "energy crisis." As fuel prices soared and fuel supplies plummeted, the media let out all the stops, devoting thousands of newspaper column inches and hundreds of broadcast minutes to the previously obscure topic of energy. Predictably, the stress was on the political and economic implications of the issue; most of the news was supplied by sources in government and industry. The environmental movement, which had been talking about energy conservation for decades when no one was listening, adopted a paradoxically defensive stance. Environmentalists advocated the need to "go slow" in developing new energy resources, and urged policy-makers not to forget the problems of nuclear waste, offshore oil, air pollution, threatened Alaskan tundra, endangered waterfowl, etc. These were (and are) important issues, but they did not speak directly to the major concern of the moment—reducing the gap between energy supply and energy demand. Reporters understandably came to see the environmental movement as a pressure group of secondary importance. In 1975, as energy problems continued and economic problems increased, environmental news coverage declined—perhaps permanently.

CONSUMERS

Americans devote a good portion of their lives to the art of consuming. One might think, therefore, that the mass media would take a lively interest in consumer news. One might think wrong.

Most of the main reasons for media inattention to the consumer-protection story are already familiar to us. First, there is no powerful consumer's lobby to fight for coverage. Second, advertisers prefer to retain their monopoly on consumer information. Third, the plight of the consumer has only recently reached "crisis" proportions, forcing the media to take notice.

There is a fourth reason of equal importance: The federal government often prefers to "protect" the manufacturer instead of the consumer. Until recently, the Federal Trade Commission maintained a notoriously cozy relationship with the companies it was supposed to regulate. And the other agencies of government have traditionally followed suit.

In one famous case, Consumers Union asked the Veterans Administration to release the results of its tests on hearing aids. CU planned to run the findings in its influential magazine, *Consumer Reports*. The VA turned down the request on the grounds that it wished to avoid publicizing the trade secrets of the hearing-aid manufacturers. Consumers Union took the case to court, and eventually won the right to the data. CU President Colston E. Warne commented: "It is abundantly clear that a search of Government files would reveal a considerable body of information about the performance of available goods and services on the American market. . . . The need today is to unlock that information." [20]

It is true that the government is often reluctant to release consumer information that might embarrass manufacturers. But it is also true that very few publishers and broadcasters have followed the lead of *Consumer Reports* and sought that information in court.

What little consumer news does reach the media is frequently ignored or underplayed. The *Washington Post* has traditionally consigned consumer news to the women's section; the *New York Times* often puts it on the financial pages. When Ralph Nader's book *Unsafe at Any Speed* (a critical attack on the automobile industry) was offered to the nation's press for serialization, 700 newspapers turned it down.[21] More often than not, advertiser pressure is the cause of the omission. On the CBS evening news, Walter Cronkite read an item stating that many pharmaceutical products were actually useless—but he didn't say *which* products. One was mouthwash; the CBS news was sponsored that evening by Scope mouthwash.

By the end of the 1960s, consumer protection was too big a political issue for the media to ignore. Supermarket boycotts, stockholders' uprisings, and the like were news events that simply had to be covered. The same was true of the actions and pronouncements of government officials, who did their best to capitalize on the wave of consumerism. The circulation figures of *Consumer Reports* tell the story. Founded in 1936, the magazine finally reached a circulation of a million in 1966. By 1974 it had climbed to 2,300,000—and it was still climbing.

Consumer news has a long way to go, but it is a great deal better today than it was a decade ago. Since 1970, specialized consumer reporters have become more common, "Action Line" columns have become more aggressive, and consumer exposés have become more acceptable to publishers and station managers. Unfortunately, it took a crisis in public confidence to make it that way. For decades, the media were content to ignore the plight of the consumer. Only when consumer affairs became an undeniable political issue—when they could ignore it no longer—did they show a sudden interest.

EDUCATION AND LABOR

Most educators would agree that education reporters need every bit as much specialized training as science reporters. Most labor experts would say the same for labor reporters. Most editors think they're both wrong—for different reasons.

Labor news simply isn't popular enough to justify a specialist. According to one study in the 1950s, labor news filled less than 2 percent of the average newspaper, and was read by only 17 percent of the readers.[22] The figures are certainly not higher today; in all probability they have declined. In any

event the number of specialized labor editors has gone down. In 1951, there were 154 of them listed in the *Editor & Publisher Yearbook*. In 1967, there were only 12.

Education, on the other hand, has quite obviously increased in importance since the 1950s, when it filled only 1.4 percent of the average paper and was read by only 16.6 percent of the readers.[23] And the number of education editors has risen also. Out of fifty-two major metropolitan newspapers, only ten had an education specialist in 1945. By 1966, forty-nine of them did.[24] Education is a typically "soft" beat. It generates a lot of news, and therefore deserves its own full-time reporter. But very few editors believe that reporter requires any special training.

Untrained reporters in both fields are ill-equipped to handle the technicalities of their subjects—pension fund manipulations and curriculum developments, cost-of-living raises and the theory of permissivism. Fortunately, they are seldom asked to do that kind of story anyhow. The public's interest in labor and education is severely limited. People like to read stories about controversy in the schools and crisis on the picket lines. That is mainly what they get.

Former Secretary of Labor W. Willard Wirtz notes that in his field "good news, reversing the adage, is no news." Wirtz continues: "A strike is invariably the subject of extended coverage, with pictures, and usually with accompanying editorials. The peaceful signing of a new collective bargaining agreement, even in a major industry, is at best a one-day story, usually on an inside page." [25] Similarly, in education, school riots receive sensational front-page coverage, while schools that have found peaceful solutions to their problems are rarely covered at all.

Certain favored kinds of specialized news are not required to compete for space and time with political stories and the like. Instead, they are organized into special sections of a newspaper, magazine, or broadcast news program, and are granted regular allotments of space and staff. Usually these special sections are popular, though the news they offer is often substandard.

BUSINESS

The mass media in America pay an impressive amount of attention to the world of business and finance. The average daily newspaper allots at least three or four pages a day to this subject—more than it gives to foreign affairs, science, environment, consumers, education, and labor combined. Almost every paper has a business editor, and the average metropolitan daily employs a business staff of half a dozen or more. Broadcasting, meanwhile, devotes several minutes a night to news of commerce and finance—more time than it gives to any other specialized topic except sports and weather. And there are more magazines devoted exclusively to business than to any other special interest.

Why all this attention? True, there are roughly 30 million stockholders in the United States, most of whom like to check the listings every day or two. But there are more than twice that many union members in the country, and still labor news is scarce.

There are at least four explanations. First, business news has a long tradition in the mass media. The first American newspapers were begun to meet the needs of the merchant community for news of ship arrivals and the like. Though the percentage of business executives among their readers has declined, most papers have never lost their early allegiance to the world of commerce. Second, the audience for business news, though small, is very dedicated. Many readers buy an afternoon paper solely in order to check on the stock market—information they cannot get from broadcast news. Third, media owners are merchants themselves, and are therefore sympathetic to the information needs of the business community.

The fourth reason is probably the most important: Business news is cheap and easy to gather. The biggest chunk of the newspaper business section is of course the stock tables. These come direct from AP or UPI by high-speed wire, ready to be inserted into the paper. No manual typesetting is required, much less editing. National business and economic stories also come via wire. Papers that need more of this sort of news than AP and UPI provide can subscribe to the special Dow Jones and Reuters business wires. As for local business and financial news, that comes in "through the transom"— press releases by the bushel from all the firms in town. A business reporter can work for years without ever leaving the office. Some do. Many more leave the office mostly to attend lavish press luncheons, boozy retirement banquets, and free junkets to new factories in exotic places.

Good business reporting, of course, is by no means cheap or easy. For one thing, corporate information policies are far more secretive than those of government. The law permits private corporations to hide almost whatever facts they want to hide; it allows them to close their meetings—even "public" stockholder meetings—to the press. Moreover, corporate PR departments do not share the ethic of open access to news. Most government officials understand that an investigative reporter is doing an important job. Company officials, by contrast, are likely to consider the reporter a discourteous snoop. It is a paradoxical truth that the public is told more about the most trivial federal agencies (and football teams) than about industrial behemoths like Standard Oil and General Motors.

Even if business reporters could get the information they needed, they would have great difficulty imparting it to their readers. Few subjects are as complex and hard to understand as the intricacies of corporate finance—or for that matter government finance. Suppose U.S. Steel announces a 6-percent price hike. It takes an unusually well-trained business reporter to calculate the effects of the move, and to decide whether or not it is inflationary. And it takes an unusually gifted writer to translate these conclusions into language a noneconomist can understand. It can't be done in a 40-second TV spot, or even a 500-word article. But will the audience wade through anything longer?

Good business reporting, then, is extremely difficult. And it is extremely rare. Undoubtedly the best business reporting in the United States is found in the *Wall Street Journal,* a daily business newspaper so comprehensive that many nonexecutives read it for information, so elegant that many also read it for pleasure. But even the *Journal* has significant limitations. A. Kent MacDougall writes:

> In my 10 years at the *Journal* (nine of them covering the publishing beat), I never heard of any reporter being asked to write a puff piece for an advertiser, take it easy on a news

source or angle a story beyond what the facts warranted. . . . As one outsider unable to fix a story complained, the *Journal* is "rotten with integrity from top to bottom." Yet, for all its deserved reputation as a tough-minded chronicle of American business, the *Journal* seldom questions the fundamental premises of the business community it covers. It may be the best newspaper in the country at exposing rotten apples in the barrel, but the shape of the barrel itself is almost never an issue.[27]

Despite its reluctance to question the givens of American business, the *Wall Street Journal* does expose the rotten apples, and it devotes enormous effort to exploring and explaining business trends. In the 1970s, nonspecialized media belatedly began trying to copy these virtues of the *Journal.* A number of factors helped encourage this move toward investigative and interpretive business coverage—the discovery of illegal corporate contributions to the Nixon re-election campaign, the shock of the energy crisis, the emergence of the consumer movement and other "anti-business" news sources, the one-two punch of inflation and recession, etc.

In 1973, financial writer Chris Welles wrote scathingly of "the chronic blindness of journalism to the realities of business and finance—a collective self-deception that corporate power is either largely benign or not all that extensive anyway, that except for a few unfortunate miscreants businessmen have the public interest at heart. . . ." [28] By 1975, Welles' indictment seemed a little too harsh. But it was still far too early to predict whether the new-found aggressiveness of American business reporting would mature or die.

The vast majority of business news, by the way, is covered by specialized business reporters for the segregated business sections of newspapers and business portions of broadcast news shows. That is undoubtedly a reason why it is so extensive, and probably a reason why it is so unaggressive. Front-page coverage of business, on the other hand, is limited largely to major cataclysms—industry layoffs, scandals and court decisions, cost-of-living statistics, etc. As economic conditions worsened in 1974 and 1975, this sort of reporting became far more common.

But did it improve in quality? Most observers agreed that it did not—but they fervently disagreed on the nature of its defects. Many business executives complained that economic news was unnecessarily gloomy, exaggerating the recession and thereby deepening it.[29] Herbert Stein, Richard Nixon's chief economic adviser, complained that economic news was ill-informed, overdramatized, conflict-oriented, and hostile to the established economic order.[30] Consumer activists complained that economic news was overly dependent on sources in government and industry, and insufficiently attentive to basic flaws in American capitalism. And readers and viewers—almost unanimously—complained that economic news was boring, frightening, and incomprehensible.

As we said before, good business reporting is extremely difficult. For decades the media didn't try to do the job. Now they are beginning to try.

TRAVEL AND REAL ESTATE

The vast bulk of travel and real estate news seems to be pure pap, designed only to fill the space between advertisements. Perhaps this is unfair. But it is certainly the case that real estate brokers, airlines, and resorts advertise generously, and find a perfect environment for their ads in the almost uniformly enthusiastic and uncritical content of newspaper travel and real estate sections. And it can hardly be a coincidence that the "news" in these sections so often features the very same places as the ads.

Even the best newspapers regularly fall into these traps. Stanford N. Sesser offers some evidence on the *New York Times:*

A *Times* travel article on Haiti spoke of "an optimistic spirit" among the Haitian people, who "give the impression that even though they lack the material abundance of some parts of the world, they share the pride that comes with independence." Not only is this description directly contradicted by articles on Haiti in the *Times'* regular news columns, but the travel story also fails to point out that dollars spent by visitors to Haiti go into the pocket of [now deceased] dictator François Duvalier, who desperately needs hard currency to prop up his repressive regime.[31]

Perhaps you feel a travel story has no business talking about dictators and repressive regimes anyhow. But it could at least talk about poor accommodations, overcrowded airplanes, rude customs officials, or the fact that some idyllic vacation isle has just been destroyed by a hurricane. You won't find those stories, either, in the travel section of your local paper. Nor will you find them on radio or television, or in specialized magazines like *Holiday* and *Travel News*.

Real estate news is more of the same—rewritten press releases designed to persuade the reader and please the advertiser. Ads and commercials for the Potomac Electric Power Company in the 1960s featured the words "It's Flameless!" One day the *Washington Post* ran a two-page ad for the company. Ferdinand Kuhn comments:

> This time the shinplaster of pseudo-news, fore and aft, was as thick as a featherbed. On that single day the paper printed 145 column inches, almost seven columns, not labeled as advertising, about the delights of electrified home life.
>
> It told of the joys of electric heating, cooling, floodlighting, and gadgetry unlimited, including an electrically warmed birdbath. . . . When a story dealt with electric heating, the writer was careful to include the adjective "flameless." . . . Again, I suppose, any resemblance to a paid commercial in these news columns was purely coincidental.[32]

These sins are more culpable on the real estate pages than in the travel section, for real estate news includes (or should include) a number of genuinely important stories. The quality of urban life is inextricably tied to the amount and kind of new housing that is built. The issues are complex, requiring expertise in such diverse fields as architecture, economics, ecology, and sociology. Perhaps we can forgive the travel section for ignoring the problems of vacationers. But we cannot forgive the real estate section for ignoring the dangers of unplanned growth.

In all fairness, the mass media in the 1970s took housing issues much more seriously than the media in the 1960s. Many TV stations and newspapers ran thoughtful analyses on the impact of urban renewal, the problems of public housing, the effects of rent control, the economics of housing construction and maintenance, etc. In virtually every case, however, housing was covered in a single feature, documentary, or series, then ignored for months until the next feature, documentary, or series. And newspaper real estate pages, which offered the potential for real continuity and depth, kept on publishing pap instead.

SPORTS

Spectator sports are probably America's foremost recreational activity. And since most spectators can't get to the game in person, they rely instead on the mass media. Every sporting event of any significance at all is carried live on radio or television. The networks bid in the millions of dollars for the rights to the most important games. Newspapers allot more space to sports than to any other specialized topic (except perhaps the women's pages). Broadcast news programs are even more overbalanced in favor of sports, devoting up to one-third the available time to that single topic. And the specialized sporting magazines, led by *Sports Illustrated*, are among the most profitable in the country.

With all that time and space, we have a right to expect sports news as detailed and comprehensive as news of the government. In a sense, that's what we get. Certainly every game, every injury, and every trade receives wide attention in the media. But it is one-sided attention. If an athlete was traded because he couldn't get along with his teammates, we are unlikely to be told about it. If an injury resulted from simmering racial conflicts among the players, we are unlikely to be told about it. And if a game was poorly played and deadly dull, we are unlikely to be told about it. The sports pages, like the travel and real estate pages, present an almost uniformly positive and enthusiastic picture of the world they cover.

In the 1970s, it became harder and harder for sportswriters to maintain this happy optimism. Player strikes, recruiting scandals, financial problems, and courtroom battles

BROADCAST SPORTS

Newspaper sportswriters may get a few gifts and favors from the teams they cover, but at least the paper pays their salaries. Television sportscasters, on the other hand, often earn their incomes directly from the team. And television itself has a strong economic interest in the continued popularity of the sporting events it programs. Little wonder, then, that TV sports announcers and commentators have more in common with promoters than with journalists.

Typical of broadcast sports is ABC's Chris Schenkel, who even "sidesteps naming the player who commits an atrocious personal foul when it is obvious to all in the stadium." [33] But don't despair. ABC also has Howard Cosell, always ready to jump in with scandals, rumors, and informed critiques of the players and the teams. Perhaps he is the forerunner of a new trend.

---

absolutely demanded hard news coverage. Most sportswriters resented this necessity, and reverted as quickly as possible to covering the games they loved.

Sportswriters are, first and foremost, fans. As Leonard Shecter has put it: "The man who covers a baseball team year after year spends a good deal more time with the management of the ball club than with his own editors; indeed, with his own wife. He becomes, if he is interested enough in his job to want to keep it, more involved with the fortunes of the team than that of his newspaper." [34]

There's nothing so terrible about this as long as it is confined to the amateur level. Who can quarrel with a local paper that refers to the town's star Little Leaguer as a pint-sized Ted Williams, and makes excuses for the 0–23 record of the high school basketball team? But professional athletics—and much of college athletics—is big business. Working to fill a 60,000-seat stadium is not the same thing as helping to support the Little League. On that level the fans have a right to know why seat prices were raised, or why the coach kept the star halfback on the bench. And nonfans have a right to know about illegal recruiting, racial unrest, and the like. If a professional boxing match was a rotten fight, we should be told. If it was fixed, we should be told that too.

ENTERTAINMENT

Herbert Kupferberg likes to tell the story of a young reporter who was sent to interview Van Cliburn when the famous pianist arrived in town to play a Tchaikovsky concerto with the local orchestra.

The reporter begins the interview by saying: "Mr. Cliburn, there are two questions I would like to ask you at the very start: How do you spell Tchaikovsky, and what is a concerto?" [35]

The story may be apocryphal, but Kupferberg's point is obvious. The average newspaper pays so little attention to the arts that it does not bother to hire a reporter who understands them.

Yet the average newspaper does have an entertainment section, averaging several pages a day and often dozens of pages on Sundays. Entertainment magazines, from *TV Guide* to *Screen Romances* to *Rolling Stone,* are enormously popular. And entertainers are by far the most frequent guests on radio and TV interview shows.

This is by now a familiar paradox. The mass media devote a great deal of time and space to entertainment, but they publish almost no solid cultural news. What they do publish can be divided into four categories: service items, press releases, human-interest features, and reviews.

Roughly half the entertainment section of the paper is strictly service—radio and TV logs, movie listings, and such. This material is of real value to readers. It is also of real value to the entertainment industry, which shows its appreciation by advertising generously. Interspersed among the ads and the logs are PR releases, touting the virtues of this or that extravaganza. Finally, the editor tosses in a couple of wire-service features or locally written human-interest pieces. It takes a real expert to tell this stuff from the PR. It is all light, readable, and invariably glowing.

The reviews are the only entertainment articles that try to be independent. On the whole they succeed. Many a movie theater owner has complained bitterly (and fruitlessly) about unfavorable reviews. But some reviewers still feel an obligation to be kind, and some are susceptible to the subtle bribe of endless free tickets. The little theater, meanwhile, is every bit as sacrosanct as the Little League.

WOMEN

In general-interest media content (on the front page, for example), women are often ignored or mistreated. This long-standing approach began to change direction in the 1970s, but there is much progress still to be made (see pp. 446–48). For the foreseeable future, women will continue to rely on specialized media devoted to women's issues and women's interests.

To a greater extent than many men realize, women do have their own separate media. Women's magazines of all sorts are among the top sellers in the country—*McCall's, Family Circle, Better Homes and Gardens, Ladies' Home Journal, Woman's Day, Redbook, Ms., Cosmopolitan,* etc. From ten in the morning to four in the afternoon, television is aimed predominantly at women. And in newspapers there is the women's section.

What's in it? Here are the most common topics according to one 1969 survey: club news, food preparation, homemaking, recipes, beauty tips, weddings and engagements, fashion, society, decorating.[36] In addition, many editors put their etiquette and advice columns (always the most popular columns in the paper) in the women's section. And if the paper can afford to use color anywhere, this is the place—food and fashion in full color.

The content of the women's section changed very little from the 1880s to the 1970s. Editors claimed—and claim—that most women like it the way it is. Certainly most advertisers like it the way it is—a fact that many critics have noted but few have objected to. Consider, for example, the following piece of mild criticism:

> So far as food is concerned, most of the "coverage" consists of recipes. In some instances, the recipes are tied in with the foods being advertised in that day's paper. This is done particularly on Thursdays, when food advertising is heavy before the traditional shopping day, Friday. This is fine, but it isn't enough.[37]

But change is coming. In 1973, the Newspaper Food Editors and Writers Association was founded with the principal goal of eliminating commercial pressures. Two years later the Association approved a code of ethics.[38] Perhaps the food editors will eventually manage to free themselves from advertisers —and perhaps the beauty editors and fashion editors will follow their lead.

Pandering to advertisers is not, however, the worst sin of the women's section. Far more basic is the lack of serious attention to real issues of interest and importance to women. Significant progress will be made when the food editors resolve to cover the nutritional value of snack foods, the health dangers of chemical food additives, the economic impact of agribusiness monopolies, etc. This sort of change, too, is beginning—but *just* beginning —to occur. In 1975, the Women's News Service advertised in *Editor & Publisher:*

WOMEN'S NEWS SERVICE reports on such explosive issues as abortion, divorce, alcoholism, runaway children (and husbands and wives), sexual freedom, household inflation, and feminism. Nor does it neglect trendy fashion, wining and dining, home decor, and child raising (and cupcake recipes).

If your newspaper has a Women's Section, a Style Section, a Living Section, a Leisure Section, or a Family Section, then WOMEN'S NEWS SERVICE is for you.[39]

In the 1970s, many newspapers did begin including an occasional serious article in the women's section. But many more papers "modernized" the section by replacing some of the traditional fashion and society content with more general-interest entertainment stories. This move was often accompanied by a name change, from "Women" to something like "Family Life" or "Leisure." But one 1975 comparison of the two types of sections concluded: "Rather than enlarge coverage of subjects deemed important to readers, it appears that efforts to upgrade the pages have resulted instead in the replacement of traditional copy with stories about movies, books, theater, travel, arts and entertainers." [40]

The women's section, in other words, still has a long way to go.

All these special departments—women, entertainment, sports, travel, real estate, and business—have several things in common. First, they are all accorded a great deal more space than they would get if they had to compete for it on the general news pages. Second, they are all popular with specific groups of readers and more or less ignored by everyone else. Third, they are all geared to keep advertisers happy, and to that end they shy away from controversial or investigative reporting. And fourth, they are all getting away with it.

The journalistic ethic may have been designed with political news in mind, but it should not be limited to political news. Even a stamp-and-coin reporter has an obligation to be honest, aggressive, accurate, and independent. It's time to begin living up to that obligation.

Notes

1 Bernard C. Cohen, "The Press, The Public and Foreign Policy," in Bernard Berelson and Morris Janowitz, eds., *Reader In Public Opinion and Communication*, 2nd ed. (New York: The Free Press, 1966), pp. 134–35, 142.

2 Leo Bogart, "The Overseas Newsman: A 1967 Profile Study," *Journalism Quarterly*, Summer, 1968, p. 305.

3 Peter Barnes, "The Wire Services in Latin America," *Nieman Reports*, March, 1964, p. 5.

4 Frederick T. C. Yu and John Luter, "The Foreign Correspondent and His Work," *Columbia Journalism Review*, Spring, 1964, pp. 5–12.

5 Walter Lippmann and Charles Merz, "A Test of the News," *New Republic*, August 4, 1920, pp. 1–42.

6 Alexander Cockburn, "How To Earn Your Trench Coat," [*MORE*], May, 1974, pp. 24–25.

7 James R. Whelan, "The Agencies and the Issues," *Nieman Reports*, December, 1967, pp. 8–9.

8 "TV: An Eyeful of China, a Thimbleful of Insight," *Newsweek*, March 6, 1972, p. 27.

9 Chilton R. Bush, ed., *News Research for Better Newspapers* (New York: American Newspaper Publishers Association Foundation, 1967), II, pp. 37–38.

10 James A. Skardon, "The Apollo Story: What the Watchdogs Missed," *Columbia Journalism Review*, Fall, 1967, p. 13.

11 Hillier Krieghbaum, "Dr. Barnard as a Human Pseudo-Event," *Columbia Journalism Review*, Summer, 1968, pp. 24–25.

12 Hillier Krieghbaum, "Science News Coverage Changes," *Editor & Publisher*, August 24, 1974, p. 40.

13 Chuck Kraemer, "Fred Wiseman's 'Primate' Makes Monkeys of Scientists," *New York Times*, December 1, 1974, p. D31.

14 Carla Marie Rupp, "Breast Cancer Stories Have News Interest," *Editor & Publisher*, October 26, 1974, p. 22.

15 Frank Carey, "A Quarter Century of Science Reporting," *Nieman Reports*, June, 1966, p. 8.

16 "Eco-Journalism," *Newsweek*, February 1, 1971, p. 43.

17 Garrett De Bell, ed., *The Environmental Handbook* (New York: Ballantine Books, 1970), p. 265.

18 Jerry Mander, "Six Months and Nearly a Billion Dollars Later, Advertising Owns Ecology," *Scanlan's*, June, 1970, p. 55.

19 Peter M. Sandman, "Mass Environmental Educa-

tion: Can the Media Do the Job?" in James A. Swan and William B. Stapp, eds., *Environmental Education: Strategies Toward a More Livable Future* (Beverly Hills, Calif.: Sage, 1974), pp. 207–47.

[20] "The Consumer's Right to Know," *Consumer Reports,* October, 1968, p. 553.

[21] Arthur E. Rowse, "Consumer News: A Mixed Report," *Columbia Journalism Review,* Spring, 1967, pp. 30–31.

[22] Charles E. Swanson, "What They Read in 130 Daily Newspapers," *Journalism Quarterly,* Fall, 1955, p. 417.

[23] *Ibid.*

[24] C. T. Duncan, "The 'Education Beat' on 52 Major Newspapers," *Journalism Quarterly,* Summer, 1966, pp. 336–38.

[25] Sam Zagoria, "Equal Breaks for Labor News," *Columbia Journalism Review,* Fall, 1967, p. 44.

[26] Curtis D. MacDougall, *Interpretative Reporting,* 5th ed. (New York: Macmillan, 1968), pp. 433–35.

[27] A. Kent MacDougall, "Up Against the Wall Street Journal," [*MORE*], October, 1972, pp. 12–13.

[28] Chris Welles, "The Bleak Wasteland of Financial Journalism," *Columbia Journalism Review,* July/August, 1973, p. 41.

[29] Frederick C. Klein, "Are the Media Making Things Worse?" *Columbia Journalism Review,* March/April, 1975, pp. 52–53.

[30] Herbert Stein, "Media Distortions: A Former Official's View," *Columbia Journalism Review,* March/April, 1975, pp. 37, 39–41.

[31] Stanford N. Sesser, "The Fantasy World of Travel Sections," *Columbia Journalism Review,* Spring, 1970, p. 46.

[32] Ferdinand Kuhn, "Blighted Areas of Our Press," *Columbia Journalism Review,* Summer, 1966, p. 8.

[33] Frank Deford, "TV Talk," *Sports Illustrated,* December 14, 1970, p. 13.

[34] Leonard Shecter, *The Jocks* (New York: Paperback Library, 1969), p. 23.

[35] Herbert Kupferberg, "The Art of Covering the Arts," *Nieman Reports,* March, 1965, p. 3.

[36] Chilton R. Bush, ed., *News Research for Better Newspapers* (New York: American Newspaper Publishers Association Foundation, 1969), IV, pp. 28–29.

[37] Sister M. Seraphim, "The Women's Section," *Nieman Reports,* March, 1964, p. 13.

[38] Philly Murtha, "New Breed of Food Editors Rally for News, Not Commercialism," *Editor & Publisher,* October 12, 1974, pp. 17, 20, 22. Carla Marie Rupp, "Food Editors Urged to Give Advertisers a 'Fair Shake,'" *Editor & Publisher,* March 1, 1975, pp. 10, 28. "Majority of Food Editors Endorse New Ethics Code," *Editor & Publisher,* March 8, 1975, p. 19.

[39] *Editor & Publisher,* January 11, 1975, p. 37.

[40] Zena Beth Guenin, "Women's Pages in American Newspapers: Missing Out on Contemporary Content," *Journalism Quarterly,* Spring, 1975, p. 69.

Suggested Readings

BARNES, PETER, "The Wire Services in Latin America," *Nieman Reports,* March, 1964.

DIAMOND, EDWIN, "The Dark Side of Moonshot Coverage," *Columbia Journalism Review,* Fall, 1969.

FAY, STEPHEN, "Burying the Working Man," [*MORE*], February, 1972.

HARRINGTON, STEPHANIE, "Two Faces of the Same Eve," *New York Times Magazine,* August 11, 1974.

LEAR, JOHN, "The Trouble with Science Writing," *Columbia Journalism Review,* Summer, 1970.

LIPPMANN, WALTER, and CHARLES MERZ, "A Test of the News," *New Republic,* August 4, 1920.

LOVELAND, DAVID C., "A Survey of Consumer Reporting," Freedom of Information Center Report No. 264, School of Journalism, University of Missouri at Columbia, July, 1971.

MACDOUGALL, A. KENT, "Up Against the Wall Street Journal," [*MORE*], October, 1972.

POE, RANDALL, "The Writing of Sports," *Esquire,* October, 1974.

POLLOCK, FRANCIS, "Towards Protecting Consumers," *Columbia Journalism Review,* March/April, 1974.

RUBIN, DAVID M., "When the Press Puts the Pressure on Business," *Management Review,* February, 1973.

RUBIN, DAVID M., and DAVID P. SACHS, eds., *Mass Media and the Environment.* New York: Praeger Special Studies, 1973.

SANDMAN, PETER M., "Mass Environmental Education: Can the Media Do the Job?" in James A. Swan and William B. Stapp, eds., *Environmental Education: Strategies Toward a More Livable Future.* Beverly Hills, Calif.: Sage, 1974.

SERAPHIM, SISTER M., "The Women's Section," *Nieman Reports,* March, 1964.

SESSER, STANFORD N., "The Fantasy World of Travel Sections," *Columbia Journalism Review,* Spring, 1970.

WELLES, CHRIS, "The Bleak Wasteland of Financial Journalism," *Columbia Journalism Review,* July/August, 1973.

ZAGORIA, SAM, "Equal Breaks for Labor News," *Columbia Journalism Review,* Fall, 1967.

Epilogue

For the most part, this book has been highly critical of the American mass media—for two reasons. First, the media deserve and need criticism. Second, it is vitally important that future journalists (and future community leaders in all occupations) be aware of what is wrong with the media and how they must change to better serve the public.

But it is equally important to preserve a sense of perspective. With all their flaws, the American media are probably both the most independent and the most responsible media in the world. The same television system that produces soap operas by the gross has also given us Walter Cronkite and "The Selling of the Pentagon." The same newspaper system that coddles the Establishment and mindlessly attacks dissidents also exposed the Watergate scandals. The same magazine system that peddles *True Romances* also peddles *Harper's*.

The best of modern American journalism is unmatched anywhere else in history or in the world today. The rest of modern American journalism must be helped to live up to those high standards.

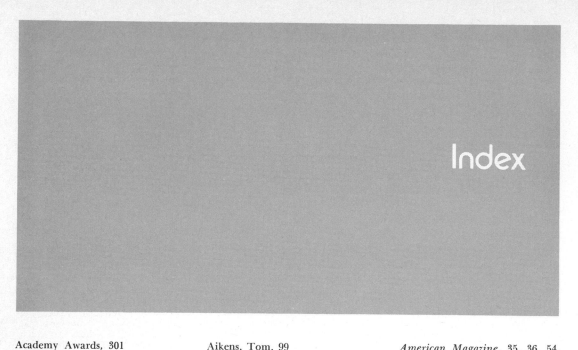